ADDICTED TO FAILURE

ADDICTED TO FAILURE

U.S. Security Policy in Latin America and the Andean Region

Edited by
Brian Loveman

ROWMAN & LITTLEFIELD PUBLISHERS, INC.
Lanham • Boulder • New York • Toronto • Plymouth, UK

ROWMAN & LITTLEFIELD PUBLISHERS, INC.

Published in the United States of America
by Rowman & Littlefield Publishers, Inc.
A wholly owned subsidiary of The Rowman & Littlefield Publishing Group, Inc.
4501 Forbes Boulevard, Suite 200, Lanham, Maryland 20706
www.rowmanlittlefield.com

Estover Road
Plymouth PL6 7PY
United Kingdom

British Library Cataloguing in Publication Information Available

Library of Congress Cataloging-in-Publication Data

Addicted to failure : U.S. security policy in Latin America and the Andean Region / edited
   by Brian Loveman.
   p. cm. — (Latin American silhouettes)
   Includes bibliographical references and index.
   ISBN-13: 978-0-7425-4097-2 (cloth : alk. paper)
   ISBN-10: 0-7425-4097-9 (cloth : alk. paper)
   ISBN-13: 978-0-7425-4098-9 (pbk. : alk. paper)
   ISBN-10: 0-7425-4098-7 (pbk. : alk. paper)
   1. Latin America—Relations—United States. 2. United States—Relations—Latin
America. 3. National security—United States. 4. National security—Latin America.
I. Loveman, Brian. II. Series.
F1418.A24 2006
355'.0310973098—dc22   2006004448

ACC Library Services
Austin, Texas

Printed in the United States of America

∞™ The paper used in this publication meets the minimum requirements of American
National Standard for Information Sciences—Permanence of Paper for Printed Library
Materials, ANSI/NISO Z39.48-1992.

Contents

Abbreviations

ACI	Andean Counterdrug Initiative
ALCA	Área de Libre Comercio de las Américas/American Free Trade Zone
ANC	Asamblea Nacional Constituyente
ASD SOLIC	assistant secretary of Defense for Special Operations and Low-Intensity Conflict
ASPA	American Service Members Protection Act
ATPA	Andean Trade Preferences Act
AUC	Autodefensas Unidas de Colombia/United Self-Defense Forces of Colombia
BIA	bilateral immunity agreement
CARICOM	Caribbean Community
CD	counterdrug
CSIS	Center for Strategic Studies
CTFP	Regional Defense Counterterrorism Fellowship Program
DCS	Direct Commercial Sales [Program]
DEA	Drug Enforcement Administration
DoD	Department of Defense (U.S.)
DSCA	Defense Security Cooperation Agency
ELN	Ejército de Liberación Nacional/National Liberation Army
EPA	Environmental Protection Agency

FARC	Fuerzas Armadas Revolucionarias de Colombia/ Revolutionary Armed Forces of Colombia
FMS	Foreign Military Sales [Program]
FOLs	Forward Operating Locations
FTAA	Free Trade Area of the Americas
GDP	gross domestic product
ICC	International Criminal Court
IMF	International Monetary Fund
LTC	lieutenant colonel
MAS	Movement toward Socialism
MVR	Movimiento Revolucionario Quinta República
NAFTA	North American Free Trade Agreement
OAS	Organization of American States
OSD	Office of the Secretary of Defense
PNAC	"Project for a New American Century"
SIVAM	Sistema de Vigilancia de la Amazonía/Amazonian Surveillance System
SOFA	status of forces agreement
SOLIC	Special Operations and Low-Intensity Conflict (DoD)
USAID	Agency for International Development
USINFO	U.S. Information Agency
USSOUTHCOM	U.S. Southern Command
WHINSEC	Western Hemisphere Institute for Security Cooperation

Figures and Tables

Figures

Tables

Preface

SINCE THE END OF THE COLD WAR the United States has officially committed itself to supporting democracy, human rights, socioeconomic development, and political stability in Latin America. As part of its national and global security strategies, the United States has spent billions of dollars to fight a war on drugs, to encourage civilian control of the military in the Western Hemisphere, and to promote judicial reform and the rule of law. U.S. civilian policy makers and military commanders have urged Latin American leaders to seek more equal distribution of income and opportunities to overcome the legacies of authoritarianism and social injustice. At the same time, the United States crusaded for "market-democracy" and committed itself to creation of a Free Trade Area of the Americas (FTAA) by 2005.

Through a series of conferences called the "Summits of the Americas," beginning in Miami in December 1994, the heads of states and governments of Latin America proclaimed their commitment to strengthening democracy, promoting prosperity through economic integration and free trade, and eradicating poverty and discrimination. They affirmed that representative democracy was "the sole political system which guarantees respect for human rights and the rule of law; it safeguards cultural diversity, pluralism, respect for the rights of minorities, and peace within and among nations."[1]

At the instance of the United States the signatories of the declaration of principles at the first Summit of the Americas also affirmed that "recognizing the pernicious effects of organized crime and illegal narcotics on our economies, ethical values, public health, and the social fabric, we will join the battle against the consumption, production, trafficking and distribution of illegal drugs, as well as against money laundering and the illicit trafficking in arms and chemical precursors. . . . We condemn terrorism in all its forms, and we will, using all legal means, combat terrorist acts anywhere in the Americas with unity and vigor."[2]

Despite contributions to the settlement of the Peru–Ecuador war (1995) and the promotion of numerous "confidence and security-building measures in the Americas," U.S. policies for the Western Hemisphere have not generally achieved their intended results. The North American Free Trade Agreement (NAFTA, 1994), and its later extension from North America to Chile,[3] was a partial success on the trade agenda. Increased military-to-military contacts and exercises, as well as expanded Latin American participation in global and regional peacekeeping missions, also could be cited as objectives attained. For the most part, however, the goals of the 1994 declaration of principles have remained unrealized.

Latin American democracies remain fragile. Human rights violations, though less pervasive than in the 1970s and 1980s, persist. Citizen security remains tenuous in much of the hemisphere. From the Southern Cone to the Caribbean and Mexico, military units have been deployed in city streets and the countryside in response to surges in violent crime. Elected civilian governments still exert little effective control over military institutions, although successful coups occurred less frequently in the 1990s and U.S. support for civilian ministries of defense provided a facade of civilian authority over the armed forces. Citizen insecurity and concern for crime and gang activities contributed to demands for militarization or remilitarization of public order missions from Mexico and Central America to parts of the Southern Cone. Notwithstanding some tactical victories against drug cartels in Colombia and reduction of acreage planted in coca in Bolivia and Peru, availability of drugs, drug consumption, and drug-related violence in Latin America and the United States have not declined.[4] Corruption, organized crime, gang violence, citizen insecurity, and social injustice and inequality have also increased since 1990.[5]

In 1999, Luigi Einaudi, at that time a visiting senior fellow at the Inter-American Dialogue (and in 2005 acting secretary-general of the Organization of American States, OAS), wrote that "the end of dictatorship has not ended poverty, social inequities or human rights abuses. With the passage of time, the failures and abuses of the democratic present can become more vivid than the dimming memories of the even greater failures and abuses of the dictatorial past."[6] With the withdrawal of U.S. forces from Panama scheduled for completion in the same year, Einaudi also called for a new security architecture in light of the persistence of threats to democracy and the rule of law, including organized crime and drug trafficking.[7] He insisted that with a reconfiguration of defense and security concepts and installations, "democracy and free trade could become a foundation for a new hemispheric bargain."[8]

Seven years later, in 2006, U.S. rhetoric and policies had changed little; the same tired calls issued from Washington, D.C., promoting democracy, human rights, and the war on drugs (and now on terror as well) and favoring free trade and increased foreign investment in Latin America. After spending billions of dollars on flawed and failed programs, and on programs that seemed often to exacerbate the woes of Latin America rather than ameliorate them, civilian and military leaders in the United States proposed more of the same: "For the second Bush term, our objectives are the same: a safer, more prosperous neighborhood—where dictators, traffickers, and terrorists cannot thrive. The hemisphere can be optimistic because we know these goals are within our reach, and we work together in a spirit of mutual respect and partnership."[9]

The same objectives included, among others, reaffirmation of more than forty years of failed policies to isolate Cuba and oust Fidel Castro as head of state in Cuba; intensification of the failed drug war; the unsuccessful campaign against guerrilla movements in Colombia and narcotics trafficking in the Andean region and elsewhere in the hemisphere; the unsuccessful, if half-hearted, efforts to control undocumented immigration; and promotion of trade policies that disadvantaged many Latin American producers and pushed migrants from the Latin American countryside to towns, cities, and the United States in increasing numbers. Even U.S. promotion of democracy, understood typically as elected governments (and regular lawful succession in office), had only limited success. Despite the transition from military to civilian governments since the 1980s, and notwithstanding Assistant Secretary for Western Hemisphere Affairs Roger F. Noriega's claim that strengthening democratic institutions, promoting prosperity through further opening of Latin American economies, and "bolstering security" were U.S. priorities, political, economic, and social conditions for millions of Latin Americans had not improved.[10]

Thus, in March 2005, Noriega told the U.S. House of Representatives Committee on International Relations Subcommittee on the Western Hemisphere,

> What the polls show is that Latin Americans by and large don't trust their governments and their institutions. The survey numbers suggest that overwhelming majorities in virtually all countries of the region have "little" or "no" confidence in their executive, judiciary, legislature, political parties, armed forces or police. I believe this can be attributed to the fact that, in many cases, political elites in the region often are perceived to exhibit an aloofness from the people they are supposed to represent and serve. That gulf is often reinforced by legal immunity granted legislators and the de facto impunity afforded many other governmental and political actors. That resultant mutual mistrust between voters and the government encourages corruption, as citizens resort to one of the few ways available to persuade government officials to actually work on their behalf—pay them directly. Many formal democratic institutions in Latin America are weak

and overly politicized. In some countries there is not one single body—not a Supreme Court, not an Electoral Commission, not a Regulatory Board—that can be relied upon to routinely make impartial, apolitical decisions in accordance with the law.[11]

More than fifteen years after the end of the Cold War, more than a decade after the first modern Summit of the Americas in which the region ostensibly committed itself to democracy, Noriega's disheartening assessment of Latin American democracy overall was much more optimistic than those of critics of U.S. Latin American policies and of Latin Americans themselves.

Why does the United States continue to pursue failed policies from past decades as if U.S. policy makers were unable to learn? What about the U.S. political system, and the systems of Latin America and the Andean region, allows a seamless connection of the Cold War, the war on drugs, and the war on terror—to the detriment of Latin Americans and the United States itself? Why do U.S. policies ostensibly designed to promote rule of law, respect for human rights, democratization, and political stability instead contribute to widespread corruption, erosion of government authority, human rights violations, increasing socioeconomic inequality, and political instability? Why do Latin American governments, the European Union, and U.S. policy makers often work at cross-purposes when they all claim to be committed to democratization, stability, and development?

The chapters in this book, written by regional and country specialists, present answers to these questions. They detail how U.S. policies toward Latin America and the Andean region evolved since the end of the Cold War and the changes in bilateral, multilateral, and regional policies. They consider, in particular, the nature of U.S. economic, security, and foreign assistance policies since the 1990s for individual countries, the Andean region, and Latin America more generally, as well as their impacts and the responses to them by policy makers, political leaders, and social movements throughout the region. They explain how policies intended to promote rule of law generate corruption and institutional decline, how efforts to promote stability have destabilized governments across the region, how the drug war (and, more recently, the war on terror), instead of reducing drug production and the narcotics trade and increasing citizen security, has had the opposite outcome. They also document the once-again expanding role of Latin American militaries in internal security missions, surveillance of civilians, and law enforcement, and the rising tensions in civil–military relations.[12]

Latin American polities and societies are diverse; generalization from Mexico to Central America and the Caribbean, to the Andean region, Brazil, and the Southern Cone necessarily glosses over this diversity. But with variation from country to country, these perverse outcomes of U.S. policies share one feature: namely, they are partially the result of a failed war on the cultivation, processing, manufacturing, and commerce of narcotics.

U.S. legislative efforts to curtail commerce and use of narcotics precede World War I. They have never been very successful. Almost six decades after the Harrison Act (1914) criminalized the nonmedical use of opium, morphine, and cocaine, President Richard Nixon declared a war on drugs in 1973. President Ronald Reagan declared the drug trade a threat to U.S. national security in 1986.[13] After the end of insurgencies in Central America in the early 1990s, the war on drugs—along with the push for a neoliberal economic agenda, particularly the opening of markets to trade and foreign capital, the privatization of public enterprises, and the "flexibilitization" of labor, safety, and environmental regulations—gradually came to dominate U.S. policy toward Latin America. In practice, however, on the ground (and also in the air and the oceans) and in the U.S. Congress, the war on drugs has overdetermined and subverted bilateral and regional policy from Mexico to the Southern Cone. In the decade of the 1990s the U.S. Department of Defense, the Drug Enforcement Administration (DEA), the State Department, and more than a dozen other U.S. agencies subordinated the dreams of Latin Americans to U.S. political shibboleths on the importance of the drug war and the connection between capitalism, democracy, human rights, and human development—political messages that were repeated ad nauseam in policy statements and formal strategy documents by Republican and Democratic policy makers alike.

Curiously, the failure of the drug war and of U.S. Latin American policy more generally has been recognized across the ideological spectrum in the United States. Libertarians and conservatives have expressed disgust with the failure of prohibitionist drug policy and U.S. interventionism.[14] Patriotic (usually retired) colonels and lieutenant colonels, like LTC (retired) Ralph Peters— who calls our policy makers committed to "instant democracy" the "ass-end of imperialism"[15]—have publicly lamented our failed policies. Policy analysts at liberal think tanks, like Adam Isacson at the Center for International Policy, have repeatedly addressed the unintended consequences of U.S. Latin American policies: "In the name of the drug war, the United States has given aid to Colombia totaling approximately US$2.4 billion between 1996 and 2002. . . . As evidence of failure accumulates, one might expect Washington to consider fundamental reconsideration of its military-dominated strategy. But U.S. officials appear to be learning the wrong lesson."[16]

Even policy makers who emphasize the achievements of Plan Colombia[17] and the progress made in crop eradication, drug interdiction, and efforts to strengthen democracy and human rights recognize that

Colombia suffers from an extraordinarily high homicide rate of 63 murders per 100,000 inhabitants each year. Surprisingly, most of these deaths are not related to the armed conflict with guerillas. Rather, they are a result of drug-related violence, weak governmental institutions and a pervasive sense of impunity before the law. The high homicide rate contributes significantly to general insecurity, lack of confidence in governmental institutions, and increasing numbers of people who resort to extra-official protection.

The presence of competing armed groups throughout Colombia creates a human rights tragedy. Threats against individuals who seek to counter terrorist influence in their community are pervasive in many areas, particularly those that involve NGOs which represent under served or exploited groups.

Colombia's internal conflict has resulted in the forced displacement of up to two million people. Most displaced people come from rural towns or villages that are contested by illegal armed groups. The majority are women and children under the age of 18, many of whom have witnessed killing of relatives and other atrocities. Displaced persons are often thought to be sympathizers of one armed group or another and as a result, established communities are often wary of providing assistance. This problem is compounded by the fact that such a large displaced population can place enormous strains on public services such as health, education, and shelters.

Security is the key element. USAID knew that security was a potential problem when Plan Colombia was designed, but it assumed that the Peace Process would be successful and that this success would result in improved security. The collapse of the Peace Talks in January 2002 demonstrates that USAID can no longer assume that there will be peace or that there will be security in many areas of Colombia. The profits from narcotics trafficking are just too large, and some of the combatants are really not interested in peace at the present time. The Colombian military needs to be significantly strengthened to resolve security-related constraints, and respect for human rights must be increased at all levels of society.[18]

In the two years that followed this testimony U.S. military assistance to Colombia increased; the war against guerrillas and paramilitaries intensified, crop eradication reduced the acreage planted in coca and poppies, and the homicide rate in Colombia declined from its world-leading level. Colombia's vice president, Francisco Santos Calderón, reported that, as a result of the government's Democratic Security policies (Seguridad Democrática), in 2003 the homicide rate was down 20 percent, forced internal displacement 52 percent, massacres 33 percent, kidnappings (an important source of income for the armed insurgents and paramilitaries) 26 percent, assassination of union leaders 57 percent, and attacks on power lines 32 percent.[19] At the same time the tactical operations of the Colombian armed forces had increased by 137 percent— placing increasing pressure on the guerrillas and paramilitaries. Santos concluded, "We are winning the war against the FARC, AUC and ELN, who are the worst violators of human rights and international humanitarian law in the Americas, and, every day, we are reducing their capability to threaten Colombians."[20] Santos added, "The results in the area of human rights, security, and social benefits are clear and impressive. There remains an immense road to travel, formidable obstacles to overcome and objectives to meet, but in light of the results and actions detailed in this report, it is indisputable that we are headed in the right direction."[21] Similar views were expressed in August 2004 by John Walters, director of the U.S. Office of National Drug Control Policy: "The example of Colombia is outstanding. I know of no other country on the face of the earth over the last two years that has had as dramatic an improvement in human rights and rule of law as Colombia."[22]

These "achievements" also required significant expansion of the Colombian police and armed forces (almost 27 percent since the Uribe administration took office in 2002), thereby increasing military, police, guerrilla, and United Self-Defense Forces of Colombia (AUC) casualties, and resulting in thousands more "displaced persons."[23] A March 10, 2004, report by the UN Office of the High Commissioner for Human Rights criticized Colombia for mass arrests, torture by security forces, and government collusion with paramilitary groups. Vice President Francisco Santos Calderón responded to the report on RCN television: "Where's the objectivity, the balance and a way of putting everything in context? . . . What we have here is a democratic government . . . and gigantic threats from armed groups full of drug trafficking money who want to defeat democracy. The United Nations may not understand that this takes work."[24]

In September 2004, *Colombia Week* reported that "forced displacement grew in the first half of 2004 throughout the country but especially in regions under Patriot Plan influence, in areas with a strong paramilitary presence and in provinces under strict control of public forces. . . . [25] Forced displacement is becoming a symptom of the failure of the government's democratic security policy, especially in rural zones where the conflict persists. The government reports displacement statistics containing only partial data that don't reflect the phenomenon's real magnitude, [hoping] to sway national and international opinion behind the security policy. But grave displacements continue."[26] Confirming the negative human rights implications of Plan Patriot and the policy of Seguridad Democrática, U.S. Secretary of State Colin Powell, speaking from Panama, said that Colombia might not be meeting congressional standards for improving protection of human rights. Previous U.S. certifications of rights progress in Colombia had been greeted with a barrage of criticism from human rights groups. Powell cautioned that President Uribe "has to keep his eye on human rights and civil rights, to make sure he is cracking down in a way that is consistent with international human rights standards." He reminded Uribe of the link that Congress has established between progress on rights protection and full funding of U.S. assistance programs.[27]

Despite upbeat speeches from the Colombian government and some U.S. policy makers, neither the war on drugs nor Plan Colombia were having the desired results for the United States, for Colombia, for the Andean region, or for other countries in the Caribbean, Central America, and the Southern Cone, where money laundering, drug transshipment, organized crime, and drug use itself became pervasive. Cocaine, heroin, and marijuana availability in the United States had not declined, nor had purity of drugs. Nor had prices increased. The internal wars in Colombia continued, as did massive displacements of civilians, and illegal armed groups maintained control over large amounts of territory (though somewhat less than before 2002). The U.S. Department of State reported that the Colombian government's human rights record remained "poor," and new security and antiterrorist legislation significantly eroded civil liberties.

Spillover effects from the Colombian war and the related war on drugs negatively affected security, human rights, and economic conditions on the borders with other Andean nations, Brazil, and Panama. In Bolivia, Ecuador, and Peru the drug war undermined support for elected governments and confronted security forces with indigenous and peasant protests. In this sense, U.S. policies unintentionally promoted grassroots democracy and social mobilization—against the U.S.-inspired drug war and the neoliberal economic agenda—but produced political instability, the exact opposite outcome of the U.S. goal of stability in the hemisphere.

In March 2005, the armed forces withdrew support for Ecuadorian president Lucio Gutiérrez and a congressional coup ousted him; he fled to Brazilian asylum. In Bolivia, President Carlos Mesa resigned in June 2005, in the face of social mobilization and street protests demanding nationalization of gas and oil reserves, constitutional change, and regional autonomy. And in January 2006, Evo Morales, an Aymara Indian leader of the coca producers' union and the Movement toward Socialism (MAS), was sworn in as the elected president. Morales had repeatedly and vociferously criticized U.S. drug eradication policy and also the neoliberal economic agenda for the hemisphere. In Peru the chief executive, Alejandro Toledo, hung on by his teeth as the impact of U.S-imposed economic, drug war, and security policies undermined government legitimacy and support. One of the leading presidential candidates, Ollanta Humala, an ex-military officer in the counterinsurgency war against Sendero Luminoso, blamed U.S.-sponsored neoliberal policies in Peru for a "social fracture without precedent in Peruvian history."[28]

The misconceived and badly executed drug war is one reason for the failure of U.S. policies. Fumigation of drug crops, interdiction, and increased military and police assistance (which comprised over 80 percent of Plan Colombia assistance), the major thrust of U.S. policies, have not produced the results desired by U.S. policy makers. But U.S. policies in Latin America and the Andean region before, during, and after the Cold War have been ensnared by partisan and bureaucratic politics and a history of policies ingrained in ignorance, disinterest, "benign neglect," and also interventionism, both covert and direct.

After September 11, 2001, U.S. Latin American and Andean region policy fused the war on drugs with the war on terror—while maintaining the legacy of what a critical CIA officer, writing as "Anonymous," calls "imperial hubris."[29]

U.S. Latin American policy, of course, was imbued with imperial hubris long before the most recent, post-1990, crusade to "make the world safe for democracy." From the time of President Theodore Roosevelt's "big stick" and the U.S. involvement in making Colombia's northern province into the independent nation of Panama—to allow construction of the Panama Canal—U.S. leaders and politicians presumed, and proclaimed, that Latin Americans need U.S. tutelage, sometimes including military occupation, to learn "good government" and "civilized" political behavior.[30]

U.S. foreign policies, like those of other powers great and small, are determined in large part by perceived self-interest. Its "special" interests in the Western Hemisphere have been explicit since before declaration of the Monroe Doctrine in 1823.[31] Greatly increased political and military intervention in Latin America after 1959, to prevent "more Cubas" and impede Soviet-communist influence in "our backyard," gave high visibility to an "Alliance for Progress" (1961–1965)—to promote democracy and prosperity as a prophylactic to revolution. This was accompanied by regionwide counterinsurgency and military assistance programs that frequently aligned the United States with military dictators and local tyrants. As Lars Schoultz has written, however, "When the Soviet Union disappeared and U.S. security interests no longer required the same level of dominance, Washington identified new problems—everything from drug trafficking to dictatorship to financial mismanagement—and moved to *increase* its control over Latin America."[32] Schoultz calls this effort "preventive hegemony"—and though it has largely failed, it remains grounded in the "pervasive belief that Latin Americans constitute an inferior branch of the human species . . . that has precluded a policy based on mutual respect."[33]

Along with misconceived and poorly designed policies, covert and direct intervention in Latin American politics, indifference to the challenges of daily survival for millions of Latin Americans, and imperial hubris, lack of mutual respect has also been part of the reason U.S. policies toward Latin America and the Andean region have reaped undesired and unintended consequences. Latin American policy makers and military leaders recognize the disdain or disregard of many U.S. leaders and citizens toward them. They also recognize that Latin America is rarely a central concern of U.S. foreign policy, whether for Congress, the Department of Defense, or other U.S. agencies. Thus, in addition to ignorance and arrogance, a not always benign neglect is a cyclical feature of U.S. policy toward the region.

Latin American politicians and military leaders are not, however, unwilling to use U.S. "assistance" to promote their own domestic and personal agendas. Elite disdain for their own citizens, corruption, racism, and authoritarianism have centuries-old roots in the region—long before misguided U.S. policies came to have important impacts. Nevertheless, poorly planned and executed programs of so-called foreign aid and military assistance lend themselves to more corruption, undermining whatever fragile legitimacy governments enjoy in most of Latin America.

The short attention spans of U.S. policy makers, military attachés, and foreign aid administrators encourage military officers, bureaucrats, and politicians in Latin America to learn how to play the U.S. game, to the detriment of their own citizens, though sometimes also to their own political demise when populist reactions to neoliberal economic policies or to excessive repression topple incumbent presidents and generally undermine governability. Lack of responsible, institutionalized political party systems to represent citizen interests, weakness and corruption in legislative and judicial branches of government, and a history of personalist politics (*caudillismo*) are exacerbated by U.S. pressure to join in the war on drugs, accept and implement the U.S. neoliberal economic project, and cooperate with the shifting security agendas proclaimed by Washington. Most recently this includes the linguistic magic that transformed druglords, arms traffickers, gangsters, and guerrillas into targets of the U.S. international war on terror. Not incidentally, this discursive innovation provided the U.S. Southern Command (USSOUTHCOM) a mission beyond engagement and counternarcotics in the Western Hemisphere that Congress could "understand" when budget time rolls around.

Melding the war on drugs with the war on terror also reinforces Washington's yearly insult to sovereign government in Latin America and around the globe with the "Annual Presidential Certification for Major Drug Producing and Transit Countries." This annual charade poisons binational relations and threatens reduction or suspension of direct U.S. foreign assistance as well as U.S. support for International Monetary Fund (IMF) or World Bank loans to countries that are "decertified." Of course, the highly politicized and largely classified process through which these decisions are made both frustrates the U.S. Congress and adds to the perception in Latin America of U.S. hypocrisy in policy application. Each year some countries are certified on the basis of "vital national interests of the United States," rather than on often questionable findings that they either are cooperating fully with the United States or taking adequate steps on their own to combat the illicit drug problem.[34] In early August 2005, as President Bush prepared to welcome Colombian president Álvaro Uribe to his Texas ranch, the Department of State certified that Colombia met the human rights conditions required by U.S. law. Since September 2004 the State Department had held up certification based on concerns regarding the performance of the Colombian army, its relationship with the paramilitaries, and several high-profile human rights cases. The transparently political decision to release funds from 2004 and 2005 subject to human rights conditionality just as Uribe came to the United States once again highlighted the arbitrariness and unilateralism that Latin Americans had come to detest.[35]

Meanwhile the U.S. House of Representatives authorized another $742 million in aid to Plan Colombia, extending it beyond its original 2000–2005 parameters. Not all congressmen supported this policy; details remained to be worked out with the Senate. Nevertheless, it was clear that the original term for Plan Colombia (2000–2005) had expired with objectives unmet and with the U.S. deeper into the Andean quagmire. Congressman Sam Farr (D-CA) declared, "Eighty percent of funds have gone for military assistance [to Colombia] and been eaten up by coca eradication. Only 20 percent of funds have gone to social and economic programs. These programs are what build local economies and communities and provide alternatives to coca production. [The current] distribution of assistance is not a recipe for permanent coca eradication. It's not a recipe for peace. It's a recipe for disaster."[36]

As I finish writing this preface, governments throughout Latin America face mounting resistance to a range of U.S.-imposed security and economic policies—from the war on drugs to the neoliberal economic agenda. Governments from Argentina to Mexico are hard-pressed to meet citizen demands for security, jobs, basic services, health care, and educational opportunities. Peasants grow coca, poppies, and marijuana, highly profitable crops in the global market economy that the United States claims to support—and their efforts are identified as a threat to U.S. national security. The United States pays for and directly participates in eradication programs that take away these opportunities, make criminals of the peasants, destroy food crops, and poison their land with fumigants.[37] The peasants in Peru, Bolivia, Colombia, Mexico, and elsewhere protest—creating grassroots organizations, democracy from below—to change their governments' policies. U.S. civilian and military leaders call these popular movements threats to U.S. national security and urge governments to use force to put them down, while threatening to cut off aid to those governments that refuse to cooperate in the drug war or who fail to negotiate bilateral immunity agreements insulating U.S. military and civilian personnel from International Criminal Court jurisdiction when operating in the Latin American host countries.

When Latin American governments respond favorably to popular pressure against neoliberal economic policies, against the drug war, against conflating the war on terror with the need for surveillance and repression of internal opposition by secret police and military intelligence units, the U.S. government characterizes them as "radical populist," "leftist," or "causes for concern." Where democratic governments reject U.S. policies or fail to join the U.S. crusade for "market-democracy," pressure is applied by various agencies of the U.S. government, linking bilateral economic and military assistance and support for particular governments in the multilateral financial institutions, such as the World

Bank and the IMF, with "cooperation" with the U.S. agenda. The U.S. government favors "democracy" (elected governments), but not governments that respond sensitively to citizen preferences and that represent their constituents when local preferences and interests conflict with U.S. policies and its global and regional agenda. The United States opposes democracy when it means that groups of Bolivians, Peruvians, Ecuadorians, Colombians, Domincans, and Brazilians exercise their rights of association and free expression to call on their governments to resist U.S. global, regional, and local hegemony.

In much of Latin America, U.S. policies contribute to political instability, renewed militarization of internal security functions, and loss of certain types of economic opportunities. For lack of opportunity, fear of repression, and flight from war zones, some Latin Americans vote with their feet, migrating north, and U.S. policy makers identify the migration as a threat to U.S. national security. In some ways massive migration may indeed be a potential threat to U.S. security, but it is a threat created, in part, by U.S. economic and security policies that uproot and displace peasants, farmers, and town dwellers in Latin America. The neoliberal economic policies, the war on drugs, and the drastic counterinsurgency campaigns create immigrants, fugitives from ill-conceived U.S. hemispheric policies.

In March 2004, the commander of the U.S. Southern Command told the U.S. Congress,

> We face two primary types of threats in the region: an established set of threats detailed in previous years and a nascent set likely to raise serious issues during this year. On the traditional front, we still face threats from narcoterrorists and their ilk, a growing threat to law and order in partner nations from urban gangs and other illegal armed groups, which are also generally tied to the narcotics trade, and a lesser but sophisticated threat from Islamic radical groups in the region. These traditional threats are now complemented by an emerging threat best described as radical populism.[38]

When did urban gangs in Latin America become threats to U.S. national security rather than law enforcement problems? Was this transformation the result—that is, "blowback"—from U.S. regional security policies since the 1980s? When did the drug traffickers and the guerrillas (who have operated since the 1960s in Colombia) become "narco-terrorists"? Was this largely the result of rhetorical and ideological spin by U.S. policy makers? Why is grassroots democracy in Latin America, represented by groups opposing U.S. drug eradication, "free trade," and pro-multinational investor policies, aka "radical populism," a threat to U.S. national security?[39]

Is it possible that U.S. economic and security policies in the region—including policies that drive peasants who cannot compete with imports of U.S. crops from the countryside, and policies that meld the war on drugs and the war on terror—undermine democracy and social welfare in Latin America while failing to make the United States more secure?

Even if most U.S. policy makers remain impermeable to feedback and addicted to failed policies and imperial hubris this volume will provide answers for others regarding the intellectual, ideological, and practical sources of U.S. policy failures in Latin America and, particularly, in the Andean region. In the chapters that follow, regional and country specialists analyze in detail the variations in implementation, outcomes, limited successes, and "collateral damage" from U.S. regional security policy in the post–Cold War era. In addition, a chapter on the European Community's policies toward the Andean region provides insight into alternative visions of the Latin American and Andean security and development dilemma in the first decade of the twenty-first century. The URL (www.rowman.com/isbn/o742540987) accompanying this volume provides for readers primary documentary material on the evolution of U.S. Latin American and Andean security policies in the post–Cold War era.

Financial support for this project came from the Ford Foundation (Andean and Southern Cone Office) and also from the Fred J. Hansen Institute for World Peace at San Diego State University. There have been many sources of intellectual inspiration. I wish to thank especially my colleague and expert on U.S.–Latin American Policy Dr. Augusto Varas, Ford Foundation representative in the Andean Region and Southern Cone, who has encouraged my research on U.S. regional security policy; has commented on ideas, drafts, and the book manuscript; and has had patience with my efforts to expand the project well beyond the original proposal. Thanks also to Judith Ewell and William Beezley for their review and comments on the draft manuscript, to Bruce Bagley for his insightful suggestions for changes in the manuscript, and to Naoko Kada, whose work on the rule of law in Latin America and editorial assistance on the manuscript have been greatly appreciated. The many other friends and collaborators who helped make this volume possible know who they are and will forgive the lack of a name-by-name rendition of their contributions.

In preparing the manuscript, the bibliography, and the accompanying URL I have had the benefit of two talented research assistants, Greg Smith and Pablo Trucco. At Rowman & Littlefield, I have been supported from the start on this project by Susan McEachern, Jessica Gribble, and Sarah Wood. Luann Reed-Siegel copyedited the manuscript, and April Leo supervised the production process.

Brian Loveman
May 2006

1

U.S. Security Policies in Latin America and the Andean Region, 1990–2006

Brian Loveman

Anti-U.S. government sentiment is present in the AOR due to a widespread and mistaken perception that the U.S. maintains a unilateralist approach and an imperialist attitude toward partner nations.

> USSOUTHCOM, *A Theater Strategy of Focused Cooperation and Mutual Security*, 2005

The stability and prosperity of the SOUTHCOM AOR are threatened by transnational terrorism, narcoterrorism, illicit trafficking, forgery and money laundering, kidnapping, urban gangs, radical movements, natural disasters and mass migration.

> General Bantz J. Craddock, commander, United States Southern Command, hearing of the House Armed Services Committee: Fiscal Year 2006 National Defense Authorization budget request, March 9, 2005

If I may make an off-the-cuff comment referencing the effect of drugs on the United States per your comment. We at U.S. Southern Command view drugs and its movement into the United States as a weapon of mass destruction, and we treat it accordingly.

> Brigadier General Benjamin R. Mixon, testimony before Congress, April 21, 2004

The new threats of the twenty-first century recognize no borders. Terrorists, drug traffickers, hostage takers, and criminal gangs form an anti-social
combination that increasingly seeks to destabilize civil societies.

> Donald Rumsfeld, secretary of defense, address to
> 2004 Conference of Western Hemisphere Defense Ministers

U.S. POLICY IN LATIN AMERICA after 1990 responded to dramatically changing
global circumstances. The Cold War was over. Whatever happened in Latin
America no longer had implications for the bipolar struggle between the Soviet
Union and the United States that had framed international politics and local
conflicts since the late 1940s. Yet Latin American policy could not avoid being
influenced by the new U.S. global security strategy, within the framework of traditional U.S. concerns in the Western Hemisphere: relative political stability; defense of economic interests, including access to markets and natural resources;
and exclusion of nonhemispheric powers from significant influence in Latin
America. This chapter traces the evolution of *official* U.S. policy, and especially
defense and security policy, toward Latin America and particularly the Andean
region since 1990, *in the words of official documents, policy statements, and analy-
ses.* To do this, the chapter includes extensive extracts from civilian policy makers and military officers charged with formulating and implementing U.S. security policy in the Western Hemisphere. Relying on the "official story," U.S. policy
objectives and instruments are made explicit, and the results of post-1990s political, economic, and security policy in Latin America and the Andean region
are assessed and views of analysts critical of U.S. policies are also surveyed.[1] The
underlying questions are: What have been the objectives of U.S. post–Cold War
political, economic, and security policy globally, in Latin America, and in the
Andean region since 1990? Have U.S. policy objectives been achieved? What
have been the unintended consequences of U.S. policy and its implementation?

In August 1991, after the first so-called Gulf War, the U.S. president announced in the "New National Security Policy of the United States" that "as we
seek to build a new world order in the aftermath of the Cold War, we will likely
discover that the enemy we face is less an expansionist communism than it is
instability itself." To confront this enemy, the United States would seek to ensure strategic deterrence, to exercise forward presence in key areas, and to respond effectively to crises around the world. Deterrence would include both
nuclear and nonnuclear forces. Forward presence would demand the permanent deployment of U.S. military forces around the globe, though it was initially thought that the effective "demonstration of our commitment to engagement" could be achieved with smaller forces than in the past. While the
United States could not be the world's policeman with responsibility for solving all the world's security problems, "we remain the country to whom others
turn when in distress."[2]

President George H. W. Bush's successor, William Clinton, adapted the 1991 security strategy document without making major changes in the U.S. vision of the new world era. Clinton insisted that to protect and advance U.S. interests in the face of the dangers and opportunities of the post–Cold War world, the United States must deploy robust and flexible military forces that could accomplish a variety of tasks: deter and defeat aggression in major regional conflicts; provide a credible overseas presence; counter weapons of mass destruction; contribute to multilateral peace operations; support counterterrorism efforts; fight drug trafficking; and address other national security objectives.

Much before the second President Bush took office and told Americans that an "axis of evil" existed, President Clinton declared that "the focus of our planning for major theater conflict is on deterring and, if necessary, fighting and defeating aggression by potentially hostile regional powers, such as North Korea, Iran or Iraq."[3] Like the first President Bush, Clinton proclaimed that the core of U.S. strategy was to "help democracy and free-markets expand," but he added the qualifier, "where we have the strongest security concerns and when we can make the greatest difference. This is not a democratic crusade; it is a pragmatic commitment to see freedom take hold where it will help us the most. Thus we must target our effort to assist states that affect our strategic interests, such as those with large economies, critical locations, nuclear weapons or the potential to generate refugee flows into our own nation or into key friends and allies. We must focus our efforts where we have the most leverage."[4]

By 1997, the Defense Department, at Congress's direction, completed the first *Quadrennial Defense Review*. Clinton's policy of "engagement and enlargement" was translated into a policy of "shaping the international environment" and "responding to the full spectrum of threats." This would require development, financing, and deployment of a "full spectrum force" that could "respond to the full spectrum of crises when it is in our interests to do so."[5] The "full spectrum force" doctrine meant retaining superiority in space, global intelligence collection, control of the seas and airspace, and the ability to project military power across great distances and to protect our interests around the world.[6]

Whether U.S. national security doctrine and policies as defined in the key 1991, 1996, and 1997 official documents would permit the exercise of sovereignty by other nations, as traditionally understood, remained to be seen. A partial answer was given in the Department of Defense (DoD)'s annual report to Congress in 1999:

> U.S. vital national interests include: Protecting the sovereignty, territory, and population of The United States; Preventing the emergence of hostile regional coalitions or hegemons; Ensuring the uninhibited access to key markets, energy supplies and strategic resources; Deterring and, if necessary, defeating aggression

against U.S. allies and friends; Ensuring freedom of the seas, airways, and space, as well as the security of vital lines of communication.

The report added, "When the interests at stake are vital—that is, they are of broad and overriding importance to the survival, security, and vitality of the nation—*the United States will do whatever it takes to defend them, including, when necessary, the unilateral use of military power.*"[7]

Thus despite the publicity achieved when President George W. Bush's "The National Security Strategy of the United States of America" (September 2002) referred to preemptive attacks against terrorists and other threats to U.S. security, the premise of unilateral and preemptive strikes was long since implicit in past U.S. security strategies and clearly present as part of President Clinton's security and defense policies.[8] What was new, perhaps, was the apparent pretension of extending doctrines and policies previously reserved for Latin America, including a broadly interpreted Monroe Doctrine, a rejuvenated Olney Doctrine (1895) and Roosevelt Corollary to the Monroe Doctrine (1904), and explicit commitments to hegemony in the global arena.[9] Yet George W. Bush himself traced the crusade to "spread democracy" in the world back to President Ronald Reagan, with the creation of the National Endowment for Democracy. He claimed, "Liberty is both the plan of Heaven for humanity, and the best hope for progress here on Earth."[10]

U.S. Post-1990 Policies and Latin America

In the early 1990s it was not entirely clear how the new U.S. global role—not the world's policeman yet determined to maintain forward presence around the world, respond to crises, and confront instability—would be applied to Latin America. U.S. policy makers celebrated the decline of insurgent and guerrilla groups that carried out terrorist activities, but they also lamented the ongoing and increasing violence associated with the drug cartels, especially in Colombia.[11] By early 1992, President George H. W. Bush's new national drug control strategy provided for further militarization of the antidrug efforts, both explicitly and implicitly, with emphasis on reducing the supply of drugs by sharpening the focus of the attack on drug trafficking organizations; identifying drug trafficking networks, determining their most vulnerable points (including leadership, operations centers, communications systems, shipping capability and transportation modes, processing facilities, chemical suppliers, and financial assets), and dismantling them *by attacking* these points simultaneously; coordinating law enforcement attacks, especially against the traffickers' home base of operations; isolating key growing areas, blocking shipment and importation of precursor and essential chemicals, destroying major processing and shipping centers, and controlling key air and riverine corridors.[12]

This policy was undertaken despite significant reservations and criticism from U.S. military officers and academics.[13] At the same time, the link between the war on drugs and terrorism, which would become much more pronounced in the 2001–2002 period, was already a topic for civilian and military reports and policy declarations.[14]

By 1994–1995, however, an emerging U.S. hemispheric security policy sought to incorporate the drug war into a more comprehensively defined range of threat scenarios in the region and in the nature of U.S. post–Cold War Latin American policy.[15] After the December 1994 Summit of the Americas and the July 1995 Defense Ministerial at Williamsburg, Virginia, the U.S. Department of Defense Office of International Security Affairs released "United States Security Strategy for the Americas."[16] The Defense Department acknowledged that after World War II, U.S. policy in the region tended to view local events geostrategically "against the backdrop of bipolar Cold War conflict." But now, a new concept of "cooperative security" was emerging, focused on "integrated approaches to shared problems." The threats to the United States were more diverse, and the line between domestic and foreign policies had blurred. The new security agenda included narco-trafficking, terrorism, immigration, and environmental degradation. For the United States' Latin American neighbors, of course, old problems remained: border disputes, political violence, internal conflicts (insurgencies in Central America, Peru, and Colombia, especially), and economic insecurity that menaced regime stability.[17]

Above all else, the United States asserted that it wished to promote democracy and open markets—in fact, "market-democracy" entered the lexicon seamlessly, as if political theorists had long taken it for granted that democracy and a particular version of capitalism were part of the same political package.[18] President Clinton's national security strategy of "engagement and enlargement" proclaimed that "the Western Hemisphere, too, is a fertile field for a strategy of engagement and enlargement.[19] Sustained improvements in the security situation there, including the resolution of border tensions, control of insurgencies, and containment of pressures for arms proliferation, will be an essential underpinning of political and economic progress in the hemisphere."[20] This document heralded the "unprecedented triumph of democracy and market economies" and pointed to the 1994 ratification of the North American Free Trade Agreement (NAFTA) as a signpost on the road to hemispheric free trade but provided only passing reference to specific regional security threats, particularly "the scourge of drug trafficking, which poses a serious threat to democracy and security."[21] More specifically, the United States' strategic objectives for the region included

support for democratic norms, including civilian control in defense matters and respect for human rights; peaceful resolution of disputes, transparency of military arms and expenditures, and development of confidence and security-building measures appropriate to the region; carrying out the Panama Canal Treaty agreements; working with our friends in the region to confront drug trafficking, combat terrorism, and support sustainable development;[22] expand and deepen defense cooperation, including international peace-keeping; prevent humanitarian crises from reaching catastrophic proportions; encourage efforts to prevent the proliferation of weapons of mass destruction.

In the mid-1995 Defense Ministerial of the Americas, "the first ever gathering of the hemisphere's civilian and military leaders," the U.S. secretary of defense announced that a consensus had been reached: "The bedrock foundation of our approach to the Americas is a shared commitment to democracy, the rule of law, conflict resolution, defense transparency, and mutual cooperation."[23] The report identified three major threats to democracy, peace, and prosperity: internal conflicts (such as guerrilla movements in Colombia, Peru, Guatemala, and Mexico); border disputes (such as the brief Ecuador–Peru war in 1995); and transnational threats (drug trafficking, terrorism, international criminal organizations). In his testimony to the House National Security Committee in March 1995, SOUTHCOM commander Gen. Barry R. McCaffrey emphasized the great diversity in Latin America ("33 nations with histories and cultural heritage that are in some cases as dissimilar as those of the countries between the English Channel and the Urals") but nevertheless stressed what had become the party line: increased economic integration, the prevalence of "market principles," democratization, and cooperative security arrangements were the wave of the future in the region.[24] Nevertheless, "widespread social and economic inequalities are exploited by insurgents, narcotraffickers and highly armed bands of criminals. Latin America also has the world's most skewed income distribution. The benefits of the recent economic turnaround infrequently trickle down to the poor. These problems can be catalysts for significant migration, both internal and international. . . . Drug production and trafficking continue to be the major regional problems which affect all the nations of the Americas."[25] McCaffrey concluded—as would military and civilian leaders in the United States for the next decade—"Our national interests in the Americas can be supported by fully engaging with all instruments of U.S. national power to achieve the objectives we share with our allies: economic growth, democratic government, regional security and control of transnational dangers such as terrorism, drug trafficking and the migration of people."[26]

Other military and civilian analysts reiterated the agenda and added various items to the list from 1995–1997: mass migration; protection of air and sea lanes, including the Panama Canal; protection of human rights; regional and international peace-making and peacekeeping missions; limitations on weapons of mass destruction, including nuclear, biological, and chemical weapons; environmental protection; control of international criminal financial and economic cartels; arms smuggling; organized crime; fighting corruption; and fighting poverty.[27]

Repeated meetings and conferences involving the region's military officers and defense ministry officials iterated and reiterated the "new" agenda for civil–military relations.[28] In November 1997, the United States Army War College joined with the U.S. Southern Command, the Inter-American Defense Board, the National Guard Bureau, and the Latin American Consortium of the University of New Mexico and New Mexico State University to cosponsor a conference entitled "The Role of the Armed Forces in the Americas: Civil–Military Relations for the 21st Century." The meeting was held November 3–6 in Santa Fe, New Mexico, hosted by the New Mexico National Guard.[29] The list of recommendations summarized from this meeting reads like a new security agenda wish list, emphasizing the role of the U.S. Defense Department in teaching Latin Americans proper civil–military relations and the role of the U.S. military in providing human rights guidelines and "coordinating" regional intelligence, antiterrorism, and antinarcotics operations. For the U.S. military, the report recommended the following:

> The U.S. Southern Command should take the lead in creating electronic communications systems to improve the sharing of security information between the hemisphere's defense establishments. The U.S. National Guard's State to State Partnership Program should be expanded to develop partnerships with more Latin American militaries in response to requests from the duly constituted civilian authorities in those countries. Human rights training for the Latin American armed forces should be continued and expanded at all levels.[30]

These recommendations formed part of a much larger politically negotiated agenda that barely disguised the discrepancies in the diverse Latin American and U.S. views of the post-1989 world—and also the discrepancies on priorities and policies *within and between* the U.S. Department of State, the Defense establishment, and the armed forces. They also made clear the unquestioned presumption that "democracy" and "markets" somehow would promote social equality and improve opportunities for most Latin Americans. Yet U.S. insistence on "opening" the Latin American economies, privatization schemes, and other dimensions of the neoliberal policies did not address the internal dislocations such measures portended, the political consequences for Latin American governments of rural unemployment or deindustrialization, nor even the frequent contradictions in U.S. policies that protected U.S. domestic markets from Latin American producers or provided subsidies for U.S. agricultural interests that discouraged Latin American exports of food, fiber, and other commodities to the United States. Freer trade definitely offered opportunities for some sectors in the region and in the United States—but it also produced millions of unemployed and displaced in the Western Hemisphere along with political and financial crises for incumbent governments.[31] Displaced peasants and rural workers formed part of the growing migrant stream heading north to the United States—and were increasingly identified as a potential security threat by citizen anti-immigrant groups and also by the Pentagon. Yet most Latin American countries, suffering the consequences of the "lost decade" and the 1980s debt crisis, were extremely vulnerable to the agenda for "structural economic reform" emanating from Washington.[32]

The Agency for International Development (USAID) expressed similar presumptions in this period, with a surprisingly direct caveat regarding U.S. national interests:

> The core of our strategy is to help democracy and free-markets expand and survive in other places where we have the strongest security concerns and where we can make the greatest difference. This is not a democratic crusade; it is a pragmatic commitment to see freedom *take hold where that will help us most.*[33] Thus, we must target our effort to assist states that assist our strategic interest. . . . We must focus our efforts where we have most leverage. And our efforts must be demand driven—they must focus on nations whose people are pushing for reform or have already secured it. By promoting and assisting the growth of democracy, the United States also supports the emergence and establishment of polities that will become better trade partners and more stable governments. Smooth transitions of power will reduce the deadly risk of nuclear weapons falling to the control of irrational agents. By facilitating citizens' trust in their government, democracy may also prevent hundreds of thousands of individuals from fleeing their homelands and contributing to destabilizing and costly refugee flows, anarchy and failed states, and the spread of disease and epidemics of catastrophic proportion.[34]

Political realism as a foundation of foreign policy was hardly a new concept, but such forthright expression of realpolitik took most of whatever gloss was left off the veneer of U.S. claims of moral leadership and humanitarian concern. U.S. security policy in the hemisphere, including its economic, environmental, and human rights components, were intended, like those of all nations, to promote national interests. For the moment, with the Cold War gone, concern for human rights and democratization were expressly made part of the regional *security agenda*, along with maintaining peace among the hemisphere's nations, improving civil–military relations, and strengthening the region's defense ministries.

Consistent with this "new" approach to hemispheric relations, the curriculum at U.S. military schools that trained Latin American personnel shifted toward the "new agenda."[35] According to the commander at the U.S. Army School of the Americas in 1999, the school's curriculum reflected the rapid democratization of Latin America. As civil wars in the region subsided, counterinsurgency was de-emphasized in favor of courses in democratic sustainment, de-mining, and counternarcotics. "'What we're doing,' says Colonel Glenn Weider, 'is giving these soldiers exposure to American ideals and proper civil–military relations. SOA courses include more hours of human-rights instruction than those at any other U.S. Army training school.'"[36]

By 1999 the list of new missions tasked to the Latin American armed forces became a litany repeated at the numerous meetings and conferences attended by military commanders, defense ministers, and other civilians and military brass. Illustratively, before departing for Bolivia to meet his counterparts in September 1999 (and shortly before a confusing civil–military coup that ousted Ecuador's president), Ecuadorian general Telmo Sandoval Barona told the press that the Latin American armed forces had become "examples to the world" in supporting democracy and overcoming poverty.[37] At the same meeting, Guatemalan general Miguel Angel Calderón made a presentation called "La Doctrina Militar en el Ejército de Guatemala" ("Military Doctrine in the Guatemalan Army") that was disseminated along with photos on the Guatemalan army Internet website. General Calderón's remarks included nearly every item on the new U.S. security agenda, from human rights to subsidiary law enforcement missions, from subordination to civilian authority to the army's commitment to consolidation of democracy. The Guatemalan army was even in the process of transforming its "axiological foundations."[38] The last frame of the website portrayed a white dove, preceded by these words: "I conclude these remarks, urging that the military camaraderie and fraternity manifested in the present conference stimulates unity and draws us closer to the Bolivarian vision, of a United America." The Guatemalan general failed to remind U.S. representatives to the conference that the "Bolivarian vision," since before the 1826 Pan American Conference in Panama, defined the United States as a principal threat to national security—at least for Spanish- and Portuguese-speaking nations in the hemisphere—and that a "United America" referred essentially to *Latin America.*

In September 1999, the Strategic Studies Institute made available "Security and Civil–Military Relations in the New World Disorder: The Use of Armed Forces in the Americas."[39] This collection better recognized the heterogenous challenges of transforming civil–military relations from Mexico, Colombia, and Venezuela to the Southern Cone but emphasized the threats of economic instability, resurgent authoritarian populism, insurgencies, and narco-politics.[40] Indeed the primary "security" focus of the volume was fighting the drug cartels, government corruption, and corruption of the armed forces themselves.

At the end of the 1990s, despite the discourse on human rights and democracy (including civilian control of the armed forces), *the operative U.S. security agenda for the hemisphere, measured in dollars and other resources committed, had become predominantly the drug wars, international terrorism,* "stability," *and* "promoting democracy," *supplemented by the commitment to trade liberalization and opportunities for private enterprise.*[41] Indeed, almost the entire policy agenda for Latin America had been "securitized": security policy encompassed everything from democratization and trade liberalization to undocumented immigration and urban gangs. Significantly, the Department of Defense had become the "lead agency" for the detection and monitoring of illicit drug smuggling into the United States, providing counterdrug support to regional military and police with counterdrug responsibilities. In principle, this lead agency function included "coordination with the State Department," but the most important missions involved support for bilateral and multilateral cross-border operations, particularly in the Andean region (between Colombia and Ecuador, Colombia and Venezuela, and Peru and Brazil).[42]

In the Department of Defense's "Annual Report to the President and Congress," the DoD claimed that "transnational threats are particularly troublesome in the Americas. Because illegal drug trafficking and associated criminal activity threaten the United States and its interests in the region, DoD will continue to support other agencies in trying to stop the flow of illegal drugs, both at the source and in transit, and will encourage and assist other nations committed to antidrug efforts. In addition, when directed by the President, the Department will defend or assist other U.S. government agencies in stemming refugee flows when they threaten U.S. interests, including its territorial sovereignty."

In short, *the only threats to U.S. security in the Western Hemisphere worthy of specific mention in 1999 were drug trafficking and its spin-offs along with undocumented immigration to the United States.* According to Gabriel Marcella, "The United States Southern Command (SOUTHCOM), in Panama and later in Miami, became the unified command par excellence for counternarcotics. *At one time, nearly 90 percent of its operations involved counternarcotics support.*"[43] None of these threats went to the traditional core mission, before 1990, of any of the U.S. armed forces, except the Coast Guard. Further, these threats referred especially to the Andean region, Mexico, and, to lesser extent, Central America and the Caribbean. This assessment was consistent with the usual marginal significance of Latin America for U.S. security planners and the armed forces, with the exception, of course, of critical moments, like the 1962 Cuban missile crisis and periods of *high salience in domestic politics* of Latin American policy, such as the Reagan administration's policies in the Caribbean and Central America in the 1980s.[44] It was also a logical, if belated, response to President Ronald Reagan's National Security Decision Directive 221 (NSDD 221) in 1986 defining drugs and the drug trade as a threat to U.S. national security.[45]

Regional Security in the New Century

By 2000, U.S. policy makers claimed that many Latin American nations had made enormous advances in democratic governance. But they also acknowledged that the reform process had been difficult and the pace of institutionalizing reform slow. Moreover, while traditional security threats continued to exist, "the principal security concerns in the hemisphere are now transnational in nature."[46] To counter these threats, U.S. policy makers reiterated their faith in democratic reform, open economies, and enhanced regional security cooperation. In practice this meant efforts to further increase U.S.–Latin American military-to-military contacts, working toward force interoperability, and engaging in cooperative security initiatives to include combating transnational crime (arms and narcotics trafficking, terrorism, extradition and prosecution of drug traffickers and money launderers, elimination of illicit drug cultivation), and general programs of law enforcement cooperation. U.S. policy included expanded counterpart visits by military personnel, military exercises and training,[47] and shifting of some U.S. assets and forward deployments to places like Honduras, El Salvador, Ecuador, and Aruba/Curaçao. Simultaneously U.S. policy sought to "advance the goal of an integrated hemisphere of free market democracies."[48] As usual, the multifaceted, multidimensional, and sometimes contradictory character of U.S. policies emanating from the State Department, DoD, Drug Enforcement Administration (DEA), and other agencies left Latin American governments puzzled and, not infrequently, frustrated.

Multilateral and bilateral components of the hemispheric security strategies were tailored to national and regional circumstances. In what was called the "Andean Ridge Nations," "expanded U.S. cooperation and interoperability with Colombian forces remains critical." More generally, in collaboration with Bolivia, Colombia, and Peru, the United States had developed "a threat-based, intelligence-driven, counterdrug interdiction strategy that focuses on air, riverine/coastal, and ground programs. Ecuador provides its air base at Manta as a forward operating location for multilateral aerial surveillance of drug-trafficking flights."[49]

What the Department of Defense did not say directly was that the United States was engaged, whether covertly or through military assistance programs, in low-intensity warfare throughout the Andean region—and had been for some time. Nevertheless, the report, in places, read like a war dispatch:

> The Department of Defense has worked closely with Colombia, Peru, and Bolivia to improve their air interdiction capability, including the provision of ground-based radars and cockpit upgrades for interceptor aircraft. . . . U.S.

ground interdiction assistance has concentrated on training selected military units in the light infantry tactics they require to support law enforcement interdiction and eradication operations. The service programs have been enhanced by the development of intelligence and communication networks. This approach has proven successful in both Peru and Bolivia.

The Colombian government has developed a comprehensive and integrated approach to address Colombia's problems. "Plan Colombia" . . . funds will, among other programs, provide equipment, training, and intelligence support to support drug eradication [*officially* extended to anti-terrorism and counterinsurgency in 2002].[50]

In practice, United States military forces were engaged in a variety of training missions throughout Latin America, often justified as part of the war against drugs. Sometimes the "training" went over the line established by Congress. Bilateral agreements and deployments put U.S. forces at risk—and potentially involved them in internal and international conflicts—on a daily basis in Mexico, Central America, and the Andean nations, though no reports surfaced of U.S. uniformed personnel engaging directly in combat with guerrilla forces.[51] In addition, numerous private subcontractors performed military and quasi-military missions, thereby overcoming congressional limits on U.S. military deployments (despite numerical caps on the contractors also) and making more difficult efforts to audit these operations or make these subcontractors accountable to Congress or anyone else.[52]

The Clinton administration's commitment of aircraft and helicopters to Colombia in mid-2000 as part of "Plan Colombia" preoccupied neighboring nations as the Fuerzas Armadas Revolucionarias de Colombia (Fuerzas Armadas Revolucionarias de Colombia, FARC) and Ejército de Liberación Nacional (ELN) military operations intensified, though delays in delivery of most of the Black Hawks and UH-1N helicopters preoccupied some members of the U.S. Congress.[53] In Brazil, Venezuela's president Hugo Chávez remarked, "That's how Vietnam started."[54] The day before, Brazil's foreign minister, Luiz Felipe Lampreia, declared that his country was "greatly preoccupied" with the potential military consequences of Plan Colombia, predicting that the war would be even worse by the beginning of 2001.[55] Notwithstanding these concerns and the deteriorating conditions "on the ground," President Clinton signed a presidential determination waiving human rights conditions in the aid package for Colombia in August 2000.[56]

By September 2000, Peru, Ecuador, Venezuela, and Brazil had deployed special units to their frontiers, anticipating the spillover from the fumigation operations and drug sweeps. Immigrants fleeing Plan Colombia created new security and humanitarian challenges for Ecuador and, to a lesser extent, Colombia's other neighbors.[57] (All this occurred well before the terrorist attacks of September 11, 2001, in the United States and before the peace nego-

FIGURE 1.1
Andean Counterdrug Initiative Countries.
Source: Map Resources. Adapted by CRS.

tiations between the main guerrilla groups and the government of President Andrés Pastrana broke down in late February 2002.) Meanwhile armed conflict intensified in Colombia itself; "The Colombian army's new aggressiveness takes advantage of improved mobility (going from eighteen helicopters in 1998 to 172 by 2002)."[58]

Even as the war in Colombia intensified and spilled over to its neighbors, and while the ongoing drug wars transformed politics in the Caribbean and Central America (in Mexico, the drug war and corruption of civilian and military sectors of government had been a long-standing problem), the premise that democracy and "free markets" were somehow linked and would benefit most Latin Americans had become a shibboleth repeated by civilian policy makers and U.S. military personnel almost ritually. But throughout the 1990s inequalities in wealth and income in the region increased; economic insecurity for millions of Latin Americans worsened, as did personal insecurity with the rise in violent crime, including contracted murders, kidnapping for hire and profit, and political violence. U.S. policies in the region were not, by themselves, responsible for these trends, but the pressures exerted on Latin American governments by the neoliberal economic model, the unrelenting war on drugs, and the lack of nuance and local knowledge by U.S. policy makers contributed significantly to these outcomes. And, in some cases, U.S. military personnel and DEA and intelligence agents participated directly in repressive operations in Latin America, ignoring formal restrictions on their activities. In other cases, fewer perhaps, U.S. civilian and military personnel directly participated in the drug trade, trafficking in arms, paramilitary activities, and human rights violations. U.S. civilian and military agency clandestine activities also conveyed mixed messages to security agency and military counterparts throughout the region.

Of course, security and stability did not depend solely on investments and freedom of markets. For U.S. civilian and military leaders terrorism and narco-guerrillas had replaced the Marxist threat of the past. Hemispheric security also depended on confronting the new threats. At the end of 1998 U.S. secretary of defense William S. Cohen told the attendees at the Defense Ministerial III in Bogotá:

> The best deterrent that we have against acts of terrorism is to find out who is conspiring, who has the material, where are they getting it, who are they talking to, what are their plans. In order to do that, *in order to interdict the terrorists before they set off their weapon,* you have to have that kind of intelligence-gathering capability, but it runs smack into Constitutional protections of privacy. And it's a tension which will continue to exist in every free society—the reconciliation of the need for liberty and the need for law and order. And there's going to be a constant balance that we all have to engage in. Because once the bombs go off—this is a personal view, this is not a governmental view of the United States, but it's my personal view—that once these weapons start to be exploded people will say protect us. We're willing to give up some of our liberties and some of our freedoms, but you must protect us. And that is what will lead us into this 21st Century, this kind of Constitutional tension of how much protection can we provide and still preserve essential liberties. And so that is a challenge that I think all of us have to address ourselves. What we need most of all is to have an understanding that we must share intelligence about terrorist activities. If you pick up information about groups that are planning attacks within your own countries

who are cross-border, then that is information that should be shared. The same is true for all of us in the hemisphere. We have an obligation to do that and I believe that it will in fact provide the kind of deterrence that we are all looking for.[59]

For Latin American military officers, however, the ideas of "shared intelligence" (such as Operación Condor, the "shared intelligence" scheme that joined the Southern Cone armed forces in international state-terrorism in the 1970s and 1980s) had very concrete reference.[60] With U.S. knowledge and indirect collaboration, Latin American military intelligence operations had attacked and assassinated "subversives" and "terrorists" in Europe, the United States, and elsewhere in the Western Hemisphere. Did U.S. policy makers really believe that monitoring by military intelligence of political and social movements across frontiers as part of counterterrorism and antidrug operations was a move that would empower civil society and encourage "democracy"? And how would Latin American officers respond to the observation that constitutional limitations on military intelligence and domestic surveillance of civilians for the United States were problems that the United States faced in combating terrorism? Perhaps they should congratulate themselves that no such inconvenient legal restrictions impeded their own operations?[61] Did Secretary Cohen mean to define this problem in a way that gave legitimacy to the Latin Americans' traditional practices: full-scale and unlimited military surveillance by military intelligence of all "potential threats"? What was the real balance between "democracy" and "security" in the "new" U.S. agenda for the hemisphere?

By 2000 it was clear that the Defense Department, the DEA, the White House Office on National Drug Control Policy, and the National Security Council had become the principal instruments of U.S. policy in Latin America, and especially in the Andean region.[62] The U.S. Department of State, weakened by temporary appointees at the highest levels for Western Hemisphere affairs and by appointment of ideologues from the Reagan years to key hemispheric positions and ambassadorships, in any case largely supported the increasingly militarized "engagement" of the United States in Latin America and the shift to the emphasis on the new security agenda of transnational threats.

Of course, official statements also continued to emphasize the commitment to democracy, human rights, and open markets.[63] Indeed, on September 11, 2001, the day that terrorists attacked the twin towers in New York and the Pentagon in Washington, D.C., the U.S.-supported Inter-American Democratic Charter, adopted by the Organization of American States (OAS) General Assembly at its special session in Lima, Peru, proclaimed, "When the special session of the General Assembly determines that there has been an unconstitutional interruption of the democratic order of a member state, and that diplomatic initiatives have failed, the special session shall take the decision to suspend said member state from the exercise of its right to participate in the OAS by an affirmative vote of two thirds of the member states in accordance with the Charter of the OAS. The suspension shall take effect immediately."[64] Revocation of the suspension would require a two-thirds vote; thus OAS decisions on exclusion of "undemocratic" governments from the regional organization might potentially affect military and civilian regimes that came to office through irregular means or that, even if legally elected, departed from democratic practices as determined by the OAS General Assembly. Given the historically preponderant influence of the United States in the OAS, this provision threatened not only military coup makers but also governments judged to have experienced an "unconstitutional interruption of the constitutional order"—an extremely ambiguous criterion given the history of irregular government succession and constitutional regimes of exception in much of the Western Hemisphere.[65] In September 2001, the members of the OAS concerned themselves less with the history of U.S. interventionism in the hemisphere and more with discouraging renewed military threats to elected civilian governments.

Yet well before the attack on the United States by Islamist terrorists on September 11, 2001, civilian and Pentagon policy makers had determined that drug trafficking, insurgency, and "instability" required further militarization of U.S. policy and actions to protect "vital interests, important interests, and other interests."[66] Democracy might serve U.S. interests, but only if it meant stability, effective law enforcement, and cooperation with the broader U.S. regional agenda. Gradually, U.S. support for democracy explicitly became a matter of security rather than an end in itself.

In October 2003 an OAS special conference on regional security identified "new threats" to security in the Western Hemisphere:

a. Terrorism, transnational organized crime, the global drug problem corruption, asset laundering, and illicit weapon trafficking;
b. Extreme poverty and social exclusion of broad sectors of the population;
c. Natural disasters, diseases, and environmental degradation;
d. Trafficking in persons;
e. Attacks on cyber security;
f. The risks of accidents during transport of hazardous materials (petroleum, radioactive materials, and toxic waste);
g. The possibility of access to and use of weapons of mass destruction.[67]

The "securitization" of poverty and social exclusion responded to the concerns of several Latin American participants; otherwise, with the possible exception of potential attacks on cyber security, it was difficult to see why any of the threats listed were considered new, corresponding more or less to the re-framed U.S. security agenda for the hemisphere, since 1990 and then 2001, with the usual nod to the commitment to democracy and markets.[68] In the course of the meetings, Colombia's ambassador to the OAS, Horacio Serpa Uribe, called on the Conference on Hemispheric Security to continue the fight on terrorism in all its forms, adding that Colombia was seeking solidarity from the member states of the OAS and the United Nations in its battle against terrorism, drug trafficking, and political violence. In Colombia, and the Andean region more generally, the U.S. regional security agenda faced its most serious challenges.

The Andean Region in Post-1990 U.S. Security Policies

As the U.S. Latin American security policies changed in the post-1990 era, the Andean region became the primary focus of defense planning and of "Latin American" policy.[69] With the peace accords in El Salvador in 1992 and in Guatemala in 1996, and the apparent defeat of the Sendero Luminoso move-ment in Peru, only in Colombia did significant Cold War–era insurgencies continue.[70] Moreover, the Andean region was the primary cultivation and processing zone for several drug crops; the base for important drug cartels; a market for the illegal arms trade; and a center of money laundering, interna-tional organized crime, and varied sorts of terrorism/violent crime. In the mid-1990s, "success" of the highly militarized U.S.–Peru antidrug strategy cut the coca air bridge from the Huallaga Valley to Colombia but had the unin-tended consequence of shifting coca cultivation from the southern Andes to Colombia (see chapters 4–6 on Ecuador, Bolivia, and Peru). Drug money gradually made the FARC, the ELN, and, later, the Autodefensas Unidas de Colombia (AUC) ever more dangerous and resilient adversaries of the Colom-bian governments. The guerrillas extended their control over territory, be-came better armed, and often outgunned the Colombian military.

In the Department of Defense's 2001 "Annual Report to the President and the Congress," prepared by the outgoing Clinton Pentagon team, the United States reaffirmed its commitment to democracy, human rights, rule of law, civilian control of the military, and peaceful dispute settlement among the re-gion's countries. The only essential security concerns mentioned reaffirmed the basic elements of the post-1990 redefinition of security policy and the par-ticular concern with the Andean region, especially Colombia.

> The United States and nations of this hemisphere share an interest in develop-ing successful counters to transnational threats such as illicit narcotics cultiva-tion, production, and trafficking; arms trafficking; terrorism, organized crime;

and illegal immigration and refugee flows in the region. Colombia is the strategic point for U.S. efforts to make a major impact on U.S. bound illegal drug traffic. Of the $1.3 billion in supplemental funding that the United States is spending in FY 2000–2001 to support Colombian counterdrug efforts, DoD programs comprise $154 million, or twelve percent of the total. These DoD programs will assist Colombia and its neighbors to develop counterdrug detection and interdiction capabilities.[71]

When the second *Quadrennial Defense Review Report* appeared (September 30, 2001), signed by Secretary of Defense Donald H. Rumsfeld, the terrorist attacks on the twin towers in New York and the Pentagon in Washington, D.C., of September 11, 2001, had somewhat refocused U.S. concerns in Latin America, making still clearer the salience of Colombia and the Andean region in U.S. regional security policy. Greater attention, understandably, was given to nonstate actors, international terrorism, and "failed" or "failing" states. The only specific mention of security concerns in Latin America in this Defense Review Report again referred to the Andean region:

> While the Western Hemisphere remains largely at peace, the danger exists that crises or insurgencies, particularly within the Andean region, might spread across borders, destabilize neighboring states, and place U.S. economic and political interests at risk. Increasing challenges and threats emanating from the territories of weak and failing states. The absence of capable or responsible governments in many countries in wide areas of Asia, Africa, and the Western Hemisphere creates a fertile ground for non-state actors engaging in drug trafficking, terrorism, and other activities that spread across borders.[72]

In 1999, the Colombian government had announced its Plan Colombia to confront the multiple security, development, human rights, drug crop cultivation, and drug-trafficking challenges it faced. Shortly thereafter, in July 2000, the United States announced its monetary, military, and normative support for the Colombian administration; Congress appropriated some $860 million dollars for support of Plan Colombia in fiscal year 2000–2001.[73] Testimony from an official of the U.S. General Accounting Office, after listing the challenges facing Colombia and the deficiencies in military, human rights, antinarcotics, and administrative aspects of Plan Colombia, concluded that if these problems were not overcome, "Plan Colombia cannot succeed as envisioned."[74]

This prediction proved more than accurate as conditions worsened in Colombia and throughout much of the Andean region during the next two years. Careful reading of the testimony in the U.S. Senate in April 2002, by Major General Gary Speer, U.S. Army, acting commander in chief of the U.S. Southern Command, provided insight into the progressive militarization of U.S. Andean region policy and the further erosion of government capabilities in Colombia. Moreover, the Colombian and Andean security concerns now merged into the global war on terrorism.[75] Even illegal immigration and other long-standing issues in hemispheric relations had been blended into the international and regional security agenda. Seemingly serious, Speer even characterized illicit drugs as "weapons of mass destruction."

> The Revolutionary Armed Forces of Colombia (FARC), the National Liberation Army of Colombia (ELN) and the United Self Defense Group of Colombia (AUC) are all on the State Department's list of Foreign Terrorist Organizations. The FARC has been implicated in kidnappings and attacks against United States citizens and interests, including the murder of three U.S. citizens in 1999. According to the Department of State's most recent "Patterns of Global Terrorism" report, 86 percent of all terrorist acts against U.S. interests throughout the world in 2000 occurred in Latin America, predominately in Colombia.
>
> . . . Illegal drugs inflict an enormous toll on the people and economy of the United States and our hemispheric neighbors, and appropriately, have often been characterized as a weapon of mass destruction. According to the latest Office of National Drug Control Policy figures, Americans spend more than $64 billion on illegal drugs while drug abuse killed more than 19,000 Americans and accounted for $160 billion in expenses and lost revenue. Most of the world's cocaine and a significant portion of the heroin entering the United States are produced in the Andean Region.[76]

Colombia deserved special attention in Major General Speer's testimony as U.S. military and civilian policy makers, and especially the DoD's Office of the Secretary of Defense (OSD) subordinate Special Operations and Low-Intensity Conflict (SOLIC) office, sought to link more explicitly the drug war and drug trade to the global war against terrorism:

> No other region is suffering the destabilizing effects of transnational threats more than the Andean Ridge countries. In Colombia, the FARC, ELN, and AUC have created an environment of instability in which the Government of Colombia does not control portions of the country. In the areas where military and police are not present and do not have control, there is lack of a safe and secure environment, which undermines the ability to govern and permits terrorism and crime to flourish. The violence in Colombia remains a significant threat to the region as the combination and links among guerrillas, terrorists, drug-traffickers, and illegal self-defense forces have severely stressed the government's ability to exercise sovereignty and maintain security. The FARC and other illegal groups cross into neighboring countries at will. In addition, neighboring countries remain transshipment points for arms and drugs entering and exiting Colombia. . . . *Simply put, the FARC is a terrorist organization that conducts violent terrorist attacks to undermine the security and stability of Colombia, financed by its involvement in every aspect of drug cultivation, production and transportation, as well as by kidnapping and extortion.*[77]

Thus the antidrug trafficking policies of the 1990s and Plan Colombia became part of the U.S. global war on terror.[78] With this in mind, USSOUTHCOM complained regarding the restrictions it faced in assisting the Colombia military and police; since the counterdrug efforts could not be easily separated from the counterinsurgency programs, it would be necessary to use Plan Colombia funds to control or destroy the guerrillas and perhaps the paramilitary forces operating in Colombia and across its borders.[79] Likewise it would be necessary to expand regional military operations: "We continue to improve our infrastructure at the Forward Operating Location (FOL) in Manta, Ecuador. Last year, operations at the FOL ceased for six months while we made runway improvements. The current construction for living quarters and maintenance facilities will be completed in June 2002. The infrastructure upgrades for the FOL at Curaçao are in progress, but Aruba remains unfunded. The FOLs are critical to our source zone counterdrug operations and provide coverage in the transit zone Pacific where we have seen the greatest increase in drug smuggling activity."[80] For SOUTHCOM, of course, the drug war had been its major mission, like it or not, for almost a decade; linking the drug war with Plan Colombia and the war on terror relegitimated its more conventional *military* missions and, just as importantly, its budget requests to Congress. Some consideration was given to direct U.S. military participation in the counterinsurgency, but political considerations blocked this option.[81]

As always in Washington, D.C., bureaucratic politics within the Pentagon and amongst the various foreign policy players, from the Department of State and the DEA to the FBI, affected U.S. foreign policy toward Latin America and the Andean region. Most U.S. policies require some sort of collaboration among departments and various agencies. Each agency seeks to put forward the best picture of its programs to Congress, to emphasize any small successes, to minimize or hide failures, and to request additional funding. Interagency coordination is rarely smooth and often conflictive. Private contractors and the foreign aid constituency, both civilian and military, add their voices to support the budget lines that feed the addiction to failure.

But Western Hemisphere policy, overall, had become increasingly militarized. In the air and on the ground, any formal restrictions separating the drug control missions from the counterterrorist missions were increasingly difficult to enforce—even for the air missions out of the FOLs.[82] At the same time, economic interests merged with security interests, especially the Colombia oil pipeline. In addition to counterdrug assistance, the Administration proposed to Congress $98 million, for FY 2003, to help Colombia to enhance the training and equipping of units to protect the Caño Limón–Coveñas oil pipeline, one of the most vulnerable elements of the economic infrastructure. According to Peter W. Rodman, assistant secretary of defense for international security affairs, funds were needed to train and equip vetted

Colombian units to protect that country's most threatened piece of critical economic infrastructure—the first 170 kilometers of the Caño-Limón oil pipeline. "This segment is the most often attacked. U.S. assistance and training will support two Colombian army brigades, National Police, and marines operating in the area. These units through ground and air mobility will be in a better position to prevent and disrupt attacks on the pipeline and defend key facilities and vulnerable points such as pumping stations. These units will also send a message that the Colombian State is committed to defending its economic infrastructure—resources that provide sorely needed employment and revenue—from terrorist attacks."[83] If approved, this training will assist the Colombians to exert effective sovereignty in the Arauca Department, where these attacks primarily occur. Through a comprehensive strategy of reconnaissance and surveillance, offensive and quick reaction operations, the Colombian military will be better able to mitigate the debilitating economic and financial effects of constant attacks on critical infrastructure.[84] U.S. Army Special Forces were deployed to Arauca in late 2002, in part to train elements of the Colombian Eighteenth Brigade as a rapid reaction force, and other soldiers as helicopter elements, thereby improving pipeline security.[85] Congress

FIGURE 1.2
With financial interests at stake in the oil fields of eastern Colombia the United States has beefed up its presence in the area by sending in Special Forces trainers to assist the local troops. Sarravena, Arauca, Colombia, February 2003. Photo courtesy of Jason P. Howe/WpN.

gave the Bush administration some $93 million for pipeline security in the 2003 budget.[86] Another $147 million was provided for the same program in 2004, and more than seventy U.S. Special Forces officers were tasked to train two elite battalions of Colombian soldiers to protect the pipeline, 50 percent of which is owned by U.S.-based Occidental Petroleum.[87] From 2001 to 2005 the number of attacks on the pipeline were significantly reduced; nevertheless, in February 2005 guerrilla attacks forced the pipeline to shut down for approximately two weeks.[88]

Beyond concern for pipeline security, Major General Speer acknowledged that U.S. counterdrug (CD) efforts to date had not been altogether successful. With regard to the drug war, in particular, cocaine supply continued to exceed demand, and "although Colombia and other partner nations are willing to work with us to counter the production and trafficking of illegal drugs, effective and sustainable counterdrug operations are beyond the capabilities of their thinly stretched security forces."[89] Moreover, "with Colombia's narcoterrorists increasingly supporting themselves through drug trafficking, it is increasingly difficult for the security forces to sustain a secure environment that allows democratic institutions to fully function, permits political, economic, and social reforms to take hold, and reduces the destabilizing spillover into neighboring countries." And, "although we have seen great progress through the military portion of the first year of Plan Colombia, the Colombian military still lacks all of the essential resources to create a safe and secure environment in Colombia. As mentioned previously, fundamental security and stability are necessary for the Government of Colombia to remain a viable, legitimate government and for other supporting programs to succeed."[90]

Speer then specifically requested that the counterdrug restrictions on U.S. military operations in Colombia regarding the drug war be formally modified.[91]

> If enacted, the Administration's FY 2002 supplemental request to expand our authorities in Colombia will provide some relief by lifting these restriction for United States funded equipment, assets, and programs for Colombia. Even, without any additional funding or resources, *this authority would allow us to look at the FARC, (AUC and ELN) not only as drug traffickers, but also as a narco-terrorist organization and to gather and share information on their activities across the board. Additionally, from an interdiction standpoint, again with the assets already provided, instead of attempting to interdict only drugs leaving Colombia, we would be able to look for the arms entering the country, which are fueling the FARC, ELN, and AUC. For Colombia, the expanded authority, if approved, would allow them to use the helicopters we provide and the CN Brigade for missions other than counterdrug.*[92]

The formal expansion of SOUTHCOM Plan Colombia missions would include intelligence operations. Speer continued, "Our ability to assist operations in Colombia is also limited by restrictions on sharing data. We are prohibited from providing intelligence that may be construed as counterinsurgency related. For the operator, it is very difficult to distinguish between the FARC as a drug trafficking organization and the FARC as a terrorist organization and the FARC as an insurgent organization. In my opinion, we have tried to impose artificial boundaries where one no longer exists."[93] Finally, "*While Southern Command's priority since September 11 has been on the planning and coordination necessary to execute the global war on terrorism, everything we are doing in Colombia and in the region supports that end. Our efforts in Colombia are not only to fight drugs but also to save democracy in that country and promote security and stability in the Andean Region.*"[94]

During the next six months various U.S. government agencies echoed the Pentagon's new characterization of the situation in the Andean region, including changes in emphasis in Plan Colombia and in the Andean Regional Initiative.[95] Illustratively, the DEA "continues to develop overwhelming evidence about the connection between the Revolutionary Armed Forces of Colombia (FARC), other terrorist groups in the Andean region, and the drug trade. The U.S. State Department has officially designated the FARC, National Liberation Army (ELN), and the United Self-Defense Groups of Colombia (AUC) as 'Foreign Terrorist Organizations.'"[96]

The FARC and ELN have routinely kidnapped U.S. citizens and attacked U.S. economic interests in Colombia. According to the 2001 U.S. State Department Annual Report on Global Patterns of Terrorism, 55 percent of all the terrorist acts in the world reportedly were committed in Colombia by the FARC or ELN. The report also claims that almost 85 percent of the terrorist attacks (219 attacks) against U.S. interests occurred in Colombia. Of these attacks, 178 reportedly were directed against the Caño Limón-Covenas oil pipeline. Since 1980, the FARC has murdered 13 U.S. citizens and kidnapped over 100 more, including the 1993 kidnapping of three U.S. missionaries, who now are believed dead. . . . Over recent months, there have been numerous reports of members and associates of the FARC exchanging cocaine or cash for weapons with arms suppliers from around the world. Although uncorroborated, these arms suppliers include criminals, revolutionary groups, and corrupt government officials from Mexico, Nicaragua, Russia, Venezuela, and other countries. Some of the weapons that allegedly have been exchanged for drugs include AK-47 rifles, M60 machine guns, rocket-propelled grenades, and MANPAD surface-to-air missiles (IGLS, STRELA, and Stinger missiles).[97]

The Department of State followed suit in October 2002. At a conference titled "Colombia at a Crossroads: Challenges Confronting the Uribe Administration," sponsored by the Center for Strategic Studies (CSIS), Thomas Shannon, U.S. deputy assistant secretary of state for Western Hemisphere Affairs, asserted that "Colombia is a democratic state under assault" by narco-terrorist organizations. Shannon added that "U.S. recognition of such factors as the

FIGURE 1.3
Fighters of the right-wing AUC militia are accused of more than 80 percent of all atrocities committed in Colombia; the group operates throughout the country and is made up of many ethnic groups. La Dorada, Putumayo, Colombia. February 2003. Photo courtesy of Jason P. Howe/WpN.

moribund nature of Colombia's peace process, the emergence of the Revolutionary Armed Forces of Colombia (FARC) as a narco-terrorist organization, the clear rejection of the FARC by the Colombian people, the increased involvement of the United Self-Defense Forces of Colombia (AUC) in drug trafficking, and that group's designation as a terrorist organization prompted 'a fundamental shift' in U.S. policy toward Colombia."

The United States now recognized that "Colombia needs to adopt a combined counter-drug and counter-terrorism approach that reflects the nation's new reality." Accordingly, "the Bush administration's request for almost $100 million for oil pipeline protection in Colombia was a 'significant' first step in supporting the nation's counter-terrorism efforts." Shannon emphasized that new counterterrorism funding approved that year by the U.S. Congress "further supports this shift by lifting the restriction that previously limited U.S. assistance to Colombia to counter-narcotics efforts and now allows counter-terrorism assistance as well." This shift would mean, among other things, "increased intelligence sharing with Colombian armed forces."[98]

More and more, Colombia and the Andean region became a part of the new U.S. global security agenda, particularly the "war against terrorism." What this

FIGURE 1.4
New solutions or means of making progress in the conflict are constantly sought out.
The results of every technological advance or new strategy are the same: more death
and destruction. Tame, Arauca, Colombia. January 2003. Photo courtesy of Jason P.
Howe/WpN.

would mean for Colombia, the region, and for the United States, in the short
run, seemed clear: subordination of democratization (except for elections)
and institution building to internal security and antidrug requirements, and
more civilian casualties.[99]

Colombia's new minister of defense, Marta Lucía Ramírez, seemed to acknowledge this prognosis as well as to welcome incorporation of Colombia,
and Plan Colombia, into the global war on terrorism. Going further, she called
for European support and United Nations' assistance in Colombia under the
provisions of resolutions condemning terrorism:

> The transnational organized crime, drug traffickers, money laundering, arms
> trafficking, and the strategic alliances within the terrorist groups are developing
> a clear path to destabilize the economies and democracies in our region, because
> the former elements weaken our institutions. In the midterm weak institutions
> mean the absence of the rule of law, which in turn makes the ruthless acting of
> these groups become some sort of "the law of the land." To stop this kind of sce-
> nario from being a reality, the Colombian people have just given a strong man-
> date to President Uribe. As you are all probably aware, Colombia is facing today
> one of the greatest challenges in its history. That challenge is in the first instance

a challenge to the very existence of the State. . . . The violence that results directly or indirectly from this conflict is unimaginable: over 34,000 homicides a year; over 3,000 kidnappings, including that of one presidential candidate, five members of Congress, and 12 deputies; 370 mayors threatened with death and the whole infrastructure of the country under permanent attack. Last year alone, one of the main oil pipelines was blown 270 times, causing irreparable damage to the environment and losses of 500 million dollars to the economy (oil accounts for a third of Colombia's exports). Colombians are tired of this violence. We want to live with peace and security. . . . This is what his [Uribe's] government intends to do, through its policy of Democratic Security. . . . We are determined to combat terrorism by all means. This is not out of opportunism on the part of the government, after the tragic events of 11 September. The opposite is true: those attacks made countries such as those of the European Union realize that the terrorist conducts that they condemned in their common anti-terrorist legislation, such as kidnapping, the destruction of infrastructure or the murder of innocent civilians, were precisely the conducts that the armed groups in Colombia had been putting into practice. That is why they and we consider them terrorists, and will continue to do so, so long as they do not abstain from killing the innocent. There is no justification for the murder of civilians. For that reason, too, we call on all countries to implement resolution 1373 of the Security Council of the United Nations. There can be no country that lends its financial system or its territory to the activities of terrorist groups. The new [September 2002] National Security Strategy of the United States expresses similar views. These are precisely the sort of problems we face in Colombia, the problems that the Democratic Security and Defense Strategy is intended to address. We will make every effort, but we cannot succeed alone. If we all agree on the transnational nature of these threats and on the need to strengthen the state to guarantee the rule of law, we must draw the consequences and act responsibly: first, by taking determined and effective measures against money laundering and the illegal trade in narcotics, chemical precursors, and weapons; and second, by helping democratic states such as Colombia, which have paid a high price combating these threats with their own resources, to strengthen its institutions and enforce the rule of law. This is not a time for finger-pointing, but for true international cooperation against threats that are a grave danger to us all.[100]

Lest it be thought that the minister of defense's linkage of Colombian and global terrorism was casual, the Colombian Embassy in Washington posted on its website reasoned arguments tying terrorism in Colombia to the events of September 11, 2001, in the United States and equating the Colombia and Afghanistan scenarios.

The question is why is Colombia's experience with terrorism relevant to America today? Why should America and the world be interested in what is going on in Colombia in the wake of these most testing of times brought about by mindless terrorism? The answer is that what is happening in Colombia is not very different from what has happened in Afghanistan. This is due to the fact that Colombia is the world's largest cocaine producer, controlling 80% of the world's coca. Afghanistan is the world's largest heroin producer, controlling 75% of the world's opium poppy, three times the output of Burma, its closest competitor. . . . Vast sums of this money are laundered each year to pay for the travel, housing, planning, weapons purchases and technical backup in terrorist operations like the devastating assault on the World Trade Center and the Pentagon. So the [drug] trade is playing a crucial role in providing such resources, both in Colombia, in Afghanistan, in Iran and potentially elsewhere in the world. Therefore, thinking that by simply eliminating Osama Bin Laden and his network will substantially curb the global terrorist threat may prove to be as misguided as the hope that the elimination of Pablo Escobar, once the leader of Colombia's most powerful and violent drug cartel, would end drug trafficking. After Colombian authorities killed Escobar, he was quickly replaced by other drug lords, with more sophisticated networks that have proven very difficult to dismantle. Colombia has learned the hard way, through more than 40 years of bloodshed, that you cannot defeat an international scourge without a balanced, carrot and stick approach. Terrorism is like a cancer that must be attacked head on, with all available sources of treatment, in very harsh and unrelenting terms.[101]

President Bush said, in September 2002, that "we know that to defeat terrorism in today's globalized world we need support from our allies and friends. Wherever governments find the fight against terrorism beyond their capacities, we will match their willpower and their resources with whatever help we and our allies can provide."[102] Colombia's new president, Álvaro Uribe Vélez, seemed to be joining forces explicitly with U.S. president George W. Bush in the global war against terror—and inviting Bush to make good on his words in Colombia.[103] On October 29, 2002, the Colombian ambassador to the United States told an audience in Washington, D.C.,

Without US assistance in continuing to finance Plan Colombia and ensuring that there are sufficient resources to fund both our military effort against terrorism and drug trafficking as well as economic development programs, it is difficult to envision a lasting, peaceful outcome in Colombia. The recent "change of authorities" that allows for US aid to be used for counter-terrorism as well as counter-narcotics is an important step in the right direction. Increased intelligence sharing and military cooperation will help us capture the leaders of the terrorist groups that threaten our democracy. And of course, both the US and Colombia are hopeful that our close cooperation will lead to a decrease in the drug trade and in terrorism.[104]

A year later, on September 10, 2003, General James Hill, head of U.S. Southern Command, directly linked Middle Eastern and Latin American terrorists, concluding, "Not surprisingly, Islamic radical groups and narco-terrorists in Colombia all practice the same business methods." President Bush included an additional US$104 million for Colombia in the "emergency supplemental" foreign aid package passed in March 2003 to pay for the war in Iraq. The requested 2004 foreign aid package included US$731 million in aid for the Andean Counterdrug Initiative destined for Colombia and six other countries.[105]

The War on Drugs and the War on Terrorism

The melding of the war against the drug trade and against international terrorism (and the authorization to allow lethal assistance to Colombia for the counterterrorism and antidrug missions, after August 2002) provided the cornerstone for the resurgence, under cover of a "new" threat scenario and with a new name (cooperative security), of the main premises of the national security doctrines that shaped Latin American civil–military relations and premised the authoritarian regimes after the coup in Brazil in 1964 until the late 1980s.[106] The war against subversion and "Castro-communism" of the Cold War era had become the war against the narco-terrorists in the Andean region and international terrorism elsewhere in the late 1990s.[107] USSOUTH-COM and the civilian defense establishment (whose careers and influence depended on the credibility of security threats in Latin America) had found the "new" enemy they required to justify convincingly their activities and funding to Congress in the post–Cold War era. SOUTHCOM, never the most important unified command, always slighted in favor of Europe and Asia, had found a way to link Western Hemisphere missions to the global focus on international terrorism.[108] In addition, there were calls for a multilateral regional security apparatus with its own rapid deployment (special forces) force, perhaps under the aegis of the OAS.[109] Everywhere the U.S. government looked in the hemisphere there were "terrorist" threats.

Not incidentally the United States also proposed creation of a rapid reaction combat force within the NATO framework. General James Jones, the first U.S. Marine to become supreme allied commander in Europe, said, "The elite force, proposed by the United States last year to adapt the Cold War alliance for new security threats, could be a tool to move NATO away from a tradition of defensive reaction to crisis prevention." The same report continued, "Jones said that if the NATO force had existed on September 11, the United States would not have had to cast around for individual allies to take its military response to Afghanistan. Some Europeans are suspicious that the NATO Response Force will become an 'American Foreign Legion,' a launchpad for the United States to project its military might. Others fear it will marginalize the European Union's emerging Rapid Reaction Force."[110]

The idea of a multilateral collective security force in the Western Hemisphere dates at least from the 1930s. Many Latin Americans, however, shared

TABLE 1.1
U.S.-Identified Terrorist Threats in Latin America, 2001–2004

Country	Threat
Argentina	Middle Eastern terrorist cells (tri-border area)
Bolivia	Drug trafficking
Brazil	Middle Eastern terrorist cells (tri-border area)
Chile	Drug trafficking; money laundering for Hezbollah
Colombia	Drug trafficking; FARC (including ties to the IRA and ETA), ELN, AUC; kidnapping; Hezbollah cells
Costa Rica	Drug trafficking
Cuba	Drug trafficking; "state-sponsored" terrorist nation (primarily for harboring terrorist fugitives)
Dominican Republic	Drug trafficking; illegal immigration (from Haiti to the United States)
Ecuador	Drug trafficking; kidnapping; weapons transshipments; Middle Eastern terrorist cells
El Salvador	Drug trafficking
Guatemala	Drug trafficking; illegal immigration
Honduras	Drug trafficking; money laundering; illegal immigration
Mexico	Drug trafficking; kidnapping; illegal immigration
Nicaragua	Drug trafficking; illegal immigration
Panama	Drug trafficking; Hezbollah cells
Paraguay	Middle Eastern terrorist cells (tri-border area)
Peru	Drug trafficking; Shining Path guerrillas
Uruguay	Middle Eastern terrorist cells (especially Brazilian border)
Venezuela	Attacks on oil pipelines; links to FARC and ELN; Middle Eastern terrorist cells

Source: Greg Weeks, "Fighting Terrorism While Promoting Democracy: Competing Priorities in U.S. Defense Policy Toward Latin America" (forthcoming), compiled from "The Western Hemisphere's Response to the September 11, 2001 Terrorist Attack on the United States," hearing before the Subcommittee on the Western Hemisphere, Committee on International Relations, 107th Congress, 1st Session, Serial No. 107-43; "Patterns of Global Terrorism 2003," United States Department of State, Office of Counterterrorism (April 29, 2004); United States Department of State, Bureau of Western Hemisphere Affairs, *Country Information*, www.state.gov/p/wha/ (last accessed October 25, 2004). By permission from Greg Weeks.

the fears of the Europeans toward the new rapid deployment force. After September 11, 2001, U.S. policy makers floated the idea of resuscitating the 1947 Rio Treaty as a collective security agreement: "The Inter-American Treaty of Reciprocal Assistance ('Rio Treaty') sets a standard whereby nations would respond in their common defense, with the ultimate goal of creating a more secure environment. Our experience since September 11th in mobilizing hemispheric support and responses to fight terrorism under the OAS Charter and 'Rio Treaty' proves that the current hemispheric security structure can address the region's security needs quite well. It also demonstrated the flexibility of our security architecture to address the new and emerging threats we face."[111]

In November 2002, U.S. secretary of defense Donald Rumsfeld hinted at the possibility of more extensive "cooperative security" initiatives in the hemisphere:

> Next May, the Organization of American States will meet to review the hemisphere's security architecture. Our objective should be to strengthen those institutions, and develop new areas for concrete cooperation. I hope that this week's conference will consider two such initiatives: First is an initiative to foster regional naval cooperation. The objective would be to strengthen the operational and planning capabilities of partner nations, upgrade national command and control systems, and improve regional information-sharing. This could potentially include cooperation among coast guards, customs, and police forces. I suggest we consider a round-table as a good way to consider and pursue this initiative. Second is an initiative to improve the hemisphere's peacekeeping capabilities. Many of you are already leaders in this field—you are sending skilled and experienced forces, with specialized capabilities, to global hot spots. We should explore the possibility of integrating these various specialized capabilities into larger regional capabilities—so that we can participate as a region in peacekeeping and stability operations.[112]

In March 2003 a major conference sponsored by the U.S. Army Strategic Studies Institute, U.S. Southern Command, and the Dante B. Fascell North-South Center of the University of Miami discussed "Building Security Cooperation in the Western Hemisphere."[113] One of the speakers had recently written, "Hegemony is not a dirty word, but its usage today often elicits negative visceral responses because it is interpreted as imperialism, when it actually connotes leadership."[114] The author, Colonel Joseph Núñez, a professor of national security and strategy at the U.S. Army War College, had also been a strong proponent for creating a new regional command within the Unified Command Plan for the Americas: "Creating an Americas Command, where homeland and hemispheric security issues are strategically merged, expands opportunity for multinational cooperation that protects our democratic community. Our neighbors are watching, hopeful that we act to provide a better framework for fighting terrorism, reassuring allies, and expanding security cooperation in the Americas."[115]

The Latin American military institutions that had feared for their relative autonomy, traditional internal security missions, and covert collaboration with their U.S. counterparts also saw opportunities in the melding of antiterrorism and the drug war.[116] In the same week of the Colombian ambassador's October 2002 speech in Washington, D.C., the commander of the Argentine army explained to a group of diplomats, economists, and businessmen in Buenos Aires that "defense must be treated as an integral matter," without the artificial distinction between internal and external security. Defense policy had to focus on the "new threats": massive flows of immigration from countries facing critical situations, armed insurgencies, organized crime and transnational threats, and overexploitation of natural resources. Lt. General Ricardo Brinzoni emphasized that it was necessary to "be prepared to defend ourselves at any moment" against various threats, and for that purpose the Argentine army was considering a "strategic system based on cooperation among the South American nations." This new system would be premised on "cooperative security" rather than "collective security"—and the basic concept would be preemption (*adelantarse a los peligros*).[117]

The Condor was again in flight in the Southern Cone and, with the cooperation of the United States, extending its hunting range into the Andean region and beyond. Simultaneously, during 2002 and into 2003 the military and human rights situation in most of the Andean region deteriorated, more U.S. military personnel arrived as "advisers," more "contractors" were hired to perform a variety of military and semi-military missions, political violence and instability increased, the number of civilian casualties mounted, and refugees from the violence fled their homes, many crossing borders. Internal opposition to U.S. insistence on crop eradication in programs in Bolivia and Peru provoked social mobilization against incumbent governments and fueled a growing anti-U.S. sentiment. Populist rhetoric swayed electorates and increasingly polarized politics from Venezuela south. Throughout the region the proclaimed objectives of U.S. policies—stability, consolidation of democracy and the rule of law, economic growth and increasing social welfare, a victory in the "war on drugs," and security itself—seemed more elusive than anytime since 1990.[118]

Resistance to the free trade and more global neoliberal economic agenda became more overt and intense in Guatemala and other parts of Central America, Ecuador, Peru, and Bolivia—to the point of forcing an elected president out of office in the latter country in October 2003 and his successor to resign as protests cut off the capital from the rest of the country in June 2005.[119] In December 2005 Bolivians elected as president Evo Morales, the leader of the coca growers union, an avid opponent of the U.S. neoliberal economic agenda in the hemisphere and likely ally of Venezuela's president Hugo Chávez. Secretary of State Condoleezza Rice had demonized Chávez as "a real problem" and "a threat to democracy in the region." She asserted that it was necessary to watch "his activities," and to "make it costly at least politically for Chávez to carry out anti-democratic activities either at home or in the region is really about where we are."[120] Morales's election added to the U.S. administration's concern regarding the tide of "radical populism" in the hemisphere. In Ecuador opponents of the Palacio's government that came to power in 2005 threatened strikes and street protests if the proposed free trade agreement with the United States was not put to a popular referendum.[121] Violent

TABLE 1.2
Unscheduled Presidential Successions, 1991–2005

September	1991	Haiti	Jean-Bertrand Aristide ousted by General Raúl Cedrás
December	1992	Brazil	Fernando Collor de Mello resigns as Senate prepares impeachment
June	1993	Guatemala	Jorge Serrano Elías resigns, under political pressure and threat of a military coup
August	1993	Venezuela	Congress ousts Carlos Andrés Pérez
February	1997	Ecuador	Congress ousts Abdalá Bucaram
March	1999	Paraguay	Raúl Cubas resigns after months of conflict with congress and the judicial branch
January	2000	Ecuador	Jamil Mahuad ousted in coup
November	2000	Peru	Alberto Fujimori resigns, after fleeing to Japan
December	2001	Argentina	Fernando de la Rúa resigns amidst social unrest
April	2002	Venezuela	Aborted coup briefly ousts Hugo Chávez, who then returns to the presidency
October	2003	Bolivia	Gonzalo Sánchez de Lozada resigns and leaves the country amidst social unrest and popular protests
February	2004	Haiti	Jean-Bertrand Aristide is removed from office and flown out of the country
April	2005	Ecuador	Lucio Gutiérrez ousted by Congress
June	2005	Bolivia	Carlos Mesa resigns as workers, peasants, and Indian leaders blockade roads and demand nationalization of gas and oil

protests in Quito and Guayaquil in early March 2006 against the free trade agreement, against further privatization of government services, and against the U.S. base at Manta coincided with strikes by petroleum workers, some demanding an end to contracts with Occidental Petroleum. As in Bolivia, Venezuela, and Peru, the U.S. neoliberal project became a focus for political opposition in Ecuador. Adding fuel to the fire, ex-Brazilian president Fernando Henrique Cardoso declared in an interview in Quito that Latin Americans should be grateful for the United States' "benign neglect" (*desprecio generoso*), since when the United States pays more attention to the region, "it is to intervene in our affairs, and we shouldn't accept its intervention." Cardoso added his criticism of the Bush administration's "backward and reactionary policies" toward South America, particularly in the areas of environmental policy and world peace.[122]

Despite such criticism, U.S. policy makers seemed ever less willing to consider the possibility that U.S. global and regional policies themselves, and the manner of their implementation, had engendered growing opposition and discontent in the Western Hemisphere. They seemed unable to fathom that aggressive, militaristic unilateralism; hegemonic pretensions; the misguided and mismanaged war on terror and its fusion with the war on drugs; and the neoliberal economic package marketed unabashedly as the region's salvation had contributed significantly to political instability, increased citizen insecurity, environmental degradation, and increased poverty—that is, to the overall failure to achieve U.S. policy objectives in Latin America during the last decade.[123]

Addicted to Failure?

Whether the unfortunate course of U.S. economic and security policies in the Andean region could be altered in the context of a more generalized and merged "war on drugs" and "war on terror" remained in doubt.[124] No major change seemed likely, especially after the reelection of George W. Bush and with the nation's civilian defense establishment in the hands of the neoconservative fraternity that had proclaimed the principles of the "Project for a New American Century" (PNAC) in 1997 and followed up with "Rebuilding America's Defenses. Strategy, Forces and Resources for a New Century" in 2000.[125] This report called for "expanding America's security perimeter" and for "new overseas bases and forward operating locations to facilitate American political and military operations around the world."[126] Within this strategic vision, the new bases and forward operating locations in Ecuador, Curaçao, Aruba, Suriname, and Central America, as well as the increased militarization of the drug war and its transformation into a war against "narco-terrorists," became part of the U.S. global mission: a crusade to make the world safe for "market-democracy."[127] Recommendations in a report by Max G. Manwaring in early 2003 included the need to "professionalize and modernize security institutions to a level where they have the capability to neutralize and/or destroy all the illegal perpetrators of violence—regardless of label."[128]

Unintended Consequences of U.S. Policies

The unintended consequences from this war on "terrorism" in the Andean Republics and in the United States itself continued to mount. After meetings between Ecuador's president, Lucio Gutiérrez, and Colombia's Alvaro Uribe in mid-March 2004, Reuters reported that Colombia had agreed to reinforce its war-torn border, where the Ecuadorians had deployed some seven thousand troops and Colombia over eight thousand. In 2003 Ecuador had requested an end to fumigation on the border due to concerns of environmental damage and displaced persons crossing the border. Official Ecuadorian army publications described the additional air, sea, and land patrols in efforts to stem the tide of drugs, arms, and "illegal combatants."[129] Nevertheless, arms smuggling, kidnapping, refugee flows, and border skirmishes increased steadily.[130] In September 2004, *El Comercio* (Quito) reported that Ecuadorian army units had encountered three FARC bases in Sucumbíos province, probably used as medical facilities and training and supply centers; the report added that battles between FARC and Colombian forces near the Putumayo and San Miguel Rivers had accelerated movement of guerrilla forces into Ecuador.[131] In the same week, *El Nacional* reported from Venezuela on a complex arms, gasoline, and drug commerce carried out on the Venezuelan–Colombian–Brazilian frontier, from which the FARC was receiving grenades and other arms.[132]

By early 2006 the conflict in the Ecuador–Colombia border region had greatly worsened as FARC and Colombian army incursions into Ecuador and Colombian military overflights of Ecuadorian territory angered Ecuadorian authorities. On February 20, 2006, the Ecuadorian defense ministry reported armed encounters between FARC units and the Ecuadorian army in Sucumbíos. FARC leader Raúl Reyes denied that combat had occurred but also offered solidarity *with Venezuela* if the United States should invade that country.[133] Reyes took the opportunity to characterize Colombian president Uribe as a "narco para military" (*narcoparamilitar*).[134] Meanwhile, repeated military and guerrilla incursions across the Colombian–Venezuelan border also exacerbated regional tensions.

But U.S. policy makers seemed immune to feedback, condemned not to learn. In 2000, Eduardo Gamarra, director of the Center of Latin America and the Caribbean at Florida International University, wrote about the Andean region, "The conflicts with guerrillas, paramilitary groups and drug traffickers seem interminable. Crumbling party systems, electoral fraud, and military coups have brought to power populist leaders of doubtful democratic vocation. Rising urban crime rates and peasant protests have created general insecurity amongst the citizenry. Further, strategies for economic growth have not bettered the living standards of the great majority of the population."[135]

Yet U.S. policy makers and military leaders continued to employ the same tired rhetoric, to provide Congress with misleading success stories and requests for more funds—for more of the same. SOUTHCOM commander James Hill visited Ecuador in February 2004 to reassure the Ecuadorian government that logistical support for troops deployed on the Colombian border would continue.[136] A month later, on March 2, 2004, Robert B. Charles, assistant secretary for International Narcotics and Law Enforcement Affairs, told the U.S. Congress,

> Drugs and crime undermine democracy, rule of law, and the stability required for economic development. The drug trade continues to kill our young people, and the bulk of the drugs arriving in the United States still come from the Andean re-

gion. The drug trade also funds terrorists in this Hemisphere and other regions. These are the stark realities. Set against them is our methodical ACI program, in its many parts. And that program is producing results. Projects in Colombia, Bolivia, Peru, Ecuador, Brazil, Venezuela, and Panama are integrated. I am making sure that our assets are being used in the most effective manner and that performance criteria for projects are strengthened in order to better measure results. We have reached a tipping point in Colombia—for the first time we may be close to delivering a lasting blow to narco-terrorists. Sustained support for President Uribe is essential. I appreciate this Committee's strong commitment to our efforts and look forward to exchanging views on how to carry this effort into the future. In all of this, there is a real mission. And in the mission, there is the real potential for lasting results that will change our world—for the better.[137]

Later in March, General Hill testified before Congress,

The security picture in Latin America and the Caribbean has grown more complex over the past year. Colombia's considerable progress in the battle against narcoterrorism is offset by negative developments elsewhere in the region, particularly in Haiti, Bolivia, and Venezuela. These developments represent an increasing threat to U.S. interests. We face two primary types of threats in the region: an established set of threats detailed in previous years and a nascent set likely to raise serious issues during this year. On the traditional front, we still face threats from narcoterrorists and their ilk, a growing threat to law and order in partner nations from urban gangs and other illegal armed groups, which are also generally tied to the narcotics trade, and a lesser but sophisticated threat from Islamic radical groups in the region. These traditional threats are now complemented by an emerging threat best described as radical populism, in which the democratic process is undermined to decrease rather than protect individual rights. Some leaders in the region are tapping into deep-seated frustrations of the failure of democratic reforms to deliver expected goods and services. By tapping into these frustrations, which run concurrently with frustrations caused by social and economic inequality, the leaders are at the same time able to reinforce their radical positions by inflaming anti-U.S. sentiment. Additionally, other actors are seeking to undermine U.S. interests in the region by supporting these movements. These traditional and emerging threats are overlaid upon states in the region that are generally marked by weak institutions and struggling economies. This resulting frailty of state control can lead to ungoverned or ill-governed spaces and people, corruption, and clientelism. The militaries we work with in the area of responsibility are feeling the brunt of both threats and weak governments, but for the most part have supported their respective constitutions, remained professional, and respected human rights. They will be under increasing pressure from these stressors over the next several years. Consequently, we must maintain and broaden our consistent military-to-military contacts as a means of irrevocably institutionalizing the professional nature of those militaries with which we have worked so closely over the past several decades.[138]

What General Hill called "radical populism" others saw as "democracy from below"—a genuinely grassroots reaction to the negative effects of neoliberal policies, the drug war, and the intensified squeeze on, and impoverishment of, millions of Latin Americans juxtaposed to the increasing concentration of wealth and income, corruption, and cynicism in hemispheric politics. The dismal failure of U.S. antidrug and "antiterrorist" policies to attain the enunciated objectives brought more and worse of the same: a harsher war on drugs, more corruption, more violence, and less security for the vast majority of the population in the Andean region, Central America, and Mexico. General Hill now expressed his concern that "radical populism" generated from frustration, inequality, and poverty threatened U.S. interests and security in the Western Hemisphere. He proposed, as U.S. military and civilian policy makers had done in the Cold War era, strengthening U.S. ties with the region's armed forces to overcome the "frailty of state control [that] can lead to ungoverned or ill-governed spaces and people, corruption, and clientelism." So-called mil-to-mil contacts might prove useful in certain circumstances, but they could not overcome the fundamentally flawed U.S. policies themselves.[139]

General Hill did not consider the possibility that while U.S. policies did not, by themselves, "cause" the Andean regional crisis or the more generalized "frustration" throughout the region, they did exacerbate them.[140] In the first years of the twenty-first century governments aligned with the U.S. antidrug and neoliberal economic agenda in Ecuador (2000, 2003) and Bolivia (2003, 2005) were removed from power, and public support for the Peruvian president, an ally of the United States in its drug war and antiterrorist agenda, reached all-time lows. The ousted president of Bolivia in 2003 blamed his fall on a narco-terrorist conspiracy organized in Cuba, Libya, and Venezuela— and told Washington policy makers that Bolivia could become the "Afghanistan of the Andes."[141] In Venezuela, the nationalist Bolivarian Revolution of ex-coup leader Colonel Hugo Chávez actively opposed U.S. policies, and tensions between Venezuela and Colombia continued rising. Indeed, in June 2004 the Colombian government announced deployment of a new military frontier brigade (the Décima Brigada), headquartered in Castilletes (Guajira); it would include special forces and, perhaps, tanks recently contracted for (but not yet delivered) in Spain.[142] Meanwhile, in Colombia, political violence, guerrilla attacks and criminality, counterinsurgency, and the drug war persisted. Only in Colombia did the country's most important newspaper, *El Tiempo*, feature a *permanent* section of the paper, like sports, travel, or business, called "Conflicto Armado" (Armed Conflict).

On August 17, 2004, the White House issued a presidential determination supporting continuing and intensified "interdiction of aircraft reasonably suspected to be primarily engaged in illicit drug trafficking":

Memorandum for the Secretary of State and the Secretary of Defense
SUBJECT: Continuation of U.S. Drug Interdiction Assistance to the Government of Colombia
Presidential Determination: No. 2004-42

Pursuant to the authority vested in me by section 1012 of the National Defense Authorization Act for Fiscal Year 1995, as amended (22 U.S.C. 2291-4), I hereby certify, with respect to Colombia, that: (1) interdiction of aircraft reasonably suspected to be primarily engaged in illicit drug trafficking in that country's airspace is necessary because of the extraordinary threat posed by illicit drug trafficking to the national security of that country; and (2) that country has appropriate procedures in place to protect against innocent loss of life in the air and on the ground in connection with such interdiction, which shall at a minimum include effective means to identify and warn an aircraft before the use of force is directed against the aircraft. The Secretary of State is authorized and directed to publish this determination in the Federal Register and to notify the Congress of this determination.[143]

GEORGE W. BUSH

According to the U.S. Information Agency website, "President Bush has authorized the U.S. Department of State to continue assistance to Colombia in carrying out an Airbridge Denial Program against civil aircraft suspected of trafficking illicit drugs. . . . The program supplies Colombia with equipment and intelligence to stem airborne drug traffic. In granting this authorization, . . . the president has determined that Colombia has appropriate procedures in place to guard against the loss of innocent lives in connection with the interdiction effort." The USINFO statement added that "the Airbridge Denial Program was suspended in April 2001 after a missionary plane was mistakenly shot down in Peru.[144] With new safety protocols in place, Colombia reintroduced the program with U.S. assistance in August of 2003, and captured or destroyed seven aircraft in the last four months of the year."[145]

Thus, the end of the U.S. summer of 2004 portended more of the same futile policies, at taxpayer expense, and also more bloodshed in Mexico, the Andean region, Central America, and the Caribbean. Never mind the conclusion of the Justice Department's National Drug Intelligence Center: "Key indicators of domestic cocaine availability show stable or slightly increased availability in drug markets throughout the country. . . . Heroin is readily available in most major metropolitan areas in the United States, and availability remains relatively stable. . . . [H]eroin availability continues to increase in rural and suburban areas."[146] Moreover, the efforts to eradicate poppy production in Colombia had produced a new "balloon effect" as cultivation increased in

Peru. According to congressman Henry Hyde, chair of the House International Relations Committee,

> We have made great progress in the eradication of opium in Colombia, as we have previously said. Now we are seeing the shift of opium to nearby Peru, and U.S. policy and strategy have not yet made the shift. . . . Recent Ministry of Peru data indicates that Peru may now have 1,400 hectares of opium, mostly in the north near the Ecuador and Colombian border, and opium latex is now being trafficked by Colombian drug dealers through Ecuador into Colombia for processing into heroin. A recent seizure of 440 kilos of opium in Peru (nearly a half ton of opium) shows how serious the growth of opium is now in that nearby nation and why Peru needs an opium eradication plan.[147]

If the Bush administration could not recognize failure of the blended war on drugs and terrorism, some American newspapers had experienced a revelation. In early May 2005, the *Pittsburgh Post-Gazette* editorialized, "U.S. policy toward Colombia, America's third-largest aid beneficiary, has turned into a sinkhole of money and military resources over the past five years. . . . Instead of pulling the plug on this unsuccessful enterprise, the Bush administration is now asking for $734 million more to finance it for yet another year. It is worth asking why."[148] The editorial continued with its explanation for the administration's enthusiasm for the drug war and its Andean security policies—and a call for a change in policies:

> One reason might be that the 800 U.S. troops and contractors now in Colombia, doubled last year, are training and supporting Colombian military forces. Those forces are, in addition to carrying out the defoliation program, also guarding an oil pipeline owned by Occidental Petroleum, near and dear to Bush administration oil industry associates.
>
> Another reason might be that the principal defoliant in use in Colombia, glyphosate, sold commercially as Roundup, is provided under a profitable contract by Monsanto. That company gave $3 million in contributions to Republicans in 2004, 75 percent of the company's overall campaign financing.
>
> A third reason might be a desire on the part of the Bush administration to support Colombia's president Alvaro Uribe, a conservative swimming against a growing tide of left-leaning presidents elected in Latin America. Mr. Uribe is seeking to amend the Colombian constitution to permit himself a second term in office.
>
> There is also talk in Latin America that the Bush administration wishes to retain its military relationship with Colombia in order to provide a base for a possible invasion of neighboring Venezuela. That country's president, Hugo Chavez, is the administration's current favorite enemy in Latin America, second only to Fidel Castro of Cuba.
>
> None of these reasons sound good enough to justify continuing to spend billions of American taxpayers' dollars in Colombia, against the clear evidence that

Plan Colombia has failed miserably in its impact on cocaine and heroin availability in the United States. The Congress should scrap Plan Colombia now, rather than throw more good money after bad. It is easy to think of better uses for $3 billion.[149]

Just as U.S. diplomatic personnel and Washington policy makers had allowed the "drug war" to overdetermine policies toward Mexico, Central America, the Caribbean, Peru, and Bolivia, including repeated indirect and direct intervention by embassy officials in local politics, the U.S. ambassador in Colombia in August 2004 publicly objected to efforts by the Uribe government to negotiate a prisoner exchange (hostages for jailed rebels) or concession of amnesties to members of the paramilitary groups engaged in the drug traffic. Reporting for the BBC on this situation, Jeremy McDermott commented, "Since the U.S. bankrolls Colombia to the tune of some $700 million a year, any comment by the American embassy cannot be ignored."[150]

Yet a little more than one week earlier the incumbent U.S. president, as had his recent predecessors, had again determined that "national security" required waiving conditions related to human rights, democratization, and rule of law—and/or cynically "certified" that such concerns were being addressed in Colombia and most of the Andean region. In early October, a House–Senate conference committee completed work on a compromise version of the 2005 Defense Department Authorization Act (H.R. 4200). The revised bill fully granted the Bush administration's request to double the number of U.S. military personnel allowed on Colombian soil, from four hundred to eight hundred. It also granted the administration's request for a 50 percent increase in the permitted presence of U.S. citizens working for private contractors in Colombia, from four hundred to six hundred.[151] As 2004 ended, the United States extended its military commitments to Colombia, moving (unofficially) closer to direct combat roles (maintaining equipment, fuel, and supply lines; planning operations; providing intelligence—and in the case of contractors, even more direct roles), while economic and humanitarian assistance failed to keep pace. Between 2002 and 2004 a doubling of military trainees from Colombia, funded mostly by the counternarcotics programs, supported the intensified counterinsurgency operations throughout the country. In 2004 and into 2005 the Colombian military, with U.S. support, activated "Plan Patriota," the largest military operation in Colombia since the early nineteenth-century independence movements. Official sources reported over eighteen thousand military personnel deployed to challenge the guerrillas in their jungle strongholds, making sure to remind readers that the government was engaged in a war against terrorism and drug trafficking with frequent references by army and navy press releases to *narcoterroristas*.[152] The FARC announced "Plan Resistencia" as its counter, and despite some tactical losses refused to be baited into large-scale battles. Guerrillas, paramilitaries, and the armed forces carried out parallel propaganda campaigns in the press and on their Internet websites.[153] The war went on; malaria, parasites, and other enemies of the soldier in dense jungle terrain took their toll. As of mid-2005 Plan Patriota had proved undecisive.[154] Undeterred by continued failures, U.S. policies further undermined Colombian democracy and rule of law by supporting a constitutional amendment that would permit President Uribe's reelection (in elections scheduled for May 2006)—a decision that flagrantly violated a longstanding constitutional tradition in the country. On November 30, 2004, an amendment to the constitution apparently permitted Uribe to run for reelection in 2006. At the very least, support for rule of law and constitutional democracy would suppose that such an amendment would not apply to the incumbent. But, as the *New York Times* wrote on December 28, 2004, "The Bush administration has quietly but steadily supported a re-election drive by government supporters who argue that Mr. Uribe needs four more years to help extricate Colombia from its long, drug-fueled conflict with Marxist rebels. Since 2000, the United States has provided Bogotá with 3.3 billion in mostly military assistance, and President Bush offered more when he visited Colombia on November 22." While there exists a long history of such amendments to promote presidential *continuismo* in the Andean region, Colombia had avoided this endemic defect of Latin American politics since the late nineteenth century.[155] The contradiction between the U.S. policy makers' repeated calls for democratization, rule of law, and transparency and their Machiavellian efforts to manipulate Andean and Colombian domestic politics further eroded credibility from the U.S. democratic crusade.

As U.S. policy makers applauded the "get tough" policies of President Uribe and melded the "war on terror" and the "war on drugs," they also pressured Peru and Ecuador to cooperate in the war against Colombian insurgents and narco-traffickers. Simultaneously they severely criticized Venezuela's refusal to join in this effort and also Venezuela's opposition to U.S. policy in Iraq.[156] Venezuelan government officials rejected the U.S. pronouncements:

> Rejecting the unilateral military actions of the United States does not mean that Venezuela or any other country that is against the military action in Iraq, is being delinquent in the fight against terrorism. Support for all of the actions that the U.S. government—or any other government—takes against terrorism simply cannot be considered a prerequisite for cooperation in the fight against the scourge we collectively face. Venezuela does not reject, and has never rejected, greater collaboration with any country, including the United States, in the fight against terrorism, so long as such efforts remain within the framework of International Law.[157]

Congress had created the Regional Defense Counterterrorism Fellowship Program (CTFP or "CT Fellowship") in the Defense Appropriations Act of

2002 by providing $17.9 million for the education and training of foreign military officers. The Defense Appropriations Act of 2004 provided $20 million to continue the program overseen by the assistant secretary of defense for Special Operations and Low-Intensity Conflict (ASD SOLIC), with support from the Defense Security Cooperation Agency (DSCA). Military officers from Argentina, Brazil, Colombia, Ecuador, Mexico, Paraguay, and Peru (and many officers from the Mideast, Mediterranean, and South Asia) were scheduled to participate in "counter-terrorism education and training" with fiscal year 2005 funding. This focus on counterterrorism and intelligence pushed the militaries of the region increasingly back into surveillance of civilians and participation in domestic politics—in direct contradiction with the early 1990s goals of distinguishing between civilian, police, and military missions. Thus the war on terrorism in Latin America undermined the objective of increasing civilian control over the military announced as part of the post-1990 U.S. agenda for democratization in the Western Hemisphere. Of course, after September 11, 2001, the same trend was apparent within the United States itself.[158]

The American Service Members Protection Act

Yet another contradiction undermined the U.S. crusade for democracy and rule of law in the region, and also threatened the long-standing military-to-military contacts that undergirded U.S. Latin American policy. In 2002, the Bush administration's allies in Congress pushed through the American Service Members Protection Act (ASPA) in response to the establishment of the International Criminal Court (ICC). In May 2002, the U.S. government "unsigned" the Rome Statute, negotiated a one-year exemption from the UN Security Council for nonstate parties to the statute whose forces were participating in UN peacekeeping missions, and embarked on a worldwide campaign to adopt bilateral immunity agreements (BIAs) to protect U.S. military forces and civilians (including civilian contractors and mercenaries[159]) from ICC jurisdiction.[160] Section 2007 of the ASPA provides that "no military assistance may be provided to the government of a country that is a party to the International Criminal Court," subject to a National Interest Waiver Section 2007 (b), whereby the president "determines and reports to the appropriate congressional committees that it is important to the national interest of the United States to waive such prohibition." Section 2007 (c) allows the president to waive the prohibition in subsection (a) if a country "has entered into an agreement with the United States pursuant to Article 98 of the Rome Statute preventing the International Criminal Court from proceeding against United States personnel in such country."[161]

While many international law experts, and the European Union, insist that the Rome Statute does not permit such bilateral agreements for signatories, the Bush administration has aggressively insisted on such agreements and has, in practice, suspended military assistance and training agreements with Latin American countries that have refused to provide U.S. personnel with immunity against human rights violations.[162] By April 2005, of twenty-two countries refusing to sign such agreements with the United States (not including those exempted by the legislation), eleven were in Latin America. Included were Costa Rica, Brazil, Paraguay, Uruguay, Peru, Ecuador, and Venezuela. The Brazilian government declared that while it wished to retain its traditionally friendly relations with the United States, a BIA agreement represented a "threat to the judicial equality of states," and further, that it would be incompatible with Brazil's international commitments and its opposition to crimes against humanity.[163] Uruguayan foreign minister Didier Opertti said that the "United States has the Pinochet syndrome," referring to the former Chilean dictator who was held in Britain in 1998–1999 on an ultimately unsuccessful extradition request from Spain to try him for the disappearance and killing of its citizens in Chile.[164] The Caribbean Community (CARICOM) issued a statement on U.S.-proposed bilateral accords, reaffirming "their strong support for the principles and purposes of the ICC" and condemning the U.S. action to withhold military assistance from the six CARICOM countries that are states parties to the ICC.[165] Other Latin American governments offered similar objections, even as U.S. officials overseas pressured them to enter into bilateral immunity agreements or face loss of economic aid in addition to severance of military assistance. Reports of this sort of pressure came from ministers of the CARICOM nations, from Barbados, the Bahamas, Honduras, and elsewhere. On July 15, 2004, an anti-ICC amendment was attached to the Foreign Operations Appropriations bill. Introduced by Rep. George Nethercutt (R-WA), it proposed cutting Economic Support Fund assistance to all country signatories of the ICC that had not entered into a bilateral immunity agreement with the United States—whether or not they collaborated in the war against terror, the war against drugs, or otherwise had friendly relations with the United States.[166] For many Latin American governments such intrusion in their domestic affairs represented an affront to sovereignty and a critical liability in domestic politics. In May 2005, the Colombian attorney general (*procurador*) announced that he would challenge the legality of the bilateral immunity agreement with the United States, claiming that it violated the 1886 and 1991 constitutions. The Colombian case was particularly sensitive not only because Colombia was the largest recipient of U.S. military assistance in the hemisphere but because U.S. military personnel had recently been arrested for arms and drug trafficking.[167]

When the U.S. Senate approved an omnibus appropriations bill for 2005 that included the Nethercutt Amendment, the Council of the European Union expressed its deep regrets and urged President Bush to make full use of his waiver powers authorized by the amendment.[168] Not only the European Union regretted the Nethercutt Amendment. SOUTHCOM commander General Bantz J. Craddock told the House Armed Services Committee,

> While the American Servicemembers Protection Act (ASPA) provides welcome support in our efforts to seek safeguards for our service-members from prosecution under the International Criminal Court, in my judgment, it has the unintended consequence of restricting our access to and interaction with many important partner nations. . . . Of the 22 nations worldwide affected by these sanctions, 11 of them are in Latin America, hampering the engagement and professional contact that is an essential element of our regional security cooperation strategy. . . . We now risk losing contact and interoperability with a generation of

TABLE 1.3
Latin American States Parties to the International Criminal Court (ICC)/Date of Adherence*

Trinidad and Tobago, April 6, 1999
Belize, April 5, 2000
Venezuela, June 7, 2000
Costa Rica, January 30, 2001
Argentina, February 8, 2001
Dominica, February 12, 2001
Paraguay, May 14, 2001
Antigua and Barbuda, June 18, 2001
Peru, November 10, 2001
Ecuador, February 5, 2002
Panama, March 21, 2002
Brazil, June 14, 2002
Bolivia, June 27, 2002
Uruguay, June 28, 2002
Honduras, July 1, 2002
Colombia, August 5, 2002
Saint Vincent and the Grenadines, December 3, 2002
Barbados, December 10, 2002
Guyana, September 24, 2004

*The official ICC website at www.icc-cpi.int/home.html&l=en (accessed May 22, 2005) describes the Court as follows:

The International Criminal Court (ICC) is the first ever permanent, treaty based, international criminal court established to promote the rule of law and ensure that the gravest international crimes do not go unpunished.
   The Court shall be complementary to national criminal jurisdictions. The jurisdiction and functioning of the Court shall be governed by the provisions of the Rome Statute. The Rome Statute of the International Criminal Court was established on 17 July 1998, when 120 States participating in the "United Nations Diplomatic Conference of Plenipotentiaries on the Establishment of an International Criminal Court" adopted the Statute. The Statute entered into force on 1 July 2002.

military classmates in many nations of the region, including several leading countries.[169]

In practice, application of the ASPA legislation reduced some contacts and programs for SOUTHCOM, creating space for other U.S. agencies to reengage in the perennial bureaucratic infighting for influence in Latin American policy, but also creating incentives for some Latin American governments to look beyond the United States for military assistance, arms, and other equipment. All of the Andean nations (except Chile) were state parties to the Rome Statute, thus complicating the U.S.-sponsored Andean Regional Initiative and also the Andean Counternarcotics Initiative. In addition, insistence on bilateral immunity agreements reinforced the perception of unreliability, unilateralism, and wrong-headedness of U.S. policy toward individual countries of the region. Finally, how could the United States claim to promote human rights in Latin America, teach about international humanitarian law and accountability for crimes against humanity in the courses offered to Latin American military personnel at the Western Hemisphere Institute for Security Cooperation (WHINSEC, ex-School of the Americas), and insist on immunity from International Criminal Court jurisdiction for U.S. military personnel who might commit gross human rights violations?[170]

In contrast to the general trend in the region against U.S. insistence on immunity for its military personnel, the Paraguayan National Congress approved an agreement on June 1, 2005, allowing U.S. troops to enter the country for eighteen months for training Paraguayan officials in nacrco-trafficking, antiterrorism, anticorruption, and some health programs. According to the Council on Hemispheric Affairs, "Jose Ruiz, Public Affairs officer for the U.S. Armed Forces Southern Command office, told COHA that 'some military training will be operational in nature,' and the goal is to better equip Paraguayans to deal with the threats of narcotrafficking, terrorism, government corruption and poverty. A contingent of 500 U.S. troops headed by seven officials arrived in Paraguay on July 1 with planes, weapons, equipment and ammunition. This group is the first of at least 13 U.S. units set to enter Paraguay until the agreement expires December 31, 2006."[171] According to the same source, "This agreement grants U.S. soldiers complete legal immunity from some of their actions while they are in the country, affording them the same privileges as diplomats as well as leaving them free from prosecution for any damages inflicted on the public health, the environment or the country's resources."[172] For many Latin American leaders and social movements, the Paraguayan decision, combined with the U.S. air base at Manta, Ecuador, was further evidence of unprecedented U.S. expansion of military presence in South America as well as its intention to evade international humanitarian law through bilateral immunity agreements.[173]

U.S. Policy and the Regional Security Dilemma

Contradictions in U.S. policies, in part originating in domestic and bureaucratic politics and in part in the evangelical righteousness of the Bush foreign policy initiatives, complicated life for USSOUTHCOM as well as for Latin American governments.[174] In 2003, USSOUTHCOM claimed that "ungoverned spaces" in the hemisphere could provide havens for terrorists, thereby threatening U.S. national security. The 2003–2004 Posture Statement of the Special Operations Forces, which reports to the assistant secretary of defense for Special Operations and Low-Intensity Conflict (SOLIC), painted an even more menacing picture:

> Many of the region's democracies remain fragile, their basis undermined by widespread economic, sociological, and political problems. They face security problems that are multidimensional and localized. Latin America has the most uneven distribution of income and wealth, where the poorest 40 per cent of the population receive only 10 per cent of the income. Poverty is widespread. Rapid population growth, proliferating transnational threats, international drug trafficking, organized crime, terrorism, environmental exploitation, illegal immigration, the proliferation of land mines, and illegal para-military forces challenge the well-being and moral fiber of every country in the Western Hemisphere. Regional domestic crime threatens U.S. economic interests and the security of our citizens abroad—over 3,000 kidnappings per year occur in Colombia, one-half of the world's abductions. The region's porous borders, the expanding influence of insurgent organizations, and the symbiotic relationship between the illicit drug industry and insurgencies combine to make the region the most complex in the world. Regional security considerations now include threats to the domestic order that challenge a state's ability to hold the country together and to govern.[175]

If conditions had not greatly improved since 1990, or indeed had worsened, cynics might at least expect that these conditions augured well for SOUTHCOM and SOCSOUTH (Special Operations) budgets. This was especially true since the mission included assisting U.S. agencies in training host-country forces to combat terrorists, to target drug production and trafficking, to assist friendly nations in *coping with internal and external threats to their security,* and "staying ready to conduct special operations *during periods of conflict and peace* in support of U.S. interests."[176] Thus internal security in Latin American nations was explicitly a regional security concern, a mission for Special Operations SOUTHCOM. It could not console critics of these programs to learn that Thomas W. O'Connell, assistant secretary of defense for Special Operations and Low-Intensity Conflict, "began his career as an Infantry Officer in Germany. He served in Southeast Asia as a field advisor to Vietnamese forces, including duties with the PHOENIX Program. . . .[177] Mr. O'Connell's career included participation in four arenas of conflict: Vietnam, Grenada, Panama, and Southwest Asia; as well as various assignments in 33 countries."[178] It was also not promising that "anti-U.S. government sentiment is present in the AOR due to a widespread and mistaken perception that the U.S. maintains a unilateralist approach and an imperialist attitude toward partner nations."[179]

In March 2005 General Bantz J. Craddock lamented that "too many of the democracies in our AOR are lacking some or all of the vital democratic institutions: a functional legislative body, an independent judiciary, a free press, a transparent electoral process that guarantees the rights of the people, security forces which are subordinate to civil authority and economic opportunity for the people." He continued,

> Because a secure environment is a non-negotiable foundation for a functioning civil society, Southern Command is committed to building capabilities of the security forces of our region. The seeds of social and economic progress will only grow and flourish in the fertile soil of security. We cannot afford to let Latin America and the Caribbean become a backwater of violent, inward-looking states that are cut off from the world around them by populist, authoritarian governments. We must reward and help those governments that are making difficult, disciplined choices that result in the long-term well being of their people. The challenges facing Latin America and the Caribbean today are significant to our national security. We ignore them at our peril.[180]

Since 2000 the United States had spent billions of dollars on Plan Colombia, a multifaceted war against drugs, transnational crime, and terrorism. The plan also included some funding for strengthening government institutions, judicial reform, economic development, and "social revitalization." A staff report to the Committee on Foreign Relations of the United States Senate concluded in December 2005 that "the lack of reliable evidence of well-documented progress in the war against drugs and neutralizing paramilitaries is disappointing considering the billions of dollars the U.S. Congress has appropriated to finance drug interdiction and eradication since 2000."[181] The report also found that despite some progress in increasing Colombian state presence throughout the national territory, "the FARC [continued to] attack indigenous towns, electrical towers, rural highways, military and police outposts. While the attacks were partially directed at military targets, civilians were also indiscriminately killed."[182] A study called "The Colombian Conflict: Where Is It Heading?" completed near the end of 2005 by Colombian and British researchers, based on a data set involving over twenty-one thousand "violence events" since 1988, concluded that "most indicators are moving in the wrong direction, although their levels are generally still good compared to the recent past," and that "paramilitary behavior has taken a sharp turn for the worse." They also found that "killing of civilians by government forces and paramilitaries increased markedly from late 2004 onward [in 2005]."[183] In short, the drug war, counterinsurgency, and paramilitary and common criminal violence continued to plague Colombia. U.S. policies, including large-scale military assistance and billions spent on drug-crop eradication and interdiction programs, had made little positive difference in the daily lives of Colombians or in reducing drug supply to the United States. While a somewhat more tolerable personal security situation in the Bogotá environs should not be discounted, endemic poverty, increases in the numbers of displaced persons (refugees of the internal war and organized crime were estimated at over three million persons from 1995 to 2005),[184] and expansion and intensification of the war to the southern provinces and the borders with Venezuela characterized the country as it faced congressional and presidential elections in March and May of 2006. Amnesty International claimed that it "has documented that there has been no substantive improvement in the human rights situation, that human rights conditions have worsened in several conflict zones, and that collusion between the armed forces and illegal paramilitary groups continues."[185] Plan Colombia and U.S. policies toward Colombia more generally have essentially failed, and in some cases made circumstances worse than before Plan Colombia was launched.

All of Colombia's neighbors, and also Bolivia, experienced political instability, population displacement, increased violence, corruption, arms trafficking across borders, and challenges to governability within their national territories.[186] In April 2005, Ecuador's president, Lucio Gutiérrez, was removed from office, after the armed forces made it known they would not oppose his ouster; he flew to asylum in Brazil. In the meantime, Ecuador's military reported increased penetration of FARC elements in the border areas, for resupply, for treatment of wounded, for acquisition of arms and chemical precursors for drug production, and for creating more permanent sanctuaries. FARC spokesperson Raúl Reyes declared to the Ecuadorian press that the fact that the guerrillas "move through territory as a clandestine organization, does not imply that they seek to upset [*"no implica ninguna acción perturbadora contra"*] the governments of Colombia's neighbors."[187]

In Bolivia, President Carlos Mesa resigned in June 2005, to be succeeded on an interim basis by the president of the Supreme Court. Opposition elements in Bolivia demanded nationalization of natural gas and petroleum resources, a constitutional convention, and an end to cooperation with the U.S. drug war. Further complicating the crisis, regional interests in Santa Cruz insisted on some sort of "regional autonomy," expressing impatience with demands by indigenous groups for increased political influence. The army commander, Cesar López Saavedra, declared that his forces were preparing to "defend democracy and national unity, ready to repress violence in La Paz."[188] The commander of the armed forces, Admiral Luis Aranda, announced ominously, "We warn those who would destroy the nation, that we are the ultimate bastion of the *patria*" and that the armed forces remain steadfastly committed to "fulfilling the sacred duty of preserving the unity of the nation."[189]

As Bolivia teetered on the brink (in the run-up to the December election of its first indigenous president, Evo Morales, who assumed the presidency in January 2006), rampant speculation in Peru questioned President Toledo's ability to survive in office. In congress, opposition deputies entered into serious discussion of impeachment—a movement that failed, bringing short-term relief that the country would avoid the full institutional crises apparent in Bolivia and Ecuador. Nevertheless, new reports on increased poppy production undercut the optimism of the U.S. DEA, while Peruvian policy makers protested the U.S. withdrawal of agricultural issues from trade negotiations. Once again, the United States sought to protect its own producers (making alternatives to drug crops in Peru less viable) and at the same time increased delivery of military assets for the drug war.

Venezuela's president repeatedly confronted the Bush administration's policies in Latin America and the Andean region. He contested U.S. hegemony in the OAS and in bilateral relations. In February 2005, Venezuela's vice president responded to U.S. secretary of state Condoleezza Rice's characterization of the country as a "negative influence" in the hemisphere by asserting that "the great danger today in the world and in the region is the United States. . . . The U.S. thinks that the Chávez government is a danger, when it is they that are the danger for the world. This is a phenomenon of psychological projection."[190] A week later, Foreign Minister Alí Rodríguez declared at the OAS, "We are sure that this forum will not entertain those who seek to impose hegemonic and unilateral criticisms upon others, though if that were the case, we would have to ask ourselves whether governments like those led by President Hugo Chávez Frías, those that propose a participatory democracy, those that oppose the neo-liberal economic model, and those that stand against the neo-colonial integration schemes for the continent, have any space in the OAS."[191]

In April 2005, Chávez ended military-to-military education programs with the United States as he escalated his anti-neoliberal and anti-Bush administration rhetoric. A U.S. media campaign insinuated that Chávez financed the opposition to Ecuador's Gutiérrez; and "U.S. intelligence sources say Mr. Chávez has financed violent indigenous groups in Ecuador, Peru and Bolivia, where a revolt in 2003 toppled pro-U.S. President Gonzalo Sánchez de Lozada. U.S. and Colombian military officials accuse Venezuela of supporting Colombian rebels, and Mr. Rumsfeld has expressed alarm over Mr. Chavez's declared plans to acquire 100,000 AK-47 rifles from Russia."[192] Christian Democratic opposition leader Eduardo Fernández, at a conference in Brazil, denounced the "militaristic, populist, and authoritarian" character of the Chávez government, claiming that it had highjacked the constitutional regime.[193] In Washington, D.C, Assistant Secretary of Defense for the Western Hemisphere Roger Pardo Maurer told journalists that U.S. Latin American policy intended to assist the region's governments to "exercise effective sovereignty over their territory," and that Venezuela's president Chávez's government had been "invaded by thousands of Cubans" who exercise influence at all levels.[194] In Colombia and Venezuela some legislators accused the Chávez government of collaborating with guerrilla forces, even allowing semi-official sanctuary for their operations in Colombia.[195] From the conservative U.S. think tank the Center for Security Policy came an overt call for the United States, either unilaterally or with allies in the OAS, to oust the Chávez government, which is characterized as a "clear and present danger to peace and security in the hemisphere."[196]

When criticized by ex–Spanish primer minister José Aznar, Chávez called him "a true fascist" and compared him to Adolph Hitler, even as he sought closer Venezuelan–Spanish relations with Aznar's successor, José Luis Rodríguez Zapatero. Rodríguez Zapatero had campaigned against U.S. foreign policy in Iraq and brought Spanish troops home after terrorist bombings in Madrid.[197] In the same week, Vice President José Vicente Rangel warned the opposition that the government was prepared for another military coup attempt, accused them of irresponsible attacks on Venezuelan democracy, and insisted that over 80 percent of the public rejected Chávez's opponents.[198]

Efforts to isolate Venezuela's nationalistic, anti-U.S. president had achieved little as Chávez sought European, Arab, Iranian, and Latin American allies—or at least collaboration—in some of his petroleum and development schemes. He found some support from Caribbean neighbors and Brazil. He also negotiated an arms deal with Russia and trade agreements with China as the U.S. government (in the executive branch, including the Pentagon, and in the Congress) flailed ineptly to rescue its Latin American policies.

According to USSOUTHCOM, instability, poverty, unemployment, mass migration, the drug war and arms trafficking, corruption, and "radical populism" continued to haunt the hemisphere.[199] Still insistent on maintaining the same course, in meetings with six visiting presidents from Central America and the Caribbean who came to Washington, D.C., in May 2005 to lobby for the Central American Free Trade Agreement (which faced some resistance in the U.S. Congress), Secretary of Defense Donald Rumsfeld's Pentagon reiterated the message: "Economic progress and security are interdependent. . . . Today, the threat to Central American and Caribbean security comes from an anti-social combination of gangs, drug traffickers, smugglers, hostage takers and terrorists. It is increasingly clear that they can be effectively combated—and are being combated—only by close cooperation among nations. . . . This trade agreement [CAFTA] could help usher in a new era of cooperation between our countries and enhanced prosperity in the region."[200]

The Bush administration proposed more of the same, addicted to failed policies like its predecessors and determined to intensify its "market-democracy" crusade, the drug war, and the Latin American variant of the war on terror, despite its many destabilizing consequences throughout the hemisphere.[201] Indeed, the global war on terror seemingly subsumed the war on drugs, the fight against organized crime, and even the efforts to consolidate democracy and respect for human rights—almost in the way that the Cold War had framed (and justified) all sorts of errant policies before 1990. In addition, the administration attempted at the OAS General Assembly at Fort Lauderdale, Florida (June 5–7, 2005), to enhance the Inter-American Democratic Charter to provide for "monitoring compliance" with the commitment to democracy in the hemisphere, an initiative clearly aimed at the Chávez government in Venezuela, though potentially a threat to the exercise of sovereignty by other governments in the Western Hemisphere that challenged U.S. hegemony or were characterized as "radical populists" (rather than "democratic") by Washington's policy elite in the State Department and the Pentagon. For the moment, Secretary of State Condoleezza Rice, in an interview preceding her address to the OAS General Assembly, limited herself to expressing U.S. concern about "some of the activities Venezuela's government has engaged in" and declared, "It's important, for instance, that we make very clear that we would expect Venezuelan cooperation on terrorism, for instance, or on counternarcotics."[202] Implied in Rice's speech was the threat that governments that refused to adhere to the failing U.S. hemispheric agenda might run the risk of covert or overt U.S. sanction. Even the weak, underfinanced, and often-ignored OAS (with a two-thirds vote) might become again an instrument of U.S. policy, if the member states were to accept the U.S. proposal for "monitoring compliance" with the Inter-American Democratic Charter. President Hugo Chávez responded to this initiative on his radio program, *Alo Presidente*: "If any member government of the OAS needs monitoring, it is the government of the United States . . . a government that supports terrorists, invades other countries, that abuses its own people and pretends to install a global dictatorship . . . a government that violates human rights around the world, a false democracy."[203] The official news agency, Agencia Bolivariana de Noticias, characterized the U.S. proposal for "certificates of democracy" as a new type of colonialism and ridiculed Condoleezza Rice's inability to separate democracy from support for free trade and capitalism.[204] In its final "Declaration of Florida," the OAS implicitly rejected the U.S. proposal for a "monitoring committee" and instead emphasized that any actions taken by the secretary-general and the OAS to reaffirm democracy in the hemisphere should be done "with respect for the principle of nonintervention and the right of self-determination of peoples."[205]

On the same day, as further indication of the crumbling of U.S. Latin American policy, Washington's ambassador to Haiti acknowledged that the UN stabilization mission to that country (MINUSTAH) had not been able to restore order nor to provide conditions that would permit peaceful elections later in the year. He requested a new U.S. military mission to Haiti to improve the security situation.[206] On June 1, the secretary-general had recommended extending the mission for a year and adding over eight hundred troops (Peruvian and Argentine) and 275 police. In effect, since the U.S.-supported ouster of elected president Jean-Bertrand Aristide in late February 2004, it had been impossible to restore order or constitutional rule. In the name of democracy, the United States, the OAS, and the United Nations maintained the country under tenuous military occupation. Whether Aristide had violated the constitution or entrenched his cronies in power, or whether he represented the possibility of some democratization of Haitian politics and society, the U.S. intervention and the subsequent international "peacekeeping" operation had not improved socioeconomic conditions in Haiti, had not increased citizen security, had not reduced drug trafficking, and had not reduced efforts to immigrate to the United States. According to Brian Concannon, Jr.,

> On June 23, the U.S. State Department briefed members of Congress on its plan to distribute thousands of handguns to the Haitian National Police, continuing a program that sent 2,657 weapons to Haiti for the police last year, despite an embargo. Haiti's citizens, especially the poor majority, are suffering under an epidemic of armed violence. Kidnappings and gun battles, between gangs, police and UN Peacekeepers have replaced the daily and nightly routine in downtown Port-au-Prince and many neighborhoods. In some areas, residents cannot leave for days, and spend nights praying that the bullets outside do not come through their thin walls. Almost everyone in the capital alters their patterns of work, school, travel or sleep, to avoid being shot or kidnapped.[207]

Whatever the justification for the intervention and no matter that over half the MINUSTAH force came from Latin American nations in a multinational operation, Haiti was another ongoing failure of U.S. policy in the Western Hemisphere. As ambassador Robert E. White had written in 1996, "There is a vast difference between the unilateral big stick and the responsible exercise of power within a multilateral framework. . . . Accountability, not nonintervention, is the basic principle of foreign policy. Once a government takes the lead in persuading the international community to impose sanctions in order to force an illegitimate regime to cede power, that nation has incurred an overriding obligation to see that policy through to success."[208] In 2005, when the Department of State proposed distribution of thousands of handguns to Haiti's notoriously unaccountable police, Congresswoman Barbara Lee declared, "If the goal is to create an environment of security and safety in Haiti, the United States cannot be complicit in arming the very criminals responsible for raping, murdering and torturing hundreds of Haitians."[209]

U.S. policies failed to achieve their intended results in Haiti, Central America, Mexico, the Andean region, and most of the Southern Cone. They often had unintended consequences directly in contradiction to official goals. They

FIGURE 1.5
Young boy mimics soldiers' goose step. With the military taking over more and more
police responsibilities and the police becoming more and more militarized, in
response to drug war demands and pressures from the U.S. Embassy in La Paz, areas
like the Chapare have taken on the atmosphere of occupied territories. Photo courtesy
of Lucian Read/WpN.

emphasized, rhetorically, the global war on terror as Latin Americans' daily concerns focused on economic insecurity, organized crime, juvenile delinquency and gangs, inequality, and unconsolidated democracy. They increased political instability, corruption, and political violence rather than reducing them. They eroded the legitimacy and support for Latin American governments that sought to collaborate with the U.S. agenda. They frustrated and embittered Latin American political leaders in Brazil and much of Spanish America. They remilitarized Latin American politics and law enforcement.

Finally, addiction to failed policies in Latin America and the Andean region also savaged the U.S. "homeland," where the blowback from failed policies contributed to increasing flows of immigrants illegally entering the country, surges of gang violence and turf wars for local control of the drug business in urban "ungoverned spaces," increasing poverty, and neglect of public services. Even as the United States proclaimed its commitment to promote democracy and the rule of law in Latin America and other world regions, public confidence in political parties, Congress, and political institutions declined. Thus addiction to failed policies in Latin America from 1990 to 2006 not only made the United States less credible abroad, but also eroded the rule of law and the quality of democracy at home.

2

Plan Colombia and the Andean Regional Initiative: Lights and Shadows

Eduardo Pizarro and Pilar Gaitán

FOLLOWING THE ADMINISTRATION of President Ernesto Samper (1994–1998), a period characterized by severely strained diplomatic relations between Washington and Bogotá, there was a radical shift in 1998 and Colombia began to play a key role in the framework of U.S. policy toward Latin America.[1]

The shift was symbolized by the approval of a broad package of U.S. assistance for the so-called Plan Colombia (2000), aid that was subsequently expanded in 2001 through the Andean Regional Initiative (ARI), focused on drug crop eradication, military assistance, alternative development projects, rule of law and judicial reform, and aid to displaced persons. In addition to Colombia, the major recipient of ARI funding, and where over 70 percent of the assistance was for police and the military, the initiative included funds for Panama, Brazil, Ecuador, Peru, Bolivia, and Venezuela.

In the space of just four or five years the U.S. assistance package underwent a dramatic transformation. It was originally intended to be a tool for combating illegal drug trafficking and its negative impacts on society and the state.[2] But in the framework of post-September 11, 2001, Washington policy favoring a worldwide antiterrorist coalition, the doors were thrown open to direct employment of the funding in the internal war against nonstate armed organizations on the political Left or Right.

Why is analysis of Plan Colombia and the Andean Initiative important within this new international context? If we subscribe to the views of Gabriel Marcella, who is intimately familiar with U.S. foreign policy toward Colombia and a professor at the U.S. Army's War College (Carlisle, Pennsylvania),

Colombia is at once a "paradigm of twenty-first century conflict and a critical test case for American strategy" (2003: 2). Between 1989 and 2003, the number of armed conflicts in the world dropped from forty-seven to thirty-three. The most entrenched conflicts were those in which the state itself was highly vulnerable (Fearon and Laitin, 2003) even as nonstate, armed actors either had control of, or were in a position to extort, natural resources such as diamonds, timber, oil, or illegal drugs (Doyle and Sambanis, 2000). So the armed conflict in Colombia, where there is significant state weakness and an abundance of illegal resources with which to fuel the internal conflict, really typifies the majority of conflicts in the world today. Given Colombia's new significance in terms of U.S. military aid (the third largest recipient, after Israel and Egypt, before the war in Iraq in 2003), it most certainly qualifies as a "test case."

Is the U.S. aid package to Colombia sufficient to address the kind of conflict this nation is facing? Opinions vary widely. According to some, U.S. intervention will only serve to escalate the conflict and the White House will find itself dealing with another Vietnam. According to others, given the sizable antidrug component of Plan Colombia and the failure of the current "war on drugs" model, the program is purely and simply inadequate for achieving the proposed objectives. It is important that we set aside such notions of "either black or white" and that we instead attempt to point out the positive features of the assistance package as well as its deficiencies.

U.S. assistance for Plan Colombia is an appropriate response to two of Colombian society's needs: the need to rebuild state institutions (particularly institutions that have to do with security and justice) and the need to debilitate drug trafficking, which is largely fueling the domestic war. At the same time, however, the package is both inadequate and questionable with regard to some of its aims. It is inadequate because important dimensions of the Colombian crisis are not being sufficiently addressed. (For example, where the fight against poverty and income disparity is concerned.)[3] It is questionable because the war on drugs model has many negative aspects, such as the environmental and social impacts of aerial fumigation, or the risk that there will be a sub-national or even cross-national "balloon effect" and that cultivation will spread into areas previously free of this plague, as has occurred in the past, when "successful" eradication programs in Peru and Bolivia pushed cultivation into Colombia.

In tackling these controversial issues we will first reconstruct the discussions and strategizing of the early years (1998–2001). Then we will briefly analyze the events of September 11 and their effects on the Colombian situation. Lastly, we will examine the positive and negative aspects of U.S. aid to Colombia.

Colombia: From "Problem Nation" to
Destabilizing Factor in the Region

In carefully reading U.S. military establishment documents from the past few years, a noticeable change in vision regarding Colombia emerges. Colombia had been classified as a "problem nation" for the world community because it was suffering institutional erosion and a grave humanitarian crisis. Change in this relatively benign vision began when political stability throughout the Andean region started deteriorating, to the point where the Andes became the most vulnerable region in all of Latin America.[4] Within this tumultuous regional scenario Colombia came to be considered a serious destabilizing factor (Marcella and Schulz, 1999).

In the last few years, various North American officials including General Charles Wilhelm, former head of the Southern Command; General Barry Mc-Caffrey, former drug czar; and General James T. Hill, commander of the Southern Command (August 2002–November 2004), have regarded Colombia as one of the Western Hemisphere's chief security problems, greater even than Cuba, which had occupied that uncomfortable spot since 1962.

Palpable examples of Colombia's significance in the framework of United States foreign policy, and the vision of the conflict dominating U.S. power circles, can be found in the new "National Security Strategy for the United States of America."

> Parts of Latin America confront regional conflict, especially arising from the violence of drug cartels and their accomplices. This conflict and unrestrained narcotics trafficking could imperil the health and security of the United States. Therefore we have developed an active strategy to help the Andean nations adjust their economies, enforce their laws, defeat terrorist organizations, and cut off the supply of drugs, while—as important—we work to reduce the demand for drugs in our own country.
>
> In Colombia, we recognize the link between terrorist and extremist groups that challenge the security of the state and drug trafficking activities that help finance the operations of such groups. We are working to help Colombia defend its democratic institutions and defeat illegal armed groups of both the left and right by extending effective sovereignty over the entire national territory and providing basic security to the Colombian people.[5]

Today (2005), Colombia is much more susceptible to various types of foreign intervention than other countries in the region. It is the only country in Latin America that has been unable to settle the most critical issue of the region's Cold War agenda (the counterinsurgency conflict) and now must simultaneously address the enormous new challenges of the 1990s international agenda (democratization, human rights, urban crime, corruption, poverty, environmental degradation, population displacement). The superimposition of new challenges on past challenges heightens the country's internal and international vulnerability to the extreme. This vulnerability is increased by various factors, geographic, political, and doctrinaire. On the one hand, there is Colombia's complex geopolitical position. It is both a Pacific and Caribbean nation, Andean and Amazonian; it lies in close proximity to Panama's Canal Zone and Venezuela's petroleum industry. It should be remembered that the North American concept of mare nostrum is no longer confined to the Caribbean and Central American basin but has been extended to include the Andean region because, among other reasons, of the production of illegal drugs (Tokatlian, 1999). With the exception of Chile, all the Andean nations are experiencing serious political, economic, and social tensions. This makes Colombia's potentially destabilizing impact on the stormy region even graver. It also explains how a new version of the old "domino theory"[6] was revived in U.S. military thinking. The theory was applied in both Indochina and Central America to justify the need for containing North Vietnam, Nicaragua, and El Salvador before they destabilized all other nations in their regions.

That Colombia's conflict might spread to its vulnerable neighbors is viewed with fear by the international community (Zackrison and Bradley, 1997). It is important to note that there are not many "living borders"—that is, borders that are active with respect to population and economic exchange[7]—on the limits between Colombia and its neighboring countries. They are rather mostly jungle borders that could be occupied by noninstitutional, armed actors as secure outposts, or used for illegal drug or arms trafficking. Colombia's lengthy land border (6,004 km) is nearly twice as long as the complex border separating the United States and Mexico (3,326 km). And unlike that border, the states on either side have only a weak (albeit increasing) presence. The 6,004 km are divided as follows: Brazil, 1,643 km; Ecuador, 590 km; Panama, 225 km; Peru, 1,496 km; and Venezuela, 2,050 km. If the United States, in spite of its enormous deployment of human, economic, and technological resources, has been unable to gain complete control over its border with Mexico, we need only imagine the implications for a border that is much longer, has little state presence on either side, and is mostly jungle.

Finally, the switch from an international doctrine of national autonomy to one that gives outsiders the right to intervene on humanitarian grounds (Dupuy, 2000) and, increasingly, because of reasons linked to global security, Colombia is a potential candidate for intervention by the international community. Most likely it is the "doctrine of preventive intervention" launched by President George W. Bush in May 2002 at West Point that may in fact be the source of the dramatic change in the international system's rules of the game.[8]

"Two-Track" Policy

By the end of the last decade, growing concern in U.S. political and military circles over the Colombian situation translated into what we have dubbed "two-track" policy. On one track, significant support for the Pastrana administration's peace initiatives was proffered by the Department of State. The meeting in Costa Rica between Philip Chicola, undersecretary for Andean Affairs, and the international head of the Fuerzas Armadas Revolucionarias de Colombia (FARC), Raúl Reyes,[9] was a clear expression of this line of behavior. On a second, subordinate track, the Department of Defense pushed to strengthen and restructure both the armed forces and the police. In a controversial article on Colombia that appeared in the *New York Times*, then secretary of state Madeleine Albright stated, "After thirty-eight years of struggle, it should be clear that a decisive military outcome is unlikely. President Pastrana was right to initiate talks; *the question is whether he can muster a combination of pressure and incentives that will cause the guerrillas to respond.*"[10] In other words, some combination of carrot and stick, peace initiatives, and, at the same time, strengthening of institutions. Although many argued these were contradictory policies, those responsible for developing policy toward Colombia defended them as complementary in nature.

In spite of the broad, polemic U.S. debate over Plan Colombia, the Clinton administration managed to put together a majority, bipartisan consensus[11] in its favor and reconciled the fundamental points of view of the agencies involved. As frequently happens in U.S. foreign policy, as an issue, country, or region becomes more important to Washington's agenda, there are efforts to overcome cross-institutional fragmentation and interagency conflict for the sake of a single, coherent agenda. This is the primary indicator of the importance an issue, country, or region has to U.S. foreign policy. The other indicator is the hierarchical level on which the issue is handled. According to Andelfo García, there is a subtle way to "figure out how sensitive the administration is to a particular country or issue, and that is the hierarchical level of the officials who are talking about it. Along those lines, Colombia is becoming increasingly important because on many occasions it has been the President of the United States himself or his Secretary of State who has made statements about the Colombian situation" (2001: 220). Therefore, the efforts of the federal government to build bipartisan, interagency consensus and the level of decision making demonstrate the degree of concern the Colombian situation has raised in Washington.

What was the core of U.S. assistance to the military and police? As previously pointed out, Colombia became the world's third largest recipient of U.S. military aid, after Israel and Egypt, in 1998. In 1999 this assistance approached three hundred million dollars. The figure has been increasing since 2000, first after the approval of the controversial Plan Colombia and again following approval of the so-called Andean Regional Initiative.

Military aid was originally designated, primarily, for the war on drugs. In spite of demands by the Pastrana government—under whom relations between Washington and Bogotá were normalized once more[12]—U.S. officials continued to emphatically insist that the fight against drug trafficking would continue to be the main issue on the bilateral Washington–Bogotá agenda. They maintained that the Colombian government's desire to "de-narcotize" the two nations' diplomatic agenda was not yet viable, and so, the bulk of assistance would go to fighting drugs and consequently, to the National Police. This decision was largely based on the fact that the number of coca-producing hectares in Colombia was increasing, as was poppy cultivation, while coca production was going down in Bolivia and Peru.[13]

Nevertheless, the doors to direct participation in the counterinsurgency war began to open gradually, in spite of resistance from many sectors in the United States that rejected their country's involvement in Colombia's politico-military conflict. In influential U.S. military and academic circles the Colombian conflict began to be defined as an "ambiguous war" because of links between the guerrillas and narco-traffickers, providing the analytical rationale for displacing the counternarcotics war with a counterinsurgency war (Downes, 1999; Marcella, 2001b; Marcella and Schulz, 1999).

Most likely the first outcome of this "ambiguous war" concept as a basis for linking the fight against drugs with the fight against the guerrillas was the decision to create three army battalions specialized in fighting drugs. Each was made up of one thousand men, artillery helicopters, and advanced communications and intelligence technology.[14] The purpose of these battalions was, chiefly, to support the Colombian National Police in eradicating coca cultivation in the Putumayo Department bordering Ecuador and Peru. This department was of fundamental geostrategic importance to paramilitary groups as well as the FARC. These two armed groups had divided the impoverished department between them, and constituted the only real "authority" in the area from which they derived the vast bulk of their economic resources, thanks to extensive coca cultivation and processing laboratories. Further, no state had any real control over this part of the Colombian border with Ecuador and Peru, so the region was conducive to drug as well as arms trafficking. This is an area of some 192,000 km², which has one of "the highest densities of illegal crops in the world."[15] Heading up the "war in the South," as it has been dubbed by the press, was the commander of the Joint Task Force South whose home base was located at Tres Esquinas in Caquetá Department.[16]

Militarization and Triangulation along the Borders

The process of militarizing the borders around Colombia started in Venezuela during the Rafael Caldera (1994–1999) administration. His government created so-called theaters for military operations to control the troubled border between the two countries. However, following his electoral victory, Lieutenant Colonel Hugo Chávez began putting his own men in charge of troops in the region, and the bases began to turn into centers for collaboration between the Bolivarian government and Colombian guerrillas, instead of instruments for the national defense.[17] The proliferation of FARC and ELN (Ejército de Liberación Nacional—National Liberation Army) guerrilla camps in Venezuelan territory came to reach critical levels for Colombian national security. After that first experience with Rafael Caldera's "theaters for military operations," and given the geostrategic importance the country's southern border had taken on for the various armed players, the U.S. government began to strongly pressure the governments of Ecuador and Peru to move troops from their common border (once the border conflict between Ecuador and Peru was over) toward the Colombian border in order to cut off drug- and arms-trafficking routes. The buildup of a military presence in these border areas has been slow and falls short of being an effective constraint on guerrilla and paramilitary forces in both cases, not only because of the geographic complexity of this region, but out of hesitancy in Ecuador and Peru to become fully engaged in the spillover of the Colombian conflict.

After much foot dragging, Ecuador mobilized around twelve thousand troops—one third of its total armed forces—toward the northern border, in accordance with the Joint Command's Strategic Plan, which called for setting up sixteen military bases on the common border (Carchi, Sucumbíos, and Esmeraldas). The militarization process would intensify under the Decreto Ejecutivo de Áreas de Reserva (Executive Decree for Areas in Reserve) signed by President Lucio Gutiérrez and published in the Registro Oficial (Official Record) on April 7, 2003. The decree established that border regions and reserves would be included in the armed forces' Plan de Guerra (War Plan) and that the armed forces would be in charge of them. Further, under the Ley de Seguridad Nacional (National Security Law), the Joint Command of the Armed Forces has the power to update, maintain, or change the status of borders and to manage restrictions imposed by the military when circumstances make them necessary (control of vehicle transit, population census, limiting freedom of movement, etc.).[18]

A similar process of militarization was taking place on the Panamanian and Brazilian borders, although each of these countries responded to its own very particular situation. Originally what was at stake in Panama's case was no more, nor less, than the future withdrawal of U.S. troops that remained stationed on bases in that country. In explosive statements made in the opening months of 1999, General Charles Wilhelm publicly declared that Panama was incapable of guaranteeing the security of the Canal, given the increasing presence of the FARC on its border. These statements were interpreted as an explicit expression of Washington's desire to keep troops stationed in the isthmus.[19] In response, the Panamanian government sent more than fifteen hundred police border guards to the frontier to show it was capable of keeping the zone secure. President Mireya Moscoso later announced that Panama was going to negotiate arms purchases with a number of countries, including the United States, in order to beef up patrols along the Colombian border.[20] In Brazil's case, the problem involved drug trafficking and the guerrilla presence, and was translated into a buildup of the Tabatinga military base on the Amazon River south of Colombia. Under this program radar stations were being installed along the more than 1,600 km the two countries share.[21] In 2002 Brazil set out to regain complete control over its airspace through the SIVAM project (Sistema de Vigilancia de la Amazonía—Amazonian Surveillance System), designed to curb arms and drug trafficking and the smuggling of rare minerals and protected species. The project included twenty-five radar stations, observation outposts, and a large fleet of aircraft (military transport, fighter-bombers, and planes equipped for radar monitoring).[22]

Another source of White House concern was the cost to antidrug policy of the 1999 closure of Howard Air Force Base in Panama. Replacement bases in Ecuador, Aruba, Curaçao, and El Salvador would only be able to carry out half of the fifteen thousand antinarcotics flights (for eradication and interdiction) that had been carried out over the area from the Panama Canal.[23] Because 80 percent of the base's activity centered on Colombia, the Southern Command drew up an emergency plan with "Forward Operating Locations" (FOLs) to configure a triangle of operations around the country.[24] It was designed to provide real-time exchanges of information for the detection of unauthorized flights in the Caribbean and Pacific and along Colombia's southern border.

On April 1, 1999, the United States and Ecuador signed an agreement granting the U.S. Air Force access to logistical installations in the country.[25] Following his July 1999 visit to Manta base at Eloy Alfaro International Airport, General Charles Wilhelm said, "The Forward Operating Locations in the Caribbean and Latin America will provide an important means of access to the region and will be an efficient, cost effective alternative to Howard Air Force base from which the US can carry out missions that are critical in the fight against drug trafficking and its ties to organized crime." He also added that the FOLs were vital in the combat against elements threatening regional security. A document similar to the one signed with the Quito government was signed by the Netherlands minister of Foreign Relations, J. J. Van Aartsen, and U.S. ambassador to The Hague Cynthia Schneider. The Dutch government would allow North American troops access "by land as well as air and use of certain airports" for "missions to detect and monitor drug traffic in the Western Hemisphere and when appropriate, interdiction."[26] U.S. bases were set up at Reina Beatrix International Airport in Aruba and at Hato Airport near Curaçao. And lastly, the U.S. and Salvadoran governments signed a ten-year agreement for use of the Comalapa International Airport in March 2000.

From Ambiguous War to International Antiterrorist Coalition

As mentioned earlier, there was a profound change in the world order following the September 11 terrorist attacks in New York and Washington, D.C. According to Stanley Hoffmann, during the 1990s the tension dominating the world was "the clash between the breaking-up of States (and the State system) and progress toward economic, cultural and political integration—in other words, globalization" (2002: 104). After the Cold War, the international community's chief concern was the harsh reality that many states were showing themselves to be pseudo-states: they lacked strong institutions, internal cohesion, and national awareness. To a great extent, attention was focused on the "failing states" and, in their most radical form, "collapsed states." This was most serious in world regions where a number of national minority groups clamored for independence, as well as in nations caught up in serious, protracted internal conflicts because nonstate armed groups controlled parts of the national territory and strategic resources. Colombia fell into the latter group.

Although that concern still exists, since September 11, 2001, the terrorism issue—and its relationship to "rogue states" and the proliferation of weapons of mass destruction—has become the focus of international debate, and above all, U.S. foreign policy.[27] Following a period of uncertainty, the international system, to some extent, again rotates around an axis of bipolar conflict where a logic of friends versus implacable enemies rules. The wars in Afghanistan and Iraq are emblematic of the new international schema.

For Colombia, the most significant *official* outcome of the tragic events of September 11 was that it cleared the way for Washington to take on the guerrillas, *who were no longer considered insurgent forces, but terrorist movements financed by drug trafficking.*[28] Throughout the Clinton administration there was—as has been pointed out—constant tension between the Department of State and the Department of Defense, the same tension that existed in U.S. public opinion. While the Department of State stated that Plan Colombia was, in terms of its military components, a counternarcotics plan, Department of Defense analysts insisted there were such fine lines between drug trafficking and the guerrillas, that one way or another, Plan Colombia would end up having an element of counterinsurgency. Analysts within the Defense Department community adopted the concept of "ambiguous war" to justify that point of view.

Terrorism and Drug Trafficking

The events of September 11 left the debate between the Departments of State and Defense in the dust. Because the FARC, ELN, and AUC (Autodefensas Unidas de Colombia—United Self-Defense Forces) were no longer considered insurgent or counterinsurgent forces but terrorist groups, direct or indirect combat against them was legitimized with a simple stroke of the pen. This perspective gained credibility as the pattern of linking illegal drug traffic with terrorism grew; after all, drug trafficking is one of the principal ways terrorist groups are financed, internationally and within Colombia.[29] Debates in the U.S. Congress over new antiterrorist legislation paved the way, such as the one spearheaded by the majority leader of the House of Representatives, Dennis Hastert (R-IL), in 2001, aimed at linking the fight against terrorism with the fight against drugs. Hastert and others pushing to control drug traffic found justification not just for maintaining, but expanding Washington's involvement in Latin America: "By cracking down on the illegal drug trade we weaken terrorists' ability to strike the United States and other democracies," Hastert pointed out in the opening press conference of a working group of forty-eight delegates for "A Drug-free America." "The illegal drug trade is the financial engine fueling many terrorist organizations around the world," he added.[30]

This new climate was also very clear in a statement Francis X. Taylor, coordinator for the State Department's Office of Anti-terrorism, made before the House of Representative's Subcommittee on the Western Hemisphere: "Today the Revolutionary Armed Forces of Colombia (FARC) are the most dangerous international terrorist organization based in the hemisphere. . . . Now more than ever, it is time to build coalitions against terrorism which are founded on pro-active diplomacy, strict application of the law, financial controls, intelligence sharing and a fierce resolve to achieve justice."[31] According to Taylor, his office was working with other agencies to formulate an antiterrorist strategy for Colombia and other countries in the Andes region that would complement Plan Colombia and the Andean Initiative. A fund of fifty-eight million dollars was originally set up for the purpose, with "emergency supplements" added by Congress following the events of September 11. Meanwhile, the Office of Budget and Management was considering a "more ambitious" program presented to Congress in 2002 directed at four fronts: curtailing money laundering, beefing up customs regulation, training officials, and increasing exchange of information.

This course of analysis and action embedded itself ever deeper during 2002 through promulgation of the "National Security Strategy for the United States of America," a policy that specifically warned—as seen earlier—of the narrowing relationship between armed nonstate groups and Colombian drug trafficking. Its corollary has been the elimination of existing restrictions on the use of U.S. assistance, which became effective October 2002. Funds could now officially be used to protect the petroleum industry's infrastructure and to fight guerrilla and paramilitary groups.

Colombia: On the Road to "Vietnamization"?

Did this shift in the designation of U.S. aid, that is, permitting resources to be used for the internal war, mean that we were *ad portas* of an escalated U.S. military presence in Colombia? Would it lead to direct intervention over the medium term?

With respect to the first question, military aid from Washington would indeed increase over the next few years, not just in the Andean Initiative arena, but in the context of the worldwide war against terrorism upon which the White House embarked. International analysts like sociologist Heinz Dieterich already believe that United States intervention in Colombia is comparable in level to El Salvador and Nicaragua between 1983 and 1984 and Vietnam in 1963. Is further escalation unavoidable?

In an interview given to *El Clarín* newspaper in Buenos Aires, Bill Perry, a Republican specialist on Latin America for Washington's Center for International and Strategic Studies, stated that, in regard to the matter of U.S. intervention, "on a scale of intervention from one to ten, we are now at two. We are sharing intelligence, satellite imaging, and intercepted communications. We are making reconnaissance and detection flights. We are also training an anti-narcotics battalion." He added that, even lacking credible policy for peace, intervention would not rise to level ten. "From a level two intervention we'll go to level three, four or five. That means we'll send more trainers and advisors, we'll arm the Colombian army better, we'll double our intelligence efforts. But we will not invade Colombia, not even the hard-liners in Congress are talking about that." He reaffirmed that in the near future the United States would rely on a combination of "good cop, bad cop policy," in other words, as we have seen, a combination of stick and carrot.[32] Now, six years later, the prescience of his analysis is stunning.

At this point, there would be two options for military intervention in Colombia: international intervention of a humanitarian nature or intervention by an inter-American army headed up by Washington. The second option can be discounted given that, in the current climate, it is highly unlikely that a South American regional consensus could be reached to support military intervention under U.S. leadership. No South American leader today would support an initiative of that type.[33] According to Argentine diplomats contacted at the time by the Buenos Aires newspaper *La Nación*, the poor reception

Washington received in Latin America for possible joint intervention led the State Department to cease its interventionist overtures, replacing them with a line of action based on increasing military aid and the number of advisors.[34] In other words, efforts were made to increase Washington's support for Plan Colombia and now, the Andean Regional Initiative.

Can a United Nations–approved humanitarian intervention also be discounted? We believe that this option is not being considered, at least for the short term. The matter, its costs and benefits, is being increasingly discussed in the halls of the United Nations. In 2002 attention was focused on the possibilities for reestablishing contacts between the government and the guerrillas, and any headway that UN Secretary-General Kofi Annan could make through his special envoy, James Lemoyne.[35]

It is our opinion that, in the short run at least, U.S. policy will follow its two present courses. First, a significant increase in military aid is foreseeable, for the drug war, and increasingly, for the counterinsurgency war. Second, neighboring countries will continue to be pressured to tighten the "sanitary corridor" around Colombia.[36]

The U.S. Assistance Package

As previously pointed out, up to 2002 only the components of the Departamento Nacional de Planeación's 7.5 billion dollar "Plan Colombia" project that were supported by the United States had been implemented. Not even the Colombian government delivered the resources it had committed, nor did the international community follow through with the resources requested by the Colombian government. Thus, while the plan's military component was originally only 7 percent of the total budget, it ended up as the bulk of the funds actually spent.

Without doubt, Plan Colombia suffered from a series of "original sins," in its conception as well as its design, that are worth pointing out. It was intended to be a global policy that was to be incorporated into the plan for national development. It included four basic components: a negotiated political settlement to the internal conflict; social and economic recovery; strengthening of institutions and social development; and an antidrug trafficking initiative. Its implementation revealed serious shortcomings.[37] To begin with, Andrés Pastrana preferred bureaucratic secrecy to public debate; further, there was no coordination or cooperation among state entities. The document, which was originally written in English, was hurriedly translated into Spanish under pressure from Congress. This created the impression that Washington was imposing itself. Second, because it was necessary to draft a document in tune with the climate in the United States at the time, the antinarcotics piece was played up, which irritated the European Union. When the Colombian government then presented a document with an alternate focus to the Europeans—one that emphasized economic and social issues—they reacted with skepticism, feeling they were being manipulated.

In this third part of our chapter we will briefly analyze the U.S. package of assistance for Plan Colombia and the Andean Initiative. As we will see, the bulk of resources have been earmarked for the armed forces and the police, although, at the same time, lesser amounts of resources have been designated for such initiatives as strengthening justice, protection for nongovernmental organizations (NGOs) and human rights activists, displaced populations, and crop substitution. Before evaluating the impact of U.S. aid to Colombia, let us briefly consider where this assistance has gone.

Plan Colombia

Of the 1,319.1 million dollar U.S. package supporting Plan Colombia,[38] only 65 percent was designated for direct investment in Colombia, as shown in table 2.1. The remainder was divided up and allocated to other nations in the area (Ecuador, Peru, Bolivia, and other, unspecified countries), various U.S. agencies, and air bases assuming the duties of former U.S. bases in the Panama Canal Zone (Ecuador, Aruba, and Curaçao), as can be seen in table 2.2. A significant amount of the resources directed specifically at Colombia ($642.3 million) was earmarked for the armed forces and the National Police. The remaining $218 million was distributed among alternative crop development (substitutes for coca, poppies, or marijuana); assistance to persons displaced due to violence; and support for human rights NGOs, judicial institutions, and the peace process (table 2.3). In other words, 75–80 percent of the resources went to military assistance and the remainder to other areas of need.

The Andean Regional Initiative

Once Plan Colombia was approved, U.S. resources began flowing into the country, year after year, without interruption into 2005. This is, without a

TABLE 2.1
Allocation of the U.S. Aid Package

Designation	Contribution (in millions of U.S. dollars)	Percent (%)
Aid to Colombia	860.3	65
Aid to other countries	180.0	14
U.S. agencies	223.5	17
Classified	55.3	4
Total	1,319.1	100

TABLE 2.2
Allocation of Resources Not Earmarked for Colombia (in millions of U.S. dollars)

Designation	Amount
Upgrades of U.S. overseas "Forward Operating Locations"($61.3 for Eloy Alfaro Airport in Manta, Ecuador; $10.3 for Reina Beatrix Airport, Aruba; $43.9 for Hato International Airport, Curaçao; $1.1 for planning and design).	$116.5
Defense Department Andean Ridge intelligence gathering	$7.0
Classified Defense Department Intelligence Program	$55.3
Radar upgrades for U.S. Customs Service P-3 aircraft	$68.0
Treasury Department "Drug Kingpin" tracking program	$2.0
Defense Department "Airborne Reconnaissance Low" aircraft	$30.0
Aid for Peru	$32.0
Aid for Bolivia	$110.0
Aid for Ecuador	$20.0
Aid to other countries	$18.0
Total	$458.8

Source: Center for International Policy, The Contents of the Colombia Aid Package (Washington, D.C., 2000).

doubt, a solid indicator of the significance that the Colombian conflict and its regional impact have acquired in the vision of the decision makers dominating formulation of U.S. national security policy. But the program underwent a change of name and went on to be called the Andean Regional Initiative. The change was a response to two circumstances. One: pressure from countries in the region troubled by the possibility that the Colombian conflict would worsen and that they—specifically Peru, Ecuador, and Panama—would not have the resources to contain it. Two: these same countries were fearful that, if the program in Colombia proved successful and there was a reduction in coca and poppy cultivation, production would increase in other nations in the re-

TABLE 2.3
Allocation of the Colombian Package

Designation	Allocation (in millions of U.S. dollars)	Percent (%)
Military assistance	$519.2	60.35
Police assistance	$123.1	14.31
Alternative development	$68.5	7.96
Aid for displaced persons	$37.5	4.36
Human rights	$51.0	5.93
Judicial reform	$13.0	1.51
Law enforcement/rule of law	$45.0	5.23
Peace	$3.0	0.35
Total	$860.3	100.00

Source: Center for International Policy, The Contents of the Colombia Aid Package (Washington, D.C., 2000).

TABLE 2.4
Andean Regional Initiative Resources (in millions of U.S. dollars)

Country	Counternarcotics and Security	Economic and Social Development	Total
Bolivia	$48.000	$74.463	$122.463
Brazil	$6.000	$12.630	$18.630
Colombia	$243.500	$137.000	$380.500
Ecuador	$15.000	$31.855	$46.855
Panama	$5.000	$8.500	$13.500
Peru	$75.000	$119.873	$194.873
Venezuela	$5.000	$0.500	$5.500
Total	$397.500	$384.821	$782.321

Source: Fact Sheet, Office of the Press Secretary, The White House, Washington, D.C., March 23, 2002.

gion to make up for it. They demanded resources to counter the threat. In other words, they feared a "reverse balloon effect": coca cultivation would return to Bolivia and Peru and perhaps move into countries previously free of the scourge, like Ecuador or Venezuela. In practice, this occurred to some extent in the period after 2003.

President George W. Bush requested a budget of 731 million dollars for the region to be delivered through the International Narcotics Control program, a combination of military, police, and socioeconomic assistance. As the number of countries benefiting from U.S. assistance grew, Colombia continued to be the chief recipient of funds, as shown in table 2.4. According to the White House press secretary, "The Andean Regional Initiative (ARI) advances the President's goal of strengthening democracy, regional stability, and economic development throughout the hemisphere."[39]

The Big Picture

If we put the resources for Colombia from Plan Colombia together with the resources from the Andean Regional Initiative and disaggregate economic and social assistance from military assistance, the overall pattern of assistance can be discerned more sharply; we get a wider view of what is going on. As table 2.5 shows, assistance for economic and social programs went from zero in 1997 to 212 million dollars in 2000 and 154.8 million dollars in 2003. The total amount of assistance, including what was budgeted for 2003, rose to 509.22 million dollars in five years. These resources came primarily from the International Narcotics Control program and were designated to support substitution of illegal crops. But socioeconomic assistance remained much lower than military and police assistance, which grew from 88.56 million dollars in 1997 to 499.02 million dollars in 2003, after peaking at 785.97 million dollars in 2000.

TABLE 2.5
All U.S. Aid to Colombia, 1997–2003 (in millions of U.S. dollars)

	1997	1998	1999	2000	2001	2002	2003
Military and Police Assistance Programs							
International Narcotics Control (INC). State Department-managed counterdrug arms transfers, training, and services	33.45	56.5	200.11	686.43	46.35	253	284.2
Foreign Military Financing (FMF). Grants for defense articles, training, and services	30	0	0.44	0.4	4.49	6	98
International Military Education and Training (MET). Training, usually not counterdrug	0	0.89	0.92	0.9	1.04	1.18	1.18
Emergency Drawdowns. Presidential authority to grant counterdrug equipment from the United States	14.2	41.1	58	0	0	0	0
"Section 1004." Authority to use the defense budget for some types of counterdrug aid to Colombia	10.32	11.78	35.89	90.60	150.04	84.99	102
"Section 1033." Authority to use the defense budget to provide riverine counterdrug aid to Colombia	0	2.17	13.45	7.23	22.3	4	13.2
Antiterrorism Assistance (ATA). Grants for antiterrorism defense articles, training, and services	0	0	0	0	?	25	?
Excess Defense Articles (EDA). Authority to transfer "excess" equipment	0.09	0	0	0.41	0.46	0.44	0.44
Discretionary funds from the Office of National Drug Control Policy	0.5	0	0	0	0	0	0
Subtotal	88.56	112.44	308.81	785.97	224.68	374.61	499.02
Economic and Social Assistance Programs							
Economic Support Funds (ESF). Transfers for the recipient government	0	0	3	4	0	0	0
Development Assistance (DA). Funds development projects	0	0.02	0	0	0	0	0
International Narcotics Control (INC). State Department-managed funding for counterdrug economic and social aid	0	0.5	5.75	208	5.65	127.5	154.8
Subtotal	0	0.52	8.75	212	5.65	127.5	154.8
Grand total	88.56	112.96	317.56	997.97	230.33	502.11	653.82

Source: Vaicius and Isacson (2003: 2).

The most significant change in U.S. military assistance to Colombia was removal of the condition, for the first time since the end of the Cold War, that military aid to Colombia be subject to its exclusive use in the war on drugs. George W. Bush crossed the "invisible line" that, formally if not always in practice, separated the counternarcotics fight from counterinsurgency programs. All Plan Colombia and Andean Initiative funding may be used for both. The "ambiguous war" theorists, made resolute by the events of September 11, ultimately prevailed in imposing their views. The change was effected in the foreign aid package President Bush submitted to Congress on February 4, 2002, which included ninety-eight million dollars for protection of the Caño Limón–Coveñas oil pipeline in Colombia. A single sentence in the bill (H.R. 4775) gave the Colombian government authority to use Plan Colombia assistance in the war against the insurgency. The law invoked the need for a united campaign "against narcotics trafficking (and) against activities by organizations designated as terrorist organizations such as the FARC, the ELN, and the AUC" (Vaicius and Isacson, 2003: 12).

Guns or Butter?[40]

To this point we have outlined the context and processes that brought about Plan Colombia and the Andean Initiative and traced changes in focus, priorities, and levels of funding. It is our intention in this last section to evaluate the positive and negative impacts of the assistance for Colombia. There are many perspectives on the matter. Analysts like Gabriel Marcella point out that "President Bush's sweeping support for Colombia underlines a remarkable turnaround in American policy. Driven for years by the ambiguity of counter-narcotics, it is now moving in the direction of a more comprehensive approach that recognizes that nation's deeply rooted and complex security problem" (2003: 1). Other points of view suggest just the opposite, that Plan Colombia falls very short of being an integrated strategy for addressing the set of problems plaguing Colombian society, exaggerating the importance of military aspects and the fight against drug trafficking.

In our opinion, Plan Colombia and the Andean Initiative correctly focus on two of the greatest challenges facing Colombian society: the need to strengthen state institutions, and the urgency of slowing the flow of resources from narco-traffic. However, as we will show later, while the approach may be correct, the ways in which measures have been implemented—referring specifically here to antinarcotics policy—have not always been the most appropriate. Moreover, other strategic dimensions of the Colombian crisis are not being addressed simultaneously, like the fight against poverty and income disparity. Other dimensions are only partially addressed, as is the case with the rebuilding of the state, where emphasis has been put on the military aspects.

On the Road toward Reconstruction of the State?

In a comparative, historic perspective, the Colombian State has always been small, poor, and weak. The historic roots of its weakness can be summed up in a few sentences. First, it is a vast territory cross-cut by a very complex geography, one of the world's most hellish. This has given rise to a multitude of markets and scattered pockets of population. That Colombia ranks third among 155 countries on the Interamerican Development Bank's "index of geographic fragmentation" says it all. Second, it was not until the first decades of the twentieth century that Colombia was able to stabilize a product (coffee) for which there was demand on the world market. In addition, industrialization was slow in coming, and the state's resource base was very shaky. Finally, it is important to stress that coffee, Colombia's strategic resource for building the nation, was privately held and generated minimal revenue for the central state. In his prologue to English historian Malcolm Deas's book on Colombia (1993: 14), former president Alfonso López Michelsen states, "The best way to understand Colombians' fate is to look at these figures. Tireless fighters, working day-in, day-out under the most adverse conditions, they have managed to survive, without, as of yet, winning the lottery; without, like Mexico, having a border with the United States; without the tourism of Cuba, in its day; or Argentina's or Uruguay's grains and cattle; or the size of Brazil. Everything conspired against the survival of the Colombian State. Only in 1975 did it begin to derive income from its patrimony—unrelated to tax revenue—from State-owned coal, surpluses of national petroleum for export, and Cerromatoso nickel." No wonder Malcolm Deas writes that, for decades, the sole patrimony of the Colombian State was the salt mines. This has been the great transformation of the twentieth century's final twenty years: to have had the fiscal or patrimonial revenues Colombia always lacked, as well as tax revenues.

Colombia's weak institutions were put to the test twice during the twentieth century, and on both occasions the country suffered a "partial collapse of the State" (Oquist, 1980). That is, while some institutions remained intact, other institutions started to crack. The first partial collapse took place at mid-century as Colombia went through the last of the bipartite civil wars of the period harshly referred to as "La Violencia" (the Violence). A similar situation at the end of the 1980s was a result of the "double war," the war against the narco-terrorism of the cartels and the war on insurgency. In the face of challenges and demands that outstrip its capacity to manage and control, a weakened and shaky Colombian State leaves exposed the deep "geological faults" of such key institutions as justice and security.

Signs of the "partial collapse" of the Colombian State became evident at the end of the 1980s. The most visible sign was, without a doubt, the growth in crime rates. *At the beginning of the 1990s, Colombia's homicide rate reached the highest in the world*: eighty homicides per one hundred thousand inhabitants, a very long way from the alarming index for Latin America (twenty), and the extremely high index in the United States (eight), not to mention light years from average rates for Western Europe (1.5). Runaway crime was just one dramatic expression of the state's diminishing capacity to carry out essential functions. The grave incompetence of the National Police was notorious. There were constant revelations of corruption at all levels; negative encounters between citizens and an authoritarian and repressive police; and evidence of police involvement in theft, "social cleansing" activity, and massacres. The police profession was on the bottom rung of the social ladder. In response to the escalation of violence and police incompetence, the Colombian elite decided to turn to private security, giving rise to unparalleled growth in private security and protection agencies. The number of private security agents was double the size of the National Police force. Along with the "privatization of security" came financing of "social cleansing"—groups who were supposed to bring down crime rates in urban centers by ridding them of undesirables: that is, selective murder of "antisocial" elements.

Privatization of security was followed by privatization in other areas. The counterinsurgency war was privatized in response to the military's inability to check the guerrilla strategy of "diffuse expansion" across national territory. First came the formation of self-defense militias, legalized under Law 48 in 1968. Even after this National Security Law was repealed by President Virgilio Barco, paramilitary groups continued to form illegally.

Justice is another state sector that has been profoundly impacted by the progressive erosion of the state. Levels of impunity are scandalously high in Colombia. While 11 percent of those convicted for homicide were sentenced in the 1970s, twenty years later the figure dropped to just 4 percent. A convicted murderer has a greater than 90 percent chance of never being punished. Moreover, judges who would not be corrupted faced death threats against themselves and their families, as did journalists who denounced political corruption, the guerrillas, and the druglords.

Lastly, erosion of the state is reflected in the growing number of arms in civilian hands, a strengthening of armed groups that challenge state authority (specifically, the FARC, the ELN, and the AUC), and the lack of a state presence in certain areas of the country, especially those settled recently. While President Uribe's aggressive military campaigns from 2003 to 2005 reasserted state authority in some parts of the country, the response of guerrillas, paramilitaries, and the drug cartels increased the levels of violence in key regions where the military penetrated. At mid-2005, though the government boasted of gains in state presence, border areas with Ecuador, Venezuela, and Panama could hardly be counted as under effective government control.

The Strengthening of Institutions

Fundamental to any country's real achievement of the rule of law and respect for human rights is a state that is capable of guaranteeing a minimum of democratic order. To do so requires that first, the state must be capable of legislating and enforcing laws, and second, power must be exercised by duly elected officials who are willing to be held accountable for their actions.

Colombia has grave failings on both counts. But the shortcoming is more acute on the level of legislation and enforcement due to the "partial collapse of the state" that the country has experienced since the end of the 1980s. The hyperviolence Colombians have had to endure since then has caused a slow but unrelenting breakdown of institutions. Most affected have been the weak agencies responsible for civilian security. As previously discussed, Colombians watched as the justice system, the prison system, the National Police, and even the military itself fell like a house of cards.

The country hit bottom in 1993. From that point forward, institutional reconstruction has yielded some encouraging results. Once the elite was able to broaden its horizon, to see beyond simple macroeconomic stability, it was possible to undertake this long-term task on several fronts, work that really began under the César Gaviria administration (1990–1994). Perhaps most outstanding is the example of the National Police, particularly because Latin America is a region where there are precious few trustworthy police institutions. In spite of the corruption in which it has recently been involved, precisely in relation to the misuse of U.S. assistance, the National Police has been somewhat cleaned up and made more professional. Justice is also making halting progress, with the creation of the Fiscalía General de la Nación (National Office of the Prosecutor General) and increased funding for the judicial system. In the last several years the overall homicide rate has dropped, largely because it declined in the primary urban centers. And over the past years, steps have been taken in relation to illegally armed groups. On the one hand, the Medellin and Cali cartels that undermined institutions through violence and corruption have been successfully dismantled. On the other, however, paramilitary groups like the AUC, and the FARC and ELN guerrillas, have widened their spheres of activity.

Even with some advances, the road to justice—a sector where it is so critical that state duties be executed flawlessly—is still long and full of stumbling blocks. Still alarming rates of impunity, backlogged courts, hundreds of thousands of arrest warrants that have not been acted on, and the dangerous work and security environment in which court officials must perform their duties are all evidence of the need for comprehensive overhaul still to be implemented. Long overdue is the drafting of a policy for broad articulation across all entities participating in the administration of justice, a policy for conducting criminal investigation that does not duplicate efforts or put individual entities' interests ahead of the general interests of the state. Institutions responsible for security, too, are in critical need of upgrading and cleanup and should be under the clear political control of civilian authority as part of a well-integrated general strategy for citizen defense and security. In short, despite some erratic and incomplete progress in a number of areas, and despite the popularity among urban elites and much of the middle class of President Uribe's *mano dura*, in other areas there has been backsliding. The Colombian State remains fragile and, at the same time, corrupt, authoritarian, repressive, and ineffective.

Finally, the Colombian military has, to some extent, recovered the offensive advantage as a result of a buildup of the armed forces (budget, number of troops, training, and technology) over the last several years, to the misfortune of the guerrillas and paramilitaries. Clearly, the process of rebuilding this institution has been slow; the country was engulfed in hyperviolence, at the mercy of the illegal drug trade and powerful armed groups who were fighting over whole chunks of the national territory. Nevertheless, the guerrillas and the AUC were far from defeated or demobilized in 2005; counteroffensives carried out by both of these groups have left numerous military personnel and civilians dead and wounded. Kidnapping remains an important business, as does arms trafficking and, of course, the drug trade. Thus the large sums spent on enhancing the capabilities of the Colombian military and the increased presence of U.S. advisers and private contractors have not won the war against the various militarized nonstate actors that challenge the authority of the Colombian State and routinely use Venezuelan and Ecuadorian territory as smuggling routes and for sanctuary.

While the immense effort to rebuild the state may have attenuated further deepening of the crisis, the effort has been oriented toward "restoration" as opposed to actual "repair." In a project of the latter type, productive employment, elimination of poverty, and efforts to increase social equity would certainly be considered crucial for attaining well-being for the majority and assuring the nation's "governability."[41]

Two things should be noted here. First, the principal goals for achieving vital macroeconomic stabilization have been met—primarily through tax, pension, labor, and financial reforms. The country has regained, to some extent, the confidence of financial markets and has garnered the support of multilateral credit institutions. Similarly, there have been encouraging signs of economic recovery. At the same time, implementation of the Plan Nacional de Desarrollo (National Development Plan) continues to raise concerns, even within sectors friendliest to the administration. Many challenge its weak social content and the viability and sustainability of the "Plan de Reactivación Social" (Social Revitalization Plan), which is supposed to reach 9.5

million Colombians and will commit estimated resources of about 3.5 billion pesos.

Public spending has been steadily redirected toward the defense and security sectors as a result of the ever-increasing financial burden of the wars against illegal armed groups and narcotics. Meanwhile, institutional energies and funding for policies designed to enhance social equity are heavily debated. Perhaps the best example is what happened in the so-called rehabilitation and consolidation zones or the former "demilitarized zone" where talks got under way with FARC guerrillas during the Pastrana–Arango administration. There has been a military recovery in these areas, if only partial in some cases, and the presence of law enforcement, once nonexistent, has been reestablished. But there has been little vital follow-up investment of a social nature, as the joint report by the Procuraduría General de la Nación (Attorney General of the Nation) and Defensoría del Pueblo (Public Defense) showed in the dramatic case of Arauca Department (*El Tiempo*, May 20, 2003). There has been no sign by the state of the administration of justice, job creation, or protection of local civilian authorities. The government faces the difficult dilemma of desperately needing to reassert its authority and to maintain the rule of law, while also having to attend to the population's basic needs, a population affected by the enormous humanitarian crisis brought on by decades of armed conflict.

This attempt at rebuilding institutions has taught us an important lesson: if Colombia is to someday attain the level of civilian security commensurate with the quality of life already enjoyed in other regions across the globe, the state must be able to institute basic democratic order. Only in such an environment can there be true respect for human rights, genuine protection for the exercise of political rights, and a climate conducive to productive investment. Who can guarantee that humanitarian standards are being met or that there is a minimum "rule of law" in states that are, or were, in a condition of collapse, such as Sierra Leone, Afghanistan, Somalia, or Sudan? Although Colombia has not sunk to such levels of institutional breakdown, it is obvious that a "partial collapse of the state" is a medium that spawns all sorts of illegitimate violence. A shaky justice system invites private parties to take justice into their own hands; the lack of protection for landholders and victims of kidnapping and extortion is an incentive for criminal paramilitary groups. The precarious condition of the state also facilitates corruption, undermines the functioning of oversight and control agencies, and impedes or makes impossible the development of necessary structural social reforms. It also diminishes the national government's autonomy and ability to negotiate in its foreign relations and to play a more positive role on the international scene.

Foreign Policy: The Other Challenge

During the last two administrations, normalization and consolidation of bilateral relations with the United States have been the centerpiece of foreign policy. Identification of the criteria and purposes underlying the fights against drugs and against terrorism during the current administration is behind this new *respice polum* guiding the country's foreign relations today. Smooth interactions and continual assistance from the United States, particularly, but not only, of a military nature, contrast sharply with the drop in political and trade activity with Europe and Asia and a marked deterioration of Colombia's relations with bordering countries.

Relations with Colombia's neighbors are going through one of their most critical periods in recent history. The primary response to collateral effects of the internal armed conflict has been increased militarization of the borders. Political instability and the poor economic performance of the Andean nations only heighten negative feelings toward Colombia. This state of affairs puts tremendous pressures on bilateral diplomacy; puts swift, effectual integration of the region at risk; and makes cooperation with other important outside parties, such as the European Union, even more difficult. The same can be said for crucial negotiations that have begun for the Área de Libre Comercio de las Américas (ALCA—American Free Trade Zone) where unified action would have great strategic advantage.

In the same vein, it is critical that existing tools for binational and regional agreement be fully exploited and that policies be reached for the various areas of common concern. It is also necessary to put concrete, viable defense and security policies for the community in place, as well as to "improve and expand measures that build trust," as called for in "La Carta Andina para la Paz y la Seguridad, Limitación y Control de los Gastos Destinados a la Defensa Externa" (the Andean Charter for Peace, Border Security, and Control on External Defense Spending) signed by the ministers of defense and foreign relations for the five countries in Lima on June 17, 2002. These accords have been severely challenged by the spillover of Colombia's internal conflicts and also by Venezuelan president Hugo Chávez's seeming sympathies for Colombian guerrillas and his anti-U.S. foreign policy initiatives, focused on diluting American influence through multilateral initiatives, both for Venezuela and the hemisphere.

It is most certainly not enough, then, to simply label Colombia as "a serious threat" to the region. And militarizing the border is not going to be effective either. On their side, Colombia and bordering states have the legitimate right to defend their sovereignty and protect their populations. But, inasmuch as the scourge of illegal drugs and transnational crime affects and involves all nations and societies on the continent, another approach is necessary: a long-term policy that turns shared responsibility and reciprocity not just into principles but into the will and the decisiveness to construct, together, an integrated regional security strategy built on consensus that is both viable and sustainable. Whether Colombia can balance its dependence and alliance with the United States with the increasingly complex and unstable political situation in the Andean region is a critical question as President Uribe comes to the end of his term in office.

Arms and munitions trafficking, the supplying of chemical components for the drug trade, money laundering, and the smuggling of goods keep feeding the cycle of struggle in Colombia and help strengthen the parties to the conflict. This obviously weakens the state and its institutions even further, diminishes security and defense capabilities, makes the illegal economy more robust at the expense of the cultivation of legal crops and alternative development programs, and undermines democracy and the possibilities for reaching a negotiated political settlement to the conflict. These types of transnational crime also augment their own capacity for growth and worsen the collateral effects of armed aggression on the borders and even within the bordering countries themselves, as demonstrated by the recurrent incursions, kidnappings, so-called vacunas,[42] roadblocks, and the bases established by various illegal groups located in countries neighboring Colombia.

The principal weapons in the global battle against these atrocities should be binational and regional cooperation among civilian and military, local and national authorities; mutual assistance between governments on judicial issues and the timely sharing of evidence; land, air, and sea interdictions; joint efforts to increase banking reserves—an effective means for controlling money laundering; the freezing of assets; and mutual control over sales of arms and chemicals. Moreover, they would be key pieces of a regional security policy designed to assure peace and good relations.

The Antinarcotics Fight

It is indisputable that the spiraling growth of illegal crop cultivation broke in 2002 and that coca leaf production in Colombia dropped recently. According to the U.S. Department of State, the decline in the first year was 15 percent. Based on the report from the director of the UN Office for the Control of Drugs and Crime Prevention (UNODC), Antonio María Costa, the decline was even greater, perhaps as high as 30 percent. Costa cites as reasons for this decline the eradication of illegal crops, the dismantling of processing labs, and peak growth in the agricultural sector, especially for cocoa and sugar cane,[43] all of which made coca planting less profitable in Colombia. According to the United Nations, illegal cultivation fell from 144,807 to 102,071 hectares between 2001 and the start of 2003, thanks particularly to declines in Putumayo (71 percent) and Caquetá (42 percent) Departments, the two regions strategically most valuable to funding the FARC and the AUC.[44] Production of coca *in Colombia* continued to decline from 2003 to 2005.

Yet even in this optimistic scenario the "balloon effect" remains operative on both the national and regional fronts. It is common knowledge that crops are being aggressively displaced, threatening even Colombia's world-famous "coffee-growing region," while coca cultivation is once again on the rise in Peru and Bolivia. Is it possible to halt the "balloon effect" without also slowing demand for drugs in industrialized nations? Skepticism is well-founded; it is precisely the asymmetrical, fragile nature of shared responsibility in the global war on drugs that has made it impossible to make solid, encouraging progress in the region.

Apropos to this situation, while demand in the principal consuming nations falls very slowly, if at all, and mandatory fumigation continues, measures that strike at the central nervous system of narco-trafficking—sea-based interdiction, curbing of money laundering, the freezing of assets, the cancellation of ownership for farmland dedicated to drugs—receive less attention.

The Colombian government's announcement that the coca and poppy aerial spraying campaign was currently at its highest level, and the U.S. State Department's report to Congress in which the Environmental Protection Agency (EPA) certified that fumigation is not toxic, put a key debate back on the table for discussion. As an editorial in the Colombian newspaper *El Tiempo* pointed out, discussion of failures and errors in judgment in relation to the fumigation policy is a matter of national interest. Even though an end to the debate will be long in coming, and consensual, multilateral solutions are not yet in sight, it is also clear that a cornerstone of Plan Colombia—fumigation—is its "Achilles' heel." The same newspaper points out,

> There is substantial evidence that peasants' food crops are being destroyed even as globalization and crop subsidies in rich nations push peasant farmers into the arms of modern agriculture's most profitable business: illegal crops. . . . Does fumigation work? Looking at it on the scale of a single country, it might look that way. . . . The issue is that on a regional and global scale, obligatory eradication policies (Colombia alone allows fumigation) serve only to re-distribute production. The market and demand are the same; only the suppliers change. When coca was eradicated in Perú and Bolivia, production shifted to Colombia. And as Asian mafias from the "Golden Triangle" have been displaced, Colombia is now supplying a large part of the US demand for opium and heroin. The fumigation campaign has cut into cultivation in Putumayo. But there is strong evidence that the crops have moved into Nariño, Arauca, Guaviare and other regions.[45]

These trends, with changes in the names of regions where eradication reduced cultivation and those into which new cultivation migrated, continued for the next three years, not only in Colombia, but in Peru, Bolivia, and even Ecuador.

There are numerous serious flaws to the logic that dynamic eradication will be able to outpace cultivation—more flaws still, taking into account that alternative development projects, difficult to implement in areas controlled by armed groups, yield extremely poor results in spite of the government's efforts. In many cases they are outright disasters, as when several trails in Orito, Putumayo, were fumigated by accident. In the absence of true agrarian development policy, the effects of preventive and punitive measures will quickly fade away amid growing rural unemployment and the collapse of agro-businesses besieged by various armed groups. It is vital that legitimate agriculture not continue to give ground to illegal cultivation and that alternative development projects, which cover only 20 percent of the families that grow these crops, hold their own over the medium and long terms, that is, beyond the year 2005, when the agreement with the United States comes to an end. An increase in multipurpose assistance from abroad, such as that given by the United Nations and several European nations; a consolidated state presence; development of integrated agrarian reform, deferred time and time again; and cooperative work with affected communities may put these programs on the road toward a viable, sustainable policy.

By Way of Conclusion

Internal and international analysts all agree that it is very hard to imagine a strictly military solution to the Colombian conflict. For that reason, all measures that are brought to bear must have achievement of domestic peace in the country on their strategic horizon. The United Nations, the European Union, and the Grupo de Países Amigos de la Paz en Colombia (Countries Who are Friends for Peace in Colombia)[46] have played, and should continue to play, an even more decisive role here. International experience shows that very few successfully negotiated settlements of civil wars have not involved a "third party" acting as mediator in the conflict. As Barbara Walter observes,

> Unlike interstate wars, civil wars rarely end in negotiated settlements. Between 1940 and 1990, 55 percent of interstate wars were resolved at the bargaining table, whereas only 20 percent of civil wars reached similar solutions. Instead, most internal wars ended with the extermination, expulsion, or capitulation of the losing side. In fact, groups fighting civil wars almost always chose to fight to the finish unless an outside power stepped in to guarantee a peace agreement. If a third party agreed to enforce the terms of a peace treaty, negotiations always succeeded regardless of the initial goals, ideology, or ethnicity of the participants. If a third party did not intervene, these talks usually failed. (Walter, 1997)

For a number of reasons (opposition to the antinarcotics piece of the U.S. assistance package, the desire to play an autonomous role in Latin America, fear of finding themselves entangled in a military conflict), the European Union nations have been very reluctant and are highly critical of Plan Colombia (Roy, 2001). Also influencing the Europeans' attitude is the fact that they have more intense interests in other regions of the world—specifically, Eastern Europe, Africa, and Asia. Thus, the European Union has opted for soft engagement, as opposed to the hard engagement approach of the United States.

Its legitimate misgivings aside, Europe's role has been invaluable, not simply because of its political support for a negotiated settlement to the conflict, but socially and economically as well. Its role is, and will be, increasingly essential. It serves to diversify foreign assistance and counterbalance the positions of the most strident, militaristic factions in the United States. It also complements U.S. aid—primarily geared toward the antinarcotics and military fight—by funneling assistance into efforts to restart the economy, bolster administration of justice, support those displaced by violence, and advance human rights. Funding from the European Union, from Japan, and from other multilateral bodies is vital to helping insure an integrated approach to the Colombian crisis.

Reconstruction of the Colombian State, then, is essential. But as recent experience shows, these efforts will fall short unless domestic peace is achieved and the requisite social changes, so often deferred, are finally instituted. This is the other side of the coin. There is awareness in the country today of the strategic importance of both courses of action. In order to take on Colombia's multidimensional crisis and overcome it, these courses of action must become state policy. It is imperative to implement policies that will withstand the coming and going of successive administrations and situations that might develop abroad, and to balance the regional strategies of the United States with the needs of Colombia, the Andean region, and Latin America more generally. Lastly, the biggest challenge is how to go about building up a democratic state, one that can provide security and create equity, when enveloped in chronic, increasingly degenerate and vile armed conflict.

Let us hope that the international community, and the United States, will realize that reconstruction of the Colombian State and peace are not antagonistic, but rather, mutually reinforcing, necessary, and interdependent policies.

3

U.S. Security Policy and
U.S.–Venezuelan Relations

Orlando J. Pérez

VENEZUELA IS A CRITICAL COUNTRY for U.S. global security interests and for its Latin American and Andean regional policies. Not only is Venezuela one of the world's largest oil producers, it is an important regional actor whose international and domestic policies can have a significant and possibly decisive impact on the conflict in Colombia. From their own perspective, Venezuelans believe that as a neighbor with a long border with Colombia their security is directly bound with that of Colombia. For the United States, this proximity also makes Venezuela a key component of U.S. strategy in the region. U.S.–Venezuelan relations since the 1990s, however, have been characterized by continual difficulties reflecting the cyclical nature of domestic and international politics in both countries.

This chapter examines the evolution of U.S.–Venezuelan relations since the 1990s, focusing particular attention on regional security issues, the reaction to Plan Colombia, and the impact of the rise to power of Hugo Chávez as president of Venezuela. The chapter begins with a brief examination of U.S.–Venezuelan relations before Chávez's rise to power. It then looks at the bilateral relations since 1998, the year Hugo Chávez won the presidency.

Before the 1990s, Venezuela was considered among the most stable and democratic countries in the region. Since the late 1950s, with the establishment of the Puntofijista system, U.S.–Venezuelan relations were based on four factors: (1) the repeated assertion by Venezuelan governments that they are a reliable partner to the United States in the hemisphere; (2) the assertion of Venezuela's political and economic stability relative to the rest of the region; (3) relations characterized by cooperation rather than conflict; and (4) the predominance of bilateral rather than regional issues in U.S.–Venezuelan relations.[1] Traditionally, economics has taken center stage in the relations between the two countries. Venezuela is the fourth largest supplier of foreign oil to the United States. The United States is Venezuela's most important trading partner, representing approximately half of both imports and exports. In turn, Venezuela is the United States' third largest export market in Latin America, purchasing U.S. machinery, transportation equipment, agricultural commodities, and auto parts. While the two countries differed on some specific issues,[2] for the most part they agreed on the broad outlines of policy, and Venezuela placed most of her attention on deepening bilateral economic relations.

Despite the long period of tranquility that had preceded the 1990s, the following decade saw some difficult years for relations between the United States and Venezuela. On the one hand, the collapse of the Puntofijista economic and political model led to the questioning of the pillars underlying U.S.–Venezuelan relations. On the other hand, the end of the Cold War led the United States to focus on an expanding array of security issues, particularly fighting drug trafficking, which tended to strain relations with Venezuela. Additionally, the increasingly "aggressive" and independent rhetoric of President Hugo Chávez strained relations further.

The Collapse of the Puntofijista System

The problems in Venezuelan politics arose from a number of sources, but the chief reason centered on the collapse of the rentier state model of development because of the downturn in oil prices and increasing corruption. The lost decade of the 1980s, when most of Latin America suffered economic problems and undertook severe adjustment programs, was particularly shocking for a country like Venezuela that had grown at a fast clip for most of the postwar period. In the 1980s, the economy destabilized, inflation skyrocketed, and government controls failed to solve the problem. The year 1989 was particularly disastrous for the Venezuelan economy. Inflation rose to 84 percent for the year, until then the highest in the history of the country. Economic output, as measured by gross domestic product (GDP), declined 8.6 percent in real terms, while salaries shrank by 11 percent.[3] In this context, Carlos Andrés Pérez, the newly elected president, implemented a harsh neoliberal restructuring policy that drastically cut state subsidies and social welfare spending.

The military was hard hit by the program in declining real wages and reduced resources for modernization. For the public, the new policies represented a clear betrayal of the "culture of entitlement." As Moises Naim states, "For most Venezuelans, such stark realities as the absence of a reliable social safety net, the near collapse of social services . . . and the persistent price increases canceled out any benefits that might eventually accrue from the successes in terms of balance of payments or economic growth."[4] On February 27, 1989, Caracas erupted into riots and looting. For junior officers in the military, the riots were a clear indication that the Puntofijista system was near collapse. Officers, whose own families were suffering from the effects of the economic crisis and the drastic neoliberal policies, identified with the plight of the population and blamed corrupt politicians of the Puntofijista system for the chaos.

By the late 1980s, the Movimiento Revolucionario Quinta República (MVR) had begun to organize among military officers, with Lieutenant Colonel Hugo Chávez Frías as its most prominent leader. Claiming to use Simón Bolivar's ideals, Chávez and his colleagues rallied the concerns of other military officers for the coup attempt of February 4, 1992. The rebellion, and another led by senior officers on November 27, 1992, shook the Venezuelan political establishment to its core, but the Puntofijista system held. However, during the next six years, the economic and political situation of the country did not improve, and by the elections of December 1998, the public was prepared to exercise an electoral coup by electing Hugo Chávez as president.

Brian Loveman and Thomas M. Davies argue, "In the 1960s and 1970s professional military officers in Latin America scanned the panorama of the hemisphere's history and blamed the ineptitude and corruption of civilian politicians as well as the imported institutions of liberal democracy for the wretched conditions in their region."[5] This appears to be the same motivation in Venezuela in the 1980s and 1990s. An alienated population fell under the charm of the charismatic paratrooper who was willing to sacrifice his life for the country in a heroic effort to take over the government and "save" the nation from a corrupt political system.

The Rise to Power of Hugo Chávez and Initial U.S. Reaction

The U.S. government did not hesitate to congratulate Chávez hours after his victory in the December 8, 1998, elections. A White House spokesperson stated that the United States "congratulated Mr. Chávez on an impressive victory." The spokesperson went on to reiterate that "we [the United States] have good relations with Venezuela and we expect to work with the Chávez government when it takes office in February."[6] Two days after the elections, the United States issued a diplomatic visa to Chávez—which had been denied the former lieutenant colonel in 1997—and U.S. ambassador John Maisto visited him and stressed that Venezuelan–American relations "would go forward from this moment along side this new, democratically-elected government."

The ambassador went on to characterize the electoral process that led to Chávez's election as an "impressive victory of democracy."[7]

Despite concerns about the precedent set by the election of a former coup leader, some of the "inflammatory" rhetoric used by the new Venezuelan president, and his denunciation of U.S. policy toward Cuba, U.S–Venezuelan relations remained cordial throughout the first few months of Chávez's administration. Between 1994 and 1998, the two governments had signed a number of treaties and memoranda related to drug trafficking, justice, defense, customs, and energy, among other matters. Cautious optimism in the United States reflected the fact that, despite the political noise, the two nations continued to share common interests, and the arrival of Chávez would not change the underlying bases of bilateral relations. President-elect Chávez visited the White House and spoke with President Clinton for a few minutes in late January 1999. The United States was now paying close attention to events in Venezuela, although maintaining a certain distance, making it clear that its willingness to maintain close relations was contingent on the preservation of democracy. Particular concern was expressed over the elections and subsequent work of the Asamblea Nacional Constituyente (ANC), charged with writing a new constitution. Given Chávez's repeated claims that all Venezuelan institutions had been corrupted and should be replaced by others through a constituent assembly, the word in Washington continued to be "wait and see."[8]

However, the Chávez "revolution" systematically removed all the checks and balances required for liberal democracy. Dismantling liberal democracy was achieved in a two-stage process: (1) eliminating the old political actors in a position to check the president and (2) securing the loyalty or subordination of the new actors. The means for the first stage was the ANC, which was authorized by a referendum in April 1999 and elected in July 1999, finished with its draft in three months, had the new constitution ratified on December 15, 1999, and disbanded itself on January 31, 2000. The old congress allowed itself to be marginalized soon after the ANC was seated, and it formally ceased to exist the day the 1999 constitution was ratified. The ANC designated an unelected National Legislative Committee to take the place of the legislature until new elections could be held and appointed a commission that purged hundreds of judges from the courts.

This transitional regime continued in power until August 2000, when new officials elected in July were seated. Chávez himself was reelected with a 56.9 percent landslide, and his allied parties won at least 99 of 165 seats in the new unicameral National Assembly. In November 2000, they granted the president sweeping powers to issue decree-laws in areas ranging from economic development to land reform. A few governors remained affiliated with opposition parties, but the federal government undermined their power by reducing funding for state and local governments. Between December 1998 and August

2000, therefore, Chávez removed, co-opted, or severely weakened all possible checks from other branches and levels of government.

Tensions in U.S.–Venezuelan Relations

The concentration of power in Chávez's hands sparked negative reactions in the United States. In early November 2000, editorials in the *Washington Post* and the *New York Times* warned about Chávez's demagogic and authoritarian political style and its potential for influencing other countries in the region. The editorials recommended that the U.S. government watch Chávez warily—avoiding unnecessary confrontations—and allay the fears of Venezuela's neighbors in the Andean region by promoting political stability through the strengthening of their judicial systems, combating official corruption, and developing closer economic ties.[9] Around the same time, another U.S. newspaper harshly criticized Venezuela's foreign and regional policies, which have been defined by Chávez's attempt to pursue a more independent foreign policy, including close ties with Cuba and a leadership role in OPEC. *Miami Herald* columnist Andrés Oppenheimer, on October 29, 2000, argued that Chávez's foreign policy has been deliberately aimed at "picking a fight" with the United States and mentioned a number of specific actions taken by Chávez in pursuit of this strategy: first, Chávez's meeting with Iraqi strongman Saddam Hussein on August 10, 2000, in clear defiance of U.S. wishes. Second, Chávez's harsh warnings, expressed at various regional meetings, against the "Vietnamization" consequences of U.S. policy in Colombia. Third, an incident surrounding the alleged foray into Venezuelan waters of the U.S. Coast Guard vessel *Reliance*. Fourth, the five-day visit to Venezuela in October 2000 of Cuban leader Fidel Castro, along with the expected "anti-U.S." rhetoric and the signing of a series of commercial agreements between Cuba and Venezuela.[10]

Despite the U.S. media's negative views of Chávez, the U.S. government maintained an officially cooperative, rather than confrontational, stance. One of the most important and revealing incidents in U.S.–Venezuelan relations was the debate over how to monitor movements of drugs in the region. The withdrawal of U.S. troops from Panama forced the United States to seek alternative bases for their counternarcotics efforts. The United States sought to replace the bases in Panama with additional Forward Operation Locations (FOLs) in the region. By March 2000, the U.S. Southern Command (SOUTHCOM) had completed agreements for three sites. An Andean region FOL is operating at the Eloy Alfaro International Airport in Manta, Ecuador. A "northern drug source zone" FOL operates at the Reina Beatrix International Airport in Aruba and the Hato International Airport in nearby Curaçao, Netherlands Antilles. A third

Central American FOL has been established at the International Airport in Co-malapa, El Salvador. However, President Chávez had announced that Venezuela would not allow U.S. aircraft to use Venezuelan airspace. This proved a significant obstacle for SOUTHCOM, which had just completed arrangements for an FOL just off the Venezuelan coast in Aruba and Curaçao. Since Venezuela sits between these islands and the Andean drug-producing region, flights from Aruba and Curaçao have had to make lengthy trips around Venezuela to reach their destinations. Chávez's refusal followed the same approach pursued by the previous government, but his rhetoric was more heated.[11] In the end, the United States decided not to insist on its request for overflights of Venezuelan territory and instead tried to work closely with Venezuela on training and common drug fighting efforts. Officials claimed that the goals of the two countries coincided completely.[12] In fact, U.S. counternarcotics assistance to Venezuela continued and, in some years, actually increased after 2001. Table 3.1 shows the total amount of military and police aid since 1996.

In addition to assistance programs, Venezuela has been one of the United States' largest arms customers in Latin America, consistently among the top regional purchaser through the Foreign Military Sales (FMS)[13] and Direct Commercial Sales (DCS) Programs. For example, in 1999 Venezuela received delivery of $31.7 million in FMS and signed agreements for another $9.5 million. In 2001, under the same program Venezuela signed agreements for over $35 million. Agreements for $20 million were signed in 2002 and 2003, with delivery of over $18 million carried out in 2002. Under the DCS program Venezuela received delivery of over $38 million worth of military equipment in 2002 and $43 million the following year.[14]

Although U.S. defense and security assistance continued to flow into Venezuela, Chávez's rhetoric and actions continued to irritate the United

TABLE 3.1
Total U.S. Military and Police Assistance to Venezuela[1]
(in millions of U.S. dollars)

1996	1997	1998	1999	2000	2001	2002	2003	2004 (est.)	2005 (req.)
>13	5.8	7.2	4.0	6.5	3.2	5.5	3.7	4.1	3.6

Source: *Just the Facts: A Civilian's Guide to U.S. Defense and Security Assistance to Latin America and the Caribbean*, Report by the Latin American Working Group and Center for International Policy, www.ciponline.org/facts.

[1] The aid encompasses ten programs run by the State and Defense Departments ranging from the International Narcotics Control (INC) program administered by the Department of State's Bureau for International Narcotics and Law Enforcement Affairs (INL), which provides aid and training to the governments and security forces of countries in which drugs are produced and transported; the International Military Education and Training (IMET), which pays for the training or education of foreign military and a limited number of civilian personnel; and Section 1004 aid, which allows the U.S. Department of Defense to spend money on counternarcotics programs in a given country. Note that the large amount in 1996 was due to "emergency drawdown" assistance, a program that allows the U.S. president to shift resources and equipment from various sources without congressional approval in cases of "emergency."

States. For instance, on October 25, 2000, President Chávez stated that Venezuela's foreign policy was aimed at promoting "a new center of political power" to counterbalance U.S. influence in the hemisphere and that "the deepening of our relations with Cuba . . . [was] part of that policy." A day later, Castro got a hero's welcome in Caracas and signed a deal to buy oil at heavily discounted prices. Likewise, Peter Romero, the former U.S. assistant secretary of state for Western Hemisphere affairs, said there were "indications of Chávez's government support for violent indigenous groups in Bolivia and ties to rebellious army officers in Ecuador."[15] Soon after, the *Miami Herald* revealed that President Banzer had asked President Chávez during the Ibero-American Summit held in November 2000 in Panama whether the latter had been aiding Felipe Quispe Huanca, indigenous leader of the coca growers' protests, and Ecuadorian foreign minister Heinz Moeller asked the Venezuelan government whether it had been aiding coup plotter Col. Lucio Gutiérrez.[16] In a February 3, 2001, article in *El Nacional*, it was revealed that the U.S. government had pressured the government of Venezuela for the removal of Miguel Quintero, director of information of the Venezuelan Foreign Ministry, due to his alleged participation in the unauthorized invitation to speak before the Venezuelan National Assembly extended to two Revolutionary Armed Forces of Colombia (FARC) members.[17]

Bush vs. Chávez: The Aftermath of September 11th

Some observers expressed concern that the election of George W. Bush as president of the United States would strain U.S. relations with Venezuela even further because of Bush's conservative ideology and the expectation that he would take a tougher stance against Cuba and the Colombian crisis. Chávez, however, reassured the new administration, "I am sure that relations with the United States will remain normal. . . . I am willing to extend my hand to the new government in the United States."[18] For its part, the Bush administration apparently had serious misgivings about Chávez's policies. For instance, an article in the Brazilian newspaper *O Estado de Sao Paulo* reported that during a meeting held in late March 2001 between President Bush and President Cardoso, the former expressed both an increasing discomfort with Chávez's constant challenges to the United States and his concerns about the impact of growing Venezuelan political instability on oil supplies. The paper reported that President Cardoso transmitted these concerns to the Venezuelan president.[19]

Another source of contention between the United States and Venezuela was the appointment of Otto Reich as assistant secretary of state for Western Hemisphere affairs.[20] Reich, a Cuban American, was a former U.S. ambassador to Venezuela and a staunch critic of the Cuban government. His confrontational style and obsession with U.S.–Cuba policy was bound to cause friction with Venezuela, particularly at a time when Venezuela under Chávez had close ties to Fidel Castro. Among the first actions taken by the new U.S. administration was a curtailment of the relationship with Venezuela's intelligence agency, the Directorate of Intelligence and Preventive Services (DISIP), because of fear that it had close ties with Cuba. A congressional aide was quoted as saying "There was a sense that anything we gave the Venezuelans would wind up in Havana."[21] Despite the differences on Cuba and the reduction of intelligence cooperation, General Speer's Posture Statement said, "In Venezuela, we seek to maintain military-to-military contacts where we can. There are more Venezuelan military students in United States schools than from any other country, this is extremely important since they will be the future leaders of the Venezuelan Armed Forces."[22]

However, Venezuelan statements made in the aftermath of the September 11, 2001, terrorist attacks caused a serious rift between the two governments.[23] Chávez condemned the attack on Afghanistan by saying, "This [speaking of the U.S. military operations in Afghanistan] has no justification, just like the attacks in New York didn't either." He went on to say, "The killing in Afghanistan must stop." In a sign of U.S. sensitivity to this issue, a State Department spokesperson responded by saying, "We [the U.S. government] were surprised and deeply disappointed by his comments."[24] The immediate reaction of the United States was to recall its ambassador from Caracas for "consultations."[25] At the height of the controversy, Tarek William Saab, a member of the Fifth Republic Movement and chairman of the National Assembly's foreign policy committee, was quoted as saying, "With the Bush administration, U.S. misunderstanding of the process of change that is going on here has gotten worse. The United States can trust this government, but they cannot intrude in our foreign policy. Trust does not mean servility. We will not be a subordinate partner in this relationship, but a strong one."[26] While Venezuelan spokespersons tried to soften Chávez's criticism and assure the United States that Venezuela supported the war on terrorism, Vice President Adina Bastidas said that terrorism was "a perverse and regrettable sub-product of Anglo-Saxon domination, which becomes unbearable for the most radical and violent of those who are dominated, and leads them to desperate, destructive and murdering outbursts."[27] Lino Gutiérrez, the acting assistant secretary of state for Western Hemisphere affairs, laid out the position of the United States in a speech to the U.S. Conference of Catholic Bishops, by saying,

> In the wake of the September 11 terrorist attacks, our historically strong relationship with Venezuela has *experienced difficulties*. President Chávez's October

29 criticisms of the U.S. and the coalition military response to international terrorism caused serious strains in our bilateral relationship. In response to
Chávez's remarks, we asked our Ambassador to Venezuela to return to Washington for consultations. In the wake of those consultations, it was decided to continue with our policy of engagement with Venezuela whereby we measure the
state of our relations by deeds, not words. However, *should Venezuelan officials
mischaracterize U.S. policy or actions, the U.S. will respond. Measuring Venezuela
by its deeds and not Chávez' words.* [emphasis added]

Gutiérrez went on to indicate "the U.S. has been generally satisfied by cooperation offered by Venezuela in its support for the war on terrorism. For example, Venezuela has promised to surge its oil production in the event of an
energy supply disruption. The Venezuelan Superintendent of Banks has provided excellent assistance searching for possible terrorist assets, and the investigative support provided by Venezuelan law enforcement and security services has been well received. These successes demonstrate that there are
practical areas in which we can cooperate in the war on terrorism." However,
in a sign of growing concern with the political situation inside Venezuela,
Gutiérrez urged the Catholic Church to remain vigilant and engaged with
human rights issues in Venezuela. Gutiérrez said, "Overall, though human
rights difficulties such as deplorable prison conditions and excessive use of
force by security forces persist, Venezuela has a generally good human rights
record. *There are, however, growing concerns about threats against freedom of
expression and of the press and undue pressure on organized labor.* We appreciate the efforts of these Catholic human rights observers [referring to Church
human rights organizations] in closely monitoring developments" [emphasis
added].[28]

Internal Dissension, Coup d'état, and U.S.–Venezuelan Relations

By the end of 2001, the internal political situation in Venezuela was at a critical moment.[29] Political opposition to the president had been mounting since
December 10, 2001, when civic groups, unions, and business organizations
staged the first nationwide strike to express discontent with the government's
decision to decree the adoption of a large package of economic reform measures on November 13. Among the forty-nine laws approved, the most controversial were a new land law and the reformed hydrocarbons law. Social unrest and union protests have persisted almost unabated since.

In a move widely seen as a sign of growing discontent within the armed
forces, during the month of February 2002 a series of high-ranking officers
publicly criticized the government. On February 7, air force colonel Pedro
Soto called the regime "fascist" and "totalitarian." While Colonel Soto claimed

to represent "75 percent of the officers, non-commissioned officers, and troops," there were no signs of a deeper move against the president. However, the next day Captain Pedro Flores called the president "undemocratic." On February 18, Vice-Admiral Carlos Molina Tamayo accused President Chávez of harming the national interest. And on February 25, Brigadier General Roman Gomez said, "There is a crisis in every sector of power. . . . They [the government] want to split us into two groups. . . . This division has been carried into the armed forces as well." The general went on to say, "Our loyalty is to the nation, not with the current administration."[30]

President Chávez's decision to dismiss several board members at the state-owned Petróleos de Venezuela S.A. (PDVSA) on April 7 and the subsequent work stoppage at key oil production facilities, due to a renewed nationwide strike on April 10, forced PDVSA to declare that it would not be able to comply with contractual crude oil and product supply commitments with its international clients. The increased prospects that the one-day nationwide work stoppage could turn into an indefinite strike, and an escalation of violence that resulted in fifteen deaths and 315 injured on April 11, prompted a military coup and the arrest of President Chávez. Even though the senior military command stressed repeatedly its respect for the democratic and constitutional order, presidential support had been undermined in the preceding months by corruption charges against senior Chávez-linked generals.[31]

Contrary to constitutional norms that would have required the vice president to assume the presidency and, upon his resignation, the president of the National Assembly, the military installed its own interim government. Pedro Carmona Estanga was designated interim president. As the former president of the country's two main industry associations, the Venezuelan Federation of Chambers and Associations of Commerce and Production (Fedecamaras, Federación Venezolana de Cámaras y Asociaciones de Comercio y Producción) and the Venezuelan Confederation of Industry (CONINDUSTRIA, Confederación Venezolana de Industriales), Carmona was expected to install a more solid framework to the economy to bolster investor confidence. Upon assuming office, the new interim president immediately appointed a new cabinet and issued a decree that temporarily dissolved all branches of government (national, state, and municipal). Activities of the National Assembly were to be suspended until new elections in December for a legislature authorized to undertake general revisions to the 1999 constitution. Furthermore, general elections (presidential, state, and municipal) were to be held no later than 365 days from April 12. Carmona also intended to establish a special committee to review and revise the forty-nine decrees signed into law by Chávez in November. Given the indiscriminate adoption of the new measures and the unconstitutional nature of the new government, along with internal military dissent over the coup and further social backlash, the new government lasted only one day, and constitutional order was reinstalled as the vice president temporarily assumed the presidency on April 13 until Chávez returned the next day.

The reaction of the United States to the coup, and the implication that the U.S. government had encouraged it, became a major source of contention between the two governments. The White House's initial reaction, expressed by the president's spokesperson, Ari Fleisher, was that "the actions encouraged by the Chávez government provoked a crisis."[32] Lino Gutiérrez, the principal deputy assistant secretary of state for Western Hemisphere affairs, stated, "The roots of the present crisis lie, we think, with the polarization that occurred under President Chávez and his confrontational policies. President Chávez has attacked freedom of the press, interfered in labor union elections, criticized the Church, stacked the judiciary, and attempted to cow any opposition."[33] The U.S. response drew fire from many in Latin America and Congress, which saw the United States as tacitly, if not directly, supporting a military coup in direct contravention of the Inter-American Charter for Democracy. The charter explicitly prohibits the recognition of a de facto regime. There were reports that Otto Reich had contacts during the coup with two influential businessmen opposed to Chávez, Gustavo Cisneros, a close friend of the Bush family, one of Latin America's richest men and owner of the largest media group in Venezuela, and Luis Giusti, a former head of Venezuela's state oil company. Reich also called Pedro Carmona the interim president.[34] A few days after the failed coup, President Bush asserted that the administration "spoke with a very clear voice about our strong support of democracy . . . and at no time did we support unconstitutional action to overthrow Chávez."[35]

Lino Gutiérrez insisted, "We oppose military coups in any democratic country. Let me be unambiguous: we oppose military coups, civilian coups, or any other kind of coup." Answering criticism that the United States had violated the Inter-American Charter for Democracy, Gutiérrez blamed Chávez for undermining democracy in Venezuela and said, "It is President Chávez who must assure the re-establishment of full democracy, guaranteeing the citizens of Venezuela the full respect for their fundamental rights, including the right to express dissent."[36]

Whether or not the United States had prior knowledge of the coup is hard to determine, although it is difficult to believe that U.S. officials, many with close ties to the Venezuelan military and business community, were not aware that something was happening. Indeed, it is also difficult to believe that Venezuelan coup plotters did not inform the United States of their intentions, particularly when one would assume that quick U.S. recognition of the new government would be essential for its ultimate success. In the end, the episode further soured U.S.–Venezuelan relations and undermined U.S. standing in the region.

The "War on Terrorism" and U.S.–Venezuelan Relations

The concerns expressed by U.S. officials following Chávez's criticism of U.S. actions in Afghanistan reflected a wider shift in policy toward the Andean region in the aftermath of September 11th. While terrorism, drug trafficking, and the connection between the two were concerns of the United States before 9/11, the subsequent globalization of the "war on terror" has added a new dimension to U.S. policy. As Brian Loveman details in his chapter in this volume, by combining the fight against drugs and terrorism the United States has given new life to the main tenets of the "national security doctrine" that formed the basis for military governments in Latin America until the 1980s.

General James T. Hill, commander of U.S. Southern Command, explained the new emphasis of U.S. policy by telling the U.S. Congress on March 12, 2003, "While the primary front in the War on Terrorism currently lies elsewhere, Southern Command plays an important supporting role. Radical Islamic Groups operating out of the region use the profits from drug, human, and arms trafficking, false documentation, and other illicit activities in our hemisphere to fund their worldwide operations." General Hill went on to argue that "narcoterrorists" were "spreading their reach throughout the region, wreaking havoc, and destabilizing legitimate governments." Venezuela and the Andean region were included by General Hill among the areas in Latin America where Islamic groups were operating, when he said, "Radical Islamic supporters have long gathered in areas such as the Tri-border region between Paraguay, Brazil, and Argentina. . . . Similarly, we continue to be concerned by *possible activities of radical Islamic groups on Margarita Island in Venezuela and Maicao, Colombia.* Precise estimates of the amount of money diverted from the region to radical Islamic groups are difficult to determine due to the illicit nature of the activity, however, the figures are likely in the hundreds of millions of dollars annually" [emphasis added].[37]

General Hill told the *Miami Herald*, "$300 million to $500 million a year, easily, goes [from Latin America] to groups such as Hamas, Hezbollah, and Al Gamaat."[38] While General Hill admitted there is little evidence that Al Qaeda has established training camps in the region, he did not completely discount the possibility. In the same article, Eduardo Gamarra, director of Florida International University's Center for Latin American and Caribbean Studies, argued that the claims about the amount of funding to Islamic groups from Latin America were "absolutely ridiculous."[39]

With little evidence that Al Qaeda is operating in Latin America,[40] and with the claim of substantial funding from the region going to Islamic terrorist groups under critical scrutiny, U.S. officials seemed to shift their focus away from Al Qaeda and emphasized the threat from regional groups. Brigadier General Galen Jackman, director of operations for the U.S. Southern Command,

and Richard Armitage, deputy secretary of state, told a Senate committee in early 2003 that the FARC guerrillas had spread their activities throughout South America. General Jackman was quoted by the *Miami Herald,* saying, "The tentacles of the FARC extend well beyond the boundaries of Colombia. . . . There is intelligence that they have worked with Sendero Luminoso in Peru, with illegal armed groups in Bolivia, and have some presence in the tri-border area in Paraguay." Armitage told the Senate that while the FARC "is not al Qaeda or Hezbollah . . . the reach of their drugs is certainly global."[41] The United States seems particularly concerned with FARC activities in Ecuador, Venezuela, and Panama. Moreover, officials also have pointed to ties between the FARC and drug traffickers in Brazil and Suriname.

In Venezuela, the opposition has used the "war on terror" to try to discredit the government. Reports in early 2003 claimed a connection between Chávez and Al Qaeda. Venezuelan air force major Juan Diaz Castillo, who sought political asylum in the United States, said that shortly following the September 11th attacks, Chávez ordered him "to organize, coordinate, and execute a covert operation consisting of delivering financial resources, specifically $1 million, to the Taliban government, in order for them to assist the Al Qaeda terrorist organization." According to Major Diaz, the transaction was carried out though Venezuela's ambassador to India, and $100,000 went for humanitarian purposes, and the remaining $900,000 ended up in the hands of Al Qaeda.[42] Such reports continue to be diffused through the Internet by regime opponents.[43] The Venezuelan government, however, has vehemently denied any links to international terrorism, and the opposition has not produced any substantial evidence to support their claims. The Bush administration does not seem to have placed much credibility on these reports, and the State Department's document on "Patterns of Global Terrorism" makes no mention whatsoever of Venezuelan ties to the Al Qaeda network, nor has any U.S. official referred to Major Diaz's charges. However, the United States does seem concerned about Venezuela's lack of commitment to the "war on terror." The State Department's report on global terrorism, in its section on the Western Hemisphere, says,

> While the Venezuelan Government expressed sympathy in the months following the 11 September 2001 attacks, Caracas made it clear that it opposed the use of force in Afghanistan and has sent mixed signals during the war on terrorism. Venezuela signed the Organization of American States (OAS) Inter-American Convention against Terrorism in June 2002, but has not yet ratified the treaty. Venezuela is a party to four of the 12 international conventions and protocols relating to terrorism. Nevertheless, Venezuelan laws do not support the efficient investigation of terrorist organization financing or activities; the United States during 2002 provided technical assistance to help the Government of Venezuela assess vulnerabilities in its financial system and to plan appropriate policy reme-

dies. The political crisis at the end of the year, however, had pushed all unrelated issues to the backburner. While Venezuela did extradite two members of the terrorist organization Basque Fatherland and Liberty to Spain, *reports abounded that the Revolutionary Armed Forces of Colombia (FARC) and the Colombian National Liberation Army were using the border area between Venezuela and Colombia for cross-border incursions and as an unchallenged safe haven for the guerrillas. Additionally, unconfirmed reports persist that elements of the Venezuelan Government may have provided material support to the FARC, particularly weapons* [emphasis added].[44]

The most recent posture statement by the commander of SOUTHCOM, General Bantz J. Craddock, delivered to the U.S. House of Representative's Armed Services Committee on March 9, 2005, continues to raise concerns about Venezuela's cooperation in the war on terror. General Craddock said, "I am also concerned with Venezuela's influence in the AOR [Area of Responsibility]. The capture of senior FARC member Rodrigo Granda in Venezuela, carrying a valid Venezuelan passport . . . is of concern." Regarding cooperation with U.S.–Colombian efforts, General Craddock said, "Among Colombia's neighbors, Venezuela's record of cooperation remains mixed. We remain concerned that Colombia's FTOs [foreign terrorist organizations] consider the areas of the Venezuelan border with Colombia a safe area to rest, transship drugs and arms, and procure logistical supplies."[45]

The Struggle for the Recall Referendum

Having failed to remove Chávez through extraconstitutional means, the United States and the domestic opposition changed tactics and sought to remove him through the constitutional process of a recall election. In December 2002, opposition parties, labor federations, and trade union representatives in Venezuela carried out their fourth national strike in less than a year, calling for the ouster of the president. The real impact of the strike was in the oil industry, where a reported 90 percent of professional employees supported the work stoppage. Oil revenues account for half of Venezuela's revenues and make up a substantial 80 percent of the country's exports. The strike in this sector weakened productivity and eventually had a devastating effect on the Venezuelan economy. Reports suggested that by the end of 2002 productivity had declined as much as 90 percent.[46] As the strike continued, the climate of political tension escalated into a full-blown political crisis. In response to clashes between government supporters and opposition demonstrators, Chávez ordered the national guard to prevent a repeat of the violence that preceded the April 2002 coup. Nevertheless, the violent clashes continued to mount. Indeed, police and military forces fired tear gas and rubber bullets at antigovernment demonstrators; several people were killed and two policemen were wounded in clashes. Finally, after eight weeks of ongoing chaos, the opposition ended the strikes. The end of the strikes coincided with the start of talks sponsored by the six-country "Group of Friends."[47] The "Group of Friends," which was made up of the United States, Portugal, Spain, Mexico, Brazil, and Chile, endorsed a proposal by former U.S. president Jimmy Carter that advocated two possibilities for ending the crisis: (1) a constitutional amendment providing for early elections would be voted upon: a majority of votes in favor of constitutional change would sanction early elections (constitutionally, Chávez was elected to serve in office until 2007); or (2) in August 2003, halfway through Chávez's term in office, there would be a binding referendum on the president's mandate, as provided for in the current constitution (according to the constitution, the earliest date for a referendum would be midway through his office in August 2003).[48] The proposal was positively received by President Chávez, as well as U.S. secretary of state Colin Powell.

However, although the "Group of Friends," other international bodies, and even President Chávez expressed support for the Carter Plan, it was clear that there was very little trust between the Venezuelan government and the Venezuelan opposition. Despite this lack of trust, on May 23, 2003, the government and the opposition signed an agreement that in part established that "resolution of the crisis should be achieved through application of Article 72 of the Constitution of the Bolivarian Republic of Venezuela, which provides for the possible holding of revocatory referenda on the mandates of all those holding positions and serving as magistrates as a result of popular election, where they have served one-half of the term for which they were elected (governors, mayors, regional legislators and representatives in the National Assembly), or will have served one-half of their term in the course of this year, as is the case of the President of the Republic."[49] However, a day after the agreement was signed violence erupted at a rally in Caracas. In June 2003, violence flared again in the streets of Caracas as battles raged between supporters and opponents of the government.

The agreement was developed after six months of negotiations and was brokered by the secretary-general of the OAS, César Gaviria, the former Colombian president. The agreement compelled President Chávez to participate in a referendum on his rule halfway through the presidential term. Opponents of the government had to gain signatures from 20 percent of the electorate in order to hold the referendum, and there would have to be some sort of National Electoral Commission established to verify the petition. The agreement called for both government supporters and opponents to end the violence, disarm the civilian population, and respect Venezuela's democracy. Opposition forces were given four days to collect 2.4 million signatures.[50] In the fall of 2003, a petition signed by three million people was rejected by the

National Election Council. The council cited the fact that the signatures had been collected several months prior to the halfway point of Chávez's term in office. After several months of protests and disputes between the government, opposition forces, and the National Election Council, the opposition was given three days, May 28–30, 2004, to "verify" signatures on the petition. On May 30, 2004, President Chávez said, "I would gladly face a referendum. . . . If they defeat me, I'll leave." The president's comments were made following a meeting with international observers, including former U.S. president Jimmy Carter.[51] After the process of verifying the signatures was completed, a date was set for the referendum—August 15, 2004. Having survived a coup d'état two years earlier, Chávez again showed his political strength by surviving the referendum. Despite opposition protests, international observers, including the Carter Center, certified Chávez's victory, with 58 percent of those voting against recalling the president and only 42 percent in favor.[52]

The victory in the referendum and the rise in oil prices throughout 2004–20066 have strengthened Chávez's hold on power and placed the United States on the defensive. The war of words between the two nations continued unabated throughout 2005 and early 2006, with Chávez claiming that the United States planned to invade Venezuela and assassinate him. Venezuela moved forward with plans to buy weapons from Russia, signed significant commercial agreements with China, and deepened its relations with Cuba. In addition, Venezuela has actively pursued alternatives to the U.S.-supported Free Trade Agreement of the Americas (FTAA). All these policies have angered the United States, with U.S. secretary of state Condoleezza Rice calling Venezuela "a bad influence" on the region.

The Colombian Crisis and Its Impact on Venezuela

In the 1990s Venezuela became increasingly concerned with Colombia's civil war and its impact on the country's security. Clashes between guerrilla forces and the Venezuelan military demonstrated a growing instability in the border region. Within Venezuela, the situation in Colombia is of course of immediate concern since the countries share a long border and the former is directly affected by refugee flows and repeated incursions into its territory by Colombian guerrillas and paramilitaries. Under President Rafael Caldera (1994–1999), relations between the two countries improved, with the armed forces sharing intelligence and coordinating some actions.

With the rise to power of Hugo Chávez, however, tensions have risen and relations between the two countries have deteriorated. Chávez's apparent sympathy with some of the insurgents' demands propelled him into the conflict as a potential mediator between the Colombian government and the guerrillas. Chávez has sought to play an active role in the diplomacy of the Colombian conflict, but Colombians, who question his motives and accuse him of intervening inappropriately in domestic Colombian affairs, view his initiatives with suspicion.[53] Both Colombia and Venezuela temporarily recalled their ambassadors in 2000 after Chávez allowed members of the FARC to speak at a forum in Caracas on Plan Colombia. Since then, Venezuela has participated as an international observer in Colombia's peace talks with the FARC and the National Liberation Army (ELN) over the objection of Colombia's privately funded paramilitary army—the United Self-Defense Forces of Colombia (AUC).

There is no evidence that Chávez's government is giving material support to the Colombian guerrillas, but weapons captured from guerrillas in 2000 turned out to have come from Venezuelan army stocks.[54] The Colombian military reported seizing 470 FAL rifles bearing the seals of the Venezuelan armed forces, or the seals of CAVIM, the Venezuelan military's arms industry, from rebels between January 1998 and July 2000.[55] In November 2000, the Colombian press reported that the ELN operated an office in Caracas and ELN representatives met regularly with Chávez and his inner circle. According to the same reports, a high-level Venezuelan military officer met clandestinely with FARC leader Marulanda in FARC-controlled territory in Colombia to arrange for the release of Venezuelan cattlemen held by the FARC and to negotiate a nonaggression agreement.[56]

Colombia charged that Venezuelan citizens were selling arms to the FARC and that its air force had violated Colombian territory. The Chávez administration responded by denying the accusations and, in turn, accusing Colombia of failing to secure its borders and violating the human rights of Venezuelan citizens.[57]

Relations between Colombia and Venezuela deteriorated still further in 2001. With increasing frequency, Colombian military and political leaders charged that Venezuela was providing arms and sanctuary to elements of the FARC and ELN. In January 2001, a Venezuelan National Guard unit seized a shipment of semiautomatic rifles apparently destined for the FARC.[58]

There were reports within the Venezuelan military of growing discontent over the government's failure to take a strong stance against the guerrillas.[59] Many in the Venezuelan military were appalled at the reports that Venezuelan arms flowed to the Colombian guerrillas. In April 2002, Colombian general Martín Orlando Carreno charged that his troops were attacked by a FARC column that entered Colombia from Venezuela.[60] In February 2003, Colombia's minister of interior, Fernando Londoño, complained that Venezuela's reluctance to declare the FARC a "terrorist" group was due to meetings between guerrilla leaders and Venezuelan officials. President Chávez responded the next day on his weekly radio and television show by chastising Colombian president Uribe for "paying too much attention to Venezuelan problems instead of his own" and suggesting that diplomatic relations between the two countries could be jeopardized.[61]

Tensions between the two countries continued to escalate, particularly after the military coup that briefly toppled President Chávez in April 2002. As mentioned earlier, Venezuelan officials suspected U.S. involvement in or, at the very least, acquiescence in the coup. Because of the close military and political relations between Colombia and the United States, along with the presence of at least four hundred U.S. military advisors in Colombian territory, Venezuelan officials feared that the United States could use Colombia as a springboard for destabilizing the Venezuelan government. In fact, in early 2004, President Chávez claimed that Venezuela had been "invaded" and faced "a serious threat to the peace, integrity and security of this republic."[62] The incident referred to by Chávez was the arrest, on May 9, 2004, of eighty-six unarmed Colombians wearing Venezuelan army uniforms in a home on the outskirts of Caracas owned by an opposition leader, Cuban-born Venezuelan Roberto Alonso. An additional sixteen Colombians were arrested, as well as a number of retired and active air force and national guard officers. Venezuelan authorities claimed the Colombians were members of right-wing paramilitary groups working with local opposition leaders, including disgruntled military officers. Chávez argued that the purpose of the "invasion" was to create the impression of divisions within the Venezuelan armed forces and push for another coup. Chávez also claimed that as a prelude to the "planned attack by paramilitaries" the United States escalated its rhetoric in order to create a climate of hostility and animosity that would serve to "justify an attack." The U.S. ambassador to Venezuela, Charles Shapiro, stated that the United States rejected "the attempts to link the arrested Colombians with our government" and "any attempt to change the government by force."[63]

In another incident, six Venezuelan soldiers and an engineer from the nation's state oil company were killed in September 2004 while inspecting a western oil field along the Colombia–Venezuelan border. Initially, it was not clear whether the attack had been carried out by paramilitaries or FARC forces, although Venezuelan newspapers later claimed that the FARC guerrillas were responsible. Colombian authorities continued to accuse their Venezuelan counterparts of ignoring or acquiescing to guerrilla movements in Venezuelan territory. The back and forth reached a new low in early 2005 in an incident that threatened to lead to the rupture of relations between the two countries.

The conflict was spurred by the arrest of a leading member of the FARC. In December 2004, Rodrigo Granda, described as FARC's "foreign minister," was kidnapped in downtown Caracas by former Venezuelan police and military agents, who were presumably paid by the Colombian government, and taken across the border to Colombia. Colombia first denied any involvement in the incident, claiming the rebel was captured in a Colombian border town, but subsequently admitted a bounty had been paid for his capture. After unsuccessfully seeking an apology from President Uribe, Venezuela recalled its ambassador from Colombia and threatened to break diplomatic relations. President Chávez said, "With much pain I have called back the ambassador in Bogotá and he will not return until the Colombia government offers us apologies." Chávez also indicated that he had "ordered all agreements and business with Colombia to be paralyzed."[64] Colombia's vice president, Francisco Santos, argued that his government's actions were "absolutely legitimate and a necessary instrument in the fight against terrorism."[65] The United States stood firmly on the side of Colombia. William Wood, the U.S. ambassador to Colombia, said Washington supported Uribe "100 percent" in the dispute. The ambassador asked Chávez to state publicly whether he considered the FARC, along with a second, smaller rebel group, the ELN, and Colombia's paramilitary forces to be terrorist organizations.[66]

The pro-Chávez leftist group Tupamaro Revolutionary Movement accused the CIA of having a hand in the abduction of Granda, citing the U.S.-funded military offensive in Colombia called Plan Patriota.[67] The group's secretary-general, Jose Pinto, said, "We believe it is part of the policy the (U.S.) Department of State and CIA have developed, in concert with puppet governments in Latin America."[68] President Chávez himself, speaking to a rally in Caracas organized to protest the incident, accused the United States of instigating the situation by saying, "I know where this provocation comes from: from Washington, not from Bogotá."[69] The U.S. Embassy denied any U.S. involvement in the incident. Many observers, however, have argued that U.S. interests in the region, and the desire of President Uribe to show the United States that he is doing everything possible to fight the FARC, precipitated the arrest of Granda. Venezuelan political analyst Carlos Romero said the kidnapping was meant to show that Colombia "[was] taking the war on the guerrillas seriously, and is now moving to bring down the leadership of the rebel groups, ending the former ambiguity of armed clashes on the one hand and tolerance on the other."[70] Another analyst, Alberto Garrido, said, "The key issue in this conflict is that it marks the launch of the Andean phase of Plan Colombia and its military adjunct, Plan Patriot, with a frontal attack on the guerrilla forces that has spilled over the Colombian borders into the rest of the region."[71]

The conflict over Granda's kidnapping was resolved on February 16, 2005, after a face-to-face meeting between Chávez and Uribe. Venezuela had already returned its ambassador to Bogotá on January 31, but Chávez insisted the conflict would not be settled unless he met personally with his Colombian counterpart; a meeting took place on February 15 in Caracas. Despite a temporary relaxation in tensions, relations between the two countries remained fragile, partly as a result of the continued hostility between Venezuela and the United States and Venezuela's stated "neutrality" in the Colombian conflict, a situation that both Colombia and the United States regard as tacit support for the FARC. For example, recent Venezuelan purchases of weapons from Russia have sparked additional conflict, with the United States questioning Venezuela's need for the weapons and Colombia worried that some weapons might fall into the hands of the Colombian guerrillas. (Of course, during the Cold War such an arms purchase might have occasioned a much more bellicose response!) As long as Colombia maintains its "special relationship" with the United States and the latter sees Chávez as a threat to regional security, Venezuelan–Colombian relations will remain precarious.

Whither the U.S.–Venezuelan Relationship?

Since the election of Hugo Chávez as president, relations between the United States and Venezuela have been characterized by verbal conflict, but ironically, in many spheres, such as oil exports and the drug war, by continued cooperation "on the ground." The main reason for cooperation is the fact that Venezuela is the fourth largest provider of crude oil to the United States, and conversely the United States is Venezuela's most important commercial partner. As stated earlier, Venezuela also has been among the largest purchaser of U.S. military equipment in the hemisphere.

Since the end of the Cold War, U.S. policy in the region has focused on security issues, primarily efforts to combat drug trafficking. After 9/11 the policy also has focused attention on terrorism. Venezuela obviously plays an important role because of its proximity to Colombia and its access to the Caribbean. Venezuela's main concern with U.S. policy in the Andean region can be summarized by four considerations. First, the overwhelming military and police component of U.S. policy, which in Venezuela's view may imply the building up of a strong U.S. military presence in Colombian territory. Second, even as an unintended consequence, the strengthening of Colombian military capabilities as an inevitable result of U.S. military assistance is perceived by Venezuela as likely to alter the balance of power in the Andean region, to the detriment of Venezuela. Third, the environmental impact of U.S. aid, as it may involve intensive fumigations likely to pollute hydrographic basins and farmland. Fourth, the fear—shared by Ecuador, Peru, Panama, and Brazil—regarding the "spillover effect," that is, the displacement of drug and guerrilla operations to Venezuelan territory. The possibilities of this fear becoming reality are based on the experiences with drug production activities during the 1980s and early 1990s, which moved from Peru and Bolivia toward Colombia after the implementation of U.S. counternarcotics strategy in the Andes.

Chávez's foreign policy seems to be guided by a number of considerations. First, there is the need to assert Venezuela's independence—both regionally and globally—vis-à-vis the United States. This is not unlike Mexico in the 1960 and 1970s but comes at a time when the United States as the sole superpower is eager to assert its power around the world, particularly in its own "backyard." Ironically, the globalization that the United States promotes opens the possibility for Chávez to court Russia, China, Iran, and other nonhemispheric powers in his effort to erode U.S. dominance over Venezuela. Another component of this independent foreign policy is Venezuela's assertion of an important role in the Organization of Petroleum Exporting Countries (OPEC) and the nonaligned nations. Venezuela has served as president of both groups during Chávez's administration. Moreover, Chávez has sought to create a "Bolivarian" bloc within the hemisphere as a counterweight to the United States. While it is far from certain this can be done, even now with President Lula of Brazil, Kishner of Argentina, and Vázquez of Uruguay, the mere mention of it has irritated the United States. In addition, as mentioned before, Chávez's independent foreign policy has included close ties to Fidel Castro and frequent denunciations of U.S. policy in the region and around the world.

The second major consideration seems to be Chávez's desire to distance himself from the U.S. military and its allies within the Venezuelan armed forces. This is one of the reasons why Venezuela refused to renew a military treaty with the United States that permitted U.S. officers to have a presence at the main military headquarters in Caracas. It also is why Venezuela refused to allow U.S. personnel to handle equipment offered for the relief of the flood victims in 2000. Historically, Venezuelan officers have had very close relations with their U.S. counterparts. This relationship makes many Venezuelan officers keen to follow the lead of the United States, particularly on security matters. This becomes a threat to Chávez's independent foreign policy and to his ability to control the armed forces. With SOUTHCOM an ever more important influence in the hemisphere, and playing a larger role in U.S. regional strategy, this independent thrust of Chávez's foreign policy (which is also a part of his domestic tactics) goes directly against the grain of U.S.–Latin American policy.

The third consideration has to do with Chávez's populist rhetoric and appeal to the marginalized sectors of Venezuelan society. On the one hand, in order to promote his policies Chávez needs to reduce the power of the economic elite. On the other hand, he requires an "enemy" against which he can rally the masses. Traditionally, the Venezuelan economic elites have had very close ties to the United States. Many have homes and investments in Miami and other major cities. Additionally, many Venezuelan businesspersons have close ties to the Cuban American and exile community. By steering a course away from the United States, Chávez may reinforce the nationalist elements of his Bolivarian Revolution and reduce the influence of the domestic and U.S.-resident economic elite on domestic and foreign policy. Of course, a source of continued conflict between the elites and Chávez is his close ties to Fidel Castro. For Castro, Chávez's policies are an opportunity to reduce the influence of the Cuban American community in an important South American country and to gain economic support for Cuba, both for energy resources and an opportunity to diversify imports through third parties.

Conversely, for the United States, relations with Venezuela seem to be conditioned by the following factors: first, and foremost, is the enormous appetite for oil and the strategic importance of having a secure source nearby. The imperative for a secure source of oil has grown as the Iraqi war drags on and crude oil prices skyrocket. This factor has forced the United States to ignore Chávez's rhetoric far more readily than it would from most other countries in the region. Second, Chávez's close ties to Castro have been a constant source of irritation to the United States. While most countries of the region have diplomatic and commercial ties to Cuba, Chávez's rhetoric and personal friendship with Castro has gone beyond what the U.S. finds acceptable. In addition, the close ties between domestic opponents of the government and the Cuban American community, the lobbying power of the latter in Washington, and the appointment of such a staunch anti-Castro personality as Otto Reich as a key Latin America advisor made this situation much more volatile. Third, as examined in detail above, Venezuela's "neutrality" in the Colombian conflict worries U.S. policy makers because they equate Venezuela's attitude with giving aid and comfort to the FARC guerrillas.

In the end, U.S. antagonism toward Chávez seems to be driven by an irrational inability to understand and accept the fact that other nations may pursue different foreign policy goals. It seems that the events of September 11, 2001, have deepened this irrationality, particularly when President George W. Bush announced that countries were now going to be judged by whether they "were with us or against us." It seems clear that while prior to September 11th the United States might have "tolerated" the populist rhetoric and the ties to countries like Cuba, Libya, and Iraq, after the terrorist attacks such policies could not be so easily countenanced. As discussed earlier, a few months after Chávez criticized U.S. policy in Afghanistan, the United States, at the very least, acquiesced to a military coup. Having survived the coup, and now a recall referendum, Chávez has emerged stronger than ever, has consolidated the hold of his supporters in congress, and looks toward reelection.

This chapter began by mentioning four factors that have shaped U.S.–Venezuelan relations since 1958: the repeated assertion by Venezuelan governments that they are a reliable partner to the United States in the hemisphere; the assertion of Venezuela's political and economic stability relative to the rest of the region; relations characterized by cooperation rather than conflict; and the predominance of bilateral rather than regional issues in U.S.–Venezuelan relations. At the dawn of the new millennium, however, relations between the United States and Venezuela have entered a period of uncertainty and animosity that have undermined previously accepted parameters. On the one hand, the future of the bilateral relationship seems to be dependent on events outside the control of either country, including the resolution or escalation of the Colombian civil war and the stability of the Middle East. On the other hand, both countries have significant economic and political interests in maintaining good relations with each another. For the United States, political and economic stability in Venezuela is vital to securing a steady and reliable source of oil and promoting its policy vis-à-vis the Colombian civil war. For Venezuela, the United States represents its most important trading partner, though Chávez and several of his ministers have threatened to use the oil weapon against the United States by sending exports to other markets.

U.S. regional security policy since the 1990s has had important and negative consequences on Venezuelan and regional politics. The increased emphasis on a "war against terror" since September 11, 2001, has converted some regional and national actors, such as Colombian drug networks and the guerrillas, into "terrorists"—thereby transforming U.S. policies in Colombia, Venezuela, and elsewhere in the region. By connecting the situation in the Andean region to the overall war against terrorism, the United States has emphasized military rather than economic assistance and increased the role of the region's militaries at the expense of civilian institutions, thus jeopardizing civilian supremacy. Even minor criticism of U.S. policy is now seen as assisting the "enemy." Venezuela's attempt to chart an independent foreign policy and its criticisms of the United States have alarmed policy makers in Washington and have led to significant levels of animosity between the two nations.

4

U.S. Andean Policy, the Colombian Conflict, and Security in Ecuador

Adrián Bonilla

Translated by Lynn Eddy-Zambrano

THIS CHAPTER DESCRIBES AND ANALYZES how U.S. security policies affect Ecuador, where the regional scenario is dominated by the fighting of the Colombian conflict and policies that aim to address it, the war on drugs strategy, and the political turmoil that has plagued Andean institutions for a decade. The United States has promoted a regionalized concept of the Colombian conflict, one that gives preeminence to the conflict's military dimensions. It has integrated this concept into a strategy that encompasses all the Andean countries. Starting in 2001, the issue of drug trafficking also began to be linked to the Colombian insurgency—characterized as "narco-terrorism."[1]

Ecuadorian governments, meanwhile, have done their best to pursue a policy of containment and prevention as they try to distance themselves from the Colombian conflict and its impacts. This policy, pursued at least until President Gutiérrez came to power in January 2003, flies in the face of U.S. concepts. Given this context, a central question is whether a small, vulnerable country can protect its own security interests when they do not coincide with those of the hemisphere's hegemonic power. First, this chapter attempts to identify principal issues and trends in U.S. policy and how Ecuador and the rest of the Andean countries respond to them. It underscores how Bogotá's policies have symbiotically aligned Colombian interests with those of Washington. It reflects specifically on the repercussions of the implementation of U.S.-backed Colombian security policy articulated first in Plan Colombia, and then in Plan Patriota, on Ecuador's vulnerabilities, and on its options for dealing with the U.S. security agenda in the region.

Second, the chapter reflects on how the Colombian conflict directly impacts Ecuador. It considers the environmental and social effects of fumigation and eradication, how the war impacts border areas, military and security policies, and measures aimed at controlling migration to check the spread of what the Ecuadorian government sees as the potential "contagion" of violence.

Finally, this chapter outlines how Ecuadorian security and foreign policy institutions perceive the threat raised by the Colombian conflict and U.S. policy. Issues on Ecuador's national security agenda vis-à-vis the Colombian conflict are detailed, and the country's containment and prevention strategy is described. It also details changes in policy during the government of Lucio Gutiérrez (2003–2005), which more closely aligned Ecuador with strategies from Washington and Bogotá—and have been reversed after Gutiérrez's ouster in April 2005 and his replacement by Alfredo Palacio. An effort is also made to review how the Colombian war is viewed in Ecuador, what military actions are being taken, how social decline is impacting the border region, and what the reactions are to changes on the Colombian political scene, specifically elimination of the demilitarized zone, the policies of Álvaro Uribe in Colombia, and the implementation of Plan Patriota.

The concluding section offers reflections on the influence of U.S. policies and their destabilizing effects in the Andean region and Ecuador and foreseeable patterns in international policy toward Ecuador.

U.S. Security Policy in the Andean Region and Ecuador

The Andean Community countries, and Ecuador specifically, have not been a strategic priority for the United States after the Cold War, except in matters relating to drug trafficking and the conflict in Colombia.[2] This was generally affirmed, if not more pronounced, following the events of September 11, 2001. While U.S. foreign policy toward Ecuador is constructed around a regional agenda, it is carried out in a bilateral fashion. Concern for drug trafficking has shaped U.S. policies and dictated decision making.[3] Throughout the 1990s U.S. foreign policy toward Latin America was characterized by a lack of knowledge about security issues. This led to the Clinton administration's initiative for the Americas, which was an agenda drawn up by earlier Republican governments. Relations with Ecuador were set within the framework of the routine handling of those issues.[4] U.S. interests and policies in the region were defined predominantly by the war on drugs.

The end of the Cold War brought no major changes in U.S.–Andean relations because the same security issues that had been priorities for Washington since the end of the 1980s continued to dominate in one form or another. A strategy aimed at accomplishing drug interdiction and control objectives provided continuity for the policies. While they did shed their anticommunist ideological slant during the 1990s, policies retained, in essence, the same mechanisms for countries' relations with one another and the same hierarchy of agenda issues.[5]

Securitization of the agenda with Ecuador and the Andes precluded the United States from opting for multilateral dealings, even though there were noteworthy attempts to do so at the beginning of the 1990s. The San Antonio and Cartagena summits during the George H. W. Bush administration, for example, outlined common issues, but the way policies were implemented "bilateralized" the relationship even though the United States did, at times, adopt a somewhat regional outlook.

A surprising outcome of the aforementioned summits for Ecuador was that it would now be included in a strategy that had previously involved only Bolivia, Colombia, and Peru. For Ecuador, inclusion in the war on drugs strategy meant getting additional resources, but most significantly, the chance to become a member of the Andean System of Preferences. This had been, to some extent, a national foreign policy objective of the Rodrigo Borja administration (1988–1992).[6]

U.S. perspectives on Latin America have become highly differentiated in recent years. Moving from Mexico down to the Southern Cone, the agenda changes. While common issues were laid out at the 1994 Presidential Summit in Miami and later ratified in Santiago and Quebec, the emphasis they are given varies, depending on the subregion concerned. Mexico, the Caribbean, Central America, the Southern Cone, and Brazil may represent five distinct visions of U.S. policy,[7] but it is in the Andean region that the most politically complex issues appear to be concentrated: democratic governability—which is a central theme that takes precedence over the ideas of representation or participation in the visions of security—drug trafficking, terrorism, migration, and foreign trade.

Ecuador's institutions have addressed all of the security-related issues[8] taken up at the Hemispheric Summits, Washington's most important tool for foreign policy in the region.[9] Ecuador has adopted a position that oscillates between compliance and consensual acceptance on foreign policy, owing to its weak institutional structure and absence of consistent agendas, and dissent, expressed in Ecuador's reticence to become further involved in the Colombian conflict or to share a regional vision of this issue.[10] Ecuadorian dissent on policy is not insignificant for the United States since it calls into question the central priorities of U.S. policy: the fight against terrorism. No Ecuadorian government, including the government of Lucio Gutiérrez, has acknowledged officially that Ecuador faces a terrorist threat, and all have refused to label the irregular armed forces and guerrillas in Colombia as terrorists.[11]

Over the last decade, Ecuadorian drug-trafficking policy has taken concrete shape through reform of the criminal justice system, changes in financial laws to control money laundering, restructuring of law enforcement, and, militarily, through deployment of thousands of troops on the Colombian border and the granting of an air base to the United States. The base functions out of the port at Manta where air monitoring and control are carried out over Ecuadorian territory, southern Colombia, northern Peru, and South America's Pacific Northwest. Base rights at Manta were granted in 1999 for a period of ten years, but not without serious opposition in Ecuador.[12] Base rights were conceded on specific request by the United States, but this action was not consistent with the strategic plans of the Ecuadorian armed forces.[13]

The defining characteristic of relations between the United States and Ecuador and the Andean region is their enormous asymmetry. This expresses itself in the priority given to drug issues—and, since 2002, to control of the border and counterinsurgency—above all other issues on the agenda, and in that capacity the United States has to set the rules of the economic game. Not only is the United States the single most important trading partner for each individual country in the region, it unilaterally sets the terms of trade. For example, Ecuador was temporarily excluded from the Andean System of General Preferences at the end of 2002.[14] The State Department offered no explanation for the action, though conflicts with U.S. companies seemed to play a role. The decision was taken despite the fact that Quito unquestionably met all its anti-drug trafficking commitments. Ecuador had been "certified" year after year with flying colors.[15] The process of reincorporation into the Preference system, which took several months, was quite complex and not altogether transparent.

The September 11 terrorist attacks on the United States indirectly influenced reorganization and refocus of U.S. foreign policy toward the Andean region and Ecuador. The U.S. bureaucracy that handles Latin American affairs was not even fully staffed until 2002.[16] The United States was without an ambassador in Ecuador for more than a year, from 2001 to 2002, following a year and a half of uncertainty about the chain of command at the Department of State and U.S. National Security Council, agencies that had been run by interim officials for almost half of the George W. Bush administration.[17] Until then Ecuador was of no strategic importance to the United States. It regained some importance once implementation of Plan Colombia began and the strategy for the Andean region was articulated.[18]

The asymmetry of relations between Ecuador and the United States is played out in terms of vulnerability. All matters of Ecuadorian, U.S., and Andean interdependence potentially involve conflict: the war in Colombia, drug trafficking, migration, and even trade, for which, since 2003, simultaneous negotiations regarding free trade with Ecuador, Peru, and Colombia have been difficult. The interests of the Andean peoples and their states have little impact on Washington decision making. At the beginning of the century the Andean region had less than 13 percent of Latin America's gross domestic product (GDP) while it accounted for 22 percent of the population; it received less than 10 percent of U.S. investments in the region and under 15 percent of U.S. trade exchange south of the Rio Grande.[19]

Because of the preeminence of security issues and the emphasis put on mechanisms to control and coerce, the U.S. presence in the region can be characterized as behavior that is guided by the hegemonic presumption that the North American nation has the option—indeed the right or responsibility—to intervene in the affairs of a backward country.[20] At the same time, foreign policy of the Andean countries has been reactive.[21] While their joint body, the Comunidad Andina de Naciones (CAN—Andean Community of Nations), has a common rhetoric on foreign policy, it has been incapable of putting into place a single, efficient mechanism that unites Andean interests, vis-à-vis the United States. Nor has it developed the institutional tools necessary to create a space for cooperative security. Relations among the countries on security and defense issues have been essentially bilateral. Moreover, it must be emphasized that despite its pioneering role in subregional integration, with its origins in the Andean Pact in the late 1960s, the CAN has been ineffective in generating viable common political, economic, and security agreements.

Ecuador's concerns and priorities in defense matters are distinct from those of its most important regional counterpart at this time: Colombia. While Bogotá, in alignment with Washington, proposes a regional approach to deal with drug trafficking and the conflict in its territory, Ecuador has made clear it prefers not to get involved with its neighbor's internal conflicts,[22] at least until the presidency of Lucio Gutiérrez, when an approximation to U.S. policy occurred.[23] Given the nature of the agendas and the difference in regional security interests, relations have to be bilateral, and decision makers are forced to work within a conventional realist scenario, especially where the implementation of policies is concerned. The structural weakness of the Andean states prevents them from creating regional institutions to handle matters jointly that would strengthen their position vis-à-vis the U.S. agenda, or that of its allies, on specific issues, such as the policies of the Colombian government.

U.S. hegemony cannot be explained entirely by the asymmetry of resources and political power. Also a factor was the consensual environment created by the Andean societies themselves. Beginning in the 1980s, at a time when many countries were hit by economic crisis, a wave of liberal reforms brought governments to power that were ideologically compatible with the idea of a harmonious, mutually advantageous relationship with the United States. Generally speaking, and with the exception of the government of President Hugo Chávez in Venezuela, the United States has enjoyed the—at times obedient—friendship of nearly all the Andean governments, beginning, emblematically, with Alberto Fujimori's coming to power in Peru (1990–2000).

U.S. Regional Security Policy and Ecuador

The concept of regional conflict frames U.S. national security strategy where Colombia is concerned. The issues that have been identified are violence on the part of the drug cartels; narcotics trafficking, which is still viewed as a health problem as well as a national security issue; and the ties drug trafficking activities create between extremist and terrorist groups. This is the vision that underlies contemporary policy of the Department of State after 2001.[24] Regardless of the foregoing, stated U.S. security objectives for 2000[25] did not change substantially in 2002, although by 2004 preoccupation with new security threats, such as "radical populism" and social movements encompassing indigenous peoples, are apparent in U.S. policy declarations on the Andean region.[26] These new concerns have been reiterated in subsequent declarations, indicating a consolidation of this diagnostic on present hemispheric security threats. Despite changes in the list of security threats, in emphasis, and in priorities, there exists the implicit possibility that Washington might resort to intervention and coercive methods.

The vision of the United States has permanently linked its security interests to the idea of democracy. This vision, however, has amplified the political option of interference or intervention in Latin American domestic affairs by U.S. diplomatic and military personnel, if necessary to promote the democratic agenda as defined by the United States.[27] Within this agenda a number of themes are especially sensitive in Ecuador.

The idea of civilian control over armed forces, which is associated with the image of subordination of the armed forces, as well as the redefinition of their appropriate size and structure, has been on the U.S. hemispheric agenda since the early 1990s. In Ecuador, where the armed forces have had great political influence and relative autonomy, this theme is highly controversial. More generally, Washington has been unable to achieve its proclaimed goal of effective civilian control over military and security forces in Latin America. With the possible exception of Bolivia, the armed forces in all the Andean nations have been highly involved in domestic politics and enjoy great autonomy. They staged a coup in Venezuela (and a countercoup in 2002). In Colombia tensions between President Pastrana and the armed forces rose to critical levels over concession of a demilitarized zone to the FARC.[28] In Ecuador, the armed forces took part in coups in 1996, 2000, and 2005. In Peru the military played a key role in the formation of the authoritarian Fujimori regime (1990–1992; 1992–2000): the high command remained in place and some thirty officers were indicted after the fall of the dictatorship.

In Ecuador, the possible spillover of the Colombian conflict and its direct implications for the country keep alive the sense of need for adequate military budgets, along with the need for redirection of the same. In the past, the

Ecuadorian armed forces were structured with the ever-present eventuality of a conventional struggle along the Peruvian border in mind. Until 1999, deployments and capabilities on the northern border were very limited. Neither the infrastructure nor the logic underlying intelligence and arms systems were sufficiently developed to handle operations by potential adversaries who might be mobile, clandestine, irregular, and have bases of support abroad. From a military standpoint then, maintaining and increasing levels of spending are a direct consequence of the Andean regional conflict and, particularly, of collaboration with the United States in its regional strategy. Moreover, it is necessary to increase investment in the armed forces and develop new combat doctrines.[29]

Another one of Washington's objectives was to establish systems of effective mutual confidence among the region's armed forces. Peru and Ecuador have clearly made progress toward formulating cooperative military agreements following the signing of peace treaties with one another. But once again, as far as mutual trust goes, Colombian armed forces have been responsible for several serious incidents with their Ecuadorian counterparts involving intelligence. They even sparked an armed confrontation on Ecuadorian territory in 2002 when the Colombian army mistakenly attacked an Ecuadorian military post in Carchi province, on the Andes border between the two nations. A forty-five-minute battle ensued.[30] While not always overt, the way the militaries of Colombia's neighbors have reacted to the Colombian conflict betrays their distrust for government forces, the insurgents, and other armed actors.

This distrust became even more evident as a result of the operation carried out to capture FARC leader Simón Trinidad, who was then transferred to Colombia and deported to the United States. The operation of Colombian and U.S. intelligence agents on Ecuadorian soil alarmed the armed forces, who were unaware of these operations and of the support for them provided by the National Police.[31]

With this kind of history, one of the ultimate goals of the U.S. strategy for the Americas—the need to involve the region's armed forces in international pacification or peace keeping initiatives—will be exceedingly difficult to achieve. The idea of a cooperative, international Andean unit conjures up the possibility that it might be deployed in Colombia. All of the Andean countries reject this possibility. Ecuador would not even entertain a suggestion by Colombian authorities that joint military exercises be held. Collaboration between the armed forces and the police of both countries is limited to information exchange and some cooperation on intelligence.[32]

When the newly appointed Colombian defense minister unilaterally suggested the idea of joint military operations in August 2002[33] the immediate response from all the neighboring countries was a resounding "no." A similar proposal by a Colombian senator close to President Uribe in June 2005 provoked a series of declarations by diplomats that distanced the Ecuadorian and Colombian governments.[34] All of the countries reinforced their military presence on Colombia's borders from 2000 to 2006; Venezuela's and Ecuador's buildups were the most significant. The Ecuadorians were explicit in their rejection of the idea of joint operations when negotiating with Colombian president Álvaro Uribe just after he took office. Ecuador has, in fact, limited its military commitments to peacekeeping operations (and not peace making) outside of South America.[35] For the time being, military cooperation among the Andean nations is limited to exchanges of intelligence. Increased Ecuadorian involvement in the Colombian conflict seemed highly undesirable from the standpoint of the country's own security, even though pressure from the outside, the United States, and Colombia has not let up. Pressure has been exerted in all spheres, military, economic, and developmental assistance/cooperation, and through intense political and diplomatic pressure, while Colombia's neighbors, including Ecuador, have become more concerned about the spillover of the Colombian violence across frontiers, especially since Uribe's ascent to power.[36]

U.S.–Ecuadorian Relations

Ecuador has no history of a hostile or distant relationship with the United States. On the contrary, all governments have sought to establish a special relationship with that power. But turbulent domestic politics in Ecuador; military activity; the emergence of especially active social movements, especially of indigenous peoples; and the country's peripheral importance for Latin America and the Andes have kept Washington relatively removed from Ecuador's affairs until the presidency of Colonel Lucio Gutiérrez (2003–2005) and the period after his ouster.

The U.S. economic agenda for the hemisphere has been problematic for Ecuador. Ecuador was temporarily locked out of the Andean System of Trade Preferences (ASTP) during the Gustavo Noboa administration (2000–2003). Several petroleum companies refused to pay the Value Added Tax, asserting they were exempt from it. The companies lobbied the United States Congress and won the ASTP sanction. The case went to arbitration despite the disposition of the government of Colonel Lucio Gutiérrez to arrange a favorable settlement for the companies. President Gustavo Noboa also doggedly tried to reach an agreement with the International Monetary Fund (IMF), blaming the difficulties he was encountering on the United States government.

During the Gutiérrez government relations with the United States improved, despite significant internal opposition to the U.S. economic and security agenda. Free trade negotiations and closer cooperation in the security realm marked this change. An agreement with the IMF was finally reached in

the first month of the Lucio Gutiérrez administration (January 2003), following trips to the United States where he avowed his friendship and solidarity
with White House policies.[37] The U.S. Embassy in Ecuador freely expressed itself about Ecuadorian domestic and foreign policies. Yet Ecuadorian society
has been particularly resistant to liberal reforms favored by Washington, not
only because of strong opposition from the lower social strata but because regional elites openly oppose them as well. Gutiérrez's policies of closer cooperation with the United States also contributed to his eventual ouster and to his
successor's (Dr. Alfredo Palacio) apparent reversal of these policies in 2005—
and to uncertainty about the bilateral relationship.

The recent evolution of various themes related to commercial and security
issues between Ecuador and the United States has heightened U.S. interest in
social and political problems faced by the Ecuadorian government. Negotiations to achieve a free trade agreement have progressed slowly, not only because important social groups oppose such an agreement but because
Ecuadorian governments have lacked a clear policy agenda in this regard.
Moreover, the coup d'état that ousted Gutiérrez from power, quite apart from
the rationale used to legitimate this unscheduled regime change, profoundly
affecting central U.S. policy objectives for the region: stability and democratic
government transitions. It also provided a dangerous precedent in a region
seemingly menaced by instability.

The issue of the military base at Manta, as well as drug eradication through
fumigation and maritime interdiction, have generated serious opposition and
resistance within Ecuador, and not only from radical groups and social movements, but also expressed, eventually, by certain elite sectors and even government authorities, once Gutiérrez was deposed.[38] In July 2005 Washington's
fears regarding radical populism were reinforced as Ecuador's minister of
economy questioned agreements previously reached with the IMF and the
World Bank as the country experienced rising social pressures from indigenous movements and other opponents of the neoliberal agenda sponsored by
the United States.

In regard to Ecuador's role in the Andean region and the Colombian violence, commitments to Colombia are officially covered under the terms set
down at the Guayaquil Summit of South American presidents. Basically these
provide for the establishment of multilateral bodies to handle all issues relating to armed groups in Colombia to preclude the possibility of bilateral agreements on terrorism, be they with Colombia or the United States. They also
imply Ecuador's opposition to the latter nation adopting unilateral policies.
The three relevant articles are:

*2. e) Their commitment to fight the global drug problem and other associated crimes,
based on the principle of shared responsibility and an approach that is comprehensive,*

balanced and cooperative in nature. In this regard, they highlighted the efforts being made by several countries to curtail consumption and money laundering, protect the environment and promote alternative development, sustainability of the last requiring broader opening of markets to substitute products.

4. The Heads of State reiterated their most forceful condemnation of terrorism in all its guises and shapes for the threat it poses to international peace and security, human life and dignity; peaceful, civilized coexistence; and because it endangers nations' stability, the strengthening of democracy and socio-economic development. They reaffirmed the need for countries to work together to eliminate it while strictly respecting human rights, in observance of the United Nations Charter and international law in general. They also recalled their profound condemnation of the terrorist attacks on September 11, 2001, their immediate recourse to the Interamerican Security System and specifically the TIAR, and their full support for applying the resolutions of the United Nations Security Council and the General Assembly. They also highlighted adoption of the Interamerican Convention on Preventing, Combating and Eliminating Terrorism at the XXXII General Assembly of the OAS and the work carried out by the Interamerican Committee Against Terrorism.

32. The Heads of State expressed their solidarity with the people and government of Colombia who defend democracy, a cause which has been strengthened as a result of the successful elections just held. They reject terrorist actions and violations of International Humanitarian law by groups acting outside the law.[39]

The declarations agreed upon by the South American presidents at the Guayaquil Summit are a departure from the Brazilian initiative's views on the Colombian conflict, which are based on a strategy of isolation.[40] At the summit responsibility for the multilateral handling of South American security issues was handed over to the Organization of American States (OAS). This measure has several implications. First, as this chapter has already intimated, any international intervention in Colombia will have to be multilateral in nature. This is meant to stymie bilateral or unilateral actions, such as a decision by Washington either acting on its own or together with a bordering country whose government bows to U.S. pressure. Second, the summit avoids identifying the armed Colombian players as "terrorists"; it labels them "groups outside the law." The intention here is to prevent the global war on terrorism from pressuring the countries in the region into joining forces and getting directly involved in the conflict. Finally, in order to reduce the emphasis put on security, drug trafficking is separated from terrorism; at the same time, economic issues are linked to the agenda. The politics of the South American Summit are certainly not Washington's politics, but neither are they confrontational.

U.S. views on Colombia formulated under the Clinton administration have been supported with increases in funding by the George W. Bush administration. These views regionalize both the Colombian conflict and the battle against drug trafficking. A variety of resources has been made available for distribution among all the countries to support Plan Colombia military activities under the Andean Regional Initiative. This initiative reinforces the primacy of Plan Colombia's military dimension and mounts a strategy that is regional in scope. So it is U.S. views, then, that are responsible for regionalizing the Colombian conflict, and none of the Andean nations can ignore them. In 2002 Ecuador received eighty million dollars in U.S. military aid. A sizable chunk of these resources has been used to outfit the base at Manta for U.S. purposes.[41] As other chapters in this book have indicated, Ecuador continued to receive military and other assistance as part of the Andean Regional Initiative to the present (2006).

The 2002 U.S. security strategy suggested that "failed states" are a potential threat to United States' security. It is precisely this concept of the state failure or partial failure that is at stake in the Andes region. Colombia is perceived as a threat not because it is a society with subhegemonic designs for the region, but rather because it is fragmented and the state is incapable of governing its space and territory.[42] Colombia is a country where the rule of law cannot be guaranteed, society is divided, and the state borders on collapse. This is a case of "defective" globalization.[43]

The sense among Andean states, especially Colombia, is that drug trafficking is not an issue that can be handled through foreign policy or by the Colombian State alone. It is, rather, a global issue that calls for policies that are equally global. The realist approach that goes hand in hand with State Department antinarcotics practices centering on interdiction and enforcement cannot be successful, then, because it presupposes capabilities the Andean States do not have.

In 2002 and 2003, Ecuadorian governments made various attempts to offset U.S. policy and formulate initiatives that would at once allow them to play a more active role yet avoid having to take a position on Colombia. There are differing perceptions of the dimensions of the threat, but for Ecuador the most serious problems derive from armed operations, population displacement, and illegal migration. All these problems worsened for Ecuador from 2003 to 2006.

From Colombia's perspective, Ecuador is a source of insecurity because the border is vulnerable to drug and arms trafficking and the criminal activities associated with them. Colombian authorities have disseminated the idea that the Ecuadorian army and police are reluctant to take on guerrilla groups; a dangerous modus vivendi has been established between illegal Colombian forces, that is, guerrillas, and Ecuadorian law enforcement.[44] This perception intensified in 2003 when various cases came to light of supposed involvement by Ecuadorian military personnel in arms trafficking into Colombia. While the type of arms and quantities reported seemed relatively insignificant, the incidents did cause political scandal.[45] The United States took the matter more seriously, as did other external actors, who urged the Ecuadorian government to take much more aggressive policies to curtail trafficking across borders of chemical precursors for the drug trade, arms, and explosives.[46]

Although Ecuador is not a "failed state," that perception sometimes exists, and its ability to control the borders with Colombia has limits.[47] In the case of Ecuador, the failed state image arises from the stereotyping of ethnic and regional differences.[48] The historic rivalry between Quito and Guayaquil, the instability of civilian governments, and the social unrest stirred up by demands from indigenous groups create this image. Nevertheless, Ecuadorian institutions do extend throughout its territory. While a "premodern" social fabric crosscuts society, it is capable of dealing with conflict via clientelist or patrimonial devices that perpetuate inequality but that have been highly successful, when compared with the experience of Ecuador's neighbors, at preventing political violence from being used for purposes of political or social vindication.[49] Nevertheless, Ecuador is not entirely capable of controlling the border with Colombia; operations of Colombian guerrillas, narco-traffickers, and the Colombian armed forces in Ecuadorian territory greatly complicate bilateral relations with Colombia, relations with the United States, and Ecuadorian domestic politics and civil–military relations.

Relations with the United States have been strained since implementation of Plan Colombia. The relationship certainly deteriorated in the absence of a U.S. ambassador from June 2001 to October 2002, but policy on Colombia has clearly been a source of friction. The U.S. government has several distinct avenues for negotiating with the Ecuadorian state where it can more strongly exercise its influence. For example, the U.S. report *Patterns of Global Terrorism, 2001*,[50] criticized Ecuador's supposed lack of control over the Colombian border. This was immediately denounced by the president, the minister of defense, and the Ecuadorian Chancellery.[51] In various arenas and through a variety of mechanisms the United States and Colombia have pressured the Chancellery and the Ministries of Foreign Trade, Economics, Government, and Defense to convince Ecuador to become more actively involved in the conflict. During the Gutiérrez presidency this policy had some overt and covert "successes." Gutiérrez initially proposed that he act as a "mediator" between the Colombian government and the guerrilla forces, but that stance was replaced quickly by a position much more favorable to a military solution, as set out in the Rio Group Summit in Cuzco in May 2003.[52]

Gutiérrez's proposals, both to mediate the conflict and the following about-face in which he offered support to the Colombian government in its fight against the guerrillas, took the ministers of defense and foreign relations by surprise. They had no prior warning of these initiatives and of the advice given to the president by Patricio Zuquilanda, who would subsequently become minister of foreign relations.[53] Both responded negatively and publicly. These events revealed that foreign and security policy, including Ecuador's role in the regional conflict, were being made in the presidential palace rather than passing through normal and proper institutional channels—where policy had been designed to limit Ecuador's involvement and to contain spillover of the Colombian conflict across its borders.

Economic assistance to build up the northern border is a key issue for the Ecuadorian armed forces, which takes a "multidimensional and holistic" view of the regional security situation.[54] Obviously the zone is a security challenge, but Ecuador's actions appear to be aimed at substantially improving its own control capabilities so as to avoid getting caught up in the conflict, as would like occur if a strictly or largely military approach were taken. The Ecuadorian military would like to assure a less porous border, without committing itself to further engagement in the Colombian conflict, and thereby help to stabilize the situation and minimize, to the extent possible, the threat of the conflict spilling over into Ecuadorian territory.

An additional source of tension in the Ecuador–U.S. relationship was Washington's proposal to exempt its troops from the terms of the International Criminal Court agreement to which Ecuador is signatory. (For more on this see Brian Loveman's chapter in this book.) A U.S. proposal for a bilateral agreement with Ecuador received a rather cold reception from the Chancellery.[55] Other key issues for the United States are the Colombian conflict and drug trafficking. Ecuador is strategically positioned on both of these interrelated fronts. The United States and Colombia are anxious to get Ecuador's support for the strategy outlined by Washington and Bogotá. On various occasions since September and October 2002, both Colombia (a meeting in Bogotá on September 5)[56] and the United States (visits by the undersecretary of the army and the commander of the Southern Command in October) strongly pressured Ecuador to become part of joint binational or multinational operations for the war in Colombia. This pressure has been applied repeatedly into 2006. The Manta air base figures prominently in these matters since the activities permitted for aircraft based in Ecuador might significantly influence logistics and combat in Colombia.

The 2002 changes in the global security agenda, especially the U.S. security agenda, are extraordinarily significant for what happens in the Andes. Security is a universal issue once more, perhaps as intense as before the end of the Cold War. The settlement or understanding of the world's regional conflicts cannot escape the U.S. war on terrorism strategy, just as the U.S. containment policy and its anticommunist vision influenced "domestic" politics around the world from the late 1940s until 1990. Deactivating the conflict in Colombia, which seems to be an explicit objective of the new strategy, is part of a worldview that contemplates alternative ways of structuring international power, alternatives that presage construction of hegemonic relationships beyond the Western Hemisphere.

The change in U.S. strategic doctrine and policy also contributes, thinking theoretically, to revival of the realism that is most conventional and most rudimentary in its analysis of the world. This type of realism, as a frame for foreign policy, finds expression in a doctrine that seeks a balance of power favoring the United States and an approach that relies on political pressure, even on potential allies, rather than a framework that emphasizes linkage politics and multiple agendas. The selection of national security decision makers comes out of these ideas and reinforces them.[57] Of course, this kind of realism as a foundation of U.S. policy already has a long history in the Andes region.[58]

The immediate effect of these views on the conflict, inside Colombia, has been a buildup of the military and emphasis on military solutions, but it has also meant the militarization of neighboring countries (see below). Colombia's neighbor states, not just the United States, have resorted to playing the realism game to deal with the situation. As a consequence, alternatives and strategies for solution or negotiation are diminished (but this in no way implies, of course, that any of the existing options might actually be effective).

It was in this global context that President Uribe, who during his first presidential campaign distanced himself from the negotiations going on with the FARC and called for strong military response, won a first-round election victory in Colombia in May 2002. He repeated this message and strong support for U.S. strategy for the region on the occasion of his first visit to Washington: Colombia is a hemispheric problem; the conflict affects stability throughout the region; what happens there will have repercussions for politics in the hemisphere for the next ten years.[59] U.S. concerns in the Andean region revolve around one central objective: fighting terrorism—which now seems conveniently to meld with the war against drugs and the defense of democracy (understood as periodic elections and legal government succession) and human rights.

Effects of the Colombian War on Ecuador

Most analysts and policy makers agree that Plan Colombia, and then Plan Patriota (a large military offensive against guerrillas in southern Colombia initiated in April 2004), radically altered the security picture and negatively impacted the Ecuadorian border region, and beyond.

In 1999 a number of nongovernmental organizations (NGOs) working on refugee and human rights issues and Amazonian research put a group together to monitor Plan Colombia. They mobilized public opinion, especially around the presence of the Forward Operating Location (FOL) at Manta air base.[60] The agreement made with the United States allowed several hundred American troops (up to 475) to operate out of the base. Further, it allowed naval operations at sea and use of Ecuadorian airspace. U.S. citizens operating out of the base are protected by their own laws; they require neither a passport nor a visa and are exempt from taxes on all imported goods. The accord includes a clause that waives Ecuador's right to sue for damages for damages incurred.[61]

The Manta base agreement is probably the most controversial piece of the plan that is intended to bring the country into line with the U.S.-backed antidrug policy. The base has been re-outfitted to meet technical and logistical specifications for intelligence operations tracking planes and crop plantings in Colombia's southeastern Amazonian plains. As an international agreement, many Ecuadorians believe that the base agreement should have gone through the required institutional channels for approval (the congress), but it did not; this gives rise to periodic political problems in the National Congress.[62] To this is added the controversial naval interdiction operations that includes the sticky issue of illegal immigration and claims that numerous boats have been sunk and that Ecuadorian fishermen have been mistreated in the country's own territorial waters by U.S. military forces.

Because Ecuador has been in a reactive mode vis-à-vis U.S. proposals on antinarotics policy since the end of the 1980s,[63] Ecuadorian politics has accepted inclusion in international antitrafficking agreements without major difficulty. Ecuador has been a loyal partner to these agreements. For that reason, U.S. antinarotics policy was not been seen as particularly problematic for the country until Plan Colombia was implemented and the FOL was installed at Manta.[64]

Since the end of the 1990s, and increasingly since the September 11, 2001, terrorist attacks put their mark on U.S. policy, the alarm raised over alleged security problems and the risk that the Colombian conflict might spill into the rest of the region are impacting the views of the opinion media, political elites, civilian groups, and academics. The situation is increasingly seen as highly problematic and threatening.

Environmental concerns also developed as Ecuador became more involved in the antidrug and regional conflict policies of the United States. A report released in October 2002[65] by a verification mission made up of various social organizations determined gliphosate fumigation had taken place inside the Ecuadorian border; the *fusarium* mold was detected as well. Problems affecting the chromosomes have been found among populations in the region, and there have been serious problems with livestock and crop damage on the Ecuadorian side of the border.[66] Such information is highly alarming to growing sectors of national society, particularly because Sucumbíos,[67] which borders on Colombia's Putumayo Department, is among Ecuador's least developed provinces; its population has historic ties to Colombia and the border there is extremely porous.

Despite all this, the Gutiérrez government lowered the profile on these issues, taking pressure off Colombian president Uribe to honor an informal agreement to avoid dispersion of gliphosphate in an area of approximately 10 kilometers around the border to prevent contamination on Ecuadorian soil. This agreement, made by Gutiérrez's first minister of foreign relations, was "frozen" by Chancellor Zuquilanda and then reasserted firmly after Gutiérrez's ouster at the MERCOSUR presidential summit in 2005.[68]

Thus, at the regional level, Plan Colombia's impacts on the border region are deemed extremely serious and complex. Military sources have observed irregular Colombian combatants in areas far removed from the border region, in the Amazonian provinces south of the border (in Napo and Orellana), all along the border, in the provinces of Carchi (in the mountains) and Esmeraldas (on the coast), and even in Imbabura and Pichincha, where the capital, Quito, is located.[69] These intrusions, both by Colombian government forces and guerrillas, periodically complicated Colombian–Ecuadorian relations and seriously impacted Ecuadorian internal politics and civil–military relations.

In the eyes of the Ecuadorian military, the Uribe government perceives Ecuador as a negative influence in the Colombian conflict. A Washington–Bogotá axis is imagined to be pressuring the country diplomatically, commercially, and politically to engage in binational joint military operations. The armed forces respond that the Colombian State should be responsible for controlling its border with Ecuador; Ecuador should not be asked to do it for them.[70]

The Ecuadorian armed forces' lack of equipment and logistical and operational capacity in the border region has not been sufficiently addressed with international cooperation. Reports have placed the number of Ecuadorian troops on the northern frontier (provinces of Esmeralda, Carchi, and Sucumbíos) at approximately eight thousand (2005), but it is very difficult, nonetheless, to control such an extensive area (620 kilometers of border). Estimates were made that a minimum of eighty-two million dollars is needed to gain effective control over the Ecuadorian border region. The United States delivered eight million dollars for development in 2001, ten million in 2002, and proposed sixteen million for 2003. Funding allocated for security amounted to just 1.65 million in 2001 and 14.3 million (a substantial increase) in 2002, of which 5.8 million went to a security program for the northern border. An allocation of 20.25 million dollars was proposed for 2003, 15.2 million of which was allocated to security on the northern border.[71] Despite significant increases in U.S. aid for border defense and "development," these resources are apparently insufficient to meet the existing needs, especially considering that not all of these resources are used for military purposes.

In terms of the question of resources, there are disagreements as to the figures. However, the Washington Office on Latin America (WOLA) and the Center for International Policy (CIP) publication *Just the Facts* (September 2004) provided the following disaggregated estimates for military/police and socioeconomic assistance from 1996 to 2005 compiled from diverse government sources and other publications. (See table 4.1.)

In any case, Ecuador has received less aid than other countries in the Andean region, as shown in table 4.1, largely, as indicated earlier, because only recently has the United States identified the country as a strategic actor in the region, although its importance is rising.[72]

In some ways, Ecuador's situation can be compared to that of Honduras during the Central American civil wars of the 1980s. Ecuador is the most vulnerable and least economically developed of all of Colombia's neighbors, just as Honduras was the poorest country in its region. While Bolivia is even less developed than Ecuador, it does not share a border with Colombia, but it receives more U.S. assistance because of its involvement in growing and processing cocaine, notwithstanding some reduction in production before 2004. The Honduran government ultimately gave in to U.S. demands to locate military bases there and allowed itself to be used as a refuge for the Contras, the anti-Sandinista paramilitary forces of the 1980s. Honduras submitted to U.S. policy at a time when it was emerging from a decade of political instability and military governments. It fell easy prey to U.S. military needs.

Ecuador faced a similar domestic political situation in 2003. Since 1995 three governments were brought down as a result of parliamentary and judicial maneuvering and coups. Six governments followed in just eight years; Ecuador is extremely fragmented socially, and its governments are weak.[73]

Throughout the latter half of the twentieth century, Ecuadorian foreign policy focused on the border conflict with Peru. After the two nations made peace the foreign policy agenda diversified, but there was an implied consensus to stay out of the Colombian conflict. Ecuadorian rhetoric on the issue changed in 2003, however, but this did not lead to hard and fast decisions. The president declared the United States his country's greatest ally.[74] And then, in July, he announced his intention to join the Colombian government's effort and agreed to that country's agenda. But in congress and in the press it was apparent that these public decisions were controversial. Thus foreign policy from 2003 until the fall of the Gutiérrez government in April 2005 continued to be characterized by its lack of definition and contradictory statements, appearing to have fallen victim to the fragmentation that also defines domestic policy.[75]

Returning to the parallels with Honduras in the 1980s, U.S. military aid to Honduras increased dramatically in the 1980s, translating into a buildup of the

TABLE 4.1

U.S. Military/Police and Socioeconomic Assistance to Andean Region Initiative/ACI Countries, 2000–2005 (in millions of U.S. dollars)

| | Year | | | | | | | | | | |
| | 2000 | | 2001 | | 2002 | | 2003 | | 2004 est | | 2005 req | |
Country	Mil/Pol	SocEc	Mil/Pol	SocEc	Mil/Pol	SocEc	Mil/Pol/	SocEc	Mil/Pol	SocEc	Mil/Pol	SocEc
Bolivia	48.98	159.77	35.12	75.33	51.26	105.67	57.24	108.96	59.56	102.28	58.48	107.68
Brazil	5.20	12.87	20.66	15.40	6.80	14.42	7.74	18.77	11.46	18.23	10.36	14.63
Colombia	765.32	214.31	224.68	5.65	371.74	120.30	605.10	149.20	551.33	150.00	574.15	150.00
Ecuador	24.43	24.19	18.71	16.37	33.99	36.76	33.13	40.52	44.10	38.01	29.79	38.98
Panama	5.61	6.30	2.04	6.92	11.55	11.14	5.85	11.04	10.75	11.58	8.60	11.82
Peru	57.63	107.08	25.47	108.63	77.66	160.67	68.38	143.00	75.73	102.12	70.60	104.83
Venezuela	6.48	0.58	3.18	0.20	5.41	2.12	3.69	0.89	4.06	2.75	3.58	1.83

Source: Data from "Diluyendo las divisiones. Tendencias de los programas militares de EEUU para América Latina," LAWGEF, WOLA, CIP, 2004: www.wola.org/publications/military_diluyendo_las_divisiones.pdf (accessed September 20, 2005).

country's armed forces. The country owed its political vitality to the amount of aid the armed forces had at their disposal, thanks to the bargain over use of Honduran territory and protection for the Contras. While U.S. military aid to Ecuador has increased, the amounts are proportionally quite different from the quantities received by Honduras. Between 1999 and 2003, Ecuador received just 104.23 million dollars. It was estimated that it would receive 29.72 million dollars in 2003,[76] which was less than 7 percent of Ecuador's nearly 450 million dollar defense budget for the year. After an important increase in aid in 2004, levels returned to those of 2003 for 2005. It must also be noted that assistance for the northern frontier is only part of the assistance provided by USAID, but it constitutes 37 percent of the aid package.[77]

Unlike what happened in Honduras, Ecuadorian armed forces became weaker after the war with Peru. This was mainly because of the intensity of domestic political conflict and its inevitable links to the three classic types of Ecuadorian political relationships: clientelism, patrimonialism, and regionalism. Moreover, from 2000 to 2006 the armed forces were embroiled in several corruption scandals and internal shakeups, eroding their prestige and legitimacy.[78]

Yet Ecuador's vulnerability to Washington–Bogotá regionalization policy is not attributable to the armed forces. Their explicit interests are to avoid involvement in the Colombian conflict:

> In accordance with Ecuadorian State foreign policy, all diplomatic efforts to achieve peace *in the Colombian civil conflict* will be supported; the country will maintain its position of *no military intervention* and draw on all necessary, sovereign measures to prevent the perpetrators of the violence from coming into and acting on national soil.[79] [emphasis added]

U.S. power to influence the Ecuadorian government derives its strength, rather, from the urgent needs facing the country and the government's expectations that it will get the funding or U.S. political support to take care of a host of problems, the most important of which are economic. Ecuadorian governments have always sought a special relationship with Washington, often allowing their agendas to be subordinated to immediate needs. One of the most common explanations behind the granting of Manta air base to the United States is that the discredited, then ousted, Jamil Mahuad administration hoped to win U.S. backing for negotiations with the IMF.[80]

In the same way that the Hondurans dealt with the spillover of both the Sandinista revolution and the Salvadoran insurgency onto their territory during the Central American crisis, Ecuador is significantly militarizing its border to stave off the Colombian contagion. In 2000, the Northern Frontier Development Unit was created, which aimed at generating dialogues between local governments bordering Colombia and the central government by creating a fund financed by, among other things, oil revenue. The idea was to invest in this area and create state presence. Similarly, the military created a division aimed at controlling the northeastern Amazon region. Its headquarters is 150 km from the border, and many battalions have transferred from the center of the country. And like Honduras, it cannot escape U.S. political influence. After his visit to the United States in February 2003, President Gutiérrez announced substantial increases in both U.S. military aid and assistance to improve living conditions in the area around the Colombian border. Ecuador expected to receive extraordinary assistance amounting to one hundred million dollars for alternative development, fifteen million to fortify border security, and an additional one hundred million dollars between 2003 and 2004 for bilateral aid through AID.[81]

The militarization of the border means that there is a defense apparatus made up of about ten thousand troops permanently stationed along the 600-kilometer extension. There is, in theory, a counterpart Colombian force of roughly the same size made up of armed forces and police. They do not have the capability to establish permanent posts but operate as mobile units. In actual practice they do not have control over the line dividing the two countries. These deployments are not, however, strictly comparable because the military situations confronted are different. The Ecuadorian troops attempt to control the border and national territory, but the Colombian troops must be highly mobile to engage guerrillas in an irregular war.

Economically speaking, the United States is Ecuador's principal trading partner.[82] Honduras was in a similar situation when it was used for U.S. purposes. Ecuador depends heavily on U.S. markets to keep its economy afloat. Unlike Honduras, however, U.S. aid is not indispensable to Ecuador's economy. This difference between Honduras and Ecuador explains, in part, why Ecuador has managed to keep its foreign policy relatively autonomous of Washington influences for much longer than Honduras was able to do so. Other political factors not related to the economy also play a part. First there is a difference in the importance the United States attached to the Central American conflict as compared to that ascribed to the Colombian conflict. Because the civil wars in Nicaragua, El Salvador, and Guatemala were viewed from the standpoint of anti-Soviet Cold War strategy they became a top priority issue for U.S. national security. The Colombian conflict is a somewhat peripheral concern at this time, despite its significance for the Andes region. Second, Ecuador is not hostile toward either Colombia or the United States, nor is it a potential ally for unlawful armed groups in Colombia. Its own interests dictate not getting involved, precisely because its security is subject to the actions of such groups. Finally, Ecuador is not quite as susceptible to economic pressures as was Honduras—and Ecuador exports oil.

Nevertheless, the structural asymmetries that exist between Ecuador and the United States do not leave the South American nation with much room to maneuver. Washington possesses the tools to bargain and pressure that will ultimately reshape Ecuadorian strategy. Indeed, already in 2003, President Gutiérrez was much more open to U.S. pressure to cooperate with the Bogotá government than was his predecessor. Ecuadorian rhetoric changed during this government, but there were various moments of tension with Colombia, despite the good relations with Washington. The border was temporarily closed; the Ecuadorian ambassador was recalled from Bogotá; and a certain xenophobia, encouraged by the authorities, accompanied these developments.

It is not inconceivable that Ecuador will permit installation of additional military bases by the United States, assigning air and sea interdiction duties to its forces,[83] or put its armed forces and police under joint Colombian and U.S. command. This is especially likely if conditions in the conflict do not change radically as a result of stepped-up government action against the guerrillas. In the absence of a force to counterbalance the situation, like the Contadora initiatives in the Central American conflict, Ecuador is at risk of succumbing to the well-coordinated and well-structured Washington–Bogotá policy designed to get all neighboring nations not hostile to the United States to collaborate directly with the Colombian government in its expanded "war on drugs and terror." Of course, domestic political events may prevent this outcome; the election of Evo Morales as president in Bolivia and the upcoming elections in Peru and Venezuela in 2006 may also constrain Ecuadorian foreign and domestic policy choices.

Security Institutions' Impressions of the Challenges Presented by Plan Colombia and Plan Patriota

Conventional logic underlying strategic planning for Ecuadorian national security decisions provides for contingencies involving violent actors from Colombia, humanitarian disaster and social conflict touched off by massive migrations, ecological disaster, or the spread of illegal crop cultivation into the country's territory. The government's potential for handling these scenarios is constrained, however, not simply because the state itself is weak, but because incurring the hostility of the United States would be a worse scenario yet. Decision making is constrained by the need to maintain harmonious relations with that nation.

The threat to national security, conventionally understood as a threat against the state and its institutions, is clear and imminent. It is not a long-range threat; it comes with the deployment, right on the Ecuadorian border, of five thousand Colombian army troops and police equipped with cutting edge technology and the latest weapons to eradicate 120,000 hectares of illegal crops. They will come face-to-face with seven thousand FARC combatants. There are also numerous paramilitary battalions in the region and unknown numbers of armed groups that occasionally engage in criminal activity.

Just as the Colombian government insists on distinguishing the guerrillas from the drug traffickers to legitimize its policies for a negotiated peace, Ecuadorian security holds fast to its antinarcotics rhetoric, even as it assesses the threats to Ecuador of the various parties to the Colombian violence. This is reflected in both Ecuador's support for the Guayaquil Summit declaration—a vital document for the Ecuadorian government—and the Chancellery's repeated statement of the Ecuadorian position. The commitment of the latter, however, is always linked to the need for more resources.[84] Nevertheless, Ecuador deployed ten thousand men to the Colombian border, practically quadrupling the number of troops that were there prior to Plan Colombia's implementation.

Ecuador's national security interests, as they relate to the Colombian conflict, are first and foremost *to contain the violence within Colombia's borders and to mitigate any possibility that local actors might be swept up in it*. All the bordering countries have declared their support for the established regime and the idea of a democratic Colombia.

In 2001 Ecuadorian immigration policy toward Colombia relaxed, thanks to the signing of the Convenios y Acuerdos de Integración Fronteriza (Border Integration Conventions and Agreements) drafted by the Comisiones de Vecindad (Neighbor Commissions) that have been meeting since 1989. In the heat of activities to promote economic integration and the opening of mar-

TABLE 4.2
Ecuador's National Security Interests, as They Relate to the Colombian Conflict

Threats[1]	Interests	Objectives
Armed operations of any origin	Prevention, neutralization	To uphold sovereignty
Humanitarian disasters	Getting resources and the appropriate infrastructure for the circumstances	To bring in resources
Colombian-style sociologization	Supporting a stable social structure	To maintain order, civility, and a culture of peace
Environmental catastrophe	Prevention	To protect
Spread of illegal cultivation	Prevention and eradication	To keep Ecuador from becoming a producer country

[1] This matrix was discussed among politicians, businesspeople, diplomats, the military, and academics attending a workshop in June 2001.

kets, there was a notable decline in border crossing enforcement. There are large numbers of migrant Colombians in Sucumbíos, but very few of them choose to be designated refugees. In 2004 it was estimated that once Plan Patriota (which began in 2004) was in full operation, an estimated two hundred thousand people would be impacted by what happened in the border region. The Ecuadorian government claimed that it would be able to handle only some five thousand of them.

There has also been persistent talk about the increase of criminal activity and violence in the border region. Accounts of *boleteos, vacunas,*[85] and kidnappings in all of the provinces bordering Colombia, not just Amazonia, have been documented by academic institutions and human rights organizations. Kidnappings of personnel working for foreign companies in the petroleum industry have captured public attention. Generally it is criminal groups disguising their acts as political who are responsible, but irregular armed troops using these methods to raise money cannot be discounted.

The AUC's (Autodefensas Unidas Colombianas—United Colombian Self-Defense Forces) presence is felt in Sucumbíos, particularly in the area around the bridge over the San Miguel River. Activities relating to the trafficking of precursors, the setting up of small laboratories, arms trafficking, and so forth[86] are common. These groups have spread into the General Farfán y Cháscales region, about 40 kilometers inside Ecuadorian territory and, of course, into the capital of Sucumbíos province, Nueva Loja or Lago Agrio, where Colombian-style summary executions were on the rise since 2001.[87]

FARC's Front 48 is located on the eastern edge of Sucumbíos Province, and the FARC is a strong presence in the region. According to numerous reports gathered, "the boys" (as the locals know them) carry out "control activities" inside Ecuadorian territory.[88] FARC Front 32 is located closer to the jungle corridor; the Colombian army is on the mountain border and in the Esmeraldas, Tumaco, and Mataje region, towns on Ecuador's northwestern border. There is also evidence of a limited ELN (Ejército de la Liberación Nacional—National Liberation Army) presence. The AUC and FARC maintain a presence in the coastal region as well.

Relations between armed Colombian and Ecuadorian groups have been close historically, particularly during the 1980s. This affiliation has not been a serious security issue for Ecuador, as their dealings have played out in an internal Colombian context, for example, in the enlistment of combatants from the Ecuadorian "Alfaro Vive, Carajo" (AVC—Alfaro Lives, Damn it) group in the Coordinadora Guerrillera Simón Bolívar (Simón Bolívar Guerrilla Movement Coordinating Body), associated with the M-19 movement in the 1980s.

There has also been talk of the alleged formation of the Fuerzas Armadas Revolucionarias Ecuatorianas (FARE—Ecuadorian Armed Revolutionary Forces). They supposedly have links to the FARC, which is reputed to have

provided them with training and support.[89] The group is said to have been detected a couple of years ago and is reported to have four hundred combatants,
but this information has not been confirmed. It should be pointed out that no
Ecuadorian political group, not even on the most radical Left, has expressed
support for, or solidarity with, the Colombian guerrillas. The ties that may
exist with Ecuador are more likely logistical, along the lines of a network of
suppliers, rather than some sort of politico-military construct.

The Ecuadorian armed forces claim these groups do not present a real security problem for the country, but according to the national police, between
six and eight cells may have already been activated. These divergent takes on
the situation touched off a debate between the minister of defense and the
commanding general of the police at the end of September and beginning of
October 2002. The debate exposed the widely differing views the two institutions have on security, which may prove problematic in the future.[90]

Neither the country's internal stability nor its political process appears
threatened by these isolated activities by irregular armed forces within
Ecuadorian territory. Basically, the FARC's ties are with arms, supply, and munitions traffickers and other sources of logistical support in the country. They
generally go about their business quietly, firm about their intention to preserve Ecuador's neutrality in the ongoing conflict. The AUC may be moving
into the country, especially in Sucumbíos, to settle scores with the guerrillas
who cross over the border. And it is assumed that national paramilitary
groups are also forming. Despite the lack of an immediate threat to the
Ecuadorian State from these activities by armed groups in the north, tension,
violence, and anomie are steadily taking hold in border communities. The
border's porosity and the difficulties of controlling it effectively are critical
factors that became ever more apparent as intensive implementation of Plan
Colombia and Plan Patriota began.

These developments have generalized a perception of imminent, increasing
danger, not just in the border region, but in other parts of the country as well.
The security agencies see different shades of threat; the perspectives of the police differ from those of the armed forces. The media, however, began to give
much greater attention to information coming in from the border region,
providing growing awareness of the situation there. Development projects,
like the one initiated by the Unidad de Desarrollo del Norte (UDENOR—Unit
for Northern Development) cannot get off the ground, and external aid agencies have transferred resources and have doubts about these projects' viability;
meanwhile the situation becomes more critical and ever more conflictive, as
violent acts, kidnappings, *boleteos*, summary executions, and other alarming
crimes are on the rise.

The Ecuadorian government's response to Colombian president Uribe's
pressures—before mid-2003—had been, in a word, cold. During his visit to

Quito before taking over the government and in repeated statements since, the Colombian president called upon his neighbors to join the fight against narco-trafficking, even intimating that the scope of Manta air base's duties should be broadened in the war on terrorism.[91] As indicated earlier, during the Gutiérrez administration, Ecuador moved closer to the U.S. and Colombian positions but did not overturn traditional security policies (which have not been reaffirmed by President Palacio in 2005).

Two weeks after Uribe's visit in August 2002, the Ecuadorian government unilaterally decided to close the Colombian border at night and require additional documentation from Colombian citizens who had enjoyed free entry privileges with Ecuador for decades. After the Colombian president's inauguration, the ministers of defense and foreign relations from both countries met, accompanied by the heads of their military and police. Trade issues were at the top of the meeting's agenda, followed by immigration. Ecuador reaffirmed its decision to restrict Colombian citizens' entry. Security was the third item on the agenda, and migration last. That order of priorities was imposed by Ecuador.

Security officials insisted that multilateral organizations were the right arena for dealing with the war on terrorism. Channels for exchanging information were broadened, and commissions were created, but there were no great breakthroughs.[92] It was learned extra-officially that Colombian authorities suggested holding joint military exercises but the idea was rejected by the Ecuadorians.

Subsequently, regarding the question of fumigations and the presence of Colombian police and military intelligence on Ecuadorian territory, Gutiérrez tacitly favored the Colombian agenda, even when the spokesperson for the FARC, Raúl Reyes, called the Ecuadorian president a "traitor" to supposed agreements previously reached with the guerrillas. After Gutiérrez's ouster, the new government seemed initially to reaffirm Ecuador's opposition to fumigation operations that affected its territory and also its concern for intrusions by Colombian armed forces into Ecuadorian territory in pursuit of the guerrillas and drug traffickers.

What Next?

In 2006 Ecuador's greatest defense and security concern remained the conflict in Colombia. It was a threat because globalization in that country and the rest of the region was "defective," a defectiveness that expresses itself in the state's inability to control its territory and the violent political acts taking place on its soil. Threatening, too, was the possibility that the country could be drawn into the conflict as a result of its "social" regionalization and a U.S. policy to consolidate action around a strategy that put the military at the forefront in a regional and *regionalized* conflict. Another issue was continuation and further intensification of the antidrug strategy based on control, interdiction, and suppression of illegal psychotropic substance production in source countries. The strategy has not proved effective, but it has produced intense social and political conflicts in much of the subregion.

The events of September 11, 2001, in the United States opened the door on the possibility that conflicts in the Andean region, specifically the one in Colombia, could fall under a global security strategy involving use of the military in the "war against terrorism." Colombia's political climate has changed; negotiated alternatives or "societal" concepts of the conflict have given way to conventional realist perspectives of security. Since Uribe took office in Colombia the military dimension of the Colombian crisis has assumed even more importance in the speeches of Colombian civilian and military leadership as well as of policy makers in Washington, D.C. This trend is ominous for Ecuador and the rest of the region.

Ecuador is in a very vulnerable position internationally with regard to its security and defense. Political turmoil in the region, economic weakness, and the complexity of the issues in conflict make setting autonomous policy extremely difficult. The primary conflicts going on in the Andes region are all transnational in nature, yet the only rules for handling them are the ones handed down by Washington. As a result, the region lacks initiative and bows to U.S. devices, vision, and strategy, despite resistance from minority political movements in all the Andean countries and of the government of President Hugo Chávez in Venezuela.

The setting of security policy by the Andean states has been reactive vis-à-vis U.S. influence. But common to the process in each country has been the seeking out of multilateral venues in which to take up regional security matters. The countries of the region have sought alternative venues in which to deal with the intensifying conflicts and challenges facing them. One such venue would be the South American presidential summits. Hopefully, traditional venues—the OAS and the United Nations—will not be overlooked.

For Ecuador, the issue of the Manta military base is crucial because newly designed U.S. security policy inextricably links what the country views as its two main security challenges in the region: terrorism and drug trafficking. As one of three FOLs replacing the Southern Command in Panama, Manta air base performs key functions in this new security design. It would be naïve to believe that antinarcotics and antiguerrilla operations could be kept neatly separate from one another, so as to abide by the letter of the signed agreements. On the contrary, it should be expected that in the future, American operations at the base will provide the Colombian State with intelligence and logistical support for the conflict, if not eventually for offensive operations against "terrorist organizations." This will turn the base into a medium-range strategic target for the FARC.

The diagnosis of Ecuador's security needs is not necessarily compatible with the strategy currently being executed in Colombia. It is in Ecuador's national interest to steer clear of the conflict, for its neighbor country to regain sovereignty and control over the border by its own means, and for Ecuador to comply fully with agreements in the fight against drug trafficking. It is not in its interest to get involved in joint or multinational military operations as part of some long-term U.S. regional strategy.

The United States National Security Strategy (2002, 2005) makes it clear that the United States will call upon all the resources, devices, and power at its disposal to achieve its objectives, whether it be with the approval of the international community or acting autonomously and unilaterally. The Department of State and the Embassy in Quito will position themselves accordingly. A certain inflexibility on the part of U.S. diplomacy is to be expected.

The Colombian–U.S. pressures being brought to bear on Ecuador weigh heavily on the country, distance it from the United States (at the same time as they "bring it closer"), and create in the country a general atmosphere of opposition to U.S. diplomacy and policy. Since Plan Colombia's implementation, fighting in the conflict has worsened living conditions on the Ecuadorian border and led to violence and upheaval, conditions that stress Ecuador's weak institutional structure. As in much of the Andean region, the war on drugs, U.S. security policy, economic interests, and diplomacy are a growing source of tensions and insecurity in Ecuador in 2006.

5

A "Medicine of Death"?
U.S. Policy and Political Disarray
in Bolivia, 1985–2006

Kenneth Lehman

IN LATE AUGUST OF 1985, Bolivian president Víctor Paz Estenssoro went before
the Bolivian people to announce a new economic plan. Inflation had reached
24,000 percent—at the time the seventh worst hyperinflation in history—and if
it were to continue on its current course for another twenty days, it would become the highest in history. Bolivia had just defaulted on its international obligations and the previous president had been forced to resign. Elections to replace him were muddled, providing Paz no clear mandate. Nonetheless, he
knew he had to act. "Either we have the moral courage to make the sacrifices
necessary to put in place a radical new policy," he told his fellow citizens that
night, "or quite simply, Bolivia will die."[1]

Just over twenty years later, as these words are being written, Bolivia is back on
its deathbed, and Venezuelan president Hugo Chávez recently charged that the
remedy prescribed by Paz that night in 1985 is the cause. Market reforms and free
trade are "a medicine of death" that has brought Bolivia to the verge of civil war,
claims Chávez.[2] Reforms heavily promoted by the United States and the International Monetary Fund (IMF) over the past two decades have made Bolivia relatively market lean but without enough counterbalancing economic growth to
offset the political, class, and ethnic tensions they have aroused. Those tensions
have torn Bolivia asunder and now align with deep historical, racial, and regional
cleavages to produce the potential for a "perfect storm" of disorder, civil war, or
even the dissolution of the country itself. Bolivia's neighbors fear its "Lebanon-
ization"; Washington worries it is a failing state, ripe for narco-terrorists who
would "support uncontrolled cultivation of coca," and observers inside the country and out wonder whether Bolivia can any longer be governed.[3]

In light of Bolivia's current difficulties, it is already easy to forget that as recently as 2002 it was considered a success story; an example of how democracy, when coupled with "Washington Consensus" policies of privatization, trade liberalization, and market reforms, could positively reshape a developing country.[4] In early 2002 the PBS special on globalization *Commanding Heights* featured Bolivia as an example of how making hard decisions can turn a country around. It was, as Gonzalo Sánchez de Lozada, Paz's planning minister and head of the stabilization team, told his *Commanding Heights* interviewer, a "reinvention of Bolivia." Bolivia became a trailblazer and a model. The segment on Bolivia closed with a statement by Jeffrey Sachs, the young Harvard professor who had been the chief outside consultant to the stabilization team. "In late 1985, as we were struggling late into the night with a problem, [Sánchez de Lozada] said, 'you know, this is extraordinarily hard, but what's happening here, this is going to have to happen all through Latin America.' [And then] I watched it unfold, one country after another."[5] Bolivia's economic about-face made it a harbinger of changes that were to occur all over the hemisphere.

By the mid-1990s Bolivia had become a showcase of Washington Consensus orthodoxy; democracy seemed well-established, inflation was low, and growth was solid, if unspectacular. Only coca and cocaine kept Bolivia from being Washington's poster child. Then, in 1997, Hugo Banzer Suárez took office, pledging to take Bolivia out of the coca-cocaine circuit before his term ended in 2002. Because of cancer, Banzer was forced to leave the presidency a year early, but not before he declared victory in the war on coca. In only three years his campaign had reduced illegal coca production by 40,000 hectares (officially only 600 hectares remained) and substituted 115,000 hectares of alternative crops.[6] Bolivia had also now become one of Washington's most compelling success stories in the perennially frustrating war on drugs.

In April 2001, two months after Banzer announced "victory" in Bolivia's drug war, the George W. Bush administration unveiled its Andean Regional Initiative. The program built upon and extended President Clinton's Plan Colombia by devoting more assistance to economic and social programs and by making the initiative regional so as to reduce the spillover effects of "successes" in Colombia. At a mid-May briefing on the initiative, administration officials set out three overarching objectives for the Andean region—what they called "The 3-Ds": democracy, development, and drug control. Since then President Bush has requested and Congress has funded nearly $4 billion to support broad regional policies that were first tested in Bolivia. But just as the initiative was launched, the Bolivian model began to come apart. The spiral toward anarchy that has followed makes observers wonder if Bolivia is again a harbinger, but of a very different trend.

This chapter examines two decades of U.S. policy in Bolivia, though it focuses primarily on the last five years. It suggests that Bolivia is a particularly striking example of the flawed application of the central postulates of post–Cold War U.S. policy in the Andean region. The fundamental problem has been that while officials identified the "3-Ds" in one order—democracy, development, and drug control—actual policies reversed those priorities. Drug control almost always came first, development assistance was made conditional on effective drug control measures, and too often the advancement of democracy—beyond the technical matter of holding regular elections—received little more than lip service.[7] Further sabotaging democracy was the degree to which policies were imposed in Washington. Too often, when initiatives did come from La Paz, they did not receive enough U.S., IMF, or World Bank support to guarantee success.

Bolivia's current dilemmas are too complex and their historical roots too deep for responsibility to be exclusively or even largely attributed to the United States as Chávez would have it. But any medicine can be a poison if overprescribed or wrongly administered. This chapter suggests that the problem is not necessarily the medicine that was prescribed, but that the application and the bedside manner must change. Other chapters in this book will provide broader comparative context to make both Bolivia's uniqueness and its similarities to its neighbors more clear, but the evidence found in this chapter suggests that Bolivia is something of an Andean "mine canary" warning of basic U.S. policy flaws in the region.

Problem 1: Putting Drug Control before Development

The contradiction between U.S. counternarcotics policies and the economic tenets of neoliberal development have been obvious to the most outspoken champions of Bolivia's reinvention. Soon after he became president in his own right in 1993, Gonzalo Sánchez de Lozada (better known to Bolivians as "Goni") told a Voice of America interviewer in a moment of candor that the war against drugs should shift focus. Prohibiting substances for which there was high demand did not work, Goni said, and it would be better to legalize and regulate cocaine.[8] Jeffrey Sachs was more blunt: "The one competitive advantage [Bolivia] has is producing cocaine for the U.S. market. And rather than give 'Entrepreneur of the Year' awards there, we go in and shoot the entrepreneurs."[9]

In fact, Bolivia has one of its few comparative advantages in the production of coca and has been an important supplier of the leaf since precolonial times. Coca is an ideal crop for small farmer production in Bolivia's eastern foothills. It produces high yields of high value on small acreages, is easy to transport over inadequate roads, flourishes in acidic rain-leached soils, requires little up-front investment or maintenance, and—contrary to the claims of U.S. drug agents—does little ecological damage. Beginning in the 1970s, Bolivia became a key supplier of the raw material for cocaine, a growing U.S. addiction. In the late 1970s and early 1980s coca grew in value as the prices of legal exports collapsed and, by late 1985, it was Bolivia's only growth industry, providing sustenance to thousands of small farmers in the Chapare and Yungas regions.[10]

That same year the U.S. Congress passed a measure as part of the 1985 Foreign Assistance Act authorizing the president to decertify and terminate aid to any country considered out of compliance with U.S. antidrug objectives. Aware of coca's importance to Bolivia's economy and cocaine's importance to the United States, Víctor Paz made coca eradication a bargaining chip to enlist U.S. support for his economic reforms. Then, under the threat of sanctions, Paz in 1988 agreed to eradicate all coca beyond that devoted to traditional use. This commitment was codified into Law 1008, which has regulated Bolivia's antidrug policies since. While in some ways an imposed and draconian measure, Law 1008 nonetheless determined that eradication would be gradual and accompanied by indemnification and assistance to the affected small farmers. The use of herbicides was prohibited, and 12,000 hectares of coca in the Yungas were protected for traditional and legal uses. All coca in the newer Chapare region was eventually to be destroyed.[11]

The burden of implementing Law 1008 fell on the presidents who followed Paz. His successor Jaime Paz Zamora wore a coca-leaf pin on his lapel while campaigning to highlight the legitimate uses of coca. Paz Zamora also tried to emphasize the reciprocal nature of the anti-coca campaign by linking coca eradication more closely to the provision of adequate development assistance—*coca por desarrollo*. If the United States and other consuming nations would reduce the demand for cocaine or would ante up sufficient development assistance to truly give coca farmers an alternative, the problem would disappear, Paz Zamora argued. Any other approach unfairly placed the costs of a U.S. problem on Bolivian shoulders. But with the Cold War ending, Congress and the administration of George H. W. Bush instead reconfirmed that drugs were a security issue and launched a new war on drugs with all the implications of military solutions to foreign threats that "war" implies.[12]

The realities of power meant that the U.S. position prevailed and that peasant coca producers, the easiest to locate and most defenseless link in the production chain, would face the heavy state intervention required to counter market signals. Soon after he took office, Paz Zamora signed a secret annex to a U.S. assistance package agreeing to bring Bolivia's military into the eradication campaign. In the furor that followed public exposure of the annex, the president tried to retreat, which opened a stormy relationship with the aggressive new U.S.

ambassador, Robert Gelbard, who had been sent by Washington to keep the Bolivians on task. Soon after Paz Zamora left office, charges surfaced that he had fraternized with a notorious Bolivian druglord and had accepted nearly $500,000 in campaign contributions from traffickers. One close associate was jailed, and though Paz Zamora escaped a similar fate, the State Department publicly revoked his visa.[13]

By the 1993 elections, drug policies had become a campaign issue that pushed all serious candidates—even Sánchez de Lozada, Washington's favorite and the eventual winner—to call for the reduction or removal of U.S. military and drug personnel from Bolivia. Armed with a bold and innovative plan to complete Bolivia's reinvention by deepening and spreading the benefits of neoliberal reforms, Goni made clear that he considered coca reduction a secondary objective until enough dynamism had been brought to the economy to give coca producers true alternatives. However, in early 1995, after Goni missed eradication targets set in Law 1008 by a wide margin during his first year in office, Bolivia was decertified, endangering the U.S. and multilateral assistance upon which his reform plans hinged. Bolivia was granted a national interest waiver but was warned of full decertification if coca eradication targets were not met by midyear. Under duress, Sánchez de Lozada sent the army into the Chapare to forcibly root out enough coca to restore Bolivia to Washington's good graces. In 1996 Bolivia was declared in full compliance, but at a steep cost in domestic support for Goni's reform package. The following year Sánchez de Lozada—whose public approval ratings now stood at 19 percent—again fell behind schedule and left the bulk of that year's eradication to his successor.[14] By the time Goni left office, it was apparent that U.S. preoccupation with eradication targets had helped to undermine his legitimacy and thus the success of his program. By further militarizing the conflict, U.S. policy had also exacerbated social tensions in Bolivia and placed peasant producers back in the crosshairs of the drug war.

Yet to what effect? As Sánchez de Lozada left office, the United Nations Drug and Crime Prevention Agency reported that coca/cocaine still constituted half of Bolivia's export revenues. The U.S. Embassy estimated that the area under coca cultivation had actually increased 27 percent in the decade since Law 1008 was promulgated. When U.S. drug czar Barry McCaffrey visited Bolivia after the transfer of power he reminded officials in the incoming Banzer government that while Bolivia had received $500 million in U.S. aid in the past seven years, coca output had increased.[15] The market logic behind these statistics is easy to understand. Bolivian governments sought U.S. assistance provided by the drug war but were cautious to take the politically difficult steps that U.S. policy makers demanded in return. Small producers were happy to take the compensation they received for destroying their illegal coca but reserved some of that windfall to plant new coca as insurance against the marketing uncertainties of alternative crops. It is also easy to understand why these dynamics were increasingly unacceptable to the United States.

The election of Hugo Banzer Suarez in 1997 sent mixed signals to Washington. During the campaign he promised to remove Bolivia from the coca/cocaine circuit, but he had been military dictator of Bolivia in the 1970s when coca production exploded, and rumors continued to circulate that members of his family were cocaine traffickers.[16] Officials in Washington were also concerned with Banzer's political pact with Paz Zamora. Because Banzer had received a bare plurality of the popular vote, the State Department did its best to steer him into an alliance with Sánchez de Lozada, warning "that it would be very difficult to work productively with an administration that had somebody with a record of drug connections among its senior members."[17] The status quo could not continue, but Washington was uncertain whether the new administration would be more cooperative or more defiant than the one that had just left office.

In fact, Banzer quickly made his position clear. Placing coca eradication in the hands of the person in his administration Washington most trusted—his young, Texas-educated vice president, Jorge Quiroga—Banzer reconfirmed his desire to remove Bolivia from the coca/cocaine circuit. Quiroga brokered a deal with coca producers that allowed Bolivia to meet and exceed that year's eradication targets, despite the hole in which Sánchez de Lozada had left them. Then early in 1998, Banzer announced Plan Dignidad—a comprehensive attack on the coca/cocaine industry at every level, but focusing on eradication of all coca designated as illegal by Law 1008. Eradication would be voluntary if possible, but forcible when necessary. Since monetary compensation had too often been used in the past to replant coca, it was phased out, and instead farmers who volunteered to eradicate their coca would receive assistance to grow new crops. The projected cost over five years was $923 million including $700 million for alternative development. The Banzer government pledged to meet at least 15 percent of the cost from its own limited resources and went hat in hand to the United States, the European Union, and the multilateral agencies to gather the rest.[18] The reception in Washington was not initially what they had hoped. In March 1998, Quiroga was forced to make an emergency trip to Washington to head off plans to cut antidrug aid to Bolivia from $21 million to $12 million. The snafu actually had little to do with Bolivia and much more to do with bureaucratic infighting in Washington. In effect, aid to Bolivia was held hostage by several U.S. congressmen who were lobbying to upgrade helicopters provided to the Colombian police. Until a compromise was reached, not only was Bolivia's antidrug aid frozen, but two Black Hawk helicopters were reassigned to Colombia, a clear sign of where Bolivia stood in Washington's priorities.[19]

Nonetheless Banzer forged ahead to eliminate an unprecedented 11,600 hectares of coca over the balance of 1998—the first substantial net reduction since the onset of the drug war. Eradication jumped to 17,000 hectares in 1999 and, while it fell somewhat in 2000, it was still the second largest net reduction in history. Equally successful was a plan to intercept chemicals crossing the borders from neighboring countries that were used to process Bolivian coca leaf. The rising shortages of such chemicals forced cocaine producers to use inferior substitutes that reduced purities to as low as 37 percent and made their product harder to sell.[20]

Still, international support remained disappointing. At a June 1999 donors' meeting in Paris, only the United Nations Drug Control Program anted up its full quota. A second donors' meeting in November was canceled due to lack of interest.[21] In a further irony, success only raised the expectations of U.S. drug officials while the simultaneous explosion of coca production in Colombia made it easy to shift resources to that less successful front in the drug war. Nonetheless, in early 2001, and a year ahead of schedule, Banzer announced that only 600 hectares of illegal coca remained in the Chapare. He invited visitors from over thirty nations to attend ceremonies marking the symbolic completion of Plan Dignidad. By now, Washington was fully convinced of the old general's sincerity and eager to take some of the credit. The State Department's 2000 Narcotics Control Strategy Report called Bolivia a "model," and more effusively, a U.S. Agency for International Development (USAID) website titled "Success Stories" stated that with U.S. assistance the Dignity Plan had converted the Chapare, "a haven of lawlessness and narco-trafficking," into "a home to thousands of hectares of legal crops and pastureland, well-maintained farm-to-market roads, breathtaking natural beauty and tourism opportunities and an increasingly vibrant economy."[22]

But "success" that continued to defy market realities also exacted costs, and like any war, this one had body counts. Under Plan Dignidad, thirty-three coca growers and twenty-seven members of security forces died.[23] It confiscated a lucrative crop from thousands of already marginal peasant farmers without offering a truly viable alternative. The *Washington Post* quoted a priest in the Chapare soon after Banzer announced "success" who instead called it a "tragedy." "Coca was taken away and the farmers were abandoned—this is not a battle won. It is a human tragedy for thousands of poor families with no way to support themselves now."[24] Both Bolivian and U.S. officials conceded this point. The Banzer government remained frustrated that support for alternative development was so limited. Of the $700 million they requested for alternative development, they eventually received $128 million.[25] The State Department's *International Narcotics Control Strategy Report* covering the year 2000 admitted that "the aggressive eradication program of 1999 and 2000 outpaced the counternarcotics alternative development program in the Chapare by a wide margin."[26] Meanwhile Bolivia's economy stagnated, at least in part because of the roughly $700 million annually the country lost as a result of Plan Dignidad's success.[27]

When Banzer left office for health reasons in August of 2001 the contradictions between coercive drug policies and neoliberal economic development policy were obvious on both the macro and micro levels. Jeffrey Sachs had foreseen them and claims later that when Banzer decided to pursue Plan Dignidad he advised the president's team "to insist on adequate aid to finance economic development" that would benefit "the hundreds of thousands of displaced peasant farmers and their dependents."[28] Instead Washington relied on sanctions and threats. Never far from the minds of the designers of Plan Dignidad was the idea that decertification loomed if they failed to satisfy U.S. drug warriors and would endanger nearly $3 billion in assistance and credits upon which the country depended.[29] Still, as the name implies, Plan Dignidad was never entirely about economic self-interest or dependency. For Hugo Banzer and Jaime Paz Zamora it was the dignity that came from clearing their names; for Jorge Quiroga the dignity impugned when Americans inevitably linked his country to drugs; and for all these men it doubtlessly had something to do with the dignity that would come from no longer having to play the duplicitous game the U.S. drug war required them to play.[30]

But market incentives to grow coca were never removed. The plan's "success" came from the application of force and perhaps more significantly from the fact that coca production in Colombia was more than tripling from 50,000 hectares to 169,800 hectares at the same time coca production in Bolivia was declining by 40,000 hectares.[31] Even so, U.S. assistance and alternate cropping schemes were never sufficient to remove the economic incentives to grow coca, meaning the plan's "success" came with increasing social and political as well as economic costs. Sachs is blunt:

> Yet such is the blundering power of the U.S. that it pressed Bolivia to do its bidding without providing for any realistic alternatives. Tiny programmes of substitute crops that the U.S. authorities on the ground knew to be wholly inadequate were cynically implemented. Real economic alternatives, especially urban employment in export-oriented sectors, are a much tougher proposition given that Bolivia is a mountainous and landlocked country 12,000 feet above sea level. Without big investment in transport, communications and plant, only a few products such as coca leaf can bear the transport costs entailed by this rugged geography.[32]

Because they did not address market issues, drug policies effectively undermined Bolivia's development and ultimately its ability to control drugs. U.S. drug policies and Bolivia's sputtering economy also undermined the elitist technocratic version of democracy that U.S. officials preferred and stirred powerful popular democratic forces that Washington feared.

Problem 2: Putting Drug Control before Democracy

The word *democracy* has multiple definitions. A bit of history will provide clues to its shades of meaning in Bolivia. The country was technically a democracy prior to 1952, in the sense that elections were held regularly, but it was a "democracy" dominated by the great tin interests that effectively excluded 80–90 percent of Bolivia's people. The same Víctor Paz Estenssoro who instituted neoliberal reforms in 1985 revealed the crisis of elitist democracy when he was elected as a reform candidate in 1951. A military coup kept him from office, but a year later a popular uprising accompanied by a general military collapse brought Paz and his Movimiento Nacionalista Revolucionario (MNR) to power and ushered in one of Latin America's most profound social revolutions. For twelve years the MNR carried out the first installment in its "invention" of Bolivia, this one largely based on the quasi-socialist economic nationalism popular on the Latin American left at the time.

Immediately after the revolution, Paz's government nationalized Bolivia's major tin mines, initiated land reform, and enfranchised all Bolivians. The MNR's model was Mexico, where corporate entities like labor and peasant unions provided grassroots support to a powerful national revolutionary party that rationed and doled out benefits through state mechanisms. However, in Bolivia a corporatist single-party "democracy" never worked that well. The MNR remained weak, and often political initiative stayed with well-organized pressure groups pushing it from below. Labor unions—especially the militant mine workers union—now bargained directly with the state; all workers, including the mine workers, formed an umbrella organization, the COB (Central Obrero Boliviano), that gave them a powerful voice in the revolutionary government; and land reform created peasant *sindicatos* that also combined in umbrella organizations to give peasants a new political influence. While the failures of Bolivia's revolution are manifest, it did succeed in creating one of the most politically mobilized populations in Latin America. In this one crucial element of democracy—citizen organization—Bolivia is arguably more advanced than the apathetic, interest-run polity of the United States itself.[33]

These features also explain one of the central paradoxes of postrevolutionary Bolivia. Though Bolivia remained of marginal importance to the United States, the United States became a central and often dominating influence in Bolivia. The military collapse that accompanied the revolution led the United States to assist this revolutionary nationalist government when it was simultaneously undermining and overthrowing similar governments in Guatemala, Iran, and British Guiana.[34] Bolivia was of low importance and low priority and thus a good place to launch a quiet experiment. The purpose of the U.S. experiment was to support and channel nationalist revolutionary impulses in directions consistent with U.S. interests. The fact that there was no acceptable alternative to the moderate leftists who led the MNR meant that another U.S. goal was to assist in recreating a military that could support the experiment so long as it stayed on track and could end it in an acceptable way if it didn't.[35]

For twelve years the United States simultaneously nurtured Bolivia's moderate leaders and its reconstituted military so that together they could contain the popular forces that the revolution had unleashed—particularly Bolivia's powerful and often radical tin miners. Finally in 1964 the experiment ended. With the recently reelected Paz palpably losing his grip, the military intervened and ruled the country for most of the next two decades. For the United States, security trumped democratic ideals and Washington was complacent with, if not actively complicit in, the change.[36] During the two decades of military rule that followed, Bolivia and the United States remained on friendly terms, with several short but notable exceptions. However, the military repeatedly failed to rein in the popular democratic forces unleashed by the revolution and in multiple ways failed to bring either long-term political stability or sustained economic growth. By the early 1980s military rule had degenerated into corruption under a junta so deeply involved in the drug trade that it lost U.S. support. For a second time in thirty years, the power and legitimacy of the Bolivian military had largely collapsed, this time beneath its own corruption, incompetence, and internal schisms. Bolivia returned to civilian rule.

In 1982 Bolivia became one of the first nations in South America to make a successful transition from military to elected civilian rule. However, prices of key legal exports were falling (petroleum from $30/bbl in 1980 to $10/bbl in 1985, tin from $6.80/lb. to $2.40/lb. overnight in mid-1985), and popular demand unleashed by the end of military repression created powerful inflationary pressures.[37] By 1985 Central Bank credits covered 93 percent of Bolivia's domestic expenditures, the government defaulted on its international obligations, the IMF and World Bank cut the country adrift, and Bolivia's first elected civilian government since the 1960s collapsed. The inability of the new government or popular mobilization to provide a solution to the escalating economic crisis opened the way to the second great revolution led by Victor Paz Estenssoro—this one from above, this one reversing the economic nationalism he had earlier championed, and this one dismantling the state system his first revolution had helped to create.[38]

Economic collapse, the trauma of hyperinflation, the government's dismantling of the state mining company as a result of the free fall of tin prices, the resulting impotence of the previously powerful mine workers union—all occurring against a backdrop of international events that discredited the socialist option—made this an abrupt and radical turnaround. Under these conditions, a new manifestation of democracy emerged in Bolivia—elitist, increasingly technocratic, and built on a series of pacts among Bolivia's leading parties.[39]

Bolivians were ambivalent about the change. At each election after 1989 they would repudiate the party in power—a sign of their growing unhappiness, but reconfirm the model by voting for candidates who would reconstruct a new pact and continue neoliberal policies—a sign of their patience and their lingering hope that new leaders and new political coalitions might bring elusive success. Meanwhile social mobilization remained relatively quiescent.

Washington lauded the emerging political stability. U.S. influence and involvement in Bolivia had declined during two decades of military rule but now rapidly reemerged with the country's restoration of constitutional government. With the Cold War ending and under the new mantra of "3-Ds" (democracy, neoliberal development, and drug control) the U.S. Embassy, the IMF, and the World Bank became central policymaking actors in Bolivia. Therefore it is ironic that U.S. drug policies systematically undermined the "democracy of pacts" (*democracia pactada*) that Washington favored, while reawakening the "democracy of social mobilization" and "old-style populism" that neoliberal development was expected to contain and redirect. U.S. drug policies weakened *democracia pactada* in several ways: first by pressuring fragile coalition governments to take politically difficult stands; second by regularly revealing the weakness and dependency of those governments whenever they attempted to assert a degree of independence from Washington; third by failing to provide sufficient assistance to assure the success of bold Bolivian initiatives like Goni's political and social reforms or Banzer's Plan Dignidad; and finally by pushing coercive rather than market-oriented policies to fight the drug war.

Because of Bolivia's history of troubled military–civil relations, a small digression on the final point is necessary. The return to civilian government in 1982 marked the end of a brutal and corrupt narco-military regime. Nonetheless, since then the United States has consistently worked to strengthen and reinsert the military as an ally in the war on drugs. In 1986 Victor Paz authorized "Operation Blast Furnace," an unprecedented joint exercise supported logistically and with troops from the U.S. Army Southern Command (SOUTHCOM). The purpose was to net traffickers, but "Blast Furnace" was an exercise of dubious constitutionality with no congressional clearance. Four years later, Jaime Paz Zamora signed a secret agreement with the United States to involve Bolivia's military in the drug war. Then in 1996, under heavy pressure from Washington, Gonzalo Sánchez de Lozada sent the military into the Chapare to carry out forced eradication. Plan Dignidad coalesced these precedents into a policy of forced eradication by Bolivian police and military forces that won heavy military support from Washington, even while support for alternative cropping lagged.[40]

In mid-2001 when Plan Dignidad bogged down and resistance in the Chapare began to escalate, a special quasi-military expeditionary task force (ETF) was created to reinvigorate the eradication drive. The initiative apparently came from the Quiroga government but the U.S. Embassy provided funding; U.S. military advisors vetted the participants, and the embassy even paid their living expenses and a monthly salary. A U.S.-trained officer of the ETF explained that the force was designed "to do the dirty work." Called "America's Mercenaries" by a Bolivian human rights spokeswoman, the ETF was responsible for at least four killings and more than fifty cases of reported abuse during its first few months of existence. The most controversial case occurred in December 2001 when the task force was sent to clear the highway of peasants carrying rotted fruits in what began as a peaceful protest of low prices and lack of markets for legal crops. In the ensuing melee one peasant union leader was badly injured and a second, Casimiro Huanca, was killed.[41]

Domestic Bolivian critics and human rights officials argued that not only did the task force violate Bolivia's constitution, it also risked spawning the kind of paramilitary forces that have created problems in Colombia or, for that matter, in Bolivia itself under the "coca generals" of the early 1980s.[42] A U.S. counternarcotics official who spoke to the *Washington Post* discounted the charges of human rights abuses and assured that "this is not a paramilitary group and it won't become one." However, videotape of the incident leading up to Huanca's death showed an armed unit running dangerously amok.[43] But even if the task force was kept on a short leash by the embassy and U.S. military advisors, there is little doubt that its very presence, its ties to a foreign power, and its dubious legality combined to undermine both Plan Dignidad and the Quiroga government. The irony is that until Bolivia's economy began to sputter, there is evidence that Plan Dignidad was receiving increasing support from many Bolivians—precisely because it was bold and Bolivian.[44] What the plan needed was an economic environment to succeed, not additional militarization or scolding from Washington. The result was a widening social crisis and failing support for democracy itself.[45] The frank assessment of Walter Albarracín, then president of the Permanent Human Rights Assembly of Bolivia, was that the United States "talks about human rights, then pressures the Bolivian state to carry out forced eradication that results in violence, death, murdered campesinos, and torture by soldiers and police. They put up the funds and we offer up the dead."[46]

Meanwhile, as it slowly undermined *democracia pactada,* U.S. drug policy also helped resurrect the "democracy of popular mobilization." Evo Morales, as many commentators have noted, is a political phenomenon created almost entirely by U.S. drug policies.[47] Son of an impoverished Aymara farmer, Morales holds political views shaped by his indigenous cultural background as well as by the syndicalist socialism of mine workers who had relocated to the Chapare after the mines were closed. Morales emerged as the organizer of several marches by coca farmers on La Paz in the early 1990s. In 1995 he created the

MAS (Movimiento al Socialismo) to run a slate of candidates in the first municipal elections authorized under the Popular Participation Law. He was elected to Bolivia's Chamber of Deputies in 1997 and his political stature continued to grow due to the coercive features of Plan Dignidad.[48]

During the Banzer and Quiroga years, Morales and MAS became advocates and representatives not only of coca producers but also of a growing group of Bolivians dissatisfied with neoliberal policies. His national stature was only further enhanced in early 2002 when he was expelled from congress and deprived of immunity so that he could be brought up on charges that he was the "intellectual author" of the murders of several policemen in the Chapare. Rumors circulated that the U.S. Embassy was behind the maneuver, and the public rallied behind Morales. In February, to the obvious displeasure of the embassy, the Quiroga government signed a pact addressing a laundry list of grower complaints and allowing Morales to return to congress.[49]

Morales parlayed his enhanced national stature into a run for the presidency later that year, and to the shock of nearly everyone, he came in second—only a little over a percentage point behind Gonzalo Sánchez de Lozada, the eventual winner. Though the State Department denied the connection, there is little doubt that Morales received a late surge from a public statement made by U.S. ambassador Manuel Rocha just before the election: "I want to remind the Bolivian electorate that if they vote for those who want Bolivia to return to exporting cocaine, that would seriously jeopardize any future aid to Bolivia from the United States."[50] Several years earlier, in an interview with the *New York Times*, Morales claimed that his "life-defining epiphany" came in 1978 when, as a member of the army, he took part in a military action against a coca growers' march. "When ordered to shoot, I shot over the heads of the protestors. I saw that the biggest defenders of democracy were the *cocaleros*."[51] Whatever else they reveal, these juxtaposed quotes suggest that Morales had a better grasp of the essential contradictions between U.S. support of democracy and the ways it waged its war against coca than did the ambassador, who was content to reinforce old patterns of Bolivian dependency. The larger phenomenon of Morales's growing national support and status also illustrate an even more essential contradiction underlying U.S. policies since the end of the Cold War: its promotion of neoliberal orthodoxies has stirred strong populist and nationalist reactions. This was particularly the case because popular forces had little to do with the setting of policy and did not receive the benefits they were promised.

Problem 3: Putting Neoliberal Development before Democracy

Brian Loveman observes in the preface to this volume that to most North Americans democracy and market economics are intimately connected. Between the end of the Cold War and September 11, 2001, the conflation of the two was the central foreign policy tenet of the United States. For two decades Bolivia's leaders fell in line, and for two decades most Bolivians waited patiently for the results—partly out of hope, partly out of residual memories of the corrupt brutality of the last years of authoritarian rule and of the chaos that accompanied the first several years of democracy prior to neoliberal reforms.

The results of those reforms are in fact more mixed and their impact more complex than either the champions of neoliberal development or its detractors often assert. Social indicators—literacy rates, mortality rates, infant mortality rates, access to public health—have generally improved, sometimes by substantial margins.[52] The result is a larger and a generally healthier and better-educated population searching for meaningful employment in a stubbornly sluggish economy. Meanwhile, political reforms have had just as complicated an impact. Power and resources have been distributed downward by a series of reforms carried out by Sánchez de Lozada's government in the mid-1990s. The Popular Participation Law of 1994 created municipalities with greater local autonomy and control of resources. The Education Reform Law, passed that same year, provided bilingual education to indigenous communities and granted greater local control of education. A 1994 revision to the preamble of Bolivia's constitution also officially recognized for the first time the "multiethnic and pluri-cultural" nature of the Bolivian nation. These changes opened channels to greater social and political participation for all Bolivians including critics of the regime and fostered a new identity politics among indigenous Bolivians who discovered that they were a majority. But reforms were top-down, designed by technocrats and presented as faits accomplis. The changes were often resented by those they were designed to assist because they ignored traditional institutions and seemed—with justification—products of political elites whose agenda was not always clear. Merilee Grindle writes,

> Indeed, one common description of the Popular Participation Law is that it was neither popular nor participatory. The political lessons that could be drawn from the experience of the NPE (Paz's 1985 economic reform package) and the major reforms of [the Sánchez de Lozada government] were stark: centralization of power, technocratic decision-making and repression of opposition were important ingredients of neoliberal policy changes.[53]

Where reforms have most clearly failed, however, is in the area they most explicitly were designed to correct—economic performance. During the first half of the 1980s, while returning to constitutional rule, Bolivians endured an economic calamity that citizens in more wealthy democracies would not have tolerated. The human costs behind the statistics are difficult to grasp: in 1986 the purchasing power of the average Bolivian salary was down 70 percent from the beginning of the decade. Per capita income fell from $1,178 in 1980 to $789 in 1987, with rural Bolivians averaging only $140 annually. Urban unemployment rates pushed 25 percent. One source calculated that even with annual growth rates of 3.5 percent, it would take forty years just to restore per capita incomes to 1978 levels.[54] In fact, as the IMF admits in a recent report, trend growth under the neoliberal model since 1985 has never exceeded 4 percent, and average per capita income growth has averaged less than 1.5 percent per annum. By 1997 real per capita GDP had recovered only about half of what it had lost since 1978, then after 1998 it went back into decline.[55] Per capita gross national income fell from $990 to $855 between 1998 and 2003, and the gap between Bolivia's wealthiest and poorest citizens further widened.[56] The IMF report acknowledges that income inequality rose sharply during the 1990s as it did in all Latin American countries undergoing neoliberal reforms. Then with the slowdown, "the distributional effects of the 1999-2002 recession were particularly pronounced." Except in the top urban decile, where incomes rose, incomes declined for all Bolivians, and "the decline in per capita income was largest in the lowest deciles." Today nearly 35 percent of Bolivians live in extreme poverty at less than $2.00 a day, and the percentage of Bolivians defined as poor reaches nearly 70 percent.[57] The social facts behind these figures are not lost on the people who live them.

Cochabamba's "water war" in 2000 first revealed that patience had run out and that the popular democratic tide was ready to turn against the neoliberal model. Water privatization was an aspect of the package of structural adjustments required of Bolivia by the World Bank and IMF. Privatization, went the logic, would eliminate public subsidies (easily manipulated by political forces) and require market discipline and efficiency over what was seen as an increasingly important resource—water. In 1998 the Banzer government auctioned Cochabamba's water system SEMAPA to the sole bidder, Aguas del Tunari, a consortium controlled by International Water, a British-owned subsidiary of multinational conglomerate Bechtel. By the terms of the contract, Aguas del Tunari gained control of all water in the supplying aquifer and was guaranteed a minimum annual return of 15 percent on its investment. The first monthly bills from the newly privatized water service arrived in January of 2000 with rate increases of from 35 percent to 300 percent. Many poorer Cochabambinos were now required to pay up to a quarter of their income for water.[58]

Protest was immediate, if initially peaceful; Indian peasants joined workers, businessmen, middle-class housewives, and the residents of Cochabamba's surrounding ring of shantytowns. Protests escalated in February when police responded with tear gas. In early April the Banzer government deployed military forces to Cochabamba in response to rising violence, and a seventeen-year-old boy was killed by an army officer in the ensuing confrontation. Police, angry at the army's insertion into the affair and protesting low wages, mutinied in Bolivia's major cities. Bolivians had found their voice, and issues now ranged from general discontent with the economic malaise, to frustration with specific wage and employment issues, to unhappiness with U.S.-supported drug policies. On April 10, the Bolivian government agreed to turn control of Cochabamba's water over to the ad hoc cooperative that had coordinated the protests. Water privatization was reversed.[59]

The London-based newssheet *Andean Group Report* immediately saw the larger implications of the events:

> Observers were shocked at the speed with which Bolivia's prized political and so-cial stability appeared to collapse after protests against increased charges by Cochabamba's privatized water company, Aguas del Tunari, broke out for the second time this year on April 2. Some believe that the protests are the beginning of the end of neoliberal experiments begun in 1985. Bolivians are tired of mak-ing sacrifices for the sake of the future when the future never seems to come. For-eign investors have certainly taken the consortium's fate as a warning of what might happen in the future.[60]

The water war brought neoliberal economic policy into direct conflict with grassroots democracy and popular mobilization. The decision to privatize the water had virtually nothing to do with the will or consent of the people of Cochabamba and a great deal to do with the mandates of the IMF and World Bank and decisions by a few powerful people in La Paz, Washington, London, and San Francisco—the corporate headquarters of Bechtel. Cochabambinos were asked to wait for the long-term payoffs that would come from market ef-ficiencies while their water bills immediately doubled and tripled. Turning water over to a consortium led by one of the world's wealthiest and most pow-erful corporations also triggered powerful historical memories of silver, tin, and other nonrenewable resources that made fortunes for powerful *elites* in-side and outside the country but left little or nothing for most Bolivians. De-mocracy (in the sense of citizen empowerment and consent) and market eco-nomics might seem natural partners to most North Americans, but to Bolivians they, quite reasonably, seemed in conflict, and this time democracy won. It was a heady experience; a powerful example of popular participation that was, at once, more authentic and more potent than anything envisioned by Sánchez de Lozada, the technocrats who had devised the Popular Partici-pation Law, or Bolivia's patrons in Washington. With the water war, Bolivia's great neoliberal experiment, never really owned or fully endorsed by the ma-jority of Bolivians, began to come apart.[61]

Support for Plan Dignidad and the drug war began to disappear at about that same time. In February 2001, immediately after announcing success in the Chapare, Banzer made the fateful decision to take the campaign against il-legal coca to the Yungas. A coca survey in 2002 by the United Nations Office on Drugs and Crime identified about 13,800 hectares of coca bush in the Yungas—1,800 hectares above the 12,000 hectares of legal coca authorized by Law 1008.[62] Eduardo Gamarra succinctly describes the results:

> It is still a source of disagreement about who gave the orders to send eradication forces into the Yungas. U.S. embassy officials claim that they did not pressure the Bolivians into pursuing a Yungas strategy so soon after the Chapare, especially in the context of other social tensions in Bolivia. Bolivian government officials argue that extensive U.S. pressure to take advantage of the momentum gained from the Chapare experience forced them to move decisively in the Yungas. Regardless of who led the charge, the results were almost catastrophic. When eradication forces moved into the Yungas in mid-June, they were immediately surrounded by coca growers. Government forces held their fire and the coca growers controlled their lot. In the end, and much to the disappointment of U.S. embassy officials, an agreement was signed in which the government pledged to never forcefully eradicate coca in the Yungas.[63]

It was the first serious reversal for Plan Dignidad, and when it came it seemed to sap all momentum built to that point. Popular discontent with Plan Dignidad now merged with growing general discontent with neoliberal policies and was nurtured by the sudden resurgence of popular mobilization rooted in Bolivia's turbulent past.

In July, Banzer left for the United States to receive treatment for an advanced stage of cancer, and in August, Jorge Quiroga, at age thirty-seven, became the youngest president in Bolivia's history. Quiroga, a charismatic young *cruceño*, graduated summa cum laude in engineering from Texas A&M University, earned his MBA at St. Edwards University in Austin, worked several years for IBM, and speaks fluent English with a Texas drawl. Quiroga was a favorite in Washington, and most Bolivians were ready to give him a honeymoon.[64] But the new president's problems began less than a month after he came to power. During the same week in September 2001 that planes flew into the World Trade Center towers in New York, Quiroga's minister of interior announced to the press that a misinterpretation of satellite data—an error in the transcription of *un cerito* (just one little zero)—meant that instead of 600 hectares of coca remaining in the Chapare, there were actually 6,000.[65] The *cerito* was an embarrassment to Quiroga, disconcerting and troubling to the United States, and the second serious reversal for Plan Dignidad in less than three months. As with U.S. foreign policy after the attack on the twin towers, nothing was quite the same with Plan Dignidad after the discovery of the missing zero. Quiroga was forced to remobilize troops in the Chapare, and confrontations escalated through the remainder of the year until he called a recess to the eradication campaign and restored Morales to his position in congress.

The election of 2002 revealed the growing disjuncture between the popular will and the neoliberal policies of *democracia pactada*. As had been the case in every election since 1989, Bolivians repudiated the ruling party. Banzer and Quiroga's ADN (Acción Democrática Nacional) received less than 5 percent of the vote. Its coalition partner, Jaime Paz Zamorra's MIR (Movimiento de Izquierda Revolucionaria) finished a disappointing fourth. Sánchez de Lozada's MNR received a bare plurality of 22 percent, with the big winner, Evo Morales, only a percentage point behind. MAS and the radical indigenous MIP (Movimiento Indigenista Pachicuti) controlled almost one third of the seats in the lower house. Their secrets, other than Ambassador Rocha's indiscreet remark, were organization and grassroots responsiveness, making them—for all their antisystem rhetoric—the political movements best able to take advantage of recent reforms to the system.[66] Finishing third was the pre-election favorite Manfred Reyes Villa of the Nueva Fuerza Republicana, the vaguely populist mayor of Cochabamba who had changed positions in the water war just in time to pose as a champion of the people. There is little doubt that Ambassador Rocha's remarks only days before the election convinced many Bolivians that a vote for Evo was a more authentic vote of protest than one for the opportunistic Reyes Villa.[67]

Morales admitted in an interview immediately after the election that the thought of being so close to the presidency made him a little nervous, even frightened.[68] He need not have worried. Once again *democracia pactada* worked, though only after intense brokering by Ambassador Rocha convinced Jaime Paz Zamora to bury his old rancor and ally with Sánchez de Lozada. The irony was not lost on many Bolivians that the man Goni had visited Washington to lobby against in 1997 and to whom the United States had denied a visa soon after now provided Sánchez de Lozada and U.S. policy one more chance to succeed. In any case, Sánchez de Lozada, the man most associated with the neoliberal model, again took power, and in a second irony would be in power when the model fully unraveled. A final irony of the 2002 election was that Sánchez de Lozada took office on the fiftieth anniversary of the MNR revolution of 1952, and the fulfilled and unfulfilled promises of the two revolutions his party had championed were about to come into stark relief.

This was to be a sterner test for Goni than his first administration had been. In 1993 the economy was rebounding and hopes for the new model were still alive. He ran that year with indigenous leader Víctor Hugo Cárdenas as his running mate and won by the largest plurality of any president since Bolivia's return to democracy. Xavier Albó remarks that "the marked cultural, social, and ideological differences between the two men created synergy instead of conflict, above all in the joint search for a new political and social order, expressed in a series of laws which aimed to humanize the neoliberal model without, however, questioning its basic precepts."[69] By 2002 the contradictions in such a quest were more apparent. Goni governed by the slimmest of margins, the country had suffered through three consecutive years of negative growth, and the opposition led by Morales was both more coherent and more radically oppositional than at any time since 1985. Coca production was again on the rise, and government deficits mushroomed from 3.3 percent of GDP in 1997 to 8.7 percent of GDP in 2002. Neither the United States nor the IMF was willing to allow such "slippage" to continue.[70]

The drug war was at a crucial stage. There was no doubt that reversals marked Quiroga's year in office. The State Department's "International Narcotics Control Strategy Report" covering 2001 noted that "changes in leadership and rising domestic disturbances had led to an overall increase in the cultivation of coca that year." It specifically criticized Quiroga for failing to pursue Plan Dignidad more relentlessly.[71] Washington, desperate to salvage a rare "success story" in the war on drugs, pressured tirelessly to finish the job laid out by Plan Dignidad. U.S. officials remembered Goni's ambiguous record in the drug war from 1993 to 1997. During the 2002 campaign he had promised to pull the military from the Chapare and revisit the whole question of legal coca quotas. The proximity of Morales to the presidency forced the State Department and the U.S. Embassy to embrace Paz Zamora, but only after intense bargaining, the full details of which are still not known.[72]

Once in office, Sánchez de Lozada suspended the eradication drive and opened negotiations with Morales and the coca growers; his minister of government observed that "zero coca" was probably unattainable. But U.S. officials expressed their displeasure at the suspension of eradication, and under pressure from the embassy Goni neither withdrew the military nor did he pursue his campaign promise to survey the legal demand for coca.[73] Talks stalled, and after a visit to Washington in November 2002, Goni reconfirmed the objective to eradicate all illegal coca. Tensions in the Chapare again escalated, and by January 2003, Morales and the coca growers were actively seeking the ouster of the president. In September, only a month before it fell, Sánchez de Lozada's government announced that the "zero coca" target set by Plan Dignidad was unattainable and that the government had officially shifted its strategy to "virtual zero"—a policy to contain illegal coca below 4,000 hectares. The announcement did not come in time to save Goni's government, and subsequent events were to make even that commitment moot.[74]

Sánchez de Lozada's primary purpose for traveling to Washington in November 2002 was to ask the Bush administration for patience and assistance. Specifically, Goni sought $150 million to tide his government over through the difficult period until a pipeline deal to transport Bolivia's newly discovered gas resources to the Pacific could be completed. However, his meetings with State Department and other officials made clear that assistance was still linked to satisfactory progress in the drug war. Nor did Bush officials seem to sense the urgency of his predicament; in a personal audience with President Bush, Goni warned that continuing poverty, growing ethnic conflicts, and declining support for the neoliberal model might soon bring him back as a political refugee unless he received more assistance. President Bush reportedly smiled, patted Goni on the back, and said that they all had it tough. The meeting was over, and Sánchez de Lozada was sent home empty-handed and with orders to complete eradication. It was a strange way to treat a "model" and "success story," Michael Shifter notes in an article in *Foreign Affairs*.[75] Only after protests and violence erupted from an IMF mandated tax increase did the United States find an extra $10 million for Bolivia.[76]

Concerned by mounting government deficits, the IMF pushed a series of cost-saving and revenue-enhancing proposals that set in motion the chain of events that would lead to Sánchez de Lozada's ouster. The IMF's own *Ex-Post Assessment* concludes that lingering government inefficiency, waste, corruption, and lack of discipline were key factors, but the evidence the report provides is more complicated.

> Beginning in 1998, the economy was hit by four shocks: spillovers from the 1998 Russian crisis to Latin America, which led Brazil to devalue in February 1999; the acceleration of Bolivia's coca eradication program by the new government of President Banzer; changes in regulations and take-over of the country's largest bank by a Spanish bank, leading to a reduction in credit; and the Argentine crisis of late 2001, which further strained competitiveness and lowered the dollar value of remittances by Bolivian workers in Argentina.[77]

The report further expands on the impact of coca eradication:

> Despite efforts to encourage crop substitution, coca eradication has resulted in a large negative income shock to the economy. Coca trade as a percentage of GDP fell from a peak of 5.6% in 1988 to about 0.7% in 2003, with significant effects on economic activity, particularly in the informal sector.[78]

In other words, coca eradication had not only negatively impacted the growers and contributed to the general fiscal crisis, it also worsened the economic conditions of the "informal sector," a euphemism for the many Bolivians who earn a living on the street instead of at steady full-time jobs (perhaps 40 percent of Bolivia's burgeoning urban population). The result was escalating social and political tension in Bolivia's largest cities.

The deficit also resulted from a new hydrocarbons law passed in 1996 by the Sánchez de Lozada government that took the state oil company YPFB (Yacimientos Petrolíferos Fiscales Bolivianos) out of direct production and turned new exploration and production over to private foreign companies. To attract investors the new law lowered royalties on oil and gas to "an internationally competitive" 18 percent.[79] The new law attracted $2.5 billion in new investments between 1997 and 2002 with Petrobras of Brazil, Repsol-YPF of Spain, British Petroleum, and Total E&P of France leading the way. By 2003 Bolivia's proven and potential reserves reached 53.3 trillion cubic feet and were the second largest in South America after Venezuela's.[80] Gas production more than doubled between 1996 and 2003, but revenues to the state did not recover their 1994 levels. An excise tax designed to make up for the reduction in royalties fell short because of "relatively generous" admissible deductions and the fact that "oil companies have learned to exploit loopholes" in the new tax system.[81]

Confronted with this series of shocks, Bolivia's deficit rose from 3.3 percent of GDP in 1997 to 8.7 percent of GDP in 2002. With no domestic debate, with a single IMF representative in La Paz exercising more influence than all of the Bolivians who were living through these difficult times, with bureaucrats in Washington exerting more power than Bolivia's own congress or his own cabinet, Goni was confronted with two options—raise taxes or cut revenues. It is instructive to remember that when the United States faced its own internal and external shocks in 2001, its deficits grew at a greater rate in less time than Bolivia's: a surplus of 2.4 percent of GDP in 2001 became a 3.7 percent deficit in 2004. The George W. Bush administration proceeded to increase defense and health care spending while cutting taxes and going to war. The result was a burgeoning deficit and a recovering economy. Bolivia tried its own countercyclical measures in 2001: freezing the price of fuel, creating employment programs to counter rising unemployment in the informal sector, and increasing capital spending. But the IMF deemed the resulting marginal increase in the deficit unacceptable. When Goni returned empty-handed from Washington in November 2002, no viable alternative remained for him other than to take the first in a series of escalating steps that have led to Bolivia's current crisis.[82]

Consequences

According to those who participated in discussions between the Sánchez de Lozada government and the IMF in early 2003, the initial deficit reduction plan under discussion would have increased excise taxes on gas and petroleum exports and created a new progressive income tax on the wealthiest 4 percent of Bolivians—those whose income had actually increased since 1998. At the urging of his oil and gas minister, Goni quickly took the tax on petroleum exports off the table. At the time, Bolivia was negotiating with Pacific-LNG, a consortium backed by several European petroleum firms, to build a $5 billion pipeline and a gas liquefaction plant on the Pacific, and both Goni and the IMF saw this as the best long-term solution to the deficit problem. The president then made the fateful decision to instead back an income tax on all Bolivians earning twice the minimum wage (any salary over $110 a month). The tax still affected only a minority of Bolivians, but now included the well-organized teachers, police, and health workers.[83] The response was the worst rioting since the return to democracy. In a second fateful decision, Goni turned to the military to control the situation.[84] Police in La Paz, unhappy not only with the tax and their pending salary negotiations but also with the prominent new role the military had been given in drug and riot control, also joined the protests. A tear gas exchange between police and troops escalated into live fire. Looting and rioting spread, and when it was over the death toll stood at thirty-four.[85]

The riots and the resulting withdrawal of U.S. dollar deposits from the banking system by nervous Bolivians worsened the deficits and forced both Sánchez de Lozada and the IMF to adjust their plans. The government removed the controversial income tax, and the IMF accepted a plan that would lead to a phased reduction in the deficit. Whether the current crisis in Bolivia would be less acute if both parties had accepted this position *before* the rioting is impossible to determine. Certainly, however, the sequence of events underscored to many Bolivians that the place to alter policies in which they had little voice was in the streets. In April the IMF authorized a $118 million standby loan with hopes that gas pipeline negotiations then in progress would resolve Bolivia's underlying fiscal problems. At a second review of the standby on October 6, 2003, first deputy managing director of the IMF Anne Krueger reported that Bolivia's economic program was broadly on track "despite a difficult political and social environment." Eleven days later Sánchez de Lozada fell, the gas pipeline negotiations having proved his undoing instead of his salvation.[86]

The "gas war" that brought down Sánchez de Lozada began in September 2003 when a peasant strike, only tangentially connected to the gas issue, trapped eighty tourists in the mountain town of Sorata. Sánchez de Lozada again used troops to free them, and in a clash at the town of Warisata, four protestors and one policeman were killed. The symbolic significance of Indian deaths in an armed effort to rescue Western tourists, at the site of Bolivia's first indigenous school, fanned the flames of that confrontation into a larger protest that drew the support of Bolivian students, workers, teachers, and the coca unions. Two powerful unifying issues bound together this disparate coalition—repudiation of plans to sell gas through Chile (the country that had seized Bolivia's coastline in a late nineteenth-century war) and the resignation of Sánchez de Lozada.[87]

On September 30, thousands marched in La Paz, keeping the capital city at a standstill for over a week. Support for the strike was particularly strong in the satellite city of El Alto, a sprawling metropolis of 750,000 that had mushroomed over the last thirty years on the rim of the canyon above La Paz. No single, easy motive explains the fury of the residents of El Alto. Mostly recent Aymara migrants from the rural altiplano, they combined long-held indigenous resentments with new frustrations evoked by their marginal status in the urban world. Their nationalist fury was stirred by the idea that Bolivia's gas would be shipped by foreign companies through a Chilean port and their class resentments were stirred by their awareness that the gas would heat the homes of foreigners when many of them had no heat.[88] Although they were in many ways powerless, the people of El Alto controlled three strategic assets: the major roads connecting La Paz with the rest of the country, the international airport at the edge of their city, and the fuel refinery that supplied the capital. On October 12—Columbus Day—*alteños* clashed with military units sent to guard a convoy of gasoline trucks that were to resupply La Paz from the refinery in El Alto. More than twenty indigenous civilians died.

Over the next several days, violence spread down into La Paz. As the toll in lives mounted, President Sánchez de Lozada found himself increasingly isolated. By mid-October the death toll during Goni's fourteen months in office had nearly reached the level of political killings under the dictatorships of the 1970s, and human rights advocates in Bolivia called the October killings the bloodiest repression of civilians by a Latin American government since the end of the Cold War. Nonetheless, Goni still had the support of the United States and the Organization of American States, and the president remained defiant, saying his resignation would "spell the end of democracy, the disintegration of Bolivia, and the establishment of a narco-terrorist dictatorship." On October 16, Argentina's president Nestor Kirchner and Brazil's Luiz Inácio "Lula" da Silva sent personal emissaries to "seek a peaceful solution that respected the rule of law." A day later, after intense negotiations involving U.S. ambassador David Greenlee, Sánchez de Lozada boarded a plane for Miami.[89]

The man who replaced him, Carlos Mesa Gisbert, was a film buff, historian, and radio commentator who had been invited to join Goni's ticket in 2002 precisely because he was a fresh face. Mesa eschewed both politics as usual and the use of violence, and because he was essentially a man without a party, he was left few governing tools except dialogue. In his speech to the nation on January 4, 2004, Mesa set out his agenda: a new hydrocarbon law and a constituent assembly to draft a new constitution.[90] His primary goal, he often told those who interviewed him during his year and a half in office, was to serve as a bridge "between a corruption-rife political system and one in which everyone—including the long-neglected indigenous majority—is given a chance to participate."[91] Because he quickly disassociated himself from Goni's repressive response to the public manifestations in October, Mesa enjoyed high public approval once in office.

However, it did not take long for the weaknesses of a president with no political tools to become manifest. Mesa's single political success—his ability to hold a referendum on gas policies in July 2004—in fact set in motion the chain of events that led to his resignation. A boycott organized by several indigenous and labor leaders failed, and the five questions on the referendum received from 55 to 92 percent support, allowing Mesa to claim a "mandate" after the vote.[92] He had nothing of the sort. It had taken four ministers of hydrocarbons and several postponements before Mesa and his team could formulate a set of carefully redacted questions that were acceptable even to those within the administration. Greatest public support went to the most ambiguous of the five questions: "Do you favor restoring state ownership of all hydrocarbons at the well-head?" Mesa attempted to clarify that this could not be applied retroactively since Bolivia lacked the resources to pay compensation, and to simply withdraw concessions already granted "would be equivalent to declaring economic war on the world." However, Evo Morales urged his followers to take the question at face value and to vote for it as a proxy for restored national control and for the revision of existing contracts. Morales vowed to take the fight to congress, and the La Paz daily, *La Razón*, editorialized, "the mother of all battles" loomed.[93]

In the aftermath of the vote Mesa told the press that "the mandate of the Bolivian people is for a strong government that takes back ownership of its resources and levies many more taxes and royalties."[94] However, the president's next steps made that statement sound insincere and escalated the conflict over exactly what the referendum had "mandated." The first hydrocarbons bill Mesa sent to congress came far short of restoring state control. Mesa's proposal not only left existing contracts untouched but provided for taxes and royalties in the 25 percent range, only marginally higher than those in the abrogated law and far below what they had been prior to 1996—or, for that matter, what had been authorized by question 5 of the referendum. Aware that he was perhaps the only president in the world with "zero legislators," Mesa turned to Goni's old "megacoalition," the final remnant of *democracia pactada*, to shepherd his proposal through congress.[95]

It was a fateful step. Evo Morales had provided Mesa's chief support to this point, shielding him from opposition on the Left and providing the president with his most dependable support in congress. After the October 2005 uprising, Evo was off meeting with Castro, Lula, Kirchner, Hugo Chávez, UN Secretary-General Kofi Annan, former U.S. president Jimmy Carter, and a host of antiglobalization groups on three continents. Those who met him were impressed with the coca union leader's increasing political maturity and sense of responsibility. Soon after Mesa took power, Morales told an interviewer that Mesa "needs time, and we'll give him time." Evo warned, however, that "a lot will depend on some clear signs that he is trying to change the economic model and political system."[96] Now the speed with which Mesa abandoned Morales and turned to the megacoalition, so deeply associated with the old economic model and political system, assured a split. Evo patched relations with more radical labor and indigenous groups that had outflanked his anti-neoliberal stance while he was cooperating with the government.[97] None of those groups constituted a voting bloc in congress equal to the megacoalition's, and none was as connected to power centers outside the country as the politicians who had dominated *democracia pactada*; but each was able to bring a sector of Bolivian society to a standstill, and reunited with Morales and the MAS, they were finally able to drive the agenda.

Increasingly buffeted from the Left in late 2004, Mesa made concessions. When he yielded to demands that Goni be charged for the February and October 2003 killings, Mesa lost the support of the MNR and his leadership increasingly lost direction. Rhetorically, Mesa continued to try to position himself within the growing chorus of critics of neoliberalism emerging in Latin America, but he also worked to maintain the economic liberalization model with only minor adjustments. "Bolivia has to insert itself into a world that is open and globalized, we're not going to be able to change these rules," he told reporters.[98] His personal views were perhaps best revealed in the welcoming speech he made to an international seminar sponsored by the Inter-American Development Bank a year before he came to power. Acknowledging the superior economic logic of the prevailing model, Mesa questioned whether neoliberalism could meet the ethical challenges that accompanied the rapid changes it so efficiently spawns.[99] Even though Mesa sincerely sought a gas law that would assure greater benefits to Bolivians from the new gas bonanza, it was this acceptance of the "superior economic logic" of the market as well as pressures from the U.S. Embassy, the IMF, and the oil company lawyers that convinced Mesa that he could not rescind the contracts already signed. His position was both moderate and reasonable, but Mesa had neither the political coalition to advance it nor—thanks to the confusing wording of the referendum—the moral authority to support his claim that he represented the will of the Bolivian majority.

Instead of finding common ground through dialogue the country splintered and positions polarized during Mesa's twenty-month administration. The most dangerous division that appeared is actually quite old: the long-existing regional cleavage reexposed by the "gas war." Many residents of Bolivia's *media luna*, a crescent of territory stretching from the Pando in the north through the large eastern department of Santa Cruz and south into gas-rich Tarija, resent the perceived "bureaucratic parasitism" of governments in La Paz and the "ignorant obstructionism" of highlands Bolivians whose economic nationalism and opposition to the gas deal they believe thwarts their region's progress. The center of these resentments is Santa Cruz, a bustling city of 1.4 million, larger than the capital and source of one third of Bolivia's GDP, where long-held separatist leanings have reemerged. A taxi driver in Santa Cruz succinctly summarizes the growing tide of opinion among *cruceños*. "We will become independent; that's what people want in Santa Cruz. We are sick and tired of financing an entire country. We don't want to know what happens in the *altiplano*, because the country's problems always, *always* originate there."[100]

The racial and ethnic attitudes that undergird such views were revealed in statements by "Miss Bolivia" (a *cruceña*) at the "Miss Universe" pageant in mid-2004. She reportedly told the press that it was unfortunate that people don't know much about Bolivia. "They think of La Paz and believe all Bolivians are poor, short, and Indian. I am from the other side of the country where it is warm. We are tall and white, we know English, and this idea that Bolivia is only an Andean country is wrong."[101] Such sentiments make it easy for the Left both inside and outside Bolivia to portray eastern resentments as the grasping self-interest of an overprivileged, tiny white minority. It is more complicated than that. First, the eastern belief that it is irrational to oppose a lucrative gas deal that could provide revenues to meet Bolivia's obligations and restore modest growth; that would encourage foreign investors to risk new capital in Bolivia; and that would enable the country to join the global economy is seconded by a chorus of influential voices outside Bolivia and seems no less than common sense. The *New York Times* in two separate editorials asserts that Bolivia's resistance to the gas deal is an unfortunate manifestation of "economic ignorance" and "a sign of how anti-globalization can end up advocating economic suicide for the poor."[102]

There is historical legitimacy behind the complaints from the east as well. All *cambas* (native *cruceños*) remember that until the national revolution of 1952 their region was a national backwater, isolated for most of the year except by air, and sharing none of the wealth the west reaped from mineral exports. Easterners could not even market their agricultural products in the west because it was cheaper and easier to import sugar, rice, alcohol, corn, and fruits from Peru and Chile by rail than by oxcart from Santa Cruz. Easterners also remember that it was only a century ago, in 1899, that a rising tin-mining elite centered in La Paz outmaneuvered the old silver-elite centered in Sucre and moved the capital to its current location. For more than a half a century, the *media luna* has been at the center of Bolivia's development strategy, and now many easterners feel it is time to wrest control from the "antiquated and protectionist . . . rent-seeking bureaucrats" in La Paz and again shift the locus of power to Bolivia's most dynamic region. The International Crisis Group (ICG), an independent, nonprofit, multinational organization headquartered in Brussels, in its provocative report on Bolivia, "Bolivia's Divisions: Too Deep to Heal?" comments that there is a double discourse at work in the region:

> While many Santa Cruz and Tarija elites have separatist tendencies, they also stress that their mission is nationalist. Santa Cruz elites paint themselves as the

productive, internationally minded mestizo part of Bolivia. In some ways they regard the indigenous as less than Bolivian: separatist, obstructionist, and backwards.[103]

Complicating matters is that since 1952 there has been a heavy influx of indigenous highlanders into eastern Bolivia as agricultural laborers, recipients of land under Bolivia's 1952 agrarian reform law, and more recently as urban migrants.[104] Indigenous Bolivians have their own historical memories. They may remember how, in 1899, La Paz-based Liberals appealed for the support of the Aymaras in their quest to wrest control of the country from the Sucre Conservatives and how afterward the Liberals turned on their indigenous allies and restored them to subordination. But they certainly remember that the areas from which they were forced to emigrate were once Bolivia's richest regions. As Laura Carlsen of the Interhemispheric Resource Center has noted, they may "understand the real, on-the-ground workings of the global economy" better than their critics.[105] Gas might be Bolivia's last bonanza and the paucity of long-term benefits from earlier silver, rubber, nitrate, and tin bonanzas make Bolivia's original inhabitants justifiably suspicious.

Indigenous Bolivians also speak a double discourse of nationalism and separatism. Their trust in the political elites that have traditionally ruled Bolivia is not deep and their distrust of neoliberal principles is not irrational. Through a century of "progress," Bolivia's per capita GDP fell from 15 percent of U.S. per capita GDP in 1900 to 7 percent in 1998 and continues to shrink.[106] Thus, as the ICG report notes, while "Santa Cruz fancies itself a risk-taking modern melting pot, conservative indigenous culture in the highlands is strong and taking increasingly radical forms." Radicals in both regions are feeding off of legitimate local resentments and are cultivating separatist sentiments that have only increased since October 2003.[107]

Regional hostilities came to focus in January 2005 when the Mesa government relaxed the freeze on fuel prices and raised gasoline prices 10 percent and diesel prices 23 percent. Protests exploded all throughout the western highlands and in Santa Cruz, *cruceño* organizers took advantage of the general disorder and the broad discontent with the fuel hike to push for regional autonomy.[108] The president without a party responded in an increasingly bizarre ballet of concessions, assertions, and retreats to the welter of competing pressures. The ballet culminated finally in Mesa's multiple resignations and withdrawals of resignations in March without the president winning a single concession. Meanwhile, the hydrocarbons law finally emerged from congress as a compromise that satisfied no one. The law retained the 18 percent royalty but added a nondeductible 32 percent direct tax on production and required companies to bring existing contracts into compliance in 180 days. Oil companies immediately protested and promised legal action. Mesa announced he would sign the law, then refused to sign it, then made clear that neither would he veto it, and finally just stepped aside and allowed the law to pass without his signature.[109]

With foreign oil companies, the IMF, and the U.S. Embassy obviously influencing Mesa's vacillations, Morales now joined the popular groups that demanded complete nationalization. He organized a march of coca farmers from the Chapare and Yungas who joined the already massive demonstration taking place in La Paz in late May. In the city, coca growers and Aymaran protestors from El Alto and small rural communities beyond were joined by non-indigenous students and workers, but this—even more than the protests twenty months earlier against Goni—was a direct indigenous challenge to the Europeanized elite that had dominated the country since the Spaniards arrived. Bolivia's many deep divisions had come sharply to focus, and with rumors of military coups swirling through the country, only one narrow issue remained on which there was anything close to consensus—Mesa had to go. He did so, and to his credit, managed to avoid bloodshed. For several tense days the country waited. Forced out of La Paz by the popular mobilization, congressional leaders met in Sucre with the military threatening to use force to maintain constitutional order. The leaders of the senate and the Chamber of Deputies, next in the constitutional order of succession, reluctantly withdrew from contention when it was clear that the ascension of either might lead the country to explode. The agreement to pass the mandate to the president of Bolivia's supreme court, Eduardo Rodríguez, who was constitutionally empowered to call new elections, only postponed the potential explosion, it did not avert it.[110]

Social peace was temporarily restored, but it is safe to assume that Bolivia's eastern departments are no more likely to retreat from their demands for autonomy than the indigenous majority is likely to return to quiescence. In few countries is the collision between pro and antiglobalization forces more pronounced or have views become more polarized. If there is one certainty it is that two decades of U.S. policy in Bolivia is in shambles.

What Now?

Shambles is a strong word, but not unwarranted. Judged by its own 3-D objectives, it is difficult to find U.S. policy successes in Bolivia. Coca production increased in 2005 for the third straight year, and aggressive coca eradication is on indefinite hold.[111] Two decades of neoliberal development strategy have failed to bring sustained growth and have only exacerbated ethnic, racial, and regional tensions to the point that democracy itself is in danger. Perhaps because failures are so obvious, U.S. officials initially seemed determined to publicly deny them. Ambassador Greenlee told the *New York Times* in the immediate aftermath of Goni's ouster in October 2003 that he saw no problem for ongoing U.S. policy nor did he see any need for increased assistance. "I think we currently provide substantial resources and it's possible that this new government can be more efficient," Greenlee stated.[112]

In public statements since, the Bush State Department has stressed continuity and "avoiding backsliding" rather than serious reassessment. In a May 2004 statement, the State Department's deputy director for Andean affairs, John Creamer, used the word *continue* multiple times and emphasized that the 3-Ds that have guided U.S. policy in Bolivia since 1985 remained its centerpieces. Creamer gave no public indication that Washington had given serious consideration to the degree that flawed application of the 3-D objectives had contributed to Bolivia's crisis. In fact, he went out of his way to stress how little basic policies have changed or needed to change. U.S. assistance to Bolivia has remained steady at about $150 million a year—the majority channeled through the Andean Counterdrug Initiative and with the largest single portion still devoted to coca eradication ($49 million).[113]

An even more complacent analysis came two months later from Assistant Secretary of State for Western Hemisphere Affairs Roger Noriega:

> Democratic governments . . . need to publicize their successes. Citizens need to know when their government is effective—when new schools are inaugurated or inoculation programs are undertaken. Last year, the president of Bolivia, Gonzalo Sánchez de Lozada, resigned under pressure. Yet Bolivia had come a significant way out of poverty because of his policies. The problem is, he didn't tell anybody about his successes and his plans for social development—and the pot boiled over.[114]

If Noriega's statement is taken at face value, U.S. policy had *succeeded*, and it was Goni's poor public relations and the obtuseness of a Bolivian populace unable to realize that things were getting better without being told that were to blame.

Jeffrey Sachs is less content to blame the victims or to accept Washington's low-key stress on staying the course. He offers a scathing critique of U.S. policy, particularly since 1999 when the Bolivian model that he had helped construct began to come apart. His views carry extra weight because he predicted much of what has happened in advance. In recent years Sachs has become a fierce critic of IMF orthodoxies and of what he considers stingy and heavy-handed U.S. policies. He now suggests that it is ludicrous to assume that sustained development results simply from adopting the proper economic policies within a correct institutional and legal framework. By Sachs's calculations, lack of direct access to the sea alone costs Bolivia a figure each year that is virtually equal to the most optimistic revenue projections for gas exports.[115] He has suggested that deeply indebted impoverished countries like Bolivia receive not only debt reduction, but that they repudiate their debts until they receive enough international assistance to assure a reasonably level playing field. He further suggests that the IMF adopt policies that are as concerned with protecting the fragile economies of developing countries as they are with protecting investors and a stable investment climate. Finally he challenges the United States—currently dead last among the major donor nations in terms of percentage of GDP devoted to development assistance—to back its words with more money.[116]

In an April 2003 article in *Financial Times*, Sachs warned of what lay ahead if Sánchez de Lozada did not receive more assistance and less rigidity from Washington. His predictions proved remarkably accurate, and after October 2003 he wrote:

> The forced resignation of Bolivia's President Gonzalo Sánchez de Lozada, following a month of violent demonstrations, marks a tragic milestone whose significance extends far beyond his impoverished country. The breakdown of civil and political order in Bolivia provides another vivid example of the poverty of U.S. foreign policy. Sánchez de Lozada is one of Latin America's true heroes, a leader who helped usher in democracy and modest economic growth during the past 20 years, including two terms as president. Yet now he has fled Bolivia in fear for his safety. The arrogance and neglect of U.S. foreign policy played a large part in this stunning reversal.[117]

Whatever their public complacency, U.S. officials are not unaware of the crisis brewing in the hemisphere and particularly in the region most impacted by U.S. drug policies. Since 2000, popular uprisings have ousted eight Latin American presidents—five of them in just three Andean countries. Governments critical of the neoliberal fundamentalism of U.S. policy since the end of the Cold War now include Argentina, Chile, Uruguay, Brazil, Venezuela, Cuba, and—most likely—will soon include Ecuador and Bolivia. It is obvious that the region is entering a new and volatile period with important implications for U.S. policy. In the absence of either public statements or access to documents that reveal a U.S. reassessment, since October 2003, one must instead evaluate actions.

Certainly there have been adjustments. Conditions have remained too chaotic since October 2003 to complete the task of eradicating excess coca set out by Plan Dignidad. Coca cultivation increased 23 percent in 2002, another 17 percent in 2003, and 17 percent in 2004. In the last year alone, Bolivia's cocaine output rose 35 percent to 107 tons.[118] The 2005 Narcotics Control Strategy Report states that "the besieged Mesa Administration, at times, seemed more concerned with containing possible confrontations with *cocaleros* through negotiation and concessions than with the consistent application of the rule of law."[119] Still, U.S. officials remained relatively patient. Despite lack of progress in the drug war, President Bush did not target Bolivia in his Annual Narcotics Certification Report. Nor has the United States removed trade preferences under the Andean Trade Promotion and Drug Eradication Act (ATPDEA) that have allowed Bolivia's textile exports to the United States to increase 80 percent since 2002.[120]

Another adjustment is that USAID's 2005 budget justification for Bolivia emphasizes measures to increase the state presence, particularly in city barrios and rural areas. For two decades the United States—backed by the World Bank and the IMF—advocated downsizing the public sector, privatizing state enterprises, and reducing state expenditures. The result was a weakened state with little to offer a frustrated populace except repression. Now "USAID is adjusting its current program to help address, in an expedited manner, the causes of the recent violent conflict." It will focus on key conflict areas like El Alto to foster "the presence of the government as a legal authority and arbiter, service provider . . . and maintainer of law and order."[121]

In January 2004, the United States and Mexico hosted an international conference of eighteen nations and six international organizations to form a Bolivia Support Group. By May 2004, that group had raised $74 million for direct budgetary support tied to "sound fiscal policy."[122] In addition, Bolivia was one of three Latin American countries and sixteen nations worldwide made eligible for the Millennium Challenge Account (MCA). This gives President Bush discretion over the allocation of $1 billion in assistance to countries considered sufficiently poor but sufficiently successful in their fight against corruption and their promotion of social welfare and economic reform to merit the assistance.[123] Bolivia just barely cleared the anticorruption benchmark that is an absolute requirement for support, and the new hydrocarbon law and resulting disorder probably take it out of the running for the MCA for the near future.[124] Nonetheless, in the midst of the May 2005 crisis, the World Bank approved two interest-free loans totaling $43.4 million to help Bolivia meet the Millennium Development Goals.[125] Perhaps the boldest and potentially most useful action by the United States came too late to save either Sánchez de Lozada or Mesa. Just as Mesa was resigning, the United States and Great Britain announced that eighteen countries, including Bolivia, would be eligible to cancel their debts to the World Bank, the IMF, and other multilateral lenders so that they could focus on economic development and social spending rather than simply repaying existing loans. The conditions are still not clear, though eligible countries need to show "that they have acted to improve governing, reduce corruption, and pursue what international lenders consider sound economic policies."[126]

Conditions such as these are understandable and probably inevitable. Wealthy nations do not want their resources to be squandered, and better governance, reduced corruption, and sound economic policies are as beneficial to the recipient nations as to international financiers and great powers. But bureaucrats tasked with assessing such conditions when backed by the power of the United States and the multilateral lending institutions often wield more influence in a small dependent country like Bolivia than elected representatives. This undermines democracy, builds resentment, and ultimately thwarts development. Several examples since the October 2003 wake-up call will illustrate that for all the patience and generosity Washington has displayed, the application of U.S. and multilateral lending-agency policy continues to be sufficiently flawed to have done little to stop or even slow Bolivia's drift into anarchy.

The basic dynamics of U.S. drug policies are now so deeply entrenched that it is difficult for either side to step away from them. In a moment of frustration, one of Mesa's closest advisors told the Bolivian press in April of 2004 that his government was under a great deal of pressure "from the other side," even though the political conditions of the country were precarious and any provocation could lead to violence. "They tell us, you are incompetent and you can't control drug trafficking, if you can't put a base [in the coca zone] to control the quantity of drugs or the coca leaf that goes out."[127] After Mesa's "victory" in the July 2004 gas referendum, U.S. officials apparently convinced him that he was sufficiently secure to reinitiate eradication. Instead violence broke out immediately. One peasant leader died, and the aborted campaign only widened the rift between Mesa and Evo Morales that had been opened by their differing interpretations of the gas referendum.[128] Morales reminded Mesa that he had promised to resign if the killing began again and said he would hold the president to that pledge. Instead, with the grudging acceptance of the U.S. Embassy, the government worked out an agreement with Morales to create a reserve of 3,200 hectares of coca in the Chapare pending an independent study to determine the actual legal demand for coca.[129]

A 2005 report to the U.S. Congress on the Andean Counterdrug Initiative acknowledges that "for some 20 years, U.S. relations with Bolivia have centered largely on controlling the production of coca leaf and coca paste." The report lists the successes and the levels of U.S. support but closes the paragraph, "Others, however, view the forced eradication as a social and political disaster that has fueled popular discontent and increased the political support for opposition candidates."[130] It is past time for policy makers in Washington to listen to the others. Back in 2001, Ambassador Rocha acknowledged that very little Bolivian cocaine then entered the United States. Most was destined for Brazil or for Europe providing the opportune moment for the United States to declare success, gracefully disengage from counterproductive policies, readjust priorities, and seek more creative long-term solutions to the problem.[131] Instead U.S. officials continued to stress "conditions" that contributed to Bolivia's current crisis.

"Conditions" can also be counterproductive when imposed from outside without subtlety or awareness of local conditions. In 2003, as his government faced growing popular discontent, Sánchez de Lozada signed an Article 98 agreement with the United States granting immunity from International Criminal Court jurisdiction to U.S. personnel in Bolivia. Bolivia was one of the 139 countries to sign the Treaty of Rome creating the ICC, and a highly respected Bolivian judge, Rene Blattman, sits on the court. As Bolivia's human rights spokesman pointed out, Bolivia was "the only country in the world to agree to [U.S. immunity] that also has a judge on the court."[132] Goni's rising chorus of critics saw this decision as yet another indicator—along with denationalizing gas, selling that gas through Chile, and speaking Spanish with an English accent—that he was more *gringo* than Bolivian. In the heated political environment of late 2003, Bolivia's congress refused to ratify the agreement, meaning that under the American Service Members Protection Act (ASPA) passed by the U.S. Congress in 2002, the Pentagon was mandated to suspend most kinds of military assistance. From July 2003 to July 2004, President Bush granted a national interest waiver to allow Bolivian legislators to ratify the agreement. However, as that grace period ran out and armed with new leverage provided by the Nethercutt Amendment, which mandates further cuts in economic assistance, the United States upped the pressure on Bolivia.[133] The Bolivian senate narrowly ratified the agreement in May 2004 against the backdrop of daily news reports out of Iraq on the Abu Ghraib Prison scandal. The senate's decision further reduced the legitimacy of that body in the eyes of many Bolivians just as it was about to deliberate on a hydrocarbons bill and hardened resistance in Bolivia's lower house to signing the immunity agreement. In July 2004, mandatory sanctions went into effect just as Mesa sought to rally public opinion around his moderate interpretation of the gas referendum. Then as conditions turned increasingly chaotic in early 2005, and desperate to maintain U.S. support, the Mesa government began to lobby for ratification. To charges that this was an affront to Bolivia's dignity, a Mesa advisor responded, "You can't eat dignity."[134]

In his March 2005 testimony before the House Armed Services Committee, SOUTHCOM commander Bantz J. Craddock stated that while he supported ASPA, the inflexible sanctions mandated by Congress were counterproductive and hampered military-to-military relations in eleven strategically significant countries in the region, including Bolivia. Not only did the suspension of International Military Education and Training (IMET) reduce vital contact between U.S. and regional military personnel, suspension of military aid opened the door to China. Chinese military officials made twenty visits to Latin America in 2004, according to Craddock, and "an increasing presence of the People's Republic of China in the region is an emerging dynamic that must not be ignored."[135] (Thus the globalization policies promoted by the U.S. have the unintended consequence of further opening Latin American markets and politics to other global powers.) That dynamic is perhaps illustrated by a story from Bolivia. In December 2004, a member of Bolivia's lower house from El Alto charged that he was under government pressure to ratify the immunity agreement and was told that unless he did so, there would be no funding to install household gas in his city. He responded, "Installation of household gas can be financed by the Chinese; we don't need U.S. aid."[136]

Bolivia's most committed antiglobalists could care less that U.S. military assistance is suspended. The same is true of the Andean Free Trade Agreement talks where Bolivia has been relegated to observer status until the issues of immunity and guarantees to investors are clarified. Conditions like the ones imposed by ASPA and the Nethercutt Amendment play directly into the hands of the opposition and undercut the government and the institutions the United States wants to support. A deeper problem is the fiction in Washington that these are not requirements or demands but rather simple concomitants to assistance agreements. No nation is forced to take assistance, goes the argument, nor are donors required to provide it free of conditions. However, this ignores the disparities of power and access to resources between donor and recipient and the degree of recipient dependency. Sheer need and undeniable dependency on these resources easily truncates or short-circuits the domestic dialogue on which democracy itself is based. The case of Carlos Mesa is instructive.

When Mesa took office in late 2003, he clarified that his primary goal was to find national agreement on a series of thorny issues through dialogue and citizen participation. Mesa sought the middle ground between extremes, and Bolivian political commentator Jorge Lazarte pointed out early in Mesa's presidency that he possessed valuable assets to achieve his objectives. He was a political outsider who was not part of the political class that had disillusioned so many Bolivians. He had also revealed his courage by quickly breaking with Sánchez de Lozada over the use of repressive measures and his commitment to dialogue by meeting indigenous radicals on their own turf and speaking to them in Aymara immediately after taking power. Lazarte noted Mesa's "empathy": his ability to see all sides of an issue, to convince everyone who spoke to him that they had been heard, and his faith that there were reasonable solutions to every conflict. Mesa also brought an understanding of Bolivia's history to the job, combined with a sincere desire to find what Lazarte called the *justo medio* (happy medium) between the extremes at play in that historical moment.[137] There is also evidence that he was not alone in seeking a middle ground. Polls are perhaps suspect, particularly in a country like Bolivia, but the consistency of Mesa's high levels of support cannot be denied. Beginning in October 2003 with an approval rating of 66 percent, Mesa's support rose to 82 percent in December and hovered in the 70–80 percent range through most of 2004.[138] Even with things collapsing around him his approval rating in early May 2005 was still over 60 percent and did not drop below 50 percent until later that month when his government was so crippled that he could no longer govern.[139]

Yet Mesa abjectly failed to identify or consolidate support around a middle position, and when he left office, Bolivians were more polarized than at, perhaps, any time in their history. Certainly it can be argued that this was a personal failure—that Mesa lacked both the tools and the skills to identify and consolidate a middle position. By the time of the gas referendum Lazarte was convinced that Mesa lacked vision as well and that his only goal was to stay in office. By the end, Lazarte considered Mesa completely adrift and charged that he now only made matters worse with his resignation threats, constant vacillation, and lack of direction. "Sadly the government is part of the problem," Lazarte charged. "No one is leading; it is a big game of chess in which the pieces move on their own accord."[140]

Without access to internal memos for evidence, one suspects that similar assessments were floating around Foggy Bottom by the end of Mesa's period in power. Yet, despite the relative patience and generosity that Mesa received from Washington, the one thing he never received was an environment of international support for true Bolivian dialogue. What passed for dialogue was Mesa trying to broker the immense gap between his most vocal and militant critics and the conditions set in Washington.[141] In the case of the hydrocarbons law he had to find a middle position between irreconcilable opposites: the U.S. government, the IMF, and the oil companies dictated that the basic outlines of the old law must be maintained if Bolivia expected further assistance or investment, even as a majority of Bolivians clearly demanded that the law be repudiated. This is why the gas referendum resolved nothing except to make Mesa seem insincere, drive Morales into resistance, and polarize positions. Dialogue never began: instead the participants staked out positions with Mesa increasingly buffeted from all sides.

There was also no dialogue on the deficit at the end of 2004, even though Mesa had managed to reduce it to a more manageable 5.5 percent thanks to new taxes on investments and soaring oil prices.[142] But Bolivia's fuel prices were frozen, and as the world price of oil rose, the subsidy increased. Cheap Bolivian fuel was black-marketed to neighboring countries while the cost of the subsidy became another drain on the national treasury. For many sound reasons, ending the oil subsidy became a condition for continuing and augmenting the IMF standby. But again there was no dialogue, no public discussion of the problem, why it was a problem, whether it was a problem, or how it might best be addressed. Instead the decision was sprung on the Bolivian people on the final day of 2004. The result was an explosion of demands, government retreats, and a return to the politics of roadblocks and strikes.

Unlike the State Department, the IMF has made its own soul-searching on Bolivia a matter of public record, and its report deserves careful reading by all who are interested in recent events in Bolivia. The guiding question of the assessment is simple and pertinent:

> How could a country that undertook one of the boldest and most celebrated economic reform programs of the 1990s and was among the first to benefit from debt relief under the HIPC (Highly Indebted Poor Countries) Initiatives find itself, only a few years later, in a situation of large deficits, sharply increasing debt, declining per capita income, financial instability and social unrest?[143]

The further "puzzle," the report continues, is how a country "perceived as having one of the best structural reform records in Latin America" made so little progress in either growth or income-based poverty measures? The study devotes over fifty pages to the collection and analysis of data, and much of its evidence has been used to support the thesis of this chapter. But because of its mandate and constituency, the Fund draws quite different conclusions: "Trend growth did not take off because successive structural reforms did not succeed in fundamentally altering the character of the state and improving the business environment which is hampered by governance problems, corruption, poor infrastructure, and high cost of operating in the formal sector." The Fund's main failing in Bolivia "was its willingness to accommodate the authorities' political constraints even when important reforms had stalled."[144]

The study concludes,

> In order to address Bolivia's main economic problems, a new medium term program should be focused on fundamental institutional and structural reforms that improve governance, reduce and better manage public expenditure, create a more equitable and efficient tax system, improve fiscal and institutional relations between central and subnational governments, strengthen the banking system, and begin a process of financial de-dollarization. However, most of these reforms will not succeed unless backed by a strong social and political consensus.[145]

In other words, the same Bolivian government that launched "one of the boldest and most celebrated economic reform programs of the 1990s" was also chiefly responsible for its disappointing results and for Bolivia's growing social inequities. The primary IMF failing was that it was too flexible. The solution, therefore, is a new and more carefully delineated set of conditions—fortified by a strengthened Fund backbone. Then, improbably, the Bolivian people must look past the bad governance, the low growth, the rising social inequities, and the increased external inflexibility to develop "a strong social and political consensus" in support of reforms they do not own and from which they may or may not benefit. The Bolivian people took this risk once. They are not likely to take it again.

One suspects that the IMF officials who wrote this report know they are presenting an implausible and impossible solution just as U.S. counterdrug officials understand that under current conditions the official eradication goals are unattainable. An important shift of attitude and power has taken place in Bolivia since 1985, and neoliberal reformers can no more turn the clock back to that date than drug warriors can turn it back to 1997 when Plan Dignidad was launched. Thus the solutions they pose are not solutions at all but continue to be part of the problem. To become part of a solution, Washington (the U.S. government, IMF, and World Bank that are centered there) must begin to trust in the process they claim to have encouraged since 1985 and begin to truly support democracy in Bolivia. Washington must be less content to exert its power and more willing to allow Bolivians to exert theirs. Instead of setting parameters, Washington must provide opportunities. This means placing fewer conditions and instead becoming more adept at encouraging democratic participation. These suggestions become particularly pertinent if Evo Morales is elected to the presidency, but hardly less so if the winner is someone more to Washington's liking. As argued above, U.S., IMF, and World Bank policies have consistently undercut the legitimacy of leaders they intended to support. It will help if the recently announced debt cancellation wipes the slate relatively clean and if Bolivia is given access to new funding through the Millennium Challenge Initiative, despite its recent problems. The outside assistance cannot stop, but the micromanaging that often accompanies it must. Bolivians must be allowed to find their own solutions but with the assurance that Washington and the world community will stand behind them so long as the process itself remains—or finally, truly becomes—democratic.

This is a tall order and perhaps a naively idealistic one. It is perhaps already too late for Bolivia to find a satisfactory solution through the democratic process, although those who know the resilience of Bolivians are aware that the finest qualities of this long-suffering people have yet to be tapped. Still, with policies in such disarray, one wonders what Washington's fallback position really is. Michael Shifter, writing in *Foreign Affairs* before presidents were recently ousted in Ecuador and Bolivia, observed, "Washington has responded to the prospect of renewed turbulence with a mix of indifference and fatalism: indifference because Peru, Ecuador and Bolivia are considered largely unimportant to U.S. interests; fatalism because all too many view them as hopeless anyway."[146] Indifference and fatalism lead easily into oversimplification. It was such an oversimplification when Roger Noriega blamed the crisis in Bolivia on meddling by Hugo Chávez. While Chávez responded with an equally polemical and oversimplified attack, he is correct that the United States is far more responsible for the current crisis in Bolivia than is Venezuela.[147]

The official rhetoric out of Washington continues to champion the democratic process. However, the recent refrain that governments in Latin America "must not only be elected democratically but must also govern democratically" and the U.S. proposal before the OAS to create a committee that would monitor the quality of democracy and the exercise of power in Latin America suggest new conditions and rising rigidity when increased flexibility seems more in order.[148] Democracy is messy and there is always the danger that Latin Americans will choose leaders that are not to U.S. liking. That danger looms now in Bolivia and the election of Evo Morales as president in late 2005 will test the limits of U.S. flexibility and the depth of U.S. support for democracy.

Back in the mid-1960s when democracies in Latin America seemed too messy, the United States quietly withdrew its calls for democratic social reforms and backed de facto governments that seemed to promise order. There were calls in Bolivia for military intervention during the chaotic days of May–June 2005 when the capital was choked with indigenous protestors.[149] And with indifference and fatalism toward Latin America as common outside the beltway as in Washington itself, voices suggesting that policies centered on the preservation of democracy are naïve and that security and order are again becoming paramount can be seductive. An article in the *Washington Times* by William Hawkins, a senior fellow for national security studies at the U.S. Business and Industry Council, suggests that Latin America is again in "full play." He concludes,

> Simple U.S. homilies about democracy and trade have failed to stem the rise of regimes whose alignments are taking an increasingly dangerous turn. The Bush administration must consider Latin America a power politics area that is in full play. It must respond with more vigor in what is essentially a political contest over who will rule in the major capitals and how will they behave.[150]

Conservative columnist Robert Novak refers more specifically to Bolivia. Citing intelligence sources and "Latin American specialists" in Washington, Novak warns that U.S. preoccupation with the Middle East ignores the rising security threat next door. Calling the leaders of the popular forces in Bolivia "a clique of leftist, Anti-American[s]" with ties to narco-terrorists, Novak alerts,

> Here is a latter-day domino effect. Dissenting officials in the U.S. government believe Bolivia is becoming what the Pentagon calls an "ungoverned area." They fear that Colombia's narcoterrorists will switch their growing and processing operations to Bolivia, making irrelevant U.S. counter-drug policy in Colombia. That prospect is privately viewed by Colombian officials as fully realistic and as a catastrophe, returning the situation in the Andes to where it was in the bad old days of the 1980s.[151]

Novak quotes a "classified National Intelligence summary" stating that "there is not any scenario under current conditions that will continue aggressive eradication in Bolivia." He goes on to suggest, however, that such a scenario could be created if the drug war in Bolivia were treated as a counterinsurgency.[152] To the good fortune of all involved, Bolivia thus far has been spared the cocaine-supported insurgencies that have affected Colombia and Peru. This is primarily because Bolivian producers have political power, a political voice, and the ability to bargain with the state. Democracy already works in Bolivia and needs to be encouraged rather than thwarted. It can best be strengthened by providing the state with greater resources, not by setting even greater conditions that limit its authority.

Bolivia has many unique features, but the story that has played out there over the last two decades requires careful analysis, not only so that future U.S. policies in Bolivia can be assured of greater success, but also because the Bolivian story warns of deeper flaws in policies the United States pursues in the region. Drug policies that ignore market realities and coercive methods that undermine democratic governance are counterproductive. Remilitarizing Latin America is playing with fire, as is ignoring the mixed legacy of neoliberal policies and the widening social end economic gaps that threaten regional stability. Policy must be patient and proceed from democratic dialogue to development to drug control and not the reverse.

The dangers increase that analysis will be truncated and that patience and the search for lasting solutions will end on all sides. In Bolivia, radical indigenous leaders hint at guerrilla war; Santa Cruz rumbles with threats of secession; in several recent cases Bolivia's military has flexed its muscles; and there are voices in Washington that call for a firm response to Bolivia's problems. For Bolivia to come apart, to be Lebanonized or become the failed state that some already fear it to be, would be a tragedy. To return full circle to the de facto governments that ruled Bolivia from 1964 to 1982, whose only merit was the coerced stability they provided domestically and their friendliness to U.S. economic interests, would be equally a tragedy. And for the Bolivia story to be repeated on a regional scale would be an avoidable tragedy—the worst kind.

The drama in Bolivia continues to unfold as this volume goes to press. Evo Morales stunned virtually all observers by taking nearly 54 percent of the vote in the December 2005 elections—the first election since the return of democracy in 1982 that did not require a congressional runoff. Since the election, Morales has essentially brought coca eradication to a standstill and on May 1, 2006, placed Bolivia's natural gas industry under national control. The boldness of these acts continues to keep U.S. policy off balance, though for how long and to what end is, as yet, uncertain.

6

U.S. Policy toward Peru:
At Odds for Twenty Years

Enrique Obando

Translated by Lynn Eddy-Zambrano

Narcotized Policy

Harsh as it to say, an analysis of U.S. policy toward Peru must examine not development assistance nor the battle against poverty, but U.S. anti-narcotics policy, as this has been the United States' number one interest in the country for the last twenty years. U.S. policy has been "narcotized," shall we say, given that all other issues, even the fight against the terrorist group Sendero Luminoso (Shining Path), which, according to military sources, left twenty-five thousand dead, while the Peruvian Truth Commission (2003) reports a death count of sixty-nine thousand from the political violence from 1980 to 2000, were subordinated to Washington's desire to control illegal drug trafficking.[1] When analyzing U.S.–Peruvian relations, there is no other recourse but to focus on drug trafficking.

The Scenario

Peruvian farmers have been growing coca for seven thousand years. The plant is part of their culture; workers in the fields have been chewing it to give them energy since time immemorial. Coca's energizing properties have been known since ancient times; the Inca considered it a sacred plant. Today it is sold in Peru as an infusion and it is used to fight off "*el soroche*" (mountain sickness), an ailment that affects lowlanders when they go high into the Andes.

Coca was never a problem in the Andes. But modern science processed it into cocaine and turned it into a powerful drug. Even then it was sold openly in pharmacies and drugstores for years. It was only at the end of the 1970s that cocaine became a real problem, thanks to the considerable increase in drug use in the United States and Western Europe. Suddenly Peruvian farmers' traditional coca harvests were being bought up by foreigners at very high prices. In a farming economy marked by extreme poverty, it was a godsend for traditional crops to bring such high prices. Naturally, farmers began to plant more and more coca until, over time, they realized it was not profitable to grow anything else.

Coca brought about a migration of small farmers who left their small, tired plots in the Andean highlands for areas more suitable to coca cultivation, like the rim of the Amazonian jungle. Moreover, coca had a very special quality: it required almost no care and was highly resistant to pests and diseases. All a farmer had to do was plant and harvest it, unlike other crops that can be raised on the jungle's edge, such as coffee or cacao, which require great amounts of care.

Supply increased to meet the demands of developed countries, and by 1982 Peru had a serious drug-trafficking problem. By the late 1970s Peruvian middlemen were buying coca leaves from the farmers, turning them into basic cocaine paste, and selling it to Colombian drug traffickers who flew in and out of clandestine airports, mostly in the Alto Huallaga area in the eastern Andes. The narco-traffickers then processed the paste into cocaine and smuggled it illegally into Europe and the United States, via a bridge comprised by several countries. This created an international division of labor: the Peruvians grew the coca leaves and turned them into paste; the Colombians processed the paste into cocaine and merchandised it. The most important part of the business, obviously, was in the Colombians' hands, as there were no Peruvian drug traffickers on a level with the Cali and Medellin cartels. In the early 1990s Peruvian farmers were taking in some three hundred million dollars a year, the middlemen and paste processors around sixteen hundred million dollars, the Colombian exporters some seven million dollars, and street sales in the United States were about seventy-nine million dollars a year.[2]

The Players

Many different players can be identified in this drama about drugs. One of them is the farmer who grows coca because he sees it as a way out of poverty. Another is the drug trafficker, who, as indicated above, processes the drug (cocaine) and smuggles it into consumer countries. A third is the Peruvian government, which has tried to control narco-trafficking since the beginning of the 1980s but has been hindered by two major obstacles: (1) it has had very few resources to invest in the war on drugs; and (2) it has always been very easy to corrupt government officials with drug money, especially given the poor salaries they earn as a result of the country's recurrent economic crises. Finally, the leading player in the drama is the U.S. government, which has pressured the Peruvian government to eradicate illegal coca cultivation and narco-trafficking.

The First Counternarcotics Efforts

As a result of U.S. pressures on the Peruvian government at the beginning of the 1980s, two special projects were created in Peru with U.S. economic aid. CORAH (Proyecto Especial de Control y Reducción del Cultivo de la Coca en el Alto Huallaga—Special Project to Control and Reduce Coca Cultivation in Alto Huallaga) was created in 1981, and PEAH (Proyecto Especial del Alto Huallaga—Special Project for Alto Huallaga) was started in 1982. The former was aimed at eradicating coca cultivation. This was carried out by hiring hundreds of farm workers to manually pull up, one by one, the illegal coca crops. Manual eradication of the fields was not effective. Thirty men, working by hand, could eradicate 1 hectare of coca per day; working very intensively, they might eradicate 2. That is an average of 1.5 hectares. From 1983 to 1985 CORAH eradicated only 8,666 hectares with the assistance of 450 workers, while it had committed to eradicate 15,000 hectares. At that rate it would have taken sixty-nine years to eradicate the 200,000 hectares of coca that existed at the time, provided not one more hectare was planted.[3]

Then policy makers considered the use of chemicals. This led to a confrontation between the Peruvian and U.S. governments. The American government suggested using the herbicide Spike 20p (tebuthiuron) in the Peruvian coca-growing regions. The Peruvian government pointed out that use of the herbicide would have serious ecological repercussions in the area, as it would not only wipe out the coca crops but, upon washing into rivers, destroy jungle foliage as well, causing irreparable damage for hundreds of kilometers. The U.S. government maintained that experiments with Spike showed it was safe and did not cause any of the effects the Peruvian government feared. Discussion came to an abrupt halt when Lilly and Company, the American manufacturer of Spike, informed the U.S. Department of State on March 20, 1988, that it would not supply its herbicide for the South America coca eradication program. Before discussions began over the use of Spike, the Peruvian government had been using 2-4-D, a commercial pesticide used to control growth in the Peruvian jungle. That chemical proved inefficient for eradication purposes and its use was abandoned.

In 1991, after ten years, CORAH had destroyed 18,000 hectares of coca. New plantings, however, more than doubled the amount eradicated. In 1991 coca acreage was more than twelve times what it had been in 1969. The 1969 level is documented in the very accurate registry of lands carried out in 1969 by the military government under General Juan Velasco Alvarado for purposes of agrarian reform; it confirms there were only 18,000 hectares of cultivated coca at the time.

PEAH's purpose, in turn, was to identify new crops that could replace coca once it was eradicated. This project did not work either, for two reasons. To begin with, it was never funded at a level necessary for it to perform efficiently. Further, while it focused on identifying alternative crops appropriate for the regional ecology, there was little concern for whether or not there were significant markets for such crops, or whether prices paid for them were high enough to make substitution attractive to farmers. This caused the two projects to fail. The first thing that farmers demanded, whether they agreed or were obliged to eradicate their coca crops, was the assistance promised by the Peruvian government for crop substitution. PEAH personnel, however, could not keep up with the cases requiring their attention. CORAH was eradicating at a faster rate than PEAH could come up with substitute crops. Consequently, the farmers perceived that the state was eradicating by force, that there was no crop substitution, assistance, or compensation whatsoever. This first brought protests from the coca farmers, then threats were made against CORAH and PEAH. Drug traffickers, then the guerrillas and politically subversive elements, took advantage of this state of affairs; finally attacks led to fires and deaths in Aucayacu and Tulumayo and other areas. PEAH was forced to move out of Tingo María.

In September 1985 the mayor and other officials from Aucayacu and the Agrarian League from Leoncio Prado province denounced PEAH for not developing agriculture in Alto Huallaga, and demanded the resignation of PEAH's regional heads. They were relieved of their duties.[4] The new leaders tried to repair the situation but were hindered primarily by the lack of adequate funding. PEAH continued to make some progress, but its snail's pace stalled CORAH, which could not continue eradication without support for crop substitution from PEAH. CORAH had another problem: there were too few police forces (UMOPAR, Unidad Móvil de Patrullaje Rural—Mobile Rural Patrol Unit, the specialized counternarcotics police financed by the U.S. in charge of protecting CORAH personnel).

Thus the projects under discussion never achieved the objectives for which they were designed, but they did have an undesired outcome: they completely alienated the coca growers from the government. Coca farmers began to identify the government as the enemy who sought to destroy their economic livelihood. This continued to be a very serious issue, as over time there were some 250,000 coca farmers located in the Huallaga region, counting family members. That added up to one million people estranged by government eradication policies. Ultimately, the region's entire eradication scenario would change drastically as a result of the presence of Peru's leading subversive group during those years: Sendero Luminoso (Shining Path).

Subversive Activity in the Huallaga Valley

Sendero Luminoso moved into the Huallaga Valley in 1984 and found that farmers looked upon the police and government officials as the enemy engaged in trying to destroy the coca fields. It was an easy task for Sendero Luminoso to find allies among the coca farmers. Even while the United States refused to support Peru in its struggle against Sendero Luminoso, U.S. eradication policy was pushing farmers at the jungle's borders into the arms of the *senderistas* (followers of Sendero Luminoso). *It would not be the first or last time the Peruvian government found itself confronting a serious political situation as a consequence of U.S. policy.*

The Peruvian army moved into the Huallaga Valley in response to the situation, with the intention of breaking up the alliance between the subversives and the coca farmers. It elected not to take part in counternarcotics activities, but to focus exclusively on the *senderista* subversives. This tactic ultimately convinced farmers that the army was not the enemy and they came to trust it. The effort was successful, and Sendero was run out of the valley. But it led to an undesired outcome: tension increased between the army, with its hands-off policy toward activities involving drug trafficking, and the police, whose mission it was to fight such activities.

The years passed and Sendero Luminoso moved back into the valley in 1987. This time it encountered another subversive group that had settled there, the Movimiento Revolucionario Túpac Amaru (MRTA, the Tupac Amaru Revolutionary Movement.) A struggle erupted between the two groups for control of the valley; Sendero eventually won out. MRTA retreated to nearby areas in San Martín Department, like Alto Mayor. The army moved in once more to fight Sendero.

In the interim the police had switched their counternarcotics tactics. Instead of going after the coca farmers to eradicate their crops, the strategy was to leave them alone, in favor of focusing efforts on the middlemen and drug traffickers. A series of search and destroy missions was carried out on cocaine paste processing labs and clandestine airports. The most important one was Operation Condor, supported by the U.S. government. The strategy worked at the beginning. Following the destruction of private airports and labs, by the end of 1985 and the first few months of 1986, the supply of coca leaves in the valley was greater than demand and prices fell. In some places they fell by 50 percent.[5] While it was the traffickers, not the growers, who were targeted this time, in the end the impact on state–grower relations was the same: although they were no longer the ones being harassed or pursued, farmers identified the state and the police as the enemy. As operations against the middlemen and drug traffickers drove down the price of coca leaves in the Huallaga Valley, farmers held the police responsible for seeking to destroy their livelihood without providing them with a viable alternative. Once more, Sendero Luminoso easily won allies among the coca farmers. It was then clear that the war on drugs was counterproductive in the fight against Sendero. Sendero was indeed financing itself off drugs, but it was more important that the army not create any more militants for the *senderistas* in that huge region of mountains and tropical rain forests. It was determined that fighting Sendero took priority over the war on drugs. The latter would be taken up once Sendero Luminoso was defeated.

By 1988 the Sendero Luminoso practically owned the Huallaga Valley again. In response, the government created Emergency Subregion Number 8 in 1989 and sent the army into the valley once more. Brigadier General Albert Arciniega Huby was made political and military head of the subregion. Just as in 1984, the army realized the only way to break up the alliance between Sendero, the drug traffickers, and the growers was to go on the offensive against Sendero, but not attack the other two. Arciniega's first objective was to win over the population. The worst possible tactic was to hunt down the coca growers or destroy the source of their income. The army focused exclusively on fighting the subversives, while allowing the drug traffickers to continue operations. The strategy was highly successful in the valley. The army inflicted heavy losses on Sendero, which had broad domination of the region, but more importantly, drew away the surrounding community's support for the *senderistas*. When the army transferred General Arciniega out of the valley in December 1989 as part of a routine change of command, Sendero had taken a heavy pounding in the area. The fight against drug traffickers continued to be a job for the police; the army did not take part in those operations. The police, however, were supported by the U.S. Drug Enforcement Administration (DEA), which had begun to make an appearance in the valley in conjunction with the war on drugs.

A DEA counternarcotics base opened at Santa Lucía in 1989. The army had to carry out thirty-two cleanup operations against the subversives to get it built. But the fact that the army would not get involved in the fight against drug trafficking, thereby allowing such activities to continue, began to create frictions with both the police and the DEA.

The View from Washington

DEA agents sent reports to Washington about General Arciniega's leniency toward drug trafficking. In October 1989 the U.S. Senate accused General Arciniega of colluding with the drug traffickers. From that moment on, Washington's view of the Peruvian army was negative. Compounding it was a report by the RAND Corporation[6] that underscored the Peruvian armed forces' lack of effectiveness in the war on the insurgents. A high-ranking official at the U.S. Embassy in Lima appeared on Peruvian television in May 1990 and issued statements about alleged human rights violations committed by the Peruvian army in the war on the insurgents after Amnesty International brought forward cases of such violations. On August 20, 1990, a report by the U.S. Congress House Committee on Governmental Operations blamed the failure of DEA counternarcotics operations on corruption and lack of cooperation from the Peruvian military.[7] It was clear that things were very tense between the Peruvian army and the U.S. government. At this point serious conversations began between the Peruvian and U.S. governments.

The Proposal for a Military Agreement

The United States offered the Peruvian government $35,945,000 (U.S.) in military equipment and training for six battalions (five for the army and one for the navy, for a total of 4,200 troops). The terms of the agreement contradicted the Peruvian army's strategy, which was to give priority to the war against the insurgency and shelve the war on drugs until such time as Sendero was defeated, in order to avoid fostering an alliance among Sendero, the drug traffickers, and the farmers. The United States offered assistance only for the war on drugs, clearly specifying that resources could not be used against the insurgents. For the army, acceptance of the agreement meant being drawn into a battle it believed was counterproductive and did not yet want to undertake. Further, the assistance was exclusively for military purposes. No allowances were made for bringing in substitute crops that would yield growers a decent living, once the coca was eradicated. If the coca were wiped out, but not replaced by crops that provided inhabitants with an acceptable income, enormous social and economic problems would develop in the valley, and conditions would be ripe for insurgency.

While the Peruvian armed forces were not unanimous in their opinion of the agreement proposed by the United States, those who opposed it in favor of staying the course with the war against insurgency strategy ultimately won out. The armed forces persuaded the Fujimori government not to sign the agreement. Washington's reaction was not exactly calm. A U.S. official quoted by the *Washington Post* indicated that the Peruvian government's refusal to sign the agreement raised serious concerns about possible ties between the Peruvian military and drug traffickers opposed to the U.S. program.[8] Drug Czar William Bennett, director for the Office of National Drug

Control Policy, proposed declaring Peru ineligible to receive U.S. assistance. The idea was to have Peru decertified by reporting before the U.S. Congress that it was not cooperating in the war on drugs. This meant U.S. assistance would automatically be reduced by half and the United States would vote "no" on loans to Peru in multilateral lenders' meetings.

The Department of State, however, took a calmer approach. It opposed such sanctions. Spokesperson Richard Boucher pointed out that Peru's cooperation in the war on drugs was vital and that nothing would be gained by breaking off relations with the Peruvian government. He suggested negotiations continue until the problems were ironed out. That is precisely what happened; in 1991 a counternarcotics agreement with the United States was finally ready to be signed.

Meanwhile, the situation in Huallaga was changing. The DEA was carrying out helicopter support operations for the Peruvian police from the base at Santa Lucía. This prompted coca production to shift northward into Bajo and Medio Huallaga and into Alto Mayo, all located in the same basin but somewhat removed from the base of antinarcotics operations.[9] The advances that had been made against the insurgency up until December 1989 began to reverse themselves, partly because the army was plagued by a lack of logistical support as a result of the country's serious economic crisis. The insurgency made a powerful reappearance with attacks on the army. Further, the region was now in the hands of two separate subversive groups. Territory from Juanjui al Sur to Tingo María, that is, the Alta Huallaga, belonged to Sendero Luminoso. Juanjui el Norte to Tarapoto and Moyobamba, the newer coca growing areas in Medio Huallaga and Alto Mayor, were dominated by the MRTA.[10]

The Fujimori Doctrine and the U.S. Antinarcotics Agreement

In response to U.S. plans for a strictly military approach to the drug problem, the Peruvian government developed a counterproposal that became labeled the "Fujimori Doctrine." These suggestions were largely based on the ideas of Hernando de Soto, then presidential advisor on drug issues. Underlying the Peruvian proposal was the idea that the problem was not criminal in nature, but attributable to poverty, and the proposed solution was alternative development. The stumbling block seemed to be that coca was Peru's only hassle-free crop. Credit for planting coca was delivered right to the farmer's doorstep; he didn't have to leave home to sell the harvest, either. No licenses, no permits, and no bookkeeping were necessary. There were no worries about processing paperwork for export or the logistics of exporting his goods. Nor did he have to pass agricultural inspections. To grow legal crops, on the other hand, a farmer had to jump through thirty-six bureaucratic hoops before beginning production. With coca, all he had to do was plant it, confident that the entire crop would be purchased from his doorstep at very lucrative prices. Given these terms, how could farmers be persuaded not to plant coca?

The Peruvian proposal made the case that it was not possible to eradicate coca without the cooperation of the producers—the farmers. If a farmer were harassed or antagonized, all he had to do was pick up, move to a new place, and continue planting. If coca were going to be eradicated, three steps had to be taken:

1. Enlist the farmers' support for eradication.
2. To accomplish the above, new crops had to be identified to replace coca once it was eradicated.
3. In contrast to PEAH, this meant not only identifying alternative crops, but first and foremost, creating the market conditions necessary for such crops to be profitable. This had several implications:
   a. Granting the farmers titles to their lands so they would be eligible for bank loans;
   b. Creating transportation networks to give alternative crops access to markets; and
   c. Getting multinational food companies behind the effort since they control the markets for certain products, that is, they set the prices.

The role of the multinationals would be to:

- Guarantee purchase of a set quantity of the alternative crop;
- Guarantee payment of special prices for it;
- Guarantee tariff advantages; and
- Guarantee reductions in bureaucratic red tape on imports of the alternative crop.[11]

To the extent that this new plan did not consider farmers criminals, and therefore, they were not to be harassed, it was in fundamental alignment with the Peruvian army's assessment of the situation. Eradication should be carried out with the farmers' cooperation, and not by force. This has been the official position of the Peruvian government since 1990.

The problem is that this was not what the U.S. government had in mind. The U.S. government decidedly favored military and police solutions. It wanted the physical eradication of coca, with or without the consent of the farmers; it wanted airborne antinarcotics interdiction operations, destruction of clandestine airfields and labs, and control of the chemical substances used in drug manufacturing. There was not a great deal of interest in funding alternative development for the coca farmers. The U.S. Army's Southern Command had its own ideas, too. General Maxwell R. Thurman, chief of the Southern Command, proposed conducting a military operation against the drug traffickers. Unlike earlier operations in coca-producing countries where coca would be wiped out in one area, only to spring up in another, this plan proposed a full, simultaneous assault on drug trafficking's most critical locations in three countries: Colombia, Peru, and Bolivia. The operation would be carried out by the armies of those countries, under close supervision of the U.S. Army.[12] As none of the region's armies accepted this strictly military plan, the idea was abandoned.

The United States finally listened to Fujimori's alternative development idea. Peru signed an antinarcotics agreement with Washington in 1991, signaling Washington's acceptance of the alternative development proposal and its commitment for economic assistance to support it. This was an important victory for the Peruvian government. But one more difficult task remained for the government: How to persuade coca farmers in the Huallaga Valley to cooperate in eradicating the coca crops?

The Rural Coca Farmers

The rural coca farmers are well organized. This is the outcome of two situations. First, the farmers organized to defend themselves against eradication policy. Second, they organized to defend themselves from Sendero Luminoso. They did ally with Sendero in a number of areas but did so because Sendero opposed eradication policy. In actual fact, the farmers favored neither Sendero nor the state over the other. All they wanted was to be left alone. In an environment where everyone was armed—Sendero and MRTA insurgents, drug traffickers, the police, and the military—the farmers took up arms to protect themselves from anyone who disturbed them. When the military's hands-off drug-trafficking policy began yielding results, the farmers had no further interest in alliances with Sendero. Sendero was perceived as a dogmatic power that intended to keep the farmers under control through force. This prompted the farmers to take up arms against the *senderistas* and organize patrols to command respect for themselves. Sendero, moreover, made a practice of levying farmers to replace the losses inflicted on them by the army. The only way for farmers to escape being impressed into terrorist ranks was to organize militarily. The army supported their patrols to the extent they were useful in the fight against Sendero.

The Peruvian government had to win over coca growers who were not, then, weak or disorganized, to enlist their collaboration on eradication. On the contrary, they were organized, and in many cases, armed. One hundred and seventy-five committees of farmers were organized under the Frente de

Defensa contra la Erradicación de la Coca del Alto Huallaga—FEDECAH, the Defensive Front against Coca Eradication in the Alto Huallaga. The name itself clearly expresses the farmers' sentiments on eradication. A second organization was the Federación Agraria de Selva Maestra (FASMA, the Selva Maestra Agrarian Federation). These groups were supported by the Confederación Nacional Agraria (CAN, National Agrarian Federation), a national growers organization. Then there were the patrols, organizations of armed growers created for protection from Sendero Luminoso; their arms could also be used in defense against government eradication policies. Backed up by the economic support for alternative development built into the agreement signed with the United States, the government managed to persuade the coca farmers to cooperate on eradication, in exchange for its assurance that they would receive advice on raising alternative crops, which the government guaranteed would be purchased at good prices.

The Setback

But then all kinds of strange things began to happen. First, the 1991 agreement only provided for $94.9 million (US) in support, of which $34.9 would go to the military. This was not a particularly impressive amount to take on a mafia that moved around more than $79 million, but it was a start, and in the coming years more money would be directed at the counternarcotics effort.

Then the U.S. Congress reduced military assistance in response to alleged human rights violations on the part of the Peruvian armed forces and reports that the Peruvian army was collaborating with the drug traffickers. This was the first setback. The United States ended up providing only $29.4 million of the $94.9 million that had been promised.

The situation worsened in 1992. At the next drug summit in San Antonio, Texas, President George H. W. Bush tried to put the focus on repressive policies rather than alternative development. At an earlier meeting in Quito, the U.S. envoy recommended an eradication system that included

- a multilateral police and military intervention force,
- common legislation on drug-trafficking issues, and
- a supranational, autonomous judicial and prison system.

All the Latin American countries rejected these ideas on the grounds of national sovereignty. Peru had to fight in San Antonio just to keep the idea of alternative development alive, at least on paper. But in reality the new agreement on drug control signed with the United States in 1992 was an agreement about repression. This time the U.S. government approved only $11 million in assistance to Peru for counternarcotics initiatives. The reasons underlying approval of such paltry sums need to be sought in the U.S. Congress. Congress was led by Democrats who felt the Bush administration's counternarcotics program was a failure; therefore, no additional funds should be allocated to it. The problem was the split Republican executive and Democratic congressional branches failed to realize that the Peruvian government had already offered alternative development to the coca farmers, and to raise the farmers' expectations only to fail to deliver could be extremely dangerous, particularly in a country experiencing insurgency. When funds promised by the United States did not materialize, the Peruvian government abandoned the coca farmers to their fate.

The Military Strategy

Alternative development was an important piece of the 1991 counternarcotics agreement signed with the United States, but it was not devoid of a military angle. Once implementation began, greater amounts of assistance went to the military than to alternative development. The core of the military strategy was aerial interdiction. This amounted to using American AWACS[13] in the air and American land-based radar to track down planes engaged in drug trafficking. Once picked up, U.S. spotter aircraft would guide Peruvian pursuit aircraft to intercept and force them to land or shoot them down, if they did not comply. Similarly, destruction began of the clandestine airports where the small aircraft landed. This strategy was employed between 1991 and 2002. Originally it was disliked by Peruvian authorities because their chief concern, alternative development, was cast aside. However, one of the objectives of alternative development, that is, to circumvent confrontation with the farmers, was being met indirectly, a by-product of the military strategy. Aerial interception managed to artificially lower demand for coca leaves in Peru: buyers were prevented from reaching sellers; that, in turn, caused coca leaf prices to fall for lack of demand. Demand fell so sharply that coca cultivation ceased to be profitable and farmers began to abandon the fields of their own volition. This strategy did not bring development but it did stave off direct conflict with the farmers and, over time, it was adopted wholeheartedly by Peruvian authorities. The military strategy reduced the farmers to poverty as narco-trafficking was destroyed with no economic alternative to take its place, but it did not entail direct eradication and averted a standoff. Under this scenario forced eradication was not necessary; instead, the strategy led to crop abandonment and prevented a dreaded confrontation between eradicators and cultivators in a country where, rocked by eleven years of terrorism from Sendero Luminoso and the MRTA, there could have been unforeseeably violent consequences.

Peru's drug-trafficking scene saw important change in 1995. The state's defeat of Sendero Luminoso and the MRTA weakened the ties between drug trafficking and terrorism. And the success of the military strategy—thanks to the efficient job done by the Peruvian Air Force, with U.S. support—broke up the air bridge that supplied cocaine paste to Colombian drug traffickers. The price of coca leaves plummeted from $4.00 (US) a kilo to $0.40 (US) a kilo. The price remained under a dollar per kilo between July 1995 and May 1998, that is, below the profit index, leading to an 18 percent reduction in cultivated land in 1996, 26 percent in 1997, and 27 percent in 1998. Total cultivated land dropped to just 51,754 hectares. Toward the end of 1998, the "cocologists," as a group of Peruvian drug-trafficking analysts came to be called, began to talk about a post-coca Amazonia. The militarization of the fight on coca seemed to have yielded results. More importantly, the Peruvian government had adopted it as an acceptable way to take care of the problem, without having to take on the coca farmers. U.S. authorities held Peru up as a shining example to the Bolivians and Colombians. But Peruvian authorities did not anticipate all the incongruities U.S. counternarcotics policy would bring, ultimately spelling failure for what seemed, at the time, a successful strategy.

A List of Incongruities

Radar

In 1990 the U.S. government set up two TPS-43 radars, one in Iquitos and the second in Andoas, to support aerial interdiction. The Andoas radar was moved to Yurimaguas from June to September 1991 and then to Pucallpa from September to April 1992. The Peruvian congress was shut down by President Fujimori in April 1992, leading to a U.S. decision to withdraw the radars. The withdrawal lasted nine months. It was not until January 1993 that both radars were functioning again from Iquitos and Pucallpa. Radar support was interrupted again in May 1994 following an incident in the Persian Gulf: a U.S. destroyer mistakenly shot down an airliner carrying Iranian passengers. This incident on the other side of the world had repercussions for drug policy: Washington lawyers contended it was illegal to shoot down civilian aircraft, even if they were involved in drug trafficking.

Fearful they would become embroiled in cases stemming from illegally downed aircraft, the radars were withdrawn again. This time it was for seven months; finally in January 1995 one radar alone was reinstalled in Iquitos, only to be removed almost immediately after war broke out between Peru and Ecuador in February 1995. Then it was withdrawn for eleven months, until January 1996. A TPS-43 was put into operation out of Iquitos; it was only in

July that a new TPS-63 radar was installed in Pucallpa, and subsequently replaced with a TPS-59 in 1997.

On April 12, 2001, a small airplane belonging to the Association of Baptists
for World Evangelization was shot down by error, causing the death of an
American missionary and her daughter. The two radars were withdrawn once
more and were not put back into operation between 1991 and July of 2004
(174 months). The radars had been withdrawn four times for a total of sixty-
six months, or 38 percent of the period. Worse yet, Peruvian authorities maintain that even during the time the radars were supposedly operational, in reality they often malfunctioned. Further, the radars were older models, not the
most technologically advanced equipment. In light of this evidence the question emerges as to whether or not the United States is really serious about
combating drug trafficking.

The AWACS and P-3s

Then there were the North American AWACS and P-3 aircraft the Peruvian
Air Force received to support interdiction operations. The aircraft provided the
air force with radar information on the exact location of small drug-trafficking
planes. The AWACS and P-3s followed the same pattern of withdrawal the
radars did, but worse yet, were withdrawn definitively during the last six months
of 1998, at the height of the success of the aerial interception operations. Need-
less to say, there were no more major interdictions after that time. The aircraft
were withdrawn in conjunction with the closing of U.S. bases in Panama under
the terms of the Carter–Torrijos accords for turning the Panama Canal over to
Panama. The planes were called back to Texas. It was surmised that security concerns precluded operation of the aircraft out of Peruvian airports. Much later
they began to fly out of Cuenca (Ecuador), where the United States had its own
air base, and continued to do so until the incident with the Association of Baptists plane, when the flights were suspended.

The Halting of Interception Activities

The shooting down of the Baptist plane in 2001 brought aerial interception
to a halt, but when the AWACS and P-3 Orion aircraft stopped flying in 1998,
the price of coca leaves began to rise again (see table 6.1.) The price was $0.80
(US) a kilo in 1998, $3.50 a kilo in 1999, and $4.00 per kilo by 2000. That is
still the price in 2005. The gains made when farmers voluntarily gave up cultivating coca because prices were low eroded until they disappeared altogether. The last year coca planting fell was 1998. Cultivation picked up again
in 1999, rising to 2,433 hectares. As 14,733 hectares were eradicated that year,

coca-cultivated land decreased overall by 12,300 hectares. The drop in cultivated land in 2000 was significantly less: only 6,206 hectares were eradicated and 1,706 new hectares were planted, for a balance on the plus-side of 4,500 hectares. There was almost no positive balance in 2001: 6,436 hectares were eradicated while 6,236 hectares were planted, leaving only 200 hectares in the plus column. In 2002 the balance was negative by a wide margin: 7,134 hectares were eradicated, 9,700 new hectares were planted; coca-cultivated land increased by 2,566 hectares.

According to the Peruvian Ministry of the Interior, the figures for 2003 were surely higher still.[14] Not even considered is the significant opium poppy cultivation now going on in the Marañón and Huallaga basins. A report from the Ministry of the Interior states, "No techniques for locating and measuring cultivation, like those used to quantify coca cultivation, have yet been put into place in these areas. But judging by the size of the 2003 seizures, they would have come from 94 cultivated hectares. Add that to the 57.8 hectares that have been eradicated and/or destroyed, for a total 151.8 hectares. Statistical extrapolation of that figure using international parameters yields the estimate that *one thousand two hundred and sixty-five (1265) hectares* of opium poppy were cultivated in Perú in 2003."[15] Opium poppy gives higher returns than coca, by a margin of seven to one.[16]

As bad as these figures are, they might be even worse, because statistics on coca leaf–cultivated lands may have been falsified. The Peruvian government accepts figures issued by the U.S. Department of State as official. The United Nations Office on Drugs and Crime (UNODC), however, has a different set of numbers, raising doubts as to what the actual figures are. While the Peruvian Ministry of the Interior's Dirección Anti-Drogas (DIRANDRO, Counternarcotics Directorate) and the U.S. Department of State claim there were 31,500 hectares of coca planted, the UNODC claims it is 46,721 hectares, a not so trifling difference of 15,221 hectares, nearly 50 percent.[17] The figures released by UNDOC for 2004 report 50,3000 hectares in coca cultivation.[18]

An Upside-Down World: The United States Opposes Aerial Interception

Even stranger things were yet to happen. Despite the fact the United States had supported Peru's alternative development proposal, it focused mainly on the military strategy to wipe out drug trafficking through aerial interception. Interception was quite successful between 1995 and 1998 and, as indicated above, ultimately embraced enthusiastically by Peru. Nevertheless, the program suffered a major setback in 1998 when the AWACS and P-3 Orion aircraft were withdrawn; then it was suspended in 2001 after the downing of the Baptist plane. In 2001 the United States began opposing aerial interception. The 2001 accident had been particularly costly because the Baptist Church

TABLE 6.1
Estimated Costs to the Peruvian Government of the War on Drugs, 2002
(in U.S. dollars)

Institution	Current Expenditures	Capital Expenditures	Total
		Entries	
Ministry of the Interior, National Police	67,973,681		67,973,681
Ministry of Production, Directorate of Controlled Chemical Substances	775,429	71,429	846,878
Ministry of Education	561,714	670,286	1,232,000
Ministry of Justice, National Penitentiary Institute	8,773,925	483,452	9,257,377
Ministry of Defense, Peruvian Air Force	5,177,203		5,177,203
Ministry of Defense, Peruvian Navy	6,061,480		6,061,480
Ministry of Women	1,304,479		1,304,479
Ministry of Foreign Relations	923,135		923,135
Attorney General	713,148	113,880	827,028
Superintendency of Banking and Insurance	1,639,893	33,385	1,673,278
Customs	580,248		580,248
DEVIDA	2,428,571		2,428,571
State presence in coca growing regions			
• Regional governments	92,250,240	8,021,760	100,272,000
• Public sectors	46,924,410	22,055,811	68,980,221
Total	236,087,556	31,450,003	267,537,579

Source: Ministry of Foreign Relations

sued the CIA for fifty million dollars; the latter ended up paying eight million. Peru did not get off either as it was ordered to replace the Baptists' airplane. Following the 2001 mishap it was decided that operations ought to be turned over to the Peruvians so the United States would not be blamed in the event of another mistake. Peru was to be given four radar-equipped C-26s to detect drug-trafficking aircraft, as well as two Citation spotter planes to lead fighters to the illegal aircraft once found. Two old A-37Bs were also donated, and eight more belonging to the Peruvian Air Force were outfitted for interception. Flight training was planned for Peruvian crews on all of the aircraft. The program started up in 2002 but was frozen in 2003. The reason for this suspension is a legal saga.

The United States is signatory to the 1944 Chicago Convention prohibiting the downing of civilian planes by military aircraft. This in itself presented difficulties for intercepting and occasionally shooting down planes running drugs. Nonetheless, in 1984 the United States signed onto the Montreal Protocol as well. It was a response to the 1983 Soviet downing of a Korean Air Lines flight that had flown over a Russian air base. Two hundred and sixty-nine lives were lost, including many Americans. In a move to prevent future incidents of this nature, the Montreal Protocol made the downing of civilian aircraft a criminal offense.[19] This presented theoretical legal questions about interdiction, but no one publicly raised them; the drug traffickers certainly were not going to benefit from the protocol. It was when a U.S. destroyer shot down an Iranian airliner over the Persian Gulf that the alarm sounded on the legal implications of shooting down civilian aircraft and the first moratorium on interceptions was declared. The mistake in 2001 halted operations a second time. At that point U.S. officials decided that problems could be averted by turning operations over to the Peruvians. However, U.S. lawyers argued that the United States could still be held liable if there were an accident, simply because it provided Peru with the means to bring civilian aircraft down.

In August 2003 Washington instituted a new procedure for monitoring antinarcotics activities that placed additional restrictions on activating the so-called deadly force phase of aerial interceptions, actions that could bring a civilian plane down. The procedure has proven very complicated and unwieldy. When the United States put its signature on the Montreal Protocol it became U.S. law. This means that the Department of Justice is called upon to safeguard against violations. The legal interdiction of an airplane trafficking drugs requires having a "presidential determination" (*estatuto de inmunidad*) in hand, a decision that comes out of the White House. To win such a determination the Peruvian government must ascertain drug trafficking represents an extraordinary threat to the country, then demonstrate it has the appropriate safeguards in place to guarantee force will only be applied when there is reasonable suspicion an aircraft is trafficking drugs. With that in place the United States can then join the interdiction program.

Yet the matter gets even more complicated: as of 2001 the U.S. Congress now requires the president to prepare a report and complete the entire presidential determination process every year. This new procedure was presented to Peruvian authorities in October 2003 by Deborah McCarthy, deputy assistant for the Bureau of International Narcotics and Law Enforcement Affairs in the Department of State.[20] Now the U.S. government is asking Peruvian authorities to create an Antinarcotics Coordination Center to determine what kind of threat drug trafficking actually poses for the country and the role air transport plays to decide whether or not it makes sense to resume interdiction. The center would also be charged with gathering the intelligence necessary to be reasonably certain planes are carrying drugs before they are intercepted. Then Peru will need to declare that aerial departure of drugs is a national security issue in order for the United States, in theory, to lend its support. But McCarthy could not guarantee that, even after meeting all those conditions, the program would resume.

The current (2005) debate surrounds financing for the Antinarcotics Coordination Center; everything seems to indicate the United States is not willing to contribute substantially. The message from the U.S. Embassy in May 2004 was that during the election year, no major decisions would be made on important issues.[21] But an aerial interdiction program is under way in Colombia. The civil war and the fact that both the FARC (Fuerzas Armadas Revolucionarias de Colombia) and the ELN (Ejército de Liberación Nacional) use drug money to finance their terrorist activities make it easy to demonstrate drug trafficking is an issue of national security. This is not the case in Peru where Sendero Luminoso and the MRTA do not represent an imminent threat to the state at this time.

The U.S. refusal to support interdiction programs impacts not only Peru. In Brazil's case opposition has been taken to extremes. Brazil is not a coca-producing country; it is an important consumer. Therein lies the Brazilian authorities' interest in starting an aerial interdiction program. Contrary to what one would expect, the United States, rather than supporting Brazil's antinarcotics initiative, threatened to cut off military aid if Brazil began intercepting illegal aircraft. The world had truly been set on its head. Brazil does not need U.S. interdiction assistance. It has its own Sistema de Vigilancia de la Amazonia (SIVAM, Amazonian Surveillance System), a broad system of primary and secondary radar, radar and monitoring aircraft, and a satellite, built at a cost of $1,500 million (US), that gives Brazil a capacity to patrol Amazonia unmatched by any other country in the region. (See Monica Herz's chapter on Brazil in this volume.) But the company that built SIVAM was Raytheon, a U.S. firm. Funding was Brazilian, the technology was U.S. And the credit used to finance construction came from Eximbank, which is dominated by U.S. capital. Washington lawyers said this was enough to be able to press charges against the United States for the erroneous downing of a plane. Nevertheless, on October 17, 2004, Brazil approved regulations that permit shoot downs of drug-trafficking aircraft.[22] At the end of May, U.S. pressures on Brazil increased to comply with U.S. law on this matter. Richard Boucher, spokesperson for the Department of State, informed Brazil that the United States might be obligated to suspend antidrug assistance if the country implemented its program to shoot down civilian planes engaged in the drug trafficking—even though the United States supported this policy in Colombia.[23] Brazil responded that the aircraft radar and attack technology would be exclusively Brazilian. But then, from another source, Human Rights Watch, Reed Brody suggested that this policy would violate the constitution and also international human rights norms against the use of lethal measures against civilian aircraft. He recommended that lethal force be used solely in self-defense against an imminent threat or death or injury.[24]

Peruvians and Brazilians trying to implement aerial interdiction programs faced, oddly enough, active opposition from the United States. The United States even began to question whether or not drugs were actually being moved by air. Brazilian sources replied that in 2003 they had records on 2,117 unregistered flights, and until May of 2004, records on another 1,036, and it was believed that the majority corresponded to drug trafficking.[25]

In the Peruvian case, as a result of the Peruvian Air Force's interdiction successes between 1995 and 1998, significant amounts of drugs began to be moved by sea, through ports, coves, and rivers. The United States mounted the Riverine Program to address river trafficking and donated watercraft to the Peruvian navy and police to patrol the rivers. Yet the United States did nothing to help the Peruvian navy acquire coastal radar or coast guard vessels, even though it is well-known that drugs hidden in export goods leave through the ports of Callao, Chimbote, Salaverry, Ilo, and Paita by various means, such as small craft, which move the drugs into the high seas, then transfer them to higher tonnage international vessels.[26] While it may well be that most Peruvian drugs are trafficked by sea, the fact that aerial interdiction has been suspended means air transport will start to pick up. Drugs move where there is no surveillance, and at this moment air surveillance is zero. At the same time, interceptions in Colombia will cause what is known as a balloon effect: Peru will begin producing the drugs that can no longer be produced in Colombia. Between 1991 and 2001 production in the three countries (Bolivia, Colombia, and Peru) remained steady at about two hundred thousand hectares. When pressure was put on Peru in the mid-1990s, production shifted to Colombia; with pressure now being put on Colombia, drug production will return to Peru, where neither effective air nor sea interdiction is in place.

Simply because there is no interdiction policy does not mean the United States will stop pressuring Peru to wipe out coca. All U.S. pressure is now directed at forced eradication, something the Peruvian government considers politically dangerous. When forced eradication began in January 2003 the coca farmers marched on Lima to pressure the government into stopping it. The government is fearful that what happened in Bolivia with Evo Morales and the fall of the Bolivian government could also happen in Peru. Morales organized Bolivian coca growers into a political force to reckon with; he ran for the presidency and got a large vote then won the presidency in late 2005. The Peruvian government conceded in response to the farmers' mobilization and made promises to carry out eradication in a "concerted, gradual" fashion. The program began in June 2003. Under this program each farmer was offered 100 kilograms of foodstuffs and a daily wage of twenty-five Peruvian *soles* for eradication work. Farmers were also promised a $180 bonus per family (20 percent when the agreement was signed, 30 percent at the midway point, and the remaining 50 percent when 100 percent of the coca in the community was eliminated). Communities accepting eradication were promised that two projects to improve the social or economic infrastructure and two projects aimed at improving productivity would also be undertaken. Those who were undocumented would also receive assistance in processing their Documento Nacional de Identificación (DNI, National Identification Papers) and processing the titles to their lands.[27]

But this program progressed very slowly, and fell short in the eyes of both Deborah McCarthy in the Department of State and Barry Crane from the Office of National Drug Control Policy. In a September 5, 2003, letter to Nils Ericsson, executive director of DEVIDA (Comisión Nacional para el Desarrollo y Vida sin Drogas—National Commission for Development and Life without Drugs), a Peruvian institution dedicated to controlling narcotics, Crane wrote, "Eight thousand hectares eradicated out of the approximately 37,000 presently growing in Perú means that growers run less than a 25% risk of losing any of their four coca harvests in a year. This is probably not sufficient to convince them to stop planting coca."[28]

The Coca Farmers Come Back

The policy of swift, forced eradication being pushed by the United States could have grave consequences for Peru's political stability. The majority of coca farmers live in areas of extreme poverty, have little schooling, and do not own the lands they farm.[29] Apart from raising coca, they have few economic alternatives. The Programa Nacional de Desarrollo Alternativo (PNDA— National Program for Alternative Development) may get Washington lip service, but as a strategy it is secondary to forced eradication. The PNDA was relatively successful at first; coca cultivation was substantially reduced. In recent years, however, it has not yielded satisfactory results, as the prices of the coca-growing region's chief export products (coffee and cacao) have fallen in international markets, while the price of coca leaf has risen. This had prompted farmers to take up coca cultivation again and radicalized their rejection of eradication and alternative development programs.[30]

Coca farmers are well-organized, too, and have formed the Confederación Nacional de Productores Agropecuarios de las Cuencas Cocaleras del Perú (CONPACCP—National Confederation of Agricultural Producers in Peru's

Coca Growing Valleys), which unites all the country's coca-growing regions, with the exception of the Asociación de Productores Agropecuarios del Valle de Monzón (APAVM—the Monzón Valley Association of Agricultural Producers). CONPACCP's general secretary is Nancy Obregón. In addition to the confederation there are seven associations or federations that unite producers according to region.[31] Those organizations completely opposed to coca eradication within their jurisdictions include the Federación de Productores Agropecuarios del Valle de los Ríos Apurímac y Ene (FEPAVRAE—the Federation of Agricultural Producers for the Apuríma and Ene River Valleys), comprising the Ene-Apurímac (Ayacucho), La Convención (Cuzco) and Satipo (Junín) Valleys, and the APAVM. FEPAVRAE's general secretary, Nelson Palomino, is in prison. FEPAVRAE and two other federations comprising Uchiza and Tocache (San Martín), Tingo María (Huánuco), and Aguaytía-Padre Abad Provinces are trying to secure his unconditional release. These organizations have harassed, attacked, and wounded personnel from CORAH and the national police. They have blocked highways, called strikes, and expelled the UN's CARE-Peru. They were responsible for the 2003 march on Lima.

The Peruvian government does not want to clash head-on with organizations of coca producers made up of thousands of farmers and their families. Not only are they organized, but in many cases, armed; it was they who formed patrols to fight off Sendero Luminoso. A clash over forced eradication could lead to an explosive situation, with the state not only alienating a significant part of the farming population but generating permanent instability in the region adjacent to the armed conflict. Clashes could spark involvement from the Colombian FARC, Bolivian coca-growing organizations, Peru's far-left Patria Roja, and fascist-like groups such as the Humala brothers' Etno-Caceristas who travel throughout Peru with uniformed thugs and discharged members of the military, selling the newspaper *Ollanta* and defending coca cultivation. Ollanta Humala's emergence as a nationalist-populist presidential candidate in 2006—after Evo Morales, leader of Bolivia's coca growers union, was elected as Bolivia's first indigenous president—further complicated Peruvian government policy and its relations with the United States. Humala campaigned in the Ayacucho and Cusco regions amongst coca growers, promising an end to foreign military (read: U.S.) involvement in the drug war—though he indicated he would be willing to receive economic and financial assistance from the United States if elected president.

To avoid an uprising the government has adopted a "gradual and concerted" policy on eradication. The process is necessarily deliberate because it involves negotiating with the farmers. Communities are contacted, a letter of invitation to gather information is signed, lands are measured and geo-referenced, a workshop is held with the farmers to identify and prioritize the two community projects that will be carried out, a communal agreement to reduce coca planting is signed upon approval by 80 percent of the community, and finally, reduction begins in two hundred days.[32] Meanwhile Colombian eradication successes increase the pressure from the U.S. Congress for Peru to adopt a similar policy. The difference is that Colombia destroys coca plants by fumigating them with chemical substances that Peru has banned in order to protect Amazonian ecology. Moreover, Colombia is in the throes of a civil war, while Peru is not. Peru has endured seventeen years of terrorism and was doing everything possible not to touch off a new cycle of social violence that could spin out of control as the country approached presidential elections in April 2006.

The Peruvian government is fighting to keep the coca-growing region from destabilizing. This is plain to the U.S. Department of State, which pointed out in the "2002 Report on International Strategy to Control Drugs" that the Peruvian government was "reluctant to eradicate in areas where confrontation with coca growers might occur."[33] Yet the United States, which did not support aerial interdiction and provided little assistance for gradual, concerted eradication, continued to push for forced eradication and poured most of its funding into Peru's Secretary of the Interior for eradication of this type. Eight UH-2H helicopters were delivered to the police in February 2004; eight more were scheduled for delivery at the end of 2004 and another eight in 2005, making a total of twenty-four helicopters. The police already had sixteen UH-1H helicopters. These helicopters were carrying out forced eradication operations in Masisea (two) and Monzón (eight). Monzón is a valley that had no police posts for several years.

The conflict between the coca farmers and the Peruvian State began to intensify in 2000. Resistance to eradication by the coca growers forced both the Fujimori and transition governments into negotiations at a *mesa de diálogo* (an ad hoc "dialogue table" between the government and growers). A Supreme Decree was issued in 2001 giving the *mesa de diálogo* status. As a result of the resistance CORAH restricted access to certain areas of the Alto Huallaga and Huallaga Central. CORAH cannot access, without compromising the safety of its personnel, large areas of coca cultivation, including the Valle de Monzón, Aguaytía, and the Valle del Río Apurímac-Ene, where resistance from organized coca farmers is extremely intense. A crisis erupted in Aguaytía in February 2003 when the Federico Basadre highway was closed, barely one month after a crisis with Bolivian coca growers began in Chapare. This brought eradication to a standstill. The coca farmers marched on Lima in April 2003. The pressure of 3,200 growers in the public square in front of the Palacio de Justicia gave rise to the concept of "gradual, concerted" eradication.[34] Finally, in February 2004, the Confederacion Nacional de Productores Agropecuarios de las Cuencas Cocaleras del Perú (CONPACCP), along with the AAAPHCPA (coca growers from Ene-Apurímac, Alto Huallaga and Federación de Productores Agropecuarios del Valle del Río Apurímac-Ene [FEPAVRAE], AAAPHCAH

Ucayali), marched on Lima again, where they held the Second National Congress of Peruvian Coca Growers.[35] They organized marches over several weeks even as the Ministry of the Interior warned there was a coordinated maneuver underfoot involving Bolivian and Colombian coca growers that aimed to first destabilize, then bring down the government. Obviously this has not transpired, but it is eminently clear that Peru's coca growers are one pressure group that can force the government to the negotiations table.

In 2004 it became clear, however, that the coca cultivators' organizations were divided and in conflict with each other. But this was not necessarily good news, since these divisions brought the appearance of extremely radical groups opposed to any dialogue at all with the government. On the one hand there were Nancy Obregón and Elsa Malpartida of CONPACCP who represented the moderate position—"concerted" or agreed upon eradication but opposition to forced eradication; Iburcio Morales, on the other hand, represented the Monzón coca cultivators opposed to all dialogue with the government. (The hymn of the Monzón *cocaleros* resonates: "Oh beloved mother earth, in your breast flowers coca, blessing the humble and cursing the bourgeoisie" / "*Oh tierra madre querida, en tu seno florece la coca bendiciendo a los mas humildes y maldiciendo a la burguesía.*")

At the end of 2004 and the beginning of 2005 relations between the government and the *cocaleros* deteriorated further. In response to eradication campaigns carried out by DIRANDRO (Dirección Anti-Drogas de la Policía) and the DEA in the province of Carabaya, a strike and social movement initiated by approximately one thousand *cocaleros* seized the hydroelectric station at San Gabán, and left three dead and nine wounded. Damage to the plant was estimated at more than one million dollars. A mob attacked the police station at Shuana.

The attack on the power station forced the government to negotiate with the *cocaleros*. Yet, in mid-April the government initiated a large-scale eradication operation in Tocache Province in the Department of San Martín. Police helicopters were met with gunfire; damage to the craft forced suspension of the operations. When operations resumed in June, protests by the *cocaleros* closed roads and shut down commerce in the region, affecting also the tourist trade and the normal provisioning of the area. Under these conditions, regional politicians began to see how they could take advantage of the situation to their own benefit and to that of their clientele.

Politicians and *Cocaleros*

Peru has recently embarked on a process of "regionalization"—a dream since the decade of the 1970s, if not before. Finally, this process is under way, but perhaps not at the most propitious moment. The centrifugal forces that are operating in the country threaten it with the sort of division, if not disintegration, that is currently affecting Ecuador and Bolivia (see chapters 4 and 5 in this volume). Recently, elected regional presidents have sought to consolidate support from their constituents and create a more permanent popular base; in the coca regions this means serious pressure to legalize coca cultivation. On June 21, 2005, Carlos Cuaresma, president of the Cuzco region (which produces 25 percent of the country's coca), signed a decree that declared the coca leaf part of the natural, biological, cultural, historical, and botanical patrimony of the region, integrated into the culture and cosmovision of the Andean world. He proclaimed freedom to cultivate coca in the La Convención, Yanatile, and Kosñipata Valleys. While these valleys are already part of Peru in which specified quantities of legal production of coca are purchased by the National Coca Company (Empresa Nacional de la Coca, ENACO) for industrial and traditional use, of the 12,700 hectares of coca in these valleys, only 10,000 are legal. Outright legalization of all coca cultivation would exempt these valleys from eradication operations.

A month later, on July 20, 2005, the Cuzco example was followed by the regional president of Huánuco, who also declared coca cultivation legal within his regional jurisdiction. The same thing was about to occur in the Puno region in mid-July, but since the regional president, David Jiménez, was a fugitive from justice, his interim replacement did not feel authorized to make this decision official.

In response to these decisions regarding the legalization of coca cultivation in two important regions, the president of the Council of Ministers asked the Constitutional Tribunal to declare the measures in Cuzco and Huánuco unconstitutional. On August 1, the Cuzco regional government, whose president, Carlos Cuaresma, is a member of FIM (Frente Independiente Moralizador), a political party allied with the government of President Toledo, sought to amend the regional regulation so that the "legal" coca cultivation could not exceed the limits established by national legislation and would apply only to those cultivators properly registered with the government. This would solve the impasse between the Toledo government and Cuzco, but not that with Huánuco.

It is not without consequence, however, that the president of FIM, a principal ally of the government, defended the ordinance legalizing coca cultivation and demanded the resignation of Nils Ericsson, president of DEVIDA, the principal government drug control agency. This implies that the *cocaleros* not only can force the government to the negotiation table, as with the protests and power station incidents in 2004 and 2005, but that they have become a significant electoral base for politicians in the newly "regionalized" political system.

One more point must be added. The country would not be required to suffer these complicated and difficult relations with the *cocaleros* if an effective aerial and maritime interdiction strategy were in place. And this difficulty comes on top of an extremely complicated relationship between the peasant population and mining concessionaires, with repeated road blockages and peasant protests over agrarian issues, and the increasing number of confrontations of social movements with government authorities across the country. At the same time, extremist political organizations of the Left, such as Patria Roja, and of the Right, such as the Movimiento Etnocacerista,[36] led by the ethno-nationalist Humala family (with military contacts), prod the people to oppose the government and resist its policies. Meanwhile, the Colombian FARC offers support to Patria Roja and some workers' organizations to provoke disorder.

Two obvious questions emerge: Why does Perú find itself in a relationship of almost absolute dependency on the United States where drug trafficking is concerned? Why doesn't it handle and pay for aerial and maritime interdiction on its own, as Brazil is currently doing? There are several issues here. For a start, Peru already contributes $267,537,579 (US) to the war on drugs[37] (see table 6.1). Second, Peru is a state that has only limited resources for all sectors, including education, health, and agriculture. Its capacity to fund interdiction, therefore, is also limited. Third, the costs for interdiction are picked up by the air force, or more accurately, the Department of Defense; that budget has been slashed by a government whose new ideas on balancing the budget simply do not make allowances for defense spending. Indeed, almost all the air force's aircraft have been grounded for lack of maintenance. And lastly, making those aircraft operative would upset the fiscal balance. In a January 18, 2002,[38] Letter of Intent signed with the International Monetary Fund, Peru made a commitment to hold the deficit to 1.9 percent in 2002 and 1.4 percent in 2003. Negotiations are currently under way for signing a new Letter of Intent that sets the deficit at 1.4 percent for 2004 and 1.0 percent for 2005 and 2006. The 2003 deficit came in at 1.7 percent, which did not leave much of a margin to invest in operationalizing aircraft for the war on drugs.

The current situation can be summed up this way: the U.S. government is pressuring Peru to wipe out the coca fields but will not allow it to employ aerial interdiction, the one method that will avert confrontation with the coca growers. The Peruvian government's approach, "gradual and concerted," is considered too slow, as it requires negotiating community-by-community before eradication can proceed, conflict-free. The country is headed toward a situation where it will either be unable to meet eradication goals or, in striving to meet them, will touch off further conflict with the coca growers. That threatened to increase the instability of Toledo's administration even further as the country looked toward elections in April 2006. It will also put in question the stability of any government that comes to power after Toledo in 2006.

The situation could get even more complicated should Peruvian, Bolivian, and Colombian coca growers, who are already coordinating with one another, organize a regional alliance in opposition to eradication. Alternatively, there will be a showdown between the Peruvian government and the American government over the impossibility of achieving 100 percent coca eradication without generating unwanted social conflict.

The Most Recent Clashes: The Rome Protocol and the G-21

U.S. opposition to the interception of planes trafficking drugs is not the only strange thing going on in this mixed-up world of ours. Opposition to the International Criminal Court is another, and one of the most transcendent. During the 1980s and 1990s, when Peru was fighting Sendero Luminoso with no help from the outside, pressure was coming out of Washington to uphold human rights in the war against the insurgents. The pressure was successful; Peru adopted a human rights defense policy at the end of the 1990s. In the aftermath of war crimes committed by Slobodan Milosevic under his policy of "ethnic cleansing" during the 1990s, and the genocide of Tutsi populations by Jean Kambanda in Rwanda in 1994, the United States pushed for creation of an International Criminal Court to prosecute criminal human rights violators. An agreement was reached and Peru, consistent with its new policy protecting human rights, signed the Rome Protocol institutionalizing the court's creation, together with dozens of other countries.

Following the invasion of Afghanistan, and with planning of the invasion of Iraq already in the works, Washington reversed its position completely. It was feared U.S. soldiers could be accused of human rights violations and become vulnerable to prosecution because the Rome Protocol obliges signatories to take those accused of violations before the court. In October 2002 the Peruvian government received the clear message that because it was a signatory to the Rome Protocol, it was expected to enter into a bilateral agreement with the United States stipulating not to turn representatives of the American government over to the International Criminal Court. Should it refuse, the United States would cut off all military assistance to Peru without notice. Peru tried out a number of intermediate positions, even one allowing all U.S. military personnel to enter the country with diplomatic status, thereby making them immune to arrest by Peruvian authorities, but Washington refused to accept anything less than a formal bilateral agreement. Peru refused to sign, as a matter of principle and to save face in the eyes of world opinion. The Peruvian position ultimately prevailed. The United States has not yet cut off military assistance, but it has been frozen at the current level, and the granting of any new assistance is subject to signature of the agreement.

On another front, the Fifth Ministerial Conference of the World Trade Organization was held in Cancun, Mexico, from September 10 to 14, 2003. After years of negotiations between developed and developing countries to achieve better terms of trade for the latter, Cancun was a letdown for everyone. A group of developing countries then decided to coordinate trade policies in order to put collective pressure on the developed countries. Peru and a number of other Latin American countries were among them. Once again, U.S. pressure was not long in coming. A simple visit by a Washington official was enough to make Peru drop out of the G-21. This occurred despite the fact that one of the G-21's most visible leaders was Brazil, with whom Peru had signed a strategic alliance a month earlier.[39]

Ancient History

Clashes between Lima and Washington are nothing new. They date back to the 1960s and the conflict over the 200-mile limit demanded jointly by Peru, Chile, and Ecuador that led to the capture of U.S. fishing boats by the Peruvian navy. They date back to the 1940s and an old grudge over unpaid taxes between Peru and the International Petroleum Company, a Canadian subsidiary of Standard Oil of New Jersey. They go back to the military junta under Juan Velasco Alvarado (1968–1975) that expropriated the aforementioned oil company, established relations with socialist countries, and acquired Soviet arms. They go back to the fight against Maoist terrorist group Sendero Luminoso, a fight Peruvian authorities expected Washington to support, but significant assistance never materialized because the end of the Cold War was near. The only thing the governments that fought Sendero got from the United States were accusations of human rights violations. The clashes, clearly, are nothing new.

Whither Peru–U.S. Security Relations?

1. U.S. policy toward Peru in recent years has been characterized by a lack of consistency, as illustrated by U.S. positions on Sendero Luminoso and counternarcotics and human rights policies.

2. Peru has a policy of maintaining good relations with the United States; this is still stipulated in its official defense policy. However, being a friend to the United States is no easy task because Washington's policies are inconsistent and sometimes contradictory, and the United States often resorts to open pressure, as it has in the cases of counternarcotics policy, the Rome Protocol, and the G-21.

3. The United States puts concerns regarding its own domestic legal and political issues above winning the war on illegal drug trafficking and above good relations with an ally like Peru. If it had maintained its policy on aerial interception and accepted the risk associated with mistakenly downing another aircraft (there was only one such incident in ten years), there would be much fewer illegal coca crops growing in Peru and the Peruvian government would not be in conflict with the coca growers. The United States now claims that most drugs do not leave Peru by air, which is a half-truth. Drugs leave from wherever there is no surveillance; presently there is no effective aerial or maritime surveillance of drugs leaving Peru. In any case, the United States has not made significant efforts to provide Peru with maritime interdiction capabilities, though no legal bar exists to prevent this from taking place.

4. Concerns over domestic legal issues are also more important to the United States than the potentially destabilizing consequences forced eradication could bring to a weak democratic government facing organized, armed groups of coca growers.

5. The American government's message that it will pressure countries not to utilize U.S.-supplied military resources, for example, by halting aerial drug-traffic interdictions in Peru and pressuring Brazil not to employ SIVAM in interception operations, so as to escape domestic legal entanglement, encourages nations to look, instead of to the United States, to Western Europe, Russia, and even China for military material support.

6. Recent periodic demonstrations of U.S pressure have generated anti-American sentiments among the population. The progress Washington made during the 1990s toward creating an image of the United States as a protector of human rights and democracy may be eroding, giving way to the old "ugly American" image of the 1960s and 1970s.

Finally, U.S. policy has undermined consolidation of democracy in Peru by eroding support for the country's elected president, stressing civilian–military–police relations, and making heroes of populist leaders and movements supporting coca producers and the related drug industry. U.S. domestic political concerns, translated into contradictory and perverse policies toward Peru, have left Peruvian democracy at risk and undermined efforts to promote socioeconomic development.

7

Brazil, Andean Security, and U.S. Regional Security Policy

Monica Herz

B RAZIL IS THE INEVITABLE but silent actor in the Colombian crisis. As the
most powerful country in South America, sharing a long (1,645 kilometers) and porous border with Colombia, it faces both the consequences of the
war itself and of the policies of the U.S. government. The policy of choice of
the Brazilian governments during the last two decades has been one of denial
of the gravity of the crisis and reactive criticism of U.S. intervention.

In this chapter I shall argue that, although the Brazilian state has systematically abstained from playing an active role in trying to solve the most prominent security crisis in the Americas, there are objective and subjective conditions that favor greater involvement of the Brazilian state and wider
cooperation with neighboring countries at the present time. These conditions
will only lead to a change in policy if international and regional arrangements
permit and if the Brazilian state can dispose of the needed resources to fully
engage in diplomatic, military, and economic efforts to deal with this multidimensional crisis. Fundamentally, U.S. policy toward the region undermines
the prospects for greater Brazilian involvement, establishing a model for regional cooperation that is not acceptable to the Brazilian ruling elite.

The international cultural environment in which national security policies
are embedded is constituted by security regimes, world political culture, and
international patterns of amity and enmity.[1] This environment has changed
significantly both in the region and the world, and the Brazilian security policies, being embedded in this environment, also were altered, through a
process of adaptation and reaction. The domestic cultural environment underwent impressive changes as well, most notably the democratization of

Brazilian politics and globalization in both the economic and cultural dimensions. Any effort to understand Brazilian security policies regarding the Andean region and the impact of U.S. regional security policies since 1990 in Brazil must take this broader context into account.

The social construction of the idea of security involves defining threats and specifying referent objects, that is, what is being secured. As Ronnie Lipschutz puts it, "Policymakers define security on the basis of a set of assumptions regarding vital interests, plausible enemies, and possible scenarios, all of which grow, to a not-insignificant extent, out of the specific historical and social context of a particular country and some understanding of what is 'out there.'"[2]

In the post–Cold War environment, the Brazilian perspective on security has been changing in the process of interaction with other actors. The most obvious revisions of the country's security policy since the 1980s are a result of the new context of its relationship with Argentina and the priority given to new aspects of regional security, such as drug trafficking and the control over the Amazon Basin. On the other hand, the elected governments have sought a new international strategy of "inclusion," which includes the acceptance of international regimes, the incorporation of the hegemonic values of liberal democracy, the growing participation in UN operations, and the incorporation of the tenets of cooperative security in the regional sphere.

The prospect for a wider engagement in Andean security issues will be analyzed, taking into account the change in the concept of security itself, which I suggest has been both internationalized and extended; relations between Brazil and the regional hegemon, the United States; the inevitable spillover effect of the Andean crisis; the links between Andean and Amazonian security; and the presence of ideas and interests regarding Brazilian regional leadership.

A number of factors stand out as serious impediments to greater engagement in hemispheric security management and the production of the domestic security plan that matches it: economic difficulties, particularistic interests of sectors of the state apparatus, the defensive posture regarding the concept of state sovereignty, the choices made by other regional actors, and the lack of institutional arrangements adapted to the new security environment.

The Concept of Security in Post–Cold War International Politics

The features of international politics that conditioned and oriented security policies and practices during the Cold War have, for the most part, changed. Apart from the demise of the bipolar strategic structure, we are faced with increasing intrastate violence and growing activism of nonstate actors. It has been acknowledged that there is a growing complexity in the security environment stemming from an array of "new" potential threats, often defined as "threats to security," such as environmental degradation, illicit drugs, unregulated movement of large amounts of capital and people, epidemic diseases, terrorism, human right abuses, and failing or failed states. These problems overlap to some extent with traditional concerns, such as the spread of both conventional and nuclear weapons or acts of territorial invasion and plunder. The growing interdependence among societies has reached the security dimension, though we must acknowledge that frontiers are less porous in this sphere. This is apparent in the discussions on the menace posed by nuclear, chemical, and biological weapons; the flow of refugees from domestic conflicts, terrorism, and transnational crime; environmental crises; and violations of human rights.

The "interaction capacity," that is, the flow of goods and information, has gained speed and range. At the same time, the growing web of international norms that constitute international society, in Hedley Bull's terms,[3] significantly limits the autonomy of most states in the security sphere, as well as in other dimensions of international coexistence. In the case of the main capitalist countries, we can perceive the formation of a security community in the sense that none of them is faced with the military threat from others. Furthermore, military industries are somewhat more integrated and less exclusively national.[4]

It is possible to depict the academic debate and the flow of transformations in the security sphere in terms of the internationalization and the expansion of the concept of security. The aspects of the debate of the redefinition of security that express a process of "internationalization" of the concept are the role played by collective security, the new scope of interventionism, and the growing web of international norms.

Interventionism[5] and the discussion of the new nature of the collective security system are at the center of the debate on security today. Although nonintervention is still a core value of the international society, commitment to this value is eroding rapidly. Human rights and humanitarian crises, nuclear nonproliferation, environmental protection, and terrorism are some of the issues that have been used to justify interventionism in the present context. Another important aspect of the internationalization of security is the growing web of norms that frame the use of force. The major international instruments on disarmament, from the 1925 protocol for the prohibition of the use in war of asphyxiating, poisonous, or other gases and of bacteriological methods of warfare to the 1997 convention on the prohibition of the use, stockpiling, production, and transfer of antipersonnel mines (Ottawa Convention), represent a move away from the lack of governance in this sphere—notwithstanding the unilateralist tendencies of the United States from the late 1990s. Security regimes, as systems of principles, norms, rules, and procedures regulating certain areas of security relationships between states, generate "islands" of co-operative security.[6]

Since the 1970s, the extension of the concept of security has been on the agenda of political leaders, having been discussed in several international commissions headed by Willy Brandt, Olf Palme, Gro Harlem Brundtland, and Julius Nyrere.[7] During the first decade, the relevance of including economic issues was stressed, while during the 1980s, environmental issues were incorporated in this effort in reconceptualization. Richard Ullman[8] called for the broadening of the concept of security as early as 1983, although the second cold war did not provide a favorable political climate for the idea that the degradation of quality of life threatens national security, particularly in the United States. But in the 1990s, this theme was pervasive in political and academic debates.

The incorporation of economic, social, and environmental issues to the security agenda stems, on the one hand, from the violent conflicts and major disruptions to normalcy that may result from the dispute over resources, while on the other hand, from a conceptual redefinition of threats to life and the "acknowledgement that threat and response are no longer within the sole or even primary purview of the military."[9] Epidemics, global warming, environmental pollution, energy supply, and demographic growth are some of the issues that have been "securitized."[10] Since 2001, terrorism has given renewed strength to the move toward the expansion of the concept of security.

The Internationalization of the Concept of Security in Brazil

The internationalization of the concept of security has been incorporated into the Brazilian ruling elite's political culture, given the limits established by a legalist tradition. Brazil signed the Nonproliferation Treaty, decided to become a full member of the Treaty of Tlateloco, accepted full-scope safeguards on its nuclear installations, and adhered to both the Missile Control Technology Regime and the Nuclear Suppliers Group. Moreover, the 1988 Brazilian constitution prohibits the development of nuclear technology for nonpeaceful purposes. The support for a collective security system is expressed in the country's active participation in UN peace operations.[11] The difficulty in establishing a clear distinction between international and national security has slowly been included in the national debate on security. Accordingly, issues such as drug traffic, terrorism, money laundering, and arms smuggling are not viewed exclusively in terms of internal or external threats.

A legalist and traditional interpretation of sovereignty has limited acceptance of the concept of internationalization of security in Brazil. As a nonpermanent member of the Security Council, the country has not been supportive of the resolutions that involve the UN in coercive interventions. Indeed, the strategic orientation included in both the 1996 and the 2005 "National Defense Policies" stresses the search for peaceful solutions to disputes and the use of force only as a means of self-defense. Brazilian representatives and diplomats favor resolutions based on Chapter VI of the charter and view with concern the move toward Chapter VII resolutions. Significantly, the Brazilian government abstained from sending troops to the Persian Gulf War in 1991 and has not supported the American and British drive for war in Iraq since 2002. As stated by Ronaldo Sardenberg, then and now again the Brazilian representative at the UN, in the context of a Security Council debate on Somalia, "It has been rightly pointed out that the United Nations cannot impose peace in Somalia or anywhere else if the parties involved are not willing to make peace themselves."[12]

This reaction can be understood in terms of the protective attitude toward the flexibilization of the concept of sovereignty and the defense of universalistic principles. The defense of the principles of a lawful international society based on universal principles and the support for the role of reason and mediation has influenced the diplomatic establishment since the beginning of the twentieth century when the new republican government set up the institutional framework for foreign policymaking.[13] Furthermore, the preference for diplomacy and legality is seen as a mechanism for exercising influence in the international system by a medium power such as Brazil. This was particularly clear in the 1990s, in the context of the generation of a concert of great powers, based on a growing consensus on human rights, democracy, collective security, free market, and sustainable development.[14]

Interventionism, whether bilateral or multilateral, in matters such as human rights, ecology, drug traffic, and terrorism encounters fierce antagonism, particularly in the military establishment. In 1989, for example, when Brazil presided over the Security Council, the Brazilian delegation opposed the proposal of the United Kingdom to include problems concerning drug trafficking in the council's agenda. The Brazilian representative objected on the grounds that this would extend the jurisdiction of the council and touch upon sensitive issues regarding intervention.[15]

The extended view of security has been largely incorporated by the ruling elite. The securitization of social development has been added to the securitization of economic development, a trend that can be detected as early as the 1950s. The systematic presence of the state in all parts of the national territory is a core objective. Spatial and social marginalization are presented as "existential threats." Despite the track record of President Cardoso's government in the social sphere, his foreign minister stated in 1996, "It has become evident that social development is the condition for economic development and constitutes the first line of national defense and of maintenance of sovereignty."[16] The 1996 document on defense policy clearly articulates the security of the state to the welfare of society, development, and democracy. The creation of the Office for Food Security at the time and the establishment of the fight against hunger as a national and international banner by the government of Luis Inacio da Silva (Lula) are examples of this trend.

Furthermore the position expressed by the former minister of defense, Geraldo Magela da Cruz Quintão, in August 2002, indicates that the concern with "new threats" had become part of the official view of security priorities:

> The probability of inter state war with neighboring countries is low as South America lives a period of greater integration and consolidation of regional peace. . . . On the other hand, the emergence of non-orthodox threats, such as terrorism, organized crime, narcotraffic and internal instability, as well as the presence of a growing number of transnational actors make the analysis more complex. Such aspects, associated with the revolution in information, that allow the flux of data and capital, without efficient control by the government, expose countries with economies in a phase of consolidation, such as ours, to great risks.[17]

The ongoing debate on the reorganization of the state and in particular of the security apparatus expresses a tendency toward a more integrated view of the threats to the state. The threat posed by drug trafficking is at the center of this debate, thus in 1998, the government created the National Antidrug Secretariat for coordinating counternarcotics activities nationwide. The redefinition of the role of the military in particular can be understood in the context of the expanded view of security.

Since the end of the Cold War, a search for the redefinition of the role of the armed forces has been taking place in Brazil. This debate has faced both the international debate on security mentioned above and the specific project delineated by the American government for Latin American armies in the post–Cold War environment, apart from the domestic discussion on the reorganization of the armed forces.

In line with the focus on drug trafficking in the definition of security threats by the United States, its own armed forces became heavily involved in counternarcotics activities in the 1990s. George H. W. Bush transferred the task to the armed forces in 1989, the Department of Defense having become a "lead agency" in the war on drugs.[18] In 1989, the Department of Defense became the leading agency in drug interdiction abroad, and in 1991, legislation authorized the Pentagon to use its funds to train military and police forces, as well as to transfer equipment, in the context of the war on drugs.[19]

In this context, pressure has been exerted on the Latin American governments to further engage their armed forces in interdiction of drug traffickers and eradication operations.[20] Relations between Latin American and U.S. militaries have intensified as a result of the war on drugs.[21] In addition, since 1999, greater emphasis has been given to assistance to regional armies, not police forces, in the context of the war on drugs.[22]

The pressure exerted by the United States for a greater involvement of the armed forces in internal missions or police missions,[23] although resisted by the armed forces, has been generating some changes. In fact, during President Fernando Henrique Cardoso's tenure the army was increasingly involved in internal tasks, of which Operation Rio[24] was the most notorious. President Cardoso established guidelines for the armed forces to support the fight against drug-trafficking organizations, in line with Article 142 of the Brazilian constitution that allows for the armed forces to guarantee law and order.

The Brazilian armed forces have not accepted this new task easily, fearing subordination to the regional hegemon should the classic role of external defense be marginalized.[25] The incentive for Latin American forces to take part in operations usually under police jurisdiction, in the context of the fight against drug trafficking, contrasts with the traditional self-image of the military as guarantors of national territorial integrity. The discussion on the new role of the armed forces in the Third World and in the Western Hemisphere in particular puts the deterrent role of the Brazilian armed forced in question.[26] A related problem that is yet to be tackled is the dispute between the Federal Police and military units over responsibility for counternarcotics operations.

One central question relevant to the consolidation of democratic regimes is civil–military relations. The change of the U.S. posture regarding the traditional autonomy of the military in Latin American societies can be observed as early as the late 1980s. Even the curriculum of training institutions for Latin American officers was modified: new themes such as the functioning of democratic regimes and respect for human rights having been included. The U.S. government stimulated strengthening (or formation, where they did not exist) of ministries of defense throughout the hemisphere. In the domestic sphere, the debate on human rights continued, and legislation was passed that prohibits U.S. military aid to units that violate human rights with impunity. (The Leahy Amendment, in section 570 of H.R. 2159 (1997), provided, "None of the funds made available by this Act may be provided to any unit of the security forces of a foreign country if the Secretary of State has credible evidence that such unit has committed gross violations of human rights, unless the Secretary determines and reports to the Committees on Appropriations that the government of such country is taking effective measures to bring the responsible members of the security forces unit to justice.")

The creation of the Ministry of Defense in Brazil was part of the process of subordination of the military apparatus to civilian authority and was in line with the trend, in the hemisphere—strongly supported by the United States. The first move in this direction was the creation of the Secretary for Strategic Affairs, directly subordinated to the presidency during Fernando Collor de Mello's administration, and the project was taken on by President Fernando Henrique Cardoso, the ministry having been established in 1999. Nevertheless, real subordination of the three armed forces to the ministry has not taken place, generating lack of coordination and ongoing budgetary disputes. The national debate on defense policy is only in its infancy. Corporate interests related to special prerogatives of the military and even local interests where the forces are stationed have impeded progress in this area. In addition, most political representatives and academics have shown little interest in the subject, but this scenario is slowly changing.

In summary, then, the incorporation of an extended concept of security took place in an environment, post-1989, in which the definition of the role of the armed forces faced internal and external pressure and has not yet found a clear path ahead. A growing number of Brazilians are increasingly conscious of the transnational nature of security problems. In general, appreciation of the links between domestic and international issues appears to be growing. This process is a direct result of the crisis in public order and the growing levels of violence related to the illegal drug trade, thus linking Brazilian security policies to hemispheric and regional (Andean and South American) security concerns.

Brazil is not a large-scale drug producer; it is, however, an important producer of precursor chemicals. The country is a major transit area for drugs shipped to the United States and Europe, and the domestic drug problem is huge and growing. The highly developed financial network makes the country vulnerable to money-laundering activity. Since the consumption, production, and trafficking of drugs in Brazil has been rising in recent years, drugs are increasingly seen as the fuel for the country's urban violence. In addition, Brazilian traffickers benefit from the country's large chemical industry, which can provide drug-processing chemicals.

In 2001, members of Brazilian criminal organizations were captured in Colombia; this event generated extensive media coverage. A congressional investigation has demonstrated the connection between Brazilian narco-traffickers and the FARC (Fuerzas Armadas Revolucionarias de Colombia) and the existence of a drug and arms trade directly involving Brazilian citizens.[27] Moreover, there have been reports of the presence of Colombian guerrillas in the slums of Rio de Janeiro. Recent research on the positions of the "Brazilian foreign policy community" shows that the third most important international threat to the country, according to this group, is international drug trafficking (52 percent), after commercial protectionism and economic and technological inequality.[28]

The Brazilian state is slowly responding to this important shift in perception. For example, the previous government sponsored development of Mutual Assistance Accords on Penal Matters, based on the Palermo Convention model,[29] the Ministry of Justice and Foreign Relation having worked together on this matter. On the other hand, the growing public perception of the transnational nature of the threat that affects the everyday life of citizens generates pressure from civil society for greater action on the part of the state. Voices emanating from social movements, political parties, and the church and the impact of this issue on the representative system have led to a growing public debate that has yet to generate significant results.

Relations with the Regional Hegemon

The special relation between Brazil and the United States that characterized the post–World War II period changed after the mid-1970s in the context of the diversification of economic relations, the search for new suppliers of assistance and material and weapons systems, the development of projects for defense-related industries, and a more independent foreign policy. Henceforth several contentious issues would mark the bilateral agenda, such as trade issues, nuclear nonproliferation, environmental protection, human rights violations, delimitation of territorial waters, access to sensitive technologies, and intellectual property regulations. In fact, the special alliance between the United States and Brazil endured only until the early 1960s. After this period, the United States was no longer the focal point for Brazilian foreign policy.

Brazilian redefinition of the concept of security since the 1970s involved a process of detachment from the inter-American security system. The definition of an arms export policy by the Geisel government in 1974, the nuclear agreement signed in 1975 with Germany, the renunciation of the 1952 military accord with the United States in 1977, and the development of a parallel nuclear program were part of this movement.[30] The 1980s can be depicted as a period marked by the debt crisis and the aggravated nature of disagreements about environmental policies and the need to liberalize the economy, at the same time that a relative rapprochement in military relations was taking place. Since 1982, the creation of working groups has represented a reaffirmation of the military and strategic ties between the United States and Brazil.[31]

The 1990s were characterized by significant changes in the relations between the United States and Latin America. The lack of a clear hemispheric policy, the stress on the universalization of the neoliberal model, and a limited, although emerging, emphasis on multilateral institutions[32] could be observed. After a period dominated by the Central American crisis, the initiatives of the George H. W. Bush administration concentrated on strengthening economic links, the negotiations of the North American Free Trade Area, and the launching of the Initiative for the Americas. The changes that took place were paradigmatic; a coercive and ideological policy was substituted by a perspective that emphasized cooperation, greater investments, and commerce. The two following administrations under the leadership of President Bill Clinton maintained similar objectives. The negotiation of the Treaty for Free Trade of the Americas would be the next step in this process. Until the post–September 11, 2001, "war on terrorism," the U. S. governments concentrated on two strategic issues during the period: the promotion of neoliberal reforms and the war on drugs.

The war against drugs in the Andean region represented a shift toward greater military involvement in the hemisphere.[33] We can observe that the diversification of American military presence is a consistent strategy.[34] Since American troops operate radar systems, monitor the region in the air, supply operational support and intelligence, and train local troops, an area of control on land, air, and through waterways was established in the Andean region, in line with the redefinition of threats mentioned earlier.[35] Hence, although troops have not been sent into battle, or, at least, their participation in combat is not acknowledged publicly, American military presence in the Andes is very significant.

During the 1990s, the negative agenda that had marked U.S.–Brazil relations during the 1970s and 1980s was left aside, and adjustment of policies in the economic, security, human rights, and environmental spheres led to better relations. The decade began with liberal reforms under the aegis of International Monetary Fund (IMF) standards. Fernando Collor de Melo applied economic measures in line with the "Washington Consensus," and Fernando Henrique Cardoso pursued a set of economic reforms according to this same framework. Although the presidency of Itamar Franco (1992–1994) was an exception, the acceptance of international regimes and the neoliberal economic model facilitated the rapprochement between the two countries.

Since the 1990s, considering that the proliferation of weapons of mass destruction (WMD) was one of the main threats posed to the security of the United States, Brazil seemed to be moving in the right direction. The international regimes that generate the principles, norms, and rules in this sphere were respected, and projects for the acquisition of nuclear weapons were abandoned. Moreover, regarding the threat posed by criminal and terrorist organizations the two countries were able to define significant spheres for cooperation. In the wake of the September 11 attacks, Brazil proposed the convening of the Consultative Body of the Inter-American Treaty of Reciprocal Assistance in a gesture of support for the United States of symbolic significance.

The presence of a leftist government in Brazil since 2003 did not change this reality. In spite of the tendency to diversify political and economic ties and a more activist posture regarding several aspects of international politics, the government of Luis Inacio da Silva has maintained a very cordial and smooth relationship with the United States.

Fulfilling the role of regional security administrator, in line with the American view of regional powers, Brazil took partial responsibility for the operation in Haiti. For the first time in the country's history Brazil is leading and providing the largest troop deployment for a UN mission. Furthermore the resolution that created the mission is based on Chapter VII of the UN charter, and President Aristide left power under considerable pressure. Thus a change in policy can be detected, the Brazilian view always having been that peace operations require consent. The motivations that explain this policy change are clearly related to the search for a leading position in the Latin America and the quest for a place in the Security Council as a permanent member, but it suited U.S. interests perfectly.[36]

But, at the same time, important points of tension can be detected. The extension of the immediate zone of influence of the United States toward the Andean region, as is indicated by the distribution of bases, the military accords signed, and the military assistance granted, generated both prospects for cooperation and conflict, as Amazon and Andean security are intertwined.

Brazilian policy choices are far from the automatic alignment of previous periods. As Maria Regina Soares puts it, "Diplomats begin with the premise of U.S. power, especially within the hemisphere, a premise that calls for a non-confrontational strategy. However, in their scenarios for a new world order, they stress multi-polarity and the opportunities it affords for Brazil's international ascent."[37]

In the regional sphere, the convergence and disagreements between the two countries can be most clearly pinpointed. While Brazil accepted the expressions of the norms of the international order in the Americas in terms both of the liberal economic paradigm and of the democratic paradigm, disagreements centered on mechanisms for regional integration and the nature of the process of reform of the inter-American security system. Brazilian policy makers have been reluctant to engage in the debate about the reform of the hemispheric security system or to establish a strategic alliance with the United States, preferring to treat economic, security, and other issues separately. Moreover the inclusion of the Andean region in Washington's immediate zone of influence represents an extra difficulty for the project of integrating MERCOSUL and the Andean countries.

There is significant resistance to a free trade area among several relevant political actors in Brazil, and the divergences regarding the timetable for negotiations and the scope of an agreement have stalled the movement toward greater integration. After the election of Lula, negotiations within South America were prioritized and the debate on the formation of the free trade area of the Americas was marginalized. The project for greater integration in South America is a potential source of tension, particularly in the sphere of energy.

The construction of the American democratic paradigm throughout the 1990s, finally leading to the adoption of the 2001 Democratic Charter, was supported by Brazilian representatives. The Brazilian elite embraced the concept of cooperative security and the confidence-building agenda received wide support. On the other hand, although the debate on the reform of the inter-American security system was stillborn, a clear split regarding the role to be played by the Organization of American States (OAS) can be observed. The OAS is widely viewed with great skepticism, and the prospect of a standing force allocated under the OAS or some other pan-American regional control is not acceptable to the Brazilian decision-making elite. Similarly, the recent move toward a more robust regime for the protection of democracy within the OAS was strongly opposed by the Brazilian government. In June 2005, during the General Assembly of the OAS, Condoleezza Rice proposed the creation of a mechanism to monitor the quality of democracy in Latin America, but the proposal was rejected and withdrawn.

Brazil's involvement in inter-American affairs can become a source of tension as Brazil tends to adhere to multilateral norms and institutions and the United States seeks greater flexibility in its foreign policy. In the case of Venezuela's political crisis under President Hugo Chávez, for example, this became clear. One of the important tests to the Inter-American Democratic Charter emanated from Venezuela when an attempted coup d'état took place in April 2002. There is widespread debate about U.S. indirect involvement in planning the coup. The United States accused Chávez of supporting terrorism in Colombia, Bolivia, and Ecuador after a two-day gathering of the National Security Agency, the Pentagon, and the State Department in November 2001,[38] and contacts between the embassy in Caracas and groups involved in the coup had been reported. In testimony before the Senate Foreign Relations Committee on February 5, Secretary of State Colin Powell expressed concern about democracy in Venezuela and complained about Caracas's response to the war on terrorism; CIA Director George Tenet made remarks in the same vein.[39] Assistant Secretary of State Otto Reich—who served as ambassador to Venezuela during the Reagan administration—seemed to endorse contacts with the opposition to the Venezuelan government. Conversely, the Brazilian government at the time supported the view that the coup d'état breached the OAS's Democratic Charter—and lent support to a negotiated way out of the crisis in accord with the Venezuelan constitution. During the initial phase of the Lula tenure, Brazil was involved in forming the group of friends of the Secretary-General of the OAS facilitating the negotiations between Hugo Chávez and the opposition that finally led to the referendum that allowed the president to remain in power.

While the rationale guiding America's security policy in the hemisphere was traditionally based on the perception of extrahemispheric threats, after the Cold War, threats emanating from the region itself acquired growing relevance. As indicated in the introduction to this book and other chapters on various Andean countries, the issues that mobilized attention in Washington were illegal migrations, drug trafficking, and in general loss of control by the state of the flow of arms, drugs, and people. These issues acquired the status of core threats when the Cold War rationale died out and the hemispheric security agenda was redefined.

As mentioned earlier, the definition of threats by the Brazilian decision-making elite focused on the situation in the Amazon region during the period in question and tended to progressively incorporate the presence of transnational criminal organizations. This generated prospects for cooperation, given the convergence in the definition of threats, but also created conditions for tensions to arise, as the strategies adopted by the two countries differed.

In 1995, a new agreement for cooperation in counternarcotics was signed. The State Department's International Narcotics Control program would work to improve the Brazilian Federal Police's intelligence and investigative capabilities. The U.S. Drug Enforcement Administration (DEA) would cooperate with the Federal Police in several counternarcotics efforts, particularly in training and in information sharing. DEA agents would also teach at the Federal Police School outside Manaus. The George W. Bush administration's Andean Regional Initiative called for Brazil to receive $6 million in counterdrug assistance and $12.6 million in social development funds in 2001. In September 2001, Brazil signed a bilateral letter of agreement with the United States for counternarcotics activities that called for mutual cooperation and U.S. aid for Operation Cobra and other counter–drug-trafficking operations. In March 2001, Brazilian military officers visited the Pentagon where they discussed border security and development programs.[40]

On the other hand, Brazil seeks to maintain autonomy in making policy and in operational matters, seeking cooperation and coordination with the American agencies, but resisting subordination. The tension has practical results, such as the lack of coordination of interdiction efforts between the Brazilian and American agencies as occurs with Bolivia, Colombia, and Peru.

The search for foreign policy autonomy is apparent in the Colombian conflict. The American involvement in the conflict, the presence of combatants across the border, and the effect on regional stability have been the main concerns of the Brazilian government. The transfer of drug laboratories and plantations and the flow of refugees also worry the Brazilian authorities.[41] The transfer of combatants and drug-related activities to Brazil and the ecological consequences of eradication operations[42] are the main themes discussed by members of the government, the military, and within society in general.

The U.S.-supported Plan Colombia generates antagonism across the political spectrum, and there is a strong feeling that it is part of the process of internationalization or/and of incremental U.S. intervention in South America. Brazil has been the plan's loudest South American critic, fearing greater American presence and loss of control over its drug policy. As the United States intensified its efforts to fight drug production in Colombia, Peru, and Bolivia by air detection and interception of suspect aircraft, the Brazilian president issued a directive in 1996 to impede access of nonauthorized flights across Brazil's northwestern border, and the 1992 project for the surveillance of the region became a reality.[43]

The definition of the FARC as a terrorist organization by the U.S. government generates increased concern, given the context in which the war against terrorism has been waged, disregarding international law in general and borders in particular. The activities of this organization within Brazilian territory could justify the presence of the U.S. Army and Colombian forces in "hot pursuit." Thus enhancing the presence of the Brazilian state in the area has acquired new urgency. The Brazilian governments have refused to define the FARC as a terrorist organization, alleging that this would impede a future role for Brazil as a mediator in the conflict.

Regarding the core issue of terrorism, the conjunction of cooperation, acceptance of the American agenda, and tension regarding autonomy for state policy also occurs. The Cardoso administration introduced the terrorist threat to Brazil's international discourse, although on the periphery of the foreign policy agenda. Terrorism has been defined as a crime, and domestic legislation establishes that where terrorism is involved, privacy protections for bank and financial transactions may be removed. In 2001, the Brazilian government signed the Convention for the Suppression of the Financing of Terrorism and issued decrees for enforcing resolutions 1333 (2001) and 1373 (2001) of the United Nations Security Council. In a speech, during the opening debate of the Fifty-Sixth United Nations General Assembly in November 2001, President Cardoso stressed the connection between drug trafficking, arms smuggling, and terrorism.[44] In addition, more attention has been given to the "triple frontier" (Brazil, Paraguay, Argentina), an area where terrorist activity takes place, according to the American government. In this region, police and intelligence activities have been intensified. In 1996, Brazil, Argentina, and Paraguay created the Tripartite Command for the Triple Frontier to coordinate police action and intelligence gathering. Nevertheless, the Brazilian government publicly denies any knowledge of terrorist activity in this region and has not redefined its foreign policy discourse, as have other countries, in terms of the war on terrorism.

Cooperation and contact in the military sphere take place on a continuous basis between Brazil and the United States. Brazilians are trained through the

International Military Education and Training Program (IMET) and Brazil takes part in SOUTHCOM regular multilateral military exercises. Brazilians attend the School of the Americas, the Center for Hemispheric Defense Studies, the Inter-American Air Forces Academy, and other schools offering education, training, and networking possibilities for Latin American military.

The role Brazil should or could play in the Western Hemisphere is the main source of tension between the two countries. On the one hand, the United States expects greater leadership from the Brazilian government, but on the other hand, the level of autonomy and specificity the Brazilian decision-making elite pursues is not generally appreciated by U.S. policy makers. The response from the Brazilian side is to search for protection in the realm of legality, especially traditional notions of sovereignty, and to be cautious regarding more active regional initiatives.

The Brazilian Perspective toward
Regional Security Institutions and the Colombian Crisis

The regional security environment during the Cold War was marked by the terms of the Rio Treaty (Interamerican Defense Treaty—TIAR), the OAS Charter, and bi- and multilateral protocols involving the United States. An explicitly anticommunist collective security system was fostered, linking the East–West conflict with "internal enemies." Modern Latin American geopolitical thought reflects this reality. The regional security institutions were conceptualized based on concern for regional stability dealing with two different sources of threats: interstate conflict and extra-hemispheric interference based on the Cold War conceptual framework.

The Inter-American System was severely hit by its failure to deal with the crisis over the Malvinas/Falklands Islands and by the 1980s Central American crisis. In addition, the United States made unilateral decisions to intervene both in Grenada in 1983 and in Panama in 1989. Greater emphasis placed on ad hoc regional arrangements such as the Contadora Group[45] and Contadora Support Group and later the Rio Group;[46] the Summit of the Americas process, which began in Miami in 1994; the Meeting of Defense Ministers; and the Guarantors of the Peru–Ecuador Treaty marked the most recent period.

The institutions that originally formed the inter-American security system were gradually transformed during the post–Cold War period incorporating the democratic paradigm, the concept of cooperative security, and generating, on the periphery, mechanisms for cooperation in the sphere of the so-called new security agenda. This trend developed in congruence with the move toward greater regional multilateralism by the Bush and Clinton administrations. Thus new forms of cooperation were stimulated. The creation of ad hoc mechanisms and the changes in the OAS during the 1990s reflect this tendency. As Jorge Dominguez notes, although multilateral and unilateral postures coexisted, one can identify a disposition toward regional multilateralism during this period.[47]

Subsequent to the Cold War, one can observe a collective desire to redefine the role of the OAS in the sphere of security in particular. Several resolutions on cooperation in this sphere were passed, two important conventions were signed,[48] and a debate on the redefinition of the concept of hemispheric security was launched. The Hemispheric Security Commission was created in 1991, and the Committee on Hemispheric Security was made a permanent component of the OAS Permanent Council in 1995, with a mandate to review the hemispheric security system.

Regarding one of the most pressing security threats in the region—narco-trafficking—a drive toward greater activism can also be observed. The Inter-American Drug Abuse Control Commission (CICAD, from its initials in Portuguese) was created in 1986 and implemented its first projects in 1988. CICAD has dealt with legislative and preventive measures. Its activities included the dissemination of information, research on drug problems, and forging links with other international organizations such as the UN. In 1992, the OAS General Assembly approved regulations on money laundering and asset forfeiture. In 1993, CICAD launched a project aimed at strengthening the ability of governments to stop the international trade in firearms meant for narcotics traffickers, and in 1996 it was the forum for the negotiation of the Hemisphere Antidrug Strategy. The Multilateral Evaluation Mechanism generated its first round of evaluation for the 1999–2000 period, publicizing information about the state of the drug problem and efforts to overcome the problem in each country and making specific recommendations. The transparency on acquisition of conventional weapons convention (1999) and control of traffic of light arms convention (1997) are closely related.

More cooperation between the hemispheric countries in the antidrug struggle should be expected in the longer term as a result of this process. Nevertheless, enforcement cooperation has been meager and U.S. bilateral supply-side strategies have dominated measures against drug-related crime and the terrorism–drug connection in the region.

In spite of these and other changes to the regional security institutions, they are not capable of dealing with the growing institutional and social crises in many countries of the continent, in particular in the Andean region. Moreover, most Latin American countries opted for a pragmatic foreign policy in the 1990s, focusing on their bilateral arrangements with the United States.

The Brazilian government has incorporated the cooperative security agenda and has supported the gradual inclusion of the new themes into multilateral arrangements, so long as they acquire a functional dimension and do not create norms or legislation seen to impinge on national sovereignty. The Brazilian ruling elite tends to adopt a status quo attitude toward the inter-American system that, in fact, favors its continuous ineffectiveness. The maintenance of a central role for the UN Security Council in the context of multilateral action is stressed,[49] and the transference of collective security functions of the UN to regional organizations, in line with the regionalization of security proposals, generates significant concern.[50] According to the legalist posture adopted by Brazil, the cooperation between regional organizations and the UN should follow the parameters established in Article 53 of the UN Charter.[51]

The Colombian crisis has been largely absent from the regional security institutions and forums. This is a consequence of the meager international involvement in the crisis, of the nature of the hemispheric security system geared toward interstate conflict and the protection of state sovereignty, and of the policy toward the region adopted by the hegemonic power. Colombian foreign policy focused on bilateral cooperation with its neighbors, although it did overcome the international isolation that marked the Samper (1994–1998) administration. A group of "friends of Colombia" was formed, and in December 1999, in the context of the peace process, the UN secretary-general nominated, responding to a request from President Pastrana, the first special adviser for international assistance to Colombia, Jan Egeland (and later, James Lemoyne). The UN good offices were established during the Pastrana presidency, and the newly elected president, Alvaro Uribe (2002), immediately requested an enhanced role for the UN. Thereafter, UN Secretary-General Kofi Annan made the good offices efforts official.

The Brazilian government has not shown any interest in opening the debate on this question in regional forums, accepting the flow of events as they were geared by U.S. and Colombian foreign policies. The call for a Contadora for Colombia did not receive any response.[52] Conversely, the move toward greater UN participation in the Colombian crisis finds support among the Brazilian authorities. In sum the status quo attitude toward regional institutions does not allow the country to contribute toward a creative endeavor that would start to tackle this regional and domestic crisis.

Brazil and Andean Security

In order to understand the Brazilian perspective toward Andean security, two tendencies in the formulation and implementation of the country's foreign policy need to be considered: first, the redefinition of the geopolitical scenario, the main source of threat having shifted from the Southern Cone to the Amazon region. Second, the ambiguity of the country's policies toward South

America, which oscillate between aspiration for regional leadership and a tendency to accept the American designs for the region, whilst assuming a defensive posture regarding its own territorial sovereignty.

Brazil's Oscillating Policy toward South America

After the transition toward democracy and the choice of neoliberal economic policies for insertion in a globalized economy, the concept of a South American region under Brazilian leadership gained favor. The diplomatic discourse substituted the term *Latin America* for *South America* when Fernando Henrique Cardoso was heading the Itamaraty.[53] If Brazil were to position itself on the international stage as a relevant actor, it would have to abandon its relatively distant posture in regional affairs. This objective is most clearly expressed in the country's candidacy for a permanent seat in the UN Security Council and its role in commercial multilateral negotiations. Brazil's policy toward South America must be understood in the context of a building block strategy regarding regional integration. In this context, MERCOSUL could become part of a wider integrationist project.

In August 2000, Brazil sponsored the first meeting of South American presidents in an effort to forge a unified regional front in negotiations with the United States regarding a hemispheric free trade zone. In reality, the South American presidents meet five times every year in the context of multilateral fora—Rio Group (once a year), MERCOSUL summits (twice a year), Iberian-American Summits (once a year), and the Meetings of South America Presidents. In December 1992, Brazil announced the launching of the Amazon Initiative, aiming to negotiate accords for economic complimentarity with the member states of the Treaty for Amazon Cooperation (Bolivia, Ecuador, Colombia, Venezuela, Peru, Suriname, and Guyana). One year later, the project for the creation of a Free Commercial Area of South America was launched, seeking to join the MERCOSUL countries, the Andean Group, and Chile. This project would be shelved in 1994, when Brazil accepted, although reluctantly, the American proposal to initiate negotiations for the creation of the Free Trade Area of the Americas. Fear of isolation in the hemispheric context prevailed at that juncture.

Thus the idea of a South American region, under Brazilian leadership, remained in the shadows, having been launched once again in the context of the 2002 election campaign. The government of Luis Inácio Lula da Silva in the first months of its tenure indicated that Brazilian foreign policy would be geared toward South America. The president has met his counterparts in the region frequently and has tailored a coherent discourse regarding the decision to prioritize the region. The foreign minister, Celso Amorim, has for many years defended a focus on South America. In fact, during his first term in office

(1993–1995), the project for a South American free trade area was launched. On the other hand, the new government did establish domestic security as a central objective, and the institutional fragility of some of its neighbors directly affects domestic security through arms smuggling and drug trafficking activities, apart from the economic interests of private and state companies in several countries.[54]

The Lula government attached renewed relevance to policies that are anchored in the region. Despite the continuing difficulties in building a strategic alliance with Argentina, stronger ties with South American nations have been generated. The South American Community of Nations was created, an accord between MERCOSUL and the Andean Community was signed, and the BNDES (National Bank for Development) has been investing heavily in the regional infrastructure. During the June 2005 MERCOSUL meeting, the Fund for Structural Convergence and Strengthening of the Institutions of MERCOSUL, aiming at development projects in the poorer areas, and a regional strategy for cooperation in the energy sphere were launched. This emphasis should be understood in the context of a foreign policy that stresses the potentialities of south–south cooperation.

Changing Perception of Threat: From Argentina to the Amazon

Historically, the Brazilian ruling elite considered Argentina the greatest external menace to its security. The two nations were at war between 1825 and 1828, having finally signed the Treaty of Montevideo, which recognizes the independence of Uruguay. The creation of a buffer state between the countries did not end the competition for political and military hegemony in the region and for access to Bolivian, Paraguayan, and Uruguayan markets and resources. During the 1960s and the 1970s, the exploration of hydroelectric power fueled the rivalry. Relations with Argentina remained competitive and unfriendly for most of the twentieth century. Nevertheless, force was never used between the two neighbors. Since the southern corner of the country was perceived as a main source of threat, defense policies expressed this reality.

Only during the 1980s did the relation change substantially in the context of redemocratization in both countries and growing contacts between the military establishments. Significantly, since the mid-1980s, an informal system of nuclear inspections has been in place. Finally, in 1991, the two countries signed a trilateral agreement with the International Atomic Energy Agency that puts all nuclear installations in both Brazil and Argentina under the supervision of the IAEA. Between 1985 and 1988, a nuclear regime was built, laying the institutional foundations for verified nuclear nonproliferation in the 1990s. Argentina and Brazil engaged in nuclear confidence-building measures and sought to integrate their national nuclear programs.

A clear shift toward the definition of the Amazon region as the core security problem of the country can be observed since the 1980s. By the end of that decade, the army was modernizing and transferring units from the south to the north. In 1985, the Calha Norte project was launched, aiming to intensify the presence of the Brazilian state in the area, although it never fully reached its objectives. The 1996 "National Defense Policy" mentions that the region is the most important strategic priority for the country, and President Fernando Henrique Cardoso referred to the presence of armed groups and organized crime in the region as he launched the country's defense policy in November of that same year.[55] All three armed forces consider the region a priority. Even the navy, which focuses its attention on the South Atlantic, has plans to enhance its operational capability in the Amazon basin. The military journals in particular treat the region as a central concern.[56]

The vast Amazon region constitutes 61 percent of the country, and its porous borders became a main concern of the ruling elite during the twentieth century. The region's fledgling infrastructure, the relations between local power and the federalist system, and the characteristics of the environment explain the absence of effective state sovereignty in the region.

Several threats are defined by the Brazilian armed forces and civilian security policy makers under the heading of lack of control, such as disrespect for the borders, illegal or predatory economic activities, and even the presence of international nongovernmental organizations (NGOs). Drug trafficking; invasion of the national territory by insurgent movements or the armed forces of neighboring countries fighting against insurgencies; unauthorized mining and minerals trade; logging without proper registration and smuggling of precious wood, gold, and diamonds; capture and trade of bio-assets; small arms trade; and nonstop border crossing by planes carrying illegal cargo take place without control by the state. In a perverse way, one could say the Amazon region has been "internationalized," with transnational and international actors gaining more presence.

The internationalization of the Amazon region has been defined as a threat by important sectors of the Brazilian elite, most importantly the military.[57] Indeed, since the nineteenth century, the perception that foreign powers or agents covet the resources of this vast area has been part of the ruling elite's approach toward the northern portion of the country. The exposure to geopolitical thinking during the twentieth century led to the view that this physical space should be valued in terms of national power. The national security doctrine of the military dictatorship (1964–1985) associated security with development and launched a program to "integrate" the region into the rest of the country. Criticism of the Brazilian government by environmentalists and the debate on the creation of reservations for native Indians fueled this threat perception during the 1980s.[58] After the redemocratization of the country the idea that there was a demographic void was abandoned and the inhabitants of the region were considered legitimate actors. After the 1992 conference, NGOs also became legitimate actors in the debate on the future of the region.

In contrast to the 1980s, when the pressure exerted by NGOs and international organizations was perceived as a threat to national sovereignty in the region, today the role played by transnational crime is increasingly seen as a major threat. The connection between urban violence and the activities of these transnational actors, as mentioned earlier, has been incorporated into the wider debate on the great social problems faced by the country.

The discussions on the United States' new security strategy since the end of the Cold War, concentrating on "new security threats" such as drug trafficking and environmental issues, raised concern among the Brazilian military. The redefinition of the concept of sovereignty and the criteria for intervention by the international community in domestic affairs during the 1990s further emphasized the potential threat of "internationalization of the Amazon region."

Brazilian policy regarding the Colombian strife and conflict in the Andean region more generally is related particularly to doctrine and concern for the impact on the Amazon region. The Brazilian government set up the Amazon Protection System (SIPAM) and Amazon Surveillance System (SIVAM) in 2001 to deal with the perceived threats to this region. They also aimed at answering the criticism of environmental degradation in the region due to unauthorized logging, mining, and other activities. The projects aim to produce information, particularly on biodiversity and illegal activities; generate a strategic and integrated governmental action; stimulate development; and enforce sovereignty. In 1998, a new law was enacted giving the president authority to order the destruction of any aircraft that does not respond to procedures to identify itself or obey air traffic control instructions.[59]

SIVAM consists of the infrastructure of technical and operational resources (sensors of various types such as fixed and mobile radar, stations for gathering environmental, weather, and other data) aimed at collecting, processing, compiling, and providing data that are of interest to the organizations that make up SIPAM (public institutions within the municipal, state, and federal structure, such as universities, agencies for environmental protection and the prevention of illegal activities, among others). It is intended to facilitate rural telecommunications and should aid in tracking aircraft entering the country.

SIPAM consists of organizations whose links are the various federal, state, and municipal agencies that carry out governmental activities in the Amazon region, and its objective is to integrate, evaluate, and provide data needed for the performance of general and coordinated activities in the Amazon region.[60] These are the largest projects ever to be implemented in the region. The main financier was EXIMBANK; this partnership marked a return of support by this U.S. entity to Brazilian projects, interrupted since the external debt moratorium.

The move toward greater integration of the Amazon countries, in line with the ideas on Brazilian leadership in the region mentioned earlier, can also be understood in this light. Brazil has given special attention to the realm of infrastructure, such as initiatives for road and power integration. Within the context of attempting to increase Latin American integration, Brazil has sought to expand and improve cooperation with all Amazon countries. The completion of the surfacing of the Manaus–Boa Vista–Caracas highway and the Brazil–Bolivia gas pipeline are examples of this policy. As mentioned earlier, an accord between the Andean Community and MERCOSUL was negotiated. In 1995, the countries that had originally joined the Amazon Cooperation Treaty in 1978 (Brazil, Bolivia, Colombia, Ecuador, Guyana, Peru, Suriname, and Venezuela) decided to create a permanent secretariat based in Brasilia. In April 2000, at the sixth meeting of Foreign Ministers of the Treaty, President Cardoso validated the treaty as a mechanism for countering illegal activities in the region.[61]

In this context, Plan Cobra (Colombia–Brazil) seeks to reinforce Brazilian military and police forces along its Amazon border with Colombia. The armed forces, the Brazilian Intelligence Agency (ABIN), and the Federal Police take part in this plan. The mission of the regional intelligence center at Tabatinga is to sort through intelligence on border activities that should be shared with Peru, Ecuador, and Colombia. New police installations along the border stretching from Tabatinga to Vila Bittencourt were created. In addition operations Pebra (Peru–Brazil) and Vebra (Venezuela–Brazil) were created in 2003 to combat drug trafficking through the borders with Peru and Venezuela.[62] In May 2005, for example, the air forces of both Colombia and Brazil conducted Operation COBRA I in the Amazon region as a joint test of their drug interdiction capabilities and the detection of drug flights.

When Plan Colombia was announced in 1999, Brazil began bolstering its border security, and several new military installations can now be seen on the bilateral border. Among them are a new air force base, a naval base, and a set of border platoons stretching from Tabatinga through an area known as Dog's Head, where the borders of Colombia, Venezuela, and Brazil meet. A jungle brigade based in the city of Tefe renders support for the troops stationed along the border. The ground forces are complemented with naval and marine units as well as aircraft at the São Gabriel da Cachoeira air base.[63]

Brazil and the Colombian Crisis

Reaffirming the principle of noninterference, the Brazilian government has opposed any direct involvement in the Colombian crisis. In particular, the presence of American troops in Latin America generates concern, the militarization of the Colombian conflict has been widely criticized, and the spread of American bases in the region did not include the Brazilian territory. Although attempts were made to reach an agreement with the United States on the use of the Alcântara Spatial Base in northeastern Brazil, the present government chose not to pursue this option, and signed an agreement on the use of the base with Ukraine. Brazilian officials have stressed that they are not interested, officially, in becoming part of Plan Colombia, although the sharing of information generated by SIVAM is planned. The presence of any multinational military operation in the Brazilian Amazon region is not acceptable to Brazilian officials, and the development of resistance strategies in case of foreign military presence in the area has been under way.

According to research produced by the Instituto de Estudios Socio Econômicos (INESC) in 2002, most Brazilian congresspersons are concerned with the threat posed by Plan Colombia, perceiving it either as a segment of a wider geopolitical objective (63 percent of the ruling coalition and 100 percent of the opposition—since 2003 the ruling coalition) or as an indication of a possible international occupation of the Amazon region.[64] The same research indicates that most members of congress perceive the war in Colombia as a threat to Brazilian sovereignty (58 percent of the ruling coalition and 92 percent of the opposition).

The war in Colombia has a spillover effect in all the border countries and beyond. The Brazilian Amazon region is less vulnerable than some Venezuelan, Ecuadorian, and Peruvian border regions, given the geography of the area and the power of the Brazilian state.[65] Nevertheless, the war has had direct repercussions within Brazilian territory. Since 1991 encounters between FARC fighters and units of the Brazilian army have been taking place. Colombian troops did transit Brazilian territory in the Traíra region (near the village of Bittencourt) in February 1991, and at Iauarete in November 1998, as part of their response to a FARC assault on Mitu (Colombia). This generated tension in bilateral relations, as a landing strip within Brazilian territory was used without authorization from the Brazilian government. Colombia issued a diplomatic note affirming that this would not happen again, and favoring the existing tendency to strengthen border protection.[66] This was one incident when illegal activities did "spill over" to the legal sphere, pointing toward the possibility of further tension in the future. In August 1999, a plane was intercepted loaded with weapons traveling from Suriname to Colombia. In March 2002, an encounter with a FARC unit took place.[67] Refugees fleeing the violence in Colombia cross borders, and guerrilla forces search for safe bases and supply areas in Brazil. Finally, the control by the FARC of areas bordering Brazil is of particular concern.

Nevertheless, most analysts would agree the greatest threat to security in the area stems from transnational criminal activity. Thus the spillover effects should be carefully characterized. Although the illegal commerce of drugs and arms is a serious concern, the transnational connections of Brazilian criminals having increased and become more evident, the incidents on the border are of a limited nature, not yet posing a serious security threat to Brazil or to its sovereignty.

The Brazilian government supported the peace process in Colombia, having favored a negotiated solution to the crisis. Although President Fernando Henrique Cardoso endorsed Colombian President Andrés Pastrana's decision to terminate the demilitarized zone granted to the FARC, the end of the peace negotiations and the stance adopted by President Uribe has left the Brazilian administrations in a vacuum regarding the war in Colombia. Particularly since the second semester of 2002, the Brazilian government chose to wait and observe the results of Uribe's military advance and his request for UN involvement in the crisis. Furthermore the present Colombian administration's emphasis on bilateral cooperation with the United States creates great difficulties for direct cooperation and policy coordination with Brazil. In late 2002 even the sale of Embraer planes accorded with the Pastrana government was abandoned due to U.S. pressure.[68] Bilateral technical cooperation and an initial dialogue with multilateral initiatives are the limits of Brazilian effective support for the Colombian government.[69] Moreover, Brazil has not joined the ten countries that form the group of facilitators.

In general the lack of a coherent strategy for cooperation and leadership in South America has resulted in weak links and meager cooperation with the Andean countries. Nevertheless some moves in this direction can be detected. The presidents of Brazil, Peru, and Ecuador joined together to request $1.3 billion from the Inter-American Development Bank for use in border social programs, aimed at dealing with the spillover from Plan Colombia. Working groups for defense cooperation were created on a bilateral basis with Peru and Ecuador. On March 11, 2003, Colombia, Peru, Bolivia, Venezuela, Ecuador, Brazil, and Panama signed an accord aimed at the fight against terrorism and drug trafficking. Also to be noted is the Brazilian government's understanding that SIVAM should be an instrument for greater regional cooperation.[70]

Brazil and Colombia do cooperate in the destruction of clandestine airstrips in the border region, in the judicial sphere, and in police operations. Several mechanisms were created in order to enhance coordination of activities in the border region: the neighborhood commission, the permanent group on consular cooperation, and the commission for Amazon cooperation, among others.

The prospect for closer ties between Brazil and Colombia stems from the security concern, but also from other important areas of common interest. Relations between the two countries are marked by distance and lack of knowledge. Nevertheless during the 1990s the perception of common interests increased. In 1993, a concerted effort by the two governments led to the creation of the Association of Coffee Producing Countries. In 1999, an accord on tariff preferences was signed and commerce between the two countries increased. A binational plan in metallurgy has been on the agenda since 1996. A neighborhood commission was created in 1993. Colombia is considered, according to Amaury de Souza's research, cited earlier, as a country where Brazil has vital interest by 61 percent of the interviewees. Among the Latin American countries, only Argentina is considered in these terms by a higher number of respondents (96 percent). The conflict in Colombia is understood to be a critical threat by 27 percent of interviewees and an important but not critical threat by 52 percent of the group in focus. Colombia seems to be on the radar scope of many citizens and policy makers in Brazil, despite this nation's traditional detachment from most of its neighbors beyond the Southern Cone.

The Brazilian Role in the Region

As we analyze the Brazilian policy toward the security crises in the Andean region, we can clearly delineate an attitude and a behavior marked by detachment and a defensive position regarding national sovereignty. The Brazilian governments have not shown the necessary initiative to activate existing or new multilateral forums and have shown interest primarily in preserving the integrity of territorial sovereignty. Preventing the country from sinking into the regional security quagmire has been a mantra repeated by politicians, military commanders, academics, and journalists alike. The statement by General Luiz Gonzaga Schroeder Lessa, former commander for the Amazon region, expresses this view clearly: "The defense policy should necessarily privilege the protection of the national territory, at the expense of international operations that result from policies in which Brazil did not, does not or will not have any participation."[71]

The nature of United States' policy toward the region, enlarging its direct zone of influence; establishing a military presence in Colombia, Ecuador, Paraguay, and elsewhere; and choosing the bilateral sphere as the focus for American support for the Colombian government in that country's civil war, raises concern in Brasilia. Although cooperation between the United States and Brazil in the security sphere should continue and even be intensified given common perceptions of threat, the two countries' positions toward the war in Colombia are at odds regarding the importance of returning to the negotiating table with the rebel groups and regarding American military presence in the Andean region. In general there is a low level of tension between the Brazilian leadership's fear of loss of autonomy over specific policies and of disrespect for national sovereignty and U.S. preference for maximum flexibility in its foreign policy.

The difficulties encountered in establishing the role of the military and a well-defined defense policy are an additional impediment for a significant Brazilian contribution. On the political front, the lack of a peace process in Colombia at present does not allow the Brazilian government to play the mediation card and support a peaceful solution to the crisis, as it so often does in its foreign policy initiatives. This leaves the Brazilian government, including the military, somewhat marginal in the overall Andean regional security crisis.

Furthermore, the institutions of the inter-American system are not geared to deal with intrastate conflict, their reform in the post–Cold War period having been stillborn. Brazil has adopted a status quo policy toward regional security institutions, allowing the United States to establish an agenda. Thus no effort to bring the issue to a wider debate in hemispheric forums has taken place.

The tension between the economic agenda and the security agenda should also be mentioned. At the same time that pressure gathered for governments to adopt neoliberal reform programs, the importance of the creation of institutions and resources to deal with criminal activities was stressed. While on one hand, the model of a minimalist state was put forward, on the other the need for the state to control the national territory was emphasized. If in other countries the U.S. military and other agencies could be expected to breach the gap, for the ruling elite in Brazil this is not a reasonable solution.[72]

Academics and politicians throughout the hemisphere have become critical and skeptical regarding the Brazilian contribution toward a solution to the crisis in the Andean region. Nevertheless, a confluence of subjective and objective factors creates favorable conditions for greater Brazilian participation in dealing with this multidimensional threat to the Andean nations and, to lesser extent, to the Brazilian state, its citizens, and the environment.

The change in the concept of security itself should be highlighted. The absence of a clear divide between internal and external threats, in a context of a growing web of international norms and institutions, has been acknowledged. The threat posed by nonstate actors and the institutional fragility in neighboring countries have put in question the "status quo attitude" stemming from the experience of frontier stabilization through peaceful negotiations. The link between transnational criminal organizations and the alarming erosion of public order in the country has entered the public debate. In this context, the entanglement between Andean security and Amazonian security becomes clear, at the same time that the Amazon is the focus of strategic considerations.

Moreover, the spillover effect of the conflict in Colombia is present on the Brazilian side of the border, generating concrete problems on the ground. In addition, Colombia has received greater attention from both policy makers and the media. On the other hand, the Brazilian government has invested in projects such as SIVAM and SIPAM that are generating results and create conditions for regional cooperation.

It is not clear if there will be a regional forum where the security of the Andean region can be seriously discussed. At present, if a proper institutional context is generated, Brazilian participation will most certainly be significant. The question is, of course, whether Brazil will take any initiative to create such a regional forum. In any case, no Brazilian presence should be expected across its borders except in the unlikely request for a *postconflict* peacekeeping force.

The government of Luiz Inácio Lula da Silva adopted a very discreet posture regarding the Colombian crisis. Cooperation in the fight against transnational criminal activities and in safeguarding control of the state over national territory has been the hallmark of the government's policies toward the region. On the other hand, regarding political stability in the Andean countries and economic integration, greater investment can be detected. This is particularly clear in the attention given to the political crises in Venezuela and Bolivia and in the energy sector. A drive toward greater participation in international decision-making processes is not compatible with a meager involvement in the security and political difficulties facing the Andean region. This contradiction cannot be hidden by a discourse and practice that stressed national sovereignty and noninterference.

Of course any policy toward any part of the hemisphere is linked to the options made in Washington. The Brazilian government will continue to refrain from subordinating its regional security agenda to the U.S. policy in the region. American intervention in the war in Colombia and military presence in the region will add to the threat perception produced by interventionism in the post–Cold War period, fostering the maintenance of a more traditional defensive posture.

The question opened by the prospects for greater involvement delineated in this chapter is whether greater activism and the preservation of autonomous policies are possible in the present regional and international environment. Faced with the unilateralist approach of the current U.S. government and the choices made by the Colombian government to focus on U.S. support, the Brazilian government finds itself with very little room to maneuver. Nevertheless the failure of governance in the Andean region, the low priority of Latin America in the current war on terrorism, and the Brazilian government's new will to make the difficult decision to bear the cost of regional leadership may allow for creative policies in the years ahead.

8

The European Union and Security and Defense Policy in the Andean Region

Philipp Schönrock-Martínez

THE EUROPEAN UNION (EU) and its member states, each of which has its own national agenda, represent a broad range of political interests where foreign policy and common security issues are concerned.[1] To accommodate this reality, attempts are being made to create new political and military institutions to help ensure that EU operations manifest both a political orientation and strategic focus that reflect its unique multinational framework. In December 1999 the European Council in Helsinki[2] set a general objective for the year 2003:[3] to be prepared to deploy and maintain some sixty thousand troops for at least one year. Said troops should be "independent, militarily speaking, and have the command, control, intelligence, logistical and other combat operations support capabilities they will need, as well as air and naval support, should they be required."

Further, the European Council in Nice[4] in December 2000 approved establishment of these permanent political and military bodies:

I. The Permanent Political and Security Committee (PSC)
II. The European Union Military Committee (EUMC)
III. The European Union Military Staff (EUMS)

Washington's executive and legislative branches have voiced concern in response to these initiatives; in their judgment the Europeans may have their priorities wrong. They believe that these initiatives could lead to the creation of new military bureaucracies and not to increased investment in the training of existing armed forces.[5]

Part of what underlies the emphasis Europe is putting on establishing new political and military institutions is a strong desire to establish increased autonomy to resolve subregional conflicts without relying on outside assistance from, for example, the United States and NATO.[6] Apparently, the U.S. position, that Europe should be more firmly committed to protecting common interests outside of its territory, is not Europe's number one priority.

A number of factors need to be considered in a discussion of the differences between U.S. and European positions on security and intervention in third countries. First, World War II (1939–1945) was fought primarily on European soil. It is impossible to know the exact number of deaths that resulted, but it could very possibly be as high as sixty million. Second, nearly all European countries were occupied during the war in some form or another. This was not the experience of the United States. Third, Europe has had a long history of asymmetric wars over the last century, sustaining and combating terrorist attacks on its territory by such groups on the legal fringe as the RAF (Red Army Faction), ETA (Euskadi ta Askatasuna), and IRA (Irish Republican Army). In the case of the United States, the 1993 attacks on New York's World Trade Center, the attack on the Alfred P. Murrah Building in Oklahoma in 1995, and the bombing at the 1996 Olympic Games in Atlanta were relatively novel, if despicable, acts of cowardice on civil society. But not until September 11, 2001, did the United States sustain the bloodiest attack of its entire history, a blow to the very heart of its territory. One of the many consequences of this attack was that the United States had to come to terms with the very real threat of terrorist acts taking place on its own soil.

Unlike the Americans, who opted for adopting a policy of preventive warfare following September 11, the great majority of Europeans felt that to combat terrorism, its underlying causes would have to be attacked at their roots. And that meant, among other things, alleviating world poverty and economic inequalities. It was an ideal moment for the Europeans to link official development assistance (ODA) together with a democratic security agenda as a political priority. As a result there would be a stronger political and economic commitment to developing countries or nations in transition. In this context links were established between foreign policy, security, and ODA policy.

In summary, most of the differences between the United States and Europe on issues relating to common security and defense policy are not attributable to opposing positions as to the main objectives, but rather, are in regard the means to achieve peace and security in the post–Cold War era, including the battle against terrorism (to the extent possible, prevention before intervention). Before presenting a detailed analysis of the position of the European Union and its member states on Plan Colombia it is important to understand the history of European assistance in the region and to identify some of Europe's interests in Colombia and the Andes region today.

European assistance in the Andes region today (2006) is marked by three significant historical patterns. First, Europe played a weak political and economic role in Latin America throughout most of the twentieth century. It was only in the 1980s that Europe decided to play a broader political role in the region and supported the Central American peace process.[7] Second, the rapid pace of globalization has revealed both how severely limited states are in their ability to confront global problems alone as well as the possibility that Latin America could become an important market for Europe. Third, during the 1990s countries like Colombia were classified as middle income, so theoretically they were no longer priority recipients for assistance.[8] Under this system, assistance would be poured into relatively lower-income countries and countries in the throes of grave humanitarian emergencies.

Over the last decade there has been a significant rethinking of the agenda as well as the objectives, players, and types of assistance Europe extends to the Andes region. Insofar as the agenda is concerned, emphasis shifted from eradicating poverty to such cross-cutting issues as drug trafficking, settling internal conflicts, human rights, and environmental protection.

European interest in Colombia centers much more on the Andean region as a geopolitical focus; it does not look at the country in isolation. There are trade interests at stake,[9] but it is important to keep in mind that the Colombian market is only of secondary interest to the EU.[10] Important too are its interests in fighting terrorism and issues relating to narco-trafficking, money laundering, the environment, strengthening institutions, arms smuggling, and Colombian emigration to European countries.[11]

Since the end of the 1990s, the priorities on Europe's Colombian agenda have specifically centered on

i. the peace process
ii. the fight against drug trafficking
iii. reinforcing the "rule of law"
iv. defending human rights and international humanitarian law
v. eliminating the causes of violence and providing help to its victims
vi. protecting biodiversity and the environment
vii. ensuring assistance and regional coordination

In addition to the above shifts, there are new players on the assistance scene, such as public and private foundations and nongovernmental organizations, which have altered the framework of relations between the state, assistance providers, and potential recipients. This new framework has the potential to combine as well as augment state and civilian activities directed at developing priority objectives. In practice, a certain rivalry has developed between the government and nongovernmental organizations over their work, their priorities, and their assistance programs. Given limited resources, this rivalry and the limits on European assistance programs have had unintended consequences, sometimes further weakening the Colombian State instead of strengthening it.

Europe's Position on Plan Colombia

Ten months after work began on Plan Colombia in the United States,[12] the EU received formal notification of it, provoking bewilderment about procedures for a project that aimed to secure funding from the Europeans without having negotiated with them first.[13] According to Joaquín Roy, director of the Miami European Union Center, "When the original Plan Colombia was unveiled, the European attitude towards helping to settle the crisis of endemic violence swung from alarm to hopefulness (although with no great expectations) and ultimately gave way to a feeling of powerless frustration and realism. But the commitment to help bring about peace was not abandoned. Initially the Europeans were extremely wary of the plan, believed to have been inspired by the U.S. but which was being peddled as an authentic Colombian product. Plan Colombia was soundly rejected and support was thrown behind the Peace Process."[14]

The European Parliament (EP) expressed its position on Plan Colombia and established a frame of reference for its support of the peace process in a twenty-two-point resolution approved on February 1, 2002, with 474 votes in favor, one against, and thirty-one abstaining.[15] The EP's vision of reaching a negotiated political settlement[16] and establishing lasting peace in Colombia is not compatible with Plan Colombia. This was reflected in the resolution and in the thoughts of Eurodeputies as revealed in their comments to journalists:

- "Plan Colombia is not the product of dialogue amongst the various social partners."
- "[The EU] believes that stepping up military involvement in the fight against drugs risks sparking an escalation of the conflict in the region, and that military solutions cannot bring about lasting peace."
- "Plan Colombia contains aspects that run counter to the cooperation strategies and projects to which the EU has already committed itself and jeopardizes its cooperation programs."

From the beginning the Europeans centered their attention on one chief concern: Plan Colombia's military dimension. Among other reasons, it became the focus of attention after numerous statements were made by nongovernmental organizations emphatically opposed to it.[17] From the Europeans' perspective, the potential consequences of the military dimension, such as an intensification of the internal conflict, forced commitments on them: once the military option was exhausted, the Europeans would have to chip in to pay for the effects of measures they had not supported.

Support for the Peace Process

Rather than support Plan Colombia, the Europeans chose to support the peace process, parallel to Plan Colombia, through negotiations, dialogue, and a strategy aimed at strengthening institutions and social development. While figures vary from source to source, according to one of the most rigorous studies undertaken as of 2003, it is estimated that the European Union as a block expended no less than 556 million euros in the period 1998–2002 in support of the peace process.[18] Add this to contributions from individual member states and the European Commission, and they become the chief generator of Official Development Assistance (ODA) in Colombia. Joint European efforts to support the peace process are particularly important here. The European Union committed significant funding to the peace process, estimated at 338 million euros as a result of meetings in Madrid on July 7, 2000; Bogotá, D.C., on October 24, 2000; and Brussels on April 30, 2001.

Commitments and concrete contributions are shown in detail in the following charts.

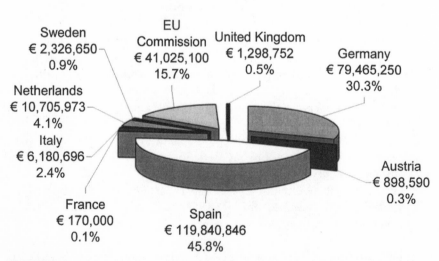

FIGURE 8.1
Breakdown of EU Investment, by Country, for Major Projects Associated with the Peace Process.
Source: Report on Cooperation in Colombia. Contributions to the Peace Process by the EU Commission and Member States, June 2002.

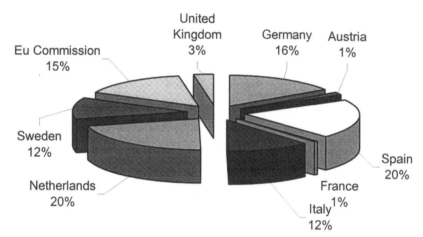

FIGURE 8.2
Percentage Breakdown of the Number of EU Projects Associated with the Peace Process.
Source: Report on Cooperation in Colombia. Contributions to the Peace Process by the EU Commission and Member States, June 2002.

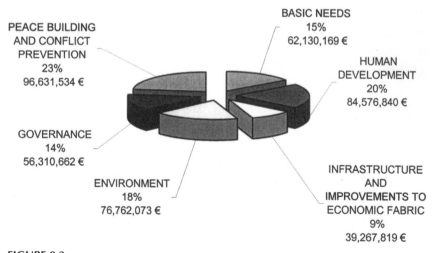

FIGURE 8.3
Total Euros, by Area of Intervention.
Source: Report on Cooperation in Colombia. Contributions to the Peace Process by the EU Commission and Member States, June 2002.

TABLE 8.1
Contributors' Roundtables (Madrid, Bogotá, and Brussels)

Country	Madrid Contributors' Roundtable			Bogotá D.C. Contributors' Roundtable			Brussels Contributors' Roundtable			Total from Contributors' Roundtables		
	Credit	Contribution	TOTAL	Credit	Contribution	TOTAL	Credit	Contribution	TOTAL	Credit	Contribution	TOTAL
Spain	70.00	30.00	100.00	—	—	—	—	—	—	70.00	30.00	100.00
Norway	—	20.00	20.00	—	—	—	—	—	—	—	20.00	20.00
Inter-American Development Bank	100.00	—	100.00	—	—	—	—	—	—	100.00	—	100.00
World Bank	100.00	—	100.00	—	—	—	—	—	—	100.00	—	100.00
Corporación Andina de Fomento	100.00	—	100.00	—	—	—	100.00	—	100.00	200.00	—	200.00
United Nations	—	30.00	30.00	—	—	—	—	—	—	—	30.00	30.00
European Union	—	—	—	—	90.00	90.00	—	—	—	—	90.00	90.00
Switzerland	—	—	—	—	12.00	12.00	—	—	—	—	12.00	12.00
Portugal	—	—	—	—	0.25	0.25	—	—	—	—	0.25	0.25
Japan	70.00	—	70.00	100.00	5.00	105.00	—	—	—	170.00	5.00	175.00
Canada	—	—	—	—	40.00	40.00	—	—	—	—	40.00	40.00
Italy	—	—	—	10.00	5.00	15.00	—	—	—	10.00	5.00	15.00
Sweden	—	—	—	—	16.00	16.00	—	9.50	9.50	—	25.50	25.50
Finland	—	—	—	—	2.20	2.20	—	1.80	1.80	—	4.00	4.00
United States	—	224.00	224.00	—	—	—	—	146.00	146.00	—	370.00	370.00
Germany	—	—	—	—	—	—	—	18.00	18.00	—	18.00	18.00
France	—	—	—	—	—	—	—	18.00	18.00	—	18.00	18.00
Austria	—	—	—	—	—	—	—	0.66	0.66	—	0.66	0.66
Ireland	—	—	—	—	—	—	—	0.45	0.45	—	0.45	0.45
Holland	—	—	—	—	—	—	—	8.00	8.00	—	8.00	8.00
England	—	—	—	—	—	—	—	1.80	1.80	—	1.80	1.80
Total	440.00	304.00	744.00	110.00	170.45	280.45	100.00	204.21	320.71	650.00	678.66	1,328.66
	59%	41%	100%	39%	61%	100%	33%	67%	100%	49%	51%	100%

Funds will be distributed through nongovernmental channels.
Totals in millions of U.S. dollars
Source: Agencia Colombiana de Cooperación Internacional

A highly placed government source who wishes to remain anonymous revealed, however, that

> when announcements were made about financial support coming out of the contributors' roundtables, they were interpreted to mean fresh resources would be forthcoming for programs aimed at strengthening institutions and social development. But these resources got mixed up with funding that had been agreed on previously through ordinary mechanisms for official assistance. And because of the widespread understanding in Europe that Plan Colombia was an eminently military strategy designed with the concurrence of the US, European Union member countries found the cooperation agreements a convenient way to avoid political pressures that could have been brought to bear by European bodies, had they supported Plan Colombia strategies.[19]

The Peace Process

The search for a negotiated political settlement to the Colombian conflict was well-intentioned on the part of the European Union and several of its member nations. The Colombian State had neither a coherent nor long-term policy. This made the European task difficult. The political toll of the breakdown in peace negotiations (in which several European countries—Spain, France, Switzerland, and Norway—were part of the Group of Friendly countries) between the Andrés Pastrana government and the FARC-EP (Fuerzas Armadas Revolucionarias de Colombia—Ejército del Pueblo/Revolutionary Armed Forces of Colombia—The People's Army) was devastating and eventually gave way to feelings of powerless frustration—and realism. The "Common Agenda for Change in a New Colombia"[20] was signed by the Colombian government and the FARC-EP before peace negotiations broke down. It contained important points that aligned with European policies toward Colombia where European nations could have played a pivotal role in implementation. Some of them were the following:

Point 9: Agreements on International Humanitarian Law
9.1. Removal of children from the armed conflict
9.2. Antipersonnel mines
9.3. Respect for the civilian population
9.4. Rule of international standards

Point 11: International Relations
11.1. Respect for self-determination and nonintervention
11.2. Latin American regional integration
11.3. Foreign debt
11.4. International treaties and agreements by the state

Ultimately, the behavior of the FARC-EP and the absence of a clear strategy by the Pastrana government (1998–2002) during peace negotiations impeded the European countries from playing the role of true mediators and monitors. The parties to the conflict were not ready for "peace"; this made the European initiatives virtually a dead letter.

Europe's Position on Illegally Armed Groups in Colombia

The FARC-EP, the ELN, and the AUC on the List of Terrorist Organizations

At the insistence of the Colombian executive, the European Union decided to add the FARC-EP[21] and the AUC (Autodefensas Unidas de Colombia—Colombian United Self-Defense Forces) to its list of terrorist organizations. The decision was adopted by the fifteen EU member nations at the Commission of Permanent Representatives on June 13, 2002.[22] At first it was thought that the Ejército de Liberación Nacional (ELN—National Liberation Army) would also be put on the list, but the EU member countries postponed their decision on the ELN in light of possibilities for moving the peace process forward with that guerrilla group. However, President Uribe urged, during his tour of various European countries, that the ELN be included in the list of terrorists. His request was accepted, and the ELN was included in the list. This decision was published on April 3 in the official bulletin of the European Union, and it demands that the member states freeze the assets of the organization and that they open the way to trials of the members of the ELN on charges of terrorism.

Post–Peace Process with the FARC-EP and the ELN

The high commissioner for the peace, Luis Carlos Restrepo, affirmed on June 22, 2005, that the international community was widely receptive to the justice and peace project being prepared in the Colombian congress.[23] The government of President Uribe has taken its chance with the peace process with the AUC. Before he took office as the president of Colombia, the paramilitary groups had already publicly expressed their desire to participate in a negotiation process with this administration. This highly controversial process aims to demobilize all the AUC blocs that participate in the negotiation.

The Colombian conflict is worsening, and no solution appears in sight for the near future to reach a peace agreement with guerrilla groups and to really dismantle the paramilitary activities. The attitude of Europe is that of serious reservation about the so-called politics of peace of the current administration. Nevertheless, Europe should insist on supporting a negotiated political solution to the confrontation, just as the United States should evaluate the results of its war against drug trafficking. Without the support of both, it would be difficult to find a solution to the Colombian conflict, or the implementation of a coherent and effective European–U.S. policy to fight drug trafficking.

Statements about collaborating on common objectives have been heard from both U.S. and European spokespersons. John Walters, director of the Office for National Policy on Drug Control, a White House agency, stated that "we must try to cooperate more boldly" with international partners in the fight against drugs.[24] Spain, for its part, recently contributed US$150,000 to CICAD (Inter-American Drug Abuse Control Comisión), the OAS counternarcotics agency, to provide equipment and technical training to antidrug units in Bolivia, Colombia, Ecuador, and Peru that will upgrade their drug data gathering and analysis systems. This donation follows an earlier one in the amount of $350,000 to support CICAD's institutional development.[25]

The Presidency of Presidente Álvaro Uribe (2002–2006)

On May 26, 2002, with 5,774,732 votes (52.88 percent of total votes), Alvaro Uribe, the actual president of Colombia, was elected in the first round of voting, for the four-year term of 2002–2006. He assumed office on August 7, 2002. In his electoral campaign Uribe proposed, in his Democratic Manifest, one hundred points that would be the guidelines for his government. Of these points, five merit special attention:

1. Democratic security and recovery of sovereignty over the entire territory;
2. Efficiency of the state through institutional reform;
3. Growth and sustainable development through job creation;
4. Social equity; and
5. Proposal to the FARC-EP to return to the negotiation table with international mediation, cease-fire, and a possible reintegration into civil society.

This Democratic Manifest served as the base, along with other, later proposals of the government, for the drafting of the 2002–2006 National Development Plan, "Toward a Communitarian State."

The Foreign Policy of the Uribe Administration

"The cornerstone of the foreign policy of Colombia is respect for principles and norms of International Law, enshrined in the Constitution and in the United Nations Charter. Among them, the most important ones are the equality of sovereign states, the non-intervention into the internal affairs of other

States, the good faith in the fulfillment of international obligations, the peaceful solution of controversies, and the abstention from threat or actual use of force."[26] For the Uribe administration, the management of foreign policy must be inspired, in addition, by three key concepts: democratic governability, shared responsibility, and solidarity.

Under the principle of shared responsibility, priority is being given to issues in which the international community should have a prominent role for their solution, such as the worldwide problem of drugs and related crimes—money laundering; illicit trade of arms, munitions, explosives, and chemical precursors, among others—terrorism, environmental problems, and the protection of the human rights.

Also, as a part of the development of its foreign policy, the Colombian government expressed its willingness to call on the international community, seeking its support to obtain human, environmental, and institutional recovery from the effects produced by the problem that the sum of the drugs, violence, terrorism, and other malaise associated with these illicit activities presents.

The Uribe administration considers that since the start of its mandate, it has taken important steps toward engaging the support of the international community in the new Colombian government's security efforts. On August 30, 2002, in Cartagena, President Álvaro Uribe confirmed that the so-called democratic security piece of Plan Colombia would be supported by several European Union nations. Spanish, French, and British support would include promoting programs for assistance to the Colombian police, for citizen protection, and for investment in Colombia.[27] At a conference organized in Washington, D.C., in October 2002, then defense minister Marta Lucía Ramírez stated that the international community was contributing to a worsening of the Colombian conflict through drug consumption, money laundering, and the trafficking of arms and chemical components. She emphasized that these were transnational problems that would be impossible to solve without cooperation from the international community.[28]

Despite the affirmations about good performance in its international relations, the Uribe administration has had some unfortunate initiatives. The following text is from an editorial, published on June 15, 2005, in the newspaper *El Tiempo*, that speaks for itself:

> By its style and its nature, the document about "guidelines for the focus of projects of international cooperation" that the Presidential Advisor, Luis Alfonso Hoyos, sent to the foreign ambassadors residing in Colombia appears as a misguided step of the government.
>
> The document, with the signature of the Commissioner, and which establishes certain strict parameters for international cooperation projects, is yet another step in the official line that in Colombia there is no armed conflict. But its effect

can be counterproductive. Not only was it unfortunate to suggest, without more explanation, to the foreign sources of assistance money, what is politically correct in the matter (which is actually what high-ranking officials, including the Foreign Minister, acknowledged in their clarifying statements hurriedly made to the ambassadors, who were surprised by the unusual email from Hoyos through which they received the document). Furthermore, the list of semantic prohibitions and the tone that it sets has quite a few repercussions.

The instructions begin stipulating that "no public official or private citizen" can establish contacts with illegally armed groups. They prohibit regional dialogues without presidential permission. They declare unacceptable as the objectives of cooperative projects any "statement or activity whose recipient totally or partially" may be these groups. They reject the use of terms "armed actors," "actors of conflict," and "non-state actors." They ask to specify the reach of concepts such as "community or territory of peace," "humanitarian region or camp (sic)." They prohibit the inclusion "of humanitarian activities that imply contact with armed groups." They call for not accepting the existence of internal armed conflict and emphasizing not only rights but "duties" of citizens. They limit the validity of the constitutional assemblies and set the orientations that the so-called peace laboratories have to have.

In theory, as the Commissioner says, a government has the right to negotiate the terms of the projects in which it serves as a counterpart. But quite another thing is to try to impose, in addition to the language, conditions that, in effect, automatically exclude dozens of valuable initiatives that at the local and regional levels address the armed conflict.

Projects like those of the Paeces (or Nasa) Indian peoples to negotiate life outside the conflict between the Colombian army and the FARC, and to resist with their Guardia Indígena would border on illegality.[29] A successful policy of returning the displaced persons, such as the one in the Valle del Cauca, would lose its moorings. How would the more than 15 "programs of development and peace" function under these conditions when their leaders are obligated to speak with armed actors to save lives or to preserve the projects against threats? And what would become of the "peace laboratories" that the European Union is financially supporting? How would the road in Micoahumado have been demined without the ELN's participation in the dialogue? The list is as long as the benefits of dialogue. How is it that, despite the fact that "corrections" were imposed on Magdalena Medio's Program of Development and Peace, the Commissioner himself acknowledges that he had to make an "exception" with its director, the father Francisco de Roux?

It is not clear that the government has the legal authority to impose such prohibitions. As to a "private citizen," would every journalist who interviews guerrillas and paramilitaries go to jail? For what would there be agencies such as Acnur, a vast presence of the United Nations, or international financing, if the armed conflict does not exist? What will happen when the foreign cooperator finds him/herself required to talk about "armed conflict" in order to justify the support provided, and the Colombian government says no? How far, sometimes, the presidential strategists appear from the war that whips so many regions of the country! As if the problem were linguistic-semantic, or as if it suffices to say in the Palace that there is no conflict in order to convert Cundinamarca into Denmark.

Unless the intent is to reduce the international presence and vigilance, the initiative that has led the government to write such a document does not appear opportune. The effect could be to isolate Colombia and make it even more difficult to have an exit to our most protuberant and shameful reality. The one that, outside the Casa de Nariño, everyone calls "internal armed conflict."

What Next?

In a country like Colombia, European cooperation is indispensable for economic and political reasons. On the economic side, if such cooperation adequately complements domestic efforts, it could produce positive effects on development, the well-being of vulnerable populations, and the strengthening of the state. On the political side, in the development of foreign and diplomatic policy, this cooperation allows for the principles of reciprocity and corresponsibility for problems with global causes and effects to be put into effect. In the particular case of Colombia, the dimension and the extensive interrelation of the problems that must be resolved such as drug trafficking, the internal armed conflict, the weakening of human rights, and the degradation of the environment make it impossible to resolve them if Colombia cannot count on financial, technical, and political support from the international community through frameworks of cooperation.

During the administration of President Andrés Pastrana, a very important political effect was produced: the internationalization of the Colombian situation. This meant a better understanding of the Colombian conflict and a stronger commitment from the Europeans in the search for the solution of the problems that the Colombian State confronts. The change of perception can be sensed in the declarations made by the then subsecretaries of International Relations in charge of Latin America from Germany, Ludger Volmer, and from the United Kingdom, Denis Macshane, who said, "Illegal armed groups routinely kidnap, take hostages, commit assassinations and extortions, and demonstrate a complete disrespect for international humanitarian law, both against the civilian population and against their political adversaries. In the past, the FARC-EP and the Ejercito de Liberación Nacional (ELN) proclaimed leftist socialist goals, but today these groups exist for their own interest in maintaining its leadership oligarchy. They do not have democratic legitimacy and sustain their level of life through an open complicity in the trafficking of drugs and illicit activities, at the same time maintaining and extending their military power through the flow of smuggled arms."[30]

Nevertheless, it is important to point out that internationalization of the situation in Colombia also implies a challenge for the country. In the first place, this phenomenon increases the number of actors that participate in the process, and as a result the state must have a high capacity for institutional and political management, otherwise it cannot achieve a true coordination between said actors. In addition, this internationalization reduces, to a certain extent, the autonomy of the government because its policies become permeable to the international decision-making networks.

During the Uribe administration, the political support that the Colombian government received in the Preparatory Meeting of the International Coordination and Cooperation Roundtable in London (2003) is noteworthy. In the Declaration of London (and afterwards in Cartagena, February 2005) the representatives of the states reaffirmed their political support for the Colombian government and for its efforts to find solutions to the threats to democracy, increasing terrorism, drug trafficking, violations of human rights and of international humanitarian law, and the humanitarian crisis of the country. In this aspect, however, it is necessary to point out the importance of the fulfillment, on the part of Colombian government, of recommendations of the Office of the United Nations High Commissioner for Human Rights in Colombia. This can affect the political support and cooperation that Colombia may receive in the coming years, given that this is a fundamental theme for many cooperating states and organizations of the civil society.

Another political aspect that is important to point out is that the donor states, especially those member states of the European Union and the United States, have different notions of time (medium- to long-term vision in the case of the former, and a short-term vision in the case of the latter) and different perceptions of cooperation and the manner in which the situation in Colombia should be resolved.

This element needs to be taken into consideration at the time of designing and implementing a strategy for international cooperation that must seek to integrate the different perceptions and mentalities of the donors in order to obtain the best results. It is necessary to avoid conflict of visions among the donors, so that cooperation offered by some does not have negative impact on the flow of resources (human, technical, and financial) offered by others.

In addition, it is fundamental to understand the bureaucratic procedures, the notion of time of the donors, their visions, and their interests in Colombia. In this way, it would be possible to have a clearer understanding of how to interact with each state and to present, with more transparency and justification, the core themes defined by the Colombian government that require economic, political, and technical assistance.

Many of the European offers, made during the Contributors' Roundtables, did not materialize, which proved the weak capacity of the Colombian State to successfully convert announcements into actual resources. The contributions depend on the will of the states, the understanding they have about the problems that they would like to resolve, and the political context in which cooperation unfolds. The study of these factors is a task that must be undertaken with maximum care by the national government. In addition, there is a need for higher technical and managerial capacity in order to materialize European support.

In this sense, and especially in the process that took place during the Uribe administration, it is clear that international cooperation offered by the United States is influenced, among other reasons, by the events of September 11, 2001, and by the war against terrorism waged by the government of President George W. Bush. It is important that Colombia take this aspect into account and take advantage of opportunities that the conjuncture offers; it also should be mindful that the context can change and that it is necessary to come up with a strategy for the long term (with issues such as the fight against poverty, attention to vulnerable populations, and alternative development) that assures the continuity of the offers of resources that complement national efforts.

Because Colombia is classified as a middle-income country, assistance providers tend not to include it among their priorities, primarily because resources are scarce and the need for international aid is so great. That said, given that the problems facing the Andean region overlap with priorities on the international agenda, and that the magnitude of these problems is so critical that prospects for development and democratic stability are threatened, the question of whether or not Europe should make the region a priority on its assistance agenda has to be addressed.

The most important factor in weighing Colombia's case for designation as a priority for European assistance is the scale of the armed internal conflict and how it prevents achievement of such global objectives as enforcement of human rights, fighting drug traffic, and protecting the environment. Europe's recognition of Colombia and the Andes as priorities for aid would contribute significantly to the resolution of critical global problems by making the region a focal point of international efforts. Moreover, it would mean broader recognition of, and appreciation for, the tolls Colombian society sustains in battling these problems.

9

After Iraq: Next Colombia?
The United States and
(In)Security in South America

Juan Gabriel Tokatlian

> One provocation that could incite a more deliberate US drive toward hege-
> mony, and mute domestic and foreign antagonism to such drive, is some
> major escalation of international terrorism.
>
> David Wilkinson, "Unipolarity without Hegemony," 1999

THE CRUCIAL GEOPOLITICAL NOVELTY about Washington's post–September 11
design to reorder the world is that the United States is becoming a major
leading power in Asia. The first war on Afghanistan in Central Asia and the second war on Iraq in the Middle East have brought the United States to unprecedented prominence in a part of the world where it wielded influence but never
the control and military presence that it now has deployed. The establishment of
de facto neo-protectorates in Kabul and Baghdad, the buildup of military bases
stretching from the heart of Central Asia to the Horn of Africa—in Uzbekistan,
Turkmenistan, Kyrgyzstan, Tajikistan, Oman, Bahrain, Qatar, United Arab Emi-
rates, Saudi Arabia, Kuwait, and Djibouti—and the actual control over the region's energy resources may be transforming the United States into a genuine
global superpower. In fact, at the turn of the twentieth century the United States
became a hemispheric power; following World War II it became an Atlantic
power; with the Cold War it extended its power over the Pacific. Its increased involvement in Africa during the post–Cold War era, and now its expansion into
Asia, have placed Washington still closer to the imperial dream.

The imperial dream is intrinsic to world primacy. In the quest for world
primacy, the United States has abandoned, if not made a mockery of, multilateralism. In the aftermath of the horrors of World War II, the international

community as a whole, and the United States in particular, patiently put together a set of world regimes, multilateral organizations, and binding global
commitments that effectively averted the outbreak of a devastating bipolar
war and preserved a fundamental peace among major powers. When the Cold
War ended the world entered an era of optimism, expecting that the dividends
of peace would be the allocation of more resources and efforts in favor of economic development, social justice, political pluralism, and strengthened international law. However, even before September 11, 2001, it was becoming
clear that inequality was widening worldwide, that fundamentalism of different types was emerging aggressively, and that global rules, processes, and
agreements was breaking up. The most worrisome signs came from Washington. Rejection of the Kyoto Protocol and the International Criminal Court
were, in effect, attempts by the George W. Bush administration to undermine
multinational instruments for dealing with environmental and human rights
issues. Furthermore, the Republican government seemed determined to avoid
principles and procedures that had been agreed upon. For example, in the area
of nonproliferation, the United States abandoned the Antiballistic Missile
Treaty prohibiting defensive weapons that was signed with the Soviet Union
in 1972. In December 2001, the administration presented its Nuclear Posture
Review, which expressly considered the deployment of nuclear weapons
against Russia, China, Iraq, Iran, North Korea, Libya, and Syria. By early 2003
Washington moved a step further: not only did it undermine and circumvent
international commitments, it embarked on the destruction of multilateral
institutions. Washington's aggressive policy on Iraq provoked a divisive foreign policy in the European Union between a London–Madrid axis (including
Eastern European countries) and a Paris–Berlin axis (including mainly Western European countries). Afterwards, the United States brought NATO to an
unprecedented crisis over a vote on the organization's support for Turkey in
the event of war on Iraq (France, Germany, and Belgium initially rejected the
proposal). The next institution that suffered U.S. destructive tactics was the
United Nations Security Council: Washington pushed ahead for a largely illegitimate and illegal policy against Baghdad. Decades of dedicated, hard, and
careful work invested in creation of broad international regimes and collective
consultation mechanisms were placed in jeopardy.

It is evident that a Washington that grows more recalcitrant out of its own
rigidity and more reactionary in its ideology does not seem interested in a benign leadership. It looks like it is time for relentless dominance. However, the
attempt to consolidate the United States as the sole preeminent military power
might well lead to greater instability and insecurity. It could even incite increasingly lethal terrorism against the United States as a challenge to the nation's resolve to keep its territory impenetrable. The quest for primacy
through military dominance also presents a serious challenge to the U.S. econ-

omy and Washington's moral stature in the world community. Furthermore, the United States' intention to build a defensive system (for example, an antimissile shield) that would theoretically render its territory invulnerable to attack may provoke the dissatisfied powers or the risk takers to attack in advance with less sophisticated weapons. It may also encourage a greater proliferation of nuclear armaments, or even first use of weapons of mass destruction, either by the United States or its adversaries. In essence, Washington and the international community as a whole may be witnessing a potentially tragic security dilemma: the search for individual and unilateral security by the United States may provoke a broader and global insecurity. This, in turn, will create more insecurity in the United States, something that may tempt the threat and employment of unrestricted military might on the part of Washington.

The basic point is that embedded in a primacy strategy—and regardless of whether the administration in Washington is Republican or Democrat—is an aggressive approach toward foreign and defense policy. The underlying rationale of unchallenged primacy is the demonstration and deployment of a muscular policy. In addition, primacy politics demands huge defense budgets, which, in turn, may unintentionally produce a civilian–military imbalance with more autonomy for the armed forces.[1]

Finally, this strategy has essentially relied upon creating ad hoc coalitions to confront Washington's enemies, both new and old, in place of the traditional Cold War alliances. This option is directed toward bringing about regime change or intimidating governments, by the recourse to a persistent coercive diplomacy, into compliance with U.S. policies. Thus, it is very likely that Washington will continue to assert the right to use force whenever it deems necessary, without much regard for the standards of legitimacy, legality, and morality that are crucial whenever the military means are applied. Paradoxically, the White House believes that it is going to win over allies for the global war on terrorism by repeatedly threatening its good friends and harshly punishing its weak opponents.

In short, it is fundamental to determine if the omnipotence Washington's behavior apparently displays is a demonstration of its true power (verging on vigorous hegemony), temporary hubris (the sign of a superpower that lacks self-control), or a concealing of the erosion of U.S. global power (meaning that it will gradually but markedly fade from its position as sole power).

The Hemispheric Puzzle

Periods with no clearly identified foreign threat were also periods of division and disorientation in US foreign policy. . . . American strategy in the

future will only be effective if it can once again focus upon a particular foreign threat, especially one that can be analogous to the old Soviet one.

—James Kurth, "American Grand Strategy," 1996

Following the September 11, 2001, attacks, Washington identified in the Western Hemisphere three areas of varying concern that might affect its vital interests. Today the Caribbean basin, which encompasses the Caribbean islands,
Panama, Central America, and Mexico, is definitely part of the defense
perimeter of the United States, and therefore it is perceived as a natural extension of its domestic security.[2] Autonomy in this subregion will begin to decline and tensions between the United States and Cuba may very probably
rise. The pursuit of full invulnerability along this perimeter, together with the
Republican government's steady movement to the Right, and the considerable
influence of southern neoconservatism (particularly from Texas and Florida),
will most likely make Fidel Castro, along with his ally president Hugo Chávez
of Venezuela, the foremost loci of uneasiness. This tense situation between
Washington and Havana and Caracas should be resolved, according to the
most hardened hawks in the United States, through a regime change on the island and in Venezuela. This ideological fixation will probably mean a distorted understanding of the Caribbean basin's more dramatic problems:
weakening institutions, massive unemployment, rampant criminality, extensive corruption, and growing mafia power.

In addition, Washington has identified Colombia, the Colombian–Venezuelan
frontier,[3] and the tri-border region between Argentina, Paraguay, and Brazil as
potential risk spots regarding terrorism. The Andean ridge is a very critical, problematic subregion, while the Southern Cone is a less threatening zone. In this
context, the basic challenge for South America as a whole is to retain relative autonomy in order to deal with these two locations (the one in the Andean ridge
and the other in the Southern Cone), which are still highly controllable and less
deadly in comparison with other hot spots of terrorism around the Middle East,
Asia, and Africa.

Notwithstanding Washington's continuing commitment to preemptive war
on transnational terrorists with global reach and on tyrants with weapons of
mass destruction—the two leading enemies, according to the September 2002
National Security Strategy—it is evident that these overwhelming threats are
not currently present in the Western Hemisphere. There have been terrorist
acts in the area and there are groups that practice terrorist tactics—for example, the Revolutionary Armed Forces of Colombia (FARC), the National Liberation Army (ELN), and the United Self-Defense Forces (AUC), all located in
Colombia—but there are no major terrorist groups with the capacity to have
critical international impact. There are also populist or even radical leaders in
the region, but there is no dictator or authoritarian ruler with the capacity to

seriously threaten the United States or to exercise a regional counterbalance to Washington's hegemony. The third source of concern for Washington—failed states—is perhaps more probable in Latin America and the Caribbean. In that sense, it may become a central focus of attention for the United States in Latin America as recent events in Haiti, Bolivia, and Ecuador suggest.

Overall, however, it was evident that U.S. officials did not think that Latin America posed an immediate or significant security threat to the United States. In March 2005 the U.S. Department of Defense released "The National Defense Security Strategy of the United States of America." The March 2005 document begins dramatically: "America is a nation at War. We face a diverse set of security challenges." From the standpoint of this chapter it is important to note that according to the March 2005 document, South America is not one of the potential arenas for war scenarios, but it does figure conceptually in the section regarding the conduct of "lesser contingencies" such as small-scale combat operations, peace operations, humanitarian missions, and noncombatant evacuations.

Yet, even though Latin America does not pose overwhelming threats to U.S. national security, security issues, defined in a global framework, once more dominate the inter-American agenda, just as occurred during the Cold War. Even economic issues seem dictated by military considerations. In that sense, the evolution of the discussion on the Americas Free Trade Area will probably be linked to the notion of achieving an Area Liberated from International Terrorism.

The extensive and excessive "securitization" of inter-American relations may help to deepen and widen already existing tensions. One of them is the gap between an increasingly conservative, xenophobic, and self-centered United States (both at the level of the government and the society) and a more nationalistic, mobilized, and demanding South American citizenry. Another is the fracture, in many cases, between mostly pro-U.S. Latin American governments and societies that are slowly growing anti-American. Regardless of the official rhetoric in the Western Hemisphere, the beginning of the twenty-first century appears to be quite unstable in terms of U.S.–Latin American and Caribbean relations.

U.S. Policy and Instability in the Andes

A prime example of this instability is what is occurring regarding Washington's Andean policy. A fast-moving political blight is spreading across the Andes, which if left unchecked, will fuel chronic instability in the Western Hemisphere. Fixing the region is not the United States' responsibility alone; it requires a long-term, joint effort from the continent's largest countries. The first administration of George W. Bush either neglected or manipulated the geopolitical value of this region by "deinstitutionalizing" the U.S.–Andes agenda and orienting it too much toward fighting narcotics. The second Bush administration should search for a collective solution to regional unrest. Today, the five Andean countries—Bolivia, Colombia, Ecuador, Peru, and Venezuela—epitomize the dark side of regional politics. They are the poster children for massive poverty, a growing drug industry, gross violations of human rights, rising organized crime, environmental exhaustion, and rampant corruption. As they descend into turmoil, the Andean area is becoming a serious security concern.

Several key questions regarding the Andean ridge area have been either downplayed or distorted by Washington. First, the forces behind the Bolivarian Revolution led by Venezuelan president Hugo Chávez will continue to make themselves felt in the area—similar to other Latin American experiences such as the Peronist revolution of the 1950s, the Castro revolution of the 1960s, and the Sandinista revolution of the 1970s. Chávez's 2004 referendum victory provided additional momentum to his very particular "revolutionary" aspiration. It is essential for external powers to develop a modus vivendi with him until he understands that his revolutionary ideals should be restricted to Venezuela. Stigmatizing Chávez as the "Saddam Hussein of the Andes" or encouraging the most extreme elements of the opposition will merely end up triggering a civil war in Venezuela.

Second, the Colombian armed conflict is barely "stabilized," contrary to claims by some Western officials. Notwithstanding President Alvaro Uribe's hard-line policies, the radical guerrillas of the Revolutionary Armed Forces of Colombia are not strategically defeated in mid-2006 and the so-called peace process with right-wing paramilitaries is extremely fragile. Dozens of Colombian drug traffickers have been extradited to the United States, and hundreds of thousands of hectares of illicit crops have been chemically fumigated, but with limited impact in terms of drug use in the region. Colombians do not generally welcome the overwhelming amounts of U.S. assistance and presence. The potential direct involvement of U.S. troops in countering guerrilla forces there would likely ignite more troubles in the country and its vicinity. The temptation by Washington to transform Uribe into a sort of Ariel Sharon of the Andes—to balance the growing power of Chávez—may internationalize Colombia's domestic conflict.

Third, Peru, Bolivia, and Ecuador are becoming critical examples of partially collapsed states, unable to cope with increasing social and ethnic demands after more than a decade of neoliberal reforms. There is no domino effect among them and each country, individually, is witnessing a crisis in its traditional leadership with an open outcome: uncertainty. It remains to be seen whether replacement of the current elites will be peaceful or violent. Choice and circumstance may interact virtuously or viciously.

Meanwhile, trade negotiations between some Andean countries and Washington will not necessarily be an insurance against institutional turmoil, social fragmentation, or ethnic violence. Thus, for example, the United States, Canada, Mexico, Brazil, and Argentina must come together to lead a fresh, sustained effort to address the underlying social, economic, and political issues driving the widespread chaos and lack of governance on the Andean ridge. The administrations in Washington, Ottawa, Mexico City, Brasilia, and Buenos Aires share responsibility for stabilizing the Andean region by peaceful and positive means. If the politics of denial prevail, as they have since the late 1990s, a mixture of territorial, ethnic, and political "balkanization" of the Andean region looms on the horizon. The result will be a fast and frantic export of violence, volatility, narcotics, and migrants to the north and south of the Western Hemisphere.

This part of South America has become of increasing concern to the United States. As during the Cold War, Washington fears that the sum of uncontrolled individual crises in a convulsed region might produce a negative domino effect, thereby exacerbating existing tensions in the Southern Cone and Central America. To this is added, likewise as during the Cold War, an ideological component; instead of the inexorable communist enemy, now it is "radical populism" that supposedly haunts Latin America. As pointed out elsewhere in this volume, General James Hill warned the U.S. Congress of the growing threat of radical populism in March 2004. The more concrete referent for this threat, for the moment, was Venezuelan president Hugo Chávez.

Until recently, this thesis, presented by General Hill and reaffirmed by the next SOUTHCOM commander, General Brantz Craddock, had not been taken up energetically by the U.S. civilian leadership. The appointment of Condoleezza Rice as secretary of state, after the reelection of President George W. Bush, seems to have also meant that the concern for radical populism in Latin America now is shared by foreign policy makers at the Department of State and the Department of Defense.

The return of an ideological framework for hemispheric politics that emphasizes security policy, in some ways similar to the Cold War era, can also be seen in concrete policies toward the Andean region. The case of Colombia resembles others where the United States used indirect intervention, that is, massive military assistance, an active military presence (with advisers), and a muscular diplomatic offensive, but without (officially) direct U.S. participation in combat. Colombia now has the second-largest U.S. embassy in the world, after Iraq. Eight hundred U.S. military advisers are officially in the country; six hundred private contractors participate in the military and diplomatic efforts. Colombia is the principal recipient of U.S. aid in Latin America and fifth on a global scale (after Israel, Egypt, Afghanistan, and Iraq).

Past trends are manifested likewise in policies toward the rest of the Andean nations. In Bolivia the United States insists on a ruinous "war against drugs" that has neither permanently disrupted the narcotics trade nor enhanced the sovereign capacity of the Bolivian state. Indeed, those who have emerged on top, at least for now, are the peasants who grow coca leaf, on the one hand, and the drug mafias that control and profit from the drug trade, on the other hand. In Peru and Ecuador, the usual disdain combined with a certain tolerance for an outright coup (Fujimori in 1992) or camouflaged coups (Bucaram in 1997, Mahuad in 2000, and Gutiérrez in 2005) have contributed to deepening erosion of government institutions.

The renewed interests of the United States in the Andean region have borrowed from the principles, objectives, and instruments of the past. If previously such policies produced no better social orders, today they may produce increasing disorder. South America is not in a condition to relive the Cold War, with new "axis of evil" (then Cuba, now Havana plus Caracas) "regime changes" (as in Guatemala in 1954, and elsewhere in Latin America until 1990), or preventive attacks. The strategy of primacy, applied to Latin America and the Andean region, will assure fulfillment of a self-fulfilling prophecy: more failed or failing states.

The key tests of how primacy operates in South America will be Brazil, Colombia, and Venezuela. Brasilia is no match for Washington; however, Brazil not only wants to increase and improve its influence in the region but also to become an influential middle power worldwide. The essential question is whether the United States intends to prevent this by undermining Brazilian projection in South America or if it is willing to live with a Brazil that searches for more visibility, recognition, and prestige. At the same time, Colombia is critical because it is the only remaining locus of an armed conflict in South America. Lastly, Venezuela is relevant due to its geopolitical value (with outlets to the Andes, the Amazon, and the Caribbean) and abundant energy resources; it is also a potential test case for regime change—something already attempted, indirectly, in the failed coup of April 2002.

The failed attempt to oust Venezuela's President Hugo Chávez was a major mistake and a demonstration of an amateurish role by the United States. The result was that Washington had, de facto, created a whole new political life-form: the benevolent coup d'état, by which it becomes acceptable to topple distasteful but democratic governments in the Americas. On April 12, White House spokesman Ari Fleisher asserted that "the Chavez administration provoked the crisis in Venezuela," that Chávez "resigned," and that before doing so, Chávez "dismissed the vice president and the Cabinet." Besides explicitly blaming Chávez for his own downfall and self-imposed dismissal of his government, the spokesman refused to define Chávez's downfall as a coup d'état. The White House's version of events is the political equivalent of the "tumble" cycle—the coup gets blamed on the victim instead of the perpetrator.

The notion of the benevolent coup d'état is supported, if tacitly, by officials outside the White House as well. Otto Reich, assistant secretary of state for Western Hemispheric affairs, and John Maisto, the National Security Council's senior director for Western Hemisphere affairs—both of whom are former U.S. ambassadors to Venezuela—and Roger Noriega, the U.S. ambassador to the Organization of American States, kept remarkably silent. The joint United States–Spain statement on Venezuela issued the same day expressed both governments' hope that the "exceptional situation" in Venezuela could be normalized as soon as possible. Consequently there was no official U.S. censure of the coup d'état.

Nor was there a clear inter-American condemnation of the coup. The heads of state of the Rio Group, the largest and most important Latin American mechanism for political cooperation, met in Costa Rica. On April 13, the group issued its final declaration of thirty-eight points without mentioning Venezuela. In a separate communication it condemned the interruption of the constitutional order in Venezuela, adding that the rupture "was generated by a process of growing polarization." Consequently, the Rio Group—in line with the United States—opted to imply a sort of justification for the coup. Latin America's preeminent international organization—the Organization of American States—was also unable to put forward a principled argument against the coup and in favor of democracy. Unless things change, many in the hemisphere will see their hopes that George W. Bush's government would be a U.S. administration that finally focuses and cares about Latin America mutate into despair. Indeed many may ask themselves if Bush's presidency is itself becoming a security concern for Latin America's still fragile democracies.

From Baghdad to Bogotá?

> Autistic power politics: that is a self-regarding concern for the perceived needs of a state (often generated by internal problems) without concern for the impact on others.
>
> —Christopher Hill, "What Is to Be Done? Foreign Policy as a Site for Political Action," 2003

It is evident by now that Colombia's violent conflict is no longer only a domestic matter; it is an international phenomenon. Both Colombia's current war[4] and future peace are conditioned by external factors such as the high levels of drug consumption and money laundering in the industrialized countries and offshore paradises; the globalization of drug networks and terrorist structures; the unconstrained growth of the light weapons market; Washington's antinarcotics, security, and foreign policies toward Bogotá; the expansion of transnational organized crime throughout the continent; and the escalating institutional turmoil in the Andean region.

Colombia's situation is, probably, the most critical one in terms of regional insecurity. It should be pointed out that Colombia was already a focus of U.S. attention and concern before September 11, 2001. The U.S. Commission on National Security/Twenty-First Century, cochaired by Gary Hart (Democrat) and Warren Rudman (Republican), corroborates this. Between the years 1999 and 2001, the commission was charged with thoroughly evaluating those dimensions of insecurity that seem to be defining the world picture in the twenty-first century and drafting a list of specific recommendations for how the United States should handle military, institutional, and diplomatic threats to its condition as a superpower. The lengthy study dedicated a special place to the discussion on "failed states." The commission emphasized that this phenomenon represented a major threat to U.S. security, and that, in the face of the increasing numbers of failed states, Washington needed to set some priorities: "*Not every such problem must be primarily a US responsibility, particularly in a world where other powers are amassing significant wealth and human resources. There are countries whose domestic stability is, for differing reasons, of major importance to US interests (such as Mexico, Colombia, Russia and Saudi Arabia). Without prejudging the likelihood of domestic upheaval, these countries should be a priority focus of US planning in a manner appropriate to the respective cases. For cases of lesser priority, the United States should help the international community develop innovative mechanisms to manage the problems of failed states.*"

The U.S. National Security Strategy has identified three principal threats for Washington: international terrorism on a global scale, "rogue states" capable of obtaining weapons of mass destruction, and locations that facilitate the presence of organizations that resort to terror, thanks to the lack of a viable state. Colombia may eventually fall into the last category. The country has been witnessing the violence of organizations that have employed terrorist tactics. However, it is not an epicenter of some kind of mega-terrorism that generates an imminent danger to United States.

At this time (mid-2006), the major players in the Colombian conflict face serious dilemmas. One of the greatest challenges is the one confronted by President Álvaro Uribe.[5] On one hand, he faces a domestic dilemma: how to recover the state's authority without falling into authoritarianism (and how to get reelected). It was indeed necessary to build up the military capacity of the state by increasing both domestic budget allocations and foreign aid. However, this is not the only requirement for attaining and securing a more legitimate state. A state that is institutionally absent, socially retracted, and economically anemic has been and will be incapable of overcoming the multiple sources of violence—guerrilla, paramilitary, drug trafficking, criminal—

regardless of the level of spending on defense and security. On the other hand, Uribe must deal with an external dilemma: how to settle the domestic war given his limited autonomy; that is, how to achieve national peace without foreign intervention. Colombia's president opted for unrestricted alignment with the United States, hoping that it would consolidate a "special relationship" between Bogotá and Washington.[6] However, there is no such thing as a partially symmetrical, "special relationship" between the United States and a peripheral country, much less after September 11. Clearly, it is not a matter of defying and molesting the United States: that is both foolish and immature. But neither should Bogotá let itself become Washington's vassal; this could run counter to the country's vital national interests. Colombia needs its *own* peace, not someone else's.

The insurgent Revolutionary Armed Forces of Colombia stand at a critical crossroads: either they continue to fight for a political cause and become a counterpart with whom the armed conflict can be negotiated, or they transform themselves entirely into a criminal machine, in which case it would be easier for Washington and Bogotá to portray them as terrorists with whom nothing can be settled. After more than forty years of existence and struggle, the FARC—which began as a rural guerrilla movement that was poorly equipped and largely unaffected by the Cold War—has been losing much of its revolutionary ethos. It has been able to increase its resources by means of its taxing of, and participation in, the drug business; its active involvement in the kidnapping industry; and its capacity to extort landowners and entrepreneurs alike. This allowed it to increment its recruitment among the needy rural sectors and the poor urban youth, while simultaneously it avoids facing the changes provoked by the collapse of the Soviet Union. Rather than improving its influence and political legitimacy, it opted to expand its military might and its capacity to carry out cross-border operations. The alternatives are, thus, apparent: either the FARC re-politicizes its project or it lets its members be turned into criminals.

The crucial dilemma for the United States is how to assist Colombia to simultaneously eradicate the lucrative drug emporium (which has its roots among consumers in the United States itself), roll back the military advances made by the guerrillas (and their expansion into urban areas), and deal politically with the paramilitary (which began a "peace process" with the Uribe government), without getting directly involved in fighting these phenomena. Washington prefers that the Colombians themselves, first and foremost, fight the "war on drugs" (of American origin) and the "war against the insurgency" (of Colombian origin). The United States is committing resources, advisors, and technology to both—which are now part and parcel of the "war on terrorism"—with the understanding that Bogotá is no Baghdad, something that Colombian elites (together with President Uribe) have yet to grasp.

Rather than another "El Salvador" or "Vietnam"-style paradigm, the United States appears to be following in Colombia a model deployed in the Philippines, a new style for open intervention.[7] A sort of "intervention by imposition"—that is, a unilateral military intervention in a nation's internal affairs regardless of the political regime in consideration—dominated during the Cold War: the United States in Vietnam and the Soviet Union in Afghanistan were typical examples. The kind of "intervention by consent" emerged in the post–Cold War era: a military intervention becomes justifiable for humanitarian reasons and, with some basis in international legitimacy, is carried out via collective actions. Haiti and Bosnia were two emblematic examples.

Lastly, a type of "intervention by invitation" seemed to emerge following September 11: democratic governments call upon foreign actors to settle militarily domestic problems. President Edward Shevardnadze arranged for a small contingent of U.S. Special Forces to be sent to train Georgian troops in the fight against Chechen rebels. In 2002, President George W. Bush and President Gloria Arroyo of the Philippines agreed that 650 U.S. soldiers would be dispatched to back up Philippine armed forces in the fight against the Abu Sayyaf group. Early in 2003 Washington allocated US$100 million dollars in antiterrorist assistance for the Philippines and sent an additional 1,750 troops to the country. U.S. military assistance continued thereafter, including logistical and operational assistance in the field.

The Colombian situation has many interesting parallels to that of the Philippines. Plan Colombia, which began in 2000, at an initial cost of US$1,319 million,[8] authorized the presence of four hundred U.S. military (lately, the cap has been placed at eight hundred) advisors and the involvement of four hundred private contractors (the new cap is at six hundred).[9]

Just following September 11, the U.S. Congress approved US$98 million for U.S. troops to train Colombian soldiers with regards to the protection of the country's oil pipeline. Once the Iraq invasion was under way, the White House asked Congress for an additional US$104 million for Colombia (the legislature had already approved nearly US$500 million for Bogotá for 2003) as part of the US$80 billion package for the war on Saddam Hussein.[10]

There are other similarities with the Philippines example. Three facts about Washington's military commitment to the Philippines' anti-insurgency policy should be highlighted. First, Abu Sayyaf has been linked to international terrorism, particularly to Al Qaeda. Second, Abu Sayyaf regularly carries out kidnappings (among them, of foreigners). And third, the Philippines' conflict has been centering in the south of the country. In Colombia, the FARC is increasingly portrayed as a movement with ties to international terrorists, like the IRA (Irish Republican Army). Second, the FARC is the most active group in terms of kidnappings. And third, even though the FARC abandoned in 2002 the demilitarized zone set up in 1999–2002 during the failed peace process, it is still in control of several areas of the south of the country.

Should the current intervention model being employed prove inadequate, it is probable that Washington may attempt to form a "coalition of the willing"—a coalition called for by Colombia and promoted by the United States—geared toward "solving" the Colombian armed conflict. President Uribe has already called on the United Nations (by arguing that the Colombian case is even more dramatic than that of Iraq) and the Organization of American States (by promoting the review of the 1947 Inter-American Treaty of Reciprocal Assistance) for more assistance in solving Colombia's internal conflicts.

South American Response: A New Contadora?

South America's quick and unchallenged acceptance that Colombia has become the epicenter of the "war on terrorism" deserves closer assessment. Three points merit some analysis. First, terrorism, as a phenomenon, is in need of a thoughtful, rigorous, and detailed evaluation. To begin with, it should be stressed that terrorism is not an objective (no one achieves or holds power indefinitely via terror), nor is it an ideology (either of the Right or Left). Terrorism is a method. Insurgencies, regardless of their orientation, any time, and everywhere, combine three modes of warfare: guerrilla warfare, intended to produce casualties among state security forces and to erode the enemy's morale; conventional warfare, aimed at creating a parallel regular army whose large and organized units will have the capacity to fight major battles; and terrorism, which directs the violence against the noncombatant civilian population. Terrorism is not a random form of conflict; it is used to achieve political aims, which, over the long term, will facilitate the takeover of power. Even so, more than a demonstration of strength, terrorism is an expression of strategic disadvantage. Terrorism is ineffective, militarily speaking, as a form of urban warfare, even though it may have symbolic effectiveness. With the exception of South Yemen in 1967, there are no other known cases of urban terrorism being effective in ousting a government.

Bearing that in mind, the FARC has noticeably stepped up its reliance on terrorism—particularly urban—although it does not yet reach the proportions that some label "mega-terrorism" (or "super-terrorism"). So what may be a definition of the FARC today? Use of one term or another creates significant conceptual and practical consequences and problems. Echoing Stepanova, I suggest the FARC be classified as an "organization involved in terrorist activities, rather than a terrorist organization."[11] This concept better conveys the range of the movement's armed activities while leaving open the possibility of engaging in future political negotiations.

Second, the current Colombian administration is involved in concluding a peace agreement with the far-right paramilitary AUC. This group is one of the thirty-six terrorist organizations on the U.S. State Department's international terrorism list. Up to now (mid-2006) Washington has actively supported this negotiation. This leads to an uncomfortable question about the situation in Colombia: why has the recourse to terrorism been so successful there? It gave a boost to the M-19 (Movimiento 19 de Abril), the most nationalistic of the armed groups: Virgilio Barco's government (1986–1990) negotiated with M-19 after they destroyed the Palace of Justice in the heart of downtown Bogotá in 1985. Drug traffickers' indiscriminate use of terrorism at the end of the 1980s helped them reach a Colombian-style plea bargain with the incoming César Gaviria administration (1990–1994). Terror tactics deployed in the late 1990s helped the Marxist FARC guerrillas to start a dialogue (which ultimately failed) with President Andrés Pastrana (1998–2002). The recourse to terror—epitomized by the massacring of thousands of civilians over the last fifteen years—allowed the paramilitaries to reach an agreement with the Uribe government. Thus terrorism seems to pay in Colombia without forceful criticism from Washington.

And third, it is important to mention what may be called the paradox of interventionism. It should be pointed out that it is the U.S. Southern Command[12] based in Miami (instead of the civilian decision makers in Washington) that is more outspoken about pushing for a larger, regional involvement in the Colombian war, in contrast to Colombia's armed forces (although some Colombian civilians do dream about a foreign military intervention against the FARC). Former SOUTHCOM commander General James Hill and Colombian president Álvaro Uribe have referred to external intervention in Colombia much more than Rumsfeld and Powell in Washington or the Colombian military commanders in Bogotá. In that sense, it is fascinating to review the U.S. Department of State's 2003 report *Patterns of Global Terrorism* and turn to the voluminous appendix chronicling the most significant acts of terrorism throughout the world in 2002. According to the list, there were only five noteworthy acts committed in Colombia: three involved kidnappings of foreigners; the other two correspond to the blowing up of oil pipelines. In fact, thousands of Colombians were massacred in 2002, there were nearly three thousand kidnappings in the country that year, and a direct attack was made on President Uribe on the day of his inauguration.

Under these circumstances, the question, then, is whether South America understands the interests it has at stake in Colombia and whether or not it is capable of promoting a peaceful settlement to the armed conflict in that Andean country. Colombia should not be the object of a military intervention; it requires political involvement. Colombia is in need of a new Contadora-style[13] peace initiative.

Like the experience in Central America in the 1980s, a Contadora for Colombia should offer a realistic diagnosis of the country's situation and provide an accurate picture of the existing threats. There have recently been some fragmented and biased studies and reports in the United States on Colombia. However, an updated and honest inquiry on Colombia is imperative. Before the Contadora was created the United States unilaterally produced and promoted the Kissinger Report on Central America; now Latin America—with the acknowledgment of Washington—must call for a consensual Report on Colombia.

Similarly, as the Contadora for Central America tried in the midst of the Cold War to preserve a political and diplomatic space so that Nicaragua and El Salvador were not lost for the West, the new post–Cold War Contadora should seek to avoid a potential destruction of Colombia in democratic terms. Although it is fragile and limited, Colombia's democracy should be the central concern. Also, as the original Contadora defined procedures and policies to escape from a low-intensity conflict in Central America, the Contadora for Colombia must establish rules and processes to avoid an Andean explosion: no party in Colombia or abroad should be allowed to promote a domino effect in the heart of South America.

However, the new Contadora should transcend the previous one in several respects. First, it should not target the United States; on the contrary it must incorporate Washington. A Contadora for Colombia should be understood both as a forum where the United States can participate and as an alternative to an uncontrolled militarization inherent in Washington's current policy toward Bogotá.

Second, the Contadora for Colombia should contemplate the use of a variety of legitimate instruments in the search for peace: political persuasion alone will not change the current level of war in Colombia. The new Contadora will have to guarantee real power sharing. Colombia needs a new democratic pact, and that means putting an end to political violence as well as to elitist rule.

And third, in the Colombian case a new Contadora must contribute to the resolution of a different kind of a domestic war—a war worsened by the drug issue. Consequently, this new Contadora should broaden the agenda of interest: for example, by proposing and debating a serious and innovative approach to controlling the narcotics trade.

To sum up, Colombians alone will not be able to solve their catastrophe—a catastrophe that is basically national but has many international dimensions and influences. Colombia needs help and understanding, not intervention or more war. Colombia needs a new Contadora. Colombia needs the hemispheric solidarity that once proved so helpful in solving the Central American crisis.

The Failed U.S. Counternarcotics Policy

Narcotics still pose a pressing problem in the United States more than four decades after the current policy to tackle them was first developed. The drug war has not worked, and although the blight of drugs is getting worse, most politicians shy away from discussing the issue. This is a big mistake. The politics of denial ends up justifying a continuous futile crusade. Nearly $400 billion of public money has been devoted to different antidrug activities during the past twenty years, with limited success. After spending so much to control the drug phenomenon, what went wrong?

In essence, the national and international drug control strategy promulgated by the United States during the last four administrations has been flawed. If abstinence is the most important target of prohibition, the figures regarding new use and more abuse of drugs and the data on drug-related criminality and youth drug-initiation reveal a costly failure. Notwithstanding the efforts and the unprecedented percentage of federal and state inmates incarcerated for drug offences, the truth is that this policy is close to collapse. And most illegal drugs are now more easily available, purer, and cheaper than in the early 1980s.

The U.S. drug strategy is double-edged. First, it seeks to reduce the price at the production stage and to improve eradication methods, discouraging peasants from cultivating illicit crops. Second, it seeks to strengthen interdiction at the processing and transit countries, to reduce the availability and potency of drugs in the United States, and to enhance seizures at U.S. borders, thus elevating the domestic price of narcotics and deterring potential new consumers.

In contrast to what was expected and desired, and as an unintended effect of the tactics on drugs, American organized crime at home and transnational criminal organizations in Latin America and the Caribbean, in particular, have become richer and more powerful, while U.S. citizens have become less safe and more victimized. Prohibition has provided the incentive for a well-organized narco-criminality to diversify the market for drugs, to channel the proceeds through financial havens, and to extend strategic partnerships with other illegal businesses. The drug phenomenon has created enormous social, political, ecological, and military difficulties throughout the Americas. Human rights abuses, environmental catastrophes, imbalances in civil–military relations, institutional corruption, massive civil rights violations, concentration of power in drug mafia, and law enforcement failures are some of the legacies left by a mistaken war that has concentrated on the supply side of the narcotics question.

The notion of a Pax Americana used to convey the sense of a single hegemony by a superpower such as the United States. But we may now be witnessing the gradual consolidation of a hemispheric Pax Mafiosa: the growing power, and even legitimacy in some cases, of a new criminal social class with the ability, commitment, and opportunity to lead. Some rural portions of Colombia and Mexico, some urban ghettos in Los Angeles and Rio de Janeiro, some municipalities in Paraguay, and some islands in the Caribbean provide a preview of what may happen if the Pax Mafiosa becomes consolidated nationally and continentally in the years to come. The Pax Mafiosa would have dire consequences: the establishment of kleptocratic governments, the breakdown of the rule of law, highly violent environments, extended social polarization, potential sanctuary for terrorist activities, and, very probably, collapsed states.

An Undesirable Ending

> Prosperity fosters hubris—ambition and the wish to have more than one's share—and disaster soon follows.
>
> —Jacqueline de Romilly, "The Rise and Fall of States According to Greek Authors," 1977

The United States has radically modified its grand strategy (see table 9.1). Washington has transformed its strategies, doctrines, and their corresponding diplomatic instruments. Containment was the leading strategy of the Cold War era. It was supposed to halt expansion of the Soviet Union, and whenever possible, roll back its sphere of influence. Deterrence, the prevailing doctrine at the time, meant that the costs would be dear for the adversary that initiated forceful action: retaliation would be annihilating should the Soviet Union decide to launch a nuclear attack. Strategy and doctrine were supported through the structuring of a network of alliances representing firm, decisive commitments. Within the Western Hemisphere the grand strategy was complemented by a subaltern doctrine formulated under the rationale that the armed forces

TABLE 9.1
The U.S. Grand Strategy

	Cold War	*Post–September 11*
STRATEGY	Containment	Primacy
DOCTRINE	Deterrence	Preemptive War
SUPPORTING MEANS	Alliances (NATO, etc.)	Flexible or Ad Hoc Coalitions (Coalition of the Willing)
SUBALTERN HEMISPHERIC RATIONALE	National Security Doctrine	Doctrine of National In-security (?)

in the region were not going to have an active, fundamental role in a potential direct fight against the Soviet Union. Thus, the so-called national security doctrine was devised and imposed in order to fight "the enemy within" (local communism, which, according to this line of thinking, turned out to have links to the international communist movement).

After September 11 and more and more clearly after the second Iraq war, the United States has drastically altered its grand strategy. The new strategy is geared toward primacy. This means that Washington will not tolerate any peer competitor—be it a traditional ally (the European Union) or a potential foe (China).

The new doctrine is preemptive warfare, designed to make it clear that the United States will employ anticipatorily its military muscle (including nuclear attack) against another country, regardless of the fact that the attacked country is not capable and willing to carry out an imminent attack against the United States. Further, the solid alliances of the past have been replaced by new forms of diplomatic support—the self-styled coalitions of the willing—whereby Washington alone defines the mission and then creates a coalition to carry out the operation.

A subaltern doctrine linked to this substantially redefined grand strategy has not yet been fully developed. There are clear signs, however, of changes on the horizon. Two things point in that direction. First, Washington has managed to implant the idea, which the different countries accept to varying degrees, that there are critical "new threats" in the region. These new threats involve the expansion of global terrorism, transnational organized crime, and worldwide drug trafficking, all of which are intertwined and operate in the context of the territorial vacuum created by weakened states. Second, the Pentagon has been insisting that the new threats demand removing the separation between internal security and external defense: the work of the police, security agencies, and armed forces should overlap and be interchangeable, and the lines between police and military functions effectively erased.

In a way, a sort of "doctrine of national in-security" is gradually emerging. Washington demands that these new threats (which involve domestic groups or movements that may be part of larger organizations devoted to violence) be coped with, without making a distinction between police and military forces, and without carefully distinguishing between radical, reformist, and other opposition groups and real threats to domestic and hemispheric security. If this logic evolves, without modification, then its repercussions on the evolution of peace and democracy in the Western Hemisphere may be enormously significant, producing the sort of unintended consequences, mostly negative, that have characterized U.S. intervention in other areas of the world.

There is no existing animosity or conflict between the United States and South America, nor does the region represent a serious threat to Washington.

However, the United States itself is becoming a source of problems that affect Latin American interests and values. But rather than thinking in terms of alignment or nonalignment vis-à-vis the United States, or subordination to or confrontation with Washington, the time has come to look at the United States as an extremely powerful world player that simultaneously generates global order and chaos. Consequently, analyzing relations with Washington and the future structure of security in the Western Hemisphere calls for an approach that is neither dogmatic nor naive.

That said, we must acknowledge that South America's leading security-related issues continue to stem from a dwindling rule of law, growing institutional weakness, increased political illegitimacy, economic vulnerability, and social inequity: these are the key sources for understanding and resolving our most critical reality. For the United States, the central question is whether it will continue to insist on policies toward the region that have failed to address these pressing problems for decades, or worse, policies that have contributed to making insecurity rather than security the daily condition for millions of Latin Americans. Will the United States overcome its addiction to failed policies, for its own sake and for the sake of its neighbors in the Western Hemisphere?

Notes

Preface

1. "Declaration of Principles," First Summit of the Americas, Miami, Florida, December 9–11, 1994: www.summit-americas.org/miamidec.htm (accessed May 2, 2005).

2. "Declaration of Principles," First Summit of the Americas.

3. See, for example, Summit of the Americas Information Network, U.S. Arms Control and Disarmament Agency, "Confidence and Security-building Measures in the Americas: A Reference Book of Hemispheric Documents": www.summit-americas.org/Hemispheric%20Security/CSBM-main.htm.

4. See Coletta A. Youngers and Eileen Rosin, eds., *Drugs and Democracy in Latin America: The Impact of U.S. Policy* (Boulder, Colo.: Rienner, 2005).

5. For a summary of threats and challenges in the region from the Commander of US-SOUTHCOM in 2005 see Testimony of General Bantz J. Craddock, commander, United States Southern Command, hearing of the House Armed Services Committee: "Fiscal Year 2006 National Defense Authorization Budget Request," March 9, 2005: http://ciponline.org/colombia/050309crad.pdf (accessed May 11, 2005).

6. Luigi R. Einaudi, "The Common Defense of Democracy in the Americas," policy brief, based on testimony before the Subcommittee on the Western Hemisphere, Peace Corps, Narcotics and Terrorism of the Senate Foreign Relations Committee, May 12, 1999: www.iadialgo.org/publications/Brief%20-%20Einaudi.html (accessed May 12, 2005).

7. For a brief discussion of base reconfiguration after 1999 see John Lindsay-Poland, "U.S. Military Bases in Latin America and the Caribbean," *Foreign Policy in Focus* 9(3) (August 2004): www.americaspolicy.org/briefs/2004/0408latammil.html (accessed May 9, 2005).

8. Lindsay-Poland, "U.S. Military Bases in Latin America and the Caribbean."

9. Roger F. Noriega, assistant secretary for Western Hemisphere Affairs, statement before the Senate Foreign Relations Committee, Washington, D.C., March 2, 2005: www.state.gov/p/wha/rls/rm/2005/q1/42885.htm (accessed May 11, 2005). Much the same: in more detail, was repeated in the testimony of Adolfo A. Franco, assistant administrator, Bureau for Latin America

and the Caribbean, United States Agency for International Development, before the Committee on Foreign Relations, United States Senate, March 2, 2005. For example, "USAID is assisting LAC countries to enact legal, policy, and regulatory reforms that promote trade liberalization, hemispheric market integration, competitiveness, and investment. [but] Narcotics trafficking, guerrilla and paramilitary violence, human rights abuses, corruption, crime, and a lack of effective government presence in the coca-growing areas in the Andes pose a threat to democracy in the region." usunrome.usembassy.it/UNISSUES/sustdev/docs/a5030205.htm (accessed May 11, 2005).

10. Roger F. Noriega, assistant secretary for Western Hemisphere Affairs, statement before the Senate Foreign Relations Committee, Washington, D.C., March 2, 2005. www.state.gov/p/wha/rls/rm/2005/q1/42885.htm (accessed May 11, 2005).

11. Roger F. Noriega, assistant secretary for Western Hemisphere Affairs, "The State of Democracy in Latin America," statement before the U.S. House of Representatives Committee on International Relations Subcommittee on the Western Hemisphere, Washington, D.C., March 9, 2005. www.state.gov/p/wha/rls/rm/2005/q1/43221.htm (accessed May 15, 2005).

12. See also Raúl Zibechi, "El nuevo militarismo en América del Sur," Informe especial del IRC Programa de las Américas, 10 Mayo, 2005. www.americaspolicy.org www.americaspolicy .org/reports/2005/sp_0505militar.html) (accessed May 12, 2005).

13. National Security Decision Directive 221, April 8, 1996, stated, in part: "The expanding scope of global narcotics trafficking has creation a situation which today adds another significant dimension to the law enforcement and public health aspects of this international problem and threatens the national security of the United States."

14. See Ted Galen Carpenter, *Bad Neighbor Policy. Washington's Futile War on Drugs in Latin America* (New York: Palgrave, 2003).

15. Ralph Peters, *Fighting for the Future: Will America Triumph?* (Mechanicsburgh, PA: Stackpole Books, 1999): 30.

16. Adam Isacson, "After Plan Colombia: Why Doesn't Washington Learn from Failure in Colombia?" Focal Point. Spotlight on the Americas. December 2002, Volume 1, Number 5. www.focal.ca/fpoint/focalpoint_dec02.pdf.

17. According to the U.S. Department of State,

The Government of Colombia developed "Plan Colombia" as an integrated strategy to meet the most pressing challenges confronting Colombia today—promoting the peace process, combating the narcotics industry, reviving the Colombian economy, and strengthening the democratic pillars of Colombian society. Plan Colombia is a $7.5 billion program. President Pastrana has pledged $4 billion of Colombian resources and has called on the international community to provide the remaining $3.5 billion to assist this effort. . . . In response to Plan Colombia, and in consultation with the Colombian Government, the United States is providing a $1.3 billion total U.S. interagency assistance package to Colombia. (Bureau of Western Hemisphere Affairs, Washington, D.C., March 14, 2001)

18. Extracts from Testimony of Adolfo A. Franco, assistant administrator, Bureau for Latin America & the Caribbean U.S. Assistance to Colombia and the Andean Region, April 10, 2002.

19. A document measuring the effectiveness of the plan on a number of dimensions from August 2002 to December 2003 was released by the Ministry of Defense: "The Effectiveness of the Colombian Democratic Security and Defense Policy. August 2003–December 2003": www .mindefensa.gov.co/politica/documentos/effectiveness_cdsdp_upto_200312_eng.pdf

20. FARC, Fuerzas Armadas Revolucionarias Colombianas; ELN, Ejército de Liberación Nacional; AUC, Autodefensas Unidas Colombianas (frequently identified as paramilitaries or "paras"). All three of these groups, in 2005, were on the United States' government list of terrorist organizations.

21. "Importantes avances del Estado Colombiano en DDHH y DIH en 2003," Bogotá, D.C., March 4, 2004 (SNE). Colombian Ministry of Defense website.

22. "U.S. Drug Czar Outlines Western Hemisphere's Counternarcotics Progress," August 10, 2004. Bureau of International Information Programs, U.S. Department of State website: usinfo .state.gov/xarchives/display.html?p=washfileenglish&y=2004&m=August&x=20040810183324 ASrelliM0.7423059&t=livefeeds/wf-latest.html.

23. See Martha Nubia Bello, ed., *Deplazamiento Forzado: Dinámica de guerra, exclusión y desarraigo* (Bogotá: Universidad Nacional de Colombia, 2004).

24. "Gigantic Threats from Armed Groups," *Colombia Week*, March 10, 2004: www.colombia week.org/20040315.html#lastword.

25. Plan Patriota, initiated in late 2003, was a military offensive and counterinsurgency operation in southern Colombia, stronghold of the FARC guerrillas, involving more than twenty thousand troops, supported by U.S. military logistics and intelligence, along with "civilian contractors." It was the largest military operation in Colombia since the mid-1960s. For descriptions of the guerrilla movements of the 1960s and 1970s see Brian Loveman and Thomas M. Davies, Jr., *Che Guevara on Guerrilla Warfare* (Wilmington, Del.: Scholarly Resources, 1997), 244–52.

26. "A Symptom of Failure," *Colombia Week*, September 13, 2004: www.colombiaweek.org/ 20040913.html#lastword (accessed May 8, 2005).

27. "Colombia This Week, September 6, 2004": colhrnet.igc.org/newitems/sept04/ctw.906.04 .htm (accessed October 12, 2004).

28. "Peru Election 2006": http://weblogs.elearning.ubc.ca/peru/archives/023485.php (accessed February 28, 2006).

29. Anonymous, *Imperial Hubris: Why the West Is Losing the War on Terror* (Washington, D.C.: Brassey's Inc., 2004).

30. Part of the so-called Roosevelt Corollary to the Monroe Doctrine (http://teachingamerican history.org/libary/index.asp?document=671), which figured in the president's speech to Congress on December 6, 1904, proclaimed:

It is not true that the United States feels any land hunger or entertains any projects as regards the other nations of the Western Hemisphere save such as are for their welfare. All that this country desires is to see the neighboring countries stable, orderly, and prosperous. Any country whose people conduct themselves well can count upon our hearty friendship. If a nation shows that it knows how to act with reasonable efficiency and decency in social and political matters, if it keeps order and pays its obligations, it need fear no interference from the United States. Chronic wrongdoing, or an impotence which results in a general loosening of the ties of civilized society, may in America, as elsewhere, ultimately require intervention by some civilized nation, and in the Western Hemisphere the adherence of the United States to the Monroe Doctrine may force the United States, however reluctantly, in flagrant cases of such wrongdoing or impotence, to the exercise of an international police power.

31. Proclaimed by President James Monroe, December 2, 1823, the doctrine (www.our documents.gov/doc.php?doc=23&page=transcript) stipulated, in part: "The American continents, by the free and independent condition which they have assured and maintain, are henceforth not to be considered as subjects for future colonization by any European powers. We should consider any attempt on their part to extend their system to any portion of this hemisphere as dangerous to our peace and safety."

32. Lars Schoultz, *Beneath the United States: A History of U.S. Policy toward Latin America* (Cambridge, Mass: Harvard University Press, 1998), xiv.

33. Schoultz, *Beneath the United States*, xv–xvi.

34. Enacted by Congress in 1986, the certification process was intended to pressure governments around the world to take tougher counternarcotics measures. Each year, the U.S. president must produce a list of major drug-producing and drug-transit countries. Countries included in

the "majors" list face mandatory sanctions unless the administration certifies that a country is fully cooperating with U.S. antinarcotics efforts or is taking sufficient steps on its own to meet the terms of the 1988 UN drug control convention. The sanctions include the withdrawal of most U.S. foreign assistance not directly related to counternarcotics programs and U.S. opposition to loans those countries seek from multilateral development banks. The administration can also waive sanctions against a country that is not fully certified, if it determines that doing so is in the "vital national interests" of the United States. For a brief critique of this process see "Drug Certification," *Foreign Policy in Focus* 3(24) (September 1998): www.fpif.org/briefs/vol3/v3n24fpo.html.

35. "Colombian Military Aid Released for Ranch Visit. Aid Frozen for Half a Year over Human Rights Abuses," Latin America Working Group: www.lawg.org/ (updated August 3, 2005).

36. Cited in "House Votes Down Military Aid Cut to Colombia," Latin America Working Group: www.lawg.org/ (updated August 3, 2005).

37. Virginia M. Bouvier, "Evaluating U.S. Policy in Colombia," policy report from the IRC Americas Program, May 11, 2005: www.americaspolicy.org/reports/2005/0505colombia.html (accessed May 12, 2005).

38. Testimony of General James T. Hill, United States Army commander, United States Southern Command, before the House Armed Services Committee, United States House of Representatives: www.globalsecurity.org/military/library/congress/2004_hr/04-03-24hill.htm, March 24, 2004.

39. The boundary between national security (protection of the state, territorial integrity and sovereignty, and essential state functions from other states or nonstate actors) and law enforcement is always blurry. But defining gang violence, drug trafficking, illegal immigration, organized crime, environmental degradation, etc. as threats to national security extends the concept beyond previous usage and "securitizes" much of public policy. Of course, contagious disease can also be defined as a national security issue instead of a public health issue, as might inflation. If almost everything is a national security concern, however, that implies a "militarization" of domestic politics—as occurred in much of Latin America from the early 1960s until the late 1980s.

Chapter 1

1. Copies of key policy statements and official documents from the 1990–2006 period are included on the accompanying URL (www.rowman.com/isbn/0742540987) provided to readers with this book.

2. Citations in this paragraph from The White House, "New National Security Policy of the United States" (Washington, D.C.: USGPO, August 1991).

3. The White House, "A National Security Strategy of Engagement and Enlargement" (Washington, D.C.: USGPO, February 1996).

4. The White House, "A National Security Strategy of Engagement and Enlargement."

5. U.S. Department of Defense, *Quadrenniel Defense Review Report* (Washington, D.C.: USGPO, 1990, conclusion.

6. U.S. Department of Defense, QDR, 1997.

7. U.S. Department of Defense, "Annual Report to the President and Congress, 1999" (Washington, D.C.: USGPO), chapter 1, emphasis added.

8. In the early 1980s the creation of a "rapid deployment force" to protect global strategic interests, especially in the Persian Gulf, anticipated both the policies of George H. W. Bush and William Clinton. The rapid deployment force eventually provided the foundation for CENT-

COM, one of the regional unified commands into which the United States divided the world for purposes of defense planning. See Maxwell Orme Johnson, *The Military as an Instrument of U.S. Policy in Southwest Asia: The Rapid Deployment Joint Task Force, 1979–1982* (Boulder, Colo.: Westview, 1983); Jeffrey Record, *The Rapid Deployment Force and U.S. Military Intervention in the Persian Gulf* (Cambridge, Mass.: Institute for Foreign Policy Analysis, 1981); United States Congress, House Committee on the Budget, "Military Readiness and the Rapid Deployment Joint Task Force (RDJTF)," Hearings before the Committee on the Budget, House of Representatives, 96th Congress, 2nd session, September 30 and October 1, 1980 (Washington, D.C.: USGPO, 1980).

9. The Monroe Doctrine (1823) asserted a unique "American sphere" that should be free of undue European ("old world") ideological, economic, and military influence. In 1895, U.S. secretary of state Richard Olney declared, regarding the Caribbean, "Today, the United States is practically sovereign on this continent, and its fiat is law upon the subjects to which it confines its interposition." The Roosevelt Corollary (1904), issued by Theodore Roosevelt in the first era of American imperialism, asserted that the United States had the obligation to intervene, unilaterally, in the affairs of Latin American countries when disorder, inability or unwillingness to pay debts, or threats to foreigners' lives and property might bring intervention by "non-hemispheric powers." Roosevelt affirmed that "in the Western Hemisphere . . . the Monroe Doctrine may force the United States . . . to the exercise of an international police power."

10. Office of the Press Secretary, November 6, 2003. President Bush Discusses Freedom in Iraq and Middle East, Remarks by the President at the 20th Anniversary of the National Endowment for Democracy. United States Chamber of Commerce Washington, D.C.: www.whitehouse.gov/news/releases/2003/11/20031106-2.html (accessed April 30, 2005).

11. U.S. Department of State Office of the Secretary of State, Office of the Coordinator for Counterterrorism, "Patterns of Global Terrorism: 1992," released April 30, 1993: "There have been notable counterterrorism successes in Latin America in 1992, particularly in Peru and Bolivia, where insurgent groups suffered major blows with the capture of top leaders. Insurgent groups have steadily become more isolated politically in Colombia, as a violence-weary public supported stronger counterterrorism measures." Almost half of the "terrorist" actions in Latin America for this period occurred in Colombia (68 of 142), including "nearly 50 attacks on the oil pipeline jointly owned by Ecopetrol of Colombia and a consortium of US and West European countries, a traditional Colombian guerrilla target": www.fas.org/irp/threat/terror_92/latin.html. Attacks on the pipeline were not only symbolic expressions of anti-U.S. and antiforeign investment agendas by the guerrillas but occasioned important losses of revenue to the Colombian government, further decreasing its ability to provide a range of services to Colombian citizens.

12. George Bush, The White House, "National Drug Control Strategy" (Washington, D.C.: USGPO, January 1992), 3–4, 9. See also, John T. Fishel, lieutenant colonel, USAR, "Developing a Drug War Strategy, Lessons Learned from Operation Blast Furnace," *Military Review* 139(15) (June 1991): 61–69; Bruce M. Bagley and William O. Walker III, *Drug Trafficking in the Americas* (Coral Gables, Fla.: University of Miami, North-South Center; New Brunswick, N.J.: Distributed by Transaction Publishers, 1994).

13. See, for example, William W. Mendel, "Counterdrug Strategy—Illusive Victory: From Blast Furnace to Green Sweep," *Military Review* 72 (December 1992): 74–87; Michael H. Abbott, colonel, U.S. Army, with Murl D. Munger, "U.S. Army Involvement in Counterdrug Operations—A Matter of Politics or National Security?" U.S. Army War College Military Studies Program Paper (Carlisle, Pa.: U.S. Army War College, March 30, 1988). The author was the aviation battalion commander who deployed assets to Bolivia in support of Blast Furnace. His conclusion is that "the introduction of U.S. military forces into the sovereign territory of a source country is neither an effective nor appropriate approach."

14. See Alvin D. Cantrell, "Drugs and Terror: A Threat to U.S. National Security" (Carlisle Barracks, Pa.: U.S. Army War College, 1992); Jeffrey G. Schuller, "The Military's Role in the Drug

War: To Just Say No Is Not Enough!" (Newport, R.I.: Naval War College, 1989); Daniel N. Steward, "Counter-Terrorism Joint Task Force: A Paradigm for Counter-Narcotics" (Newport, R.I.:
Naval War College, 1993); Patrick F. Webb, "Narcoterrorism: A Threat to the United States,"
USAWC Military Studies Program Paper (Carlisle Barracks, Pa.: U.S. Army War College, 1992),
34 pp.

15. The modern "drug war" began with Richard Nixon's presidency in 1973 and the creation
of the Drug Enforcement Administration (DEA). President Ronald Reagan's National Security
Decision Directive 221 declared the drug trade a threat to U.S. national security in 1986. During
the Reagan presidency military assets were directed against drug production and trafficking.
Shortly after taking office in the George H. W. Bush presidency, Secretary of Defense Dick
Cheney issued a memorandum calling the drug trade "a direct threat to the sovereignty and security of the country" (Department of Defense "Guidance for Implementation of the President's
National Drug Control Strategy," 1989). A second memorandum stated that curtailing the flow
of drugs into the United States is a "high priority security mission of the Department of Defense" ("Memorandum for the Commanders of the Unified and Specified Combatant Commands, Subject: *Elevation of the Mission Priority of Counternarcotics Operations*," 1989). President William Clinton also followed this policy. In 1998 a document prepared under the direction
of the Chairman of the Joint Chiefs of Staff ("Joint Counterdrug Operations," February 17,
1998) stated, "Those who contribute to the production, transport, sale and use of illegal drugs
and laundering of drug money present a threat to the national security of the United States." The
Clinton administration, in the 1999 "National Security Strategy," designated drug trafficking a
transnational threat to U.S. interests. For an overview of U.S. drug policy with country studies
see Coletta A. Youngers and Eileen Rosin, eds., *Drugs and Democracy in Latin America* (Boulder,
Colo.: Rienner, 2005).

16. This document is included on the URL (www.rowman.com/isbn/0742540987) that accompanies this volume.

17. In some ways, the so-called new security agenda of the 1990s was not markedly different
in concept from the agenda in the 1970s at the Tenth Conference of American Armies in Caracas: "El tema central de esta Reunión, que generalmente se manejaba dentro de esquemas de seguridad militar, fue el relativo a la 'seguridad económica colectiva', basada en la interdependen-
cia de los conceptos vinculados a la seguridad y el desarrollo y, por ende, a la idea de que
cualquier sistema de seguridad a nivel continental debe ir acompañado de una acción tendiente
al progreso de los pueblos del Hemisferio, ya que, las causas del subdesarrollo son las que origi-
nan principalmente las amenazas a la seguridad." According to the official website (in April 1999,
www.ejercito.gub.uy/viccomea/index.html), the Conference of American Armies "*es un Organ-
ismo Militar de carácter internacional integrado y dirigido por los Ejércitos del Continente Ameri-
cano con la autorización del gobierno de sus respectivos países . . . que funciona desde 1960, tiene
como finalidad alcanzar una estrecha integración y cooperación para el estudio conjunto de problemas de interés mutuo dentro América, con el objetivo de salvaguardarlo de todas las amenazas a la
paz, a la democracia y a la libertad de los países miembros.*" Thus while particular items on the
agenda, such as narco-trafficking, sustainable development, and migration, had changed in the
1990s, the underlying focus on stability, economic growth, and "fighting poverty" as aspects of
"security" and "democracy"—and therefore of concern to defense planners and the armed
forces—remained constant. On the 1997 II Conferencia Interamericana de Directores de Insti-
tutos de Altos Estudios Estratégicos meeting in El Salvador, see apc.nicarao.org.ni/pieca/
contenidos/reg12_4.htm; www.mundolatino.org/i/politica/EUA_Amla/capit_15.htm#(11)a)
(accessed November 19, 1999). Luis Dallanegra Pedraza, *Relaciones políticas entre Estados Unidos
y América Latina ¿Predominio monroista o unidad?* luisdallanegra@pinos.com.

18. A more sophisticated version of this viewpoint conflating democracy and capitalism, discussing the links between economic integration and hemispheric security, is Patrice M. Franko,

Toward a New Security Architecture in the Americas: The Strategic Implications of the FTAA, foreword by Georges A. Fauriol (Washington, D.C.: Center for Strategic and International Studies, 2000).

19. This language survived well into the George W. Bush administration, as reflected in the SOUTHCOM website: USSOUTHCOM Mission. "USSOUTHCOM shapes the environment within its area of responsibility by conducting theater engagement and counterdrug activities in order to promote democracy, stability, and collective approaches to threats to regional security; when required responds unilaterally or multilaterally to crises that threaten regional stability or national interests, and prepares to meet future hemispheric challenges" (www.southcom.mil/home/mission.cfm).

20. The White House, "A National Security Strategy of Engagement and Enlargement."

21. The White House, "A National Security Strategy of Engagement and Enlargement."

22. The report claimed that of 321 international terrorist incidents worldwide in 1994, fifty-eight were in Latin America. But anti-U.S. attacks numbered forty-four, putting the region ahead of the Middle East, which ranked second and had only eight such attacks (p. 15).

23. U.S. Department of Defense, Office of International Security Affairs, "United States Security Strategy for the Americas," 1995. It should be noted that Mexico and some other governments in the hemisphere did not "sign on" to this agenda; officially, Mexico sent only civilian observers to the meeting.

24. Prepared statement of Gen. Barry R. McCaffrey, commander in chief, U.S. Southern Command, before the House National Security Committee, March 8, 1995: www.defenselink.mil/speeches/1995/t19950308-mccaffrey.html (accessed May 2, 2005). McCaffrey described SOUTHCOM in 1995 (still in Panama) as "a battalion-sized headquarters of 700 men and women of all services. It is the smallest of all the unified commands. The headquarters includes representatives from the Department of State, CIA, DEA, DIA [Defense Intelligence Agency], NSA [National Security Agency], the Coast Guard and U.S. Customs Service."

25. Prepared statement of Gen. Barry R. McCaffrey.

26. Prepared statement of Gen. Barry R. McCaffrey.

27. Max G. Manwaring, "Latin American Security and Civil-Military Relations in the New World Disorder," *Low Intensity Conflict & Law Enforcement* 4(1) (Summer 1995): 29–43; Gabriel Marcella, ed., *Warriors in Peacetime: The Military and Democracy in Latin America—New Directions for U.S. Policy* (London: Frank Cass, 1994); Richard Millett and Michael Gold-Bliss, eds., *Beyond Praetorianism: The Latin American Military in Transition* (Miami: North-South Center, 1996).

28. At times, U.S. officers, civilians, and Latin American officers seemed excessively optimistic in describing the success of the post-1990 security agenda. Lieutenant Colonel (USAF, Ret.) Russell Ramsey wrote in 1994 that "shared linguistic training, and operations experiences between US and Latin American military officers today contribute to democratically obedient armed forces relationships" (Russell W. Ramsey, "U.S. Strategy for Latin America," *Parameters*, Autumn 1994, 70–83). As evidence for this assertion Ramsey cites his articles "U.S. Military Courses for Latin Americans Are a Low-Budget Strategic Success," *North-South, the Magazine of the Americas* 2 (February–March 1993): 38–41; "A Military Turn of Mind: Educating Latin American Officers," *Military Review* 73 (August 1993): 13; and Berry L. Brewer, "United States Security Assistance Training of Latin American Militaries: Intentions and Results," Wright-Patterson Air Force Base, Ohio, September 1995: www.benning.army.mil/usarsa/main.htm.

29. See Donald E. Schulz, "The Role of the Armed Forces in the Americas: Civil Military Relations for the 21st Century," Strategic Studies Institute, April 1998.

30. For insights into the missions and views of SOUTHCOM, see "Diálogo, El foro militar de las Américas" at www.allenwayne.com/dialogo/. Of course, missions mean budgets or at least

justification for budgets, and SOUTHCOM was hard-pressed to find traditional military missions in Latin America in the 1990s.

31. On some of the negative side effects of the U.S./International Monetary Fund/World Bank policy agenda, see Joseph E. Stiglitz, *Globalization and Its Discontents* (New York: Norton, 2002). For his part, the USSOUTHCOM commander, General Bantz J. Craddock, told the U.S. Congress in March 2005:

> Although Latin America and the Caribbean is generally free of the prospect of cross-border conventional military attacks between nations, it is the world's most violent region, with 27.5 homicides per 100,000 people. This lack of security is a major impediment to the foreign investment needed to strengthen Latin American and Caribbean economies to pull more of the population above the poverty line. . . . The roots of the region's poor security environment are poverty, inequality, and corruption. Forty-four percent of Latin America and the Caribbean are mired in the hopelessness and squalor of poverty. The free market reforms and privatization of the 1990's have not delivered on the promise of prosperity for Latin America. Unequal distribution of wealth exacerbates the poverty problem. The richest one tenth of the population of Latin America and the Caribbean earn 48% of the total income, while the poorest tenth earn only 1.6%. In industrialized countries, by contrast, the top tenth receive 29.1%, while the bottom tenth earn 2.5%. Uruguay has the least economic disparity of Latin American and Caribbean countries, but its unequal income distribution is still far worse than the most unequal country in Eastern Europe and the industrialized countries. A historical climate of corruption siphons off as much as 10 percent of the gross domestic product and discourages potential foreign investment. (Testimony of General Bantz J. Craddock, commander, United States Southern Command, hearing of the House Armed Services Committee: "Fiscal Year 2006 National Defense Authorization Budget Request," March 9, 2005)

32. On the debt crisis and its aftermath in Latin America according to economists supportive of the Washington Consensus, see Sebastian Edwards, *Crisis and Reform in Latin America: From Despair to Hope* (New York: Oxford University Press, 1995); John Williamson and Pedro-Pablo Kuczynski, *After the Washington Consensus: Restarting Growth and Reform in Latin America* (Washington, D.C.: Institute for International Economics, 2003).

33. This idea was a reaffirmation of President Clinton's "A National Security Strategy of Engagement and Enlargement."

34. U.S. Agency for International Development, "Democracy and Governance" (www.info .usaid.gov/democracy/). Italics added.

35. Joseph C. Lear, "School of the Americas and U.S. Foreign Policy Attainment in Latin America," information paper, School of the Americas (www.benning.army.mil/usara/ACADEMIC/ leru.htm); Ramsey, "A Military Turn of Mind: Educating Latin American Officers," 10–17.

36. This was available at www.benning.army.mil/usarsa/main.htm. U.S. Army School of the Americas, Ft. Benning, Georgia. For a description of new courses and objectives at the School of the Americas see Russell W. Ramsey, "The Democratic Sustainment Course at the U.S. Army School of the Americas," July 1999. For a strong defense of the U.S. Army human rights record and the importance of training U.S. military personnel see Russell W. Ramsey, "Forty Years of Human Rights Training," *Journal of Low Intensity Conflict & Law Enforcement* 4(2) (Autumn 1995): 254–70. See also, Gregory Weeks, "Fighting the Enemy Within: Terrorism, the School of the Americas, and the Military in Latin America," *Human Rights Quarterly* 5(1) (October–December 2003): 12–27.

37. "Militares de América se reúnen hoy en Bolivia," *El Telégrafo* (Guayaquil), November 15, 1999. In mid-2000 the Ecuadorian congress legislated an amnesty for civilians and military personnel, authors, and participants in the events of January 21, 2000, and events related to the change in the constitutional government.

38. Guatemala army Internet website, www.mindef.mil.gt/noticias/. Axiology is the branch of ethics dealing with the relative goodness or value of the motives and end of actions: "*Quiero de-*

*cirles que el Ejército de Guatemala, está en pleno proceso de reconversión, realizando las transfor-
maciones necesarias en su estructura, y en sus funciones y especialmente en su orientación axiológ-
ica.*" The Ecuadorian *Libro de la Defensa Nacional* (2002) (www.libroblancoecuador.org/index
libroblancodef1.htm) also contained a list of "new security threats" that paralleled to great extent the new U.S. agenda: 29–31.

39. Max G. Manwaring, ed., *Security and Civil–Military Relations in the New World Disorder:
The Use of Armed Forces in the Americas.* Anthology from a symposium cosponsored by The
Chief of Staff, United States Army, The George Bush School of Government and Public Service,
U.S. Army War College, September 1999.

40. See especially Donald E. Schulz, "The United States and Latin America: A Strategic Perspective," in Manwaring, *Security and Civil–Military Relations in the New World Disorder*, 1–19.

41. As President William Clinton put it in a speech to the Council of the Americas, translated
in the Ecuadorian military magazine *Revista Fuerzas Armadas de Ecuador* (Tenemos que ganar
en Colombia. Tenemos que ganar la lucha por el Area de Libre Comercio de las Américas. Tenemos que demostrar que la libertad y los mercados libres van de la mano. Eso es en lo que ust-
edes creen, y vamos a tener una oportunidad de demostrarlo): www.fuerzasarmadasecuador
.org/espanol/publicaciones/revistamdndic2000/textoclavesobreplancolombia.htm.

42. U.S. Department of Defense, "United States Security Strategy for the Americas" (1995),
22–24.

43. Gabriel Marcella, "The United States and Colombia: The Journey from Ambiguity to
Strategic Clarity" (Carlisle, Pa.: Strategic Studies Institute, May 2003), 51. Emphasis added.

44. Lars Schoultz has written that U.S. (military) relations with Latin America are character-
ized by cycles of attention and neglect, that the cycles are not random, reflecting the rise and fall
of the perception in Washington of extra-hemispheric threats. "U.S. Values and Approaches to
Hemispheric Security Issues," in *Security, Democracy and Development in U.S. Latin American
Relations*, ed. Lars Schoultz, William C. Smith, and Augusto Varas (Miami: North-South Center,
University of Miami, 1994), 34.

45. "National Security Decision Directive 221, April 8, 1986." Electronic Resource. An online,
declassified and vetted, facsimile of this NSDD is found at www.fas.org/irp/offdocs/nsdd/
23-2766a.gif. See also the Digital National Security Archive with the NSDDs from President Tru-
man to Clinton (nsarchive.chadwyck.com/pdintro.htm).

46. U.S. Department of Defense, Office of the Secretary of Defense, Inter-American Affairs,
"United States Security Strategy for the Americas" (Washington, D.C.: USGPO, October 2000), 2.

47. According to the SOUTHCOM website, beginning in 1995, exercises "shifted from bilateral
events featuring conventional combat scenarios to multilateral exercises focusing on peacekeeping,
humanitarian assistance, counter narco-trafficking, and other more appropriate post–Cold War
missions." U.S. Southern Command, "Profile of the United States Southern Command," Miami,
October 1997. Between 1995 and 2002 such exercises numbered fifteen to twenty-two each year.
For descriptions of these exercises see ciponline.org/facts/exe.htm#6 (accessed May 13, 2005).

48. U.S. Southern Command, "Profile of the United States Southern Command," 3–8.

49. U.S. Southern Command, "Profile of the United States Southern Command," 28.

50. U.S. Southern Command, "Profile of the United States Southern Command," 28–29. The
report further describes the U.S. commitment to human rights and democracy, as well as the bilateral and regional strategies for Mexico, Central America, the Southern Cone, and Brazil.

51. On the missions being flown out of Ecuador see, for example, "Comandante de la FAE
revela varios 'problemas' en la Base Aérea de Manta," *Diario Hoy* (Quito) (electrónico), September 6, 2000; "Ajustan operaciones en base de Manta," *El Telégrafo* (Guayaquil) (electrónico), September 6, 2000.

52. Many of the U.S. civilian contractors were ex-military personnel, some from other Latin
American countries. Several have been taken prisoner by the FARC and at least one murdered.

Congress did establish numerical limits on these contractors, but rigorous control on the ground was difficult and accountability lacking. For an assessment of the role of contractors in the Colombian conflict before the Uribe administration see "U.S. Contractors in Colombia," compiled by CIP Colombia Program Intern Sara Vins, November 2001, www.ciponline.org/colombia/contractors.htm. Until 2004, the law restricted the U.S. presence in Colombia to four hundred military personnel and four hundred contractors. This limit was increased in 2004. Non-U.S. civilian contractors do not count toward this cap, whether flying fumigation missions or providing other services for the Colombian or U.S. armed forces. Major U.S. corporations provide such civilian personnel and sell equipment for these programs, making the Andean conflict a source of profit as well as a high-pay opportunity for ex-military personnel and corporations.

53. For an extensive summary and analysis of Plan Colombia in Spanish see Ingrid Vaicius, "El Plan Colombia: El Debate en los Estados Unidos," *International Policy Report*, August 2000 (www.ciponline.org/colombia/aid/ipr0800/ipr0800.htm); "Helicópteros Black Hawks, en el 2002," *El Tiempo* (Bogotá) (electrónico), September 22, 2000.

54. "Chávez lanza nuevas críticas a Plan Colombia 'Así empezó Vietnam'," *El Colombiano* (Medellín) (electrónico), September 6, 2000. Of course, Chávez was merely repeating what many newspaper articles and political opponents of Plan Colombia had been saying for months.

55. "Plan Colombia, protagonista en Cumbre Suramericana," *El Tiempo* (Bogotá) (electrónico), August 31, 2000.

56. August 22, 2000, Presidential Determination No. 2000-28 Memorandum for the Secretary of State: SUBJECT: Presidential Determination on Waiver of Certification Under Section 3201 "Conditions on Assistance for Colombia," in Title III, Chapter 2 of the Emergency Supplemental Act, FY 2000, as Enacted in Public Law 106-246: www.ciponline.org/colombia/082301.htm (accessed August 23, 2004).

57. "Colombianos huyen a Ecuador por fumigación de plantaciones," *El Mostrador* (electrónico), September 13, 2000; "Destruyen 5 mil hectáreas de coca y 90 laboratorios en Colombia," *El Mostrador* (electrónico), September 14, 2000; "5 mil hectáreas de coca fueron eliminadas," *El Comercio* (Quito), September 14, 2000. In this last article the director of the DEA in Colombia is quoted as saying that "nothing will stop the Police in their fight against the narcotics traffic." In Peru, Minister of Defense General Carlos Bergamino announced that his country was sending military reinforcements to the Colombian border, expecting Colombian guerrillas and drug traffickers to flee to neighboring countries in response to the fumigation, supported by attack helicopters.

58. Marcella, "The United States and Colombia," 44.

59. U.S. Department of Defense, "Hemispheric Cooperation in Combating Terrorism," Defense Ministerial of the Americas III, Secretary of Defense William S. Cohen, Cartagena, Colombia, Tuesday, December 1, 1998. Emphasis added.

60. For a brief description of "Operation Condor," see "Archives Unearthed in Paraguay Expose U.S. Allies' Abuses," *New York Times*, August 11, 1999:

> Intelligence sharing between Washington's allies in South America did not begin with Operation Condor, but the plan formalized and deepened cooperation among police and military forces that had taken power in six countries: Brazil, Argentina, Chile, Paraguay, Uruguay and Bolivia. After Gen. Manuel Contreras of Chile invited security chiefs to create "the basis of an excellent coordination and improved action" at a meeting in November 1975, police forces from member countries began to operate in each others' jurisdictions. Their new ties allowed security officials to take part in joint interrogations, to pursue people across borders and to order surveillance on citizens who sought asylum in other nations.

See J. Patrice McSherry, "Operation Condor Clandestine Interamerican System," *Social Justice* 26(4) (Winter 1999): 144–74; "Analyzing Operation Condor: A Covert Inter-American Structure," paper presented at the XXII International Congress of Latin American Studies Association (LASA), Miami, March 2000; *Predatory States: Operation Condor and Covert War in Latin America* (Lanham, Md.: Rowman & Littlefield, 2005). See also John Dinges, *The Condor Years: How Pinochet and His Allies Brought Terrorism to Three Continents* (New York: The New Press, 2004). For links to Internet websites treating Operation Condor see larcdma.sdsu.edu/humanrights/rr/Latin%20America/PLA.html.

61. In fact, despite "democratization" in Brazil after 1985, the armed forces refused to provide information on domestic and international intelligence operations during the military dictatorship to civilian authorities, even after direct requests from the president in 1993. See "Ejército habría ocultado la existencia de la O. Cóndor," *Diario El Sur* (Concepción, Chile), May 23, 2000 (Internet version):

> La administración del presidente Itamar Franco solicitó en 1993 información. Los documentos obviaron supuestamente datos de importancia. SAO PAULO, (AFP). El Ejército brasileño ocultó presuntamente información pedida por el gobierno del ex presidente Itamar Franco en 1993 sobre la Operación Cóndor, referida a colaboración de los regímenes militares de Argentina, Brasil, Bolivia, Chile, Uruguay y Paraguay para aniquilar a la izquierda opositora, según indican documentos divulgados ayer en la prensa local. El gobierno de Franco investigó en 1993 el tenebroso plan y solicitó información al Ejército que, a pesar de haber terminado el régimen militar en 1985, habría ocultado datos importantísimos.

62. In the late 1990s, the U.S. Department of State continued to play an important role in Colombia, both officially and covertly, as illustrated by secret meetings with the FARC in and out of Colombia. See Cynthia Arnson, "The Peace Process in Colombia and U.S. Policy," paper presented at the Conference on "Democracy, Human Rights, and Peace in Colombia," University of Notre Dame, Helen Kellog Institute for International Studies, March 26–27, 2001, 5–12.

63. See, for example, U.S. Department of State "U.S. Support for Plan Colombia," press release presented by Marc Grossman, under secretary for Political Affairs, Bogotá, Colombia, August 31, 2001 (www.state.gov/p/wha/rls/rm/2001/august/4798.htm).

64. Inter-American Democratic Charter (Article 21), OAS General Assembly, Lima, Peru, September 11, 2001. Full text available at www.oas.org/main/main.asp?sLang=E&sLink=/xxxvga (accessed May 15, 2005).

65. See Brian Loveman, *The Constitution of Tyranny. Regimes of Exception in Spanish America* (Pittsburgh: University of Pittsburgh Press, 1993).

66. Richard J. Koucheravy (major, U.S. Army), "The United States Military and Plan Colombia: A Direct Combat Role? Combat Forces and the U.S. Role in Plan Colombia" (Fort Leavenworth, Kans.: School of Advanced Military Studies, 2001), 30.

67. "Presentation of the Rapporteur of the Special Conference on Security," Édgar Gutiérrez, minister of Foreign Affairs of Guatemala, to the Permanent Council of the OAS (presented to the Permanent Council at its regular meeting of December 3, 2003), CES/doc. 14/03 add. 1: http://scm.oas.org/doc_public/ENGLISH/HIST_03/CE00359E07.doc.

68. Of course, "securitization" of public policy issues implies an "upgrading" of concern by suggesting that sovereignty and public welfare are *threatened* in a fashion that requires more than routine policy responses, and perhaps justifying extraordinary measures to confront the threats identified. In some cases, these extraordinary measures may include going beyond normal constitutional constraints and even to suspending civil liberties and rights, due process, and other citizen guarantees against government abuse. And, as recent debates in the United States have revealed, when the threats are of great enough concern, some policy makers may even justify torture (or "torture light"). See Barry Buzan, Ole Weaver, and Jaap de Wilde, *Security: A New Framework for Analysis* (Boulder, Colo.: Rienner, 1998).

69. The term *defense planning* is used here broadly. In principle, the Department of State is the lead agency, overall, within the interagency group that defines and implements U.S. policy. This group includes the Department of Defense, DEA, CIA, and other agencies with counter-drug and counterterrorism tasks. Even some arms transfers and sales formally go through the Department of State, though the DoD "administers" the program.

70. Intervention in Haiti in 1994, ostensibly to support democracy and carry out a humanitarian mission, created a tangential component to Latin American policy—one based on almost a century of occasional deployments of troops to Haiti in moments of crisis. While for domestic political reasons President Clinton threatened to invade the country to overturn a military junta and to "restore democracy," officials in the CIA, the Pentagon, and other U.S. agencies resisted Clinton's decision. In any case, Haiti was certainly not a main focus of U.S. Latin American policy. See Robert E. White, "Haiti: Policy Lost, Policy Regained," *Cosmos Journal*, 1996: www.cosmos-club.org/journals/1996/index.html (accessed May 30, 2005). White claimed that Clinton's 1994 invasion of Haiti was a benchmark in U.S. policy: "For the first time in the history of our relations with the Caribbean and Central America, the United States used armed force clearly and unambiguously on the side of a democratically elected president. For the first time, America intervened not to shore up an unpopular, military-dominated regime but on behalf of an elected government pledged to change and reform."

71. U.S. Department of Defense, "Annual Report to the President and the Congress" (Washington, D.C.: USGPO, 2001).

72. U.S. Department of Defense, *Quadrennial Defense Review Report* (Washington, D.C.: USGPO, September 30, 2001), 5.

73. The Colombian government's official document on the plan is posted on the Nizkor website at www.derechos.org/nizkor/colombia/doc/planof.html. The Colombian Embassy in Washington, D.C., has a website that posts a description and justification of Plan Colombia, seeking to emphasize the nonmilitary elements of the plan:

> The Government of Colombia has developed a multi-year, comprehensive strategy designed to bring about lasting peace by reducing the production of illegal drugs, revitalizing the economy and strengthening government institutions. This is known as Plan Colombia.
>
> The international press tends to refer to Plan Colombia as only a military operation, but this is inaccurate. Because Plan Colombia is a social and political strategy to bring government presence to the country's frontier territories and re-unite them with the rest of the country. In other words, it seeks to strengthen public institutions and the rule of law in an area overwhelmed by lawlessness. And at the same time, bring about economic reform and sustained growth to an ailing economy, which in 1999 had negative GDP growth of 4.3%.
>
> Of course, Plan Colombia also seeks to fight against the drug trade, because a significant portion of the multi-billion dollar profits from drug-trafficking are funding the activities of guerrillas and paramilitaries, while thousands of innocent civilians are caught in the crossfire. A final peace agreement, probably the most important of the four main objectives of Plan Colombia, will remain illusive as long as the rebel groups maintain an unlimited source of funding from drug trafficking. So it is in Colombia's national interest to crack-down on this illegal industry. (www.colombiaemb.org/plan_colombia.htm)

74. U.S. General Accounting Office (GAO), "Statement of Jess T. Ford, Director, Testimony before the Subcommittee on Criminal Justice, Drug Policy and Human Resources, Committee on Government Reform, House of Representatives, "Drug Control: Challenges in Implementing Plan Colombia,'" October 12, 2000.

75. See DEA, Drug "Intelligence Brief, 'Drugs and Terrorism: A New Perspective,'" September 2002 (www.usdoj.gov/dea/pubs/intel/02039/02039.html).

76. Major General Gary Speer, U.S. Army acting commander in chief of the U.S. Southern Command (SOUTHCOM), before the Senate Foreign Relations Committee Subcommittee on

Western Hemisphere, Peace Corps, and Narcotics Affairs, "Ayuda de EE.UU. a Colombia," usembassy.state.gov/colombia/wwwsgs02.shtml (English version also online). Apparently, the notion that drugs were "weapons of mass destruction"—at least for purposes of congressional testimony and generating budgets—became accepted at high levels at SOUTHCOM, as it was repeated by Brigadier General Benjamin R. Mixon in his testimony before Congress, April 21, 2004.

77. Speer, "Ayuda de EE. UU," italics added.

78. Of course, Plan Colombia included nonmilitary and non-antidrug components, administered mostly by the Agency for International Development (AID). AID's official website explained its role in Plan Colombia as follows:

> Presented by the Government of Colombia in 1999, Plan Colombia is an integrated, balanced proposal to promote the intertwined objectives of peace, the rule of law, prosperity and respect for human rights. Recognizing the significance and urgency of these goals, USAID has developed several activities to directly support Plan Colombia. Specifically, USAID's expanded program will foster an effective justice system, observance of basic human rights, increased democratic participation, stronger local governments, a decline in government corruption, improved social infrastructure, a reduction of illicit crop production, and assistance for internally displaced persons. These activities represent a significant component of the US government's support for Plan Colombia and its efforts to support peace and prosperity in this Andean nation. (http://usembassy.state.gov/bogota/wwwsaidc.shtml)

79. For the evolving U.S. military and think-tank view of the Colombian and Andean region conflicts, see the following posted online by the United States Army, Strategic Center Institute: Max G. Manwaring, "U.S. Security Policy in the Western Hemisphere: Why Colombia, Why Now, and What Is to Be Done?" June 2001 (http://carlisle-www.army.mil/usassi/ssipubs/pubs2001/westhem/westhem.pdf); Judith A. Gentleman, "The Regional Security Crisis in the Andes: Patterns of State Response," June 2001 (http://carlisle-www.army.mil/usassi/ssipubs/pubs2001/andes/andes.pdf); "Plan Colombia: Some Differing Perspectives" (Gabriel Marcella, Charles E. Wilhelm, Alvaro Valencia Tovar, Ricardo Arias Calderon, Chris Marquis), June 2001 (www.carlisle.army.mil/usassi/ssipubs/pubs2001/pcdiffer/pcdiffer.htm; Joseph R. Nuñez, "Fighting the Hobbesian Trinity in Colombia: A New Strategy for Peace," February 2001 (www.carlisle.army.mil/usassi/ssipubs/pubs2001/trinity/trinity.htm); Gabriel Marcella, "Plan Colombia: The Strategic and Operational Imperatives," April 2001 (www.carlisle.army.mil/usassi/ssipubs/pubs2001/pcimprtv/pcimprtv.htm).

80. Written statement of Major General Gary D. Speer, United States Army acting commander in chief United States Southern Command, before the 107th Congress Senate Foreign Relations Committee Subcommittee on Western Hemisphere, Peace Corps, and Narcotics Affairs, April 24, 2002.

81. See Major Richard J. Koucheravy, "The United States Military and Plan Colombia: A Direct Combat Role?"

82. The FOLs were later renamed Cooperative Security Locations (CSLs).

83. *U.S. Policy toward Colombia* Hearing before the Subcommittee on the Western Hemisphere of the Committee on International Relations House of Representatives 107th Congress 2nd Session April 11, 2002. Testimony of Peter W. Rodman, assistant secretary of defense for international security affairs, United States Department of Defense: http://commdocs.house.gov/committees/intlrel/hfa78682.000/hfa78682_0.HTM (accessed February 27, 2006).

84. *U.S. Policy toward Colombia* Hearing.

85. For background on the pipeline protection project and a critique of U.S. policy see "The Real Costs of Pipeline Protection in Colombia: Corporate Welfare with Deadly Consequences," A Witness for Peace Report from Arauca, July 2002 (www.w4peace.org/pdf/arauca.pdf).

86. Marcella, "The United States and Colombia," 55.

87. Winifred Tate, "No Room for Peace? United States' Policy in Colombia," *Accord* (2004), special issue on Colombia's Peace Processes (www.c-r.org/accord/col/accord14/noroomforpeace .shtml) (accessed February 5, 2004).

88. "Reabierto oleoducto Caño Limón en Colombia tras ataques," Yahoo Noticias, February 25, 2005 (http://espanol.news.yahoo.com/050225/2/y98v.html); Daniel Leal Diaz claimed that attacks on the pipeline went from 170 in 2001 to 17 in 2004 ("Colombia & Iraq: Halliburton Makes the Connection," World War 4 Report, January 17, 2005, http://globalpolicy.igc.org/ empire/intervention/2005/0117coliraq.htm).

89. "Testimony of Major General Gary D. Speer," http://usregsec.sdsu.edu.docs/GeneralSpeer April2002.pdf.

90. "Testimony of Major General Gary D. Speer."

91. In practice (and in secret), the distinction between counterinsurgency and the drug war had long since been blurred. According to an interagency paper written by the National Security Council in June of 1989, military aid for Colombia was in fact intended for counterinsurgency in addition to counternarcotics activities: "Better counternarcotics operations require the military to deal with insurgents; better law enforcement and counterinsurgency efforts require better intelligence; successful counternarcotics and counterinsurgency operations require economic assistance to offset lost narcotics dollars." At the highest levels of strategic planning in the United States, counternarcotics meant counterinsurgency just before the end of the Cold War (United States National Security Council, "Strategy for Narcotics Control in the Andean Region," June 30, 1989 (electronic resource), available online at the George Washington University National Security Archive: www.gwu.edu/~nsarchiv/NSAEBB/NSAEBB69/col11.pdf).

92. United States National Security Council, "Strategy for Narcotics Control in the Andean Region," emphasis added.

93. United States National Security Council, "Strategy for Narcotics Control in the Andean Region."

94. United States National Security Council, "Strategy for Narcotics Control in the Andean Region," emphasis added.

95. It is not always easily discernible whether the State Department, National Security Council, or another agency "took the lead" in establishing a new policy agenda and discourse. But the gradual transformation of the guerrillas into "narco-terrorists" in this period is evident in official discourse from the various agencies engaged in Andean policy formation and implementation: Plan Colombia (P.L. 106-246). From 2001 to 2003 the Andean Regional Initiative budget requests included the Andean Counterdrug Initiative (ACI), child survival and health, development assistance, economic support funds, and foreign military financing. For fiscal year 2004, the ACI budget requests were separate, with other categorical programs also being discussed individually, that is not part of an "Andean Regional Initiative" program. These changes make somewhat more difficult strict comparisons by "program" for the 2001–2003 period and the post-2004 years. ACI is managed by the State Department (Bureau of International Narcotics Control and Law Enforcement Affairs). For detailed analysis of the resources committed to Plan Colombia, ARI, and ACI from 2000 to 2005 see Connie Veillette, "Andean Counterdrug Initiative (ACI) and Related Funding Programs: FY 2005 Assistance, Updated December 9, 2004," Congressional Research Service (CRS), www.au.af.mil/au/awc/awcgate/crs/rl32337.pdf (accessed May 12, 2005); and "Colombia: Issues for Congress," updated, January 19, 2005, Congressional Research Service (CRS), p. 24 (www.fas.org/sgp/crs/row/RL32250.pdf).

96. Yet in June 2005, U.S. ambassador William Wood supported, if not wholeheartedly, the Colombian "Justice and Peace Law," intended to provide incentives for guerrillas and the paramilitaries to disarm in exchange for reduced prison sentences. The law also provided, in principle, some reparation for victims. (See "Ambassador William B. Wood's Remarks before the Cali Colombian American Chamber of Commerce," June 24, 2005, http://bogota.usembassy.gov/

wwwsww56.shtml#English.) Although the law was criticized by human rights organizations as an example of impunity for crimes against humanity, Colombia's vice president, Francisco Santos Calderón, vigorously defended it in editorials published in U.S. newspapers. See "Colombia Grasps at Peace," *Los Angeles Times*, July 26, 2005, B13.

97. "Overview—Plan Colombia/Andean Regional Initiative, DEA. Antinarcotics Summary, Sept 17, 2002. Statement of Asa Hutchinson, administrator, Drug Enforcement Administration before the Senate Caucus on International Narcotics Control, Executive Summary, DEA Congressional Testimony," September 17, 2002 (www.usdoj.gov/dea/pubs/cngrtest/ct091702 .html).

98. Scott Miller, writer/editor, "U.S. State Dept. Official Examines Evolution of U.S. Policy toward Colombia," The Washington File, October 9, 2002 (product of the Office of International Information Programs, U.S. Department of State: http://usinfo.state.gov).

99. For a detailed budget analysis of the Bush administration FY 2002 aid request for the Andean counterdrug initiative and for Plan Colombia, see the Center for International Policy, Colombia Project, website, especially www.ciponline.org/colombia/2002request.htm. Analysis includes requests by Department of Defense, Department of State, and related agencies for Andean region countries.

100. "Minister of Defense: Democratic Security, Transnational Threats and the Rule of Law," *Colombian View*, October 8, 2002, Washington, D.C., Center for Strategic and International Studies. Posted on official website of the Colombian Embassy in Washington, D.C., "Presentation by Minister of Defense Marta Lucía Ramírez, at the Center for Strategic and International Studies, Washington, D.C.," October 8, 2002 (www.colombiaemb.org/).

101. "Colombia: 40 Years of Experience Fighting Terrorism," official website, Embassy of Colombia, Washington, D.C., www.colombiaemb.org/terrorism.htm (this article was posted before President Uribe assumed office).

102. The White House, "The National Security Strategy of the United States of America," Washington, D.C., September 2002.

103. President Uribe and other Colombians also urged the United Nations and the Organization of American States to play a more active role, given the international nature of the Colombian conflict—a post–Cold War conflict touching on key aspects of the U.S. post-1990s security agenda: drug trafficking, human rights, environmental security, democracy, international crime, and corruption. See, for example, Jaime Zuluaga Nieto, "El necesario apoyo político de la ONU y de la comunidad internacional," III Encuentro Nacional de Mesas Ciudadanas, Bogotá, 2002.

104. Talking Points for Ambassador Luis Alberto Moreno, Luncheon Series, School of Advanced International Studies, John Hopkins University, October 29, 2002 (www.colombiaemb .org/statements.htm#POINTS).

105. Tate, "No Room for Peace?"

106. The DEA opportunistically linked the drug war to the war on terrorism as soon as the Bush administration provided the opening: "'The War on Terror and the War on Drugs are linked,' a high-ranking DEA official recently told the Senate Judiciary Committee. 'Thirty-nine percent of the State Department's current list of designated foreign terrorist organizations have some degree of connection with drug activities,' he said. In his May 20th testimony, Steven Casteel, Assistant DEA Administrator for Intelligence, said that 'whether a group is committing terrorist acts, trafficking drugs or laundering money, the one constant to remember is that they are all forms of organized crime'" (DEA home page, June 3, 2003: www.usdoj.gov/dea/). See also, text: "U.S. Official Lauds Colombian Efforts to Combat Narco-Terrorism," U.S. Department of State, Washington File: Paul E. Simons, Acting Assistant Secretary of State, International Narcotics and Law Enforcement Affairs, Hearing Before Senate Drug Caucus: "The narco-terrorist threat is among the greatest the United States and Colombia face, and success against the drug trade and terrorism in

Colombia will improve security in both countries, and in the Andean region as a whole. The ongoing internal strife that Colombia has suffered has hampered its economic progress, severely strained both military and civil institutions, and wreaked havoc on the civilian population who must live with the constant threat of terrorist violence. It has also resulted in a flood of illicit drugs into the United States" (http://usinfo.state.gov/cgi-bin/washfile/display.pl?p=/products/washfile/ geog/ar&f=03060302.lar&t=/products/washfile/newsitem.shtml).

107. Not incidentally, key personnel from counterinsurgency and counterdrug operations in the Department of Defense migrated to the Department of Defense's Special Operations and Low-Intensity Conflict (SOLIC) under the authority of the assistant secretary of defense for Special Operations and Low-Intensity Conflict. The melding of the drug war and the war on terror for the Andean region is illustrated well by the following excerpt from the SOLIC mission statement:

> Colombia is of particular importance to the US because illegal drug trafficking there and its connections to terrorists and other armed groups that threaten US interests in a peaceful and secure Colombia and Andean region. The US Government has made it a matter of national priority to support the creation or enhancement of Colombian CN [counternarcotics] capabilities. Congress affirmed this priority by appropriating $1.7 billion over two years Colombia's comprehensive CN effort, *Plan Colombia*. Further supplemental budget action in Fiscal Years 2003 and 2004 provided the Department with additional authority to support Colombia's unified campaign against narcotics traffickers and terrorist organizations. (Department of Defense Counternarcotics Mission Statement, at www.defenselink .mil/policy/solic/cn/mission.html)

108. For a critical assessment of SOUTHCOM's role and missions see Tom Barry, "U.S. Southern Command Confronts Traditional and Emerging Threats," IRC Americas Program Policy Brief, July 24, 2004 (www.americaspolicy.org/briefs/2004/0407militar_body.html) (accessed March 27, 2005). In its 2005 document, *A Theater Strategy of Focused Cooperation and Mutual Security*, SOUTHCOM declared that "transnational terrorism and organized crime constitute the primary threats to U.S. interests in the hemisphere."

109. See Colonel Joseph R. Núñez, "A 21st Century Security Architecture for the Americas: Multilateral Cooperation, Liberal Peace and Soft Power" (Carlisle, Pa.: Strategic Studies Institute, 2002), 57 pp. Earlier in the decade, a CATO Institute-based critic of the Clinton administration's regional policies had issued the following forecast:

> The desire to defend democracy wherever it is threatened in the Americas offers a potentially unlimited number of opportunities for OAS intervention. Worse, if OAS member nations are willing to implement that doctrine through military force, Washington could soon find itself risking American lives in parochial struggles that are at best only peripheral to U.S. security interests. Avid interventionists would see no end to the hemispheric "threats" that could be resolved by military responses. And proponents of a multinational peacekeeping force for the Americas would see no end to the good that such an institution could do throughout the hemisphere. (Ian Vasquez, "Washington's Dubious Crusade for Hemispheric Democracy," *CATO Policy Analysis*, No. 201 (January 12, 1994), www.cato.org/pubs/ pas/pa-201.html)

110. "NATO Plans 5,000-Strong Strike Force by October," Reuters (online), May 30, 2003.

111. U.S. Department of State "Cooperative Hemispheric Security Architecture for the 21st Century," Ambassador Roger F. Noriega, U.S. permanent representative to the Organization of American States, remarks to the Conference at the Inter-American Development Bank, Washington, D.C., September 20, 2002 (http://usinfo.state.gov/topical/pol/arms/csbm/csbmam06.htm).

112. U.S. Department of Defense "Defense Ministerial of the Americas," statement by Secretary of Defense Donald H. Rumsfeld, Santiago, Chile, November 19, 2002 (www.defenselink.mil/ speeches/2002/s20021119-secdef.html).

113. Conference agenda and speaker topics at www.miami.edu/NSC/pages/RegSecurity.html.

114. Núñez (April 5, 2002): 4.

115. Joseph Núñez, "Homeland and Hemisphere," *Christian Science Monitor* (online), December 20, 2001 (www.csmonitor.com/2001/1220/p9s1-coop.html).

116. See George Kourous, "Return of the National Security State?" background paper from the IRC's Americas Program, November 18, 2002 (www.americaspolicy.org/briefs/2002/0211 security.html).

117. "Para Brinzoni, 'la seguridad debe ser tratada como un todo,'" *La Nación* (electróncio), November 1, 2002 (www.lanacion.com.ar/). Of course, the desperate economic situation of the Argentine army in this period also may have influenced Brinzoni's eagerness to adopt the "cooperative security" discourse.

118. Between 1997 and 2005 ten Latin American presidents were forced from office or resigned before their elected terms ended.

119. Jeffrey Sachs, "Call It Our Bolivian Policy of Not-So-Benign Neglect," Washington Post.com, October 26, 2003, B02. Sachs wrote: "[President] Bush was following the standard, failed script handed him by the State Department, Treasury Department, National Security Council and Pentagon. It is a script I know well. As an economic adviser to Bolivia and dozens of other poor countries during the past 20 years, I have watched the United States fumble and founder as friendly, impoverished governments have collapsed. As a result, the mutual interests of the United States and these countries have been squandered."

120. "Rice Assesses a Troubled World," *Pittsburgh Tribune Review*, interview with Bill Steigerwald, October 23, 2004, http://pittsburghlive.com/x/tribune-review/trib/pittsburgh/s_265031 .html (accessed February 2, 2006).

121. "'Ecuador Decide' anuncia confrontación con Gobierno Si no incluye en consulta popular tema del TLC," Ecuadorinmediato.com (accessed July 14, 2005).

122. "Mucho mejor que Bush ignore a SudAmérica," *Diario La Hora*, March 9, 2006, at www.lahora.com.ec/frontEnd/main.php?idSeccion=403010.

123. A special issue of *Accord* in early 2004 (editor Mauricio García-Durán) was dedicated to "Colombia's Peace Processes." The authors reviewed the history of the Colombian conflict and its spillover into the Andean region, Brazil, and the Caribbean.

124. For a libertarian critique of the U.S. drug war see Ted Galen Carpenter, *Bad Neighbor Policy: Washington's Futile War on Drugs in Latin America* (New York: Palgrave, 2003).

125. These documents are included on the URL (www.rowman.com/isbn/0742540987) accompanying this volume.

126. Thomas Donnelly (principal author), "Rebuilding America's Defenses. Strategy, Forces and Resources for a New Century," 2000: 74 (www.newamericacentury.org/RebuildingAmericas Defenses.pdf).

127. Concern for opening new markets and opportunities for trade has been an element of U.S. foreign policy since independence in the late eighteenth century. Andrew Bacevich (*American Empire. The Realities and Consequences of U.S. Diplomacy* [Cambridge, Mass.: Harvard University Press, 2002], 88) argues that "the Big Idea guiding U.S. strategy is openness: the removal of barriers to the movement of goods, capital, people, and ideas, thereby fostering an integrated international order conducive to American interests, governed by American norms, regulated by American power, and, above all satisfying the expectations of the American people for ever-greater abundance."

128. Max G. Manwaring, "The Strategic Effects of the Conflict with Iraq: Latin America" (Carlisle, Pa.: Strategic Studies Institute, U.S. Army War College, March 2003), 10.

129. *Revista de las Fuerzas Armadas de Ecuador*, "Gestión de las Fuerzas Armadas" Edición 136, August 2003 (www.fuerzasarmadasecuador.org/revistaagosto2003/art.gestionfuerzasarmadas.htm).

130. Reuters, March 19, 2004 (www.alertnet.org/thenews/newsdesk/N17106959.htm).

131. Reported in *abc.es*, September 12, 2004 (abc.es/abc/pg040912/portada.asp).

132. "Confiscan armas y gasolina en frontera de Brasil con Venezuela y Colombia," *El Nacional* (September 10, 2004).

133. "FARC niega enfrentamiento con el ejército ecuatoriano," *Diario La Hora*, February 28, 2006: www.lahora.com.ec/frontEnd/main.php?idRegional=1 (accessed February 28, 2006).

134. "FARC ofrecen 'solidaridad incondicional a Chávez," El Universal.com (accessed February 28, 2006).

135. Eduardo Gamarra, "La crisis andina y la política de los Estados Unidos," *Foreign Affairs en Español*, Edición Especial (December 2000): 112.

136. *Diario La Hora*, February 10, 2004: www.fuerzasarmadasecuador.org/novedades/showarticle.php?id=184.

137. "U.S. Policy and the Andean Counterdrug Initiative (ACI)," Robert B. Charles, Assistant Secretary for International Narcotics and Law Enforcement Affairs, Testimony before the House Government Reform Committee Subcommittee on Criminal Justice, Drug Policy, and Human Resources, Washington, D.C., March 2, 2004 (www.state.gov/g/inl/rls/rm/30077.htm).

138. Testimony of General James T. Hill, United States Army commander, United States Southern Command before the House Armed Services Committee, United States House of Representatives, March 24, 2004.

139. Of course, certain aspects of the SOUTHCOM activities, such as the Humanitarian Assistance Program, focused on disaster relief and emergency preparations for the hemisphere—missions for which affected populations were usually grateful. For an official slide-show overview of these activities see http://68.166.42.251/southcom/documents/1 (accessed May 12, 2005). However, SOUTHCOM framed the HA program in broader regional security and developmental language:

> HA activities meet two key requirements; to maintain a robust overseas presence aimed at shaping the international security environment in a manner that deters would-be aggressors, strengthens friends and allies, and promotes peace and stability in regions of tension, and when called upon assist the victims of storms, earthquakes and other natural or manmade disasters. This fraction of the program is also tailored to help underdeveloped countries; particularly those that have been affected by disaster or hardship, to improve healthcare, education, and agricultural development ensuring sustainable community development. The ultimate goal is to build the capacity of community members in order to meet existing and future challenges and mitigate the need for U.S. assistance.

140. See Tate, "No Room for Peace?"

141. See Fredy Rivera Vélez, "Partidos, fuerzas armadas y crisis institucional en tiempos de incertidumbre," 151–61; Juan Ramón Quintana, "Dilemas y desafíos del gobierno de 'transición histórica': A propósito del poder político y las Fuerzas Armadas en Bolivia," 17–41 in Comisión Andina de Juristas, *El control democrático de la defensa en la región andina: Escenarios para un integración civil-militar* (Lima: 2004).

142. "Crean primera brigada de frontera en límite con Venezuela," *El Tiempo*, June 18, 2004 (http://eltiempo.terra.com.co/coar/ACC_MILITARES/accionesarmadas/ARTICULO-WEB-_NOTA_INTERIOR-1713827.html).

143. The White House, "Presidential Determination: No. 2004–42," August 17, 2004 (www.whitehouse.gov/news/releases/2004/08/20040817-8.html).

144. See Michael Evans, ed., "Shoot Down in Peru—The Secret U.S. Debate over Intelligence Sharing in Peru and Colombia," National Security Archive (www.gwu.edu/~nsarchiv/NSAEBB/NSAEBB44/).

145. August 18, 2004, "U.S. Continues Assistance for Colombian Aerial Interdiction Program," www.allamericanpatriots.com/m-news+article=storyid-2720.html.

146. "National Drug Threat Assessment 2005, Summary Report," National Drug Intelligence Center, February 2005 (www.usdoj.gov/ndic/pubs11/13846/index.htm#Overview) (accessed May 15, 2005).

147. Background memo to committee members from Chairman Rep. Henry Hyde (R-Illinois), Hearing of the House International Relations Committee: "Plan Colombia: Major Successes and New Challenges," May 11, 2005, Committee on International Relations U.S. House of Representatives, Memorandum, May 10, 2005.

148. *Pittsburgh Post-Gazette,* "Editorial: Junk This Plan/The U.S. Drug War in Colombia Isn't Working," May 2, 2005 (www.post-gazette.com/pg/05122/497563.stm) (accessed May 21, 2005).

149. *Pittsburgh Post-Gazette,* "Editorial: Junk This Plan/The U.S. Drug War in Colombia Isn't Working."

150. Jeremy McDermott, "US Slams Colombia Prisoner Plan," BBC News, World Edition, August 27, 2004: http://news.bbc.co.uk/2/hi/americas/3600556.stm.

151. Adam Isacson, Center for International Policy, "Congress Doubles the Limit on U.S. Troops in Colombia," www.ciponline.org/colombia/041008cap.htm.

152. For example (May 20, 2005) the Colombian navy Internet website reported that it was continuing its battle against the narco-terrorists (*"La Armada Nacional continúa con el desarrollo de operaciones ofensivas tendientes a neutralizar el accionar delictivo de los grupos narcoterroristas, que pretenden atacar a la población civil y la infraestructura nacional."*), www.armada.mil.co/index .php?idcategoria=75985&PHPSESSID=3cea4496589d86e3bd1d875bdcbea10d; the army website reported also on its victories over terrorists: *"Combates militares propinan nuevos golpes a grupos terroristas"* (www.ejercito.mil.co/index.php?idcategoria=78668) (accessed May 20, 2005).

153. In April 2005, a statement on the FARC website, signed by Iván Márquez, integrante del Secretariado del FARC-EP, invited the government forces to stay forever in the jungle, leaving the jungle clearings blasted for the helicopters as monuments to the failure of Plan Patriota. "Los resultados del 'Plan Patriota,'" www.farcep.org/novedades/coyuntura/editorial/abril_11_2005.php (accessed May 21, 2005). In contrast the Comando General, Fuerzas Armadas de Colombia multilingual Internet website (www.fuerzasmilitares.mil.co/) provided updated accounts of operations against the "terrorists," listing dead, wounded, captured, and war materiel decommissioned. Likewise the Colombian army home page offers the latest news from the battlefront and features articles on the strategy to defeat the guerrillas, for example, "Dura ofensiva contra el terrorismo en Colombia," www.ejercito.mil.co/index.php?idcategoria=78571&PHPSESSID= 4eda881194c66f73f83374c90c42e6c5 (accessed May 19, 2005).

154. María Alejandra Villamizar, "Análisis noticioso: El Plan Patriota es la apuesta por ganar la guerra," El Tiempo.com, May 4, 2004, http://eltiempo.terra.com.co/coar/ACC_MILITARES/ planpatriota/ARTICULO-WEB-_NOTA_INTERIOR-2056612.html. Official statistics on dead, wounded, and captured, along with equipment, weapons, and vehicles captured through April 29, 2005, can be found at: "Las cifras son otro campo de batalla del Plan Patriota," El Tiempo.com, May 2, 2005, http://eltiempo.terra.com.co/coar/ACC_MILITARES/planpatriota/ ARTICULO-WEB-_NOTA_INTERIOR-2056681.html).

155. See Loveman, *The Constitution of Tyranny,* especially chapters 5 and 6.

156. For a more critical view of Uribe's "Democratic Security" policies see Gustavo Gallón Giraldo, director, Comisión Colombiana de Juristas, "'Seguridad Democrática': El traje nuevo de un imperador en ciernes," paper presented at a conference in Cartagena, September 17–19, 2004 (www.coljuristas.org/archivos/ponencia.pdf).

157. Embassy of the Bolivarian Republic of Venezuela in the United States of America, Washington, D.C., April 30, 2004, Venezuelanalysis.com (www.venezuelanalysis.com/docs.php ?dno=1012) (accessed May 25, 2005).

158. On this program see the official website at http://ctfellowship.org/pages/whatCTFP/ countryPART/country05.htm (accessed May 13, 2005).

159. Some sources use the terms *contractors* and *mercenaries* interchangeably. However, some civilian contractors working for various foreign governments and U.S. government agencies do not conform to the traditional, limited meaning "hired to serve in a foreign army." Since, in general, the term *mercenary* is used pejoratively, this is not simply a matter of proper definition but

also of characterization and normative judgment. In any case, the U.S. government sought to protect its nationals, to the extent possible, from ICC jurisdiction.

160. Both the Clinton and Bush administrations objected to certain aspects of the ICC and insisted on modifications before U.S. ratification. A clear and detailed defense of the U.S. position regarding the ICC is Brett D. Schaefer, "The Bush Administration's Policy on the International Criminal Court Is Correct," Heritage Foundation, Backgrounder # 1830, March 8, 2005 (www.heritage.org/Research/InternationalOrganizations/bg1830.cfm) (accessed May 11, 2005). A chronology of the Bush administration's anti-ICC efforts, from Under Secretary John Bolton's letter (May 6, 2002) to UN Secretary-General Kofi Annan, announcing the U.S. decision to nullify its signature of the Rome Statute until late 2003, is found in American Nongovernmental Organizations Coalition for the International Criminal Court, "Chronology of U.S. Opposition to the International Criminal Court," at www.iccnow.org/pressroom/factsheets/FS-AMICC-US-Timeline.pdf (accessed May 16, 2005).

161. Subsection (d) exempts NATO member countries; a major non-NATO ally (including Australia, Egypt, Israel, Japan, Jordan, Argentina, the Republic of Korea, and New Zealand); or Taiwan.

162. For an initial list of countries entering into such bilateral immunity agreements with the United States see Human Rights Watch, "Bilateral Immunity Agreement, June 20, 2003." In the summer of 2003, the Bush administration threatened to suspend $5 million in nondrug military aid, and possibly raise it to $150 million, if Colombia did not enter into a bilateral immunity agreement. Colombia signed an agreement with the United States on September 17, 2003. This agreement became extremely controversial in May of 2005, when U.S. military personnel were arrested for engaging in arms trafficking to the paramilitaries and drug smuggling (Juan Forero, "Colombia Accepts a U.S. Deal on Exemptions in Human Rights Cases," *New York Times*, September 19, 2003).

163. "U.S. Military Aid and the International Criminal Court," July 2, 2003 (www.amicc.org/docs/Brazil_BIA.pdf) (accessed May 14, 2005).

164. Bill Vann, "US Retaliates over War Crime Immunity Demand," World Socialist Website, July 5, 2003 (www.wsws.org/articles/2003/jul2003/icc-j05_prn.shtml) (accessed May 15, 2005).

165. Irune Aguirrezabal Quijera, "The United States' Isolated Struggle against the ICC," August 4, 2003, Global Policy Forum, www.globalpolicy.org/intljustice/icc/2003/0804usicc.htm (accessed May 14, 2005).

166. Nethercutt was also a great proponent of trade liberalization—including unrestricted sale of food and medicine to Cuba in order to "support American farmers and American values"—as evidenced by a successful amendment he proposed to an agriculture appropriations bill (FY 2001). He also was given a perfect 100 percent scorecard for his votes on issues of concern by the Christian Coalition of Washington State in 2001 (www.christiancoalition.us/voter-guides/congressional_scorecard.htm) (accessed May 13, 2005).

167. "Procuraduría demandará convenio de inmunidad a militares de EEUU," Noticias RCN Radio, www.rcn.com.co/noticia.php3?nt=9185 (accessed May 18, 2005).

168. Council of the European Union, "Declaration of the Presidency on Behalf of the European Union on the Nethercutt Amendment," December 10, 2004 (www.iccnow.org/documents/otherissues/impunityart98/2004/EUStatementNethercutt10Dec04.pdf) (accessed May 14, 2005).

169. Testimony by General Bantz J. Craddock, commander, House Armed Services Committee, March 9, 2005 (www.amicc.org/docs/Craddock%20Statements%203-05.pdf) (accessed May 13, 2005). A regionally focused U.S. military officer who requested to remain unnamed when consulted on his views of APSA and U.S. Latin American policy told me: "It is a congressionally-driven self-inflicted head wound to our regional U.S. security interests." In general, military officers preferred to deal with such issues through bilateral status of forces agreements (SOFAs),

the usual way to handle most problems arising from military basing and operations in foreign countries.

Status-of-forces agreements are not basing or access agreements. Rather, they define the legal status of U.S. personnel and property in the territory of another nation. The purpose of such an agreement is to set forth rights and responsibilities between the United States and the host government on such matters as criminal and civil jurisdiction, the wearing of the uniform, the carrying of arms, tax and customs relief, entry and exit of personnel and property, and resolving damage claims. . . . Most SOFAs recognize the right of the host government to "primary jurisdiction," which is to say the host country exercises jurisdiction for all cases in which U.S. military personnel violate the host country's laws. There are two exceptions, however, which generally apply only in criminal cases involving U.S. forces personnel: When the offense is committed by Americans against Americans ("inter se" cases), and when the offense is committed by Americans in carrying out official duty. In these situations, the United States has primary jurisdiction over the accused American. (Global Security.Org: www .globalsecurity.org/military/facility/sofa.htm [accessed May 14, 2005]).

170. On WHINSEC (ex-School of the Americas), see the official website at www.benning .army.mil/whinsec/ (accessed May 23, 2005); descriptions of the human rights courses taught at the institute are online at: www.benning.army.mil/whinsec/democracy.asp?id=96 (accessed May 23, 2005). For a highly critical study of SOA/WHINSEC see Lesley Gill, *The School of the Americas. Military Training and Political Violence in the Americas* (Durham, N.C.: Duke University Press, 2004).

171. Mary Donohue and Melissa Nepomiachi, "Washington Secures Long-Sought Hemispheric Outpost, Perhaps at the Expense of Regional Sovereignty," Council on Hemispheric Affairs, July 20, 2005, www.coha.org/NEW_PRESS_RELEASES/New_Press_Releases_2005/05.78_ Washington_Secure_Long_Sought_Military_Outpost_Perhaps_At_the_Expense_of_ Regional_Soverignty.htm) (accessed July 20, 2005).

172. Donohue and Nepomiachi, "Washington Secures Long-Sought Hemispheric Outpost."

173. In mid-July 2005, despite the seeming disapproval of his minister of Foreign Affairs, Ecuador's new president, Alfredo Palacio, who replaced the ousted Lucio Gutiérrez (2005), promised to honor the agreement that had conceded base rights to the United States at Manta for ten years (1999–2009). The United States not only used the air base but facilities at the nearby port; controversy continued over whether the base was being used solely for counternarcotics activities or also as a counterinsurgency platform to monitor and attack the Colombian insurgents. See "Nueva controversia: Presidente contradice a Parra Gil sobre Base de Manta," Ecuadorin-mediato.com, July 16, 2005.

174. Domestic politics were also influenced by Secretary of Defense Rumsfeld's base-closing and relocation initiatives. Surely by coincidence, Florida did not suffer. Governor Jeb Bush remarked in 2003:

Florida welcomes Special Operations Command South (SOCSOUTH) to Homestead and our state's military community. This is a decision by U. S. Special Operations Command and U. S. Southern Command that will bolster the military value of the Homestead Air Reserve Base, as well as strengthen Florida's already robust military composition. The state is proud of our military presence, with 21 active installations and three unified commands contributing significantly to the $44 billion defense industry impact to Florida's economy, and the addition of SOCSOUTH is welcomed news. Approximately 150 military and civilian personnel and their families assigned to the command will relocate to the Homestead area before the end of March 2004, increasing the value of the military in Florida. We place defense as a top economic priority and must do all that we can to protect Florida's military installations from the 2005 Base Realignment and Closure (BRAC) process. (Statement by Governor Jeb Bush Regarding the United States Special Operations Command's Decision to Relocate Special Operations Command South to Homestead from Puerto Rico: www.myflorida.com/eog_new/eog/ library/releases/2003/November/puerto-rico_11-19-03.html [accessed April 29, 2005])

175. U.S. Special Operations Forces, Posture Statement 2003–2004: www.defenselink.mil/policy/solic/2003_2004_SOF_Posture_Statement.pdf (accessed May 16, 2005), 53.

176. U.S. Special Operations Forces, Posture Statement 2003–2004, 53–54, emphasis added. The official language in the Special Operations mission for supporting friendly governments is "Foreign Internal Defense, which is the action taken to counter subversion, lawlessness and insurgency, and address causes of host-nation's instability." Interview with Thomas W. O'Connell, assistant secretary of Defense for Special Operations and Low-Intensity Conflict, May 25, 2004. Special Operations Technology Online Archives (www.special-operations-technology.com/article .cfm?DocID=485) (accessed May 10, 2005).

177. In the late 1960s, during the Vietnam War, the Central Intelligence Agency (CIA) initiated the Phoenix Program, which was aimed at destroying the Viet Cong infrastructure by "neutralizing" its supporters. It is claimed that the program led to the execution, without trial, of about twenty thousand South Vietnamese who were suspected of collaborating with the Viet Cong. See: "United States Involvement in the Vietnam War," Britannica Student Encyclopedia, 2005. Encyclopædia Britannica Online, May 31, 2005 (http://search.eb.com/ebi/article?tocId= 9314143).

178. SOLIC official website: www.defenselink.mil/policy/solic/asd_bio.html (accessed May 13, 2005).

179. USSOUTHCOM, *A Theater Strategy of Focused Cooperation and Mutual Security, 2005.* (This document is available on the URL [www.rowman.com/isbn/0742540987] accompanying this book.)

180. Testimony of General Bantz J. Craddock, commander, United States Southern Command, hearing of the House Armed Services Committee: "Fiscal Year 2006 National Defense Authorization Budget Request," March 9, 2005 (http://ciponline.org/colombia/050309crad.htm) (accessed February 28, 2006).

181. "'Plan Colombia': Elements for Success." Staff Trip Report to the Committee on Foreign Relations, United States Senate. 109th Congress, 1st Session. September 2005 (Washington, D.C.: USGPO, 2006), 3.

182. "'Plan Colombia': Elements for Success,"11

183. Jorge A. Restrepo and Michael Spagat, "The Colombian Conflict. Where Is It Heading?" Bogotá: Centro de Recursos para el Análisis de Conflictos (CERAC), November 3, 2005: 70–71. Online power point slide presentation at: www.cerac.org.co/pdf/CSISPresentationwithtext-V10_Low.pdf (accessed February 24, 2006).

184. La Conferencia Episcopal de Colombia y la Consultoría para los Derechos Humanos y el desplazamiento (Codhes), "Alrededor de 3 millones de Colombianos se han desplazo en los últimos 10 años": www.codhes.org/index.php?option=com_content&task=view&id=192&Itemid=1 (accessed February 18, 2006).

185. Amnesty International, "Colombia. Human Rights Concerns": www.amnestyusa.org/countries/colombia/index.do (accessed February 28, 2006).

186. See "Colombia and Its Neighbours: The Tentacles of Instability," Bogotá/Brussels: International Crisis Group, April 8, 2003; interview with Colombian army commander, General Martín Orlando Carreño, *El Universal* (Cúcuta), March 21, 2004: "There are some things difficult to control, especially in the very active borders with Ecuador and Venezuela. Our objective is to impede passage of the terrorists in either direction. . . . Arms trafficking across these borders is extensive. It's good business and control is not easy. . . . Drug trafficking is very active and Cúcuta is a place where it germinates. . . . We must fight aggressively against this cancer."

187. "Las FARC extienden sus nexos en Ecuador," *El Comercio,* May 19, 2005 (www.elcomercio .com/noticias.asp?noid=128724).

188. "FF AA se preparan," Los Tiempos.com (Cochabamba), May 20, 2005.

189. "FF.AA. advierten que actuarán de ser necesario," *El Universo* (Guayaquil), June 10, 2005 (http://200.105.240.202/2005/06/10/14/e98c8bd1af5e46fdbe0c1d3892a01020.html?EUID=").

190. "Venezuela's VP Says US Has Isolated Itself with Its Foreign Policy," Venezuelanalysis .com, February 17, 2005 (www.venezuelanalysis.com/news.php?newsno=1511) (accessed May 10, 2005).

191. "At OAS Venezuela Says US Interventionism Is Prelude to Aggression," Venezuelanalysis.com (www.venezuelanalysis.com/news.php?newsno=1520) (accessed May 22, 2005).

192. Martin Arostegui, "Evidence Emerging of Role in Ecuadorean Revolt," *Washington Times*, May 1, 2005 (www.washingtontimes.com/functions/print.php?StoryID=20050430-113324-8610r) (accessed May 1, 2005).

193. "Gobierno venezolano se fundamenta en un esquema autocrático-populista," Prensa de Copei, 2000.com.ve (www.2001.com.ve/20050520/Política/Política9.asp?tp=7) (accessed May 20, 2005).

194. Dimitri Barreto, "Populismo radical, el otro rival de EE.UU," El Comercio.com, May 15, 2005, www.elcomercio.com/noticias.asp?noid=128532.

195. "Denuncian plan rebelde en frontera con Colombia," El Universal.com, May 27, 2005, www.eluniversal.com/2005/05/27/pol_art_27105H.shtml.

196. J. Michael Waller, "What to Do about Venezuela?" The Center for Security Policy, Washington, D.C., May 2005 (www.centerforsecuritypolicy.org/What_to_Do.pdf) (accessed May 27, 2005).

197. "Chávez tacha de fascista a Aznar y dice que 'Hitler se queda corto a su lado,'" www .analitica.com/va/vpi/3246632.asp (accessed May 20, 2005).

198. "Militares no apoyarán un golpe," El Universal.com, May 20, 2005 (www.eud.com/2005/ 05/20/pol_art_20106A.shtml).

199. See USSOUTHCOM *Theater Security Command Strategy*, August 13, 2004.

200. "Rumsfeld Meets with Six Latin-American Presidents," USDOD Defense Link, May 11, 2005 (www.defenselink.mil/news/May2005/20050511_1022.html) (accessed May 12, 2005).

201. General James Hill, commander of the U.S. Southern Command, Miami, North-South Center, March 3, 2003.

202. Text of Secretary of State Condoleezza Rice's interview with *Miami Herald* correspondent Pablo Bachelet, Friday June 3. Posted on Sun, June 5, 2005 (www.miami.com/mld/miamiherald/ news/world/americas/11822113.htm?source=rss&channel=miamiherald_americas).

203. "Chávez: Si hay que monitorear algún gobierno de la OEA sería a EEUU," El Universal.com, June 5, 2005, www.eud.com/2005/06/05/pol_ava_05A566513.shtml.

204. "Condoleezza Rice: Las democracias deben estar a favor del libre mercado," Agencia Bolivariana de Noticias, www.abn.info.ve/go_news5.php?articulo=9523 (accessed June 5, 2005).

205. Declaration of Florida, Delivering the Benefits of Democracy, June 7, 2005 (www .oas.org/main/main.asp?sLang=E&sLink=http://www.oas.org/OASpage/eng/latestnews/latest news.asp).

206. "La embajada de EE UU en Haití pidió el envío de marines," El Nacional.com, June 5, 2005, www.el-nacional.com/# (15:30:10, minuto a minuto). See the MINUSTAH website (www.un.org/Depts/dpko/missions/minustah/) for details on the background to the MINUS-TAH mission at www.un.org/Depts/dpko/missions/minustah/background.html. The basic justification of the mission reads: "Having determined that the situation in Haiti continued to constitute a threat to international peace and security in the region and acting under Chapter VII of the UN Charter, the Security Council, by its resolution 1542 of 30 April 2004, decided to establish the United Nations Stabilization Mission in Haiti (MINUSTAH) and requested that authority be transferred from the Multinational Interim Force (MIF), authorized by the Security Council in February 2004, to MINUSTAH on 1 June 2004."

207. Brian Concannon Jr., "Throwing Gasoline on Haiti's Fires," IRC Americas Program, July 14, 2005 (http://americas.irc-online.org/am/159) (accessed July 26, 2005).

208. Robert E. White (1996) *Cosmos Journal*, www.cosmos-club.org/journals/1996/index.html (accessed May 30, 2005).

209. News HaitiAction.net: www.haitiaction.net/News/BL/6_9_5.html (accessed February 28, 2006).

Chapter 2

1. According to the Center for International Policy, beginning in 2000, numerous debates and news articles "had put Colombia near the top of Washington's list of international priorities" (Ingrid Vaicius and Adam Isacson, "The 'War on Drugs' Meets the 'War on Terror'," *International Policy Report*, 2003), 1.

2. The antinarcotics piece of the U.S. assistance package to Plan Colombia contained a counterinsurgency component from the outset, because weakening the financial base of the FARC (Fuerzas Armadas Revolucionarias de Colombia—Revolutionary Armed Forces of Colombia) and the AUC (Autodefensas Unidas Colombianas—United Self-Defense Forces)—which depended 50 percent and 70 percent, respectively, on income from illegal drug trafficking—was considered a principal objective of the package. "The central premise of the US component of Plan Colombia was that money from the trade in illegal drugs feeds the coffers of the guerrillas. . . . If the narcotics funds could be stopped or drastically diminished, the guerrillas could not mount their ambitious military campaigns against the state" (Marcella, 2003: 23).

3. According to former ambassador to Bogotá, Myles Frechette (2003), Plan Colombia was stripped down to just its antinarcotics dimension because only the United States contributed significant resources to it. Not even Colombia invested the amount it had promised; nor did the international community, starting with the European Union, give the resources that would have been necessary to effectively address other dimensions of the Colombian crisis besides drug trafficking, such as restarting the economy or fighting poverty.

4. During the 1970s the international community focused its attention on the Southern Cone in response to institutional instability there and military coups. During the 1980s attention shifted to Central America and its civil wars. Today the "storm zone" is now located, without a doubt, in the Andean region.

5. The complete document published in September 2002 is on the URL (www.rowman.com/ isbn/0742540987) that accompanies this book and may also be viewed on the following web page: http://usinfo.state.gov/topical/pol/terror/secstrat2.htm.

6. Sam Tanenhaus, "The Rise and Fall and Rise of the Domino Theory," *New York Times*, March 23, 2003. This theory, originally coined by President Dwight Eisenhower shortly after the French were defeated at Dien Bien Phu Valley in Vietnam in 1954, was picked up by the Kennedy administration in its readings on Indochina, and later, it was widely applied to Latin America (Chile, Nicaragua, El Salvador, and Granada). Undersecretary for Defense Paul D. Wolfowitz has recently tried to give the formula a positive spin, affirming that democratizing Iraq could generate a democratizing domino effect throughout the Middle East.

7. With the exception of some areas bordering Venezuela where there is significant commercial and cultural activity and important movements of the population, the remainder (including the entire border region with Brazil, Panama, and Peru) are sparsely populated jungle regions.

8. John Podhoretz, "The Bush Revolution," *New York Post*, May 2, 2003; James Atlas, "A Classicist's Legacy: New Empire Builder," *New York Times*, May 4, 2003.

9. These conversations took place in spite of the fact that the FARC (as well as the ELN— Ejército de Liberación Nacional—National Liberation Army) appeared on the biannual list of terrorist groups put out by the Department of State in 1997, which expressly prohibits such

meetings. The talks were suspended after the killing of three North American Native American activists (Ingrid Washinawatok, Larry Lahe'ena'e Gay, and Terrence Freitas) by the FARC.

10. "Colombia's Struggles and How We Can Help," *New York Times*, August 10, 1999, 17; "Los Estados Unidos y otros amigos deben ayudar a Colombia," *Clarín*, August 11, 1999, 15. The secretary of state added a third axis to Washington policy: economic support: "Any nation interested in helping Colombia fight drugs or achieve peace will have an interest in helping it recover economically. The United States has been working with the International Monetary Fund, the World Bank and other partners to insure that needed assistance is available." Up to this point the most important economic tool for restarting economies in the Andean region (with the exception of Venezuela) has been the Andean Trade Preferences Act (ATPA), which President George W. Bush renewed on August 6, 2002. The ATPA is a unilateral benefit granted by the United States to Ecuador, Peru, Colombia, and Bolivia. It exempts certain key exports of those countries from customs regulations. The aim of this benefit package is to create economic alternatives to illegal drug production. Colombia has been, by far, the primary beneficiary.

11. This interbureaucratic agreement across party lines contrasted with the firm opposition to Plan Colombia on the part of numerous influential NGOs and in academic circles, as well as from various newspapers such as the *New York Times*.

12. Because narco-funds found their way into the financing of his Partido Liberal campaign for the presidency, during Ernesto Samper's administration Colombia was subjected to the worst international ostracism in its history and was decertified by Washington in the war on drugs. Colombia is still paying the price of the infiltration, and of Washington's misguided response, both of which led to a deepening collapse of the country's institutions and deterioration of the internal public order.

13. Furthermore, this was the only issue that had any real possibility of getting congressional support. Few members of the U.S. Congress were willing to involve the country in a confusing armed Colombian conflict.

14. The United States preferred to create these three units rather than risk supporting already existing units that might have been blocked under Section 570 of the Foreign Operations Appropriation Act, better known as the Leahy Amendment. This amendment forbids giving funds to the security forces unit of a foreign state if the Department of State has credible evidence that said unit has committed human rights violations.

15. *Hoy*, Quito, August 25, 2000.

16. The so-called Pentágono Criollo (Hybrid Pentagon) at Tres Esquinas (Caquetá) opened on August 24, 2000. This advanced center of operations functions on satellite communications; webcam; and an interactive program run by satellite from seven points within Colombia (military and police units), the DEA, CIA, U.S. Southern Command, and the Pentagon's Section for Latin American Affairs. It is expected that all military and police units in Colombian territory will be networked by 2005.

17. "Presentan prueba de vinculación de la FAN con la guerrilla colombiana," *El Universal*, January 30, 2002; Roberto Guiusti, "Las FARC entrenan a las FBL en centro de instrucción zuliano," *El Universal*, April 28, 2003.

18. Marcelo Larrea, "Ecuador: ¿Lucio se hunde en el Plan Colombia?" *Agência de Informação Frei Tito para a América Latina*, May 5, 2003: www.adital.org.br.

19. A few months before, the president of the Subcommittee on Criminal Justice and Drug Policy of the U.S. House of Representatives stated he was "frankly worried that the FARC . . . might make the situation in Panamá more unstable and that the US would have to return to Panamá at sometime, at great expense and sacrifice, to maintain the Canal's security and to protect our national interests" (*El Espectador*, May 5, 1999).

20. *El Tiempo*, August 9, 1999.

21. In response to Plan Colombia's approval, which has raised tremendous concern throughout the entire region, Brazil put "Operation Cobra" into effect, a name that combines the initials of both countries (cf., *El Tiempo*, August 25, 2000). The capture of the notorious Brazilian drug trafficker Fernandinho by Colombian troops during Operation "Gato Negro" exposed the dangerous ties between the Brazilian mafia and the FARC.

22. President Lula da Silva promised the Colombian government Brazil would fight drug and arms trafficking along their common border and agreed to share information captured by the SIVAM with Colombian authorities. See Patricia Zimmerman, "Uribe vai usar informaçoes brasileiras para patrulhar traficantes," *Folhe Online*, March 7, 2003.

23. *El Espectador*, May 5, 1999.

24. See U.S. Military Facilities, Forward Operating Locations, www.ciponline.org/facts/fol.htm.

25. "El cerco a Colombia," *Clarín Digital*, August 1, 1999.

26. *Cambio*, No. 231, August 9, 1999.

27. In Latin America links are made between at-risk states and terrorism via the idea that terrorist or criminal groups can easily take root in regions that have a weak state presence. In a speech during the most recent meeting of the American ministers for defense held in Chile, U.S. secretary of defense Donald Rumsfeld made reference to the risks to regional security "ungoverned spaces" or "lawless areas" represent. In turn General James Hill, director of the Southern Command, stated at a recent Miami conference, "Today the threat to the countries in the region is not the military force of the adjacent neighbor or some invading foreign power. Today's foe is the terrorist, the narco-traffickers, the arms trafficker. This threat is a weed that is planted . . . and nurtured in the fertile ground of ungoverned spaces, such as coastlines, river and unpopulated areas" (quoted in Andrés Oppenheimer, "Terrorists, Traffickers Find Haven in Latin America's 'Ungoverned Spaces,'" *Arizona Daily Star*, March 12, 2003). The main "ungoverned spaces" being, according to the Department of Defense, the border between Brazil, Paraguay, and Argentina; the borders between Brazil and Colombia (the Tabatinga and Leticia corridor); the border between Colombia and Ecuador (the Lake Agrio area); the Darién region between Colombia and Panama; and lastly, Suriname.

28. Gerardo Reyes, "Washington, impaciente con el proceso de paz," *El Nuevo Herald* (Miami), October 18, 2001. It should be noted that covert U.S. policy had long since recognized the nexus between guerrillas and the narcotics trade and that counterinsurgency and counternarcotics activities had been melded in practice, if not acknowledged publicly.

29. "EEUU elabora primer plan antiterrorista para los países andinos," *El latinoamericano*, www.latinoamericano.05c.net/. Cass Ballenger, president of the Subcommittee on the Western Hemisphere, stated, "Terrorism and drugs cannot be treated as two different things. Income from drugs is used to finance terrorist activities and to protect drug traffickers. They go hand-in-hand and must be fought." After a meeting with President Andrés Pastrana, Representative Mark Souder, president of the Antidrug Action Group of the House of Representatives, stated unambiguously, "The line that may have existed between insurgency, drug traffic and terrorism has completely disappeared" and therefore resources contributed by his country could be used to fight the FARC, ELN, and the AUC, if that was what the Colombian government needed. "They crossed the line to becoming terrorists a long time ago. It is becoming increasingly clear that Colombia not only has a drug problem but one where terror is being used to impose policy. We're trying to show Americans that drug trafficking has turned into terrorism and we have to fight it in this hemisphere just like we are in the Middle East" (*El Tiempo*, November 8, 2001).

30. Dennis Hastert, quoted in Marcela Sánchez, "Terror and Drugs: The Same Battlefield," *Washington Post*, October 3, 2001.

31. Transcript of House Western Hemisphere Subcommittee Hearing, October 10, 2001, "The Western Hemisphere's Response to the September 11, 2001 Terrorist Attack on the United States": at www.ciponline.org/colombia/101001.htm (accessed July 28, 2005).

32. Ana Barón, "El cerco a Colombia," *Clarín Digital,* August 1, 1999.

33. There was a point when Washington hypothetically could have counted on support from Alberto Fujimori and Carlos Menem. But resistance from Brazil—a country that has a penetrating vision of its geopolitical interests—would have paralyzed any decision coming out of Buenos Aires to take action along its border, far from Argentine territory.

34. *La Nación,* July 27, 1999.

35. Jan Engeland was originally appointed special adviser to the secretary-general on International Assistance to Colombia on December 1, 1999. James LeMoyne took over the position in January 2002.

36. As long as militarization of the borders is the product of policy mutually agreed upon by the Colombian armed forces and neighboring countries to take concrete action (e.g., to fight illegal drug or arms traffic), it could have a dissuasive effect that would be positive for all nations in the region.

37. The original Plan Colombia was drafted in English by officials in charge at Planeación Nacional (National Planning) following long working sessions with officials from the Department of State. The idea was to take advantage of Andrés Pastrana's scheduled visits to the United Nations and the White House to launch the plan for Colombian assistance on an international scale. Because of time pressures the government committed enormous errors of management and presentation that compromised the project's credibility domestically and internationally (from an interview with the former U.S. ambassador in Bogotá).

38. The following statistics were taken from the Web page for Washington's Center for International Policy: www.ciponline.org/Colombia/aid/aidsumm.htm.

39. Fact Sheet, Office of the Press Secretary, The White House, Washington, D.C., March 23, 2002 (www.state.gov/p/wha/rls/fs/8980.htm) (accessed July 20, 2005).

40. At a Foro Social conference in Bogotá, Alejandro Santos, director of the magazine *Semana,* seized on Professor Paul Samuelson's famous dilemma and asked: "The dilemma that brings us together today is how to go about breaking the vicious cycle of war and poverty. Should we promote security to get the economy re-started and do away with poverty that way? Or should we promote social investment in order to get at the 'objective causes' underlying violence and re-start the economy that way?" (Alejandro Santos, "Cañones o mantequilla," Semana.com, February 6, 2003).

41. See Juan Tokatlian's highly interesting article, "Estados Unidos y Latinoamérica, más distanciados," *El Tiempo,* September 10, 2002.

42. Literally, "vaccination." This colloquial euphemism with roots in cattle ranching refers to the practice of regularly paying off drug traffickers in exchange for protection against the "viruses" of kidnapping, theft, and plundering.

43. The record is likely associated with increased cultivation of alternative crops on about 46,000 hectares formerly planted with illegal crops, according to the Latin American head of the UNODC, Aldo Lale-Demoz ("Colombia reduce plantaciones de coca en un 30%," *El Espectador,* March 18, 2003).

44. Rachel Van Dongen, "Fall in Amount of Coca Grown in Colombia," *Financial Times,* March 22, 2003.

45. *El Tiempo,* September 10, 2002.

46. During the Pastrana administration, there were two "groups of friendly countries": one friendly to the FARC, the other friendly to the ELN. Some countries were members of both groups, who agreed to get along. The group of countries working alongside the FARC in the peace process consisted of seven European nations (Spain, France, Italy, Norway, Sweden, and Switzerland), three from Latin America (México, Cuba, and Venezuela), and Canada. This group of countries later became the Comisión de Facilitación Internacional (International Facilitation Commission) through an agreement between the government and the FARC negotiating team signed on February 7, 2002.

Chapter 3

1. For more details regarding the evolution of U.S.–Venezuelan relations, see Carlos A. Romero, "Las Relaciones entre Venezuela y Estados Unidos: Realidad Histórica u Opción Política?" *Política Internacional*, vol. 1, no. 2 (April–June 1986): 11–14; Judith Ewell, *Venezuela and the United States: From Monroe's Hemisphere to Petroleum's Empire* (Athens: The University of Georgia Press, 1996); Janet Kelly and Carlos A. Romero, *The United States and Venezuela: Rethinking a Relationship* (New York: Routledge, 2001).

2. The most notable differences revolved around relations with Cuba and Central America; by the 1970s Venezuela had restored diplomatic relations with the Caribbean island and played an important role in pressuring the ouster of Anastasio Somoza in Nicaragua.

3. Moises Naim, *Paper Tigers and Minotaurs: The Politics of Venezuela's Economic Reforms* (Washington, D.C.: Carnegie Endowment for International Peace, 1993), 59–60.

4. Naim, *Paper Tigers and Minotaurs*, 59–60.

5. Brian Loveman and Thomas M. Davies, Jr., eds., *The Politics of Antipolitics: The Military in Latin America* (revised and updated) (Wilmington, Del.: Scholarly Resources, 1997), 3.

6. *El Universal* (Caracas), December 8, 1998 (www.eluniveral.com).

7. *El Universal* (Caracas), December 10, 1998 (www.eluniveral.com).

8. *El Universal* (Caracas), August 28, 1999 (www.eluniveral.com).

9. "The Next Fidel Castro," editorial, *Washington Post*, November 2, 2000, A28; and "The Ambitions of Hugo Chávez," *New York Times*, November 6, 2000. President Chávez reacted to the Oppenheimer article and to the two editorials, arguing that there was an "ongoing conspiracy orchestrated by minority, but influential, economic and political sectors in Washington and their allies in Venezuela, to try to damage the relationship with the U.S., which the Venezuelan government strongly valued." Chávez stated, "we are obliged to maintain and nurture our relationship with Washington, which is condemned to be good" (Cenovia Casas, "Chávez: Las relaciones con EEUU están condenadas a ser buenas," *El Nacional* [Caracas], November 7, 2000).

10. See Andrés Oppenheimer, "Is Chávez Picking a Fight with U.S.?" *Miami Herald*, October 29, 2000, p 6-A; "Las bofetadas de Chávez a Estados Unidos," *El Nuevo Heraldo*, October 30, 2000.

11. Gioconda Soto, "No habrá marcha atrás en materia de sobrevuelos," *El Nacional* (Caracas), June 1, 1999.

12. "EE UU propone a Venezuela fortalecer inteligencia y entrenamiento antidrogas," *El Nacional* (Caracas), July 9, 1999.

13. FMS involves government-to-government sales of defense articles, training, and services. DCS are sales from U.S. companies licensed by the U.S. government.

14. See *Just the Facts: A Civilian's Guide to U.S. Defense and Security Assistance to Latin America and the Caribbean* (www.ciponline.org/facts).

15. Cited in John Marshall and Christian Parenti, "New World Order . . . but Venezuela's 'Revolution' Faces Many Obstacles": www.blythe.org/nytransfer-subs/2001-South_America/Venezuela's_revolution_faces_many_obstacles (accessed August 1, 2005).

16. Christian Hoag, "Chávez Rebuts U.S. Official, Denies Link to Violent Groups," *Miami Herald*, December 8, 2000; Andrés Oppenheimer, "Neighbors Say Chávez Aids Violent Groups," *Miami Herald*, December 5, 2000, p. 1A; Andrés Oppenheimer, "Venezuela's Chávez Need Only Listen to His Neighbors," *Miami Herald*, December 10, 2000, p. 6A.

17. Gioconda Soto, "La CIA Siguió los pasos de alto funcionario de la Cancillería," *El Nacional* (Caracas), February 3, 2001.

18. "Chávez Says Venezuelan–U.S. Relations Will Remain 'Normal' under Bush," CNN, December 31, 2000 (www.cnn.com).

19. "Bush expresó preocupación sobre escenario venezolano," *El Nacional* (Caracas), April 3, 2001.

20. More will be said later regarding Reich's alleged role in the April 2002 coup against Chávez.

21. Juan O. Tamayo, "U.S. Is Wary of Chávez's Cuba Ties," *Miami Herald*, June 10, 2001.

22. "Posture Statement of Major General Gary D. Speer, United States Army, Acting Commander in Chief United States Southern Command," 107th Congress, Senate Armed Services Committee, 5 (March 5, 2002), p. 18.

23. Concern was also raised by Venezuela's canceling, in early September 2001, of an agreement that allowed U.S. military personnel to maintain an office at Fuerte Tiuna, the headquarters of the Venezuelan Ministry of Defense.

24. Tim Johnson, "Chávez Condemns Bombings by U.S.," *Miami Herald*, October 31, 2001.

25. Nicholas Kralev, "United States Recalls Emissary to Venezuela," *Washington Times*, November 3, 2001.

26. Scott Wilson, "Chávez Turns Caracas from U.S. Ally to Critic," *Washington Post*, November 22, 2001, p. A42.

27. Fabiola Sánchez, "Vicepresidente Venezolana arremete contra los EU," *El Nuevo Herald*, November 10, 2001.

28. "U.S. Policy in the Western Hemisphere, Ambassador Lino Gutiérrez, Acting Assistant Secretary, Bureau of Western Hemisphere Affairs Remarks to the United States Conference of Catholic Bishops," Washington, D.C., December 17, 2001 (www.state.gov/p/wha/rls/rm/2001/6950.htm).

29. The discussion of the political situation before and after the April 2002 coup draws heavily from Orlando J. Pérez, "*Chavismo* and the Transformation of Civil–Military Relations in Venezuela," *South Eastern Latinamericanist*, vol. XLVI, no. 1–2 (Summer 2002): 12–33.

30. "Chávez Unmoved as Officers Desert," *BBC News* (http://news.bbc.co.uk/hi/english/world/americas/), February 26, 2002.

31. A. Keller y Asociados, Análisis del entorno sociopolítico venezolano, en base a los resultados de la Encuesta Urbana Nacional de Opinión Publica del II trimestre de 2002, July 2002.

32. Tim Weiner, "A Coup by Any Other Name," *New York Times*, April 12, 2002.

33. "'Venezuela's Uncertain Future: Challenges for U.S. Policy,' Lino Gutierrez, Principal Deputy Assistant Secretary for Western Hemisphere Affairs, Remarks to North-South Center Roundtable, Carnegie Endowment for International Peace," Washington, D.C., April 17, 2002 (www.state.gov/p/wha/rls/rm/9573.htm).

34. "Tales from a Failed Coup," *The Economist*, April 25, 2002; Christopher Marquis, "Bush Administration Met with Venezuelans Who Ousted Leader," *New York Times*, April 16, 2002; Karen De Young, "Bush Officials Defend Their Actions on Venezuela," *Washington Post*, April 18, 2002, p. A01.

35. Tim Johnson, "Bush: U.S. at No Time Supported Overthrow," *Miami Herald*, April 19, 2002.

36. Gutiérrez, "Venezuela's Uncertain Future."

37. Statement by General James T. Hill, United States Army Commander, United States Southern Command, before the House Armed Service Committee, United States House of Representatives on the State of Special Operations Forces, March 12, 2003.

38. Andrés Oppenheimer, "General: Islamists Find Latin America Funds," *Miami Herald*, March 9, 2003, p. 1A.

39. Oppenheimer, "General: Islamists Find Latin America Funds," p. 1A.

40. The State Department's report *Patterns of Global Terrorism* said, "At year's end [2002], there was no confirmed, credible information of an established al-Qaida presence in Latin America," United States Department of State, *Patterns of Global Terrorism, 2002*, Office of the Secretary of State and Office of the Coordinator for Counterterrorism, Washington, D.C., April 2003, p. 66.

41. Tim Johnson, "Colombian Rebel Groups Seen as Regional Danger," *Miami Herald*, September 18, 2002, p. 11A.

42. Ivan G. Osorio, "Chávez Bombshell: A Defector's Testimony Links the Venezuelan Strong-man to International Terror," *National Review Online,* January 8, 2003 (www.nationalreview .com).

43. A group of dissident military officers have set up a web page (www.militaresdemocraticos .com) in which they continue to report the alleged connection between Chávez and Al Qaeda.

44. U.S. Department of State, *Patterns of Global Terrorism, 2002,* p. 74.

45. United States Southern Command, Posture Statement of General Bantz J. Craddock, United States Army Commander, United States Southern Command, before the 109th Congress, House Armed Services Committee, Washington, D.C., March 9, 2005, www.house.gov/hasc/ testimony/109thcongress/FY06%20Budget%20Misc/Southcom3-9-05.pdf.

46. Dudley Althaus, "Strike Cripples Venezuelan Oil Industry," *Houston Chronicle,* December 8, 2002; Frances Robles, "Banks, Supermarkets Shut Down in Venezuela Strike," *Miami Herald,* January 9, 2003.

47. "Lula: Alliance Needed to Aid Venezuela," United Press International, January 9, 2003.

48. Frances Robles, "Former President Carter Offers Venezuela Solution," *Miami Herald,* January 22, 2003.

49. "Agreement between the Representatives of the Government of the Bolivarian Republic of Venezuela and the Political and Social Groups Supporting It, and the Coordinadora Democratica and the Political and Civil Society Organizations Supporting It," Embassy of the Bolivarian Republic of Venezuela, Washington, D.C. (www.embavenez-us.org/).

50. Tom Carter, "U.S. Hails Step toward Venezuela Vote; 5-Member Electoral Council Sworn In," *Washington Times,* August 28, 2003.

51. Alice M. Chacon, "Venezuela's President Tells Former U.S. President Jimmy Carter He Would Be Happy to Face Recall Vote," AP Worldstream, May 30, 2004.

52. An audit of the election conducted by the Carter Center discovered some minor problems, but not nearly enough to reverse the outcome. See, "Audit of the Results of the Presidential Recall Referendum in Venezuela," Final Report, The Carter Center, August 26, 2004; and "Report on an Analysis of the Representativeness of the Second Audit Sample, and the Correlation between Petition Signers and the Yes Vote in the Aug. 15, 2004 Presidential Recall Referendum in Venezuela," The Carter Center, September 16, 2004. These and other reports, including the full observation report, can be found at the center's Web page, www.carter center.org.

53. See Scott Wilson, "Venezuela and Colombia Square Off over Rebels," *Washington Post,* March 17, 2001, p. A16; "Nuevas denuncias sobre relación Chávez-Farc," *El Espectador* (Bogotá), March 8, 2002; Hoag, "Chávez Rebuts U.S. Official, Denies Link to Violent Groups."

54. "El silencio sobre las armas," *Venezuela Analítica* (Caracas), July 24, 2000.

55. Tamayo, "U.S. Is Wary of Chávez's Cuba Ties."

56. "La mano de Chávez," *Cambio* (Bogotá), November 21, 2000.

57. Tim Johnson and Andrés Oppenheimer, "Tensions Rise between Colombia, Venezuela," *Miami Herald,* July 24, 1999; Giocando Soto, "Las FFAA de Colombia son el fuente de armas," *El Nacional,* Caracas, August 21, 1999.

58. Andy Web-Vidal, "Venezuelan Guns Aiding Guerrillas," *Financial Times,* January 25, 2001.

59. Personal interview with General (r) Boris Saavedra, Washington, D.C., September 8, 2002.

60. "Rebel-Camp Allegations Fuel Tension in Venezuela," *Miami Herald,* April 5, 2002.

61. Humberto Márquez, "Colombia–Venezuela: Tensions Grow over Iraq and Guerrillas," Inter Press Service English News Wire, March 13, 2003.

62. Humberto Márquez, "Venezuela: Chávez Says "Invasion" Planned in Miami and Colombia," Inter Press Service News Wire, May 12, 2004.

63. Márquez, "Venezuela."

64. Christopher Toothaker, "Venezuela Suspends Ties with Colombia," AP Online, January 14, 2005, www.ocregister.com/ocr/2005/01/15/sections/nation_world/mexico_latinamerica/article_377775.php.

65. Toothaker, "Venezuela Suspends Ties with Colombia."

66. Gary Marx, "Colombia, Venezuela Relations Chill Further over Guerrilla Accusations," *Chicago Tribune*, January 18, 2005.

67. The Plan Patriota, initiated in the summer of 2003, seeks to take the offensive against the FARC. With U.S. tactical and logistical support, about fifteen thousand Colombian troops have been dispatched into the FARC stronghold of southern Colombia, in an effort to decapitate the seventeen thousand–strong rebel army.

68. Fabiola Sanchez, "Venezuela Says Colombian Police Involved in Rebel's Capture, Recalls Ambassador over 'Violation of Sovereignty,'" AP Worldstream, January 14, 2005.

69. "Venezuela's Chávez: U.S. behind Colombia Rebel Arrest," Agence France Presse English, January 24, 2005.

70. Humberto Márquez, "Colombia–Venezuela: Lula Steps in to Ease Bilateral Tensions," www.IPSterraviva.net, January 21, 2005.

71. Márquez, "Colombia–Venezuela."

Chapter 4

This chapter was written with the assistance of Alexei Páez, who organized much of the information on Ecuadorian points of view regarding the threat of the Colombian conflict. Claudia Donoso and Hernán Moreano assisted with gathering data from news sources.

1. In the 1980s U.S. ambassador to Colombia Lewis Tambs, appointed by President Ronald Reagan, had used the term *narcoguerrilla*, linking the guerrilla movements with drug trafficking.

2. Some analysts suggest that this is more the result of neglect than myopia, with the U.S. and Andean elites sharing responsibility for the "increasing risk that the region will suffer fiscal, political, and security collapse." See Julia E. Sweig, "Andes 2020. Una nueva estrategia ante los retos que enfrentan Colombia y la región andina," Friederich Ebert Stiftung and Council on Foreign Relations, Bogotá (October 2004): 37.

3. This conclusion can be drawn from a review of the literature on drug trafficking from the last twenty years. See Bruce Bagley, ed., *Drug Trafficking Research in the Americas: An Annotated Bibliography* (Miami: North-South Center, 1997).

4. See Peter Smith, *Talons of the Eagle: Dynamics of U.S.-Latin American Relations* (New York: Oxford University Press, 2000), 247. See Adrián Bonilla, "Estados Unidos y Ecuador," in *Estados Unidos y los Países Andinos, 1993–1997: Poder y desintegración*, ed. Andrés Franco (Bogotá: CEJA, 1998).

5. See Jorge I. Domínguez, "U.S.-Latin American Relations during the Cold War and Its Aftermath," in *The United States and Latin America: The New Agenda*, ed. Victor Bulmer Thomas and James Dunkerley, David Rockefeller Center for Latin American Studies (Cambridge, Mass.: Harvard University and Institute of Latin American Studies, University of London, 1999), 33–50.

6. Adrián Bonilla, "National Security Decision-Making in Ecuador: The Case of the War on Drugs," PhD dissertation, University of Miami, October 1994.

7. See Abraham Lowenthal, "Los Estados Unidos y América Latina después del 11 de septiembre," *Diplomacia* 89 (October–December 2001): 73–76.

8. The conferences of the hemispheric Ministers of Defense have taken on increased importance; the VI conference took place in Quito in November 2004, as a continuation of a process, now institutionalized, intended to discuss topics related to hemispheric security (Williamsburg,

1995; Bariloche, 1996; Cartagena, 1998; Manaus, 2000; and Santiago, Chile, 2002). At the 2004 conference a central theme was "the new hemispheric security architecture."

9. See Joseph Tulchin, "Redefinición de la Seguridad Nacional en el Hemisferio Occidental. La función del multilateralismo," in *Diplomacia de Cumbres*, ed. Francisco Rojas, 19–33 (Santiago: FLACSO Chile, Wilson Center, 1996).

10. Jeanne Hey, *Theories of Dependent Foreign Policy and the Case of Ecuador in the 1980s* (Athens: Ohio University Center for International Studies, 1995).

11. Ecuador expressed this position in the South American Summit in Guayaquil in 2003, and this served as a precedent for other meetings of this sort, despite explicit requests from the Colombian government to foreign ministries in the region to label these groups as terrorists.

12. From a legal position, see Teodoro Bustamante Ponce, *¿Es la lógica algo obsoleto?: Un análisis de los acuerdos sobre la base de Manta* (documento de Trabajo, FLACSO-Ecuador, 2004).

13. Author interview with a very high-ranking retired military officer.

14. See Trade Act of 2002: www.sice.oas.org/Trade/tradeact/act10.asp.

15. See Ecuadorian news reports for the months of September and October, 2002.

16. To this should be added the complicated interplay of foreign policy actions by the Departments of State, including AID, Commerce, and Defense, the Southern Command, the DEA, and other U.S. agencies. See Daniel W. Christman and John G. Heimann, *Andes 2020: A New Strategy for the Challenges of Colombia and the Region* (Council on Foreign Relations, 2004), 18.

17. John Maisto was the advisor to the National Security Council, and Otto Reich was the undersecretary of state for Latin American affairs.

18. The Regional Andean Strategy was enacted in 2001. Ecuador's importance is reflected by increases in funding for international assistance; the unusual terms offered by international credit agencies, especially the Monetary Fund, with which an agreement was reached in February 2003 after ten years of problems; and the fact that a U.S. president again received an Ecuadorian president after a lapse of twelve years.

19. Connie Veillete, *Andean Counterdrug Initiative (ACI) and Related Funding Programs: FY 2005 Assistance CRS Report for Congress*, updated December 8, 2004, CRS Report for Congress, www.ndu.edu/library/docs/crs/crs_rl32337_09dec04.pdf#search='ANDEAN%20REGIONAL%20INITIATIVE%202003.

20. This is Russell Crandall's thesis on the relationship between the United States and Colombia, but it can be applied to security issues in general, especially drug trafficking. See *Driven by Drugs* (Boulder, Colo.: Rienner, 2002).

21. Adrián Bonilla, "Multilateralismo en la Región Andina," in *Diplomacia de Cumbres*, ed. Francisco Rojas (Caracas: FLACSO-Academia Diplomática Mexicana, Nueva Sociedad, 1999).

22. Interview with the government minister, Quito, October 3, 2002.

23. Declarations made by Minister of Government Mauricio Gándara (June 20, 2005, Radio La Luna) indicated that at the end of the Gutiérrez government an agreement was under consideration for joint Colombian–Ecuadorian military operations by army and police. Negotiations on the agreement were frozen by the government that succeeded Gutiérrez.

24. The White House, "The National Security Strategy of the United States of America," 2002, Internet version, www.whitehouse.gov/ncs/nss.html, PDF file, p. 10.

25. U.S. Department of Defense, "The United States Strategy for the Americas" (Washington, D.C.: USGPO, 2002).

26. "The security picture in Latin America and the Caribbean has grown more complex over the past year. Colombia's considerable progress in the battle against narcoterrorism is offset by negative developments elsewhere in the region, particularly in Haiti, Bolivia, and Venezuela. . . . We still face threats from narcoterrorists and their ilk, a growing threat to law and order in partner nations from urban gangs and other illegal armed groups, which are also generally tied to the narcotics trade, and a lesser but sophisticated threat from Islamic radical

groups in the region. These traditional threats are now complemented by an emerging threat best described as radical populism, in which the democratic process is undermined to decrease rather than protect individual rights" (Testimony of General James T. Hill, Commander of the Southern Command before the House of Representatives Committee on Armed Forces, March 24, 2004).

27. "In a visit to Miami last April, the spokesperson for the Southern Command, Colonel David McWilliams, was emphatic: (We confront threats such as terrorism, narcotrafficking, radical populism) 'Nos enfrentamos con amenazas como terrorismo, narcotráfico, populismo radical.'" See *El Comercio*, June 21, 2005, A7. In his visit to Ecuador in July 2005, General Bantz Craddock, commander of the Southern Command, emphasized the theme of democracy as one of the most important elements of U.S. security in the region.

28. See Edgar Téllez and Oscar Montes, *Diario Íntimo de un Fracaso* (Bogotá: Editoria Planeta, 2002).

29. Operational capacity has been enhanced through advanced training and acquisition of materiel for jungle fighting. This has required purchase of new equipment, while at the same time traditional conventional forces must be maintained for strategic and economic reasons.

30. Someone by the name of Diego Serna, who was later arrested as a FARC guerrilla fighter, is alleged to have been a member of Hugo Chávez's security team when he visited Colombia on May 4, 2001. See Téllez and Montes, *Diario Íntimo de un Fracaso*, 314–15. The incident occurred on June 27 on Ecuadorian soil on the border between Tulcán and Ipiales, far from Amazonia. See *BBCMundo.com* for June 28, 2001, or *El Comercio*, Quito, June 28, 2001, 1.

31. "[La] captura de Trinidad tiene serias consecuencias para el Ecuador en los aspectos de Seguridad Nacional, por lo que se requiere de esbozar, aunque sea de manera somera, los posibles efectos para el país de esta situación, para, asimismo, tratar de articular una política coherente, que permita minimizar los potenciales problemas que podría acarrear esta situación. También, y primeramente, se debe analizar la captura en términos de lo que significa política e institucionalmente para el país" (*Informe del Gabinete Ministerial del Ministerio de Defensa*, January 4, 2004).

32. See Mama Coca, "Informe de Fronteras del Mes de Septiembere 2002-09-09," at www .mamacoca.org/informes_fronteras/informe_fronteras_septiembre_2002.htm.

33. "Colombia anuncia operaciones militares conjuntas con países vecinos," *El Tiempo* (Bogotá), August 20, 2002, 1.

34. Senator Jimmy Chamorro suggested joint operations by Colombian and Ecuadorian armed forces and severely criticized the Ecuadorian government for its permissive approach to the FARC. See *El Comercio* (Quito), July 2, 2005.

35. Minutes of debates taken from the *Libro Blanco Ecuador*.

36. See International Crisis Group, "Colombia y sus vecinos: Los tentáculos de la inestabilidad," *Informe sobre América Latina* No. 3, April 8, 2003.

37. Speech by President Gutiérrez at the White House on February 11, 2003. See *El Comercio*, February 12, 2003, A1.

38. The current (July 2005) minister of government, Mauricio Gándara, is known for his firm opposition to concession of the Manta base and the agreement that made this possible. The current foreign minister has questioned fumigation operations and also maritime interdiction. See *El Comercio*, April 21–23, 2005, and *El Comercio*, June 20 and 21, 2005.

39. "Consenso de Guayaquil sobre integración, seguridad e infraestructura para el desarrollo," www.cumbresur.com/novedades/, October 10, 2002.

40. See Jose Genoino, "Uma nova politica externa," *O Estado de Sao Paulo*, July 5, 2003.

41. Socorro Ramírez, "La internacionalización del conflicto y de la paz en Colombia," in *El Plan Colombia y la internacionalización del conflicto*, ed. Luis Alberto Restrep et al. (Bogotá: Planeta, 2001), 103–14.

42. For example, see Daniel Pécault, *Guerra contra la sociedad* (Bogotá: Planeta, 2001), chapters 5–8.

43. I borrow this idea from Juan Gabriel Tokatlian, *Globalización, narcotráfico y violencia* (Bogotá: Editorial NORMA, 2000), chapter 1.

44. International Crisis Group, "Colombia y sus vecinos: Los tentáculos de la inestabilidad."

45. Public accounts referred to a few high-caliber machine guns, rifle ammunition, grenades, uniforms, medical supplies, and other nonlethal items. See *El Comercio*, various editions in February and March 2004.

46. International Crisis Group, "Las fronteras de Colombia: El eslabón débil de la política de seguridad de Uribe," *Informe sobre América Latina*, no. 9, September 23, 2004.

47. See Christman y Heimann, *Andes 2020, op.cit*, Conclusiones "Una región hacia el colapso."

48. See CIA scenarios for 2010.

49. Despite three recent irregular changes in government provoked by social movements and political opposition, only two deaths occurred (in the last one, in 2005).

50. United States Department of State, Office of Counterterrorism, "Patterns of Global Terrorism, 2001," May 21, 2002, www.state.gov/s/ct/rls/pgtrpt/2001.

51. *El Comercio*, May 22, 2002, "Terrorismo: Unda rechaza informe de EE.UU."; ANSA. *El Comercio*, May 28, 2002, "Canciller destaca esfuerzos por controlar la frontera"; *El Comercio*, August 29, 2002, "Moeller: Colombia debería tener más presencia militar."

52. After meeting with Colombian president Alvaro Uribe, Gutiérrez dropped his offer to act as mediator and proposed that if the FARC did not accept the ideas for peaceful settlement coming from the United Nations "the world would be disposed to collaborate with Colombia with more forceful means ("el mundo estaría dispuesto a colaborar con Colombia en otro camino"). Uribe applauded Gutiérrez's about-face. See *El Tiempo*, May 23, 2003.

53. Author interviews with high-ranking Defense and Foreign Relations officials, June 2003.

54. Author interview with General Oswaldo Jarrín, commander of the Joint Forces (Comando Conjunto) of the Ecuadorian Armed Forces in the first phase of the Gutiérrez government.

55. U.S. pressure on this issue has been persistent and powerful. On June 20, 2005, the issue arose again, when during SOUTHCOM commander General Bantz Craddock's visit to Ecuador, it was reported that the United States would suspend a substantial part of its programmed military assistance to the country if a bilateral accord on this issue were not signed (*El Comercio*, June 21, 2005).

56. Ecuadorian Ministry of Foreign Relations press release, "Reunión de alto nivel entre los Ministros de Relaciones Exteriores, Defensa Nacional, Interior, Gobierno y Policía y Comercio Exterior de Colombia y Ecuador," Bogotá, September 5, 2002.

57. Donald Rumsfeld: Offensive Realist; Colin Powell: Defensive Realist; Paul Wolfowitz: Democratic Imperialist; Condeleezza Rice: classic Realpolitik. These images are British in origin. See "Unprecedented Power, Colliding Ambitions," *The Economist* 150(30) (September 26, 2002).

58. See works written by Bruce Bagley and Juan Gabriel Tokatlian during the 1990s.

59. Marc Grossman, "Joining Efforts for Colombia," paper presented by the undersecretary for political affairs, the U.S. Department of State, at Georgetown University, June 24, 2002.

60. On his June 2005 visit to Ecuador, General Craddock told the press that "Ecuador is a key player in the fight against drug trafficking. The base at Manta facilitates our work, although we need to improve our operations and inter-military relations" (*El Comercio*, June 21, 2005, A7).

61. See the text of the accord in the Registro Oficial No. 326, Función Ejecutiva, Decreto 1505 (www.ecuadorpaisdeleyenda.com/encrucijada/convbaseman.htm) or a summary in "La Base de Manta, enclave de Estados Unidos en Ecuador," by Marcelo Larrea at www.vialaterna.com.co/omun_26ago.htm (accessed September 2, 2002).

62. Sandra Edwards, "Colombian Conflict Impacts Ecuador," Washington Office on Latin America, 2002: www.wola.org/d&d_ecuador_update.htmp.p4 (accessed September 2, 2002).

63. Ecuador is not classified as a producer country, but rather as a country through which chemical precursors and substances are moved, and as a base for money laundering.

64. Bonilla, "Estados Unidos y Ecuador."

65. Verification Mission report, "Impactos en Ecuador de las fumigaciones realizadas en Putumayo dentro del Plan Colombia," Acción Ecológica, ALDHU, Asociación Americana de Juristas, CEDHU, Ecociencia, INREDH, Laboratorio de Suelos LABSU, RAPAL, SERPAJ, Acción Creativa, Comité Andino de Servicios, Quito, October 2002.

66. There are reports of 2,560 hectares of crops affected by the fumigations and about 11,828 animal deaths attributable to them. See the Verification Mission report, 4, table 1-c.

67. Sucumbíos, one of Ecuador's largest provinces, faces Colombia along the country's northeastern border. Colombia's largest coca leaf plantations and the FARC's Blocks 32 and 48 are found across the border. The most intense fighting between government troops and the guerrillas has taken place on the Colombian territory adjoining Ecuador. A network supporting and supplying the illegal Colombian forces is assumed to operate on the Ecuadorian side, even though the military presence there is one of the largest in the country. See the International Crisis Group report, "Colombia's Elusive Quest for Peace," March 26, 2002: www.intl-crisis-group.org/projects/showreport.cfm?reportid=626.

68. Chancellor Parra requested suspension of spraying until independent scientific studies could be completed on the effects of the herbicide and also requested a meeting with the Colombian foreign minister to discuss this issue (*El Universo*, July 12, 2005).

69. Interview with a member of cabinet from the Ministry of Defense, September 2002.

70. Interview with a member of cabinet from the Ministry of Defense, September 2002.

71. Edwards, "Colombian Conflict Impacts Ecuador," 3.

72. Tomado de Carla Alvarez, Ibid. Ant.

73. Felipe Burbano de Lara, "Democracia, cultura política y gobernabilidad. Los estudios políticos en los años 90," in *Democracia, gobernabilidad y cultura política*, ed. Felipe Burbano de Lara (Quito: FLACSO, 2003), 31–36.

74. President Lucio Gutiérrez's official visit to the United States on February 11, 2003, www.whitehouse.gov/news/releases/2003/01/20030117-5.html.

75. For a consideration of the nature of Ecuadorian foreign policy, see Adrián Bonilla, "Alcances de la Autonomía en la Hegemonía en la Política Exterior Ecuatoriana," in *Orfeo en el Infierno. Una Agenda de Política Exterior Ecuatoriana*, ed. Adrián Bonilla, 11–46 (Quito: FLACSO-CAF-Academia Diplomática, 2002).

76. Carrie Callaghan, "La Ayuda militar estadounidense para el Ecuador," Observatorio Internacional para la Paz, 2003: www.oipaz.or.ec/.

77. See Carla Alvarez, *La Cooperación Norteamericana para el desarrollo en la Frontera Norte*, tesis para el grado de Maestría en Relaciones Internacionales, FLACSO-Ecuador, May 2005.

78. Adrián Bonilla, "Las Fuerzas Armadas ecuatorianas y su contexto político," presentation made at the Semana Iberoamericana sobre Paz, Seguridad y Defensa at the Instituto Gutiérrez Mellado, Madrid, June 2002.

79. Ministry of National Defense, *Política de la Defensa Nacional del Ecuador* (Quito: Ministerio de Defensa, 2002). This document includes the Ecuadorian defense strategy, also called "Libro Blanco."

80. Interview with a high-ranking official from the Ministry of Foreign Relations during the Mahuad administration, August 29, 2003. In January 2000, Vice President Noboa declared: "Under the laws laid out in the constitution I find myself under the obligation of assuming the presidency of Ecuador," "I have the support of the armed forces and national police." "Ecuador's Noboa Assumes Power after Coup," CNN.com, January 22, 2000 (www.cnn.com/2000/WORLD/americas/01/22/ecuador.04/).

81. "EEUU aumentará ayuda a Ecuador en más de 100 millones," Agencia Hinhua: http://fpspa.peopledaily.com.cn/200302/13/sp20030213_61518.html (accessed September 2, 2003).

82. Thirty-eight percent of Ecuadorian exports are destined for the United States. See ALADI's (Asociación Latinoamericana de Integración) Web page at www.aladi.org/nsfaladi/estudios.nsf/decd25d818b0d76c032567da0062fec1/d93119f24e8f7af503256d8004ee2a9/$FILE/1770-3.pdf (accessed August 12, 2003).

83. During his visit to Ecuador in March 2003, the commander of the US Southern Command, James T. Hill, urged expanding the Manta air base agreement to include an agreement on air and sea interdiction. See "Alista acuerdo de interdicción," *El Universo,* March 18, 2003.

84. "Canciller destaca esfuerzos por controlar la frontera," *El Comercio,* May 28, 2002.

85. Colloquially, *boleteos* are anonymous written threats, and *vacunas* (literally, "vaccinations") refer to the practice of regularly paying off drug traffickers in exchange for protection against the "viruses" of kidnapping, theft, and plundering [translator's note].

86. According to military intelligence sources who asked not to be named (October 2002).

87. For statistics on violence in the border areas, see Carlos Arcos, Fernando Carrión, and Edison Palomeque, "Violencia para el BID" (Quito: FLACSO, 2001).

88. Ongoing research by sociologists and anthropologists has confirmed the presence of FARC guerrillas in Ecuadorian Amazonia who mostly confine their activities to visual reconnaissance.

89. "New Rebel Group in Ecuador Claims Ties to FARC," September 16, 2002: www.strafor.com/standard/analysis_view.php. ID.

90. As a result of the Trinidad case, a document of the Ministerial Cabinet from the Defense Ministry (January 4, 2004) stated the following: "It is evident that foreign intelligence groups are operating in the country associated with the National Police (PN). The American and Colombian services have been operating visibly and with the approval of the PN, without the knowledge patience, of the Ecuadorian security forces, violating national sovereignty and ignoring state security policy in direct relation with the American embassy and Colombian military and police intelligence, pursing a separate security agenda, based on their particular interests, and risking the overall Ecuadorian security agenda regarding Colombia."

91. "Dos posiciones sobre el conflicto en Colombia," *El Comercio,* July 27, 2002.

92. "Relatoría de resultados y compromisos, reunión de alto nivel sobre asuntos fronterizos," Bogotá, September 5, 2002 (copy of the original document).

Chapter 5

1. Carlos D. Mesa Gisbert, "Cincuenta años por los caminos del poder," in *Víctor Paz: Su presencia en la historia revolucionaria de Bolivia,* ed. Guillermo Bedregal (La Paz: Editorial Los Amigos del Libro, 1987), 174. Ironically, the man who recorded those words was the historian and former president who was just ousted, ending his own quest to stave off Bolivia's death.

2. "U.S. behind Bolivia Crisis—Chávez," *BBC News,* June 13, 2005.

3. Agencia de Noticias de MERCOSUR, "Ministro Argentino advierte Libanización de Bolivia," June 25, 2004, www.apfmercosur.com.ar/despachos.asp?cod_des=24108; Andrés Oppenheimer, "Bolivia an Example of a Nation That Needs Lots of Help to Survive," *Miami Herald,* June 10, 2004; and General James T. Hill, Posture Statement, United States Army Commander, United States Southern Command, before the 108th Congress, Senate Armed Services Committee, April 1, 2004.

4. There is no clear consensus on what is meant by the "Washington Consensus." For a brief discussion see Center for International Development at Harvard University, Global Trade Negotiations Home Page, www.cid.harvard.edu/cidtrade/issues/washington.html.

5. PBS, "Chapter 10: Bolivia at the Brink," *Commanding Heights,* April 2003, www.pbs.org/wgbh/commandingheights.html. The website also includes interesting interviews with both Gonzalo Sánchez de Lozada and Jeff Sachs.

6. *Andean Group Report* (published monthly by Latin American Newsletters), London, February 27, 2001, and U.S. Department of State, "International Narcotics Control Strategy Report: South America—2000," www.state.gov/g/inl/rls/nrcrpt/2000/883.htm.

7. Based on its analysis of U.S. General Accounting Office Reports, the International Crisis Group (an independent, nonprofit multinational organization based in Brussels) notes that the State Department "has a difficult time disentangling what is democracy assistance and what is counter-narcotics-related funding" (International Crisis Group, "Bolivia's Divisions: Too Deep to Heal?" *Latin America Report #7*, July 6, 2004, p. 14, 15 at www.icg.org//library/documents/latin_america/07bolivias_divisions.pdf).

8. Interview of Gonzalo Sánchez de Lozada with Roger Wilkinson of the Voice of America, November 7, 1994, carried at the time on the Voice of America website.

9. Jeffrey Sachs, "New Approaches to International Donor Assistance," speech presented at the International Development Research Centre, Ottawa, June 19, 2001, http://web.idrc.ca/en/ev-30635-201-1-DO_TOPIC.html.

10. Allison Spedding, "Cocataki, Taki-Coca: Trade, Traffic and Organized Peasant Resistance in the Yungas of La Paz," in *Coca, Cocaine, and the Bolivian Reality*, ed. Madeleine Barbara Leons and Harry Sanabria (Albany: State University of New York Press, 1997), 118–19; Claire Hargraeves, *Snowfields: The War on Cocaine in the Andes* (New York: Holmes and Meier, 1992), 31; and James Painter, *Bolivia and Coca: A Study in Dependency* (Boulder, Colo.: Rienner, 1994), 20. For the environmental case against coca, see "Los Andes en peligro: Consequencias ambientales del narcotráfico," March 19, 2001, on the U.S. Embassy website: www.megalink.com/usemblapaz/narcoambiente.html. Virtually all the damage this site catalogs results from the processing of coca into coca paste, not from the cultivation of coca plants.

11. Kenneth D. Lehman, *Bolivia and the United States: A Limited Partnership* (Athens: University of Georgia Press, 1999), 199–203; Government of Bolivia, *Ley del regimen de la coca y sustancias controladas No. 1008 de 19 de Julio 1988*, July 19, 1998; and National Law Center for Inter-American Free Trade, "Commentary on the *Ley del regimen de la coca y sustancias controladas*" *Interam Data Base*, vol. 6, no. 3 and 4 (1995): 278–94.

12. Lehman, *Bolivia and the United States*, 206–7. At the end of the Cold War, Maxwell Thurmon, commander of the U.S. Southern Military Command (SOUTHCOM), stated that with the Cold War over, the drug war is "the only war we've got" (Adam Isacson, "The U.S. Military in the War on Drugs," *Drugs and Democracy in Latin America: The Impact of U.S. Policy*, ed. Coletta A Youngers and Eileen Rosin [Boulder, Colo.: Rienner, 2005], 28).

13. Eduardo A. Gamarra, "U.S.-Bolivia Counternarcotics Efforts during the Paz Zamora Administration," in *Drug-Trafficking in the Americas*, ed. Bruce Bagley and William O. Walker (Coral Gables, Fla.: University of Miami, North-South Center, 1994); and Eduardo A. Gamarra "Has Bolivia Won the War? Lessons from Plan Dignidad," http://lacc.fiu.edu/research_publications/working_papers/working_paper_01.pdf. Gelbard went on to become head of the State Department's counternarcotics office and then to become a troubleshooter in the Balkans and Indonesia.

14. "U.S.-Bolivia Relations at a High Point" *Washington Times*, March 23, 1998; Lehman, *Bolivia and the United States*, 212–14; and Gamarra, "Has Bolivia Won the War?"

15. *Latin American Weekly Report*, July 1, 1997, and *Andean Group Report*, November 4, 1997.

16. President George W. Bush placed the husband of Banzer's niece, Marco Marino Diodato del Gallo, on a list of nine foreign narcotics kingpins subject to U.S. sanctions. "Bush Adds 9 Targets to Drug Kingpin List," Associated Press news bulletin, June 2, 2005.

17. Anthony Faiola and Douglas Farah, "Newly Elected Ex-Dictator Vows to Wage War on Drugs in Bolivia," *Washington Post*, August 4, 1997, and *Latin American Weekly Report*, June 17, 1997. Sánchez de Lozada sent Minister of Interior Carlos Sánchez Berzain to Washington to remind the State Department of the incongruity of working with a party and a leader implicated

in drug trafficking. Banzer's vice president Jorge Quiroga also traveled to Washington to make just the opposite case.

18. Government of Bolivia, "Plan Dignidad: Estrategia Boliviana de Lucha Contra el Nar-cotráfico: 1998–2002,"April 1998 (www.bolivia.gov.bo/).

19. *Andean Group Report,* March 3, 1998, and Douglas Farah, "Aircraft Compromise Lifts Freeze on Anti-Drug Aid to Latin America," *Washington Post,* June 26, 1998. Eduardo Gamarra provides further twists to this story (Gamarra, "Has Bolivia Won the War?").

20. U.S. Department of State, "International Narcotics Control Strategy Report—2000," *South America.*

21. George Ann Potter, "Is the War on Drugs Bringing 'Dignity' to Bolivia?" (www.coha.org).

22. Anthony Faiola, "In Bolivia's Drug War, Success Has a Price," *Washington Post,* March 4, 2001; U.S. Department of State, *International Narcotics Control Strategy Report—2000, South America;* and U.S. Agency for International Development, "USAID Helps Transform the Chapare; Remove Bolivia from the Drug Economy" (www.usaid.gov/locations/latin_america_caribbean/country/bolivia/boliviachapare.html) (May 11, 2004).

23. ICG, "Bolivia's Divisions: Too Deep to Heal?" p. 19.

24. Faiola, "In Bolivia's Drug War, Success Has a Price."

25. Kevin G. Hall, "Bolivia Challenges Washington Wisdom in the Andean Drug War," *Knight Ridder Newspapers.* Assistance under the Andean Regional Initiative continued to be skewed toward eradication: $153.5 million between 2001 and 2004 for eradication, $115.8 for alternative development. CRS Regional Report for Congress, "Andean Regional Initiative (ARI) FY 2003 Supplemental and FY 2004 Assistance for Colombia and Neighbors," updated August 27, 2003 (http://fpc.state.gov/documents/organization/24044.pdf).

26. U.S. Department of State, *International Narcotics Control Strategy Report—2000, South America.*

27. Estimates vary widely, based on differing criteria. U.S. Drug Enforcement Administration (DEA) administrator Donnie Marshall reported in 2000 that the income derived from illicit drug activity shrank from US$400 million in 1995 to US$86 million in 1999. "Within the same period, the share of the drugs economy as a proportion of gross domestic product and legitimate exports fell from 6.8% to 2.2% and from 26% to 7.3%, respectively." His figures make the $700 million figure conservative ("Donnie R. Marshall, Testimony before the House Committee on Government Reform: Subcommittee on Criminal Justice, Drug Policy and Human Resources," March 2, 2001: www.usdoj.gov/dea/pubs/cngrtest/ct030201.htm). The IMF identifies the loss of drug revenues as one of the key contributing factors in the economic downturn beginning in 2000. See IMF, *Bolivia: Ex Post Assessment of Longer-Term Program Engagement—Staff Report and Public Information Notice on the Executive Board Discussion,* IMF Country Report No 05/139 (April 2005), p. 32, available at www.imf.org/external/pubs/ft/scr/2005/cr05139.pdf.

28. Jeffrey D. Sachs, "Another U.S. Foreign-Policy Failure, *Miami Herald,* October 30, 2003.

29. Government of Bolivia, "Plan Dignidad, Lucha Antidroga, 1997–2001, Progress Report," 2002 (www.bolivia.gov.bo/.)

30. See Eduardo Gamarra's discussion of the motivations behind Plan Dignidad in "Has Bolivia Won the War?"

31. DEA, "Intelligence Brief: Changing Dynamics of Coca Production in the Andean Region," June 2002 (www.usdoj.gov/dea/pubs/intel/02033/02033p).

32. Jeffrey Sachs, "A World for Which Bush Cares Little," *Financial Times,* April 9, 2003.

33. James Malloy, *The Uncompleted Revolution* (Pittsburgh: University of Pittsburgh Press, 1970). See also Laurence Whitehead, "The Bolivian National Revolution: A Comparison"; Eduardo Gamarra, "Political Parties since 1964: Construction of Bolivia's Multiparty System"; and George Gray Molina, "Offspring of 1952: Poverty, Exclusion, and the Promise of Popular Participation," in *Proclaiming Revolution: Bolivia in Comparative Perspective,* ed. Merilee Grindle and Pilar Comingo (London: Institute of American Studies, 2003).

34. Cole Blasier, *The Hovering Giant: U.S. Responses to Revolutionary Change in Latin America* (Pittsburgh: University of Pittsburgh Press, 1976), and Kenneth D. Lehman, "Revolutions and Attributions: Making Sense of Eisenhower Administration Policies in Bolivia and Guatemala," *Diplomatic History* vol. 21, no. 2 (1997): 185–213.

35. U.S. State Department, "Memorandum, Siracusa to Bernbaum," February 2, 1956, *Foreign Relations of the United States, 1955–57*, 7:539.

36. Lehman, *Bolivia and the United States*, chapter 6.

37. Lehman, *Bolivia and the United States*, 191–98.

38. Lehman, *Bolivia and the United States*, 191–98. See the PBS interview with Gonzalo Sánchez de Lozada, March 20, 2001, in *Commanding Heights*.

39. Eduardo Gamarra has discussed these party pacts. The "pact system" allowed presidents since Paz to govern, even though all were elected by a minority of the popular vote. Essentially this has worked through a set of shifting alliances among the MNR, the MIR, and the ADN. See Gamarra, "Construction of Bolivia's Multiparty System," in *Proclaiming Revolution*, 289–91.

40. The thesis that the militarization of U.S. drug policies undermined Bolivian democracy is amply developed in a recent book that includes a chapter on Bolivia by Kathryn Ledabur. See Youngers and Rosin, *Drugs and Democracy in Latin America: The Impact of U.S. Policy*.

41. *Latin American Weekly Report*, December 11, 2001; "Bolivia: U.S.-Backed Eradication Heightens Poverty and Violence," WOLA (www.wola.org), December 11, 2001; and Anthony Faiola, "U.S. Role in Coca War Draws Fire," *Washington Post*, June 23, 2002.

42. Paramilitary forces played an important and sinister role in Bolivia between 1978 and 1982. German war criminal Klaus Barbie was an advisor to Bolivian paramilitary forces working closely with Bolivia's military.

43. Faiola, "U.S. Role in Coca War Draws Fire."

44. Evidence of Bolivian views of Plan Dignidad is incomplete, but Eduardo Gamarra suggests that public opinion surveys and anecdotal evidence both point to what he calls a growing "national consensus" shared even by many coca producers that "illicit crop cultivation and production hurt Bolivia's development prospects and international image" (Gamarra, "Has Bolivia Won the War?").

45. "An Alarm Call for Latin America's Democrats: The Latinobarometro Poll," *The Economist*, July 26, 2001. The poll showed support for democracy in Bolivia declined nearly 10 percent between 2000 and 2001.

46. Quoted in Ledebur, "Bolivia: Clear Consequences," in Youngers and Rosin, *Drugs and Democracy in Latin America*, 163.

47. Among the commentators are Roberto Laserna, "Bolivia: Entre populismo y democracia," *Nueva Sociedad*, no. 188 (November–December 2003): 12–13, and Kathryn Ledebur, "Special Update: Bolivia—Popular Protest Brings Down the Government," Washington Office on Latin America, November 2, 2003.

48. His election resulted from constitutional reforms in 1994 that determined that 50 percent of the members of the lower house would be directly elected in single-member districts rather than selected from party lists as was previously the case (Eduardo Gamarra, "Construction of Bolivia's Multiparty System," 298 and 306). See also Ledebur, "Bolivia: Clear Consequences," 174–75.

49. Ledebur, "Bolivia, Clear Consequences," 159–60.

50. "EEUU amenaza con suspender ayuda si Evo llega al poder," *El Diario* (La Paz), June 26, 2002. The State Department denied any connection between the ambassador's statement and the late surge by Morales, which confounded the pollsters: "Feds Defend Ambassador to Bolivia," *New York Times*, July 10, 2002.

51. Clifford Krauss, "A Bolivian Legislator Who Just Says 'Yes' to Coca," *New York Times*, June 13, 1998.

52. According to United Nations figures, life expectancy in Bolivia has risen from 46.7 years in the early 1970s to 63.9; infant mortality rates are less than half and mortality rates for children

under five are one-third their rates in the early 1970s (PNUD, *Informe Nacional de Desarrollo Humano, 2004*, La Paz, 2004), 273. See also data provided by the United Nations and the World Bank Group, "Bolivia Data Profile" (April 2004): http://devdata.worldbank.org/external/CPProfile .asp?SelectedCountry=BOL&CCODE=BOL&CNAME=Bolivia&PTYPE=CP. Herbert Klein also gives a good summary of recent statistical data on Bolivian social indicators in Herbert Klein, "Social Change in Bolivia since 1952," *Proclaiming Revolution* and in Lehman and Klein, *A Concise History of Bolivia* (Cambridge: Cambridge University Press, 2003), 250–52. Bolivian sociologist Roberto Laserna notes that overall, poverty rates have declined from 71 percent in 1992 to 58 percent in 2002 and are lowest in the sectors most fully integrated into the global economy, though these figures—provided by the Bolivian government—seem at odds with the figures provided by the IMF, which are cited below in this report. Interestingly, while families in the traditional rural sector are poorer, Laserna reports that they are less likely to consider themselves poor than those in the marginal urban sector. Roberto Laserna, "Bolivia: Entre populismo y democracia," and "Bolivia: La Crisis de Octubre y el fracaso del *Ch'enko*," both found at www.geocities.com/laserna_r/.

53. Merilee Grindle, "Shadowing the Past? Policy Reform in Bolivia, 1985–2002," in *Proclaiming Revolution*, 334. Chapters in *Proclaiming Revolution* by Manuel Contreras on education reforms and George Gray Molina on popular participation also provide good discussions of the issues covered here. An excellent history and analysis of the impact of popular participation on indigenous organizations is found in Xavier Albó, "Bolivia: From Indian and Campesino Leaders to Councillors and Parliamentary Deputies," in *Multiculturalism in Latin America: Indigenous Rights, Diversity and Democracy*, ed. Rachel Sieder (London: Palgrave, 2002), 74–101.

54. Washington Estellano, "From Populism to the Coca Economy in Bolivia," *Latin American Perspectives*, vol. 83, no. 21 (1994): 39.

55. IMF, *Bolivia: Ex Post Assessment of Longer-Term Program Engagement*, pp. 3, 5, and 6.

56. United Nations Development Program, *Human Development Indicators*, 2004, http://hdr .undp.org/; World Bank Group, "Bolivia Data Profile"; and ICG, "Bolivia's Divisions: Too Deep to Heal?" p. 19.

57. IMF, *Bolivia: Ex Post Assessment of Longer-Term Program Engagement*, 5 and 6, and Ledebur, "Bolivia: Clear Consequences," 144.

58. William Finnegan, "Leasing the Rain," *New Yorker*, March 8, 2002. A full account of the water war and its follow-up can be found in Oscar Olivera, *¡Cochabamba! Water War in Bolivia* (Cambridge, Mass.: South End Press, 2004).

59. Olivera, *¡Cochabamba!* and PBS, "Timeline: Cochabamba Water Revolt" (www.pbs.org/ frontlineworld/stories/bolivia/timeline.html).

60. *Andean Group Report*, May 16, 2000. In November 2001, Bechtel, taking advantage of the fact that Aguas del Tunari was chartered in the Netherlands, with which Bolivia has reciprocal trade agreements, applied to the International Centre for Settlement of Investment Disputes, asking $25 million for breach of contract and lost income. See commentaries: Jim Shultz, "Bolivia: Time to Open Up Secret Trade Courts," November 8, 2002 (www.corpwatch.org/article .php?id=4858.html) and Morrison & Foerster Update, "Quarterly Report on Water Industry Developments in Latin America," April 2004 (www.mofo.com/news/general). Recently Bechtel decided to drop its claims.

61. A "heady" popular victory does not necessarily translate into sound policy. Roberto Laserna argues that "victory" in the water war "meant that the poor still use the same dirty and expensive water" ("Bolivia, the Beleaguered Democracy," 2003, www.princeton.edu/plasweb/ news/lasernaEng.doc). Supporters of deprivatization of water admit continuing problems in water supply; see "A cuatro años de la guerra del agua: un balance de SEMAPA y la cogestación de los servicios básicos," CEDIB (Centro de Documentación e Informaciones Bolivia) (www .cedib.org/pcedib/?module=displaystory&story_id=659&format=html). See also Olivera, *¡Cochabamba!* 53–104.

62. United Nations Office on Drugs and Crime, "Bolivia: Coca Survey in the Yungas of La Paz in 2002," March 2003 (www.unodc.org/pdf/publications/bolivia_coca-survey_2002.pdf).

63. Gamarra, "Has Bolivia Won the War?"

64. Fundación CIDOB, "Jorge Fernando Quiroga Ramírez, Biografías de Líderes Políticos (Bolivia)," August 21, 2002 (www.cidob.org/bios/castellano/lideres/q-001.htm), and Gamarra, "Has Bolivia Won the War?"

65. *Latin American Weekly Report*, September 18, 2001; *Andean Group Report*, October 2, 2001.

66. Gamarra, "The Construction of Bolivia's Multi-Party System," *Proclaiming Revolution*, 304.

67. *El Diario*, July 4, July 10, July 23, 2002, and *Latin American Weekly Report*, July 2, July 9, July 16, and August 13, 2002. A fascinating recent documentary film, *Our Brand Is Crisis*, suggests Goni's U.S.-based consulting firm, Greenberg, Carville, and Shrum, also cut into Reyes Villa's support through a smear campaign designed to call his integrity into question.

68. Yvonne Zimmermann, "Entrevista con Evo Morales," *Indymedia*, July 10, 2002 (http://bolivia.indymedia.org/es/2002/07/168.shtml).

69. Xavier Albo, "Indigenous Political Participation in Bolivia," in *Multiculturalism in Latin America: Indigenous Rights, Diversity and Democracy*, ed. Rachael Sieder (Basingstoke, U.K.: Palgrave Macmillan, 2002), 78.

70. Jim Shultz, *Deadly Consequences: The International Monetary Fund and Bolivia's "Black February"* (Cochabamba: Democracy Center, 2005), 17.

71. U.S. Department of State, "International Narcotics Control Strategy Report—2001," www.state.gov/g/inl/rls/nrcrpt/2002/html/17944.htm. Kathryn Ledebur quotes an embassy cable of December 6, 2001, stating, "We are quite concerned by the agreement in November to halt eradication and withdraw troops from the front lines in the Chapare where they have been so effective" (Ledebur, "Bolivia: Clear Consequences").

72. The fact that the United States discontinued funding the expeditionary task force in late July, as these negotiations were taking place, suggests that it might have been one of the items on the table, but growing opposition to the task force in the U.S. Congress was also a factor. See Ledebur, "Bolivia: Clear Consequences," 159–61, and Andean Information Network, "Chapare Coca Growers Resist Eradication," September 2, 2002 (www.nadir.org/nadir/initiativ/agp/free/imf/bolivia/txt/2002/0902chapare_growers.htm).

73. Coca producers argued that demand was far in excess of the 12,000 hectares allowed by Law 1008.

74. *El Diario*, August 2, 2002; *Latin American Weekly Report*, September 24, 2002; October 8, 2002; January 21, 2003; and August 5, 2003. In August 2003, 50 tons of cocaine bound for Spain were seized in Santa Cruz—the largest single haul in Bolivia's history. The capture suggested that perhaps the Bolivian cocaine industry was not nearly as crippled as once thought. Ironically, events since late 2002 have led U.S. antidrug officials to embrace positions that they rejected then; the survey on the legal market for coca is currently in progress, and lower limits on illegal coca production have at least been temporarily substituted for the "zero-coca" objective.

75. Michael Shifter, "Breakdown in the Andes," *Foreign Affairs*, September/October 2004 (www.foreignaffairs.org). The story of the meeting between Bush and Sánchez de Lozada is also told by Sachs, "Another U.S. Foreign Policy Failure," and by Larry Rohter, "Bolivian Leader's Ouster Seen as Warning on U.S. Drug Policy," *New York Times*, October 23, 2003.

76. The IMF is not an agency of the United States government, of course, but with its office in Washington where 90 percent of its staff is located, a governing structure that provides voting power in proportion to the size of a country's economy (The United States' voting power is two hundred times that of Bolivia's), and the requirement of a super-majority of 85 percent to make

major decisions (the United States holds a 17.6 percent voting share, which gives it an effective veto), it is safe to assume that the United States and the IMF generally work in close agreement (IMF, "Articles of Agreement of the International Monetary Fund" (2005), cited in Schultz, *Deadly Consequences*, 11).

77. IMF, *Bolivia: Ex Post Assessment of Longer-Term Program Engagement*, appendix 1, p. 42.

78. IMF, *Bolivia: Ex Post Assessment of Longer-Term Program Engagement*, appendix 1, p. 43.

79. IMF, *Bolivia: Ex Post Assessment of Longer-Term Program Engagement*, appendix 1, p. 24.

80. U.S. Department of Energy, "Country Analysis Briefs: Bolivia," November 2004, www.eia.doe.gov/emeu/cabs/bolivia.html.

81. IMF, Bolivia: *Ex Post Assessment of Longer-Term Program Engagement*, 24–25.

82. See Shultz, *Deadly Consequences*, 17–18.

83. Shultz, *Deadly Consequences*, 18–22.

84. It is not certain whether this decision came at U.S. urging. It is clear, however, that throughout Latin America, U.S. military advisors routinely encourage Latin American militaries to engage in domestic operations that are prohibited by U.S. law. See Isacson, "The U.S. Military in the War on Drugs," 22, and Coletta A. Youngers, "Conclusions and Recommendations," in *Drugs and Democracy in Latin America*, 344.

85. "Rioting, Clashes in Bolivian Capital Kill 16," *Washington Post*, February 14, 2003, and "Economic Crisis and Vocal Opposition Test Bolivia's President," *New York Times*, February 16, 2003. Roberto Laserna observes that the income tax was progressive and if established might have allowed the reduction of more regressive value-added taxes. Unfortunately Bolivians were fast approaching a point of polarization where such nuanced arguments lost force (Laserna, "Bolivia: Entre populismo y democracia," 11).

86. IMF, "Reinvigorating Growth in Bolivia," remarks by Anoop Singh at the CAINCO Economic Forum, Santa Cruz de la Sierra, July 17, 2003; and IMF, "IMF Completes Second Review of Bolivia's Stand-By Arrangement," October 6, 2003 (www.imf.org/external/country/BOL/).

87. *El Diario*, September 23, 2003; *Latin American Weekly Report*, September 23, 2003, and October 21, 2003.

88. A book, written well before these events, provides important insights into the resentments that exploded in El Alto last October. See Lesley Gill, *Teetering on the Rim: Global Restructuring, Daily Life, and the Armed Retreat of the Bolivian State* (New York: Columbia University Press, 2000). The reformulation of culture in El Alto is complicated. An article in the *New York Times* notes the fascination of young *alteños* with U.S. ghetto-inspired hip-hop music (Juan Forero, "Young Bolivians Adopt Urban U.S. Pose, Hip-Hop and All," *New York Times*, May 26, 2005).

89. Unlike most Bolivian events, the gas war drew detailed U.S. coverage. Good summary accounts of the September and October events are found in *El Diario*, December 31, 2003; *Latin American Weekly Report*, October 21, 2003; Raquel Gutierrez Aguilar, "Recuperating Natural Resources, Rebuilding a Nation," Interhemispheric Resource Center (www.americaspolicy.org); and Kathryn Ledebur, "Popular Protest Brings Down the Government," *Special Update: Bolivia*, Washington Office on Latin America, November 2003. The role of the United States was a source of some controversy. Support for Sánchez de Lozada was strong until the end, but the U.S. Embassy denied charges that it had coordinated the military defense of Goni's doomed government. See Frances Robles, "Embassy Didn't Guide Military during Bolivian Protests," *Miami Herald*, October 21, 2003.

90. Carlos Mesa, "Mensaje de Carlos Mesa Gisbert, Presidente Constitucional de la República de Bolivia," January 4, 2004 (www.comunica.gov.bo/documentos_oficiales/discursos/20040104-mesa.html).

91. Reed Lindsay, "Bolivia's Divisions Grow Deeper," *Toronto Star*, September 22, 2004.

92. The questions (loosely translated) were as follows: 1. Are you in favor of abrogating Hydrocarbon Law 1689 promulgated by Sánchez de Lozada? 2. Are you in favor of restoring state ownership of all hydrocarbons at the well-head? 3. Do you favor restoring a role for YPFB in the

future exploitation of hydrocarbons? 4. Do you support the president's use of gas as a bargaining chip in negotiations with Chile for a sovereign port on the Pacific? and 5. Do you favor increasing royalties on currently privatized hydrocarbon production up to 50% for use in social investments (schools, health, roads, job training, etc.)? (*El Diario*, July 23, 2004). Question 2 received 92 percent support; questions one and three received 87 percent approval. Question 4 was backed by 55 percent of the voters and question 5 by 62 percent—the questions on which Morales urged a "no" vote (*El Diario*, July 23, 2004).

93. Quoted by Alistair Scrutton, "Bolivia Faces Tough Task of Interpreting Referendum," *Washington Post*, July 19, 2004. Other sources for the information in this paragraph come from Bill Weinberg, "Bolivia: Mandate or Muddle on Oil and Gas Resources," posted July 11, 2006, at www.americas.org/item_16109. Teo Ballvé, "After the Referendum," August 9, 2004, http://portland.indymedia.org/en/2004/08/294293.shtml; and Juan Forero, "Bolivians Support Gas Plan and Give President a Lift," *New York Times*, July 19, 2004.

94. "Mesa Takes Gas Fight to Congress," July 19, 2004, EFE (www.efe.es/principal.asp).

95. "Mesa Takes Gas Fight to Congress."

96. Benjamin Dangl, "Legalizing the Colonization of the Americas: An Interview with Bolivian Cocalero Leader Evo Morales, December 1, 2003 (www.americas.org).

97. The MAS did better in the December 2004 municipal elections than any of the traditional parties, but the party won no mayorships in major cities, and its percentage of the total vote was lower than in the 2002 presidential elections. This might have further convinced Morales that cooperation with Mesa was politically costly. See *Latin American Weekly Report*, December 7, 2004, and December 14, 2004. Also Franz Chavez, "New Grassroots Political Actors Emerge from Local Elections," Inter Press Service, December 6, 2004 (www.ipsnews.net).

98. Lindsay, "Bolivia's Divisions Grow Deeper."

99. Carlos Mesa, "Discurso de Apertura," Seminario Internacional "Capital Social Etica y Desarrollo: Los Nuevos Desafíos," La Paz, November 25 and 26, 2002 (www.iadb.org/etica/sp4321/DocHit.cfm?DocIndex=524).

100. Juan Forero, "In Bolivia's Elitist Corner, There's Talk of Cutting Loose," *New York Times*, August 27, 2004. The taxi driver's quote comes from Teo Ballvé, "Bolivia after the Referendum," (www.Americas.com). In 2000, Santa Cruz provided 42 percent of the nation's agricultural output, 34 percent of industrial GNP, and 25 percent of the extractive GNP (ICG, "Bolivia's Divisions: Too Deep to Heal?" 16, footnote).

101. "Comité Pro-Santa Cruz exige autonomía regional," *El Diario*, June 24, 2004. The comments by the beauty queen drew vehement reaction from the La Paz press ("Boliviana deja pésima impresión de la patria," *El Diario*, May 27, 2004).

102. Editorial, "Revolt of the Poor in Bolivia," *New York Times*, November 3, 2003, and Jim Schultz, "Bolivia's Pipeline Dreams," *New York Times*, July 17, 2004.

103. ICG, "Bolivia's Divisions: Too Deep to Heal?" 15.

104. According to the 2001 census, the indigenous population of Santa Cruz Department is 447,000 out of a total population of slightly over two million. Nearly five hundred thousand *cruceños* self-reported that they were immigrants to Santa Cruz from other Bolivian departments. See Bolivia, Insitituto Nacional de Estadística, "Bolivia: Población Total por Condición Indígena y Área de Residencia, Según Departamento Censo 2001," and "Bolivia: Población Migrante Interdepartamental" (www.ine.gov.bo/cgi-bin/Piwdie1xx.exe/TIPO).

105. Laura Carlsen, "Resources War: Lessons from Bolivia, Americas Program," Interhemispheric Resource Center, November 11, 2003, http://americas.irc-online.org/columns/amprog/2003/0311bolivia.html.

106. Andre Hofman, "Long-Run Economic Development in Latin America in a Comparative Perspective: Proximate and Ultimate Causes," *Serie Macroeconomia del Desarrollo #8* (Santiago, Chile: CEPAL/ECLAC, Economic Development Division, December 2001).

107. ICG, "Bolivia's Divisions: Too Deep to Heal?" 14–17.

108. "Indian and Leftist Groups, Seeking Reforms, Seal Off 2 Cities," *Los Angeles Times*, January 12, 2005; Carlos Valdes, "Santa Cruz Joins Anti-Government Rally," *Miami Herald*, January 12, 2005; "El gasolinazo obliga al gobierno a librar una batalla en las calles y en el Congreso," *Bolpress*, January 18, 2005 (www.americas.org); and "Water, Oil and the Mob," *The Economist*, January 22, 2005.

109. Key sources for this paragraph include: "Mesa promulgaría hoy la Ley de Hidrocarburos," *La Razón*, May 8, 2005; "Mesa Rejects Fuel Tax Proposal," *Financial Times*, May 11, 2005; "Fracasa el diálogo; Mesa al borde del abismo," *Bolpress*, May 13, 2005; "Bolivia to Lose $10 Billion in Oil, Gas Projects, Trade Group Says," *Bloomberg.com*, May 18, 2005; Juan Forero, "Foreign Gas Companies in Bolivia Face Sharply Higher Taxes," *New York Times*, May 18, 2005; and "Gas Law Signed, New Protests," May 23, 2005 (www.americas.org).

110. Key sources on this tumultuous period: "Miles de campesinos rodean la Plaza Murillo," *Bolpress*, May 24, 2005; "Coup Rumors, Peasant Protests Put Bolivia on Edge," CNN.com, May 26, 2005; Mary Milliken, "Indigenous Protesters Descend on Bolivia's Capital," *Reuters*, June 1, 2005; Héctor Tobar and Raúl Peñaranda, "President Offers to Resign Amid Mounting Crisis," *Los Angeles Times*, June 7, 2005; "Estrategia 'Vaca Diez presidente del país' se elaboró hace un mes," *El Diario*, June 8, 2005; Juan Forero, "No. 1 Quits in Bolivia, and Protesters Scorn Nos. 2 and 3," *New York Times*, June 9, 2005; and Juan Forero, "Bolivia Congress Names New President, Setting Stage for Elections," *New York Times*, June 10, 2005.

111. Documents cited by Robert Novak, in his column titled "Bolivia's Drug Crisis," January 15, 2004 (www.cnn.com/2004/ALLPOLITICS/01/06/column.novak.opinion.bolivia/).

112. Rohter, "Bolivian Leader's Ouster Seen as Warning on U.S. Drug Policy."

113. See "U.S. Supports Democracy, Development, Counternarcotics Efforts in Bolivia," statement by John Creamer, Deputy Director for Andean Affairs," May 7, 2004 (www.usinfo.state.gov).

114. "U.S. Official Outlines Progress and Challenges in Latin America," speech by Assistant Secretary of State Roger Noriega, July 30, 2004, at www.usinfo.state.gov. Since he is the senior State Department official for Latin America, one assumes that this statement does not accurately reflect Noriega's depth of understanding of the events in Bolivia.

115. "Jeffrey Sachs on the Challenges of Development," paper presented to the International Development Research Centre, June 19, 2001 (http://web.idre.ca/en/ev-25642-201-1-DO_TOPIC.html). An article in the La Paz newspaper *El Diario* claims that IMF, World Bank, and UN Conference on Trade and Development studies reinforce Sachs's calculations and that the total losses since 1998 are more than $4 billion ("Bolivia pierde más de $US 4.000 millones por enclaustramiento," *El Diario*, July 4, 2004).

116. Jeffrey Sachs, "What's Good for the Poor Is Good for America," *The Economist*, July 12, 2001; "Weapons of Mass Salvation," *The Economist*, October 24, 2002; and "World Bank and Donors Must Change to Reach MDGs," March 1, 2004 (http://info.worldbank.org/etools/bspan/PresentationView.asp?PID=1061&EID=548). The United States, even after its recently announced Millennium Challenge increase, is currently devoting less than 1 percent of GDP to economic assistance. The goal set by the UN's Millennium Challenge is 7 percent of GDP.

117. Sachs, "Another U.S. Foreign-Policy Failure," and Sachs, "A World for Which Bush Cares Little."

118. Congressional Research Service Report for Congress, "Andean Counterdrug Initiative (ACI) and Related Funding Programs: FY2005 Assistance," December 9, 2004, p. 16, and U.S. Department of State, International Narcotics Control Strategy Report—2005, March 2005, p. 4 (www.state.gov). The most recent statistics from a report by the UN Office on Drugs and Crime show that the balloon effect is still very much operative. Despite a 7 percent drop in coca production in Colombia in 2004, the overall production of coca in the Andes increased 3 percent (Mark Jon, "U.N. Drugs Chief Raises Alarm on Bolivia Crisis," Reuters, June 14, 2005).

119. U.S. Department of State, International Narcotics Control Strategy Report—2005.

120. U.S. International Information Programs, "U.S. Releases Annual Narcotics Certification Report," September 16, 2004, at usinfo.state.gov. ATPDEA is one of the fast-track concessions recently granted the president by Congress and is to be linked to drug control success. See U.S. Embassy, La Paz, "Bolivia and the Andean Trade Program" (http://lapaz.usembassy.gov/atpdea/ atpaeng.htm).

121. USAID, "Budget—Bolivia," 2005 (www.usaid.gov/policy/budget/cbj2005/lac/bo.html). Lesley Gill, in her study of El Alto, observes that factors accompanying globalization "are undermining the ability of states to maintain the political, economic, and cultural conditions that are crucial to the unity of the nation state. . . . As policies enforced by states drive more people into poverty, 'governability' increasingly becomes an issue for national and international policy makers who must devise methods to manage the tensions that erupt among the legions of unemployed and underemployed. These methods frequently rely on the use of force" (Gill, *Teetering on the Rim*, 8, with an extended discussion in chapter 9).

122. U.S. Department of State, Daily Press Briefing, Richard Boucher spokesman, "Donors Group Meeting," January 15, 2004 (www.state.gov/r/pa/prs/dpb/2004/28194.htm); Secretary Colin L. Powell, "Remarks to the Bolivia Support Group," January 16, 2004 (www.state.gov/ secretary/rm/28250.htm); IMF, "Bolivia: Third Review Under the Stand-By," IMF Country Report No. 04/193, July 2004 (www.imf.org/external/country/BOL/); and *El Diario*, April 27, 2004, May 13, 2004, July 9, 2004. The Bolivia Support Group has been noticeably silent since the middle of 2004 except to issue a joint statement in March 2005 urging Bolivians to maintain dialogue and follow constitutional norms The joint statement in March can be found at www.state .gov/r/pa/prs/ps/2005/43145.htm.

123. The White House, "Remarks by the President at Ceremony Celebrating Countries Selected for the Millennium Challenge Account," May 10, 2004; ICF, "Bolivia's Divisions: Too Deep to Heal?" footnote, p. 20; and U.S. Congress, "The Millennium Challenge Account: Congressional Consideration of a New Foreign Aid Initiative, CRS Report for Congress," March 19, 2004.

124. Marcela Sánchez of the *Washington Post* has argued that despite its problems Bolivia should be a prime candidate for the Challenge. "If [quoting President Bush] 'persistent poverty can turn nations of great potential into the recruiting grounds of terrorists,' then Bolivia's poverty rate of almost two-thirds of its people—the highest in South America—coupled with its tremendous political instability should put it directly in MCA's sights," Sanchez argues (Marcela Sanchez, "Bolivia seeks Underdog Victory in Contest for U.S. Aid," May 13, 2004, special to *washingtonpost.com*).

125. World Bank Group, "Bolivia: World Bank Approves $43.4 Million to Support Poor Rural Areas and Help Bolivia Meet the Millennium Development Goals in 2015," News release 2005/480/LAC, May 26, 2005 (www.worldbank.org).

126. Paul Blustein, "Debt Cut Is Set for Poorest Nations," *Washington Post*, June 12, 2005, and Elizabeth Becker and Richard W. Stevenson, "U.S. and Britain Agree on Relief for Poor Nations," *New York Times*, June 10, 2005. Evo Morales's response was that "Bolivia is no debtor, rather a creditor of nations such as Spain and Britain that have historically looted our resources" ("Bolivia Is 'a Creditor Not a Debtor' of G 8," *Mercopress*, June 12, 2005.

127. "Cocaleros Protest Police Base," April 10, 2004 (www.americas.org).

128. Martin Arostegui, "Analysis: Coca War Looms in Bolivia," United Press International, September 30, 2004, and "Cocalero Pact Signed," October 17, 2004 (www.americas.org). A detailed account of the death can be found at U.S. Department of State, "Bolivia: Country Report on Human Rights Practices—2004," February 28, 2005 (www.state.gov). The action in the Chapare also effectively scuttled a brief overture by U.S. officials toward Morales and the MAS. For a discussion of this brief overture, see Martin Arostegui, "Bolivia's Divided Opposition Movement," United Press International, August 9, 2004.

129. International Crisis Group, "Coca, Drugs and Social Protest in Bolivia and Peru," *Latin America Report*, vol. 12, no. 3 (March 2005): 10–11 (www.crisisgroup.org/home/index.cfm?id= 3307&l=1). In a private conversation, a State Department official told the author that U.S. officials were certain that the survey of the legal market for coca would back their position that 12,000 hectares is more than enough to meet the legitimate market. The growing weakness of the Bolivian government likely makes any results from the survey moot.

130. Connie Veillete, CRS Report for Congress, "Andean Counterdrug Initiative (ACI) and Related Funding Programs: FY2005 Assistance," December 9, 2004, p. 17.

131. Kevin G. Hall, "Coca Growers Resist Drug Troops," *Miami Herald*, February 10, 2004, and Eduardo Gamarra, "Give the New President a Breather," *Miami Herald*, October 23, 2003. The U.S. Embassy acknowledges the potential costs of taking the war to the Yungas. See "Informe del Departamento de Estado de los Estados Unidos de Norte America sobre la Estrategia Internacional para el Control de Narcóticos," March 1, 2004 (http://bolivia.usembassy.gob/InformeContrNarc.htm).

132. Background on the ICC can be found at the website of the American Nongovernmental Organizations Coalition for the International Criminal Court, www.amicc.org.usinfo/administrationpolicy_BIAs.html. Bolivia's relationship to the court is discussed in "NGOs Urge Bolivia to Resist U.S. ICC Immunity Agreement," Coalition for the International Criminal Court, June 1, 2004 (www.iccnow.org), and Luis Bredow and Jim Schultz, "U.S. Threatens Bolivia in Effort to Secure Criminal Court Immunity," *Pacific News Service*, March 3, 2005.

133. U.S. Department of State, "U.S. Allows Continuing Military Aid to Some ICC Signatories," July 1, 2003 (http://usinfo.state.gov/dhr/Archive/2003/Oct/14-479006.html). The case in support of ASPA, the Nethercutt Amendment, and Article 98 Agreements can be found in Brett D. Schaefer, "The Bush Administration's Policy on the International Criminal Court is Correct," *Backgrounder* no. 1830, March 8, 2005, the Heritage Foundation.

134. Bredow and Schultz, "U.S. Threatens Bolivia in Effort to Secure Criminal Court Immunity." A legal brief against the U.S. position was sent to the Bolivian government in January 2005, see letter from Neil Hicks, director of international programs, Human Rights First, to Carlos Mesa Gisbert, January 18, 2005 (www.humanrightsfirst.org/index.html).

135. Posture Statement of General Bantz J. Craddock, Commander, United States Southern Command, hearing of the House Armed Services Committee: "Fiscal Year 2006 National Defense Authorization budget request," March 9, 2005, found at the website of the Center for International Policy's Colombia Program, http://ciponline.org/colombia/050309crad.htm.

136. "Rechazo total a la inmunidad yanqui," *Bolpress*, December 24, 2004, www.americas.org.

137. Lazarte's comments are found in "El Estilo de Carlos Mesa," *La Prensa* (La Paz), January 11, 2004.

138. "El Estilo de Carlos Mesa," *La Prensa* (La Paz), January 11, 2004, and "La Popularidad del Presidente Carlos Mesa," *Los Tiempos* (Cochabamba), December 19, 2003.

139. The figures come from a poll of Bolivian adults carried out by Barómetro Iberoamericano de Gobernabilidad and were reported on the Angus Reid Consultants website, May 7, 2005 (www.angus-reid.com/polls/index.cfm?fuseaction=viewItem&itemID=7096).

140. José Antonio Aruquipa, "Country on the Edge," *Latinoamerica Press*, June 2, 2005 (www.latinamericapress.org). Lazarte is a political analyst, former advisor to Bolivia's central labor union (Central Obrero Boliviano), and a judge in the National Electoral Court. Currently he is an advisor to interim president Eduardo Rodríguez.

141. In his report after visiting Bolivia in December 2003, former president Jimmy Carter noted: "It was interesting that [all political leaders he spoke to] took for granted the deep involvement of the United States in the internal political affairs of Bolivia" (Jimmy Carter, "Bolivia Trip Report," December 16–21, 2003: www.cartercenter.org/doc1571.htm).

142. Data from the Bolivian Government's Ministerio de Hacienda, quoted in Shultz, *Deadly Consequences*, 28.

143. IMF, *Bolivia: Ex-Post Assessment of Longer-Term Program Engagement*, 4.

144. IMF, *Bolivia: Ex-Post Assessment of Longer-Term Program Engagement*, 3.

145. IMF, *Bolivia: Ex-Post Assessment of Longer-Term Program Engagement*.

146. Shifter, "Breakdown in the Andes."

147. Roger Noriega told reporters that "Chávez' profile has been very apparent (in the Bolivia crisis) since the beginning." Chávez's response was that it was U.S. open market policy that lay behind "the exclusion, misery, and destabilization" that had brought Bolivia "to the verge of civil war." (Jane Bussey, "Washington and Venezuela Trade Barbs over Bolivia at OAS Conference in Fort Lauderdale," *Miami Herald*, June 7, 2005; and "U.S. Behind Bolivia Crisis—Chavez," *BBC News*, June 13, 2005). The BBC cited Argentine sources who reported that in fact Chávez had played a key role in achieving a solution to the immediate Bolivian crisis by placing a series of calls to Morales urging him to accept a constitutional outcome.

148. See U.S. Department of State, "Rice Heralds Latin America's 'March toward Freedom,'" May 2, 2005, and "United States Supports Democratic Reform in Americas," May 3, 2005 (www.usinfo.state.gov). For a discussion of the U.S. proposal at the OAS, see Joel Brinkley, "U.S. Proposal in the OAS Draws Fire as an Attack on Venezuela," *New York Times*, May 22, 2005. A State Department official conversant with Bolivia told the author that increasingly events there are being filtered through a Castro/Chávez lens that tends toward oversimplification.

149. See "FFAA en estado de 'máxima alerta,'" *El Deber* (www/eldeber.com.bo/20050524/nacional2.html); "Bolivia Armed Forces Chief Says Military Backs Mesa," *Bloomberg.com*, May 25, 2005; "Bolivia President Wary of 'Coup,'" CNN.com, May 30, 2005; and Juan Forero, "Armed Forces Vow to Defend Bolivia's Democratic Succession," *New York Times*, June 9, 2005.

150. William Hawkins, "Latin America in Play," *Washington Times*, May 23, 2005. An even more vigorous call for action comes from Michael Radu, "Andean Storm Troopers," Foreign Policy Research Institute, May 4, 2005 (www/fpri.org/enotes/20050504.latin.radu.andeanstrormtroopers .html).

151. Robert Novak, "Bolivia's Drug Crisis," www.cnn.com/2004/ALLPOLITICS/01/06/column.novak.opinion.bolivia/. General James J. Hill of the U.S. Southern Command made a similar point: "If radicals continue to highjack the indigenous movement, we could find ourselves faced with a narco-state that supports the uncontrolled cultivation of coca" (Testimony of James J. Hill, United States Southern Command, before the House Armed Services Committee, www.house .gov/hasc/openingstatementsandpressreleases/108thcongress/04-03-24hill.html).

152. Novak, "Bolivia's Drug Crisis."

Chapter 6

1. See Perú, Comisión de Verdad y Reconciliación, August 2003, www.cverdad.org.pe/ingles/ifinal/conclusiones.php (accessed August 4, 2005).

2. Miguel Gonzales del Rio Vigil, "Problemática Relacionada a la Sustitución de los Cultivos de la Hoja de Coca," in Escuela Superior de Guerra Naval, Serie Editorial *Conferencias Magistrales* (Callao, 1992).

3. José Barsallo Burga and Eduardo Gordillo Tordolla, *Drogas, Responsabilidad Compartida* (Lima: J.C. Editores S.A., 1988), 157.

4. Burga and Tordolla, *Drogas, Responsabilidad Compartida*, 149.

5. Cynthia McClintock, "The War on Drugs: The Peruvian Case," *Journal of Interamerican Studies and World Affairs*, vol. 30, no. 2 &3 (Summer/Fall 1988): 127–42.

6. Gordon McCormick, *From the Sierra to the Cities: The Urban Campaign of the Shining Path* (Santa Monica, Calif.: RAND Corp., 1992).

7. *El Comercio*, August 25, 1990, and *La República*, August 21, 1990.

8. *Expreso*, September 27, 1990.

9. Francisco Reyes, "Narcotraficantes crean otro Huallaga," journalistic research paper.

10. Reyes, "Narcotraficantes crean otro Huallaga."

11. Gonzales del Rio Vigil, "Problemática Relacionada a la Sustitución de los Cultivos de la Hoja de Coca."

12. *Newsweek*, July 16, 1990, 8–11.

13. "Airborne Warning and Control System, this aircraft has both a large surveillance radar capable of detecting, classifying and tracking a large number of aircraft at distances in excess of several hundred miles and command, control and communications abilities (c3) for the tactical guidance of pursuit and other such aircraft." From Edward Luttwak and Stuart L. Koehl, *The Dictionary of Modern War* (New York: Gramercy Books, 1991), 70.

14. "The Special Project for the Control and Eradication of Coca Crops in the Alto Huallaga (CORAH) shows 11,462.85 hectares of coca were eradicated in 2003; that should reduce the 36,600 hectares currently under cultivation in the country. However. the U.S. Department of State has not yet completed its report on the numbers of hectares as of December 31, 2003. The figures might depart from mathematically extrapolated numbers, and would most likely be higher as a result of plant rehabilitation and new plantings, particularly in the Huallaga and Ene-Apurímac valleys" (Ministry of the Interior, Directorate of Intelligence, *Apreciación de Inteligencia Estratégica*, February 10, 2004).

15. Ministry of the Interior, General Directorate of Intelligence, *Apreciación de Inteligencia Estratégica* (highlighted as in the source).

16. Presentation by Nils Ericsson, executive director for DEVIDA, at a working meeting with Deborah McCarthy at the Peruvian Chancellery on October 22, 2003.

17. Ministry of the Interior, General Directorate of Intelligence, *Apreciación de Inteligencia Estratégica*, 4.

18. Informe UNODC, Brussels, June 13, 2005. This report includes, however, crops planted less than one year, which suggests that the figures for 2005 will be even higher.

19. On May 10, 1984, 107 contracting states attending the Assembly of the International Civil Aviation Organization, including the United States, unanimously adopted the protocol relating to an amendment of the Convention on International Civil Aviation (article 3 bis). Said protocol declares the following:

a) The contracting States recognize that every State must refrain from resorting to the use of weapons against civil aircraft in flight and that, in case of interception, the lives of persons on board and the safety of aircraft must not be endangered. This provision shall not be interpreted as modifying in any way the rights and obligations of States set forth in the Charter of the United Nations. b) The contracting States recognize that every State, in the exercise of its sovereignty, is entitled to require the landing at some designated airport of a civil aircraft flying above its territory without authority or if there are reasonable grounds to conclude that it is being used for any purpose inconsistent with the aims of this Convention; it may also give such aircraft any other instructions to put an end to such violations. For this purpose, the contracting States may resort to any appropriate means consistent with relevant rules of international law, including the relevant provisions of this Convention, specifically paragraph (a) of this Article. Each contracting State agrees to publish its regulations in force regarding the interception of civil aircraft. c) Every civil aircraft shall comply with an order given in conformity with paragraph (b) of this Article. To this end each contracting State shall establish all necessary provisions in its national laws or regulations to make such compliance mandatory for any civil aircraft registered in that State or operated by an operator who has his principal place of business or permanent residence in that State. Each contracting State shall make any violation of such applicable laws or regulations punishable by severe penalties and shall submit the case to its competent authorities in accordance with its laws or regulations. d) Each contracting State shall take appropriate measures to prohibit the deliberate use of any civil aircraft registered in that State or operated by an operator who has his principal place of business or permanent residence in that State for any purpose inconsistent with the aims of this Convention. This provision shall not affect paragraph (a) or derogate from paragraphs (b) and (c) of this Article. (emphasis added)

20. Working meeting with Ms. Deborah McCarthy on October 22, 2003.

21. Meeting with James Benson, director, Narcotics Affairs Section, U.S. Embassy, Lima, Peru, May 6, 2004.

22. Agencia EFE 17 de octubre del 2004, "Una ley permite a la Fuerza Aérea brasileña derribar los aviones sospechosos de narcotráfico" (www.efe.com/).

23. Prensa Latina (PL) 19 de Julio 2004, "Brasil pondrá en vigor ley que permite derribar aviones ilegales."

24. Agencia EFE, "Una ley permite a la Fuerza Aérea brasileña derribar los aviones sospechosos de narcotráfico."

25. PL, "Brasil pondrá en vigor ley que permite derribar aviones ilegales."

26. Ministry of the Interior, *Apreciación de Inteligencia Estratégica*, 11.

27. Presentation by Nils Ericsson.

28. September 5, 2003, letter from Barry Crane to Nils Ericsson.

29. Luis Piscoya, "Evaluación de la Crisis de los Agricultores Cocaleros en el Perú: Implicancia para los Intereses de Seguridad," in *Elementos de Seguridad y Defensa, Vol. II*, ed. Enrique Obando (Lima: IDEPE, 2003), 119–52.

30. Ministry of the Interior, *Apreciación de Inteligencia Estratégica*, 5.

31. The unions are:

- Asociación de Agricultores Agropecuarios y Productores de Hoja de Coca del Alto Huallaga (AAAPHCAH—Association of Coca Leaf Growers and Producers of the Alto Huallaga Valley), comprised of Uchiza and Tocache (San Martín) Provinces, Antonio Huamán, general secretary.
- Asociación de Productores Agropecuarios y Productores de Hoja de Coca de la Provincia de Padre Abad (AAAPHCPA—Association of Coca Leaf Growers and Producers of Padre Abad Province), Flavio Sanchez Moreno, general secretary.
- Federación de Productores Agropecuarios del Valle de los Rios Apurímac y Ene (FEPAVRAE—Federation of Apurímac and Ene River Valley Agricultural Producers), comprising the Ene-Apurímac (Ayacucho), La Convención (Cuzco), and Satipo (Junín) Valleys. Their secretary-general, Nelson Palomino, is currently imprisoned.
- Asociación de Productores Agropecuarios del Valle del Monzón (APAVM—Association of Agricultural Producers for the Monzón Valley), encompassing the Monzón district and the town of Cachicoto, Iburcio Morales, general secretary.
- Federación Provincial de Campesinos de la Convención, Yanatili y Lares (FEPCACYL—Provincial Campesino Federation of La Convencion, Lares and Yanatile), Avelino Quispe, general secretary.
- Asociación de Cafetaleros y Cocaleros de Chanchamayo (Association of Chanchamayo Coffee and Coca Growers), governed by the mayor of Chanchamayo, Provincial Agrarian Federation Commander Walter Mendoza.
- Federación Agraria Provincial de Satipo (Satipo Provincial Agrarian Federation) (Ministry of the Interior, *Apreciación de Inteligencia Estratégica*, 5–6).

32. Presentation by Nils Ericsson.

33. Quoted by Luis Piscoya, "Evaluación de la Crisis de los Agricultores Cocaleros en el Perú," 138–39.

34. Piscoya, "Evaluación de la Crisis de los Agricultores Cocaleros en el Perú," 131–36.

35. Ministry of the Interior, *Apreciación de Inteligencia Estratégica*, 6.

36. In January 2005, members of this group led by Antauro Humala, a retired army officer, occupied a police station, killed four officers, and wounded others. They demanded the resignation of President Toledo. Toledo declared a thirty-day state of emergency in the region. The

rebels' program focuses on establishing a nationalist indigenous movement modeled on the Inca empire. They also accuse Toledo of selling out Peru to Chilean business interests.

37. Ministry of the Interior, *Apreciación de Inteligencia Estratégica.*

38. "Peru Letter of Intent and Technical Memorandum of Understanding," Lima, Peru, January 18, 2002, https://www.imfo.org/external/np/loi/2002/per/01/.

39. The members of the Group of 21 were Argentina, Bolivia, Brazil, China, Chile, Colombia, Costa Rica, Cuba, Ecuador, Egypt, the Philippines, Guatemala, India, Mexico, Nigeria, Pakistan, Paraguay, Peru, South Africa, Thailand, Turkey, and Venezuela.

Chapter 7

1. This framework is discussed by Ronald Jepperson, Alexander Wendt, and Peter J. Katzenstein, "Norms Identity, and Culture in National Security," in *The Culture of National Security: Norms and Identity in World Politics*, ed. Peter J. Katzenstein (New York: Columbia University Press, 1996), 34.

2. Ronnie Lipschutz, *On Security* (New York: Columbia University Press, 1995), 10.

3. Hedley Bull, *The Anarchical Society: A Study of Order in World Politics* (London: Macmillan, 1977).

4. For a discussion of these systemic variables that change the security environment see Barry Buzan, "The 'New World Order' and Beyond," in Lipschutz, *On Security*, 187–209. For a recent debate on security communities see Emanuel Adler and Michael Barnett, *Security Communities* (Cambridge: Cambridge University Press, 2000).

5. For a discussion of interventionism in the post–Cold War context see James Mayall, *The New Interventionism, 1991–1994* (Cambridge: Cambridge University Press, 1996).

6. Harald Muller, "Internalization of Principles, Norms and Rules by Governments: The Case of Security Regimes," in *Regime Theory and International Relations*, ed. Volker Rittberger and Peter Mayer, 361–90 (Oxford: Clarendon Press, 1993). The author stresses that regimes do not cover the entire area of security. He suggests that the literature has been inclined to take the Concert of Europe as a paradigm, thus searching for global security regimes.

7. Willy Brandt, *North-South: A Programme for Survival* (London: Pan Books, 1980); Olf Palme, *Common Security* (New York: Simon & Schuster, 1982); Gro Harlem Brundtland, *Our Common Future* (London: Oxford University Press, 1987); The Stockholm Initiative, *Common Responsibility in the 1990s* (Stockholm: Prime Minister's Office, 1991).

8. Richard Ullman, "Redefining Security," *International Security*, vol. 8, no. 1 (Summer 1983): 129–53.

9. David B. Dewitt, "Introduction: The New Global Order and the Challenges of International Security," in *Building a New Global Order: Emerging Trends in International Security*, ed. David Dewitt, David Haglund, and John Kirton (Oxford: Oxford University Press, 1993).

10. See Lev Voronkov, "International Peace and Security: New Challenges to the UN," in *The United Nations in the New World Order: The World Organization at Fifty*, ed. Dimitris Bourantonis and Jarrod Weiner, chap. 1 (New York: St Martin's, 1995).

11. See Ivan Cannabrava, "O Brasil e as Operações de Manutenção da Paz," *Política Externa*, vol. 5, no. 3 (December 1996): 93–105.

12. See Security Council Meeting 317, November 18, 1993.

13. Luiz Felipe de Seixas Corrêa, "Introdução," in *A Palavra do Brasil nas Nações Unidas*, Fundação Alexandre Gusmão (Brasilia: FUNAG, 1995), 17.

14. Gelson Fonseca, "Aspectos da Multipolaridade Contemporânea," *Contexto Internacional*, no. 11 (January–June 1990).

15. Roberto Pereira da Silva, "Brasil—Geopolítica e Destino," *Parcerias Estratégicas*, vol. 1, no. 2 (December 1996): 103.

16. Luiz Felipe Lampreia, "O Brasil e o Mundo no Século XXI: Uma Visão do Itamaraty," *Política Externa*, vol. 5, no. 3 (December 1996).

17. Presentation at the seminar organized by the Commission on External Relations and National Defense of the Brazilian Congress, August 20, 2002.

18. For a discussion of this theme see Luís Alexandre Fuccille, "As Forças Armadas e a temática interna no Brasil contemporâneo," thesis, São Carlos University, 1999.

19. Adam Isacson and Joy Olson, "Just the Facts: A Quick Tour of U.S. Defense and Security Assistance to Latin America and the Caribbean," *International Policy Report*, December 1998, 4–5.

20. Francisco Rojas Aravena, "Introducción," in *Narcotráfico y Seguridad en América Latina y el Caribe*, ed. Paz Verónica Milet (Santiago: FLACSO, 1997).

21. Gina Amatangelo, "Militarization of the U.S. Drug Control Program," *Foreign Policy in Focus*, vol. 6, no. 17 (May 2001): 4.

22. Center for International Policy, "U.S. Security Assistance to the Andean Region, 2000–2001": www.ciponline.org (accessed August 25, 2002).

23. See Eliézer Rizzo de Oliveira, "A Defesa do Estado Democrático," in *A revisão da república: Seminários*, org. Eliézer Rizzo de Oliveria (Campinas, Brazil: Editora da Unicamp, 1994); Wendy Hunter, "The Brazilian Military after the Cold War: In Search of a Mission," *Studies in Comparative International Development*, vol. 28, no. 4 (Winter 1994): 31–49.

24. Operation Rio was a military operation against organized crime that took place in Rio de Janeiro between November 1994 and March 1995.

25. Mário César Flores, *Bases para uma política militar* (Campinas, Brazil: Editora da Unicamp, 1992).

26. João Roberto Martins Filho, "The Brazilian Armed Forces after the Cold War: Overcoming the Identity Crisis," paper presented at the LASA Congress, Chicago, September 1998.

27. Report by a special federal congressional committee charged with investigating organized crime and drug trafficking in Brazil issued in 2000.

28. Amaury de Souza, "A agenda internacional do Brasil: Um estudo sobre a comunidade brasileira de política externa" (Rio de Janeiro: CEBRI, Centro Brasileiro de Relações Internacionais, 2002).

29. Palermo Convention on Transnational Organized Crime, December 2000. State parties to the convention are required to establish in their domestic criminal law codes for criminal offenses: participation in an organized criminal group; money laundering; corruption; and obstruction of justice. Organized criminal groups are defined by the convention as follows: "Organized criminal group 'shall mean a structured group of three or more persons existing for a period of time and acting in concert with the aim of committing one or more serious crimes or offenses established pursuant to this Convention, in order to obtain, directly, or indirectly, a financial or other material benefit.'"

30. Amado Luiz Cervo and Clodoaldo Bueno, *História da Política Exterior do Brasil* (São Paulo: Editora Ática, 1992).

31. Geraldo Lesbat Cavagnari Filho, "Estratégia e Defesa (1960–1990)," in *Sessenta Anos de Política Externa Brasileira (1930–1990)* vol. III, org. José Augusto Guilhon de Albuquerque (São Paulo: Annablume, 2001).

32. Lars Schoultz, William C. Smith, and Augusto Varas, "Introduction," in *Security, Democracy, and Development in U.S.–Latin American Relations* (Miami: North-South Center, 1994).

33. For this discussion see J. Samuel Fitch, "The Decline of U.S. Military Influence in Latin America," in Schoultz, Smith, and Varas, *Security, Democracy, and Development in U.S.–Latin American Relations*, 77–113.

34. John Lindsay-Poland, "U.S. Military Bases in Latin America and the Caribbean," *Foreign Policy in Focus*, vol. 6, no. 35 (2001): 1; Center for International Policy, "Counterdrug Radar Sites," August 18, 2002: http://ciponline.org/facts/radar.htm (accessed on August 18, 2002).

35. Michael L. Evans, "U.S. Drug Policy & Intelligence Operations in the Andes," *Foreign Policy in Focus*, vol. 6 , no. 22 (2001): 1–2.

36. Eugenio Diniz, "O Brasil e a MINUSTAH," *Security and Defense Studies Review*, vol. 5, no. 1 (2005).

37. Maria Regina Soares de Lima, "Brazil's Alternative Vision," in *The Americas in Transition: The Contours of Regionalism*, ed. Gordon Mace and Louis Bélanger (Boulder, Colo.: Rienner, 1999), 7.

38. Conn Hallinan, "U.S. Shadow over Venezuela," *Foreign Policy in Focus*, April 17, 2002: www.fpif.org/progresp (accessed August 20, 2002).

39. Steve Ellner and Fred Rosen, "Venezuela's Failed Coup, the U.S.' Role and the Future of Hugo Chávez," *Foreign Policy in Focus*, June 2002, www.foreignpolicyinfocus.org/papers/venezuela .html.

40. Ronald J. Morgan, "Brazil's Escalating Role in the Drug War," *Colombia Report*, July 15, 2002, www.colombiareport.org/colombia12.

41. General Alberto Cardoso, interview for Reuters, in "Brazil Says Plan Colombia Biggest Security Risk," August 29, 2000, CNN.com (accessed on October 3, 2002).

42. Chemical agents such as glyphosate and biological agents such as fusarium oxysporum could flow into the Ica and Japura Rivers from the Putumayo and Caquetá rivers respectively (Morgan, "Brazil's Escalating Role in the Drug War").

43. Thomaz Guedes da Costa, "Brazil's SIVAM: As It Monitors the Amazon, Will It Fulfill Its Human Security Promise?" *ECSP Report*, no. 7 (2002): 47–58.

44. Statement by Mr. Alberto Mendes Cardoso, Head of the Brazilian Delegation to the Inter-American Committee on Terrorism, January 30, 2002, OEA/Ser.L/X2.2 CICTE/doc.8/01.

45. The Contadora Group (Colombia, Mexico, Panama, and Venezuela) first met in January 1983 and in July 1985 the Contadora Support Group was created (Argentina, Brazil, Peru, and Uruguay).

46. The Rio Group was created in December 1986, when the members of the Contadora and Contadora Support Group agreed to generate a Permanent Mechanism for Consultation and Political Coordination. The aim was to prevent unilateral intervention by the United States in view of the growing instability in Central America. In 1990, Chile and Ecuador joined the group. See Francisco R. Aravena, "The Rio Group and Regional Security in Latin America," in *Regional Mechanisms and International Security in Latin America*, ed. Olga Pellicer (Tokyo: United Nations University Press, 1998), 112–30.

47. Jorge Dominguez, "The Future of Inter-American Relations," Working Paper, Inter-American Dialogue, 1999, p. 3.

48. Inter-American Convention against the Illicit Manufacturing of and Trafficking in Firearms, Ammunition, Explosives, and Other Related Materials and the Inter-American Convention on Transparency in Conventional Weapons Acquisitions.

49. See Celso Amorim, "O Brasil e as Novas Dimensões da Segurança Internacional," paper presented at the Instituto de Estudos Avançadas da USP, São Paulo, September 11, 1998.

50. See, for example, Lauro Soutello Alvez (advisor to the Department of International Organizations of the Ministry of Foreign Affairs), "O Brasil e as Operações de Paz da ONU," *Carta Internacional*, no. 37 (March 1996).

51. See, for example, the argument made by Ronaldo Sardenberg during the Security Council meeting on the role played by the OAU within the Arusha peace process in Rwanda—March 12, 1993. For Sardenberg's statement, see "Statements Made to the Security Council Meeting on the International Criminal Tribunals for Rwanda and the Former Yugoslavia," December 15, 2005, www.nieuwsbank.nl/en/2005/12/15/1006.htm.

52. Juan Gabriel Tokatlian, "Colombia, el Plan Colombia y la región Andina: Implosión o Concertación," *Nueva Sociedad*, no. 173 (May–June 2001): 127–43.

53. Flávia de Campos Mello, "Política Externa Brasileira e os blocos internacionais," *São Paulo em Perspectiva*, vol. 16, no. 1 (2002): 37–43, 38.

54. See Marco Cepik, "A política Externa de Lula: Desafios do primeiro ano e a questão colombiana," International Crisis Group (2002): www.crisisweb.org.

55. *O Estado De São Paulo*, November 8, 1996.

56. See for example the special edition in 1997 of the Brazilian army magazine *Verde-Oliva* at the magazine website: www.exercito.gov.br/VO/indice.htm.

57. See for example Seminar on the Amazon Region, Escola Superior de Guerra, December 1999. Amaury de Souza's research, quoted earlier, shows that the internationalization of the Amazon is considered a critical threat by 49 percent of interviewees and an important but not critical threat by 28 percent of interviewees.

58. Luis Bitencourt, "The Importance of the Amazon Basin in Brazil's Evolving Security Agenda," in *Environment and Security in the Amazon Basin*, ed. Joseph S. Tulchin and Heather A. Golding, 53–74 (Washington, D.C.: Woodrow Wilson International Center, 2002).

59. Law 9614 (March 5, 1998) added a section paragraph to article 303 (dealing with detention and interdiction).

60. As cited on the Brazilian Ministry of Foreign Relations website: www.mre.gov.br (accessed December 23, 2002).

61. Address at the sixth meeting of the Foreign Ministers of the Treaty of Amazonian Cooperation, Caracas, April 6, 2000 (www.mre.gov.br).

62. For information on military operations in the area see www.cna.mar.mil.br (Naval Command of the Western Amazon), www.exercito.gov.br (Military Command of the Amazon), and www.abin.gov.br (Intelligence Agency).

63. Morgan, "Brazil's Escalating Role in the Drug War."

64. Edélcio Vigna, "O quê o congresso nacional pensa sobre o plano Colômbia," in *Plano Colômbia perspectivas do parlamento brasileiro*, pesquisa INESC, Brasília, 2002, 41–50, 43.

65. Richard Millet, "Colombia's Conflicts: The Spillover Effects of a Wider War," *North-South Center Agenda Papers*, no. 57 (2002).

66. Larry Rohter, "Latest Battleground in Latin Drug War: Brazilian Amazon," *New York Times*, October 30, 2000, A-1.

67. Katherine Baldwin, "Brazil Army Kills Colombia Rebels," Reuters, March 6, 2002.

68. "EUA impedem vendas da Embraer à Colômbia," *O Globo*, November 19, 2002, 27.

69. Marco Cepik, "Brasil y El Plan Colombia: Notas Sobre Ajenamiento y Diplomacia Presidencial, Seminario América Latina y El Plan Colombia: Estabilidad o Crisis?" Universidad Central Venezolana, Caracas, May 29, 30, 2002.

70. Geraldo Magela da Cruz Quintão (Minister of Defense), "Projeto SIVAM e a integração com os países vizinhos," *Carta Internacional*, no.116 (October 2002): 2–3.

71. Participation in the seminar organized by External Relations and National Defense Commission, Brazilian Congress, August 20, 2002.

72. Peter Andreas, "Free Market Reform and Drug Market Prohibition: US Policies at Cross-Purposes in Latin America," *Third World Quarterly*, vol. 16, no. 1 (1995): 75–88.

Chapter 8

1. In this chapter, the EU refers to the EU-15, or the EU before its enlargement in 2004, which had fifteen member states and a population of about 375 million. The EU also has five (5) operations institutions and five (5) support bodies. The institutions are: the Council of the European Union; the European Commission; the European Parliament; the Court of Justice; and the Court of Auditors. The bodies are: the European Economic and Social Committee; the Committee of

the Regions; the European Ombudsman; the European Investment Bank; and the European Central Bank. For more about European institutions, visit www.europa.eu.int.

2. The European Council in Helsinki, December 1999 (http://ue.eu.int/pesc/military/es/homees.htm).

3. Meeting this objective will prove difficult as many setbacks have interfered.

4. The European Council in Nice, December 2000 (http://ue.eu.int/pesc/military/es/homees .htm).

5. Gerd Föhrenbach, in Politik un Gesellschaft Online, International Politics and Society, January 2001, www.fes.de/ipg/ipg1_2001/artfoehrenbach.htm.

6. The Transatlantic Treaty signed in Washington on April 4, 1949.

7. Javier Solana, "Reencuentro en la Era de la Globalización," *El Espectador* (Bogotá), May 12, 2002, 8-A.

8. Countries in this category have annual per capita incomes between $765 and $3,035 (U.S. dollars).

9. In 2000, European commissioner Chris Patten congratulated himself because "Latin America became the most attractive developing region in the world for foreign investment." In 2002 he had to admit that "many things have changed. Latin America has been rocked by economic and political upheaval that has put at risk the considerable progress it had made" (*El Mercurio* [Santiago de Chile], May 12, 2002).

10. According to the Subdirección de Inteligencia de Mercados–Proexport Colombia (Colombian Pro-Export Market Intelligence Subdivision) Report on Colombian Exports, January–December 2004, the European Union is the third-largest destination for Colombian exports, with increase from US$1895.9 million to US$2325.1 million in 2004, or 13.9 percent of Colombian exports worldwide. According to DANE's (Departamento Admnistrativo Nacional de Estadística) March 2000 press release, traditional Colombian exports to the EU amounted to 17.3 percent, while 67.7 percent went to the United States. Figures for nontraditional exports were 11.4 percent to the EU and 31.4 percent to the United States.

Various Latin American countries get attention from the international community for different reasons. These reasons can be of two natures: attraction or concern. On the attraction side are such factors as potential markets or many shared values, such as the primacy of democracy. Sources of concern are political instability, persistent inequality, corruption, and lack of security for citizens. The MERCOSUR countries (with the exception of Paraguay) and Chile, and increasingly, Mexico, are associated with the first group of factors, while leading the second group are countries like Colombia. This oversimplified picture, which reflects current international perceptions, is what really underlies relations between the European Union and Colombia today. (Christian Freres, *La Revista* in *El Espectador*, March 18, 2001, 39 and 40)

11. According to the Departamento Administrativo de Seguridad's (Department for Security Administration) Statistical Yearbook and the International Migration Organization (IMO), overall migration, including both Colombians and foreigners, rose from 1,662,000 in 1991 to 3,280,809 in 2000. Some 280,000 Colombians did not return to their country in 2000. Spain has been particularly affected by this phenomenon. In 2002 it was estimated that 68 percent of the 400,000 Colombians in Spain were undocumented. The negative effects of this "brain drain," the loss of individuals in whom Colombia has invested through educating them, are already being felt as national development has slowed. Civil society and the Colombian State, together with European states, should rise to the challenge and find opportunities to better conditions for those Colombians who leave, live outside the country, and would like to return. Agreements with European states receiving Colombians, re-patriation policies, providing information about conditions and opportunities available in European countries, and preventing slavery are all part of an integrated migration policy.

12. The U.S. Congress approved the Plan Colombia budget on June 20, 2000.

13. Opinion expressed by Professor Pierre Gilhodes at the March 30, 2001, Universidad Militar Nueva Granada (UMNG) conference.

14. Joaquín Roy, "The European Union and Colombia: Neither Plan Colombia Nor the Peace Process, from Good Intentions to Tremendous Frustration," University of Miami, North-South Center, Working Paper No. 11, January 2003: (www.revistainterforum.com/english/pdf_en/WP11 .pdf#search='university%20of%20miami%20north%20south%20center%20publications') (accessed August 1, 2005).

The European Union's position might also be interpreted another way: it is easier to support the peace process than commit to significant economic allocations, offer bigger and better tariff preferences for products produced in conflict zones, etc.

15. For more information about the EP's position on Plan Colombia, see, "Resolución del Parlamento Europeo sobre el Plan Colombia y el Proceso de Paz," Instituto de Estudios Geoestratégicos, Universidad Militar Nueva Granada (UMNG), 2002.

16. The European Parliament expressed its willingness to President Álvaro Uribe Vélez to support a negotiated end to the Colombian conflict and to support Colombia logistically, diplomatically, and commercially in order for the peace accord to take hold ("Parlamento europeo apoya salida negociada al conflicto," *El Colombiano*, December 3, 2002).

17. Such as the petition, "Colombia Responds," backed by sixty social organizations and NGOs, fueling the environment in which the debate over Plan Colombia unfolded on January 31, 2001, and giving rise to the resolution. The move was promoted by Eurodeputy Joaquin Miranda (IUE-IVN), president of the European Parliament's Commission on Development and Cooperation. See the European Parliament's Resolution on Plan Colombia and the Peace Process, IEG, 2002, 228.

18. Data from a study by the Centro de Pensamiento Estratégico Internacional (CEPEI), Bogotá, Colombia (www.cepei.org).

19. Government source, Office of the President of the Republic of Colombia, 2002.

20. "Common Agenda for Change in a New Colombia" was signed by the Colombian government and the FARC-EP in Machaca, Caquetá, on May 6, 1999.

21. AFP, "Añade Europa a las FARC en la lista negra"; *El País*, "Bruselas incluye a las FARC en la lista negra de grupos terroristas," June 13, 2002.

22. While the FARC-EP denounced the change in status, in a July 18, 2002, communiqué to the Secretariate of the Central Military Staff, they let it be known that, nevertheless, "they hope that in the future [as a result] of the favorable political, economic, social and cultural changes that should take place in the world, you [the European Union] might play an active part in the reconciliation process once more, with the endorsement of both parties."

23. www.altocomisionadoparalapaz.gov.co/noticias/2005/junio/jun_22_05a.htm?PHPSES-SID=7c9610f9f01b7bdfdae273a944d885f1.

24. Servicio noticioso desde Washington, "Estrategia contra las drogas 2002 busca mayor cooperación internacional," February 23, 2002.

25. Servicio noticioso desde Washington, "España apoya esfuerzos antinarcóticos andinos," May 31, 2002.

26. Ministerio de Relaciones Exteriores de Colombia, "Política Exterior de Colombia 2002–2006: Gobernabilidad Democrática, Responsabilidad Compartida y Solidaridad" (Bogotá, 2003), 15.

27. Presidencia de la República, August 30, 2002 (www.presidencia.gov.co/cne/agosto/ 30/23302002.htm).

28. "La comunidad internacional debe compartir la responsabilidad de ayudar a solucionar el conflicto de Colombia," *El Tiempo*, October 8, 2002.

29. See "La guerra en el norte del Cauca tiene a los indígenas paeces en medio de todos los fuegos," *El Tiempo*, May 11, 2005 (http://eltiempo.terra.com.co/coar/ACC_MILITARES/ accionesarmadas/ARTICULO-WEB-_NOTA_INTERIOR-2063582.html).

30. Ludger Volmer and Denis MacShane. "Colombia—el momento para un nuevo acercamiento," Oficina de Prensa y Relaciones Públicas, Embajada Británica en Colombia, March 27, 2002. Denis Macshane respondió a una pregunta sobre si creía que las reclamaciones de la guerrilla eran justas: *"No sé cómo era la cosa hace 40 años, pero hoy existen para sí mismas. Son una empresa que funciona con el mercado de la extorsión. Tienen negocios con los narcotraficantes y en realidad no manejan una propuesta política, pero son parte del problema político y deben ser lidiados políticamente."*

Chapter 9

1. In March 2005 the U.S. Department of Defense released "The National Defense Strategy of the United States of America." This important document updates the various strategic visions published since September 11, 2001, including the second *Quadrennial Defense Review* (September 2001); Nuclear Posture Review Report (December 2001); "National Strategy for Homeland Security" (July 2002); "National Security Strategy of the United States of America" (September 2002); "National Strategy to Combat Weapons of Mass Destruction" (December 2002); "National Strategy to Combat Terrorism" (February 2003); and "The National Military Strategy of the United States of America. A Strategy for Today; A Vision for Tomorrow" (December 2004). The National Defense Strategy seeks to establish general objectives that orient the activities of the Department of Defense, provide direction for military strategy, and coordinate agencies responsible for national defense.

2. It is pertinent to recall that of the thirty-nine occasions on which the United States used its armed forces in Latin America in the twentieth century, thirty-eight were in the Caribbean basin and only one in South America (Operation Blast Furnace in Bolivia in 1986). See Richard F. Grimmett, "Instances of Use of United States Armed Forces Abroad, 1789–1999," CRS Report for Congress, May 17, 1999.

3. It is important to emphasize that the Venezuelan–Colombian relationship is currently the most problematical in South America. The present worsening in relations is attributable to a structure of enmity exacerbated by multiple state and nonstate actors on both sides of the frontier in addition to the growing influence of the United States. Historically, relations between Venezuela and Colombia have been complex, but generally positive, with the exception of some disputes on maritime limits in the Gulf of Venezuela (Gulf of Coquibacoa for Colombia). This dispute did not impede a prolific bilateral commerce, rich cultural exchanges, and diplomatic collaboration at key junctures, for example during the Contadora peace process for Central America. However, in the first years of the twenty-first century relations have taken a dramatic turn for the worse. Important elements of political leadership, business groups, and security forces in both countries have taken actions (and made declarations) that seriously damage the bilateral relationship—and Washington has not seemed displeased with these developments.

During the administration of President Andrés Pastrana (1998–2002), when the Colombian government unsuccessfully sought to reach agreement with the FARC, President Chávez proclaimed Venezuelan "neutrality," creating the sensation in Bogotá that, instead of contributing to a political solution of Colombia's problems, Chávez sought to promote his Bolivarian Revolution in the neighborhood. During the government of President Álvaro Uribe (2002–2006), high-ranking government officials and well-known politicians enthusiastically supported the attempted coup against the Venezuelan president in April 2002. These actions created the conviction in Caracas that Bogotá, rather than supporting democracy in Venezuela, wished to see the ouster of Chávez. From a commercial standpoint, many of the businessmen in both countries who had stimulated binational investments began to have second thoughts on Andean integration, greatly reducing Colombian–Venezuelan economic relations from 2000 to 2003.

Colombian economic elites have looked north for a free trade agreement with the United States; some Venezuelans look south to MERCOSUR. In this sense, Colombians and Venezuelans alike have declared a de facto end to the Andean Community of Nations (though it was dying gradually thanks, in part, to the actions of the rest of its members). Each Andean country has adopted a strategy of going it alone, to Washington's pleasure, as it moves forward with its policy of divide and conquer in regard to trade.

4. Colombia's irregular war—as it has often been labeled by government, international officials, experts, and observers—has changed its nature. It has become a bloody, unprincipled war, creating a dramatic human rights nightmare. At first glance, this horror has multiple and powerful origins and lacks a clear purpose. However, it is evident that all of the armed groups—guerrillas, paramilitaries, drug traffickers, criminal gangs, armed forces, and police—have created terror among the unarmed citizenry and have expanded the conflict. The country is suffering from a degraded war, not an indefinable conflict. Success depends on new mind-sets, policies, and targets. It is Colombian society and its poor that must be the center of concern, not just the state and the wealthy. The current situation is, in part, a result of the attitudes and policies of the country's elite. Unlimited support for the present style of government in Colombia will not eliminate violence. Thus, the solution for Colombia, and the United States, lies not in continuing the same policies. Any solution will require radical innovation, not more of the same.

5. The negotiations between the Colombian government and the Revolutionary Armed Forces of Colombia that took place between January 7, 1999, and February 20, 2002, taught a number of important lessons. The entire process was in fact marked by major errors, defects, and problems, of both form and substance. The two parties were responsible for the conversations' failure. Manichean points of view—one of them supposing magnanimity on the part of the government and intractability on the part of the guerrillas, or another assuming straightforwardness from the insurgents and Washington's complete manipulation of the administration—are not conducive to understanding what happened, much less learning anything from that process.

6. If President Álvaro Uribe were to take a closer look at Argentina he would realize that Colombia's foreign policy course may be strategically incorrect. Over a decade ago Buenos Aires went down the same erroneous path when it opted for automatic alignment with the United States. Guido Di Tella, Argentina's foreign minister at the time, labeled U.S.–Argentine relations as "*carnales.*" Buenos Aires was willing to give the White House most of what it wanted. But the ties between both countries never had the same significance for the United States; it enjoyed Argentina's acquiescence without having to negotiate or concede anything in return. President Carlos Menem's (Justicialista Party) choice of international alignment with the United States was absolute and profound. Argentina sent troops to the first Iraq war of 1991. At the United Nations it voted closer to Washington than no other Argentine government had done since 1945. Argentina, more than any other Latin American nation, followed U.S. policy vis-à-vis Cuba and fully adopted the so called Washington Consensus by opening up its economy, liberalizing its financial sector, and privatizing government enterprises. Argentina's bandwagoning with the United States, which continued through the administration of President Fernando De la Rúa (Radical Party), was a remarkable failure. Argentina today is, domestically, poorer, more unequal, and deeply fragmented, and externally, weaker, more marginalized, and less influential, than three decades ago.

7. We are not including in this categorization the clandestine (Chile) and quasi-clandestine (Nicaragua) interventions implemented during the Cold War.

8. Between 1989 and 1999, Colombia received US$1.388 billion in antinarcotics and security assistance. Figures on U.S. aid to Colombia in that period can be seen in Nina M. Serafino, "Colombia: US Assistance and Current Legislation," CRS Report to Congress, June 13, 2001.

9. The growth in mercenary activity is causing serious concern in the international community. During the 1980s growing uneasiness led the United Nations to draft the Convention

against the Recruitment, Use, Financing, and Training of Mercenaries (1988). The convention entered into force in October 2001 when it was ratified by twenty-two states (Azerbaijan, Saudi Arabia, Barbados, Belarus, Cameroon, Costa Rica, Croatia, Cypress, Georgia, Italy, Libya, Maldives, Mauritania, Qatar, Senegal, Seychelles, Suriname, Togo, Turkmenistan, Ukraine, Uruguay, and Uzbekistan). None of the leading powers has signed or approved this multilateral agreement. During the 1990s, the use of mercenaries in internal conflicts was fueled by the globalization of technology; the weakening of fragile states; protracted local armed struggles (even after the East–West conflict had ended); the vilification of civil wars; and the privatization of security in industrialized and developing countries. The spread of the phenomenon has been sharp in Africa, particularly in Angola, Chad, Guinea-Bissau, Ethiopia, Eritrea, Liberia, Mozambique, the Democratic Republic of the Congo, Rwanda, Sierra Leone, Somalia, and Sudan. The experiences of Nicaragua in Latin America during the 1980s, Afghanistan in Asia, and the former Yugoslavia in Europe during the 1990s were the most traumatically violent that have involved a strong mercenary presence. Civilian and military experts and nongovernmental organizations alike have issued warnings about increasing numbers of security agencies in South Africa, England, and the United States offering private military services to companies, governments, and para-institutions. The most well-known include the South African Executive Outcomes (now disbanded), the British Sandline International, and the American Military Professional Resources Incorporated (MPRI) and DynCorp. The boom of these agencies, the nature of their ties to the states where they are established, the lack of international norms regulating this activity, and the inability to control the effects of their operations have aroused genuine alarm worldwide.

10. A review of disbursements of U.S. aid to Colombia since 1997 reveals the following (figures are in U.S. dollars): 1997, 88.6 million; 1998, 113 million; 1999, 317.6 million; 2000, 977.3 million; 2001, 248.3 million; 2002, 522.2 million; 2003, 770.2 million; and 2004, 699 million. Thus, in the period 1997–2004 U.S. aid to Colombia totaled 3,736.2 million. These figures can be seen at http://ciponline.org/colombia/.

11. Ekaterina Stepanova, *Anti-terrorism and Peace-building during and after Conflict* (Stockholm: SIPRI, 2003), 7.

12. It seems that the SOUTHCOM commander is being transformed into a proconsul in the U.S. imperial project. In Rome, the proconsuls governed colonized territories. See Juan Gabriel Tokatlian, "O momento pró-consular: A América Latina depois da reeleicao de Bush," *Política Externa*, no. 13 (March–May 2005).

13. See Juan Gabriel Tokatlian, *Globalización, narcotráfico y violencia: Siete ensayos sobre Colombia* (Bogotá: Editorial Norma, 2000).

Selected References

Government Documents

Bolivia, La Paz. "Plan Dignidad, Lucha Antidroga, 1997–2001, Progress Report," (2002) www.bolivia.gov.bo/.

———. "Plan Dignidad: Estrategia Boliviana de Lucha Contra el Narcotráfico: 1998–2002" (April 1998), www.bolivia.gov.bo/.

———. *Ley del regimen de la coca y sustancias controladas No. 1008 de 19 de Julio 1988* (July 19, 1988), www.congreso.gov.bo/leyes/1008.htm.

Departamento Nacional de Planetación, Bogotá. *Hacia un Estado Comunitario: Plan Nacional de Desarrollo, 2002–2006* (2002).

Embajada de Colombia, Washington, D.C. "Presentation by Minister of Defense Marta Lucía Ramírez, at the Center for Strategic and International Studies, Washington, D.C." (October 8, 2002), www.colombiaemb.org/.

Ministerio de Defensa, Quito. "Gestión de las Fuerzas Armadas." *Revista de las Fuerzas Armadas de Ecuador* edición 136 (August 2003), www.fuerzasarmadasecuador.org/revistaagosto2003/art.gestionfuerzasarmadas.htm.

———. *Política de la Defensa Nacional del Ecuador* (Quito: Ministerio de Defensa, 2002).

———. "El texto clave sobre el Plan Colombia." *Revista de las Fuerzas Armadas del Ecuador*, www.fuerzasarmadasecuador.org/espanol/publicaciones/revistamdndic2000/textoclavesobreplancolombia.htm.

Ministerio del Interior, Lima. "Dirección General de Inteligencia, Apreciación de Inteligencia Estratégica" (Tráfico Ilícito de Drogas y Terrorismo) (February 10, 2004).

Ministerio de Relaciones Exteriores, Quito. "Reunión de alto nivel entre los Ministros de Relaciones Exteriores, Defensa Nacional, Interior, Gobierno y Policía y Comercio Exterior de Colombia y Ecuador" (Bogotá, September 5, 2002).

Organization of American States. "Presentation of the Rapporteur of the Special Con-
    ference on Security" (December 3, 2003), http://scm.oas.org/doc_public/ENGLISH/
    HIST_03/CE00359E07.doc.

———. Inter-American Democratic Charter (Lima: Organization of American States,
    September 11, 2001), www.oas.org/charter/docs/resolution1_en_p4.htm.

"Posture Statement of General Charles E. Wilhelm, United States Marine Corps Com-
    mander in Chief, United States Southern Command." Washington, D.C.: House
    Armed Services Committee (March 23, 2000), www.house.gov/hasc/testimony/
    106thcongress/00-030-23wilhelm.htm.

"Posture Statement of Major General Gary D. Speer, United States Army, Acting Com-
    mander in Chief United States Southern Command," 107th Congress, Senate
    Armed Services Committee, 5 (March 5, 2002).

Presidencia de la República de Colombia. "Documento Oficial del Gobierno Colom-
    biano sobre el Plan Colombia" (1999), www.derechos.org/nizkor/colombia/doc/
    planof.html.

Steward, Daniel N. "Counter-Terrorism Joint Task Force: A Paradigm for Counter-
    narcotics, Document No.: M-U 41662 S849c." Newport, RI: Naval War College
    (March 16, 1993).

United Nations. "Convention against the Recruitment, Use, Financing and Training of
    Mercenaries." New York: United Nations, 1988.

United Nations Office on Drugs and Crime. "Coca Surveys in the Yungas of La Paz in
    2002" (March 2003), www.unodc.org/pdf/publications/bolivia_coca-survey_2002
    .pdf.

U.S. Agency for International Development (USAID). "Democracy and Governance"
    (June 17, 2004), www.info.usaid.gov/democracy/.

———. "USAID: Bolivia, CBJ 2005" (May 24, 2004), www.usaid.gov/policy/budget/
    cbj2005/lac/bo.html.

———. "USAID Helps Transform the Chapare; Remove Bolivia from the Drug Econ-
    omy" (May 11, 2004), www.usaid.gov/locations/latin_america_caribbean/country/
    bolivia/boliviachapare.html.

U.S. Congress, House Committee on the Budget. "Military Readiness and the Rapid
    Deployment Joint Task Force (RDJTF)," Hearings before the Committee on the
    Budget, House of Representatives, 96th Cong., 2nd sess., September 30 and October
    1, 1980." Washington, D.C.: USGPO, 1980.

U.S. Department of Defense. "A Theater Strategy of Focused Cooperation and Mutual
    Security: United States Southern Command." Washington, D.C.: USGPO, 2005.

———. "The United States Strategy for the Americas." Washington, D.C.: USGPO, 2002.

———. "Defense Ministerial of the Americas." Statement by Secretary of Defense
    Donald H. Rumsfeld, Santiago, Chile (November 19, 2002), www.defenselink.mil/
    speeches/2002/s20021119-secdef.html.

———. "Annual Report to the President and Congress." Washington, D.C.: USGPO,
    2001.

———. Quadrennial Defense Review Report. Washington, D.C.: USGPO, September 30,
    2001.

———. "The United States Security Strategy for the Americas." Washington, D.C.:
    USGPO, October 2000.

————. "Annual Report to the President and Congress." Washington, D.C.: USGPO, 1999.

————. "Hemispheric Cooperation in Combating Terrorism," presented by Secretary of Defense William S. Cohen, Defense Ministerial of the Americas III, Cartageña, Colombia, December 1, 1998.

————. *Quadrennial Defense Review Report.* Washington, D.C.: USGPO, 1997.

————. "The United States Strategy for the Americas." Washington, D.C.: USGPO, 1995.

————. "Guidance for Implementation of the President's National Drug Control Strategy" (1989).

————. "Memorandum for the Commanders of the Unified and Specified Combatant Commands, Subject: *Elevation of the Mission Priority of Counternarcotics Operations*" (1989).

U.S. Department of State. "FY 2005 Congressional Budget Justification for Foreign Operations, Western Hemisphere," www.state.gov/documents/organization/28980 .pdf.

————. "U.S. Official Outlines Progress and Challenges in Latin America," statement presented by Assistant Secretary of State Roger Noriega, July 30, 2004.

————. "U.S. Supports Democracy, Development, Counter-narcotics Efforts in Bolivia," statement presented by Deputy Director of Andean Affairs, John Creamer, May 7, 2004.

————. "U.S. Policy and the Andean Counterdrug Initiative (ACI)," Robert B. Charles, Assistant Secretary for International Narcotics and Law Enforcement Affairs, Testimony Before the House Government Reform Committee Subcommittee on Criminal Justice, Drug Policy, and Human Resources. Washington, D.C. (March 2, 2004), www.state.gov/g/inl/rls/rm/30077.htm.

————. "Remarks to the Bolivia Support Group," presented by Secretary Colin Powell (January 16, 2004), www.state.gov/secretary/rm/28250.htm.

————. "Daily Press Briefing," presented by Richard Boucher (January 15, 2004), www.state.gov/r/pa/prs/dpb/2004/28194.htm.

————. "International Narcotics Control Strategy Report—2002" (March 2003), www.state.gov/g/inl/rls/nrcrpt/2002/html/17944.htm.

————. "Patterns of Global Terrorism" (2002), www.state.gov/s/ct/rls/pgtrpt/2002/.

————. "Cooperative Hemispheric Security Architecture for the 21st Century," Ambassador Roger F. Noriega, U.S. Permanent Representative to the Organization of American States, Remarks to the Conference at the Inter-American Development Bank, Washington, D.C. (September 20, 2002), http://usinfo.state.gov/topical/pol/ arms/csbm/csbmam06.htm.

————. "Patterns of Global Terrorism, 2001" (May 21, 2002), www.state.gov/s/ct/rls/ pgtrpt, 2001.

————. "'Venezuela's Uncertain Future: Challenges for U.S. Policy,' Lino Gutierrez, Principal Deputy Assistant Secretary for Western Hemisphere Affairs Remarks to North-South Center Roundtable, Carnegie Endowment for International Peace," Washington, D.C. (April 17, 2002), www.state.gov/p/wha/rls/rm/9573.htm.

————. "U.S. Policy in the Western Hemisphere, Ambassador Lino Gutierrez, Acting Assistant Secretary, Bureau of Western Hemisphere Affairs Remarks to the United

States Conference of Catholic Bishops," Washington, D.C. (December 17, 2001), www.state.gov/p/wha/rls/rm/2001/6950.htm.

———. "U.S. Support for Plan Colombia," press release presented by Marc Grossman, Under Secretary for Political Affairs, Bogotá, Colombia (August 31, 2001), www .state.gov/p/wha/rls/rm/2001/august/4798.htm.

———. "International Narcotics Control Strategy Report: South America" (2000), www.state.gov/g/inl/rls/nrcrpt/2000/883.htm.

———. "Memorandum: Siracusa to Bernbaum; Foreign Relations of the United States, 1955–1957" (February 2, 1956).

U.S. Department of State, Office of the Secretary of State, Office of the Coordinator for Counterterrorism. "Patterns of Global Terrorism: 1992" (April 30, 1993), www .fas.org/irp/threat/terror_92/latin.html.

U.S. Drug Enforcement Agency. "Intelligence Brief: Drugs and Terrorism: A New Perspective" (September 2002), www.usdoj.gov/dea/pubs/intel/02039/02039.html.

———. "Overview—Plan Colombia/Andean Regional Initiative, DEA. Antinarcotics summary, Statement of Asa Hutchinson, Administrator, Drug Enforcement Administration before the Senate Caucus on International Narcotics Control, Executive Summary, DEA Congressional Testimony" (September 17, 2002), www.usdoj.gov/ dea/pubs/cngrtest/ct091702.html.

———. "Intelligence Brief: Changing Dynamics of Coca Production in the Andean Region" (June 2002), www.usdoj.gov/dea/pubs/intel/02033/02033.html.

———. "Donnie R. Marshall, Testimony before the House Committee on Government Reform: Subcommittee on Criminal Justice, Drug Policy and Human Resources" (March 2, 2001), www.usdoj.gov/dea/pubs/cngrtest/ct030201.htm.

U.S. Embassy, Bogotá. "Ayuda de EE.UU. a Colombia," presented by Major General Gary Speer, U.S. Army Acting Commander in Chief of the U.S. Southern Command (SOUTHCOM) before the Senate Foreign Relations Committee Subcommittee on Western Hemisphere, Peace Corps, and Narcotics Affairs (April 24 2002), http:// usembassy.state.gov/colombia/wwwsgs02.shtml.

U.S. Embassy, La Paz. "Bolivia and the Andean Trade Program," http://lapaz .usembassy.gov/atpdea/atpaeng.htm.

U.S. General Accounting Office. "Statement of Jess T. Ford, Director, Testimony before the Subcommittee on Criminal Justice, Drug Policy and Human Resources, Committee on Government Reform, House of Representatives, 'Drug Control: Challenges in Implementing Plan Colombia'" (October 12, 2000).

U.S. House Armed Services Committee. Testimony of General James T. Hill, Commander, United States Southern Command (March 24, 2004), www.house.gov/ hasc/openingstatementsandpressreleases/108thcongress/04-03-24hill.html.

U.S. National Security Council. "Strategy for Narcotics Control in the Andean Region" (June 30, 1989), www.gwu.edu/~! nsarchiv/NSAEBB/NSAEBB69/col11.pdf.

The White House. "Memorandum for the Secretary of State: SUBJECT: Presidential Determination on Waiver of Certification Under Section 3201 'Conditions on Assistance for Colombia'" (August 22, 2004).

———. "Memorandum for the Secretary of State and the Secretary of Defense: SUBJECT: Continuation of U.S. Drug Interdiction Assistance to the Government of Colombia Presidential Determination: No. 2004-42" (August 17, 2004), www .whitehouse.gov/news/releases/2004/08/20040817-8.html.

———. "Remarks by the President at Ceremony Celebrating Countries Selected for the Millennium Challenge Account" (May 10, 2004), www.whitehouse.gov/news/releases/2004/05/20040510.html.

———. "The National Security Strategy of the United States of America." Washington, D.C. (2002).

———. "Joint Counterdrug Operations." Washington, D.C.: USGPO, February 17, 1998.

———. "A National Security Strategy of Engagement and Enlargement." Washington, D.C.: USGPO, February 1996.

———. "A National Security Strategy of Engagement and Enlargement." Washington, D.C.: USGPO, July 1994.

———. "National Drug Control Strategy." Washington, D.C.: USGPO, January 1992.

———. "New National Security Policy of the United States." Washington, D.C.: USGPO, August 1991.

———. "National Security Directive 221: 'Narcotics and National Security'" (April 8, 1986), www.fas.org/irp/offdocs/nsdd/23-2766a.gif.

Books, Monographs, and Theses

Ahumada, Consuelo, and Telma Angarita, eds. *Las políticas de seguridad y sus implicaciones para la región andina.* Bogotá: Observatorio Andino, 2005.

Ahumada Beltrán, Consuelo, and Telma Angarita, eds. *Conflicto y fronteras en la región andina.* Bogotá: Observatorio Andino, 2004.

Anonymous. *Imperial Hubris: Why the West Is Losing the War on Terror.* Washington, D.C.: Brassey's Inc., 2004.

Bacevich, Andrew J. *American Empire: The Realities and Consequences of U.S. Diplomacy.* Cambridge, Mass.: Harvard University Press, 2002.

Bagley, Bruce M., ed. *Drug Trafficking Research in the Americas: An Annotated Bibliography.* Miami: North-South Center, 1997.

Bagley, Bruce M., and William O. Walker III, eds. *Drug-Trafficking in the Americas.* Coral Gables, Fla.: University of Miami, North-South Center, 1994.

Barsallo Burga, José, and Eduardo Gordillo Tordolla. *Drogas, Responsabilidad Compartida.* Lima: J.C. Editores S.A., 1988.

Bernal Cuellar, Jaime, coordinador. *Estado actual de la justicia colombiana: Diagnóstico y soluciones.* Bogotá: Universidad Externado de Colombia, 2003.

Blasier, Cole. *The Hovering Giant: U.S. Responses to Revolutionary Change in Latin America.* Pittsburgh: University of Pittsburgh Press, 1976.

Bonilla, Adrián. "National Security Decision-Making in Ecuador: The Case of the War on Drugs." PhD diss., University of Miami, 1994.

Bourantonis, Dimitris, and Jarrod Weiner. *The United Nations in the New World Order: The World Organization at Fifty.* New York: St Martin's, 1995.

Brandt, Willy. *North-South: A Programme for Survival.* London: Pan Books, 1980.

Brundtland, Gro Harlem. *Our Common Future.* London: Oxford University Press, 1987.

Bull, Hedley. *The Anarchical Society: A Study of Order in World Politics.* London: Macmillan, 1977.

Cantrell, Alvin D. "Drugs and Terror: A Threat to U.S. National Security." Carlisle Barracks, Pa.: U.S. Army War College, 1992.

Cardona C., Diego, Bernard Labatut, Stephanie Lavaux, and Ruben Sánchez D., eds. *Encrucijadas de la seguridad en Europa y las Américas.* Bogotá: Centro de Estudios Politicos e Internacionales (CEPI), 2004.

Carpenter, Ted Galen. *Bad Neighbor Policy: Washington's Futile War on Drugs in Latin America.* New York: Palgrave, 2003.

Cervo, Amado Luiz, and Clodoaldo Bueno. *História da Política Exterior do Brasil.* São Paulo: Editora Ática, 1992.

Comisión Andina de Juristas. *El control democrático de la defensa en la región andina: Escenarios para un integración civil-militar.* Lima: Comisión Andina de Juristas, 2004.

Cragin, Kim, and Bruce Hoffman. *Arms Trafficking and Colombia.* Santa Monica, Calif.: Rand National Defense Research Institute, 2003.

Crandall, Russell. *Driven by Drugs.* Boulder, Colo.: Rienner, 2002.

Deas, Malcolm. *Del poder y la gramática, y otros ensayos sobre historia, política y literatura colombiana.* Bogotá: Tercer Mundo Editores, 1993.

De Souza, Amaury. *A agenda internacional do Brasil: Um estudo sobre a comunidade brasileira de política externa.* Rio de Janeiro: Centro Brasileiro de Relações Internacionais (CEBRI), 2002.

Dewitt, David, David Haglund, and John Kirton, eds. *Building a New Global Order: Emerging Trends in International Security.* Oxford: Oxford University Press, 1993.

Dinges, John. *The Condor Years: How Pinochet and His Allies Brought Terrorism to Three Continents.* New York: The New Press, 2004.

Edwards, Sebastian. *Crisis and Reform in Latin America: From Despair to Hope.* New York: Oxford University Press, 1995.

Fernández de Soto, Guillermo. *La ilusión posible. Un testimonio sobre la política exterior colombiana.* Bogotá: Norma, 2004.

Flores, Mário César. *Bases para uma política militar.* Campinas, Brazil: Editora da Unicamp, 1992.

Franko, Patrice M. *Toward a New Security Architecture in the Americas: The Strategic Implications of the FTAA.* Washington, D.C.: Center for Strategic and International Studies, 2000.

Fucille, Alexandre. "As Forças Armadas e a temática interna no Brasil contemporâneo." Thesis, Universidade Federal de São Carlos, 1999.

Fundação Alexandre Gusmão (FUNAG). *A Palavra do Brasil nas Nações Unidas.* Brasília: FUNAG, 1995.

Gill, Lesley. *Teetering on the Rim: Global Restructuring, Daily Life, and the Armed Retreat of the Bolivian State.* New York: Columbia University Press, 2000.

Grabendorff, Wolf, ed. *La seguridad regional en las Américas.* Bogotá: Fescol, 2003.

Grindle, Merilee, and Pilar Domingo, eds. *Proclaiming Revolution: Bolivia in Comparative Perspective.* Cambridge, Mass.: David Rockefeller Center for Latin American Studies, Harvard University, 2003.

Guilhon de Albuquerque, José Augusto, org. *Sessenta Anos de Política Externa Brasileira (1930–1990),* vol. III. São Paulo: Annablume, 2001.

Hey, Jeanne. *Theories of Dependent Foreign Policy and the Case of Ecuador in the 1980s.* Athens: Ohio University Center for International Studies, 1995.

Johnson, Maxwell Orme. *The Military as an Instrument of U.S. Policy in Southwest Asia: The Rapid Deployment Joint Task Force, 1979–1982.* Boulder, Colo.: Westview, 1983.

Katzenstein, Peter J., ed. *The Culture of National Security: Norms and Identity in World Politics.* New York: Columbia University Press, 1996.

Kelly, Janet, and Carlos A. Romero. *The United States and Venezuela: Rethinking a Relationship.* New York: Routledge, 2001.

Lehman, Kenneth D. *Bolivia and the United States: A Limited Partnership.* Athens: University of Georgia Press, 1999.

Lehman, Kenneth D., and Herbert S. Klein. *A Concise History of Bolivia.* Cambridge: Cambridge University Press, 2003.

Leons, Madeline Barbara, and Harry Sanabria, eds. *Coca, Cocaine and the Bolivian Reality.* Albany: State University of New York, 1997.

Lipschutz, Ronnie. *On Security.* New York: Columbia University Press, 1995.

Loveman, Brian, and Thomas M. Davies, Jr., eds. *The Politics of Antipolitics: The Military in Latin America.* Revised and updated. Wilmington, Del.: Scholarly Resources, 1997.

Luttwak, Edward, and Stuart L Koehl. *The Dictionary of Modern War.* New York: Gramercy Books, 1991.

Malloy, James. *The Uncompleted Revolution.* Pittsburgh: University of Pittsburgh Press, 1970.

Manwaring, Max G., ed. *Security and Civil–Military Relations in the New World Disorder: The Use of Armed Forces in the Americas.* An Anthology from a Symposium cosponsored by The Chief of Staff, United States Army, The George Bush School of Government and Public Service, U.S. Army War College, September 1999.

Marcella, Gabriel, ed. *Warriors in Peacetime: The Military and Democracy in Latin America, New Directions for U.S. Policy.* London: Frank Cass, 1994.

Marcella, Gabriel, and Donald Schulz. *Colombia's Three Wars: U.S. Strategy at the Crossroads.* Carlisle, Pa.: Strategic Studies Institute, 1999.

Mayall, James. *The New Interventionism, 1991–1994.* Cambridge: Cambridge University Press, 1996.

McCormick, Gordon. *From the Sierra to the Cities: The Urban Campaign of the Shining Path.* Santa Monica, Calif.: RAND Corp., 1992.

Milet, Paz Verónica, ed. *Narcotráfico y Seguridad en América Latina y el Caribe.* Santiago: FLACSO, 1997.

Millett, Richard, and Michael Gold-Bliss, eds. *Beyond Praetorianism: The Latin American Military in Transition.* Miami: North-South Center, 1996.

Naim, Moises. *Paper Tigers and Minotaurs: The Politics of Venezuela's Economic Reforms.* Washington, D.C.: Carnegie Endowment for International Peace, 1993.

Nuñez, Joseph R. "A 21st Century Security Architecture for the Americas: Multilateral Cooperation, Liberal Peace and Soft Power." Carlisle, Pa.: Strategic Studies Institute, 2002.

Nyrere, Julius. *The Stockholm Initiative: Common Responsibility in the 1990s.* Stockholm: Prime Minister's Office, 1991.

Painter, James. *Bolivia and Coca: A Study in Dependency.* Boulder, Colo.: Rienner, 1994.

Palme, Olf. *Common Security.* New York: Simon & Schuster, 1982.

Pécault, Daniel. *Midiendo fuerzas: Balance del primer año del gobierno de Álvaro Uribe Velez.* Bogotá: Planeta, 2003.

———. *Guerra contra la sociedad.* Bogotá: Planeta, 2001.

Peters, Ralph. *Beyond Terror: Strategy in a Changing World.* Mechanicsburg, Pa.: Stackpole Books, 2002.

———. *Fighting for the Future: Will America Triumph?* Mechanicsburg, Pa.: Stackpole Books, 1999.

Record, Jeffrey. *The Rapid Deployment Force and U.S. Military Intervention in the Persian Gulf.* Cambridge, Mass.: Institute for Foreign Policy Analysis, 1981.

Richani, Nazih. *Systems of Violence: The Political Economy of War and Peace in Colombia.* Albany: State University of New York Press, 2002.

Rittberger, Volker, and Peter Mayer, eds.. *Regime Theory and International Relations.* Oxford: Clarendon Press, 1993.

Rizzo de Oliveira, Eliézer, org. *A revisão da república: Seminários.* Campinas, Brazil: Editora da Unicamp, 1994.

Schoultz, Lars. *Beneath the United States: A History of U.S. Policy toward Latin America.* Cambridge, Mass.: Harvard University Press, 1998.

Schoultz, Lars, William C. Smith, and Augusto Varas, eds. *Security, Democracy, and Development in U.S.–Latin American Relations.* Miami: North-South Center, 1994.

Smith, Peter. *Talons of the Eagle: Dynamics of U.S.–Latin American Relations.* New York: Oxford University Press, 2000.

Stepanova, Ekaterina. *Anti-terrorism and Peace-building during and after Conflict.* Stockholm: SIPRI, 2003.

Stiglitz, Joseph E. *Globalization and Its Discontents.* New York: Norton, 2002.

Téllez, Edgar, and Oscar Montes. *Diario Íntimo de un Fracaso.* Bogotá: Editora Planeta, 2002.

Tokatlian, Juan Gabriel. *Globalización, narcotráfico y violencia: Siete ensayos sobre Colombia.* Bogotá: Editorial Norma, 2000.

Valencia, León. *Adiós a la política, bienvenida la guerra. Secretos de un malogrado proceso de paz.* Bogotá: Intermedio Editores, 2002.

Williamson, John, and Pedro-Pablo Kuczynski. *After the Washington Consensus: Restarting Growth and Reform in Latin America.* Washington, D.C.: Institute for International Economics, 2003.

Articles, Chapters, Internet Reports

Abbott, Michael H., Colonel, U.S. Army, with Murl D. Munger. "U.S. Army Involvement in Counterdrug Operations—A Matter of Politics or National Security?" U.S. Army War College Military Studies Program Paper. Carlisle, Pa.: U.S. Army War College, March 30, 1988.

"An Alarm Call for Latin America's Democrats: The Latinobarometro Poll." *The Economist,* July 26, 2001.

Amatangelo, Gina. "Militarization of the U.S. Drug Control Program." *Foreign Policy in Focus,* vol. 6, no. 17 (May 2001): www.fpif.org/briefs/vol6/v6n17drugmil.html.

Amorim, Celso. "O Brasil e as Novas Dimensões da Segurança Internacional." Paper presented at the Instituto de Estudos Avançadas da USP, São Paulo, November 9, 1998.

Andreas, Peter. "Free Market Reform and Drug Market Prohibition: US Policies at Cross-Purposes in Latin America." *Third World Quarterly*, vol. 16, no. 1 (1995): 75–88.

Aravena, Francisco R. "The Rio Group and Regional Security in Latin America." In *Regional Mechanisms and International Security in Latin America*, ed. Olga Pellicer, 112–29. Tokyo: United Nations University Press, 1998.

Arcos, Carlos, Fernando Carrión, and Edison Palomeque. "Violencia para el Bid." Quito: FLACSO, 2001.

Arnson, Cynthia. "The Peace Process in Colombia and U.S. Policy." Paper presented at the Conference on "Democracy, Human Rights, and Peace in Colombia," University of Notre Dame, Helen Kellog Institute for International Studies, March 26–27, 2001, 5–12.

Asheshov, Nicholas. "Bolivia's New Generation Takes Over the Helm." *Wall Street Journal*, June 11, 1993.

Baker, Pauline, and John Ausink. "State Collapse and Ethnic Violence: Toward a Predictive Model." *Parameters: US Army War College Quarterly*, vol. XXVI (January 1996): 19–31.

Baldwin, Katherine. "Brazil Army Kills Colombia Rebels." *Reuters*, March 6, 2002.

Berdal, Mats, and David Keen. "Violence and Economic Agendas in Civil Wars: Some Policy Implications." *Millennium: Journal of International Studies*, vol. 26, no. 3 (1997): 795–818.

Bernal-Meza, Raúl. "A política exterior do Brasil: 1990–2002." *Revista Brasileira de Política Exterior*, vol. 45, no. 1 (2002): 36–71.

Bitencourt, Luis. "The Importance of the Amazon Basin in Brazil's Evolving Security Agenda." In *Environment and Security in the Amazon Basin*, ed. Joseph Tulchin and Heather Golding, 53–74. Washington, D.C.: Woodrow Wilson International Center, 2002.

Bonilla, Adrián, "Alcances de la Autonomía en la Hegemonía en la Política Exterior Ecuatoriana." In *Orfeo en el Infierno. Una Agenda de Política Exterior Ecuatoriana*, ed. Adrián Bonilla, 11–46. Quito: FLACSO-CAF-Academia Diplomática, 2002.

———. "Las Fuerzas Armadas ecuatorianas y su contexto político." Presentation made at the Semana Iberoamericana sobre Paz, Seguridad y Defensa at the Instituto Gutiérrez Mellado, Madrid, June 2002.

———. "Multilateralismo en la Región Andina." In *Democracia de Cumbres*, ed. Francisco Rojas. Caracas: FLACSO-Academia Diplomática Mexicana, Nueva Sociedad, 2000.

———. "Estados Unidos y Educador." In *Estados Unidos y los países Andinos, 1993–1997: Poder y desintigración*, ed. Andrés Franco. Bogotá: CEJA, 1998.

Brewer, Berry L. "United States Security Assistance Training of Latin American Militaries: Intentions and Results." Wright Patterson Air Force Base, Ohio, September 1995: www.benning.army.mil/usarsa/main.htm.

Burbano de Lara, Felipe. "Democracia, cultura política y gobernabilidad. Los estudios políticos en los años 90." In *Democracia, gobernabilidad y cultura política*, ed. Felipe Burbano de Lara, 31–36. Quito: FLACSO, 2003.

Camacho, Álvaro. "La policía colombiana. Los recorridos de una reforma." *Análisis Político*, no. 41 (September–December 2000): 106–26 (http://168.96.200.17/ar/libros/colombia/assets/own/analisis%20politico%2041.pdf).

Campos Mello, Flávia de. "Política Externa Brasileira e os blocos internacionais." *São Paulo em Perspectiva*, vol. 16, no. 1 (2002): 37–43.

Cannabrava, Ivan. "O Brasil e as Operações de Manutenção da Paz." *Política Externa*, vol. 5, no. 3 (December 1996): 93–105.

Casas, Cenovia. "Chávez: Las relaciones con EEUU están condenadas a ser buenas." *El Nacional* (Caracas), November 7, 2000.

Cepik, Marco. "Brasil y El Plan Colombia: Notas Sobre Ajenamiento y Diplomacia Presidencial, Seminário América Latina y El Plan Colombia: Estabilidad o Crisis?" Caracas, Universidad Central Venezuelana, May 29–30, 2002.

Cervo, Amado Luiz. "Relações internacionais do Brasil: um balanço da era Cardoso." *Revista Brasileira de Política Internacional*, vol. 45, no. 1 (2002): 5–35.

Collier, Paul, and Anke Hoeffler. "Greed and Grievance in Civil War." Washington, D.C.: The World Bank, 2001 (www.worldbank.org/research/conflict/papers/greed grievance_23oct.pdf).

Collier, Paul, Anke Hoeffler, and Mans Soderbom. "On the Duration of Civil War." Washington, D.C.: The World Bank, Development Research Group, 1999.

Dávila, Andrés. "Relaciones civiles-militares en Colombia: Pautas de negociación y de subordinación en contextos desfavorables." Paper presented at the Seminario Internacional "Las Fuerzas Armadas en la región andina, ¿no deliberantes o actores políticos?" Lima, Comisión Andina de Juristas, August 9–10, 2001.

De Young, Karen. "Bush Officials Defend Their Actions on Venezuela." *The Washington Post*, April 18, 2002.

Dominguez, Jorge. "The Future of Inter-American Relations." Working Paper. Washington, D.C.: Inter-American Dialogue, 1999.

Donnelly, Thomas. "Rebuilding America's Defenses: Strategy, Forces and Resources for a New Century." A Report of the Project for a New American Century, 2000 (www .newamericancentury.org/RebuildingAmericasDefenses.pdf).

Donohue, Mary, and Melissa Nepomiachi. "Washington Secures Long-Sought Hemispheric Outpost, Perhaps at the Expense of Regional Sovereignty." Council on Hemispheric Affairs (COHA), Washington, D.C., July 20, 2005.

Downes, Richard. "Poder militar y guerra ambigua: El reto de Colombia en el siglo XXI." *Análisis Político*, no. 36 (1999): 69–81.

Doyle, Michael, and Nicholas Sambanis. "International Peacebuilding: A Theoretical and Quantitative Analysis." *American Political Science Review*, vol. 94, no. 4 (2000): 779–801.

Dunn, Lewis. "On Proliferation Watch: Some Reflections on the Past Quarter Century." *The Non-Proliferation Review*, vol. 5, no. 3 (Spring–Summer 1998).

Dupuy, Pierre-Marie. "Une évolution en quatre phases." *Défense Nationale*, no. 3 (2000).

Evans, Michael L., ed. "Shoot Down in Peru—The Secret U.S. Debate over Intelligence Sharing in Peru and Colombia." National Security Archive, George Washington University, April 23, 2001 (www.gwu.edu/~nsarchiv/NSAEBB/NSAEBB44/).

———. "U.S. Drug Policy & Intelligence Operations in the Andes." *Foreign Policy in Focus*, vol. 6, no. 22 (2001).

Faiola, Anthony. "U.S. Role in Coca War Draws Fire." *Washington Post*, June 23, 2002.

———. "In Bolivia's Drug War, Success Has a Price." *Washington Post*, March 4, 2001.

Faiola, Anthony, and Douglas Farah. "Newly Elected Ex-Dictator Vows to Wage War on Drugs in Bolivia." *Washington Post*, August 4, 1997.

Farah, Douglas. "Aircraft Compromise Lifts Freeze on Anti-Drug Aid to Latin America." *Washington Post*, June 26, 1998.

Fearon, James, and David Laitin. "Ethnicity, Insurgency, and Civil War." *American Political Science Review*, vol. 97, no. 1 (2003): 75–90.

Finnegan, William. "Leasing the Rain." *The New Yorker*, March 8, 2002.

Fishel, John T., Lt. Col., USAR. "Developing a Drug War Strategy, Lessons Learned from Operation Blast Furnace." *Military Review*, vol. 139, no. 15 (October 11, 1993): 61–69.

Fonseca, Gelson. "Aspectos da Multipolaridade Contemporânea." *Contexto Internacional*, no. 11 (January–June 1990).

Forero, Juan. "Hide-and-Seek among the Coca Leaves." *New York Times*, June 9, 2004.

———. "From Llama Trails to the Corridors of Power." *New York Times*, July 6, 2002.

Frechette, Myles. "In Search of the Endgame: A Long-Term Multilateral Strategy for Colombia." *The North-South Agenda Papers*, no. 62 (2003).

Gamarra, Eduardo. "The Offspring of 1952: Poverty, Exclusion, and the Promise of Popular Participation." In *Proclaiming Revolution: Bolivia in Comparative Perspective*, ed. Merilee Grindle and Pilas Domingo, 345–63. London: Institute of Latin American Studies, 2003.

———. "Political Parties Since 1964: Construction of Bolivia's Multiparty System." In *Proclaiming Revolution: Bolivia in Comparative Perspective*, ed. Merilee Grindle and Pilar Domingo, 289–317. London: Institute of Latin American Studies, 2003.

———. "Has Bolivia Won the War? Lessons from Plan Dignidad." Draft paper, Latin American and Caribbean Center, Department of Political Science, Florida International University, April 2002 (http://lacc.fiu.edu/research_publications/working_papers/working_paper_01.pdf).

———. "La crisis andina y la política de los Estados Unidos." *Foreign Affairs en Español*, Edición Especial (December 2000): 112–19.

———. "U.S.–Bolivia Counternarcotics Efforts during the Paz Zamora Administration." In *Drug-Trafficking in the Americas*, ed. Bruce M. Bagley and William O. Walker III, 217–58. Coral Gables, Fla.: University of Miami, North-South Center, 1994.

García, Andelfo. "Plan Colombia y ayuda estadounidense. Una fusión traumática." In IEPRI, *El Plan Colombia y la internacionalización del conflicto*. Bogotá: Editorial Planeta Colombiana, 2001.

Gentleman, Judith A. "The Regional Security Crisis in the Andes: Patterns of State Response." June 2001 (http://carlisle-www.army.mil/usassi/ssipubs/pubs2001/andes/andes.pdf).

Gil Savastano, Laura. "La Mediación de la ONU: Expectativas, Probabilidades Y Riesgos." *Analisis Politico*, no. 47 (2002): 77–85.

Gleditsch, Nil Petter, et al. "Armed Conflict 1946–2001: A New Dataset." *Journal of Peace Research*, vol. 39, no. 5 (2002): 615–37.

Gonzáles del Rio Vigil, Miguel. "Problemática Relacionada a la Sustitución de los Cultivos de la Hoja de Coca," in Escuela Superior de Guerra Naval, Serie Editorial Conferencias Magistrales, Callao, 1992.

Grossman, Marc. "Joining Efforts for Colombia." Paper presented by the Undersecretary for Political Affairs, U.S. Department of State, at Georgetown University, June 24, 2002.

Guedes da Costa, Thomaz. "Brazil's SIVAM: As It Monitors the Amazon, Will It Fulfill Its Human Security Promise?" *ECSP Report*, no. 7. Washington, D.C.: Woodrow Wilson International Center for Scholars, 2002 (wwics.si.edu/topics/pubs/ECSP7-featurearticles-4.pdf).

Hall, Kevin G. "Coca Growers Resist Drug Troops." *Miami Herald*, February 10, 2004.

Hoag, Christian. "Chávez Rebuts U.S. Official, Denies Link to Violent Groups." *Miami Herald*, December 8, 2000.

Hoffmann, Stanley. "Clash of Globalizations." *Foreign Affairs* (July/August 2002).

Hunter, Wendy. "The Brazilian Military after the Cold War: in Search of a Mission." *Studies in Comparative International Development*, vol. 28, no. 4 (Winter 1994): 31–49.

International Crisis Group. "Colombia y sus vecinos: Los tentáculos de la inestabilidad." *Informe América Latina*, no. 3 (2003).

Isacson, Adam. "After Plan Colombia: Why Doesn't Washington Learn from Failure in Colombia?" *Focal Point. Spotlight on the Americas*, vol. 1, no. 5 (December 2002) (www.focal.ca/fpoint/focalpoint_dec02.pdf).

Isacson, Adam, and Joy Olson. "Just the Facts: A Quick Tour of U.S. Defense and Security Assistance to Latin America and the Caribbean." *International Policy Report*, December 1998, 4–5.

Jeter, Jon. "A Smoother Road to Free Markets." *Washington Post*, January 21, 2004.

Johnson, Tim. "Colombian Rebel Groups seen as Regional Danger." *Miami Herald*, September 18, 2002.

———. "Bush: U.S. at No Time Supported Overthrow." *Miami Herald*, April 19, 2002.

———. "Chávez Condemns Bombings by U.S." *Miami Herald*, October 31, 2001.

Johnson, Tim, and Andrés Oppenheimer. "Tensions Rise between Colombia, Venezuela." *Miami Herald*, July 24, 1999.

Klein, Herbert. "Social Change in Bolivia since 1952." In *Proclaiming Revolution: Bolivia in Comparative Perspective*, ed. Merilee Grindle and Pilar Domingo, 232–58. London: Institute of Latin American Studies, 2003.

Koucheravy, Richard J., Major, U.S. Army, "The United States Military and Plan Colombia: A Direct Combat Role? Combat Forces and the U.S. Role in Plan Colombia." Fort Leavenworth, Kans.: School of Advanced Military Studies, 2001, 30.

Kralev, Nicholas. "United States Recalls Emissary to Venezuela." *Washington Times*, November 3, 2001.

Krauss, Clifford. "A Bolivian Legislator Who Just Says 'Yes' to Coca." *New York Times*, June 13, 1998.

Lamazière, Georges. "O impacto das processos de integraçao regional nas políticas de defesa a seguranço: o Brasil e a Cooperação político-militar na América do Sul." *Política Externa*, no. 4 (March–May 2001): 42–48.

Lampreia, Luiz Felipe. "O Brasil e o Mundo no Século XXI: Uma Visão do Itamaraty." *Política Externa*, vol. 5, no. 3 (December 1996).

Langman, Jimmy. "Bolivia's Protests of Hope." *The Nation*, October 22, 2003 (www.thenation.com/docpring.mhtml?i=20031103&s=langman).

Laserna, Roberto. "Bolivia: Entre populismo y democracia." *Nueva Sociedad*, no. 188 (November–December 2003) (www.nuevasoc.org.ve/upload/articulos/3155_1.pdf).

———. "La Crisis del Octubre y el Fracaso del Ch'enko." *Anuario Social y Político de América Latina y el Caribe*, vol. 7 (2003) (www.geocities.com/laserna_r/bolivia-heterogenea5.pdf).

———. "Bolivia, the Beleaguered Democracy, 2003" (www.geocities.com/laserna_r/).

Lear, Joseph C. "School of the Americas and U.S. Foreign Policy Attainment in Latin America." Information paper, School of the Americas, January 1996 (www.benning .army.mil/usara/ACADEMIC/leru.htm).

Le Billon, Philippe. "The Political Ecology of War: Natural Resources and Armed Conflicts." *Political Geography*, vol. 20, no. 5 (2001): 561–84.

———. "The Political Economy of War: What Relief Agencies Need to Know." *HPG Report*, no. 1 (2001).

Lehman, Kenneth D. "Revolutions and Attributions: Making Sense of Eisenhower Administration Policies in Bolivia and Guatemala." *Diplomatic History*, vol. 21, no. 2 (1997): 185–213.

Lindsay-Poland, John. "U.S. Military Bases in the Latin America and the Caribbean." *Foreign Policy in Focus*, vol. 9, no. 3 (August 2004) (www.fpif.org/briefs/vol9/ v9n03latammil.html).

———. "U.S. Military Bases in Latin America and the Caribbean." *Foreign Policy in Focus*, vol. 6, no. 35 (2001) (www.fpif.org/fpiftxt/1356).

Llorente, María Victoria. "Perfil de la Policía Colombiana." In *Reconocer la guerra para construir la paz*, ed. Malcolm Deas and María Victoria Llorente. Bogotá: Uniandes-CEREC-Norma, 1999.

Lowethal, Abraham. "Los Estados Unidos y América Latina después del 11 de septiembre." *Diplomacia*, no. 89 (October–December 2001): 73–76.

Magela da Cruz Quintão, Geraldo. "Projeto SIVAM e a integração com os países vizinhos." *Carta Internacional*, no. 116 (October 2002).

Manwaring, Max G. "The Strategic Effects of the Conflict with Iraq: Latin America." Carlisle, Pa.: Strategic Studies Institute, U.S. Army War College, March 2003.

———. "U.S. Security Policy in the Western Hemisphere: Why Colombia, Why Now, and What Is To Be Done?" (June 2001) (http://carlisle-www.army.mil/usassi/ ssipubs/pubs2001/westhem/westhem.pdf).

———. "Latin American Security and Civil-Military Relations in the New World Disorder." *Low Intensity Conflict & Law Enforcement*, vol. 4, no. 1 (Summer 1995): 29–43.

Marcella, Gabriel. "Plan Colombia: The Strategic and Operational Imperatives." In *Implementing Plan Colombia*. Carlisle, Pa.: Strategic Studies Institute, 2001.

———. "The United States and Colombia: The Journey from Ambiguity to Strategic Clarity." Carlisle, Pa.: Strategic Studies Institute, 2003.

Marquis, Christopher. "Bush Administration Met with Venezuelans Who Ousted Leader." *New York Times*, April 16, 2002.

Martins Filho, João Roberto. "The Brazilian Armed Forces after the Cold War: Overcoming the Identity Crisis." Paper presented at the LASA Congress, Chicago, September 1998.

Mason, Ann. "La crisis de seguridad en Colombia: Causas y consecuencias internacionales de un Estado en vía de fracaso." *Colombia Internacional*, nos. 49–50 (2001): 82–102.

McClintock, Cynthia. "The War on Drugs: The Peruvian Case." *Journal of Interamerican Studies and World Affairs*, vol. 30, no. 2 & 3 (Summer/Fall 1988): 127–42.

McSherry, J Patrice. "Analyzing Operation Condor: A Covert Inter-American Structure." Paper presented at the XXII International Congress of Latin American Studies Association (LASA), Miami, March 2000.

———. "Operation Condor: Clandestine Interamerican System." *Social Justice*, vol. 26, no. 4 (Winter 1999): 144–74.

Mendel, William. "Counterdrug Strategy—Illusive Victory: From Blast Furnace to Green Sweep." *Military Review*, vol. 72 (December 12, 1992): 74–87.

Millet, Richard. "Colombia's Conflicts: The Spillover Effects of a Wider War." *North-South Center Agenda Papers*, no. 57 (2002).

National Law Center for Inter-American Free Trade. "Commentary on the *Ley del regimen de la coca y sustancias controladas.*" *Interam Data Base*, vol. 6, no. 3–4 (1995): 278–94.

Novak, Robert. "Bolivia's Drug Crisis." January 15, 2004 (www.cnn.com/2004/ALLPOLITICS/01/06/column.novak.opinion.bolivia/).

Nuñez, Joseph R. "Homeland and Hemisphere." *Christian Science Monitor*, December 20, 2001 (www.csmonitor.com/2001/1220/p9s1-coop.html).

———. "Fighting the Hobbesian Trinity in Colombia: A New Strategy for Peace." February 2001 (www.carlisle.army.mil/usassi/ssipubs/pubs2001/trinity/trinity.htm).

Oppenheimer, Andrés. "Bolivia an Example of a Nation That Needs Lots of Help to Survive." *Miami Herald*, June 10, 2004.

———. "General: Islamists Find Latin America Funds." *Miami Herald*, March 9, 2003.

———. "Chávez Need Only Listen to His Neighbors." *Miami Herald*, December 10, 2000.

———. "Neighbors Say Chávez Aids Violent Groups." *Miami Herald*, December 5, 2000.

———. "Las bofetadas de Chávez a Estados Unidos." *El Nuevo Heraldo*, October 30, 2000.

———. "Is Chávez Picking a Fight with U.S.?" *Miami Herald*, October 29, 2000, 6-A.

Ortúzar, Ximena. "Adviertan sindicatos al nuevo presidente: 'Si nos valla tambien lo vamos a tumbar.'" *La Jornada de Mexico*, October 19, 2003.

Passaje, David. "The United States and Colombia: Untying the Gordian Knot." *The Letort Papers*. Carlisle, Pa.: Strategic Studies Institute, 2000.

Pereira da Silva, Roberto. "Brasil—Geopolítica e Destino." *Parcerias Estratégicas*, vol. 1, no. 2 (December 1996).

Pérez, Orlando J. "*Chavismo* and the Transformation of Civil–Military Relations in Venezuela." *South Eastern Latinamericanist*, vol. XLVI, no. 1–2 (Summer 2002): 12–33.

Piscoya, Luís. "Evaluación de la Crisis de los Agricultores Cocaleros en el Perú: Implicancia para los Intereses de Seguridad." In *Elementos de Seguridad y Defensa, Vol. II*, ed. Enrique Obando, 119–52. Lima: IDEPE, 2003.

Rangel Suárez, Alfredo. "Parasites and Predators: Guerrillas and the Insurrection Economy of Colombia." *Journal of International Affairs: Shadow Economies: Promoting Prosperity or Undermining Security*, vol. 53, no. 2 (Spring 2000): 577–602.

———. "Colombia: La guerra irregular en el fin de siglo." *Análisis Político*, no. 28 (May–August 1996).

Ramírez, Socorro. "La internacionalización del conflicto y de la paz en Colombia." In *El Plan Colombia y la internacionalización del conflicto*, ed. Luis Alberto Restrepo et al., 103–14. Bogotá: Planeta, 2001.

Ramsey, Russell W. "The Democratic Sustainment Course at the U.S. Army School of the Americas." July 1999.

———. "Forty Years of Human Rights Training." *Journal of Low Intensity Conflict & Law Enforcement*, vol. 4, no. 2 (Autumn 1995): 254–70.

———. "U.S. Strategy for Latin America." *Parameters*, Autumn 1994, 70–83.

———. "A Military Turn of Mind: Educating Latin American Officers." *Military Review* 73 (August 1993): 10–17.

———. "U.S. Military Courses for Latin Americans Are a Low-Budget Strategic Success." *North-South, the Magazine of the Americas*, 2 (February–March 1993): 38–41.

Renner, Michael. "The Anatomy of Resource Wars." *Worldwatch Paper*, no. 162 (2002).

Richani, Nazih. *The Political Economy of Violence: The War System in Colombia*. Albany: State University of New York Press, 2002.

Riedmann, Arnold. "La reforma policial en Colombia." In *Justicia en la Calle: Ensayos sobre la policía en América Latina*, ed. Peter Waldmann, 215–39. Medellín: Konrad Adenauer Stiftung-Ciedla-ISLA-Biblioteca Jurídica Diké, 1996.

Robles, Frances. "Embassy Didn't Guide Military during Bolivian Protests," *Miami Herald*, October 21, 2003.

Rohter, Larry. "Bolivian Leader's Ouster Seen as Warning on U.S. Drug Policy." *New York Times*, October 23, 2003.

———. "Latest Battleground in Latin Drug War: Brazilian Amazon." *New York Times*, October 30, 2000, A-1.

———. "Bolivian Peasant's Ideology of Fury Still Smolders." *New York Times*, October 20, 2000.

Romero, Carlos A. "Las Relaciones entre Venezuela y Estados Unidos: Realidad Histórica u Opción Política?" *Política Internacional*, vol. I, no. 2 (April–June 1986): 11–14.

Rotberg, Robert. "Failed States in a World of Terror." *Foreign Affairs*, vol. 81, no. 4 (July/August 2002): 127–40.

Roy, Joaquin. "European Perceptions of Plan Colombia: A Virtual Contribution to a Virtual Peace Plan?" In *Implementing Plan Colombia*. Carlisle, Pa.: Strategic Studies Institute, 2001.

Sachs, Jeffrey D. "The FP Memo: How to Run the International Monetary Fund." *Foreign Policy*, July–August 2004 (www.foreignpolicy.com/story/cms.php?story_id=2565&page=0).

———. "Another U.S. Foreign-Policy Failure." *Miami Herald*, October 30, 2003.

———. "A World for Which Bush Cares Little." *Financial Times*, April 9, 2003.

———. "Weapons of Mass Salvation." *The Economist*, October 24, 2002.

———. "What's Good for the Poor Is Good for America." *The Economist*, July 12, 2001.

———. "Jeffrey Sachs on the Challenges of Development." Paper presented to the International Development Research Centre, June 19, 2001 (http://web.idre.ca/en/ev-25642-201-1-DO_TOPIC.html).

Sánchez, Fabiola. "Vicepresidente Venezolana arremete contra los EU." *El Nuevo Herald*, November 10, 2001.

Sánchez, Marcela. "Bolivia Seeks Underdog Victory in Contest for U.S. Aid." *Washington Post*, May 13, 2004.

Schoultz, Lars. "U.S. Values and Approaches to Hemispheric Security Issues." In *Security, Democracy and Development in U.S. Latin American Relations*, ed. Lars Schoultz, William C. Smith, and Augusto Varas, 33–58. Miami: North-South Center, University of Miami, 1994.

Schuller, Jeffrey G. "The Military's Role in the Drug War: To Just Say No Is Not Enough!" Newport, R.I.: Naval War College, 1989.

Schultz, Jim. "Bolivia's Pipeline Dreams." *New York Times*, July 17, 2004.

———. "Behind Bolivia's Gas War." *Pacific News Service*, October 17, 2003.

Schulz, Donald E. "The Role of the Armed Forces in the Americas: Civil Military Relations for the 21st Century." Strategic Studies Institute, April 1998.

Scrutton, Alistair. "Now Comes the Hard Part for Bolivia's Leaders." *Reuters News Wire*, July 19, 2004.

Serafino, Nina M. "Colombia: US Assistance and Current Legislation." *CRS Report to Congress*, June 13, 2001.

Soares de Lima, Maria Regina. "Brazil's Alternative Vision." In *The Americas in Transition: The Contours of Regionalism*, ed. Gordon Mace and Louis Bélanger, 133–52. Boulder, Colo.: Rienner, 1999.

Soto, Gioconda. "La CIA siguió los pasos de alto funcionario de la Cancillería." *El Nacional* (Caracas), February 3, 2001.

———. "Las FFAA de Colombia son el fuente de armas." *El Nacional* (Caracas), August 21, 1999.

———. "No habrá marcha atrás en materia de sobrevuelos." *El Nacional* (Caracas), June 1, 1999.

Soutello Alvez, Lauro. "O Brasil e as Operações de Paz da ONU." *Carta Internacional*, no. 37 (March 1996).

Tamayo, Juan O. "U.S. Is Wary of Chávez's Cuba Ties." *Miami Herald*, June 10, 2001.

Tate, Winifred. "No Room for Peace? United States' Policy in Colombia." *Accord* (2004), special issue on Colombia's Peace Processes (www.cr.org/accord/col/accord14/noroomforpeace.shtml).

Tokatlian, Juan. "Colombia, el Plan Colombia y la región Andina Implosión o Concertación." *Nueva Sociedad*, no. 173 (May–June 2001): 127–43.

———. "Guerra interna, injerencia externa." *Desafíos*, no. 1 (1999).

———. "Colombia en guerra: las diplomacias por la paz." *Desarrollo Económico*. Buenos Aires, vol. 155 (October–December 1999): 339–60.

Tulchin, Joseph, "Redefinición de la Seguridad Nacional en el Hemisferio Occidental. La función del multilateralismo." In *Diplomacia de Cumbres*, ed. Francisco Rojas, 19–33. Santiago: FLACSO Chile, 1996.

Ullman, Richard. "Redefining Security." *International Security*, vol. 8, no. 1 (Summer 1983): 129–53.

"Unprecedented Power, Colliding Ambitions." *The Economist*, vol. 150, no. 3 (September 26, 2002).

Vaicius, Ingrid. "El Plan Colombia: El Debate en los Estados Unidos." *International Policy Report*, August 2000 (www.ciponline.org/colombia/aid/ipr0800/ipr0800.htm).

Vaicius, Ingrid, and Adam Isacson. "The 'War on Drugs' Meets the 'War on Terror.'" *International Policy Report*. Washington, D.C., 2003.

Vásquez, Ian. "Washington's Dubious Crusade for Hemispheric Democracy." *Cato Policy Analysis*, no. 201 (January 12, 1994) (www.cato.org/pubs/pas/pa-201.html).

Verification Mission Report, "Impactos en Ecuador de las fumigaciones realizadas en Putumayo dentro del Plan Colombia." Quito: Acción Ecológica, ALDHU, Asociación Americana de Juristas, CEDHU, Ecociencia, INREDH, Laboratorio de Suelos LABSU, RAPAL, SERPAJ, Acción Creativa, Comité Andino de Servicios, October 2002.

Vigna, Edélcio. "O quê o congresso nacional pensa sobre o plano Colômbia." In *Plano Colômbia perspectivas do parlamento brasileiro, pesquisa INESC.* Brasília, 2002, 41–50.

Wallensteen, Peter, and Margareta Sollenberg. "Armed Conflict, 1989–2000." *Journal of Peace Research,* vol. 38, no. 5 (2001): 629–44.

Walter, Barbara. "The Critical Barrier to Civil War Settlement." *International Organization,* vol. 51, no. 3 (1997): 335–64.

Webb, Patrick F. "Narcoterrorism: A Threat to the United States." USAWC Military Studies Program Paper. Carlisle Barracks, Pa.: U.S. Army War College, 1992.

Webb-Vidal, Andy. "Venezuelan Guns Aiding Guerrillas." *Financial Times,* January 25, 2001.

Weiner, Tim. "A Coup by Any Other Name." *New York Times,* April 12, 2002.

Wilson, Scott. "Chávez Turns Caracas from U.S. Ally to Critic." *Washington Post,* November 22, 2001.

———. "Venezuela and Colombia Square Off over Rebels." *Washington Post,* March 17, 2001, A16.

Zackrison, James, and Eileen Bradley. "Colombian Sovereignty under Siege." *Strategic Forum,* no. 12. Washington, D.C.: National Defense University, 1997.

Zartman, William. "The Unfinished Agenda: Negotiating Internal Conflicts." In *Stopping the Killing: How Civil Wars End,* ed. Roy Licklider, 20–36. New York: New York University Press, 1993.

Zepeda, Alexis. "Sánchez de Lozada Addresses Packed Auditorium." *Reflections/Reflejos,* Fall 2002. Washington, D.C.: Center for Latin American Studies, Georgetown University (www.georgetown.edu/sfs/programs/clas/fall02Reflejos.pdf).

Internet

Agencia de Noticias de MERCOSUR. "Ministro Argentino Advierte Libanización de Bolivia," June 25, 2004 (www.apfmercosur.com.ar/despachos.asp?cod_des=24108).

Alexander's Gas & Oil Connections. "Enron Keeps Role in Bolivian Pipeline Project." *Company News: Latin America,* vol. 7, no. 14 (July 12, 2002) (www.gasandoil.com/goc/company/cnl22892.htm).

Amazon Watch # 181. "Enron/Shell Cuiaba Gas Pipeline," July 2000 (www.amazonwatch.org/amazon/BO/cuiaba/).

Andean Information Network. "Chapare Coca Growers Resist Eradication," September 2, 2002 (www.nadir.org/nadir/initiativ/agp/free/imf/bolivia/txt/2002/0902chapare_growers.htm).

"Andean Trade Promotion and Drug Eradication Act." Organization of American States, 1991 (www.sice.oas.org/Trade/tradeact/act10.asp).

"Canciller destaca esfuerzos por controlar la frontera." *El Comercio* (Quito), May 28, 2002 (www.elcomercio.com/).

Carrie Callaghan. "La ayuda militar estadounidense para el Ecuador." Observatorio Internacional para la Paz, 2003 (www.oipaz.or.ec).

Center for International Development at Harvard University. "Washington Consensus." Global Trade Negotiations Home Page, April 2003 (www.cid.harvard.edu/cidtrade/issues/washington.html).

Center for International Policy. "U.S. Security Assistance to the Andean Region, 2000–2001," August 25, 2002 (www.ciponline.org/facts/co01.htm).

———. "Counter-Drug Radar Sites," August 18, 2002 (http://ciponline.org/facts/radar.htm).

Ceresole, Norberto. "El modelo venezolano o la posdemocracia: Caudillo, apóstoles, pueblo." *El Universal Digital*, January 11, 1999 (http://politica.eud.com/1999/03/08/ceresole.html).

"Colombia's Elusive Quest for Peace." International Crisis Group, March 26, 2002 (www.crisisweb.org//library/documents/report_archive/A400594_26032002.pdf).

"Colombia to Reinforce Borders, Ecuador Says." Reuters Foundation, Alertnet, March 18, 2003 (www.alertnet.org/thenews/newsdesk/N17106959.htm).

"Consenso de Guayaquil sobre integración, seguridad e infraestructura para el desarrollo," October 10, 2002 (www.cumbresur.com/novedades/).

"Crean primera brigada de frontera en límite con Venezuela." *El Tiempo*, June 18, 2004 (http://eltiempo.terra.com.co/coar/ACC_MILITARES/accionesarmadas/ARTICULO-WEB-_NOTA_INTERIOR-1713827.html).

CRS Regional Report for Congress. "Andean Regional Initiative (ARI) FY 2003 Supplemental and FY 2004 Assistance for Colombia and Neighbors," August 27, 2003 (http://fpc.state.gov/documents/organization/24044.pdf).

"Cúpula militar en encuentro con Jefe del Comando Sur." *El Universo* (Guayaquil), March 18, 2003 (www.eluniverso.com/core4/eluniverso.asp?edicion=1&page=noticia&id=787&tab=1&contid=5FD05B52819847E89A6AE125E44DDF12).

Dangl, Benjamin. "Evo Morales: After 50 Years of Resistance, We Are Taking Power," December 3, 2004 (www.greenleft.org.au/back/2003/564/564p16.htm).

"Dos posiciones sobre el conflicto en Colombia." *El Comercio* (Quito), July 27, 2002 (www.elcomercio.com/).

"Ecuador's Noboa Assumes Power after Coup: Increasingly Unpopular President Ousted in Military Takeover." CNN.com, January 22, 2000 (www.cnn.com/2000/WORLD/americas/01/22/ecuador.04/).

Edwards, Sandra. "Colombian Conflict Impacts Ecuador." Washington Office on Latin America, 2002 (www.wola.org/d&d_ecuador_update.htmp.p4).

"EEUU aumentará ayuda a Ecuador en más de 100 millones." Agencia Hinhua, September 2003 (http://fpspa.peopledaily.com.cn/200302/13/sp20030213_61518.html).

"Diálogo El foro militar de las Américas" (www.allenwayne.com/dialogo/).

Ellner, Steve, and Fred Rosen. "Venezuela's Failed Coup, the U.S.' Role and the Future of Hugo Chávez." *Foreign Policy in Focus*, June 2002 (www.foreignpolicy-infocus.org/papers/venezuela.html).

Energy Information Administration. "Country Analysis Briefs," October 2003 (www.eia.doe.gov/emeu/cabs/bolivia.html).

Farthing, Linda. "Rethinking Alternative Development in Bolivia." *Andean Information Network*, Washington Office on Latin America, February 2004 (www.wola.org/publications/ddhr_bolivia_memo_ad_feb2004.pdf).

Fundación CIDOB. "Jorge Fernando Quiroga Ramírez," August 21, 2002 (www.cidob.org/bios/castellano/lideres/q-001.htm).

Gollust, David. "Bolivia Receives Promises of Support at Washington Conference," January 17, 2004 (http://quickstart.clari.net/voa/art/af/5F1D9DF7-C3BC-4D67-AC05F58C06BDBDB0.html).

Gómez, Luís, and Al Giordano. "El *Mallku* Speaks: The Narco News Interview with Felipe Quispe," January 15, 2002 (www.narconews.com/felipe1eng.html).

Hall, Kevin G. "Bolivia Challenges Washington Wisdom in Andean Drug War." *Knight Ridder Newspapers*, July 7, 2004 (www.thestate.com/mld/thestate/news/world/9255805.htm?template=contentModules/printstory.jsp).

Hallinan, Conn. "U.S. Shadow over Venezuela." *Foreign Policy in Focus*, April 17, 2002 (www.fpif.org/commentary/2002/0204venezuela2.html).

International Monetary Fund. "Bolivia and the IMF" (www.imf.org/external/country/BOL/).

———. "Bolivia: Third Review under the Stand-By." *IMF Country Report*, No. 04/193, July 2004 (www.imf.org/external/country/BOL/).

"Interview with Gonzalo 'Goni' Sánchez de Lozada." Public Broadcasting System, *Commanding Heights*, March 20, 2001 (www.pbs.org/wgbh/commandingheights/lo/people/pe_country.html).

Kourous, George. "Return of the National Security State?" Background paper from the IRC's Americas Program, November 18, 2002 (www.americaspolicy.org/briefs/2002/0211security.htm).

"Llega el Jefe del Comando Sur del Ejército de EE.UU." *El Universo*, March 18, 2003 (www.eluniverso.com/core4/eluniverso.asp?edicion=1&page=noticia&id=14&tab=1&contid=D809EB50CDCE4AFD87B6CDCC473F2675).

Loveman, Brian. "Latin America: Plan Condor" (http://larcdma.sdsu.edu/humanrights/rr/Latin%20America/PLA.html).

Mesa, Carlos. "Discurso de posesión del Presidente Carlos Diego Mesa Gisbert," October 17, 2003 (www.comunica.gov.bo/documentos_oficiales/discursos/20031017-mesa.html).

Morrison & Foerster Update. "Quarterly Report on Water Industry Developments in Latin America," April 2004 (www.mofo.com/news/general.cfm?MCatID=8859&concentrationID=&ID=1161&Type=5).

Morgan, Ronald J. "Brazil's Escalating Role in the Drug War." *Colombia Journal Online*, July 15, 2002 (www.colombiajournal.org/colombia122.htm).

"NATO Plans 5,000-Strong Strike Force by October," Reuters (online), May 30, 2003.

"New Rebel Group in Ecuador Claims Ties to FARC." Austin: Strategic Forecasting, Inc., September 16, 2002 (www.strafor.com/standard/analysis_view.php).

Osorio, Ivan G. "Chávez Bombshell: A Defector's Testimony Links the Venezuelan Strongman to International Terror." *National Review Online*, January 8, 2003 (www.nationalreview.com/comment/comment-osorio010803.asp).

"Para Brinzoni, 'La seguridad debe ser tratada como un todo.'" *La Nación*, November 1, 2002.

Public Broadcasting System, Frontline World. "Timeline: Cochabomba Water Revolt," June 2002 (www.pbs.org/frontlineworld/stories/bolivia/timeline.html).

Sachs, Jeffrey. "World Bank and Donors Must Change to Reach MDGs," March 1, 2004 (http://info.worldbank.org/etools/bspan/PresentationView.asp?PID=1061&EID=548).

———. "Call It Our Bolivian Policy of Not-So-Benign Neglect." Washington Post.com, October 26, 2003.

———. "New Approaches to International Donor Assistance." Presented at International Development Research Centre, Ottawa, Canada, June 19, 2001 (http://web .idrc.ca/en/ev-30635-201-1-DO_TOPIC.html).

———. "IMF, Reform Thyself." Hoover Institution, Public Policy Forum, International Monetary Fund (www.imfsite.org/reform/sachs2.html).

Schultz, Jim. "Bolivia: Time to Open up Secret Trade Courts," November 8, 2002 (www.corpwatch.org/article.php?id=4858.html).

United Nations Development Program. "Human Development Report, 2004: Human Development Index: Bolivia," 2004 (http://hdr.undp.org/statistics/data/country_ fact_sheets/cty_fs_BOL.html).

"U.S. Aid to Colombia Since 1997: Summary Tables." Center for International Policy, Colombia Program, February 20, 2004 (http://ciponline.org/colombia/aidtable.htm).

"U.S. Committee for Refugees, Country Report: Venezuela," 2002 (www.refugees.org/ world/countryrpt/amer-carib/venezuela).

U.S. SOUTHCOM. "Mission" (www.southcom.mil/home/mission.cfm).

Witness for Peace (Report from Arauca), "The Real Costs of Pipeline Protection in Colombia: Corporate Welfare with Deadly Consequences," July 2002 (www.w4peace .org/pdf/arauca.pdf).

World Bank Group. "Bolivia Data Profile," April 2004 (http://devdata.worldbank .org/external/CPProfile.asp?SelectedCountry=BOL&CCODE=BOL&CNAME= Bolivia&PTYPE=CP.)

Zimmerman, Yvonne. "Entrevista con Evo Morales." *Indymedia*, July 10, 2002 (http:// bolivia.indymedia.org/es/2002/07/168.shtml).

Zuluaga Nieto, Jaime. "El necesario apoyo político de la onu y de la comunidad internacional." III Encuentro Nacional de Mesas Ciudadanas, Bogotá (2002).

Index

About the Contributors

Adrián Bonilla received his PhD in international politics at the University of Miami. He is currently the director of the Quito branch of FLACSO (Facultad Latinoamericana de Ciencias Sociales). He has published numerous articles in academic journals and book chapters in Ecuador, Latin America, and the United States on topics related to security and conflict. He has also published five books: *Orfeo en el infierno: Una agenda de Política exterior ecuatoriana* (editor, 2002); *Ecuador-Perú: Horizontes de la negociación y el conflicto* (editor, 1999); *Las sorprendentes virtudes de lo perverso: Ecuador y Narcotráfico en los 90* (1993); *Economía política del narcotráfico: El caso ecuatoriano* (coedited with Bruce Bagley and Alexei Páez) (1991); and *En busca del pueblo perdido: Discurso y diferenciación de la izquierda en el 60* (1991).

Pilar Gaitán is a political science graduate from the Universidad de los Andes, Bogotá, and earned a master's degree in political science at the Universidad Autónoma de México. She was research professor at the Universidad Externado De Colombia (1983–1987) and a researcher at the Instituto de Estudios Politicos y Relaciones Internacionales de la Universidad Nacional de Colombia (1987–1994). From 1991 to 1992 she was professor of political science at the Universidad de los Andes (1991–1992). She has published research in numerous magazines and journals and in 1998 authored the book *Poder local: Realidad y utopía de la descentralización en Colombia* (1998). She has also had a distinguished public service career as director of the Secretariat of Human Rights in the Colombian Ministry of Defense (1994–1995), director for special affairs in the Ministry of Foreign Relations (1995–1996), vice minister of foreign relations (1996–1998), and director of international affairs in the Fiscalía General de la Nación, Bogotá (1998–2001). From 2002 to 2003 she served as the representative in Washington, D.C., of the NGO Ideas para la Paz. From 2003 to 2004 she served in Colombia's permanent mission to the Organization of American States in Washington, D.C.

Monica Herz teaches at the Pontifícia Universidade Católica do Rio de Janeiro, Centro de Ciências Sociais, Instituto de Relações Internacionais—PUC-RJ. She received her PhD (1994) from the London School of Economics and Political Science and a master's degree in sociology from the Instituto Universitário de Pesquisas do Rio de Janeiro, IUPERJ, Rio De Janeiro, Brazil. She is the director of the Institute of International Relations. She has written on Brazilian foreign policy and Latin American security. Her most recent book is *Ecuador vs. Peru: Peacemaking amid Rivalry* (coauthored with João Pontes Nogueira, 2002).

Kenneth Lehman is Squires Associate Professor of History at Hampden-Sydney College in Virginia, where he teaches courses in Latin American history, U.S. history, and the history of U.S. foreign relations. He is author of *Bolivia and the United States: A Limited Partnership*, published as part of the "United States and the Americas" series by the University of Georgia Press. He has published research on Eisenhower policies in Bolivia and Guatemala in *Diplomatic History* and wrote a chapter comparing U.S. policy toward the Mexican and Bolivian revolutions in *Proclaiming Revolution: Bolivia in Comparative Perspective*, a collaborative study of the Bolivian revolution on its fiftieth anniversary. He became interested in Bolivia while living and teaching there in the 1970s and early 1980s and returns regularly for research. He received his MA in Latin American studies from the University of New Mexico and his PhD in history from the University of Texas at Austin.

Brian Loveman is the Fred J. Hansen Chair for Peace Studies and professor of political science at San Diego State University. He received an MA (1969) and PhD (1973) from Indiana University and a BA in history and political science from the University of California at Berkeley (1965). His major fields of interest are Latin American politics, inter-American politics, international relations, and human rights. Among his recent publications are *Strategy for Empire: U.S. Regional Security Policy in the Post–Cold War Era* (2004); *El espejismo de la reconciliación política: Chile 1990–2002* (2002, with Elizabeth Lira); *For la Patria: Politics and the Armed Forces in Latin America* (1999); *Las suaves cenizas del olvido: Vía chilena de reconciliación política, 1814–1932* (1999, with Elizabeth Lira): 2nd edition, revised and expanded, June 2000; *Las ardientes cenizas del olvido: Vía chilena de reconciliación política, 1932–1994* (2000); *Chile: The*

Legacy of Hispanic Capitalism, 3rd ed. (2001). He teaches classes in Latin American politics, inter-American relations, comparative politics, politics of the developing nations, international relations, and environmental politics.

Enrique Obando is an anthropologist who graduated from the Pontificia Universidad Católica in Peru. He received a master's degree in security policy from George Washington University in Washington, D.C. He is currently the director of the Institute of Political and Strategic Studies (Estudios Políticos y Estratégicos–IDEPE) in Lima, Peru. He is also professor of political science at the Universidad del Pacífico. He recently participated as a member of the Commission to Restructure the National Intelligence Council in Peru and representative on the National Anticorruption Commission (Comisión Nacional de Lucha contra la Corrupción y la Promoción de la Ética y Transparencia en la Gestión Pública). He also served as an advisor to the National Defense Directorate. His publications in English include "Subversion and Anti-Subversion in Peru, 1980–1992: A View from Lima," in *Low Intensity Conflict & Law Enforcement*, vol. 2 (Autumn 1993); "The Power of Peru's Armed Forces," in *Peru in Crisis, Dictatorship or Democracy?* ed. Joseph Tulchin and Gary Bland (1994); "Civil–Military Relations in Peru: 1980–1996. On How to Control, and Co-opt the Military (and of the Consequences of Doing So)," in *Shining and Other Paths: War and Society in Peru, 1980–1995*, ed. Steve J. Stern (1998); "The Impact of the 1995 Conflict on Peru and Peruvian–Ecuadorian Relations," in *Security Cooperation in the Western Hemisphere: Resolving Ecuador–Peru Conflict*, ed. Gabriel Marcella and Richard Downes (1999); "Defeating Shining Path: Lessons for the Future," in *Saving Democracies: U.S. Intervention in Threatened Democratic States*, ed. Anthony Joes (1999).

Orlando J. Pérez is associate professor of political science at Central Michigan University, where he teaches courses in comparative politics, Latin American politics, and U.S.–Latin American relations. He has carried out field research in several countries of the region, including Panama, Nicaragua, El Salvador, Guatemala, Honduras, and Venezuela. As a consultant, he has worked on public opinion surveys, democratization, civil–military relations, and corruption issues for USAID and the United Nations Development Program. His work has appeared in the *Journal of Interamerican Studies and World Affairs*, *Hemisphere*, *South Eastern Latin Americanist*, and *Political Science Quarterly*, and as numerous chapters in edited volumes. He is the editor of *Post-Invasion Panama: The Challenges of Democratization in the New World Order*. He is currently completing a manuscript on the transformation of civil–military relations in Central America. He received his MA and PhD in political science from the University of Pittsburgh.

Eduardo Pizarro is a professor at the Universidad Nacional de Colombia in Bogotá where he was cofounder and ex-director of the Instituto de Estudios Políticos y Relaciones Internacionales (IEPRI). He has published extensively on Colombian politics and internal conflict including *Las FARC (1949–1966): De la autodefensa a la combinación de todas las formas de lucha* (1991) and has been a weekly contributor to the newspaper *El Espectador* and a columnist in *El Tiempo*. He was a visiting fellow at the program in Latin American studies at Princeton University for the academic year 2000–2001. Pizarro holds a BA in sociology from the University of Vincennes, Paris; an MA in international relations from the Institute of High Studies for Development, in Bogotá, Colombia; and a PhD in political science from the Institute of Political Studies of Paris. In the United States he has taught at Columbia University and the Kellogg Institute at the University of Notre Dame.

Philipp Schönrock-Martínez is founder and director of CEPEI (Centro de Pensamiento Estratégico Internacional) in Bogotá, D.C., Colombia. He has coordinated projects for the Ecole de la Paix in Grenoble, France, and has served as a consultant to the Charles Leopold Mayer para el Progreso del Hombre Foundation in Paris, France. He has also worked for the Colombian government's commercial office in Hamburg, Germany. Schönrock-Martínez has published numerous essays in Europe and Latin America and writes periodically in the Colombian press, including in *El Tiempo* and *El Espectador*.

Juan Gabriel Tokatlian was born in Buenos Aires, Argentina (1954). He is a sociologist and received an MA (1981) and a PhD (1990) in international relations from The Johns Hopkins University School of Advanced International Studies (Washington, D.C.). He is currently director of political science and international relations at the Universidad de San Andrés (Victoria, Provincia de Buenos Aires, Argentina). He lived in Colombia for eighteen years (1981–1998). He served as associate professor (1995–1998) at the Universidad Nacional de Colombia (Bogotá), where he was senior researcher at the Instituto de Estudios Políticos y Relaciones Internacionales (IEPRI). Tokatlian was cofounder (1982) and director (1987–1994) of the Centro de Estudios Internacionales (CEI) at the Universidad de los Andes (Bogotá). He has published extensively, both books and articles, on Colombian and Argentine foreign policies; on U.S.–Latin American relations; on drug trafficking, organized violence, and terrorism in the Americas; and on global politics and dynamics. His most recent books are *Hacia una nueva estrategia internacional: El desafío de Néstor Kirchner* (2004) and *Globalización, Narcotráfico y Violencia: Siete Ensayos sobre Colombia* (2000).

Table of Contents for
Supplementary Materials URL

U.S. Government

Congressional Testimony

Congressional Research Service

U.S. General Accountability Office (USGAO)

Joint Chiefs of Staff (JCS)

Presidents

U.S. Military Officers (Ret. & Active Duty) & Civilians at Civil–Military Institutions

and Terrorism: El Salvador and Colombia," *Military Review*, March–April 2004

Colombian Government

LATIN AMERICAN SILHOUETTES

Editors: William H. Beezley and Judith Ewell

For la Patria: *Politics and the Armed Forces in Latin America*
By Brian Loveman
The Politics of Antipolitics: The Military in Latin America, Third Edition
Edited by Brian Loveman and Thomas M. Davies, Jr.
Argentine Caudillo: Juan Manuel de Rosas
By John Lynch
The Women's Revolution in Mexico, 1910–1953
Edited by Stephanie E. Mitchell and Patience A. Schell
Gringolandia: Mexican Identity and Perceptions of the United States
By Stephen D. Morris
Real Life in Castro's Cuba
By Catherine Moses
Brazil in the Making: Facets of National Identity
Edited by Carmen Nava and Ludwig Lauerhass, Jr.
Mexico in the 1940s: Modernity, Politics, and Corruption
By Stephen R. Niblo
Feeding Mexico: The Political Uses of Food since 1910
By Enrique C. Ochoa
Impressions of Cuba in the Nineteenth Century: The Travel Diary of Joseph J. Dimock
Edited by Louis A. Pérez, Jr.
Cantinflas and the Chaos of Mexican Modernity
By Jeffrey M. Pilcher
The Divine Charter: Constitutionalism and Liberalism in Nineteenth-Century Mexico
Edited by Jaime E. Rodríguez O.
Myths, Misdeeds, and Misunderstandings: The Roots of Conflict in U.S.-Mexican Relations
Edited by Jaime E. Rodríguez O. and Kathryn Vincent
The Origins of Mexican National Politics, 1808–1847
Edited by Jaime E. Rodríguez O.
Integral Outsiders: The American Colony in Mexico City, 1876–1911
By William Schell, Jr.
The French in Central America: Culture and Commerce
By Thomas D. Schoonover
The Tale of Healer Miguel Perdomo Neira: Medicine, Ideologies, and Power in the Nineteenth-Century Andes
By David Sowell
Based on a True Story: Latin American History at the Movies
Edited by Donald F. Stevens
Cuban and Cuban-American Women: An Annotated Bibliography
Edited and Compiled by K. Lynn Stoner, with Luis Hipólito Serrano Pérez
Patriotism, Politics, and Popular Liberalism in Nineteenth-Century Mexico: Juan Francisco Luca and the Puebla Sierra
By Guy P. C. Thomson with David G. LaFrance
A Parisian in Brazil: The Travel Account of a Frenchwoman in Nineteenth-Century Rio de Janeiro
By Adèle Toussaint-Samson
Edited and Introduced by June E. Hahner
Argentina: The Challenges of Modernization
Edited by Joseph S. Tulchin with Allison M. Garland
Cuba and the Caribbean: Regional Issues and Trends in the Post–Cold War Era
Edited by Joseph S. Tulchin, Andrés Serbín, and Rafael Hernández
State and Society in Spanish America during the Age of Revolution
Edited by Victor M. Uribe-Uran
Disorder and Progress: Bandits, Police, and Mexican Development
By Paul J. Vanderwood
Hacienda and Market in Eighteenth-Century Mexico: The Rural Economy of the Guadalajara Region, 1675–1820
By Eric Van Young
Latin America in the Middle Period, 1750–1929
By Stuart F. Voss
Repression, Resistance, and Democratic Transition in Central America
Edited by Thomas W. Walker and Ariel C. Armony
Vagrants and Citizens: Politics and the Masses in Mexico City from Colony to Republic
By Richard A. Warren
On the Border: Society and Culture between the United States and Mexico
Edited by Andrew Grant Wood
Revolution in the Street: Women, Workers, and Urban Protest in Veracruz
By Andrew Grant Wood